WileyPLUS

WileyPLUS is a research-based online environment for effective teaching and learning.

WileyPLUS builds students' confidence because it takes the guesswork out of studying by providing students with a clear roadmap:

- what to do
- how to do it
- if they did it right

It offers interactive resources along with a complete digital textbook that help students learn more. With *WileyPLUS*, students take more initiative so you'll have greater impact on their achievement in the classroom and beyond.

WileyPLUS

ALL THE HELP, **RESOURCES,** AND PERSONAL **SUPPORT** YOU AND YOUR STUDENTS NEED!

www.wileyplus.com/resources

1st DAY OF CLASS ...AND BEYOND!

2-Minute Tutorials and all of the resources you and your students need to get started

WileyPLUS

Student Partner Program

Student support from an experienced student user

Wiley Faculty Netwo

Collaborate with your colleagues, find a mentor, attend virtual and live events, and view resources
www.WhereFacultyConnect.com

WileyPLUS

Quick Start

Pre-loaded, ready-to-use assignments and presentations created by subject matter experts

Technical Support 24/7 FAQs, online chat, and phone support
www.wileyplus.com/support

© Courtney Keating/iStockphoto

Your *WileyPLUS* Account Manager, providing personal training and support

AUDITING
A PRACTICAL APPROACH
EXTENDED CANADIAN EDITION

Library and Archives Canada Cataloguing in Publication

Moroney, Robyn, author

Auditing : a practical approach / Robyn Moroney (Monash University, Caulfield East, Australia), Fiona Campbell (Ernst & Young, Melbourne, Australia), Jane Hamilton (La Trobe University, Bendigo, Australia), Valerie Warren (Kwantlen Polytechnic University, Surrey, British Columbia); with contributions from Luke Baxter, Darrell Jensen, Ernst & Young LLP, Toronto, Ontario. —Extended Canadian edition.

Includes bibliographical references and index.
Issued in print and electronic formats.
ISBN 978-1-118-87841-5 (pbk.). —ISBN 978-1-119-04814-5 (pdf)

1. Auditing—Textbooks.   I. Title.

HF5667.M696 2014b   657'.45   C2014-906814-X
                                            C2014-906815-8

Production Credits
Executive Editor: Zoë Craig
V.P. and Director of Market Solutions: Veronica Visentin
Marketing Manager: Anita Osborne
Editorial Manager: Karen Staudinger
Developmental Editor: Daleara Jamasji Hirjikaka
Production and Media Specialist: Meaghan MacDonald
Editorial Assistant: Maureen Lau
Cover and Interior Design: Joanna Vieira
Cover Image: © 1stGallery/Erni Brummer
Production: Jackie Henry and Dennis Free, Project Managers, Aptara Inc.
Typesetting: Aptara Inc.
Printing & Binding: Courier Printing

Printed and bound in the United States of America

1 2 3 4 5 CC 19 18 17 16 15

John Wiley & Sons Canada, Ltd.
5353 Dundas Street West, Suite 400
Toronto, ON, M9B 6H8 Canada
Visit our website at: www.wiley.ca

AUDITING
A PRACTICAL APPROACH
EXTENDED CANADIAN EDITION

Robyn MORONEY
Monash University, Caulfield East, Australia

Fiona CAMPBELL
EY, Melbourne, Australia

Jane HAMILTON
La Trobe University, Bendigo, Australia

Valerie WARREN
Kwantlen Polytechnic University, Surrey, British Columbia

With contributions from

Luke BAXTER
Darrell JENSEN
Janet JOHNSON
Stephanie LAMONT
Anilisa SAINANI
EY

Partial Adaptation of
Modern Auditing & Assurance Services, Fifth Edition

Philomena Leung, Paul Coram,
Barry J. Cooper, Peter Richardson

ABOUT THE AUTHORS

Robyn Moroney, B.Ec. (Hons), M.Com., Ph.D., CA, CPA, is an Associate Professor in the Department of Accounting and Finance at Monash University, Australia. Before commencing her academic career, Robyn worked as an auditor at Arthur Young, now Ernst & Young. With over 25 years' academic experience, Robyn has previously held positions at the University of Melbourne, the University of Auckland, the University of New South Wales, and La Trobe University. As a member of the board of the Accounting and Finance Association of Australia and New Zealand, which represents the interests of accounting and finance academics in both countries, Robyn has taken on a number of roles including co-chairing the conference technical committee and the doctoral symposium. Her areas of research are the behavioural aspects (auditor decision-making processes) and economics of auditing.

Fiona Campbell, B.Com., FCA, is an Assurance Partner with Ernst & Young in Melbourne, Australia. Fiona has been serving clients in the assurance practice since 1991 and has worked on audit clients primarily in the manufacturing, consumer, and industrial products industries, as well as not-for-profit sector organizations. She has considerable experience providing professional services to Australian and foreign-controlled companies, including large publicly listed and private companies. Fiona is also responsible for assurance methodology and technology at Ernst & Young in Australia, and has been involved in designing the firm's global audit methodology for the past 14 years, including ensuring compliance with both international and local auditing standards.

Jane Hamilton, B.Bus., M.Acc., Ph.D., is Professor of Accounting at the Bendigo campus of the Regional School of Business, La Trobe University, Australia, and previously held academic positions at the University of Technology, Sydney. Jane has 20 years' experience in teaching and has published the results of her auditing research in several Australian and international journals.

Valerie Warren, B.Comm., MBA, CPA CA is the Accounting Department Chair at the School of Business at Kwantlen Polytechnic University in British Columbia. Before commencing her academic career, Valerie worked as an auditor with KPMG. As well as teaching a variety of accounting courses, including auditing, advanced accounting, and accounting theory, Valerie also serves as a Practice Review Officer for the Institute of Chartered Accountants of BC, where she conducts practice reviews of national, regional, and small CA firms to ensure compliance with current accounting and assurance standards.

PREFACE

Welcome to the extended Canadian edition of *Auditing: A Practical Approach*. This is not just another auditing text. As the title suggests, the textbook focuses on how audits are conducted in practice. As authors, we bring our diverse experiences to this book to provide a very different approach to teaching and studying auditing. In addition to covering the essential topics of auditing, the text provides greater insight into how an audit is conducted and the issues that are of greatest concern to practising auditors.

As each chapter unfolds, students are introduced to the various stages of an audit. Key auditing concepts are addressed in a succinct manner, making them easily understandable. To underpin this approach, each chapter begins with a diagrammatic representation of the stages of an audit, with the current stage highlighted as we progress through the text. The diagram provides a useful reference point to ground the discussion in each chapter to the relevant stage in the audit process. To underpin our discussion of how an audit is conducted, we use a case study of a hypothetical client, Cloud 9. The discussion in each chapter is kept general, with our case study providing an example of how the general principles behind each audit may be applied in practice. By using this approach, students are provided with a continuing example of how the concepts discussed may apply in practice.

The Cloud 9 case study provides a flexible learning tool to be used within an auditing and assurance course. Details about Cloud 9 and its audit are provided in each chapter to give an insight into how an audit is conducted, the issues that auditors face at each stage of an audit, and the processes used to gather evidence and arrive at conclusions. The Cloud 9 case materials can form the basis of class discussions, student role plays, or online exchanges between students. At the end of each chapter, a case-study problem is set using Cloud 9 as a basis. These problems can be used as part of the weekly tutorial program, or as an assignment for students to work on individually or in groups (or some combination of the two). This textbook contains 13 chapters. An overview of each chapter is now provided, followed by a description of the structure used in each chapter.

Overview of the text

Chapter 1: Introduction and overview of audit and assurance. This chapter begins with a definition of assurance engagements, which leads into a discussion of the source of the historical and ongoing demand for audit services. This is then followed with assurance services, an explanation of how they can differ, and the different levels of assurance and opinions that can be provided by auditors. The role of the financial statement preparer is also contrasted with that of the auditor. The regulations surrounding the provision of assurance services are outlined and the expectation gap is explained. This chapter provides the background that underpins the remainder of the text.

Chapter 2: Ethics, legal liability, and client acceptance. This chapter provides an overview of the fundamental principles of professional ethics that apply to all accountants. Particular attention is given to auditor independence, including threats and safeguards. The auditor's legal liability to their client and third parties is explained, together with the concept of contributory negligence. This chapter ends with a discussion of the factors to consider in the client acceptance or continuance decision, which marks the commencement of our discussion of how an audit is conducted.

Chapter 3: Audit planning I. The first stage of every audit involves planning. This important topic is covered in two chapters. Chapter 3 begins with a discussion of the different stages of an audit. The key components of the planning stage are gaining an understanding of a client, identifying the risk of fraud, assessing the extent of related party transactions, evaluating the client's going concern assumption, gaining an understanding of the client's corporate governance structure, and evaluating how a client's information technology can impact risk. These components of audit planning are described in detail in this chapter, along with a discussion of how client closing procedures can impact reported results.

Chapter 4: Audit planning II. This chapter continues our discussion of audit planning. Specifically, this chapter includes a definition of audit risk and describes its components. The concept of materiality, the development of planning materiality, and how it is used when conducting an audit is then described. The process used by auditors in arriving at their audit strategy, which provides a blueprint for the remainder of the audit, is explained. The chapter concludes with an overview of the use of analytical procedures during the planning phase of an audit.

Chapter 5: Audit evidence. This chapter contains an overview of the different types of audit evidence and the processes used by auditors to gather that evidence throughout the audit. The audit assertions, which aid in risk identification and the design of audit procedures, are defined. The concept of sufficient appropriate audit evidence is explained. The procedures when using the work of an expert or another auditor are described. This chapter concludes with a discussion of how auditors document the details of evidence gathered in their working papers.

Chapter 6: Sampling and overview of the risk response phase of the audit. This chapter begins with a discussion of audit sampling. Sampling and non-sampling risk are explained and contrasted and then followed by a discussion of the difference between statistical and non-statistical sampling. Various sampling methods used in practice are then described. The factors that impact sample sizes when testing controls and conducting substantive tests are then outlined. Tests of controls and substantive procedures are then described. A description of the difference between tests of controls and substantive procedures and the factors that impact the nature, timing, and extent of audit testing are explained.

Chapter 7: Understanding and testing the client's system of internal controls. This chapter provides an overview of internal controls. Internal control is defined and the seven generally accepted objectives of internal control activities are outlined. Internal controls at the entity level are explained and contrasted. This chapter discusses how an auditor determines when to conduct their tests, how they identify different types of controls, how they select the techniques to use when testing controls, how they select controls to test, and how they design their tests of controls. The chapter demonstrates that once controls testing is completed, an auditor must interpret the results of their testing and the implications of the findings for the remainder of the audit. A description is provided of how an auditor documents their understanding of their client's system of internal controls. Based upon that understanding, an auditor will then identify strengths and weaknesses in their client's system of internal controls and communicate their findings to those charged with governance in the organization.

Chapter 8: Execution of the audit—performing substantive procedures. This chapter provides an overview of the substantive procedures used by auditors when testing the details of their client's transactions and account balances. This chapter includes a discussion of the link between audit risk and the nature, timing, and extent of substantive procedures conducted by the auditor. An overview is provided of common substantive audit procedures used in practice and the level of audit evidence obtained when conducting different tests. This chapter concludes with a description of the documentation of the conclusions reached by auditors as a result of their substantive procedures.

Chapter 9: Auditing sales and receivables. This chapter begins with a discussion of the audit objectives when auditing sales and receivables. It identifies the functions and control procedures normally found in the processing of sales, cash receipts, and sales adjustment transactions. The audit strategy, including the risk of material misstatement and tests of controls for these accounts, is discussed. The chapter ends with an overview of the substantive audit procedures used to audit the sales and receivables cycle, including the confirmation of accounts receivable.

Chapter 10: Auditing purchases, payables, and payroll: This chapter begins with a discussion of the audit objectives applicable to purchases, payables, and payroll. It identifies the functions and control procedures normally found in the processing of purchase, payment, and purchase adjustment transactions. The audit strategy, including the risk of material misstatement and tests of controls for these accounts, is discussed. The chapter ends with an overview of the substantive audit procedures used to audit purchases, payables, and payroll.

Chapter 11: Auditing inventories and property, plant, and equipment: This chapter describes the audit objectives applicable to inventory and property, plant, and equipment. Record keeping for these accounts is discussed. This is followed by the considerations in determining the audit strategy for inventory and property, plant, and equipment. Substantive audit procedures are discussed, including procedures relating to the client's inventory count.

Chapter 12: Auditing cash and investments: This chapter includes the audit objectives applicable to cash and investments. The audit strategy for cash and investments is discussed, as well as substantive procedures for these accounts. "Lapping" and how an auditor can detect it is described.

Chapter 13: Completing and reporting on the audit. This final chapter of the text marks the conclusion of the audit. An explanation of the procedures performed by an auditor as part of their wrap-up, including gathering and evaluating audit evidence, is provided. The going concern concept is revisited in the context of finalizing the audit. Subsequent event testing is explained. The procedures used by auditors when evaluating material misstatements uncovered during their audit are outlined. A description is provided of how auditors evaluate the conclusions drawn throughout the audit in relation to evidence gathered and its impact on the overall opinion formed on the financial statements. The form and content of the audit report is outlined. Finally, a description is provided of the types of reports an auditor will provide to the client's management and those charged with governance at the conclusion of the audit. This chapter is followed by an appendix that discusses the various types of special engagements and reports that an auditor may be asked to complete.

Structure of each chapter

Each chapter commences with an overview of the *learning objectives* addressed in the chapter. These learning objectives are highlighted throughout the chapter as the discussion unfolds. After each learning objective is covered in the text, three *before you go on* questions are set for students to confirm they recall the main issues covered. As these questions come directly from the text, it is straightforward for students to check their understanding of the key concepts covered before progressing to the next learning objective (section) in the chapter. Specific learning objectives are also linked to end-of-chapter professional application questions. This approach means that tutorial questions can be set to ensure coverage of the learning objectives considered most important.

Following the list of learning objectives is a summary of the Canadian and international *auditing and assurance standards* discussed in each chapter. The listed standards are incorporated in the discussion within the textbook. Other pronouncements and guidance statements are also listed and discussed where applicable.

The summary of standards is followed by a diagram of the *overview of the audit process*. This figure aids in understanding the structure of the textbook, which mirrors the process generally used when conducting an audit. The diagram highlights the stage to be covered in the current chapter, which aids in understanding what has come before and what is still to come.

Following the overview diagram is an *audit process in focus* section, which includes a brief overview and outline of the chapter. As *key terms* appear in the text for the first time, their definitions appear in the margin, which aids studying and revision.

The *Cloud 9* case study appears throughout each chapter. Students can choose to incorporate Cloud 9 in their reading of each chapter or to go back and read through the case study after reading the main text. As Cloud 9 is easily distinguishable from the main text, either approach can be adopted when studying a chapter.

Descriptions of the *professional environment* in which auditors operate appear in each chapter. These vignettes provide some details of the auditing profession and various challenges faced by auditors.

Each chapter concludes with a summary, list of key terms used, and end-of-chapter questions. The *summary* provides a brief recap of each learning objective covered in a chapter. The end-of-chapter questions include *multiple-choice questions*, review questions, professional application questions, a Cloud 9 case study question, and a research question.

Solutions to multiple-choice questions appear at the end of each chapter, so students can use these as part of their independent study. The *review questions* test student understanding of the key concepts covered in the chapter. The *professional application questions* are problems designed around the learning objectives set for the chapter. Each question is graded as basic, moderate, or challenging and indicates the learning objective(s) covered. A selection of the professional application questions is based upon problems published by professional bodies such as CPA Canada in their various publications including *External Auditing* and *Advanced External Auditing* as well as problems set for the Uniform Final Exam. Several professional application questions are also based on Audit and Assurance exams administered by Chartered Accountants Australia and New Zealand. The inclusion of these problems in the text helps build familiarity with the type of problems that students will encounter in their professional exams. The Cloud 9 *case study* builds from one chapter to the next and is based on the information provided in each chapter, in the case study at the end of each chapter, and in the appendix to the textbook. The use of a case study in this text aids in the appreciation of how each topic covered fits in to the context of an audit as a whole. Together with the practical approach used in the body of the text, this allows a deeper understanding of how audits are conducted in practice. *Research questions* provide an opportunity for students to gain a deeper appreciation of the role of academic research in providing greater insights into audit practice. Sample documents and forms are included in *Appendix A* at the end of the text and provide students with useful examples of the forms and templates that they would encounter during an audit.

Technology for Teaching and Learning

WileyPLUS

Auditing: A Practical Approach Extended Canadian Edition offers instructors and students a unique and comprehensive set of technology tools to aid in instruction and learning. These have been carefully developed and integrated with the text and serve to expand the educational experience.

WileyPLUS is an innovative, research-based online environment for effective teaching and learning.

WileyPLUS builds students' confidence because it takes the guesswork out of studying by providing students with a clear roadmap: what to do, how to do it, if they did it right. Students will take more initiative so you'll have greater impact on their achievement in the classroom and beyond.

WileyPLUS and the *Auditing: A Practical Approach* Extended Canadian Edition website at http://www.wiley.com/go/moroneyextended provide a wealth of online resources including quizzes, chapter PowerPoint slides, and videos for classroom use accessible to both instructors and students. Instructors also have access to the Solutions Manual and the Testbank in Word and computerized formats.

Acknowledgements

We thank the following reviewers for their valuable feedback:

Sally Anderson, *University of Calgary*

Peggy Coady, *Memorial University of Newfoundland*

Valerie Greenwood, *SAIT Polytechnic*

Cynthia Maier, *SAIT Polytechnic*

Camillo Lento, *Lakehead University*

Wendy Popowich, *Northern Alberta Institute of Technology*

Sanjian Zhang, *McGill University*

We would also like to thank the following contributors for preparing the ancillaries to the book and for their useful suggestions and comments:

Angela Davis, *Booth University College*
Robert Ducharme, *University of Waterloo*
Chris Leduc, *Cambrian College*

We would like to thank EY, specifically Luke Baxter, Darrell Jensen, Janet Johnson, Stephanie Lamont, and Anilisa Sainani for reviewing the text and for offering valuable suggestions for improvement as well as for providing us with real-world exhibits to include in the text.

We also thank the staff at John Wiley & Sons Canada, Ltd., for their support and expertise. We would especially like to thank Zoë Craig, Acquisitions Editor; Deanna Durnford, Supplements Coordinator; Luisa Begani, Media Editor; Daleara Hirjikaka, Developmental Editor; and Anita Osborne, Marketing Manager. We also wish to thank all the sales representatives for their tireless efforts in promoting this book. We would like to specially thank Jackie Henry, Laurel Hyatt, Zofia Laubitz, and Belle Wong for their editorial contributions.

We also thank our families for their support and patience. A special thanks to the "guys," Oliver, Matthew, and Nicholas.

We have tried to produce a text that is error-free and that meets your requirements. Suggestions and comments from users are always welcome.

Valerie Warren
December 2014
valerie.warren@kpu.ca

HOW TO USE THIS BOOK

Auditing: A Practical Approach has been designed with you—the student—in mind. This textbook has been designed to enhance your learning experience and is our attempt to provide you with a book that both engages you with the subject matter and encourages a greater understanding of the auditing process. We have tried to accomplish these goals through the following elements.

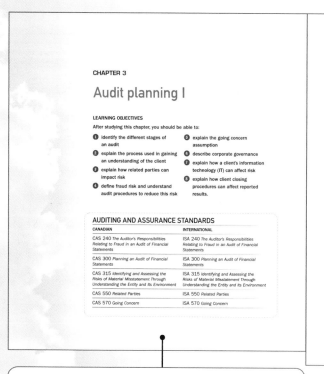

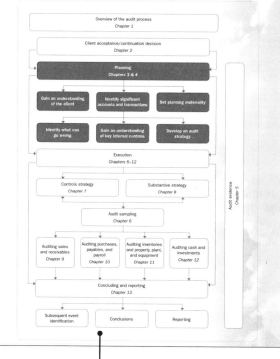

The chapter opens with the **learning objectives** for the chapter and the **auditing and assurance standards** (both Canadian and international) applicable to each chapter. Each learning objective is repeated at the point within the chapter where the concept is discussed and is summarized at the end of the chapter.

The **overview of the audit process** is a detailed flowchart that appears at the beginning of each chapter providing a schematic overview of the audit process. The relevant component to the chapter is highlighted as you progress through the text. You will find this flowchart useful to develop a holistic understanding of the audit process.

Cloud 9 is an integrated case study that aligns with the audit methodology detailed in each chapter. The case appears several times in each chapter, providing a continuing practical insight into how the topics discussed can be applied in an audit. The **audit process in focus** provides an introduction to the topics covered in the chapter.

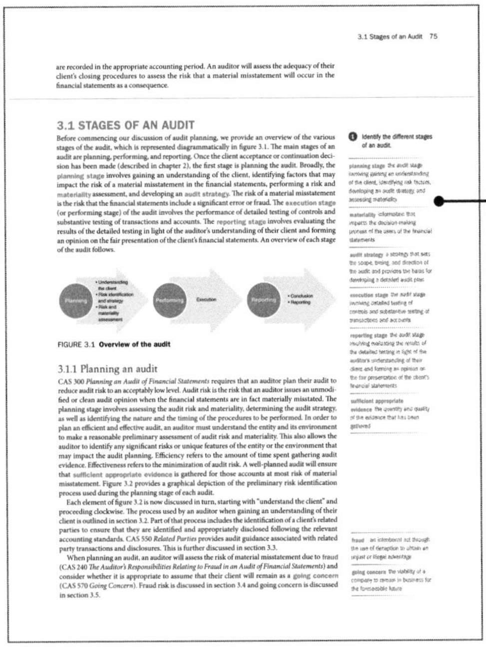

Key terms are bolded in the text at first mention and defined in the margin, listed again at the end of the chapter, and defined in the end-of-book glossary.

Professional environment boxes apply the key topics and processes discussed in the chapter to current events locally and internationally.

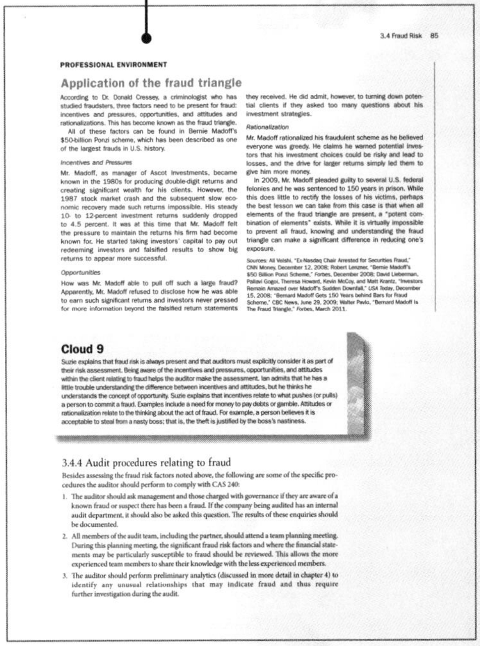

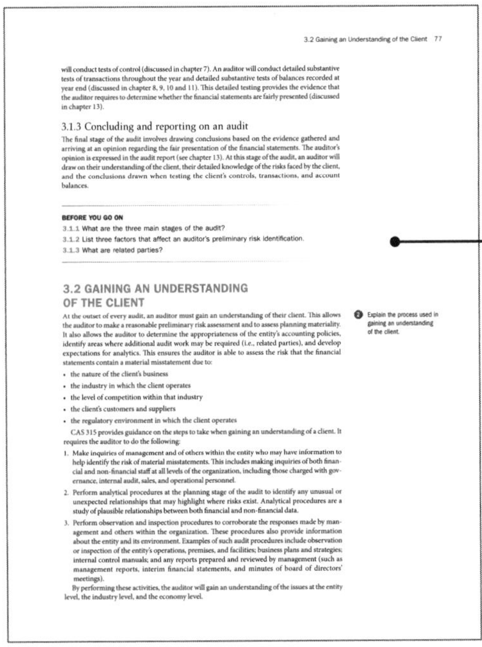

Before you go on questions are presented after each section and contain questions for review of the key points covered.

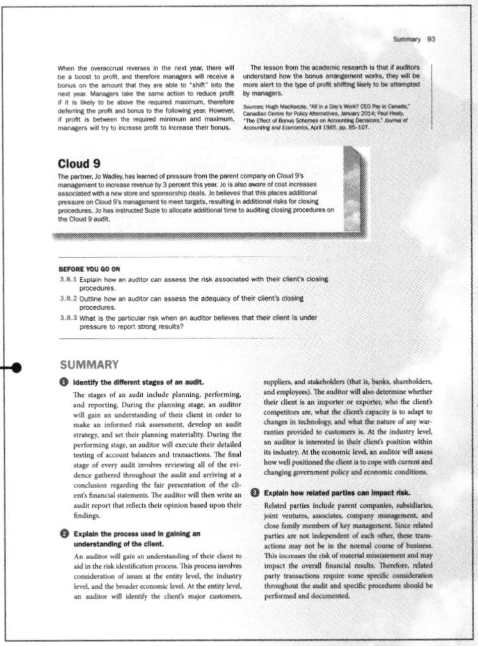

The **summary** restates and summarizes the learning objectives set for the chapter.

Excerpt 1 — page 75

3.1 Stages of an Audit 75

are recorded in the appropriate accounting period. An auditor will assess the adequacy of their client's closing procedures so that the risk that a material misstatement will occur in the financial statements as a consequence.

3.1 STAGES OF AN AUDIT

Before commencing our discussion of audit planning, we provide an overview of the various stages of the audit, which is represented diagrammatically in figure 3.1. The main stages of an audit are planning, performing, and reporting. Once the client acceptance or continuation decision has been made (described in chapter 2), the first stage is planning the audit. Broadly, the planning stage involves gaining an understanding of the client, identifying factors that may impact the risk of a material misstatement in the financial statements, performing a risk and materiality assessment, and developing an audit strategy. The risk of a material misstatement is the risk that the financial statements include a significant error or fraud. The execution stage (or performing stage) of the audit involves the performance of detailed testing of controls and substantive testing of transactions and accounts. The reporting stage involves evaluating the results of the detailed testing in light of the auditor's understanding of their client and forming an opinion on the fair presentation of the client's financial statements. An overview of each stage of the audit follows.

Margin: Identify the different stages of an audit.

planning stage the audit stage involving gaining an understanding of the client, identifying risk factors, developing an audit strategy, and assessing materiality

materiality information that impacts the decision-making process of the users of the financial statements

audit strategy a strategy that sets the scope, timing, and direction of the audit and provides the basis for developing a detailed audit plan

execution stage the audit stage involving detailed testing of controls and substantive testing of transactions and accounts

reporting stage the audit stage involving evaluating the results of the detailed testing in light of the auditor's understanding of their client and forming an opinion on the fair presentation of the client's financial statements

sufficient appropriate evidence the quantity and quality of the evidence that has been gathered

FIGURE 3.1 Overview of the audit

3.1.1 Planning an audit

CAS 300 *Planning an Audit of Financial Statements* requires that an auditor plan their audit to reduce audit risk to an acceptably low level. Audit risk is the risk that an auditor issues an unmodified or clean audit opinion when the financial statements are in fact materially misstated. The planning stage involves assessing the audit risk and materiality, determining the audit strategy, as well as identifying the nature and the timing of the procedures to be performed. In order to plan an efficient and effective audit, an auditor must understand the entity and its environment to make a reasonable preliminary assessment of audit risk and materiality. This also allows the auditor to identify any significant risks or unique features of the entity or the environment that may impact the audit planning. Efficiency refers to the amount of time spent gathering audit evidence. Effectiveness refers to the minimization of audit risk. A well-planned audit will ensure that sufficient appropriate evidence is gathered for those accounts at most risk of material misstatement. Figure 3.2 provides a graphical depiction of the preliminary risk identification process used during the planning stage of each audit.

Each element of figure 3.2 is now discussed in turn, starting with "understand the client" and proceeding clockwise. The process used by an auditor when gaining an understanding of their client is outlined in section 3.2. Part of that process includes the identification of a client's related parties to ensure that they are identified and appropriately disclosed following the relevant accounting standards. CAS 550 *Related Parties* provides audit guidance associated with related party transactions and disclosures. This is further discussed in section 3.3.

When planning an audit, an auditor will assess the risk of material misstatement due to fraud (CAS 240 *The Auditor's Responsibilities Relating to Fraud in an Audit of Financial Statements*) and consider whether it is appropriate to assume that their client will remain as a going concern (CAS 570 *Going Concern*). Fraud risk is discussed in section 3.4 and going concern is discussed in section 3.5.

fraud an intentional act through the use of deception to obtain an unjust or illegal advantage

going concern the viability of a company to remain in business for the foreseeable future

---

Excerpt 2 — page 77

3.2 Gaining an Understanding of the Client 77

will conduct tests of control (discussed in chapter 7). An auditor will conduct detailed substantive tests of transactions throughout the year and detailed substantive tests of balances recorded at year end (discussed in chapter 8, 9, 10 and 11). This detailed testing provides the evidence that the auditor requires to determine whether the financial statements are fairly presented (discussed in chapter 13).

3.1.3 Concluding and reporting on an audit

The final stage of the audit involves drawing conclusions based on the evidence gathered and arriving at an opinion regarding the fair presentation of the financial statements. The auditor's opinion is expressed in the audit report (see chapter 13). At this stage of the audit, an auditor will draw on their understanding of the client, their detailed knowledge of the risks faced by the client, and the conclusions drawn when testing the client's controls, transactions, and account balances.

BEFORE YOU GO ON
3.1.1 What are the three main stages of the audit?
3.1.2 List three factors that affect an auditor's preliminary risk identification.
3.1.3 What are related parties?

3.2 GAINING AN UNDERSTANDING OF THE CLIENT

At the outset of every audit, an auditor must gain an understanding of their client. This allows the auditor to make a reasonable preliminary risk assessment and to assess planning materiality. It also allows the auditor to determine the appropriateness of the entity's accounting policies, identify areas where additional audit work may be required (i.e., related parties), and develop expectations for analytics. This ensures the auditor is able to assess the risk that the financial statements contain a material misstatement due to:

- the nature of the client's business
- the industry in which the client operates
- the level of competition within that industry
- the client's customers and suppliers
- the regulatory environment in which the client operates

CAS 315 provides guidance on the steps to take when gaining an understanding of a client. It requires the auditor to do the following:

1. Make inquiries of management and of others within the entity who may have information to help identify the risk of material misstatements. This includes making inquiries of both financial and non-financial staff at all levels of the organization, including those charged with governance, internal audit, sales, and operational personnel.

2. Perform analytical procedures at the planning stage of the audit to identify any unusual or unexpected relationships that may highlight where risks exist. Analytical procedures are a study of plausible relationships between both financial and non-financial data.

3. Perform observation and inspection procedures to corroborate the responses made by management and others within the organization. These procedures also provide information about the entity and its environment. Examples of such audit procedures include observation or inspection of the entity's operations, premises, and facilities; business plans and strategies; internal control manuals; and any reports prepared and reviewed by management (such as management reports, interim financial statements, and minutes of board of directors' meetings).

By performing these activities, the auditor will gain an understanding of the issues at the entity level, the industry level, and the economy level.

Margin: Explain the process used in gaining an understanding of the client.

Excerpt 3 — page 85

3.4 Fraud Risk 85

Application of the fraud triangle

According to Dr. Donald Cressey, a criminologist who has studied fraudsters, three factors need to be present for fraud: incentives and pressures, opportunities, and attitudes and rationalizations. This has become known as the fraud triangle.

All of these factors can be found in Bernie Madoff's $50-billion Ponzi scheme, which has been described as one of the largest frauds in U.S. history.

Incentives and Pressures
Mr. Madoff, as manager of Ascot Investments, became known in the 1980s for producing double-digit returns and creating significant wealth for his clients. However, the 1987 stock market crash and the subsequent slow economic recovery made such returns impossible. His steady 10- to 12-percent investment returns suddenly dropped to 4.5 percent. It was at this time that Mr. Madoff felt the pressure to maintain the returns his firm had become known for. He started taking investors' capital to pay out redeeming investors and falsified results to show big returns to appear more successful.

Opportunities
How was Mr. Madoff able to pull off such a large fraud? Apparently, Mr. Madoff refused to disclose how he was able to earn such significant returns and investors never pressed for more information beyond the falsified return statement

they received. He did admit, however, to turning down potential clients if they asked too many questions about his investment strategies.

Rationalization
Mr. Madoff rationalized his fraudulent scheme as he believed everyone was greedy. He claims he warned potential investors that his investment choices could be risky and lead to losses, and the drive for larger returns simply led them to give him more money.

In 2009, Mr. Madoff pleaded guilty to several U.S. federal felonies and he was sentenced to 150 years in prison. While this does little to rectify the losses of his victims, perhaps the best lesson we can take from this case is that when all elements of the fraud triangle are present, a "potent combination of elements" exists. While it is virtually impossible to prevent all fraud, knowing and understanding the fraud triangle can make a significant difference in reducing one's exposure.

Sources: Ali Velshi, "Ex-Nasdaq Chair Arrested for Securities Fraud," $50 Billion Ponzi Scheme," CNN Money, December 12, 2008; Robert Lenzner, "Bernie Madoff's $50 Billion Ponzi Scheme," Forbes, December 2008; David Lieberman, Pallavi Gogoi, Theresa Howard, Kevin McCoy, and Matt Krantz, "Investors Remain Amazed over Madoff's Sudden Downfall," USA Today, December 15, 2008; "Bernard Madoff Gets 150 Years behind Bars for Fraud Scheme," CBC News, June 29, 2009; Walter Pavlo, "Bernard Madoff Is The Fraud Triangle," Forbes, March 2011.

Cloud 9
Suzie explains that fraud risk is always present and that auditors must explicitly consider it as part of their risk assessment. Being aware of the incentives and pressures, opportunities, and attitudes within the client relating to fraud helps the auditor make the assessment. Ian admits that he has a little trouble understanding the difference between incentives and attitudes, but he thinks he understands the concept of opportunity. Suzie explains that incentives relate to what pushes (or pulls) a person to commit a fraud. Examples include a need for money to pay debts or gamble. Attitudes or rationalization relate to the thinking about the act of fraud. For example, a person believes it is acceptable to steal from a nasty boss; that is, the theft is justified by the boss's nastiness.

3.4.4 Audit procedures relating to fraud

Besides assessing the fraud risk factors noted above, the following are some of the specific procedures the auditor should perform to comply with CAS 240:

1. The auditor should ask management and those charged with governance if they are aware of a known fraud or suspect there has been a fraud. If the company being audited has an internal audit department, it should also be asked this question. The results of these enquiries should be documented.

2. All members of the audit team, including the partner, should attend a team planning meeting. During this planning meeting, the significant fraud risk factors and where the financial statements may be particularly susceptible to fraud should be reviewed. This allows the more experienced team members to share their knowledge with the less experienced members.

3. The auditor should perform preliminary analytics (discussed in more detail in chapter 4) to identify any unusual relationships that may indicate fraud and thus require further investigation during the audit.

Excerpt 4 — page 93

Summary 93

When the overaccrual reverses in the next year, there will be a boost to profit, and therefore managers will receive a bonus on the amount that they are able to "shift" into the next year. Managers take the same action to reduce profit if it is likely to be above the required maximum, therefore deferring the profit and bonus to the following year. However, if profit is between the required minimum and maximum, managers will try to increase profit to increase their bonus.

The lesson from the academic research is that if auditors understand how the bonus arrangement works, they will be more alert to the type of profit shifting likely to be attempted by managers.

Sources: Hugh MacKenzie, "All in a Day's Work? CEO Pay in Canada," Canadian Centre for Policy Alternatives, January 2014; Paul Healy, "The Effect of Bonus Schemes on Accounting Decisions," *Journal of Accounting and Economics*, April 1985, pp. 85–107.

Cloud 9
The partner, Jo Wadley, has learned of pressure from the parent company on Cloud 9's management to increase revenue by 3 percent this year. Jo is also aware of cost increases associated with a new store and sponsorship deals. Jo believes that this places additional pressure on Cloud 9's management to meet targets, resulting in additional risks for closing procedures. Jo has instructed Suzie to allocate additional time to auditing closing procedures on the Cloud 9 audit.

BEFORE YOU GO ON
3.8.1 Explain how an auditor can assess the risk associated with their client's closing procedures.
3.8.2 Outline how an auditor can assess the adequacy of their client's closing procedures.
3.8.3 What is the particular risk when an auditor believes that their client is under pressure to report strong results?

SUMMARY

1 Identify the different stages of an audit.

The stages of an audit include planning, performing, and reporting. During the planning stage, an auditor will gain an understanding of their client in order to make an informed risk assessment, develop an audit strategy, and set their planning materiality. During the performing stage, an auditor will execute their detailed testing of every audit procedure while reviewing all of the evidence gathered throughout the audit and arriving at a conclusion regarding the fair presentation of the client's financial statements. The auditor will then write an audit report that reflects their opinion based upon their findings.

2 Explain the process used in gaining an understanding of the client.

An auditor will gain an understanding of their client to aid in the risk identification process. This process involves consideration of issues at the entity level, the industry level, and the broader economic level. At the entity level, an auditor will identify the client's major customers,

suppliers, and stakeholders (that is, banks, shareholders, and employees). The auditor will also determine whether their client is an importer or exporter, who the client's competitors are, what the client's capacity is to adapt to changes in technology, and what the nature of any warranties provided to customers is. At the industry level, an auditor is interested in their client's position within its industry. At the economic level, an auditor will assess how well positioned the client is to cope with current and changing government policy and economic conditions.

3 Explain how related parties can impact risk.

Related parties include parent companies, subsidiaries, joint ventures, associates, company management, and close family members of key management. Since related parties are not independent of each other, these transactions may not be in the normal course of business. This increases the risk of material misstatement and may impact the overall financial results. Therefore, related party transactions require some specific consideration throughout the audit and specific procedures should be performed and documented.

Multiple-choice questions provide a self-test opportunity to confirm understanding of the concepts presented in the chapter. Solutions are provided at the end of the chapter.

Review questions test your understanding of the material presented in the chapter and encourage considered comment.

Professional application questions are graded as basic, moderate, or challenging and specifically test your understanding of the material presented in the chapter on the learning objectives indicated.

Case study—Cloud 9 questions continue the Cloud 9 case presented in the textbook and encourage detailed evaluation of the scenario presented. These challenging exercises are ideal for group discussion and build professional communication skills. In addition, longer case-type questions allow students to analyze information and pull together concepts from the chapter and apply them to real-world situations.

Research questions take you beyond the text and encourage you to complete various research-based activities.

BRIEF CONTENTS

CONTENTS

13 Completing and reporting on the audit 466

CHAPTER 1

Introduction and overview of audit and assurance

LEARNING OBJECTIVES

After studying this chapter, you should be able to:

1 define an assurance engagement

2 explain why there is a demand for audit and assurance services

3 differentiate between types of assurance services

4 explain the different levels of assurance

5 outline different audit opinions

6 differentiate between the roles of the preparer and the auditor, and discuss the different firms that provide assurance services

7 identify the different regulators, legislation, and regulations surrounding the assurance process

8 describe the audit expectation gap.

AUDITING AND ASSURANCE STANDARDS

CANADIAN	INTERNATIONAL
Canadian Standards for Assurance Engagements, s. 5000–5790	*International Framework for Assurance Engagements*
CAS 200 *Overall Objectives of the Independent Auditor, and the Conduct of an Audit in Accordance with Canadian Auditing Standards*	ISA 200 *Overall Objectives of the Independent Auditor and the Conduct of an Audit in Accordance with International Standards on Auditing*
CAS 210 *Agreeing the Terms of Audit Engagements*	ISA 210 *Agreeing the Terms of Audit Engagements*
CAS 220 *Quality Control for an Audit of Financial Statements*	ISA 220 *Quality Control for an Audit of Financial Statements*
CAS 240 *The Auditor's Responsibilities Relating to Fraud in an Audit of Financial Statements*	ISA 240 *The Auditor's Responsibilities Relating to Fraud in an Audit of Financial Statements*
CAS 610 *Using the Work of Internal Auditors*	ISA 610 *Using the Work of Internal Auditors*
CAS 700 *Forming an Opinion and Reporting on Financial Statements*	ISA 700 *Forming an Opinion and Reporting on Financial Statements*
CAS 705 *Modifications to the Opinion in the Independent Auditor's Report*	ISA 705 *Modifications to the Opinion in the Independent Auditor's Report*
CAS 706 *Emphasis of Matter Paragraphs and Other Matter Paragraphs in the Independent Auditor's Report*	ISA 706 *Emphasis of Matter Paragraphs and Other Matter Paragraphs in the Independent Auditor's Report*
Canadian Standards for Assurance Engagements s.7050	ISRE 2410 *Review of Interim Financial Information Performed by the Independent Auditor of the Entity*
	IAPS 1010 *The Consideration of Environmental Matters in the Audit of Financial Statements*
CSQC 1 *Quality Control for Firms that Perform Audits and Reviews of Financial Statements, Other Financial Information, and Other Assurance Engagements*	ISQC 1 *Quality Control for Firms that Perform Audits and Reviews of Financial Statements, and Other Assurance and Related Services Engagements*
Canadian Standards for Assurance Engagements, Review Engagements, s. 8100–8600	
Canadian Standards for Assurance Engagements, Compilation Engagements, s. 9200	

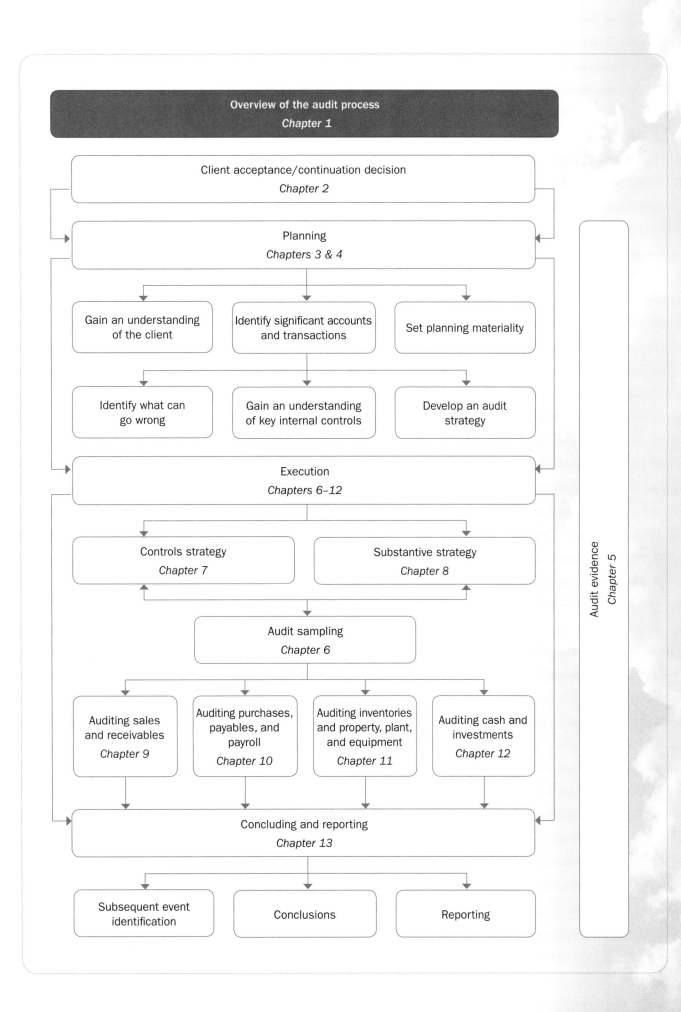

Cloud 9

This book is designed to provide students with the opportunity to learn about auditing by using a practical, problem-based approach. Each chapter begins with some information about an audit client—Cloud 9 Ltd. (Cloud 9). The chapter then provides the underlying concepts and background information needed to deal with this client's situation and the problems facing its auditor. As students work through the chapters, they gradually build up their knowledge of auditing by studying how the contents of each chapter are applied to Cloud 9. The end-of-chapter exercises and problems also provide students with the opportunity to study other aspects of Cloud 9's audit, in addition to applying the knowledge gained in the chapter to other practical examples.

Cloud 9 Ltd., a subsidiary of Cloud 9 Inc., a listed company in Canada, is looking to expand. McLellan's Shoes is seen as a potential target.

In 1980, Ron McLellan starts a business in manufacturing and retailing customized basketball shoes. Ron calls his business McLellan's Shoes. Ron borrows from the bank to start the business, using his house as security, and over the years he works very hard to establish a profitable niche in the highly competitive sport shoe market. Ron is able to repay the bank in 1990, just before the recession. As he watches interest rates soar above 20 percent, he vows never to borrow again.

As the business grows, Ron's wife and three adult children start to work for him, with responsibility for administration, marketing and sales, production, and distribution. By the early 1990s, Ron's business employs 20 people full-time, most of whom work in production. There are also several casual employees and part-time staff in the retail outlet, particularly during busy periods.

In February 1992, Ron receives a call from Chip Masters, the senior vice-president of Cloud 9 Inc. Chip expresses an interest in buying McLellan's Shoes. Ron is getting tired, and his children are starting to fight among themselves about who is going to take over from their father. Ron has had enough, but he does not want Chip to know that. He asks if Chip is ready to talk about the price. Chip says he is, but first he needs to see the audited financial statements for McLellan's Shoes.

Ron asks for some time. He tells Chip that he needs to talk to his family and will get back to him. When Ron puts the phone down he immediately rings his friend from the golf club, Ernie Black, who is a professional accountant. For years, Ernie has been quietly suggesting to Ron that his business affairs need attention. Ron is skilled at making deals and working hard, but he has never bothered with sophisticated financial arrangements. He has never had a formal set of financial statements prepared for McLellan's Shoes. Ron is in a panic—he wants to sell McLellan's Shoes, but what is he going to do about Chip's request for audited financial statements?

AUDIT PROCESS IN FOCUS

The purpose of this chapter is to provide an overview of audit and assurance services. As the focus of this book is the audit of financial statements, we begin with an overview of what an audit is, and why and how it is done. We discuss the reasons why there is a demand for audit and assurance services. We also introduce some of the assurance and audit terms that will be used throughout the text. We then go on to define assurance engagements and differentiate between the various types of assurance engagements. The assurance engagements explained in this chapter include financial statement audits, compliance audits, operational audits, comprehensive audits, and internal audits. We also discuss the emerging area of assurance of corporate social responsibility disclosures. We then provide an overview of the different levels of assurance that can be provided when conducting assurance procedures. The levels of assurance discussed in the chapter include reasonable, moderate, and no assurance engagements.

Next, we provide a brief overview of the different audit opinions that an auditor can arrive at after completing an audit. An auditor can provide either an unmodified or a modified audit opinion. Unmodified or modified opinions can include an emphasis of matter paragraph, which is intended to draw the reader of the opinion to a specific matter. If a modified opinion is used, the auditor has the choice of three types of modifications: qualified, adverse, or a disclaimer of opinion. These concepts are explained further in this chapter.

The roles of the financial statement preparer and auditor are explained and contrasted. An overview of the different firms that provide assurance services is then given. That section contains details about both accounting and consulting firms and the different services they provide. An overview of assurance regulators and their regulations is provided. The audit expectation gap is explained in the last section of the chapter.

1.1 AUDITING AND ASSURANCE DEFINED

An assurance is an engagement where an auditor or consultant is hired to provide an opinion on a subject matter. This is done to enhance the reliability of the information. According to the CPA Canada Handbook, an **assurance engagement** is an engagement where a practitioner is engaged to issue a written report and concludes on a subject matter for which the accountable party is responsible. Therefore, a prerequisite for an assurance engagement is the existence of an **accountability relationship**, where one party is answerable to another for the subject matter (s. 5025.04).

An assurance practitioner may be an auditor working in public practice providing assurance on financial statements or a consultant providing assurance about environmental disclosures. As illustrated in the triangle in figure 1.1, there must be an accountability relationship where a person or organization is responsible to the users for the subject matter. For a financial statement audit, the company is the accountable party, its shareholders are the users, and the subject matter is the financial statements. Engagements where the practitioner is hired to provide advice to clients, such as management and tax consulting, are not assurance engagements, as there is no accountability relationship between management and users.

While the audit of a company's financial statements is one of the most common types of assurance engagements and the focus of much of this book, it is not the only type of assurance engagement.

Later in this chapter, section 1.3 provides a description of some of the different types of assurance services.

 1 Define an assurance engagement.

assurance engagement an engagement performed by an auditor or consultant to enhance the reliability of the subject matter

accountability relationship a situation in which one party is answerable to another for the subject matter

FIGURE 1.1 **Parties involved in an assurance engagement**

Cloud 9

Chip Masters has asked Ron McLellan for audited financial statements of McLellan's Shoes. He has heard about tax audits, efficiency audits, and financial statement audits. Are they all the same thing? Ernie explains to Ron that there are several services that people call "audits" that are different from financial statement audits. However, all these services, including financial statement audits, can be defined as assurance engagements.

When you are acquiring a new skill, it is often necessary to become familiar with new terminology. This section presents a number of key assurance and audit terms to introduce you to the language of auditing.

TERM	DEFINITION
applicable financial reporting framework	The financial framework chosen by management to prepare a company's financial statements. For example, an applicable framework for a reporting issuer would be International Financial Reporting Standards (IFRS). An applicable framework for a private enterprise could be Accounting Standards for Private Enterprises (ASPE), or it could be IFRS.
assertions	Statements made by management regarding the recognition, measurement, and presentation and disclosure of items in the financial statements.
audit evidence	Information used by the auditor to support the audit opinion.
audit file	The file where the evidence and documentation of the work performed are kept as a permanent record to support the opinion issued.
audit plan	The list or description of audit procedures to be performed.
audit risk	The risk that the auditor may express an inappropriate opinion. This means the auditor may indicate that the financial statements are not materially misstated when in fact they are.
financial statements	A structured representation of historical financial information, including the related notes.
independent auditor's report	The auditor's formal expression of opinion on whether the financial statements are in accordance with the applicable financial reporting framework.
internal control	The processes implemented and maintained by management to help the entity achieve its objectives.
material	An amount or disclosure that is significant enough to make a difference to a user. For example, if a company reports a profit of $100,000 and the auditor finds an error resulting in an overstatement of net income by $10, this probably wouldn't affect an investor's decision. However, if the auditor finds an error overstating revenue by $50,000, or 50 percent of the profit, this likely would affect the user's decision and would therefore be considered material.
materiality	The maximum amount of misstatement or omission the auditor can tolerate and still issue an unmodified or "clean" audit opinion.
sufficient and appropriate evidence	The quantity (sufficiency) and quality (appropriateness) of the evidence collected by the auditor.
unmodified opinion	The auditor's opinion concluding that the financial statements are fairly presented. (Also called an "unqualified opinion.")
working papers	Paper or electronic documentation of the audit created by the audit team as evidence of the work completed.

BEFORE YOU GO ON

1.1.1 What are two examples of assurance providers?

1.1.2 What might an assurance provider express a conclusion about?

1.1.3 What is an accountability relationship?

1.2 DEMAND FOR AUDIT AND ASSURANCE SERVICES

In this section we will provide an overview of the key financial statement users and their requirements. This is followed by a description of why these users may demand an audit of the financial statements. Next, three theoretical frameworks that have been used to encapsulate these sources of demand are described. Finally, the demand for assurance services in a voluntary setting is explored.

2 Explain why there is a demand for audit and assurance services.

1.2.1 Financial statement users

Financial statement users include current and potential investors (shareholders if the entity is a company), suppliers, customers, lenders, employees, governments, and the general public. Each of these groups will read the financial statements for a slightly different reason. Each group of users and their reasons for reading a company's financial statement is described below.

Investors

In the case of a company, investors generally read the financial statements to determine whether they should invest in or buy, hold, or sell shares in the entity being reported on. They are interested in the return on their investment and are concerned that the entity will remain a going concern into the foreseeable future. Investors may also be interested in the capacity of the entity to pay a dividend. Prospective investors read financial statements to determine whether they should buy shares in the entity.

Suppliers

Suppliers may read the financial statements to determine whether the entity can pay them for goods supplied. They are also interested in whether the entity is likely to remain a going concern (that is, it is likely to continue to be a customer of the supplier) and continue to be able to pay its debts as and when they fall due.

Customers

If customers rely on the entity for their business, they may read the financial statements to determine whether the entity is likely to remain a going concern.

Lenders

Lenders may read the financial statements to determine whether the entity can pay the interest and principal on their loans as and when they fall due.

Employees

Employees may read the financial statements to determine whether the entity can pay their wages or salaries and other entitlements (for example, holiday pay). They may also be interested in assessing the future stability and profitability of the entity, as this affects their job security.

Governments

Governments may read the financial statements to determine whether the entity is complying with regulations and paying a fair amount of taxation given its reported earnings, and to gain a better understanding of the entity's activities. An entity in receipt of government grants may provide a copy of its financial statements when applying for a grant and when reporting on how grant funds have been spent.

The general public

The general public may read the financial statements to determine whether they should associate with the entity (for example, as a future employee, customer, or supplier) and to gain a better understanding of the entity, what it does, and its plans for the future.

1.2.2 Sources of demand for audit and assurance services

Financial statement users and their needs, as outlined in the previous section, are many and varied. There are a number of reasons why some or all of these users would demand audited financial statements. The primary reason is to reduce **information risk**, which is the risk that users will rely on incorrect information to make a decision. The causes of information risk include remoteness, complexity, competing incentives, and reliability. Each of these concepts is now explained.

information risk the risk that users will rely on incorrect information to make a decision

Remoteness

Most financial statement users do not have access to the entity under review. This makes it difficult to determine whether the information contained in the financial statements is a fair presentation of the entity and its activities for the relevant period.

Complexity

Most financial statement users do not have the accounting and legal knowledge to enable them to assess the complex accounting and disclosure choices being made by the entity.

Competing incentives

Management has an incentive to disclose the information contained in the financial statements in a way that helps them achieve their own objectives—for example, to present their performance in the best possible light. Users may find it difficult to identify when management is presenting biased information.

Reliability

Financial statement users are concerned with the reliability of the information contained in the financial statements. As they use that information to make decisions that have real consequences (financial and otherwise, such as assessing the future viability of the company), it is very important that users are able to rely on the facts contained in the financial statements.

An independent third-party review of the information contained in the financial statements by a team of auditors, who have the knowledge and expertise to assess the fair presentation of the information being presented by the preparers, aids users across all of these issues. Auditors have access to entity records, so they are not remote. They are trained accountants and have detailed knowledge about the complex technical accounting and disclosure issues required to assess the choices made by the financial statement preparers. Independent auditors have no incentives to aid the entity in presenting its results in the best possible light. They are concerned with ensuring that the information contained in the financial statements is reliable and free from any significant (material) misstatements (error or fraud).

Cloud 9

Ron tells Ernie that he has no remote users, such as shareholders or lenders, and his business is not very complex. He is the owner and the manager of McLellan's Shoes and therefore has no competing incentives. For all these reasons, he has never felt the need to purchase an audit to assure users of the reliability of his business's financial information. Ernie agrees, but points out that there is now a user who is very interested in the reliability of the financial information—Chip Masters.

1.2.3 Theoretical frameworks

The reasons for demanding audit and assurance services outlined in the previous section have led to the development of three theoretical frameworks that have been used to explain why audits occurred prior to regulations requiring that they be done, why users may demand an audit from

Cross-functional organizations

Taking a cross-functional view of the internal organization essentially means applying the concepts of supply chain management to the internal organizational structures, incentives, and metrics. It may also involve strategic-level analyses of what adds value and what does not add value in a supply chain. This can be called a **value chain analysis,** defined in the *APICS Dictionary,* 15th edition, as

> an examination of all links a company uses to produce and deliver its products and services, starting from the origination point and continuing through delivery to the final customer.

Once the organization decides who it wants to partner with and who it can omit, the next thing is to ensure that it is capable of collaborating effectively. Changing organizational structures to become more cross-functional often takes the form of focusing more on process flows than on functional areas. When processes are considered to be more important than the functions that perform them, organizations gain an overall systems perspective, which helps to ensure that each aspect of the process is value added and takes the final result and the total of all costs into account.

A process of getting a new product to market, for example, would start with research and development and then include procurement management, production, distribution, and marketing and sales (including order management). Clearly, this process, as defined, goes outside of what one department might do. However, due to inefficiencies and the need to optimize the overall process, organizations have found it necessary to develop a method of getting these departments to act as one. This unifying role was initially called materials management and is now more commonly called logistics management, and the function is called logistics. The *Dictionary* defines **logistics** as follows:

> 1) In a supply chain management context, it is the subset of supply chain management that controls the forward and reverse movement, handling, and storage of goods between origin and distribution points. 2) In an industrial context, the art and science of obtaining, producing, and distributing material and product in the proper place and in proper quantities. 3) In a military sense (where it has greater usage), its meaning can also include the movement of personnel.

Supply chain managers take the concept of a unifying role beyond even the boundaries of logistics. The most senior supply chain manager might have some degree of authority over an entire process. For example, this role could ensure that product design accounts for the needs of the later parts of the process, including ease of production and distribution. Similarly, a person in this position could ensure that overall inventory targets are maintained. When appropriate, a unifying role such as this might also work with other support functions, such as finance, information systems, or human resources, to ensure that the needs of the overall process come first. Often, supply chain managers will also be involved in risk management from an organization and/or supply

a certain type of firm (for example, an international or an industry specialist firm), and why users may demand assurance of voluntarily disclosed information (for example, environmental reports). The three theories are agency theory, the information hypothesis, and the insurance hypothesis. Each is described in turn.

Agency theory

When an individual is an owner-manager of his or her own business, there are no competing incentives. The owner (principal) and manager (agent) are one. When an owner hires a manager to run the business on his or her behalf, potential conflicts arise. The manager has an incentive to provide favourable results. If there is one owner, he or she can more easily monitor the activities of the manager. When there are several owners (such as shareholders of a large company), it is difficult for the owners to monitor the activities of the management. Agency theory tells us that due to the remoteness of the owners from the entity, the complexity of items included in the financial statements, and competing incentives between the owners and managers, the owners (principals) have an incentive to hire an auditor (incur a monitoring cost) to assess the fair presentation of the information contained in the financial statements prepared by their managers (agents).

Information hypothesis

Financial statement users require access to high-quality information to make a variety of decisions. That information is used to determine whether to hold or sell shares in the entity, whether to lend money to the entity, what rate of interest to charge the entity on money lent, and so on. The greater the perceived quality of the information contained in the financial statements, the more likely it will be relied upon by the users of that information. The information hypothesis tells us that due to the demand for reliable, high-quality information, various user groups, including shareholders, banks, and other lenders, will demand that financial statements be audited to aid their decision-making.

Insurance hypothesis

Investors take on a risk when buying shares. If the entity fails, investors could lose the money invested. According to the insurance hypothesis, an audit is one way for investors to insure against at least part of their loss should the company they invest in fail. As auditors are required to take out professional indemnity insurance policies, they are seen as having "deep pockets" (that is, access to money), should an investor be able to prove that audit failure was to blame, at least in part, for a loss. The insurance hypothesis tells us that investors will demand that financial statements be audited as a way of insuring against some of their loss should their investment fail.

Cloud 9

Cloud 9 is considering buying McLellan's Shoes from Ron. In effect, it is considering investing in the business. If the business fails, the shareholders of Cloud 9 will lose their money. The new investors have incentives that are in competition with Ron's. If Ron purchases an audit, he is providing assurance to the potential new investors about the fair presentation of the financial statements. The audit also increases the perceived reliability of the information in the financial statements. For example, the outsiders know that Ron will have to convince an auditor of the appropriateness of the reporting decisions he is making.

Purchasing an audit is also a way of taking insurance against any possible loss by creating the opportunity for investors to recover their investment from the auditor. In reality, the auditor is not guaranteeing the success of the business, only providing reasonable assurance that the financial statements comply with the relevant laws and standards and gives a fair presentation of the business's financial position and performance. There is little chance of a successful legal action against an auditor unless it can be established that the auditor failed to perform to a reasonable standard.

1.2.4 Demand in a voluntary setting

While the main focus of this book is the audit of company financial statements, assurance providers (including auditors and consultants) provide other assurance services (as outlined in section 1.3). The theories outlined above are now being used to understand more about the demand for assurance of corporate social responsibility (CSR) disclosures, including environmental, sustainability, and carbon emissions reports.

It is becoming more common for companies to voluntarily disclose CSR information in their annual reports, on their websites, and in separate stand-alone reports. This trend toward increased disclosures has been in response to stakeholder (shareholder, lender, employee, customer, supplier, and public) demand that companies be more accountable for their impact on the environment and on society. Stakeholders are concerned about more than just profits and returns on shareholder funds. They want to know what impact companies are having on our environment and what actions are being taken by those companies to reduce that impact.

Stakeholders are concerned about the reliability of environmental and other CSR disclosures. Just as the provision of these disclosures is voluntary, so is the assurance. Companies are not required to have their environmental and other CSR disclosures assured, yet several companies do. Assurance is provided to meet user demands for high-quality, reliable information and to demonstrate a high level of corporate responsibility.

BEFORE YOU GO ON

1.2.1 Who are the main users of company financial statements?

1.2.2 Why might financial statement users demand an audit?

1.2.3 What are the three most common theories used to explain the origins of the demand for audit and assurance services?

1.3 DIFFERENT ASSURANCE SERVICES

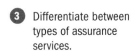
3 Differentiate between types of assurance services.

In this section, we provide an overview of the different types of assurance services that an assurance practitioner can provide. Common types of assurance engagements are financial statement audits, compliance audits, operational audits, comprehensive audits, and internal audits. We will also briefly consider assurance on corporate social responsibility (CSR) disclosures. Each will now be explained in turn.

1.3.1 Financial statement audits

financial statement audit an audit that provides reasonable assurance about whether the financial statements are prepared in all material respects in accordance with the financial reporting framework

According to CAS 200 *Overall Objectives of the Independent Auditor and the Conduct of an Audit in Accordance with Canadian Auditing Standards,* the objective of a **financial statement audit** is for the auditor to express an opinion about whether the financial statements are prepared in all material respects in accordance with a financial reporting framework (CAS 200, para. 11). Within a Canadian context, this means that the financial statements have been prepared in accordance with Canadian generally accepted accounting principles (GAAP) and any relevant legislation, such as the Canada Business Corporations Act.

This means that when a set of financial statements has been audited, the information presented has been verified by an independent auditor. To do this, the auditor methodically gathers evidence to corroborate the financial information presented by management. At the end of an audit engagement, the auditor issues a report indicating whether the financial information is fairly presented in accordance with the financial reporting framework. This lends credibility to the information.

listed entity an entity whose shares, stock, or debt are listed on a stock exchange

fair presentation the consistent and faithful application of accounting standards when preparing the financial statements

The Canadian Securities Administrators (CSA) requires **listed entities** to publish audited financial statements annually. It is the auditor's responsibility to form an opinion on the fair presentation of the financial statements. **Fair presentation** refers to the consistent and faithful application of the accounting standards. In fulfilling their role, the auditor must be independent of the company audited and exercise due professional care.

Cloud 9

Ron believes that his business has good, reliable financial records. Ron's wife helps him keep tight control of the cash and other assets, and together they prepare some simple reports on a regular basis. Ron believes he knows exactly what is happening in the business and monitors the business's cash flow and profit very closely. However, he has not prepared financial statements that comply with Canadian generally accepted accounting principles (GAAP). Is this a problem? Ernie explains to Ron that some businesses must apply the accounting standards. For example, if a company requires audited financial statements to meet regulatory requirements or form part of a loan agreement, then the financial statements must comply with Canadian GAAP.

Process of a financial statement audit

An audit is a systematic process. It involves the gathering of evidence in a logical fashion to substantiate the balances and disclosures in the financial statements. All audits should follow the same process to ensure that professional standards are met. Regardless of the size or complexity of the entity, auditing principles remain the same. Some engagements may be riskier than others, so the amount of work performed and the time spent may vary, but the sequence to be followed is the same for all audits.

The first step in this sequence is the planning stage. This involves performing an overall risk assessment. The auditor documents an understanding of the business, its environment, and its processes to determine where the greatest risks may be. The auditor then devises an overall audit strategy, taking these risks into consideration. This allows the auditor to plan when to perform the "field work" (the work to be done at the client's premises), who will do it, and what exactly needs to be done. Tasks are usually divided by business cycle or financial statement groupings (for example, purchasing cycle; cash; property, plant, and equipment). The financial statement accounts related to each cycle are divided into sections. For each section there should be an "audit working paper program" that lists the procedures to be performed for that area.

During the execution stage, the auditor typically works at the client's premises. When the auditor is not a sole practitioner, and carries out the engagement as part of a team, staff members are assigned sections to complete, which generally involves obtaining information, assessing it, and having discussions with the client's staff regarding systems, procedures, and clarification as required. As the work is done, it is documented in the audit working paper file (which may be electronic or paper). The documentation is done through the use of narrative, memos, or schedules with audit "ticks" (common conventions used by auditors to indicate the work performed). The audit programs are "signed off" or initialled by audit members once completed. Each completed section is then reviewed by a more senior auditor, as work must be properly supervised.

Once the field work has been completed, the auditor leaves the client's premises; however, there remain a number of completion procedures to be done. Once all of the required procedures have been performed, the completed file and financial statements go to the partner responsible for the audit for review. If the partner believes there is sufficient and appropriate evidence in the audit file, and the financial statements appear fairly stated, he or she will approve and issue an unmodified audit opinion on the financial statements.

Limitations of a financial statement audit

An audit is conducted to enhance the reliability and credibility of the information in the financial statements. It is not a guarantee that the financial statements are free from fraud and error.

The limitations of an audit result from the nature of financial reporting, the nature of audit procedures, and the need for the audit to be conducted within a reasonable period of time and at a reasonable cost (CAS 200).

"The nature of financial reporting" refers to the use of judgement when preparing financial statements, because of the subjectivity required when arriving at accounting estimates. Judgement is also required when selecting and applying accounting methods.

"The nature of audit procedures" refers to the reliance on evidence provided by the client and its management. If an auditor does not have access to all the information relevant to the audit, there is a limitation in the scope of the audit. If the auditor is unaware of this situation, he or she may arrive at an inappropriate conclusion based on incomplete facts. Evidence may be withheld or modified by perpetrators of fraud. It can be difficult for an auditor to determine whether fraud has occurred and documents altered, as those committing fraud generally hide evidence. Sampling is used when testing transactions and account balances. If a sample is not representative of all items available for testing, an auditor may arrive at an invalid conclusion.

"The timeliness and cost of a financial statement audit" refers to the pressure an auditor faces to complete the audit within a certain time frame at a reasonable cost. While it is important that auditors do not omit procedures in an effort to meet time and cost constraints, they may be under some pressure to do so. This pressure will come from clients wanting to issue their financial statements by a certain date, from clients refusing to pay additional fees for additional audit effort, and from within the audit firm, where there are pressures to complete all audits on a timely basis to avoid incurring costs that may not be recovered. By taking the time to plan the audit properly, an auditor can ensure that adequate time is spent where the risks of a significant error or fraud are greatest.

1.3.2 Compliance audits

compliance audit an audit to determine whether the entity has conformed with regulations, rules, or processes

A **compliance audit** involves gathering evidence to ascertain whether the person or entity under review has followed the applicable rules, policies, procedures, laws, and regulations. There are a number of examples of compliance audits. A tax audit is used to determine whether an individual or company has completed a tax return in accordance with the Income Tax Act. Within an organization, management may specify that certain processes be followed when completing a function. For example, a company may have policies and procedures for the hiring of new staff. In that case, the organization's internal auditors may be called upon to determine whether employees are following the specified processes appropriately.

1.3.3 Operational audits

operational audit an assessment of the economy, efficiency, and effectiveness of an organization's operations

Operational audits are concerned with the economy, efficiency, and effectiveness of an organization's activities. Economy refers to the cost of inputs, including wages and materials. Efficiency refers to the relationship between inputs and outputs; specifically, efficiency refers to the use of the minimum amount of inputs to achieve a given output. Finally, effectiveness refers to the achievement of certain goals or the production of a certain level of outputs. From an organization's perspective it is important to perform well across all three dimensions and not allow one to dominate. For example, if buying cheap inputs results in an inefficient production process, efficiency may be seen to be sacrificed to achieve economic goals.

Operational audits are generally conducted by an organization's internal auditors, or they may be outsourced to an external audit firm. Operational audits are sometimes referred to as value for money audits, performance audits, or efficiency audits.

1.3.4 Comprehensive audits

comprehensive audit an audit that encompasses a range of audit and audit-related activities, such as a financial statement audit, operational audit, and compliance audit

A **comprehensive audit** may encompass elements of a financial statement audit, a compliance audit, and an operational audit. For example, an auditor may report on whether an entity has met its efficiency targets. Comprehensive audits most commonly occur in the public sector, where compliance with various regulations is examined as part of the financial statement audit.

1.3.5 Internal audits

internal audit an independent service within an entity that generally evaluates and improves risk management, internal control procedures, and elements of the governance process

those charged with governance generally the board of directors, and may include management of an entity

Internal audits are conducted to provide assurance about various aspects of an organization's activities. The internal audit function is typically conducted by employees of the organization being audited, but can be outsourced to an external audit firm. As such, the function of internal audit is determined by **those charged with governance** and management within the organization. While the functions of internal audits vary widely from one organization to another, they are often concerned with evaluating and improving risk management, internal control procedures, and elements of the governance process. The internal audit function often conducts operational audits, compliance audits, internal control assessments, and reviews. Many internal auditors are members of the Institute of Internal Auditors (IIA), an international organization with more than 120,000 members that provides guidance and standards to aid internal auditors in their work. When conducting a financial statement audit, the external auditor may consider the work done by the internal auditors (CAS 610 *Using the Work of Internal Auditors*).

1.3.6 Corporate social responsibility (CSR) assurance—An emerging area

Corporate social responsibility (CSR) reporting is voluntary. However, it is becoming more widespread. (See section 1.2.4 of this chapter for a discussion of the demand for assurance in a voluntary setting.) CSR disclosures include environmental, employee, and social reporting. Some organizations choose to have their CSR disclosures assured by an independent assurance provider. For example, Vancity Savings and Credit Union, part of the Vancity Group, voluntarily issues a CSR report, and it is formally assured by an independent third party. The assurance of CSR disclosures can be carried out by both auditors and specialist **consulting firms**. As these disclosures include non-financial as well as financial information, the skill set required to conduct these assurance services is quite broad.

Whether a company chooses to provide additional voluntary environmental disclosures or not, an auditor must still consider the impact of environmental issues on a client's financial statements when conducting the financial statement audit. However, as investors demand more relevant information in this area, further guidance is expected.

corporate social responsibility (CSR) a range of activities undertaken voluntarily by a corporation; CSR disclosures include environmental, employee, and social reporting

consulting firms non-audit firms that provide assurance services on non-financial information, such as corporate social responsibility and environmental disclosures

---

PROFESSIONAL ENVIRONMENT

Assurance engagements on carbon emissions information

Many companies now present CSR information in their annual reports or in separate corporate sustainability reports. In some cases, the reports include information about carbon emissions. However, the reporting and assurance of these reports is voluntary and largely unregulated, raising concerns about the quality of the information. One of these concerns is that the information being provided in CSR reports is not sufficiently quantitative, particularly with respect to carbon emissions data.

Due to the increasing demand for assurance on greenhouse gas information, the International Auditing and Assurance Standards Board (IAASB) developed and approved the International Standard on Assurance Engagements (ISAE) 3410. In Canada, this standard was approved by the Auditing and Assurance Standards Board (AASB) and entitled the Canadian Standard on Assurance Engagements (CSAE) 3410, *Assurance Engagements on Greenhouse Gas Statements.* The goal of the standard is to provide assurance over greenhouse gas information that will give investors, consumers, and other users the comfort in knowing that the information provided by companies is reliable. The standard stipulates an auditor's responsibilities in identifying, assessing, and responding to the risks of material misstatement when engaged to report on greenhouse gas (GHG) statements. It sets out requirements and guidance on the work to be performed and the reporting responsibilities for both reasonable and limited assurance engagements.

The IAASB believes that this standard will enhance the reliability of the emissions information being reported on and as the demand for companies to disclose their emissions information increases, public confidence in assured greenhouse gases statements becomes more significant.

Sources: "IAASB Issues Consultation Paper to Enhance Reporting on Greenhouse Gases," International Federation of Accountants, news release, October 22, 2009; "The IAASB Releases the New Global Standard on Assurance on Greenhouse Gas Emissions," South African Institute of Chartered Accountants, July 2012; "International Standard on Assurance Engagements (ISAE) 3410, Assurance Engagements on Greenhouse Gas Statements, At a Glance," IAASB, June 2012.

Cloud 9

Ron is not concerned about internal audits—his business is too small for a separate internal audit function. He is also not worried about CSR reporting or compliance and operational audits. His priority at the moment is to close the deal with Chip Masters, and he still does not know what he has to do about the audit.

BEFORE YOU GO ON

1.3.1 What are the three elements of an operational audit?

1.3.2 What is the objective of a financial statement audit?

1.3.3 What are the most common tasks of the internal audit function?

1.4 DIFFERENT LEVELS OF ASSURANCE

④ Explain the different levels of assurance.

In this section we describe the different levels of assurance that a practitioner can provide when conducting assurance procedures. An assurance practitioner can provide reasonable assurance, moderate assurance, or no assurance. When providing reasonable and moderate assurance, the practitioner's report is addressed to the party requesting assurance (for example, a company's shareholders). When an assurance practitioner performs a non-assurance engagement, a report on the findings is sent to the responsible party (that is, the organization that prepared the information under consideration). The differences between reasonable, moderate, and no assurance are now explained.

1.4.1 Reasonable assurance

reasonable assurance assurance that provides high but not absolute assurance on the reliability of the subject matter

The objective of a **reasonable assurance** engagement is to gather sufficient evidence upon which to form a positive expression of an opinion regarding whether the information being assured is presented fairly. This means that the auditor has done adequate work to report with reasonable certainty that the information being assured is, or is not, reliable. This does not reflect absolute assurance, as an auditor can never be 100 percent certain that there are no errors or omissions. For example, an auditor is in the position to say whether in their opinion the financial statements are in accordance with relevant laws and accounting standards and they present fairly the financial position of the reporting entity. Auditors can make such a positive statement only if they are reasonably sure that the evidence gathered is sufficient and appropriate. The audit of a company's financial statements is one example of a reasonable assurance engagement. CAS 700 *Forming an Opinion and Reporting on Financial Statements* provides guidance on the form and elements of the audit report.

The audit opinion will depend upon the auditor's findings while conducting the audit. A brief overview of the different opinions that an auditor may form when conducting a financial statement audit is provided in the next section of this chapter. Reasonable assurance is the highest level of assurance provided; again, note that it is high but not absolute assurance. An example of an audit report is provided in figure 1.2.

1.4.2 Moderate assurance

moderate assurance assurance that provides negative assurance on the reliability of the subject matter

The objective of a **moderate assurance** engagement is to perform sufficient procedures and gather sufficient evidence upon which to express a negative assurance form of communication regarding the reliability of the information being assured. This means that the auditor has done adequate work to report whether or not anything came to their attention that would lead them to believe that the information being assured is not worthy of belief. The auditor is not in a position to say that in their opinion the financial statements are in accordance with the relevant law and accounting standards, and does present fairly the financial position and performance of the reporting entity. The auditor is able to say only that the information is plausible, in that nothing makes them believe otherwise. To make a negative statement, auditors do not need to obtain as much evidence or perform as many procedures as when they make a positive statement.

review engagement engagement in which the auditor does adequate work to report whether or not anything came to their attention that would lead them to believe that the information being assured is not fairly presented

The review of a company's financial statements is called a **review engagement**. A review engagement may be requested when the client requires some assurance over the financial statements but does not require an audit level of assurance. For example, a lender of a small business may not want to approve a loan based on financial statements with no assurance, but it may not require the same level of assurance that an audit would provide. CPA Canada Handbook sections 8100–8600 provide guidance on review engagements and the form and elements of the review report. An example of a review report is provided in figure 1.3. The review report highlights the responsibilities of the auditor to comply with Canadian generally accepted standards for review engagements and to ensure that the financial statements comply with Canadian GAAP or another appropriate financial reporting framework. An explanation of the procedures used in conducting the review is provided. The report states explicitly that an audit was not performed and therefore an audit opinion is not being expressed. Finally, the review report includes the conclusion of the auditor that they were not aware of any matter that made them believe that the financial statements were not in all material respects in accordance with GAAP or other appropriate framework (negative assurance).

Ernst & Young LLP
Ernst & Young Tower
222 Bay Street, PO Box 251
Toronto, ON M5K 1J7

Tel: +1 416 864 1234
Fax: +1 416 864 1174
ey.com

INDEPENDENT AUDITORS' REPORT

To the Board of Directors of Skyward Ltd.

We have audited the accompanying consolidated financial statements of Skyward Ltd., which comprise the consolidated statements of financial position as at December 31, 2015 and 2014, and the consolidated statements of comprehensive income, changes in equity and cash flows for the years then ended, and a summary of significant accounting policies and other explanatory information.

Management's responsibility for the consolidated financial statements

Management is responsible for the preparation and fair presentation of these consolidated financial statements in accordance with International Financial Reporting Standards, and for such internal control as management determines is necessary to enable the preparation of consolidated financial statements that are free from material misstatement, whether due to fraud or error.

Auditors' responsibility

Our responsibility is to express an opinion on these consolidated financial statements based on our audits. We conducted our audits in accordance with Canadian generally accepted auditing standards. Those standards require that we comply with ethical requirements and plan and perform the audit to obtain reasonable assurance about whether the consolidated financial statements are free from material misstatement.

An audit involves performing procedures to obtain audit evidence about the amounts and disclosures in the consolidated financial statements. The procedures selected depend on the auditors' judgment, including the assessment of the risks of material misstatement of the consolidated financial statements, whether due to fraud or error. In making those risk assessments, the auditors consider internal control relevant to the entity's preparation and fair presentation of the consolidated financial statements in order to design audit procedures that are appropriate in the circumstances, but not for the purpose of expressing an opinion on the effectiveness of the entity's internal control. An audit also includes evaluating the appropriateness of accounting policies used and the reasonableness of accounting estimates made by management, as well as evaluating the overall presentation of the consolidated financial statements.

We believe that the audit evidence we have obtained in our audits is sufficient and appropriate to provide a basis for our audit opinion.

Opinion

In our opinion, the consolidated financial statements present fairly, in all material respects, the financial position of Skyward Ltd. as at December 31, 2015 and 2014, and its financial performance and its cash flows for the years then ended in accordance with International Financial Reporting Standards.

Toronto, Canada

February X, 2016.

"Ernst & Young LLP"

Chartered Professional Accountants
Licensed Public Accountants

A member firm of Ernst & Young Global Limited

FIGURE 1.2 **Example of an audit report**

Source: EY, 2014

EY

Building a better
working world

Ernst & Young LLP   Tel: +1 416 864 1234
Ernst & Young Tower   Fax: +1 416 864 1174
222 Bay Street, PO Box 251 ey.com
Toronto, ON M5K 1J7

REVIEW ENGAGEMENT REPORT

To the Board of Directors of Skyward Ltd.

We have reviewed the consolidated balance sheets of Skyward Ltd. as at December 31, 2015 and the consolidated statements of income, retained earnings and cash flows for the year then ended. Our review was made in accordance with Canadian generally accepted standards for review engagements and, accordingly, consisted primarily of inquiry, analytical procedures and discussion related to information supplied to us by the company.

A review does not constitute an audit and, consequently, we do not express an audit opinion on these consolidated financial statements.

Based on our review, nothing has come to our attention that causes us to believe that these consolidated financial statements are not, in all material respects, in accordance with Canadian accounting standards for private enterprises.

Toronto, Canada   "Ernst & Young LLP"

February X, 2016.   Chartered Professional Accountants
                                       Licensed Public Accountants

A member firm of Ernst & Young Global Limited

FIGURE 1.3 **Example of a review engagement report**
Source: EY, 2014

In conducting a review, an auditor will obtain an understanding of the entity under review; identify potential material misstatements where effort should be concentrated; and conduct analytical procedures, enquiries of entity personnel, and other tasks to aid in the formulation of their report. The work done when conducting a review is less extensive than the work done when conducting an audit. Specifically, an auditor will make enquiries of key personnel, apply analytical procedures, and hold discussions with client staff. That is why an auditor can provide only moderate (limited) assurance after completing a review. It is also why this engagement is less time-consuming and therefore less costly.

1.4.3 No assurance

An assurance provider may perform other services for clients for which **no assurance** is provided. In such circumstances an assurance provider must ensure when reporting to users that they make clear that they are merely reporting the activities that they have performed (and in some engagements, their findings) and are not providing assurance. An example of an engagement where no assurance is provided is a **compilation engagement**, where an auditor compiles the financial information as provided by the client and arranges it into a set of financial statements. The accountant ensures that the information is mathematically correct but does not perform any procedures to assure that the information is not materially misstated, and therefore no expression of assurance is provided. However, the auditor must ensure that they are not associated with information that may be false or misleading.

To ensure that users are aware that no assurance is being provided, the auditor attaches what is called a **Notice to Reader** report to the financial statements. The Notice to Reader report explicitly states that no assurance is being provided. An example of a Notice to Reader is provided in figure 1.4.

no assurance what results when an auditor completes a set of tasks requested by the client and reports factually on the results of that work to the client

compilation engagement engagement in which an auditor compiles a set of financial statements based on the information provided by the client, ensuring mathematical accuracy

Notice to Reader the communication issued when the auditor performs a compilation engagement

Ernst & Young LLP
Ernst & Young Tower
222 Bay Street, PO Box 251
Toronto, ON M5K 1J7

Tel: +1 416 864 1234
Fax: +1 416 864 1174
ey.com

**Building a better
working world**

NOTICE TO READER

On the basis of information provided by management, we have compiled the balance sheet of Cloud 9 Ltd. as at December 31, 2015 and the statements of income, retained earnings and cash flows for the year then ended.

We have not performed an audit or review engagement in respect of these financial statements and, accordingly, we express no assurance thereon.

Readers are cautioned that these statements may not be appropriate for their purposes.

Toronto, Canada

February X, 2016.

"Ernst & Young LLP"

Chartered Professional Accountants
Licensed Public Accountants

A member firm of Ernst & Young Global Limited

FIGURE 1.4 **Example of a Notice to Reader**
Source: EY, 2014

Table 1.1 summarizes the differences among the three types of engagements.

TABLE 1.1 **Types of engagements**

CHARACTERISTIC	AUDIT	REVIEW	COMPILATION
Objective	To reduce the assurance engagement risk to an acceptably low level so that a positive opinion can be provided. Reasonable assurance means a high, but not absolute, level of assurance.	To reduce the assurance engagement risk to an acceptable level to allow the practitioner to express a negative form of expression in that nothing has come to their attention.	To compile a set of financial statements based on information provided. No assurance provided.
Procedures	Sufficient appropriate evidence is obtained as part of a systematic process that includes: • obtaining an understanding of the assurance engagement circumstances • assessing risks • responding to assessed risks • performing further evidence-gathering procedures using a combination of inspection, observation, confirmation, re-calculation, re-performance, analytical procedures, and inquiry	Sufficient appropriate evidence is obtained as part of a systematic process that includes obtaining an understanding of the subject matter and other assurance engagement circumstances, but in which evidence-gathering procedures are limited to discussion, analytics, and inquiry.	Mathematical accuracy is checked. There is no requirement for sufficient appropriate evidence; however, the auditor must not be associated with anything false or misleading.

(continued)

TABLE 1.1 **Types of engagements** (continued)

CHARACTERISTIC	AUDIT	REVIEW	COMPILATION
Financial reporting framework	Must be in accordance with Canadian GAAP or other appropriate financial reporting framework.	Must be in accordance with Canadian GAAP or other appropriate financial reporting framework.	GAAP not required.
Level of assurance	High assurance	Moderate assurance	No assurance
Report	Independent Auditor's Report	Review Engagement Report	Notice to Reader
Cost and time	Most time-consuming, highest cost	May take less time, as less work required; lower cost	Least amount of work, lowest cost

Cloud 9

As Ernie explains the differences between reasonable and moderate assurance, Ron wonders if Chip will accept a review, rather than an audit, of the financial statements. If he will, it will be much easier and cheaper for Ron. However, Ron also realizes that Chip would not get as much assurance from a review as he would get from an audit. Ron thinks Chip would know the difference between an audit and a review; because he asked for an audit, Chip must need the additional assurance it provides.

BEFORE YOU GO ON

1.4.1 What are the main differences between reasonable and moderate assurance engagements?

1.4.2 What is the level of assurance required for an annual financial statement for a reporting issuer?

1.4.3 What does negative assurance mean?

1.5 DIFFERENT AUDIT OPINIONS

 5 Outline different audit opinions.

unmodified opinion a clean audit opinion; the auditor concludes that the financial statements are fairly presented

emphasis of matter what results when an auditor will issue an unmodified audit opinion when there is a significant issue that is adequately disclosed and there is a need to draw the attention of the user to it

Chapter 13 contains a detailed discussion of the different types of audit opinions an auditor can arrive at when completing an audit. The purpose of this section is to present a very brief overview of those opinions.

The most common audit report is unmodified and contains an unmodified opinion. An **unmodified opinion** is also known as a clean opinion. The audit report in figure 1.2 is an example of such a report. Auditors arrive at this type of opinion when they believe that the financial statements are not materially misstated and that they present fairly the financial position of the company, and that the information provided is in accordance with Canadian GAAP.

An audit report may have an unmodified opinion and include an **emphasis of matter** paragraph. An emphasis of matter paragraph draws the attention of the reader to an issue that the auditor believes has been adequately and accurately explained in a note to the financial statements. The purpose of the paragraph is to ensure that the reader pays appropriate attention to the issue when reading the financial statements. The audit report remains unmodified and users of the financial statements can still rely on the information contained in the financial statements (CAS 706 *Emphasis of Matter Paragraphs and Other Matter Paragraphs in the Independent Auditor's Report*).

All other audit reports are modified. There are three types of modifications, shown in table 1.2 (CAS 705 *Modifications to the Opinion in the Independent Auditor's Report*).

Nature of the matter giving rise to the modification	Auditor's judgement about the pervasiveness of the effects or possible effects on the financial statements	
	Material but not pervasive	Material and pervasive
Financial statements are materially misstated	Qualified opinion	Adverse opinion
Inability to obtain sufficient appropriate audit evidence	Qualified opinion	Disclaimer of opinion

TABLE 1.2 Audit opinion modifications

Source: CAS 705 Modifications to the Opinion in the Independent Auditor's Report, para. AI

The first is called a **qualified opinion** and is issued when the auditor believes that "except for" the effects of a matter that is explained in the audit report, the financial statements can be relied upon by the reader. A qualified opinion is used when the matter of concern can be identified, quantified, and explained in the audit report. In this case the matter of concern is material but not pervasive to the financial statements. In this context, "pervasive" refers to misstatements that are not confined to individual accounts or elements of the financial statements, or, if confined, the misstatements affect an extensive portion of the financial statements or there are missing disclosures that are vital to a user's understanding of the financial statements. An example of this type of report is provided in chapter 13 (see figure 13.4).

More serious matters require either an **adverse opinion** or a **disclaimer of opinion**. An adverse opinion is appropriate if the auditor has evidence that identified misstatements, individually or in aggregate, are material and pervasive to the financial statements. A disclaimer of opinion is used when the auditor is unable to obtain sufficient appropriate audit evidence on which to base the opinion, and concludes that the possible effects on the financial statements could be material and pervasive. Although these opinions are used in different circumstances, in both instances the matter or matters of concern are so material and pervasive to the financial statements that the auditor cannot issue a qualified, "except for" opinion.

qualified opinion opinion provided when the auditor concludes that the financial statements contain a material (significant) misstatement

adverse opinion opinion provided when the auditor concludes that there is a pervasive material misstatement in the financial statements

disclaimer of opinion opinion provided when the impact of a scope limitation is so extreme that an auditor is unable to obtain sufficient appropriate evidence to base an opinion

Cloud 9

Ron worries that an auditor might not be able to give a clean opinion on his business's financial statements. The whole point of getting an audit would be to give Chip sufficient assurance that the financial statements give a true and fair view of his business's financial position and performance, and thus agree to pay a good price for the business. If the auditor gives a disclaimer of opinion or an adverse opinion, Chip could either change his mind about the business or offer only a very low price because he can't be sure that the business is as profitable and as solvent as Ron claims. Even getting a qualified opinion would be serious. Ernie assures Ron that disclaimers are extremely rare; in fact, he has never seen one. Adverse opinions are also rare, and if Ron's belief about his good financial records and tight control over assets is well founded, then there should not be any major problems.

BEFORE YOU GO ON

1.5.1 What are the different types of unmodified audit opinions?

1.5.2 What are the different types of modified audit opinions?

1.5.3 What type of audit opinion is unmodified and modified?

1.6 PREPARERS AND AUDITORS

In this section we explain and contrast the different responsibilities of financial statement preparers and auditors. We provide details of the role that each group plays in ensuring that the financial statements are a fair representation of the company in question. Following this discussion, there is an overview of the different firms that provide assurance services.

6 Differentiate between the roles of the preparer and the auditor, and discuss the different firms that provide assurance services.

A complete set of financial statements includes the balance sheet (statement of financial position), income statement (statement of comprehensive income), statement of cash flows, statement of changes in equity, and the accompanying notes. It is the responsibility of those charged with governance (generally the board of directors and management of an entity) to prepare the financial statements. They must ensure that the information included in the financial statements is fairly presented and complies with Canadian accounting standards and interpretations. According to CAS 200 *Overall Objectives of the Independent Auditor and the Conduct of an Audit in Accordance with Canadian Auditing Standards*, those charged with governance are responsible for:

- identifying the financial reporting framework to be used in the preparation and presentation of their financial statements
- reporting, establishing, and maintaining internal controls that are effective in preventing and detecting material misstatements finding their way into the financial statements
- selecting and applying appropriate accounting policies and making reasonable accounting estimates

1.6.1 Preparer responsibility

It is the responsibility of those charged with governance to ensure that the information contained in their financial statements is relevant, reliable, comparable, understandable, and fairly presented. Each of these concepts is now discussed.

Relevant

The information included in the financial statements should be relevant to the users of that report. Information is relevant if it has an impact on the decisions made by users regarding the performance of the entity. Users require information that helps them evaluate past, present, and future events relating to the entity. They are interested in evaluating past decisions made by management and predicting whether the entity will remain viable (that is, a going concern) into the future. Users can use current information to estimate future share price movements, like dividend payments, and the ability of the entity to meet its immediate obligations.

Reliable

The information included in the financial statements should be reliable to the users of those statements. Information is reliable when it is free from material misstatements (errors or fraud). If users perceive that the information presented is unreliable, for whatever reason, the financial statements cannot be used to make the types of decisions outlined above. The information must be unbiased; it must not be presented in such a way as to influence the decision-making process of the user. An independent audit of the financial statements is one method of improving the reliability of the financial statements.

Comparable

The information included in the financial statements should be comparable through time. Users need to be able to trace an entity's performance to identify any trends that may influence their perception of how well the entity is doing. Users also need to be able to benchmark the performance of the entity against other similar organizations to assess its relative performance. To enable such comparisons, information must be presented consistently across time and across entities. Any changes in accounting policies must be clearly disclosed so that appropriate adjustments can be made. Consistent application of Canadian generally accepted accounting principles by all entities over time aids these comparisons.

Understandable

The information included in the financial statements should be understandable. Users need to understand the information presented in order to make appropriate decisions. The notes to the financial statements are used to provide additional details to aid in the interpretation of the accounting information provided. The details included in the notes must be phrased in such a way as to impartially inform users to aid their decision-making.

Fairly presented

The information included in the financial statements should be fairly presented. "Presented fairly" or "truth and fairness" refers to the consistent and faithful application of the accounting standards or an applicable framework when preparing the financial statements.

It is the responsibility of the auditor to form an opinion on the fair presentation or the truth and fairness of the financial statements. In doing so, the auditor will assess the accounting policies selected by those charged with governance of the entity. Specifically, the auditor will evaluate whether those accounting policies are consistent with the financial reporting framework used by the entity. The auditor will also consider the accounting estimates made by those charged with governance and management to determine whether the estimates are reasonable. The auditor will assess the relevance, reliability, comparability, and understandability of the information presented in the financial statements.

1.6.2 Auditor responsibility

When undertaking an audit, the auditor should use professional scepticism, professional judgement, and due care. Each of these concepts is now defined and explained.

Professional scepticism

Professional scepticism is an attitude adopted by the auditor when conducting the audit. It means that the auditor remains independent of the entity, its management, and its staff when completing the audit work. In a practical sense, it means that the auditor maintains a questioning mind and thoroughly investigates all evidence presented by the client. The auditor must seek independent evidence to corroborate information provided by the client and must be suspicious when evidence contradicts documents held by the client or enquiries made of client personnel (including management and those charged with governance).

Professional judgement

Professional judgement relates to the level of expertise, knowledge, and training that an auditor uses while conducting an audit. An auditor must utilize their judgement throughout the audit. For example, an auditor must determine the reliability of an information source and decide on the sufficiency and appropriateness of evidence gathered, the procedures to be used in testing, and an appropriate sample size.

Due care

Due care refers to being diligent while conducting an audit, applying technical and statute-backed standards, and documenting each stage in the audit process.

1.6.3 Assurance providers

Assurance services are provided by accounting and other consulting firms. The largest accounting firms in Canada are known collectively as the "Big-4." The firms that make up the Big-4 are Deloitte, EY, KPMG, and PricewaterhouseCoopers (PwC). These four firms operate internationally and dominate the assurance market throughout the world. There were once eight international firms, but after a series of mergers and the collapse of Arthur Andersen, the Big-8 became the Big-4. These four firms dominate the audits of Canada's largest companies.

The next tier of accounting firms is known as the national accounting firms. The firms in this tier have a significant presence nationally and most have international affiliations. National firms in Canada include, among others, Collins Barrow, BDO, PKF Canada, Grant Thornton, DMCL, Myers Norris Penny, RSM Richter, and Nexia Canada. These firms service medium-sized and smaller clients.

The next tier of accounting firms is made up of regional and local accounting firms. These firms service clients in their local areas and range in size from single-partner firms to several-partner firms with professionally qualified and trained staff.

All of these accounting firms provide non-assurance (or non-audit) services as well as assurance (or audit) services. Non-assurance services include management consulting, mergers and acquisitions, insolvency, tax, and accounting services. The Rules of Professional Conduct specify a number of requirements that restrict an accounting firm from providing non-audit services to its audit clients. These rules were established to increase the transparency of the extent of services being provided by an accounting firm to its audit clients after the collapse of several high-profile companies, including Enron and WorldCom (in the United States). The collapse of Arthur Andersen (previously an international accounting firm) raised concerns that the provision of non-audit services to an audit client could affect the independence and objectivity of the auditor.

Accounting firms are not the only providers of assurance services. A number of consulting firms provide assurance services primarily in areas of corporate social responsibility, including some combination of environmental issues, carbon emissions, community engagement, charitable activities, and employee welfare as well as disclosures in other areas. Consulting firms employ staff with a variety of expertise, including, for example, engineers, accountants, sociologists, scientists, and economists.

Cloud 9

Ernie stresses to Ron that any financial statements prepared for McLellan's Shoes are Ron's responsibility, even if they are audited. The auditor has to be sceptical about the claims made by Ron in the financial statements. These claims include, for example, that the assets shown on the balance sheet exist and are valued correctly, and that the balance sheet contains a complete list of the business's liabilities. In other words, the auditor is not just going to believe whatever Ron tells him or her. Auditors must gather evidence about the financial statements before they can give an audit opinion. Ernie also explains to Ron that because his business is relatively small, he has a choice between large and small audit firms. Very large companies would be expected to select a larger audit firm because often smaller firms may be too small to effectively maintain their independence. If a small audit firm audits a large company it is open to the criticism that it will not be sufficiently sceptical because it does not want to lose the fees from that client. A large audit firm has many other clients, so the fees from any one client are a relatively small part of its revenue. Ron likes the idea that the smaller audit firms may be less costly.

BEFORE YOU GO ON

1.6.1 A financial statement must be relevant and reliable. What do these terms mean in this context?

1.6.2 What three characteristics should an auditor have when conducting an audit?

1.6.3 What are non-audit services?

1.7 THE ROLE OF REGULATORS AND REGULATIONS

7 Identify the different regulators, legislation, and regulations surrounding the assurance process.

In this section we discuss the regulators and regulations that have an impact on the audit process.

1.7.1 Regulators, Standard Setters, and Other Bodies

The accounting profession in Canada is primarily self-regulated; however, it does rely on legislation to some extent. Currently, a number of organizations have an impact on the auditing profession, either directly or indirectly. They include the Auditing and Assurance Standards Board (AASB), the Canadian Securities Administrators (CSA), and the various provincial securities commissions, the Canadian Public Accountability Board (CPAB), and the Chartered Professional Accountants of Canada or CPA Canada (which integrated the former Canadian Institute of Chartered Accountants, Certified General Accountants Association of Canada, and the Society of Management Accountants of Canada).

Auditing and Assurance Standards Board (AASB)

The purpose of the Canadian AASB is to serve the public interest by setting high-quality auditing and assurance standards.[1] To accomplish this, the AASB adopted the International Standards on Auditing (ISAs), which are issued by the International Auditing and Assurance Standards Board (IAASB). The ISAs have been redrafted by the IAASB and placed in a "clarity" format to improve the consistency of application worldwide. The Canadian version of the ISAs is now referred to as the Canadian Auditing Standards (CASs). In addition to issuing the CASs, the AASB is responsible for issuing the Canadian Standards for Assurance Engagements (CSAEs), as well as the Canadian review engagement and compilation engagement standards.

PROFESSIONAL ENVIRONMENT

International Auditing and Assurance Standards Board (IAASB)

The IAASB develops and issues International Standards on Auditing (ISAs). The IAASB claims that many countries either adopt ISAs as the national auditing standards or base their national auditing standards on the ISAs. ISAs have been recognized by securities and derivatives markets around the world, although the stock exchanges in the United States use the Public Company Accounting Oversight Board's (PCAOB) auditing standards.

The Clarity Project to redraft the ISAs began in 2003 with the objective of improving the clarity and consistent application of international auditing standards. This was seen as essential to the adoption of ISAs for statutory audits in Europe. The project has resulted in the redrafting of 36 international auditing standards. The final seven redrafted standards were released in early 2009, with application to audits for periods beginning on or after December 15, 2009.

The IAASB operates under the auspices of the International Federation of Accountants (IFAC), the global organization for the accounting profession, representing 157 associations in 123 countries (see www.ifac.org). Simnett argues that one of the hurdles that the IAASB faces in achieving greater acceptance of the ISAs is the perception that it is captured by the accounting profession. IFAC's members are accounting organizations and, in the past, most members of the IAASB have been practising auditors.

To increase the confidence of investors and others, IFAC has created a Public Interest Oversight Board (PIOB) to oversee the operations of the IAASB (and other standard-setting bodies associated with IFAC) (see www.ipiob.org). The PIOB was established in 2005 with the goal of increasing the transparency of the standard-setting arrangements in a manner that reflects the public interest. The PIOB reviews and approves the terms of reference for the standard-setting boards, evaluates the boards' due process procedures, oversees the work of the committees responsible for nominating members of the boards, and suggests projects for the boards. In an effort to increase international acceptance of the PIOB, and thus the ISAs, the members of the PIOB are drawn from a broad range of professions and regulatory agencies.

Sources: "International Auditing and Assurance Standards Board–Fact Sheet," International Federation of Accountants, May 2011; R. Simnett, "A Critique of the International Auditing and Assurance Standards Board," *Australian Accounting Review 17*, July 2007, pp. 28–36.

Canadian Securities Administrators (CSA)

In Canada, securities regulation falls under provincial jurisdiction. However, securities regulators from across the provinces and territories have joined together to form the CSA. The CSA is a voluntary umbrella organization with the objective of improving, coordinating, and harmonizing regulation of the Canadian capital markets.[2] Part of its mandate is to regulate listed entity disclosure requirements. As such, it requires the annual filing of audited financial statements in accordance with Canadian GAAP, which in Canada is now IFRS for listed entities. It also requires that the CEOs and CFOs of reporting issuers certify that the annual financial statements are fairly presented. In addition, the CSA issues staff notices to provide reporting issuers with guidance on various issues, such as environmental disclosures.

Canadian Public Accountability Board (CPAB)

CPAB was incorporated in 2003 under the Canada Corporations Act. It was formed by the CSA, Canadian Institute of Chartered Accountants, and Office of the Superintendent of Financial Institutions (OSFI) with the objective of promoting high-quality audits. The CSA requires that auditors of reporting issuers register and be a member in good standing with CPAB. To be a member in good standing, a firm must pass a CPAB inspection, which includes a review of the firm's compliance with its quality control policies and a sample of engagement files for compliance with professional standards.

Toronto Stock Exchange (TSX)

The TSX is the largest stock exchange in Canada. It aims to help listed companies raise funds, provide opportunities for investors to build wealth, and enable buyers and sellers to transact with confidence. In order to remain listed on the TSX, a company must meet the requirements of the Securities Act of Ontario, the relevant provincial securities acts, and the CSA. Companies listed on the TSX must file all required documents through the SEDAR (System for Electronic Document Analysis and Retrieval) electronic filing system.

Chartered Professional Accountants of Canada (CPA Canada)

At the time of writing, the Canadian accounting profession was undergoing a transition period. Nationally, the three main accounting bodies, the Canadian Institute of Chartered Accountants, the Certified General Accountants Association of Canada (CGA-Canada), and the Society of Management Accountants of Canada (CMA Canada), have agreed to adopt a new professional accounting designation, the Chartered Professional Accountant (CPA). CPA Canada is the national organization that has been established to support unification of the Canadian accounting profession. However, as the Canadian accounting profession is provincially regulated, decisions regarding subsequent mergers are made provincially. Across Canada, the merger is in various stages of progress, except in Quebec, where unification is complete. As a united profession, the new organization will have 125,000 professional members and 20,000 candidates and registered students, resulting in one of the largest accounting bodies in the world.[3] Training to become a CPA requires completion of an extensive training program, which combines study and mentored work experience with a focus on technical competence and skills. The successful completion of a rigorous professional exam will be required before a CPA designation is conferred.

1.7.2 Legislation

In Canada, a company can be incorporated under either federal or provincial jurisdiction. If a company is incorporated federally, then it must follow the statutes of the Canada Business Corporations Act (CBCA) (excluding banks and insurance and trust companies). The CBCA calls for audited financial statements for federally incorporated companies that are listed on Canadian stock exchanges. The CBCA statutes also require that these financial statements be in accordance with Canadian generally accepted accounting principles, and audits must be conducted in accordance with Canadian generally accepted auditing standards as defined by the CPA Canada Handbook. In addition, the CBCA provides regulation for auditor independence, auditor appointment, and auditor access to information and company records.

1.7.3 Regulation

Auditing standards are issued by the Auditing and Assurance Standards Board (AASB) in Canada. The standards provide minimum requirements and guidance for auditing engagements. The 36 Canadian Auditing Standards (CASs) constitute Canadian generally accepted auditing standards (GAAS), and apply to all audits of historical financial information where audit assurance is provided. They are based on the International Standards for Auditing (ISAs); however, they may be modified to comply with Canadian legal or regulatory environments.

The Canadian Standards for Assurance Engagements (CSAEs) are the engagement standards that apply to engagements other than audits of financial statements and other historical financial information. These standards provide general and specific guidance for assurance engagements other than historical financial information, such as the effectiveness of internal controls, where either reasonable or limited assurance is provided. Assurance engagements that comply with the CSAEs are also in compliance with Canadian GAAS. In addition, there are standards for review and related services, including compilation engagements.[4] Figure 1.5 provides an overview of the CPA Canada Handbook—Assurance.

Cloud 9

Ernie explains that, in general, the regulators and regulations that apply to companies are not relevant to McLellan's Shoes. However, any auditor Ron engages would be also performing company audits and would be a member of at least one of the professional accounting bodies. The auditor would apply the auditing and accounting standards that are relevant to an audit engagement when auditing a small business. The auditor would apply strict professional standards to Ron's audit and should perform the audit to a reasonable standard.

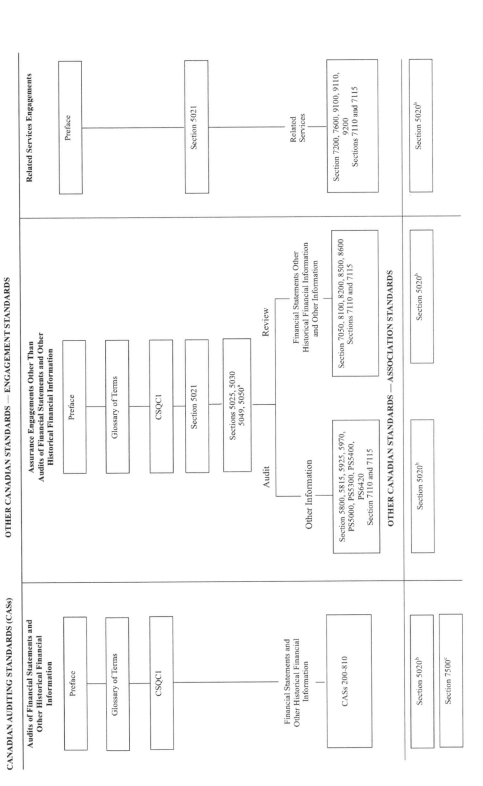

CANADIAN AUDITING STANDARDS (CASs)

OTHER CANADIAN STANDARDS — ENGAGEMENT STANDARDS

FIGURE 1.5 Overview of the Assurance Handbook

Source: Chartered Professional Accountants of Canada. "Overview of the Assurance Handbook," CPA Canada Handbook—Assurance, Part I, "Preface to the CPA Canada Handbook—Assurance, Copyright © 2001, Chartered Professional Accountants of Canada. References to the CPA Canada Handbook are reprinted with permission from Chartered Professional Accountants of Canada, Toronto, Canada. Any changes to the original material are the sole responsibility of the author and/or publisher and have not been reviewed or endorsed by the Chartered Professional Accountants of Canada.

[a] USING THE WORK OF INTERNAL AUDIT IN ASSURANCE ENGAGEMENTS OTHER THAN AUDITS OF FINANCIAL STATEMENTS AND OTHER HISTORICAL FINANCIAL INFORMATION, Section 5050, provides guidance on using the work of internal audit in carrying out an audit engagement other than an audit of financial statements and other historical financial information. The guidance may be useful for other types of engagements.

[b] ASSOCIATION, Section 5020, provides guidance on the public accountant's association with information, which may occur irrespective of the type of engagement.

[c] AUDITOR'S CONSENT TO THE USE OF THE AUDITOR'S REPORT IN CONNECTION WITH DESIGNATED DOCUMENTS. Section 7500, provides guidance on the auditor's responsibilities, after the completion of the audit of the entity's financial statements, when the auditor agrees to consent to the use of the auditor's report in connection with a designated document.

1.8 THE AUDIT EXPECTATION GAP

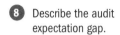

Describe the audit expectation gap.

The audit expectation gap occurs when there is a difference between the expectations of assurance providers and financial statement users. The gap occurs when user beliefs do not align with what an auditor has actually done. In particular, the gap is caused by unrealistic user expectations, such as:

- The auditor is providing complete assurance.
- The auditor is guaranteeing the future viability of the entity.
- An unqualified (clean) audit opinion is an indicator of complete accuracy.
- The auditor will definitely find any fraud.
- The auditor has checked all transactions.

The reality is that:

- An auditor provides reasonable assurance.
- The audit does not guarantee the future viability of the entity.
- An unqualified opinion indicates that the auditor believes that there are no material (significant) misstatements (errors or fraud) in the financial statements.
- The auditor will assess the risk of fraud and conduct tests to try to uncover any fraud, but there is no guarantee that they will find fraud, should it have occurred.
- The auditor tests a sample of transactions.

The audit expectation gap is represented graphically in figure 1.6.

The audit expectation gap can be reduced by:

- auditors performing their duties appropriately, complying with auditing standards, and meeting the minimum standards of performance that should be expected of all auditors
- peer reviews of audits to ensure that auditing standards have been applied correctly
- auditing standards being reviewed and updated on a regular basis to enhance the work being done by auditors
- education of the public
- enhanced reporting to explain what processes have been followed in arriving at an audit (reasonable assurance) or a review (limited assurance) opinion (significant improvements have been introduced by standard-setters improving assurance reporting)
- assurance providers reporting accurately the level of assurance being provided (reasonable, limited, or none)

FIGURE 1.6 **Audit expectation gap**

As described in this chapter, financial statement users rely on audited financial statements to make a variety of decisions. They use the statements to assess the performance of the company, the appropriateness of the remuneration paid to management, the adequacy of dividends declared, and the likely future viability of the company. Following the corporate collapses of the early 2000s (for example, Enron and Worldcom), user confidence in auditors and audited financial statements hit a low. In Canada and the United States, increased regulation was imposed on the auditing profession. The United States passed the Sarbanes Oxley Act (SOX) and created the Public Company Accounting Oversight Board (PCAOB). These organizations focus on corporate governance and accounting and audit regulations. In Canada, increased regulation resulted in the creation of the Canadian Public Accountability Board (CPAB). The standard-setters have also responded to public demands that auditors pay greater attention to the risk that a material fraud may occur. CAS 240 *The Auditor's Responsibilities Relating to Fraud in an Audit of Financial Statements* requires that auditors consider the risk of material fraud on every audit. The auditor must assess the risk that a material fraud could occur and gauge the adequacy of the client's system of internal control to prevent or detect such a fraud. If the auditor is not satisfied with the client's system of internal control, their audit procedures must be designed to aid in the detection of any material suspected frauds.

While highlighting the importance of considering fraud in every audit, standard-setters also highlight that the primary responsibility for fraud prevention and detection remains with those charged with governance (generally the client's management) (CAS 240, para. 4). They also emphasize the inherent limitation of any audit, making fraud detection less than certain (CAS 240, para. 5).

Cloud 9

Ron believes that Chip Masters would know what an audit can provide and what it cannot, because Chip is an experienced vice-president of a large international company. He would deal with auditors on a regular basis. Ron thanks Ernie for his time. Ernie has helped him to understand that preparing more detailed financial statements and engaging an auditor to perform a financial statement audit would not be as bad as he first thought. Ron now understands why Ernie thinks audits are valuable, and not just another business expense. If Chip Masters thinks that Ron's financial statements are more credible with an audit, then it is likely that he will be prepared to pay a higher price for Ron's business.

BEFORE YOU GO ON

1.8.1 Define the audit expectation gap.

1.8.2 What has caused the audit expectation gap?

1.8.3 What can be done to reduce the audit expectation gap?

SUMMARY

1 Define an assurance engagement.

An assurance engagement involves an assurance provider arriving at an opinion about some information being provided by their client to a third party. A financial statement audit is one type of assurance engagement. This engagement involves an auditor arriving at an opinion about the fair presentation of the financial statements. The audit report is addressed to the shareholders of the company being audited, but other users may read the financial statements.

Learning about auditing and assurance requires an understanding of auditing and assurance terminology, including terms such as audit risk, materiality, internal controls, listed entity, and assertions.

2 Explain why there is a demand for audit and assurance services.

Financial statement users include investors (shareholders), suppliers, customers, lenders, employees, governments, and the general public. These groups of users demand audited financial statements because of their remoteness from the entity, accounting complexity, their incentives competing with those of the entity's managers, and their need for reliable information on which to base decisions. The theories used to describe the demand for audit and assurance services are agency theory, the information hypothesis, and the insurance hypothesis.

❸ Differentiate between types of assurance services.

Assurance services include financial statement audits, compliance audits, performance audits, comprehensive audits, internal audits, and assurance on corporate social responsibility (CSR) disclosures.

❹ Explain the different levels of assurance.

The different levels of assurance include reasonable assurance, which is the highest level of assurance, moderate assurance, and no assurance. Reasonable assurance is provided on an audit of a company's financial statements. Moderate assurance is provided on a review of a company's financial statements that provides negative assurance. No assurance is provided in a compilation engagement.

❺ Outline different audit opinions.

An auditor can issue an unmodified and unqualified opinion, also known as a clean report, an unqualified opinion with an emphasis of matter opinion, or a modified and qualified opinion, which is issued when the financial statements contain a material (significant) misstatement (error or fraud).

❻ Differentiate between the roles of the preparer and the auditor, and discuss the different firms that provide assurance services.

It is the responsibility of a company's governing body to ensure that their financial statements are relevant, reliable, comparable, understandable, and true and fair. It is the responsibility of the auditor to form an opinion on the fair presentation of the financial statements. In doing so the auditor must maintain professional scepticism and utilize professional judgement and due care.

The firms that provide assurance services include the Big-4 international firms, the national firms (with international links), local and regional firms, and consulting firms that tend to specialize in assurance of CSR and environmental disclosures.

❼ Identify the different regulators, legislation, and regulations surrounding the assurance process.

Regulators of the assurance process include the Auditing and Assurance Standards Board (AASB), the Canada Business Corporations Act (CBCA), Canadian Securities Administrators (CSA) and the various provincial securities commissions, and the Canadian Public Accountability Board (CPAB). Relevant legislation includes the Canada Business Corporations Act (CBCA). The three organizations responsible for accounting designations in Canada—the Canadian Institute of Chartered Accountants (CICA), the Certified General Accountants Association of Canada (CGA-Canada), and the Society of Management Accountants of Canada (CMA Canada)—have joined CPA Canada, which is responsible for the Chartered Professional Accountant (CPA) designation.

❽ Describe the audit expectation gap.

The audit expectation gap occurs when there is a difference between the expectations of assurance providers and financial statement or other users. The gap occurs when user beliefs do not align with what an auditor has actually done.

KEY TERMS

Accountability relationship, 5
Adverse opinion, 19
Applicable financial reporting
   framework, 6
Assertions, 6
Assurance engagement, 5
Audit evidence, 6
Audit file, 6
Audit plan, 6
Audit risk, 6
Compilation engagement, 16
Compliance audit, 12
Comprehensive audit, 12

Consulting firms, 13
Corporate social responsibility
   (CSR), 13
Disclaimer of opinion, 19
Emphasis of matter, 18
Fair presentation, 10
Financial statement audit, 10
Financial statements, 6
Independent auditor's report, 6
Information risk, 8
Internal audit, 12
Internal control, 6
Listed entity, 10

Material, 6
Materiality, 6
Moderate assurance, 14
No assurance, 16
Notice to Reader, 16
Operational audit, 12
Qualified opinion, 19
Reasonable assurance, 14
Review engagement, 14
Sufficient and appropriate evidence, 6
Those charged with governance, 12
Unmodified opinion, 6, 18
Working papers, 6

MULTIPLE-CHOICE QUESTIONS

1.1 The parties relevant to an assurance engagement are:

(a) assurance practitioner, users, responsible party.

(b) assurance practitioner, responsible party, subject matter.

(c) assurance practitioner, users, criteria.

(d) assurance practitioner, subject matter, criteria.

1.2 Under the Canada Business Corporations Act the auditor has a responsibility to:

(a) form an opinion on the subject criteria.

(b) form an opinion on the independence of the company.

(c) form an opinion on the fair presentation of the financial statements.

(d) all of the above.

1.3 Performance audits are useful because:

(a) they include an internal audit.

(b) they are concerned with the economy, efficiency, and effectiveness of an organization's activities.

(c) they involve gathering evidence to ascertain whether the entity under review has followed the rules, policies, procedures, laws, or regulations with which it must conform.

(d) none of the above.

1.4 The function of internal audit is determined by:

(a) the external auditor.

(b) the Institute of Internal Auditors.

(c) those charged with governance and management.

(d) the government.

1.5 Negative assurance means:

(a) the auditor disclaims responsibility for the audit opinion.

(b) an adverse audit report.

(c) the auditor has conducted an audit and provides an opinion that the financial statements are not materially misstated.

(d) the auditor has done adequate work to report whether or not anything came to their attention that would lead them to believe that the information being assured is not fairly presented.

1.6 A "clean" audit report is issued when:

(a) the auditor has no independence issues.

(b) the audit opinion is unqualified and the auditor includes a paragraph in the audit report to emphasize something important.

(c) the audit opinion is unqualified and unmodified.

(d) the users cannot rely on the financial statements.

1.7 Those charged with governance have a responsibility to ensure that the information in financial statements is:

(a) relevant and reliable.

(b) comparable and understandable.

(c) fairly presented.

(d) all of the above.

1.8 Agency theory explains that audits are demanded because conflicts can arise between:

(a) managers and owners.

(b) managers and agents.

(c) owners and principals.

(d) auditors and owners.

1.9 The insurance hypothesis means:

(a) managers must take insurance.

(b) owners must take insurance.

(c) an audit acts as insurance.

(d) none of the above.

1.10 The audit expectation gap occurs when:

(a) auditors perform their duties appropriately and satisfy users' demands.

(b) user beliefs do not align with what an auditor has actually done.

(c) peer reviews of audits ensure that auditing standards have been applied correctly and the standards are at the level that satisfies users' demands.

(d) the public is well educated about auditing.

REVIEW QUESTIONS

1.1 What does "assurance" mean in the financial reporting context? What qualities must an "assurer" have in order for you to feel that their statement has high credibility?

1.2 Compare the financial statement users and their needs for a large listed public company with those of a sporting team (for example, a football team).

1.3 Why do audit firms offer consulting services to their audit clients? Why don't they just do audits and let consulting firms provide the consulting services?

1.4 An assurance engagement involves evaluation or measurement of subject matter against criteria. What criteria are used in a financial statement audit?

1.5 Who would request a performance audit? Why?

1.6 Are internal auditors independent? Which internal auditor would be more independent: an internal auditor who reports to the chief financial officer (CFO) of the company, or an internal auditor who reports to the audit committee?

1.7 What is an "emphasis of matter" paragraph? When do you think an auditor would use it?

1.8   What standards or guidelines are relevant to the assurance of corporate social responsibility disclosures?

1.9   Describe the expectation gap.

1.10 Explain the system of reviewing the quality of audits performed by listed company auditors.

PROFESSIONAL APPLICATION QUESTIONS

Basic ★   Moderate ★ ★   Challenging ★ ★ ★

1.1 Demand for assurance ★ ★ ★

In 2002 the audit firm Arthur Andersen collapsed following charges brought against it in the United States relating to the failure of its client, Enron. Some other clients announced that they would be dismissing Arthur Andersen as their auditor before it was clear that Arthur Andersen would not survive.

Required

Using the theories outlined in this chapter on the demand for audits, give some reasons why these clients took this action.

1.2 Assurance providers ★ ★

Most audit firms maintain a website that explains the services offered by the firm and provide resources to their clients and other interested parties. The services offered by most firms include both audit and non-audit services.

Required

(a) Find the websites for (1) a Big-4 audit firm and (2) a national audit firm. Compare them on (i) the range of services provided, (ii) geographic coverage (that is, where their offices are located), (iii) staff numbers and special skills offered, (iv) industries in which they claim specialization, (v) publications and other materials provided to their clients or the general public, and (vi) marketing message.

(b) In times of economic recession would you expect the demand for audits to increase or decrease? Would you expect clients to shift from large (Big-4) auditors to national auditors or from national auditors to Big-4 auditors? Why or why not?

Questions 1.3 and 1.4 are based on the following case.

Securimax Limited (Securimax) has been an audit client of KFP Partners (KFP) for the past 15 years. Securimax is based in Waterloo, Ontario, where it manufactures high-tech armor-plated personnel carriers. Securimax often has to go through a competitive market tender process to win large government contracts. Its main product, the small but powerful Terrain Master, is highly specialized, and Securimax does business only with nations that have a recognized, democratically elected government. Securimax maintains a highly secure environment, given the sensitive and confidential nature of its vehicle designs and its clients.

Clarke Field has been the engagement partner on the Securimax audit for the last five years.

The board of Securimax is considering changing from an audit engagement to a review engagement and has approached Clarke to discuss the implications of this change. Clarke suggests that KFP could perform the review engagement.

Securimax's financial year end is December 31.

Source: Adapted from the Institute of Chartered Accountants Australia's CA Program's *Audit and Assurance Exam,* May 2008. Provided courtesy of Chartered Accountants Australia and New Zealand.

1.3 Types of assurance engagements ★ ★

Required

What is a review engagement? Why would a review be appropriate for a set of financial statements for Securimax?

1.4 Expectation gap ★ ★   8

Required

Discuss the expectation gap that could exist for the audit of Securimax. Consider the existence of any special interests of the users of Securimax's financial statements.

1.5 Performance and compliance audits ★ ★ ★   3

Fellowes and Associates Chartered Accountants is a successful national accounting firm with a large range of clients across Canada. In 2015, Fellowes and Associates gained a new client, Health Care Holdings Group (HCHG), which owns 100 percent of the following entities:

- Shady Oaks Centre, a private treatment centre
- Gardens Nursing Home Ltd., a private nursing home
- Total Laser Care Limited, a private clinic that specializes in the laser treatment of skin defects
  Year end for all HCHG entities is June 30.

  Total Laser Care Limited (TLCL) owns two relatively old laser machines used in therapy. Recently, staff using these machines have raised concerns that they have adverse impacts on patients.

  TLCL also wishes to purchase a new, more technologically advanced machine. The Ministry of Health has agreed to fund half the purchase price on the basis that TLCL followed the ministry's "Guidelines for Procurement of Medical Equipment" when purchasing the machine. The Ministry of Health has engaged the provincial Auditor General to check that TLCL met the terms of the funding agreement.

Source: Adapted from the Institute of Chartered Accountants Australia's CA Program's *Audit and Assurance Exam,* December 2008. Provided courtesy of Chartered Accountants Australia and New Zealand.

Required

Discuss the relevant criteria against which the Auditor General will check TCCL's compliance with the terms of the funding agreement.

1.6 Types of assurance engagements ★ ★   4

DDD Motor Sales Inc. is privately owned. It wants to expand its business and has approached its bank for a loan. DDD wants the funds to purchase additional inventory and will be able to provide excellent security to the bank. The bank has agreed that since DDD can provide good security for the loan, an external audit will not be required. The bank manager has insisted that DDD hire a firm of professional accountants to examine DDD's financial records and provide some level of assurance.

Required

(a) What type of engagement is required? Explain your answer.

(b) Assume that DDD contracts with Cicak & Jones, CPAs, to perform the required services. What is the title of the report or communication that Cicak & Jones will prepare?

(c) Identify the type of procedures Cicak & Jones will be required to conduct.

Source: © CGA-Canada, now CPA Canada. Reproduced with permission.

1.7 Audit opinions ★ ★ ★   1 5

Required

What type of audit report would be appropriate in each of the following scenarios? Explain.

(a) There is uncertainty relating to a pending exceptional litigation matter that is adequately disclosed in the notes.

(b) The client's records are inadequate and the auditor is unable to obtain sufficient appropriate evidence.

(c) There is a material uncertainty that casts a significant doubt on the entity's ability to continue as a going concern and this uncertainty is adequately disclosed.

(d) There is a GAAP departure concerning a highly material item.

(e) The client will not allow the auditor to contact the client's legal counsel.

(f) The client's accounting records have been destroyed.

(g) There is a material misstatement in the client's inventory account. The misstatement is deemed to be material but not pervasive to the financial statements.

(h) Inventories are misstated. The misstatement is deemed to be material but not pervasive to the financial statements.

1.8 Types of audit opinions ★ ★

Situation 1

The accounting firm of Aschari and Di Tomaso was engaged to perform an audit of the financial statements of Pammenter Inc. During the audit, Pammenter Inc.'s senior managers refused to give the auditors the information they needed to confirm any of the accounts receivable. As a result, Aschari and Di Tomaso were not able to confirm the accounts receivable balance. However, they did not encounter any other problems during the audit.

Situation 2

The accounting firm of Jovanovic and St. Pierre has discovered, during its audit of Robson Chemicals Inc., that the client is being sued for $3 million. Allegedly, one of its products exploded and severely injured a customer. In the firm's discussion with Robson's lawyers, Jovanovic and St. Pierre ascertained that it is very likely that Robson will indeed have to pay this entire amount when the lawsuit is resolved. To provide for this, Robson's chief financial officer has included information relating to the lawsuit in the notes to its financial statements, but did not otherwise reflect it in its financial statements.

Required

For each of the independent situations presented above:

(a) state what type of audit opinion should be issued and

(b) explain your reasoning.

Source: © CGA-Canada now CPA Canada. Reproduced with permission.

1.9 Different audit opinions ★

C. D. Hodgson and Associates Chartered Accountants audited the financial statements of Tallender Company, a sporting goods retailer. As with all of his firm's audits, Carl Hodgson conducted the Tallender audit in accordance with generally accepted auditing standards, and, therefore, wrote a standard unqualified opinion in his audit report.

On Saturday afternoon, just as he was about to write the audit opinion relating to this audit, Carl received an emergency telephone call from his wife regarding an accident involving their only child. He had to leave the office immediately and was not sure when he would be able to return. Since the only other person in the office at the time was a junior accountant, Khaled Nersesian, who had also worked on the audit, Carl handed him the completed financial statements and working papers and asked him to make sure it was appropriate to issue an unqualified opinion.

Required

What should Khaled Nersesian take into consideration in deciding whether an unqualified opinion is appropriate for Tallender Company?

1.10 The expectation gap ★ ★ ★

Certek Technologies Inc. (Certek) is a biotechnology company whose stock traded on a major Canadian stock exchange. Over the 22 months following its initial public offering in May 2009, Certek's stock rose an astounding 1,350 percent. In mid-March 2000, Certek's stock began to decline. Then, in April 2000, the stock price plummeted when it was announced that Certek had stopped all research activities on its major projects due to unsatisfactory scientific results. You, CPA, are sitting with some friends who make the following comments:

Ruby: I lost a bundle on the Certek stock. The stock went up with every press release. It seemed like the company was going to solve every medical problem in the world. I thought the auditors had a responsibility to investors and the capital markets for information released to the public.

Omid: I don't understand how audited financial statements are the least bit useful. Certek was investing huge amounts of money in researching new pharmaceutical products, yet the financial statements provided no information on whether its research would develop into viable products. Couldn't the auditors take some responsibility for evaluating the research that companies are doing?

Required

(a) What is the auditor's responsibility for information released to the public?

(b) Discuss Omid's comment with reference to the expectation gap.

(c) What can auditors do to reduce the expectation gap?

Source: Adapted from the Uniform Final Exam (UFE), CPA Canada, Paper 2, 2000.

1.11 CPAB ★ ★ ★   ❼

You are a trainee auditor working for a small audit firm. You completed your accounting degree at the end of last year and although you have not yet had much experience, you are concerned about some of the practices and procedures adopted by your audit firm. You overhear the two partners, Anouk and Riley, discussing some problems they are facing with a particular client. Anouk is advising Riley to "get the paperwork right" on the audit, otherwise they will be in trouble with CPAB's inspection program. After the conversation, Riley comes to you to ask if you, as a recent graduate, know anything about the CPAB inspection. Riley confesses that he hasn't been keeping up to date.

Required

Write a report to Riley explaining CPAB's audit inspection program.

1.12 Audit reports ★   ❸ ❹ ❺ ❻ ❽

A sample audit report is provided in figure 1.2 in this chapter. A sample review engagement report is provided in figure 1.3.

Required

(a) Explain the relevance of the paragraphs "Management's responsibility for the financial statements" and "Auditor's responsibility" in the audit report to the audit expectation gap.

(b) Find the lines in the audit report that express the auditor's opinion. Is it an unqualified or modified audit opinion?

(c) Find the lines in the review report that express the auditor's conclusion. Is it an audit opinion? Is it a positive or negative statement?

(d) Make a list of the other differences between the audit report and the review report.

1.13 Being an auditor ★ ★   ❹ ❺ ❽

You have recently graduated from university and have started work with an audit firm. You meet an old school friend, Kim, for dinner—you haven't seen each other for several years. Kim is surprised that you are now working as an auditor, because your childhood dream was to be a ballet dancer. Unfortunately, your knees were damaged in a fall and you can no longer dance. The conversation turns to your work and Kim wants to know how you do your job. Kim cannot understand why an audit is not a guarantee that the company will succeed. Kim also thinks that company managers will lie to you in order to protect themselves, and as an auditor you would have to assume that you cannot believe anything a company manager says to you.

Required

(a) Write a letter to Kim explaining the concept of reasonable assurance, and how reasonable assurance is determined. Explain why an auditor cannot offer absolute assurance.

(b) Explain in the letter to Kim the concept of "professional scepticism" and how it is not the same as assuming that managers are always trying to deceive auditors.

CASE STUDY—CLOUD 9

Ron McLellan established his business, McLellan's Shoes, in 1980. Ron keeps records and his wife helps him prepare basic accounting records. As McLellan's Shoes has no outside owners, Ron has never seen the need to have his books audited.

When Chip Masters from Cloud 9 Inc. expressed an interest in buying McLellan's Shoes in 1992, Ron was asked to provide audited financial statements. Ron discussed his concerns about having an audit with his friend Ernie Black. Ernie is concerned that Ron may forget their conversations and has asked you to prepare a summary of the issues listed below for Ron.

Required

(a) What are the main differences among a financial statement audit, a review engagement, and a compilation engagement?
(b) What is the difference between reasonable assurance and moderate assurance?
(c) Why would Chip ask Ron to have the financial statements for McLellan's Shoes audited rather than reviewed?
(d) What factors should Ron consider when selecting an accounting firm to complete the McLellan's Shoes audit?

RESEARCH QUESTION 1.1

Chong and Pflugrath conducted a study of different audit report formats and their effects on the audit expectation gap. They investigated whether report length (long or short), the location of the audit opinion (at the start or the end), and plain language (instead of technical language) affect shareholders' and auditors' perceptions of the audit. They surveyed a sample of shareholders and auditors and concluded that the responses indicate that different report formats have only minor effects on the audit expectation gap.[5]

Required

(a) In your view, what should be contained in an audit report that conveys realistic explanations of the auditor's role and the assurance provided by the audit report?
(b) Do you believe that auditors are correct in dismissing users' expectations as "unrealistic"? Should auditors be trying to meet these expectations by rethinking their role and changing their approach?

RESEARCH QUESTION 1.2

Required

Access the CPA Canada Handbook and locate the following:
(a) What number is the CAS for audit documentation?
(b) How many sections are there to each CAS?
(c) What is the name of Section 5025?
(d) What numbers relate to review engagements?
(e) Where specifically can the required wording for the Notice to Reader be found?

SOLUTIONS TO MULTIPLE-CHOICE QUESTIONS

1. a, 2. c, 3. b, 4. c, 5. d, 6. c, 7. d, 8. a, 9. c, 10. b.

NOTES

1. "Auditing and Assurance Standards Board," Financial Reporting & Assurance Standards Canada, http://www.frascanada.ca/auditing-and-assurance-standards-board/ [accessed June 2, 2014].
2. "Who We Are," Canadian Securities Administrators, http://www.securitiesadministrators.ca [accessed June 2011].
3. "Uniting the Accounting Profession," Chartered Accountants of Canada and Certified Management Accountants, May 2011. "A Framework for Uniting the Canadian Accounting Profession," CPA Canada, http://unification.cpacanada.ca [accessed October 2014]. "One National Body for Canada's Accounting Profession," CPA Canada news release, October 1, 2014.
4. Ethical standards are also important regulations concerning auditors. These are discussed in detail in chapter 2 of this book.
5. K. M. Chong and G. Pflugrath, "Do Different Audit Report Formats Affect Shareholders' and Auditors' Perceptions?" *International Journal of Auditing 12*, 2008, pp. 221–41.

CHAPTER 2

Ethics, legal liability, and client acceptance

LEARNING OBJECTIVES

After studying this chapter, you should be able to:

1 describe the fundamental principles of professional ethics and list some of the specific rules professional accountants are required to follow

2 define and explain auditor association and independence

3 explain the relationship between an auditor and key groups they have a professional link with during the audit engagement

4 explain the auditor's legal liability to their client, contributory negligence, and the extent to which an auditor is liable to third parties

5 identify the factors to consider in the client acceptance or continuance decision.

AUDITING AND ASSURANCE STANDARDS

CANADIAN	INTERNATIONAL
CAS 210 *Agreeing the Terms of Audit Engagements*	ISA 210 *Agreeing the Terms of Audit Engagements*
CAS 220 *Quality Control for an Audit of Financial Statements*	ISA 220 *Quality Control for an Audit of Financial Statements*
CAS 610 *Using the Work of Internal Auditors*	ISA 610 *Using the Work of Internal Auditors*
CSQC 1 *Quality Control for Firms that Perform Audits and Reviews of Financial Statements, Other Financial Information, and Other Assurance Engagements*	ISQC 1 *Quality Control for Firms that Perform Audits and Reviews of Historical Financial Information, and other Assurance and Related Services Engagements*

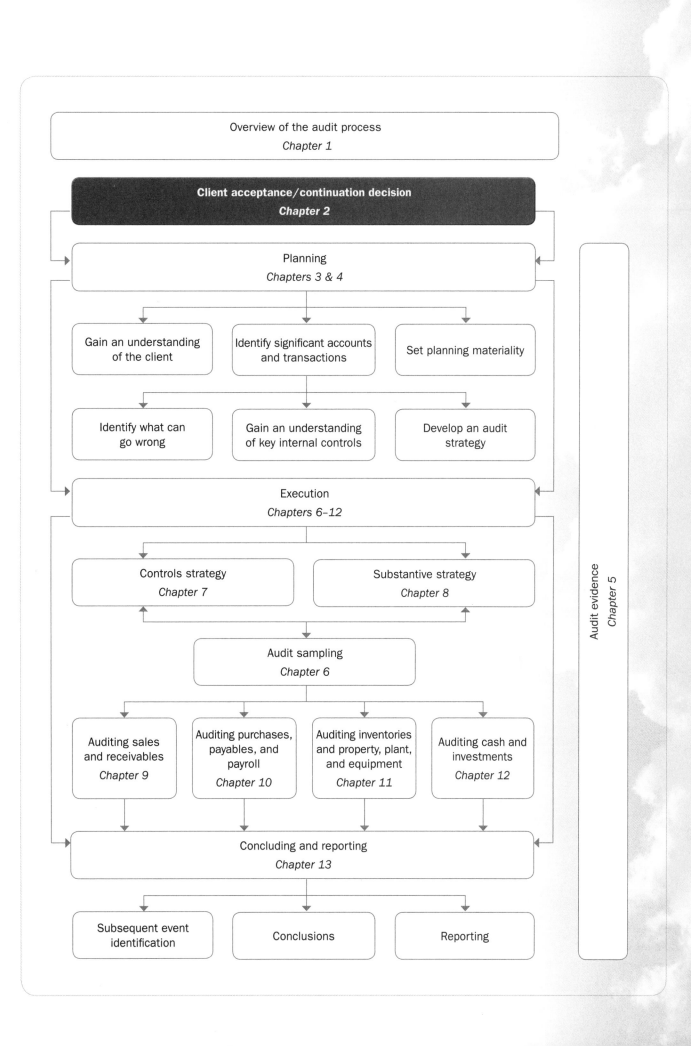

Overview of the audit process
Chapter 1

Client acceptance/continuation decision
Chapter 2

Planning
Chapters 3 & 4

Gain an understanding of the client

Identify significant accounts and transactions

Set planning materiality

Identify what can go wrong

Gain an understanding of key internal controls

Develop an audit strategy

Execution
Chapters 6–12

Controls strategy
Chapter 7

Substantive strategy
Chapter 8

Audit sampling
Chapter 6

Auditing sales and receivables
Chapter 9

Auditing purchases, payables, and payroll
Chapter 10

Auditing inventories and property, plant, and equipment
Chapter 11

Auditing cash and investments
Chapter 12

Concluding and reporting
Chapter 13

Subsequent event identification

Conclusions

Reporting

Audit evidence
Chapter 5

Cloud 9

Recall from chapter 1 that Ron McLellan was considering selling McLellan's Shoes. He came to an arrangement with Chip Masters and sold McLellan's Shoes to Cloud 9 Inc. in 1993. The new business is named Cloud 9 Ltd. (Cloud 9). As part of the sale agreement, Ron McLellan was appointed to the Cloud 9 board of directors.

It is now the present day. Cloud 9 has approached the accounting firm W&S Partners about performing the December 31, 2016 audit. If the client is accepted, the partner responsible for the audit will be Jo Wadley. She has asked Sharon Gallagher and Josh Thomas to assist with the client acceptance work. Sharon is an audit manager. Her task is to make sure that there are no nasty surprises for the audit team if they accept the audit. Sharon knows how crucial this is. She still has nightmares about an audit she worked on when she was a new graduate at another audit firm. The client in that case threatened to dismiss the auditor when the auditor wanted him to recognize an impairment loss on some assets. The client was the firm's largest account and the partner was under a lot of pressure to keep the client.

Josh is an audit senior. He has not been involved in the client acceptance process before, and needs the experience so he can be promoted to audit manager. Sharon and Josh do not know anything about Cloud 9 other than that it manufactures and retails customized basketball shoes; it is a subsidiary of Cloud 9 Inc., a publicly listed Canadian company; and it was purchased from Ron McLellan in 1993. Sharon stresses to Josh that they want to know that the client is not going to be difficult to deal with, and that W&S Partners can do a good job of the audit. Josh asks how they can know that now, before they start the audit.

AUDIT PROCESS IN FOCUS

The purpose of this chapter is to provide an overview of the current audit environment. We start by considering the fundamental principles of professional ethics. In particular, we discuss the principles of integrity, objectivity, professional competence and due care, confidentiality, and professional behaviour. We will also discuss some of the specific rules that incorporate these principles.

Auditor association is defined and how it may come about is discussed. Auditor independence is then described and its importance is explained. Independence of mind (actual independence) is compared and contrasted with independence in appearance (perceived independence). The factors that can threaten auditor independence are then explained. Safeguards that can reduce these threats are also discussed. These safeguards to auditor independence have been established in the law, in professional standards, or in accounting firm policies and procedures.

Financial statement auditors liaise with a number of groups when completing their audit. Apart from their client's management and staff, who aid the auditor directly throughout the audit, other groups are fundamental to the successful completion of an audit. These groups include the client's shareholders, board of directors, audit committee, and internal auditors. The nature of the relationship that the auditor has with each of these groups is explored in this chapter.

An overview of the legal liability of the auditor is provided next. In that summary, we explore the current status of an auditor's liability to their client and third parties. The concept of contributory negligence is also explained.

Finally, we consider the factors that impact the auditor's client acceptance/continuation decision. This section of the chapter marks the beginning of our substantive overview of how an audit is conducted, since the first step for any audit is the decision to accept a company as a new audit client or continue as the auditor of an existing client.

2.1 THE FUNDAMENTAL PRINCIPLES OF PROFESSIONAL ETHICS

1 Describe the fundamental principles of professional ethics and list some of the specific rules professional accountants are required to follow.

Generally speaking, ethics are the standards of behaviour that promote human welfare or the overall public "good."[1] When we speak of ethics with respect to professional accountants, we are therefore referring to the standards of behaviour that promote the welfare of society and the accounting profession.

2.1.1 The six fundamental ethical principles

In Canada, all professional accountants must abide by a code of professional conduct based on six fundamental ethical principles. Accounting professionals are expected to use these principles to guide their behaviour, as they reflect the values deemed critical to the accounting profession. These principles are to act with integrity, objectivity, professional competence and due care, confidentiality, and professional behaviour. Compliance with these fundamental ethical principles is mandatory for all members of the accounting profession. Non-compliance can lead to disciplinary measures by a member's professional body.

What Makes a Profession?

Many people refer to themselves as professionals; however, a true profession should encompass the following characteristics:

- There is mastery of an intellectual skill due to extensive education and training.
- Services are offered to others for a fee.
- There is an independent society or institute that sets and maintains the standards to ensure members are qualified and competent.
- There is a code of conduct established and enforced by the society or institute.

Integrity

Integrity is the obligation that all members of the profession be straightforward and honest. Members should not be associated with information that is materially false or misleading.

> **integrity** the obligation that all members of the accounting profession be straightforward and honest

Objectivity

Objectivity is the obligation that all members of the profession not allow their personal feelings or prejudices to influence their professional judgement. Members should be unbiased and not allow a conflict of interest or the influence of others to impair their decision process.

> **objectivity** the obligation that all members of the profession not allow their personal feelings or prejudices to influence their professional judgement

Professional competence and due care

Professional competence and **due care** are the obligation that all members of the profession maintain their knowledge and skill at a level required by the professional body. Members must attain a level of competence and keep up to date with changes in regulations and standards. The attainment of competence comes from education and work experience. Competence is maintained through continuing education and work experience. Members must also act diligently, taking care to complete each task thoroughly, document all work, and finish on a timely basis.

> **professional competence** the obligation that all members of the accounting profession maintain their knowledge and skill at a required level
>
> **due care** the obligation to complete each task thoroughly, document all work, and finish on a timely basis

Confidentiality

Confidentiality is the obligation that all members of the profession refrain from disclosing information that is learned as a result of their employment to people outside of their workplace. An exception is made where a client has allowed this disclosure to occur or where there is a legal requirement to disclose such information. Members are also not allowed to use information to their advantage or to the advantage of another person that has been gained as a result of their employment and is not publicly available. An example is using information learned from a client to trade shares.

> **confidentiality** the obligation that all members of the profession refrain from disclosing information that is learned as a result of their employment to people outside of their workplace

Professional behaviour

Professional behaviour is the obligation that all members of the profession comply with rules and regulations and ensure that they maintain the reputation of the profession. Members should be honest in their representations to current and prospective clients. Members should not claim to be able to provide services that they are not able to provide. They should not claim to possess qualifications that they do not possess. They should not claim to have gained experience in areas where they have little or none. Finally, members should not undermine the quality of work produced by others or question their reputation.

> **professional behaviour** the obligation that all members of the profession comply with rules and regulations and ensure that they do not harm the reputation of the profession

Cloud 9

Josh is confident that he understands the fundamental principles of professional ethics. They apply to all of their audits and to their professional behaviour as accountants. Josh and Sharon can see no reason why they would not be able to abide by these fundamental principles in the audit of Cloud 9.

2.1.2 Specific rules incorporating the principles of professional ethics

In addition to the guiding ethical principles for professional accountants, there are also a number of specific rules that incorporate these principles. These are important because the principles are not specifically enforceable, but the rules of professional conduct are. Some of these rules are described below.

Fees and pricing

A fee can be provided only when requested by the potential client. Fee quotes cannot be provided to a client without adequate knowledge of the work to be performed. Fees quoted cannot be significantly lower than the fees charged by a predecessor firm. Contingency fees (based on outcome of service) are not permitted.

Advertising

Advertising must be in good taste. It cannot be false or misleading or make unsubstantiated claims.

Contact with predecessor

Before accepting a new engagement, the new auditor is required to contact the predecessor auditor and ask if there is any reason he or she should not accept the engagement. The rules of professional conduct require the predecessor auditor to reply on a timely basis. Due to the requirement of confidentiality, the response will be limited to a yes or no unless the client gives permission to the predecessor auditor to provide more information.

Firm names

Firm names are not to be misleading. They must be in good taste, and they cannot be self-laudatory.

Professional conduct

If a public accountant becomes aware that another designated accountant has breached the rules of professional conduct or has acted in a way that would discredit the profession, the public accountant has a duty to inform the relevant institute of the breach. However, before informing the appropriate institute, the public accountant should contact the other accountant and inform him or her of the criticism and request an explanation.

PROFESSIONAL ENVIRONMENT

Ethical decision-making

Ethical dilemmas are commonplace in both life and the workplace. It is therefore likely that a professional accountant will face an ethical dilemma at some point during his or her career. While the above principles of the code of conduct guide behaviour, the resolution to an ethical dilemma usually involves making a choice between alternatives where there may not be an obvious right or wrong answer. To help make the best possible decision when facing an ethical dilemma, one should follow a structured decision-making process such as the one outlined below:

1. Obtain the relevant facts.
2. Identify the ethical issues.
3. Determine who is affected by the outcome of the dilemma and how each individual or group is affected.

4. Identify the likely alternatives available to the person who must resolve the dilemma.

5. Identify the likely consequence of each alternative.

6. Decide on the appropriate action.

This will ensure all of the issues, affected groups, alternatives, and consequences are considered before a final decision is made.

Apply the above six steps to the following scenario:

You are a recently designated accountant. As a result of having your designation, you have been hired as the controller at a national manufacturing company. Due to a recent economic slowdown, the company has been struggling to meet earnings targets. These targets are the basis for senior management bonuses. You report directly to the CFO.

This is your second month with the company; however, it is your first year end (December 31). The auditor will be coming to audit the books in three weeks. You have finalized the financial statements, and you have reviewed them with the CFO and the CEO.

The week before the auditor is expected to arrive the CFO comes to your office and explains that the financial results are very disappointing. He would like you to make the following journal entry:

> On December 31, a sales contract was signed for $500,000 of goods with delivery to take place January 3. You are asked to record the revenue for this contract on December 31, the date the contract is signed and before the work is performed. This will result in early revenue recognition and doing so, will eliminate the overall net loss for the year.

You are married with a stay-at-home spouse and two small children. To celebrate your success, you recently purchased a new home. It cost a little more than you planned to spend and the mortgage payments are pretty hefty.

What would you do? What are the ethical issues you would need to consider?

BEFORE YOU GO ON

2.1.1 What does it mean to act in the public interest?

2.1.2 List and explain the five fundamental ethical principles in the code of professional conduct for professional accounting bodies.

2.1.3 What are the rules with respect to fees?

2.2 ASSOCIATION AND INDEPENDENCE

According to the Canadian Standards for Assurance Engagements (CSAEs), **association** is the term used to indicate a public accountant's involvement with financial information. There are three ways in which association can happen:

 Define and explain auditor association and independence.

association what occurs when a public accountant is involved with financial information

1. When the public accountant performs a service or consents to the use of his or her name implying that a service was performed with the information.

2. When a third party indicates, without the consent of the public accountant, that he or she is associated with the information.

3. When a third party assumes that the public accountant is associated with the information.

When a public accountant is associated with information, he or she must comply with the rules of professional conduct and with the requirements of the CPA Canada Handbook. The level of the public accountant's involvement with the information must be clearly communicated. This is very important because public accountants must take care to ensure that they are not associated with anything false and misleading.

The concept of **independence** is essential to a public accountant. It is a requirement to comply with the ethical principles to act with integrity and objectivity. Independence is defined as acting with integrity, objectivity, and professional scepticism. It is fundamental to every audit and must be adhered to by every auditor who provides assurance services. An external auditor is often referred to as an independent auditor, which highlights the importance of independence in every audit engagement. Financial statements must be relevant, reliable, comparable, understandable, and fairly presented. (Refer to chapter 1 for a detailed description of these terms.) It is the responsibility of those charged with governance in a company (the **board of directors** and management) to ensure that the financial statements meet these requirements. It is the responsibility of the external auditor to form an opinion on the fair presentation of the financial statements. If an auditor is not independent of their client, it will affect the credibility and reliability of the financial statements. It is vital that financial statement users believe that the external auditor is independent of the company they audit. If that independence is compromised in any way, it will detract from the ability of users to rely on the financial statements to make decisions.

independence the ability to act with integrity, objectivity, and professional scepticism

board of directors the group that represents the shareholders and oversees the activities of a company and its management

There are two forms of independence:

- *Independence of mind* is the ability to act with integrity, objectivity, and professional scepticism. It is the ability to make a decision that is free from bias, personal beliefs, and client pressures. Independence of mind is also referred to as actual independence.

- *Independence in appearance* is the belief that independence of mind has been achieved. It is not enough for an auditor to be independent of mind; they must also be seen as independent. Auditors must consider their actions carefully and ensure that nothing is done to compromise their independence both of mind and in appearance. Independence in appearance is also referred to as perceived independence.

Both independence of mind and independence in appearance are important for every auditor on every assurance engagement. It is the responsibility of every auditor to consider potential threats to their independence and to seek out appropriate safeguards to reduce those threats to the extent possible. If a threat to an auditor's independence appears insurmountable for a particular client, an auditor should consider discontinuing as the auditor of that client.

The next section includes a discussion of the various threats to auditor independence for all assurance engagements as well as some of the additional threats to be considered for reporting issuers. That discussion is followed by a review of some of the safeguards that have been put in place by regulation, the profession, and accounting firms to minimize the threats to auditor independence.

Cloud 9

Sharon tells Josh about her experience at another audit firm where the client tried to pressure the audit partner into dropping a request to write down the asset values. It was an example of a threat to the auditor's independence. Although it is difficult to stop a client asking for a favour, the audit firm needs to have safeguards to prevent a simple request from turning into unreasonable pressure on the audit team to meet that request. Sharon and Josh agree that they need to consider the specific independence threats and safeguards for the audit of Cloud 9. The audit must be independent, as well as be seen to be independent.

2.2.1 Threats to independence

The rules of professional conduct identify five key threats to auditor independence. They are self-interest, self-review, advocacy, familiarity, and intimidation threats. Section 161 of the Canada Business Corporations Act also deals with the requirement of the auditor to be independent. This section focuses on independence as it applies to *all* assurance engagements. This includes all audit and review engagements but not compilation engagements (a non-assurance engagement). However, where the public accountant is not independent of the compilation client, this fact should be added to the Notice to Reader report.

Self-interest threat

self-interest threat the threat that can occur when an accounting firm or its staff has a financial interest in an assurance client

Self-interest threat is the threat that can occur when an accounting firm or its staff has a financial interest in an assurance client. Some examples include:

- assurance team members involved in the assurance engagement (and their immediate families) owning shares in the client's business

- firm members not involved in the assurance engagement (and their immediate families) owning more shares in the client than the maximum number of shares permitted by the relevant governing body

- a loan to or from the client outside of normal lending terms

- fee dependence, where the fees (from assurance and other services) from one client form a significant proportion of the total fees earned from all assurance clients

- a close business relationship with the client, unless the relationship is limited to an immaterial financial interest for the client, the firm member, and the firm

Cloud 9

Sharon's old firm had a fee dependence problem. The audit fees they earned from the client resisting the recommended accounting treatment for asset values were a significant proportion of the firm's total fees. W&S Partners is a much larger audit firm than Sharon's old firm, and Cloud 9's fees will not be a significant portion of total fee revenue.

Self-review threat

Self-review threat is the threat that can occur when the assurance team forms an opinion on their own work or work performed by others in their firm. Some examples include:

- an assurance team member having recently been an employee or a director of the client and therefore able to influence the subject matter of the assurance engagement
- information prepared for the client that is then assured, such as creating source documents, or preparing and recording journal entries without first obtaining management's approval
- services performed for the client that are then assured, such as internal audit services, information technology services, legal services, human resource services, and corporate finance services and valuations

self-review threat the threat that can occur when the assurance team needs to form an opinion on their own work or work performed by others in their firm

Cloud 9

Josh and Sharon do not know of any current work being done for Cloud 9 by W&S Partners, or of any other relationships between members of the audit team and the client's staff. However, they will check with all other departments at W&S Partners, particularly the consulting department. They will also ask any new member of the audit team to disclose their interests and relationships with the client before they join the team.

Advocacy threat

Advocacy threat is the threat that can occur when an accounting firm or its assurance staff acts, or is believed to act, on behalf of its assurance client. In such a case, the objectivity of the assurance provider may come under question. Some examples include:

- encouraging others to buy shares or bonds being sold by the client
- representing the client in negotiations with a third party
- representing the client in a legal dispute

advocacy threat the threat that can occur when a firm or its staff acts on behalf of its assurance client

Cloud 9

The partner, Jo Wadley, advises Sharon and Josh that the audit firm is not acting for Cloud 9 in any other matter.

Familiarity threat

Familiarity threat is the threat that can occur when a close relationship exists or develops between the assurance firm and the client, or between members of the assurance team and directors or employees of the client. The result can be that the assurance team becomes too sensitive to the needs of the client and loses its objectivity. Some examples include:

- a long association between the assurance firm and the client
- a long association between members of the assurance team and their client

familiarity threat the threat that can occur when a close relationship exists or develops between the assurance firm (staff) and the client (staff)

- an assurance team member with a close relative who holds a senior position of influence at the client
- a former partner of the assurance firm holding a senior position with the client
- the acceptance of gifts by members of the assurance team from the client, other than very minor tokens
- the acceptance of hospitality (for example, a meal or tickets to a sporting event) by members of the assurance team from the client, other than very minor gestures

Cloud 9

Familiarity is usually a greater issue for existing clients than for new clients, such as Cloud 9 for W&S Partners. However, there could be personal familiarity issues in any audit engagement. Josh is worried about asking the senior staff to declare their relationships with the management of Cloud 9. He thinks they might regard that question as impertinent. Sharon tells Josh that she knows the senior staff at W&S Partners are very committed to ethical behaviour. If they were not to ask this question as part of the process of accepting the new client, Sharon and Josh would be disciplined for poor performance.

Intimidation threat

intimidation threat the threat that can occur when a member of the assurance team feels threatened by client staff or directors

Intimidation threat is the threat that can occur when a member of the assurance team feels threatened by the client's staff or directors. The result can be that the assurance team member is unable to act objectively, believing that if he or she does so there may be some negative consequences based upon the threat received. Some examples include:

- the threat that the client will use a different assurance firm next year
- undue pressure to reduce audit hours to reduce fees paid

Cloud 9

The partner at Sharon's old firm was threatened with dismissal from the audit, and Sharon has heard of other clients pressuring auditors to reduce their fees. Sharon is confident that the firm of W&S Partners does not rely unreasonably on any one audit and is therefore less vulnerable to threats. She also knows that auditors at W&S Partners keep very detailed records of time spent on any audit tasks and can justify their fees if a client questions the amount.

reporting issuer a public company with a market capitalization and a book value of total assets greater than $10 million

While the above apply to *all* assurance engagements, there are additional prohibitions for auditors of reporting issuers. A **reporting issuer**, in accordance with the independence standard, is a public company with a market capitalization and a book value of total assets greater than $10 million. Some of the additional requirements to ensure auditor independence for reporting issuers include the following:

- Audit partners must be rotated every seven years, with a five-year break from the audit engagement.
- Audit committee must pre-approve all services provided to the client by the firm.
- Audit partners may not be directly compensated for selling non-assurance services to the audit client.
- Certain services are prohibited, meaning the auditor of a reporting issuer cannot perform any of the following: legal services, management functions, human resource services, corporate finance services, litigation suppport, or expert services. Neither can the auditor of a reporting issuer perform bookkeeping and accounting, actuarial, internal audit, valuation

services, and financial information systems design and implementation where the results of the services will be subject to audit.

- Where an engagement team member accepts employment in a financial reporting role with a client, the firm must refrain from being the auditor of that client for at least one year from the date the financial statements were filed with securities regulators.[2]

When any of these threats are recognized, steps should be taken to remove or reduce the threat to an acceptably low level. This can be achieved by utilizing an appropriate safeguard. Figure 2.1 shows the steps taken to minimize threats to independence in an assurance engagement.

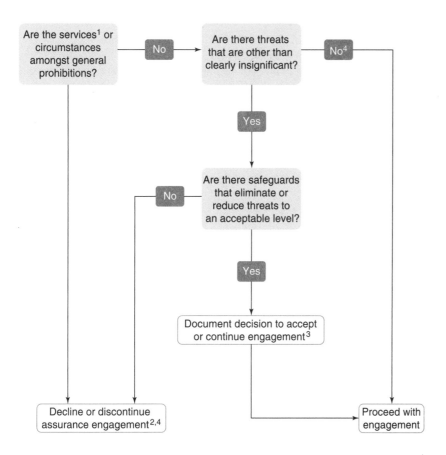

Notes

1 There are additional prohibitions to be considered for reporting issuers.
2 Consider whether a compilation engagement will meet client's needs, and whether it is appropriate in the circumstances to downgrade to a compilation. If so, disclose in the Notice to Reader the nature and extent of lack of independence.
3 Documentation should include the nature of engagement and safeguards to eliminate threats or reduce to an acceptable level.
4 Documentation of the assessment would be prudent.

FIGURE 2.1 **Overview of independence standard for assurance engagement**

Source: Adapted from the Guide to Canadian Independence Standards (2009 Update) with permission of the Chartered Professional Accountants of Canada, Toronto, Canada.

2.2.2 Safeguards to independence

Safeguards are mechanisms that have been developed by the accounting profession, legislators, regulators, clients, and accounting firms. They are used to minimize the risk that a threat will surface (for example, through education) and to deal with a threat when one becomes apparent (for example, through reporting processes within the assurance firm).

Safeguards created by the profession, legislation, or regulation

The accounting profession, legislation, and regulation have created a range of safeguards, including CSQC 1 *Quality Control for Firms that Perform Audits and Reviews of Financial Statements, Other Financial Information, and Other Assurance Engagements.* Safeguards include education of accountants about the threats to independence and the establishment of a code of ethics. For reporting issuers, legislation requires that an auditor be independent and that a communication of independence be issued to the client annually. Figure 2.2 is an illustration of the auditor independence letter.

March 1, 2016
    The Audit Committee
    Cloud 9 Ltd.
    Dear Audit Committee Members:

I have been engaged to audit the financial statements of Cloud 9 Ltd. (the Company) for the year ending December 31, 2016.

Canadian generally accepted auditing standards (GAAS) require that I communicate at least annually with you regarding all relationships between the Company and me that, in my professional judgement, may reasonably be thought to bear on my independence.

In determining which relationships to report, these standards require me to consider relevant rules and related interpretations prescribed by the appropriate provincial institute/order and applicable legislation, covering such matters as:

(a) holding a financial interest, either directly or indirectly, in a client;

(b) holding a position, either directly or indirectly, that gives the right or responsibility to exert significant influence over the financial or accounting policies of a client;

(c) personal or business relationships of immediate family, close relatives, partners or retired partners, either directly or indirectly, with a client;

(d) economic dependence on a client; and

(e) provision of services in addition to the audit engagement.

I am not aware of any relationships between the Company and me that, in my professional judgement, may reasonably be thought to bear on my independence, that have occurred from January 1 to December 31, 2015.

GAAS requires that I confirm my independence to the audit committee in the context of the *Rules of Professional Conduct of the Institute of Chartered Accountants of Ontario.* Accordingly, I hereby confirm that I am independent with respect to the Company within the meaning of the Rules of Professional Conduct of the *Institute of Chartered Accountants of Ontario* as at March 1, 2016.

This report is intended solely for the use of the audit committee, the board of directors, management, and others within the Company and should not be used for any other purposes.

I look forward to discussing with you the matters addressed in this letter at our upcoming meeting.

Yours truly,

W.J.W. Barton

CHARTERED ACCOUNTANT

FIGURE 2.2 **Sample independence letter**

Safeguards created by clients

Clients can put in place appropriate mechanisms that will reduce the threat to independence. They can introduce appropriate **corporate governance** mechanisms (discussed further in chapter 3), such as the establishment of an audit committee to liaise between the assurance partner and management to enhance independence. (See section 2.3.3 for a discussion of the role of audit committees.) Clients can ensure that the responsibility for the appointment and removal of an auditor rests with **independent directors** on the audit committee or the board.

corporate governance the rules, systems, and processes within companies used to guide and control

independent directors non-executive directors without any business or other ties to the company

Clients can establish policies and procedures dedicated to ensuring that the financial statements are fairly presented. Finally, clients can put in place policies and procedures dedicated to ensuring that the assurance team has access to all required documents and records when required. These safeguards can reduce but not eliminate the threat to independence. To ensure their effectiveness, clients must ensure that policies and mechanisms established are working effectively.

Cloud 9

Sharon explains to Josh that one of their key tasks will be to discover, document, and evaluate any independence safeguards created by Cloud 9. She explains that safeguards created by the profession and W&S Partners apply to all audits, so the relative success of an audit with respect to independence problems is significantly affected by the safeguards created by the client. The greater these safeguards, the less likely there will be any problems with the audit. The auditor needs to know that if a problem does arise, the client has committed to protect the integrity of the audit.

Sharon asks Josh to document the governance structure at Cloud 9, including background information on the directors and senior management. Sharon will investigate the structure governing the relationships between the directors and management of Cloud 9 and the parent company, Cloud 9 Inc.

Safeguards created by accounting firms

Accounting firms have in place a range of safeguards to ensure independence. They have policies and procedures to ensure the quality of their service, and they provide continuing education for their staff regarding these policies and procedures. Firms have client acceptance and continuance procedures to ensure that they identify any threats to independence on a timely basis. Firms have partner rotation policies to ensure that audit partners remain independent of their clients. They also have a policy of peer review, where audit partners review the working paper files of other partners and provide comment and feedback. Finally, firms establish procedures for staff to follow if they become aware of a threat to their independence. These safeguards can reduce but not eliminate the threat to independence. Accounting firms must ensure that policies and mechanisms established are working effectively.

Table 2.1 lists the five threats to independence, together with some of the safeguards that can help to remove or reduce each threat to an acceptably low level.

TABLE 2.1 **Summary of independence threats and safeguards**

THREATS TO INDEPENDENCE	EXAMPLES	SAFEGUARDS TO INDEPENDENCE
Self-interest threat	• An auditor has a financial interest in their client. • An audit firm relies on the fees from a client. • An audit partner is concerned about losing a prestigious client. • An auditor has a business relationship with a client.	• Policies and procedures within an accounting firm identifying any staff with financial interest in an assurance client. • Regular review of assurance and other fees earned from each client compared with total fees from all assurance clients. • Minimizing the provision of non-audit services to assurance clients. • Policies and procedures prohibiting business relationships with clients.

(continued)

TABLE 2.1 **Summary of independence threats and safeguards** (continued)

THREATS TO INDEPENDENCE	EXAMPLES	SAFEGUARDS TO INDEPENDENCE
Self-review threat	• An assurance team is asked to evaluate the effectiveness of an operating system that a colleague in their firm implemented on behalf of the client. • An assurance team audits records that were prepared by a colleague in their firm on behalf of the client. • A member of the assurance team has recently been an employee of the client in a position that impacted the subject matter being assured.	• Minimizing the provision of non-audit services to assurance clients. • When providing non-audit services, ensuring that the client is responsible for overseeing and guiding that work and making any final decisions regarding the outcomes of that work. • Having a cooling-off period before an audit partner can be employed in a senior role at an audit client.
Advocacy threat	• A firm promotes shares of an audit client. • An auditor represents an audit client in a legal case.	• Policies and procedures prohibiting business relationships with clients. • Policies and procedures prohibiting the representation of clients in any disputes or legal matters. • Rotating staff assigned to clients so they do not spend too much time at any one client's premises.
Familiarity threat	• An auditor has a family member who is a director on the board of an audit client. • An auditor has a family member involved in the preparation of the accounting information subject to audit. • An auditor accepts special gifts from their client. • A long association exists between members of the audit team and an audit client. • A director is on the board of an audit client who was until recently the engagement partner on the audit.	• Partner and staff rotation policies. • Education regarding acceptance of gifts and hospitality from assurance clients providing examples of what is and what is not acceptable. • Procedures when assigning staff to assurance clients ensuring no close personal relationships exist between assurance team members and client personnel. • Education regarding socializing with client personnel.
Intimidation threat	• A client threatens to dismiss the audit firm. • The audit firm is threatened with litigation by their audit client. • The client places pressure on the audit team to reduce the scope of the audit, to reduce audit fees, or to meet an unrealistic deadline. • A member of the client's staff places undue pressure on the audit team to allow them to use an inappropriate accounting technique.	• Avoidance of fee dependence. • Appropriate corporate governance structures within clients, such as an audit committee, to liaise with senior assurance team members and client management. • Adherence to stringent procedures regarding the removal of assurance providers.

Source: Based on Accounting Professional and Ethical Standards Board 2011, APES 110, section 290. Reproduced with the permission of the Accounting Professional and Ethical Standards Board (APESB), Victoria, Australia.

PROFESSIONAL ENVIRONMENT

Quality control

Canada adopted the CSQC 1, *Quality Control for Firms that Perform Audits and Reviews of Financial Statements, Other Financial Information, and Other Assurance Engagements*, on December 15, 2009, to complement its adoption of the CASs. The CSQC 1 deals with a firm's responsibilities to establish, document, and maintain a system of quality control if it performs audits and reviews of financial statements and other assurance engagements. The purpose of this standard is to ensure firms comply with legal and regulatory requirements and to ensure firms issue appropriate opinions.

As a result, firms that offer assurance services must have a quality assurance manual that outlines policies and procedures in the following areas:

· leadership responsibility to promote a culture of quality
· compliance with ethical requirements including a requirement to assess independence

- client acceptance and continuance to ensure firms perform engagements within their competencies and that they have adequate resources available
- human resource policies to ensure personnel are capable, competent, and ethical
- criteria for performing and documenting engagement quality reviews: while an engagement quality review (more commonly known as second partner review) is required for all listed entities, firms need criteria to assess the need for an engagement quality review for non-listed entities. An engagement quality review involves a review of the financial statements and the work performed, and an evaluation of the opinion formed.

- monitoring: there are two requirements a firm must meet with respect to monitoring. First, a firm must perform an ongoing assessment of its compliance with the policies and procedures set out in its quality assurance manual. Second, every one to three years, a firm should have a "monitor" (someone not involved in the assurance engagements) review a selection of assurance files, as well as assess the quality control activities of the firm. A report should be issued identifying any weaknesses or deficiencies.

Source: The *CPA Canada Handbook* – Assurance, Effective as of December 15, 2009

BEFORE YOU GO ON

2.2.1 What are the three ways an auditor can become associated with financial information?

2.2.2 Why is auditor independence so important?

2.2.3 What are some examples of circumstances that may cause a familiarity threat?

2.3 THE AUDITOR'S RELATIONSHIPS WITH OTHERS

The external auditor has the responsibility to form an opinion on the fair presentation of the financial statements prepared by their client. In conducting their audit, the external auditor comes into contact with client staff and management on a regular basis. The key groups that the external auditor will have a professional link with are the client's shareholders, the board of directors, the audit committee, and the internal audit team.

3 Explain the relationship between an auditor and key groups they have a professional link with during the audit engagement.

2.3.1 Auditors and shareholders

The audit report is addressed to the **shareholders** of the company being audited. This means that the shareholders are acknowledged as the main recipients of the financial statements and the attached audit report. Shareholders own the company. If the company fails, shareholders stand to lose most, if not all, of their investment. Shareholders rely on the audit report and the opinion contained within it to inform them about the reliability of the information provided by the management of their company in the financial statements. Auditors will not often meet the shareholders they report to except when they attend their client's annual general meeting. Exceptions include major shareholders, whom the auditor may meet with from time to time, and shareholding board members and client personnel, whom the auditor will meet with during the course of their audit. Shareholders are responsible for the appointment and removal of their company's auditors. The board of directors will facilitate this process on behalf of shareholders. Generally, the board will select an audit firm that they believe is appropriate or will propose when it is time to appoint a new audit firm. The board will then make a recommendation to shareholders. Shareholders generally follow recommendations made by the board of directors.

shareholders owners of the company

2.3.2 Auditors and the board of directors

The board of directors represents the shareholders and oversees the activities of a company and its management. It is the role of the board to ensure that the company is being run to benefit the shareholders. The board will generally comprise a mixture of executive and non-executive directors. **Executive directors** are also part of the company's management team; they are full-time employees of the company. **Non-executive directors** are not part of the company's management team; their involvement is limited to preparing for and attending board meetings and relevant board committee meetings. It is the directors' responsibility to ensure that the financial statements are fairly presented and provide a true and fair view. It is the responsibility of the external auditor to audit the financial statements. The audit partner will meet with members of the board when necessary throughout the audit.

executive directors employees of the company who also hold a position on the board of directors

non-executive directors board members who are not employees of the company. Their involvement on the board is limited to preparing for and attending board meetings and relevant board committee meetings

It is important that the board of directors have a mixture of executive and non-executive members; however, the majority of the board should be independent directors. The executive members have a deeper understanding of the company and its workings. Auditors meet with executive directors throughout the audit. The non-executive members are better representatives of shareholders as they are not employees of the company and can be more impartial in their dealings with management. The external auditor will read the minutes of board meetings to learn about the key decisions regarding the strategic direction the board plans to take the company in the future. Other information that may be found in the minutes includes the level of dividends declared, plans for significant asset purchases, purchases and sales of major investments, and major agreements with other companies that may be contemplated.

Boards of larger companies will also have a series of committees made up of various members of the board. It is the role of these committees to efficiently deal with specific important issues. The main board committee that the auditor deals with is the audit committee. The audit committee is described in more detail in the next section.

2.3.3 Auditors and the audit committee

audit committee a subcommittee of the board of directors. The audit committee enhances auditor independence and ensures that the financial statements are fairly presented and that the external auditor has access to all records and other evidence required to form their opinion.

An effective **audit committee** will enhance the independence of the external audit function: an audit committee acts on behalf of the full board of directors to ensure that the financial statements are fairly presented and that the external auditor has access to all records and other evidence required to form their opinion. While ultimate responsibility for the fair presentation of the financial statements rests with the full board, an audit committee can improve the efficiency of achieving this goal.

In Canada, the Canadian Securities Administrators (CSA) require that all listed companies have an audit committee. The role of this committee is to oversee the accounting, financial reporting, and audit of the financial statements. The audit committee should be established by the board and should consist of at least three independent directors who are financially literate.

From an audit perspective, it is important that the audit committee be independent of the remainder of the board and of the financial reporting function. The audit committee should consist of only non-executive independent directors. As noted earlier, a non-executive director is not part of the company's management team. An independent director is a non-executive director without any business or other ties to the company that could impede his or her ability to act impartially.

An audit committee should consist of members who can read and understand the contents of the financial statements. It is important that audit committee members have some understanding of the accounting policies used by the company and can communicate easily with the auditor about those choices. The audit partner will report to the audit committee when they have a significant disagreement with management regarding accounting choices made and/or with the content of the notes to the financial statements.

A formal charter sets out the structure, composition, and responsibilities of the audit committee. When a company does not have an audit committee, the audit partner will meet with members of the board of directors.

The responsibilities of the audit committee include the following:

- to recommend the auditor and their fees to the board
- to oversee the audit and resolve any differences between the auditor and management
- to pre-approve all non-audit services to be provided to the entity or its subsidiaries by the independent auditor

2.3.4 Auditors and internal auditors

internal auditors employees of the company who evaluate and make recommendations to improve risk management, internal control procedures, and elements of the governance process

The role of internal audit (and **internal auditors**) is determined by those charged with governance, ideally the audit committee. The role of the internal audit function was explained in chapter 1. The external auditor views the internal audit function as part of the company being audited and, as such, the internal audit function can never be wholly independent of the company. However, if a company has an effective internal audit function, the external auditor can consider modifying the nature and timing of their procedures and reduce the extent of their audit testing. The final opinion on fair presentation of the financial statements remains with the external auditor, as does the responsibility for gathering and evaluating sufficient appropriate audit evidence to form that opinion. If the external auditor intends to use the work of the internal audit function, they should consider various internal audit characteristics (CAS 610 *Using the Work of Internal Auditors*), including the objectivity, technical competence, and due professional care of the internal audit function and the effectiveness of communication between internal and external audit. These characteristics are described below.

Objectivity

Objectivity is achieved when the client organization's internal audit function has a high level of independence from the rest of the organization. The more independent the internal audit function, the more reliance that can be placed upon it by the external auditor. Ideally, internal auditors should report directly to the audit committee or the board of directors.

Technical competence

Technical competence is the skills, training, and ability of the internal audit team. The external auditor may consider the background and qualifications, the level of training undertaken, and the extent of the experience of the internal audit staff. The external auditor will also be concerned as to whether internal audit staff are appropriately qualified for their roles.

> **technical competence** the skills, training, and ability of the internal audit team

Due professional care

Due professional care is the documentation, planning, and supervision of the internal audit function. The external auditor is interested in the level of planning undertaken by internal audit. They will also want to see evidence of the procedures undertaken by internal auditors in formulating their conclusions.

Communication

Communication between internal and external auditors is achieved through the scheduling of regular meetings, the external auditor having access to internal audit documentation as needed, and the external auditor informing internal auditors of any issues affecting their work that arise during the external audit. It is important that internal and external auditors are free to communicate without interference from client management or staff.

Cloud 9

Understanding the board of directors and its subcommittees will be a part of Josh and Sharon's work in documenting Cloud 9's governance structure. In particular, they have to find out whether Cloud 9 has an audit committee and get to know the background of the directors who sit on the board. They also have to check for the existence of an internal audit department at Cloud 9, and find out what they can about the role and function of the internal audit department at Cloud 9 Inc. (the parent company) as it relates to Cloud 9.

BEFORE YOU GO ON

2.3.1 What is the difference between a non-executive and an independent director?

2.3.2 Why is it important that an audit committee be independent?

2.3.3 Why might an external auditor want to use the work of the internal audit function?

2.4 LEGAL LIABILITY

As noted in chapter 1, the external auditor must exercise due care when conducting an audit. This means that the auditor must be diligent in applying technical and professional standards, and must document each stage in the audit process. If the auditor is found to be **negligent** (to have not exercised due care), they may be sued for damages by their client or a third party.

Under tort law, to prove that an auditor has been negligent, it must be established that:

- A duty of care was owed by the auditor.
- There was a breach of the duty of care.
- A loss was suffered as a consequence of that breach.

> **4** Explain the auditor's legal liability to their client, contributory negligence, and the extent to which an auditor is liable to third parties.

> **negligence** failure to exercise due care

Tort law is a body of rights, obligations, and remedies that is applied by courts in civil proceedings to provide relief for persons who have suffered harm from the wrongful acts of others. The person who sustains injury or suffers pecuniary damage is known as the plaintiff, and the person who is responsible for inflicting the injury and incurs liability for the damage is known as the defendant.[3]

2.4.1 Legal liability to clients

An auditor can be sued by their client. When suing the auditor, the client must prove that the auditor owed them a duty of care. A client can establish that the auditor owed them a duty of care in one of two ways: (1) under contract law for breach of contract or (2) under tort law for negligence.

1. Under contract law, a client can sue the auditor for breach of contract. This action may be taken when the auditor fails to live up to their responsibility implicit in agreeing to act as the auditor and explicit in the engagement letter. For example, if the auditor withdraws from an audit without cause, before completing the audit and issuing the report, the client can sue the auditor for breach of contract.

2. Under the tort of negligence, a client can claim that the auditor failed to take reasonable care in the performance of the audit. This means that the work was below the standard that may be reasonably expected from a designated public accountant. The injured party must prove that the auditor's carelessness or unintentional behaviour caused harm and therefore breached the duty of care.

An auditor's duty of care to their client has been established and defined through case law over more than a century. In these cases, the definition of reasonable care and skill has changed over time to reflect changes in professional standards. To prove that an auditor has been negligent, a plaintiff, whether a client or a third party, must establish that an auditor did not comply with auditing standards, ethical pronouncements, or some element of the law in place at the time the auditor conducted their audit. Often-cited cases are described below.

London and General Bank Ltd. (No. 2) (1895) 2 Ch. 673

This case established that an auditor has a duty to report to the shareholders, not the directors, of the company being audited. In forming his judgement, Lord Justice Linley noted that "an auditor however is not bound to do more than exercise reasonable care and skill in making inquiries and investigations. He is not an insurer; he does not guarantee that the books do correctly show the true position of the company's affairs. What is reasonable care and skill in any particular case must depend upon the circumstances of that case." This case provided an explanation of the extent to which an auditor could be held liable for the actions of their clients.

Kingston Cotton Mill (No. 2) (1896) 2 Ch. 279

In this case, Lord Justice Lopes noted that "it is the duty of an auditor to bring to bear on the work he has to perform that skill, care and caution, which a reasonably competent, careful and cautious auditor would use. What is reasonable skill, care and caution must depend on the particular circumstances of each case. An auditor is not bound to be a detective or, as was said, to approach his work with suspicion or with a foregone conclusion that there is something wrong. He is a watchdog, but not a bloodhound." This finding indicated that an auditor is not to *assume* that the client's accounts are materially misstated.

Pacific Acceptance (1970) 90 WN (NSW) 29

This case recognized that standards of reasonable care and skill had changed considerably since the Kingston Cotton Mill case of 1896. Justice Moffit pronounced the following in his judgement in the Pacific Acceptance case:

- Auditors have a duty to use reasonable care and skill.
- Auditors have a duty to check and see for themselves rather than rely on client management and staff.
- Auditors must closely supervise and review the work of junior staff.
- Auditors must properly document procedures used.
- Auditors have a duty to warn and inform the appropriate level of management.

- Auditors have a duty to take further action where suspicion is aroused that a misstatement may have occurred.
- Auditors should be guided by professional standards.

Negligence is any behaviour that is careless or unintentional and breaches the duty of care. In proving that an auditor has been negligent, a client or its shareholders would need to prove that the auditor had not complied with auditing standards or ethical guidelines. After establishing that the auditor owed them a duty of care and that the auditor has been in some way negligent (has breached that duty of care), the client or its shareholders would need to establish that they suffered a loss as a result of that negligence. To ascertain a causal relationship between the negligent act and the loss suffered, reasonable foreseeability must be proven. This means that the auditor must have been aware that any negligence on their part could cause a loss to the client or its shareholders.

2.4.2 Contributory negligence

Contributory negligence means that where a plaintiff (the party suing) and the defendant (the auditor) can be proven to have been negligent, each party must be held accountable in proportion to their guilt. For example, management is responsible for putting in place an adequate system of internal control. However, if management fails to do this and the auditor uncovers the weakness and reports it to management, but fails to report it to the directors when management does not repair the deficient control, management, as well as the auditor, would be found to have been negligent and to have contributed to the loss of the plaintiff.

2.4.3 Legal liability to third parties

Establishing that a duty of care is owed to third parties is not straightforward. **Third parties** include anyone other than the client and its shareholders who use the financial statements to make a decision (for example, creditors). As third parties generally do not have a contractual relationship with the auditor, they must rely on tort law. The key difficulty for third parties is establishing that a duty of care was owed to them by the auditor. If they are able to prove that such a duty is owed, third parties must provide evidence that the auditor was negligent and that the third party suffered a loss as a result of that negligence. Below is a very brief summary of the key cases that have established the legal liability of auditors to third parties.

third parties anyone other than the client and its shareholders who uses the financial statements to make a decision

Ultramares Corp v. Touche (1931) 174 N.E. 441

This is an American case that has had an impact on Canadian auditors because it resulted in what is called the Ultramares doctrine. The Ultramares doctrine establishes that auditors are not liable for ordinary negligence to parties that they do not have a privity (contractual) relationship with. In this case, Judge Cardozzo ruled that an auditor cannot have "liability in an indeterminate amount for an indeterminate time to an indeterminate class." The liability of auditors would be too great, as auditors should not be required to owe a duty of care to everyone.

Hedley Byrne & Co v. Heller and Partners Ltd. (1964) A.C. 465

This is an English case heard by the House of Lords, but the outcome has had an impact on professionals in all common law countries. It introduced the concept of foreseeable third parties. The court's ruling in this case expanded the concept of auditor liability beyond the privity (contractual) relationship. The concept of liability was extended to third parties provided the auditors knew beforehand that the third party would be relying on their opinion.[4]

Haig v. Bamford (1977) S.C.R. 466

This is a Canadian case that furthered the foreseeable third-party concept. In this case, the auditor prepared audited financial statements knowing that the statements were being provided to an outside investor. The investor relied on the financial statements and subsequently the company went bankrupt and the investor incurred a loss. The court ruled that although the auditors did not know the name of the investor, they knew the audited financial statements were being passed on to unidentified members of a limited class for use in a transaction of which the accountants were aware.

Hercules Management Ltd. v. Ernst & Young [1997] S.C.R. 165

In this case, potential shareholders relied on the audited financial statements and made a share investment. They then brought a suit against the auditor claiming that the financial statements were prepared negligently. The outcome of this case reversed the trend of expanding auditor legal liability. The court dismissed the negligence claim in that it ruled the audited financial statements were prepared to evaluate management stewardship, not for individuals making investment decisions. Therefore, because the plaintiffs did not rely on the financial statements for the purpose for which they were prepared, there was no duty of care.

Livent Inc. v. Deloitte & Touche LLP, 2014 ONSC 2176

This recent case heard in Ontario may change the future landscape of auditor liability. Livent, a theatre production company that ran the Phantom of the Opera, went bankrupt in the late 1990s. After it filed for bankruptcy, the company and its management were investigated for both criminal and securities fraud. Subsequently, two of its founders, Garth Drabinsky and Myron Gottlieb, were convicted of fraud for "cooking the books" and its auditor, Deloitte & Touche, was sued for failing to detect the fraud. In April 2014, an Ontario judge ruled that Deloitte was negligent when conducting its 1997 audit and ordered the accounting firm to pay Livent creditors $84.8 million. The lawsuit was successful because it did not challenge the doctrine established by the Hercules case above, which limited auditor liability to third parties. In the Livent case, the lawsuit was not filed directly by third-party shareholders or creditors, but rather it was filed by the receiver of the bankrupt company on behalf of the creditors. The judge ruled this fit within the Hercules limitation because the plaintiff was the company itself. At the time of writing, Deloitte was appealing this decision. If upheld, it could expand auditor liability and lead to more lawsuits against auditors in which companies are sued by bankruptcy receivers on behalf of investors.[5]

In summary, to establish that an auditor owes a duty of care to a third party, the third party must demonstrate that a duty of care existed, the duty of care was breached, the audit report was relied upon, and there were quantifiable damages. The third party must also establish that the auditor was aware that the third party was going to use the financial statements and that they relied on the financial statements for the purpose for which they were prepared. Figure 2.3 illustrates auditor liability.

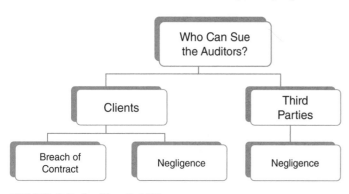

FIGURE 2.3 **Auditor liability**

PROFESSIONAL ENVIRONMENT

Self-regulation of professional accountants

The accounting profession is self-regulating. Each province has a written code of conduct that is enforced by each provincial institute. Any complaint made against a member is investigated. If the investigation leads to a formal complaint of professional misconduct, a hearing is held. Similar to a court hearing, a committee of peers hears evidence and testimony regarding the allegation. Based on the evidence presented, a determination is made as to whether the member has violated the code of conduct. When a member is found guilty of professional misconduct, consequences include being reprimanded, fined, suspended, or expelled. In some provinces, the results of such hearings may be published.

Ontario is one province where the results of professional conduct cases are published. The following is a sample of some of the cases published and the consequences. (Note: The names have been changed.)

1. Public accountant Bill Summers was found guilty of professional misconduct for attempting to obtain clients through use of a telemarketing campaign. He was fined $1,500.

2. While a partner in a professional accounting firm, Lorne Motto entered into an improper arrangement with two of his firm's clients. Without the knowledge of his partners, Mr. Motto inflated the time charged for his professional services and then discounted the fees in return for home renovations and favourable pricing on computer equipment for his personal use. Also, while engaged as the auditor of a company, he accepted two loans from the company's president. Mr. Motto was found guilty and he was expelled from the profession. Subsequent to being expelled, Mr. Motto applied for readmission to the institute after upgrading his professional credentials.

3. Theodore Chase was found guilty of failing to maintain the good reputation of the profession. The charges arose after Mr. Chase was convicted of income tax evasion under the Income Tax Act. Over a six-year period, Mr. Chase failed to report over $300,000 of income and evaded income taxes of over $80,000. He was fined $5,000 and expelled from the institute.

4. Jean Santos was found guilty of using client confidential information for personal gain. Mr. Santos received confidential information that one of his clients was about to purchase all the shares of ABC Limited. Mr. Santos acted on that information to purchase shares of ABC Limited before the proposed buyout becoming public. Mr. Santos was fined $2,314 (an amount equal to twice the profit he realized on his subsequent sale of the shares) and was suspended for three months.

5. Public accountant Kent Ray improperly removed funds from the bank account of a not-for-profit organization, of which he was a director and signing officer, and converted the funds to his own use. He then falsified the association's financial statements in an effort to cover up his misappropriation. He was fined $3,000 and expelled from membership.

Source: Chartered Professional Accountants for Ontario, Decisions, Orders and Reasons in Cases involving Disciplinary Proceedings, http://www.cpaontario.ca/Public/DisciplinaryCases/1013page1385.aspx

2.4.4 Avoidance of litigation

There are a number of ways that an auditor can avoid litigation. These include:

- hiring competent staff
- training staff and updating their knowledge regularly
- ensuring compliance with ethical regulations
- ensuring compliance with auditing regulations
- implementing policies and procedures that ensure:
  - appropriate procedures are followed when accepting a new client
  - appropriate staff are allocated to clients
  - ethical and independence issues are identified and dealt with on a timely basis
  - all work is fully documented
  - adequate and appropriate evidence is gathered before forming an opinion
- meeting with a client's audit committee to discuss any significant issues identified as part of the audit
- following up on any significant weaknesses in the client's internal control procedures in a previous year's audit

---

BEFORE YOU GO ON

2.4.1 What are the two ways a client can establish the duty of care?

2.4.2 What is contributory negligence?

2.4.3 What must be established under tort law to prove that an auditor has been negligent?

2.5 CLIENT ACCEPTANCE AND CONTINUANCE DECISIONS

The first stage of any audit is the client acceptance or continuance decision. While the decision to take on a new client is more detailed than the decision to continue with an existing client, they have much in common. CSQC 1 provides guidance on the procedures to be followed when making the client acceptance or continuance decision.

The first step involves the assessment of client integrity. When assessing client integrity, the auditor will consider:

5 Identify the factors to consider in the client acceptance or continuance decision.

- the reputation of the client, its management, directors, and key stakeholders
- the reasons provided for switching audit firms (client acceptance decision)
- the client's attitude to risk exposure and management
- the client's attitude to the implementation and maintenance of adequate internal controls to mitigate (minimize) identified risks
- the appropriateness of the client's interpretation of accounting rules
- the client's willingness to allow the auditor full access to information required to form their opinion
- the client's attitude to audit fees and its willingness to pay a fair amount for the work completed

Information relevant to the client acceptance or continuance decision can be found through:

- communication with the previous auditor (client acceptance decision) before communicating any client details to the prospective auditor (if that permission is refused, the auditor should consider declining the appointment as auditor)
- communication with client personnel
- communication with third parties such as client bankers and lawyers
- an Internet or background search
- a review of news articles about the client
- a review of prior-period financial statements

The code of professional conduct and the CSQC 1 deal with professional appointments. Before accepting a new client, consideration must be given to any threats to compliance with the fundamental principles of professional ethics (integrity, objectivity, professional competence and due care, confidentiality, and professional behaviour). Threats to the fundamental principles of professional ethics will occur if the prospective client is dishonest, involved in illegal activities, or aggressive in its interpretations of accounting rules. An audit firm should not accept an entity as a new client if it is concerned about any of these issues. Potential threats to compliance with the fundamental principles of professional ethics for existing clients should be considered from time to time.

To ensure professional competence and due care, an audit firm must make certain that it has the staff available at the time required to complete the audit (client acceptance decision). The audit firm must ensure that its audit staff have the knowledge and competence required to conduct the audit. The auditor must have access to independent experts if required.

To ensure that it is independent of prospective and continuing clients, the audit firm must review the threats to independence, described earlier, and make certain that safeguards are put in place to limit or remove those threats. An auditor should therefore assess independence before the client acceptance or continuance decision is made. See figure 2.4 for a sample of an independence assessment worksheet [form 410] from the *Canadian Professional Engagement Manual (C·PEM)*. It is important to note the C·PEM is not authoritative guidance, but rather it is a tool used by practitioners to assist in performing assurance and compilation engagements.

FIGURE 2.4 **Extract of independence assessment, C·PEM Form 410**
Source: CPEM Form 410

Are we satisfied there are no existing prohibitions that would preclude the firm or any staff member from performing the engagement? Address each of the following prohibitions listed below:

a) Financial interests in entity.
b) Loans and guarantees to/from client.
c) Close business relationships with client.
d) Family and personal relationships with client.
e) Future or recent employment with entity serving as officer, director, or company secretary of client.
f) Provision of non-assurance services such as corporate finance or legal services that involve dispute resolution.
g) Performance of management functions for the client.
h) Making journal entries or accounting classifications without first obtaining management's approval.
i) Acceptance of gifts or hospitality from client (other than clearly insignificant).
j) Fee quote that is considerably less than market price for the engagement.

(continued)

FIGURE 2.4 **Extract of independence assessment, C·PEM Form 410** (continued)

---

k) Provision of legal services.
l) Preparation of source documentation.
m) Provision of corporate finance services.

Are we satisfied there are no significant "threats" to independence? Address each of the following threats in relation to the firm and any member of the engagement team:

a) Self-interest (i.e., where loss of client fees would be material).
b) Self-review (i.e., the nature and extent of bookkeeping services required or where a judgement from a previous engagement needs to be evaluated in reaching conclusions).
c) Advocacy (i.e., acting as an advocate on behalf of client in litigation or in share promotion).
d) Familiarity (i.e., being too sympathetic to the client's interests).
e) Intimidation (i.e., being deterred from acting objectively and exercising professional scepticism).

Comment: Threats identified and safeguards (if any) to reduce the threat to an acceptable level:

If an independence threat appears insurmountable, an audit firm should consider declining an offer to act as an auditor of a prospective client or resign from the audit of an existing client. An example of such a threat is fee dependence, where the fees from a client would form a significant proportion of total fees earned. This can occur if a prospective client is much larger than an audit firm's current clients or if an existing client has grown significantly.

The final stage in the client acceptance and continuance decision process involves the preparation of an **engagement letter**. CAS 210 *Agreeing the Terms of Audit Engagements* provides guidance on the preparation of engagement letters. An engagement letter is prepared by an auditor and acknowledged by a client before the commencement of an audit. It is a form of contract between an auditor and the client. Engagement letters should be updated each year to remind management of the existing terms and for legal liability purposes. The purpose of the engagement letter is to set out the terms of the audit engagement to avoid any misunderstandings between the auditor and the client. The letter will confirm both the obligations of the client and the auditor.

An engagement letter includes an explanation of the scope of the audit, summarizes the responsibilities of management and the responsibilities of the auditor, identifies the applicable financial reporting framework, and makes reference to the expected form and content of the audit report. An example of an engagement letter for statements prepared in accordance with International Financial Reporting Standards (IFRS) is provided in the appendix to CAS 210 and is reproduced in figure 2.5.

engagement letter letter that sets out the terms of the audit engagement, to avoid any misunderstandings between the auditor and their client

FIGURE 2.5 **Example of an engagement letter**
Source: Auditing and Assurance Standards Board 2009, CAS 210 *Agreeing the Terms of Audit Engagements, App. 1*

To the appropriate representative of management or those charged with governance of Securimax Ltd.

You have requested that we audit the financial statements of Securimax Ltd. which comprise the balance sheet as at December 31, 2016, and the income statement, statement of changes in equity, and cash flow statement for the year then ended, and a summary of significant accounting policies and other explanatory information. We are pleased to confirm our acceptance and our understanding of this audit engagement by means of this letter. Our audit will be conducted with the objective of our expressing an opinion on the financial statements.

We will conduct our audit in accordance with Canadian generally accepted auditing standards. Those standards require that we comply with ethical requirements and plan and perform the audit to obtain reasonable assurance about whether the

---

(continued)

FIGURE 2.5 **Example of an engagement letter** (continued)

financial statements are free from material misstatement. An audit involves performing procedures to obtain audit evidence about the amounts and disclosures in the financial statements. The procedures selected depend on the auditor's judgement, including the assessment of the risks of material misstatement of the financial statements, whether due to fraud or error. An audit also includes evaluating the appropriateness of accounting policies used and the reasonableness of accounting estimates made by management, as well as evaluating the overall presentation of the financial statements.

Because of the inherent limitations of an audit, together with the inherent limitations of internal control, there is an unavoidable risk that some material misstatements may not be detected, even though the audit is properly planned and performed in accordance with Canadian generally accepted auditing standards.

In making our risk assessments, we consider internal control relevant to the entity's preparation of the financial statements in order to design audit procedures that are appropriate in the circumstances, but not for the purpose of expressing an opinion on the effectiveness of the entity's internal control. However, we will communicate to you in writing concerning any significant deficiencies in internal control relevant to the audit of the financial statements that we have identified during the audit.

Our audit will be conducted on the basis that management and, where appropriate, those charged with governance acknowledge and understand that they have responsibility:

(a) For the preparation and fair presentation of the financial statements in accordance with International Financial Reporting Standards;

(b) For such internal control as management determines is necessary to enable the preparation of financial statements that are free from material misstatement, whether due to fraud or error; and

(c) To provide us with:

(i) Access to all information of which management is aware that is relevant to the preparation of the financial statements such as records, documentation, and other matters;

(ii) Additional information that we may request from management for the purpose of the audit; and

(iii) Unrestricted access to persons within the entity from whom we determine it necessary to obtain audit evidence.

As part of our audit process, we will request from management and, where appropriate, those charged with governance written confirmation concerning representations made to us in connection with the audit.

We look forward to full cooperation from your staff during our audit.

Insert: appropriate reference to the expected form and content of the auditor's report.

The form and content of our report may need to be amended in the light of our audit findings.

Please sign and return the attached copy of this letter to indicate your acknowledgement of, and agreement with, the arrangements for our audit of the financial statements, including our respective responsibilities.

Acknowledged and agreed on behalf of Securimax Ltd.
by James Reynolds, CFO
Securimax Ltd.
October 1, 2016

As indicated in the engagement letter, management is responsible for the entity's accounting process, which involves the recording of transactions and events. It is management's responsibility to ensure that the information is properly recorded, classified, and summarized at the end of the accounting period. Management is considered to be responsible for the financial statements and acknowledges this responsibility when they sign the engagement letter in which the following are outlined:

• Management is responsible for the selection and preparation of the financial statements in accordance with the appropriate financial reporting framework.

- Management is responsible for ensuring that there are adequate internal controls in place so the prepared financial statements are free from material misstatement.
- Management is responsible for providing the auditor unrestricted access to personnel and documents as needed.

By agreeing to the above, management acknowledges its understanding that the auditor does not have any responsibility for the preparation of the financial statements or for the entity's related internal controls, and that these concepts are fundamental for an independent audit.

Cloud 9

Sharon and Josh have already discussed some of the specific client acceptance issues, such as independence threats and safeguards. Sharon explains that they also have to consider the overall integrity of the client; that is, the management of Cloud 9. This means they need to perform and document procedures that are likely to provide information about the client's integrity. Josh is a little sceptical. "Do you mean that we should ask them if they are honest?" Sharon suggests that it is probably more useful to ask others, and the key people to ask are the existing auditors. Josh is still sceptical. "The existing auditors are Ellis & Associates. Are they going to help us take one of their clients from them?" Sharon says that the client must give permission first, and, if that is given, the existing auditor will usually state whether or not there were any issues that the new auditor should be aware of before accepting the work. Sharon also gives Josh the task of researching Cloud 9's press coverage, with special focus on anything that may indicate poor management integrity.

Sharon emphasizes that they must perform and document procedures to test whether W&S Partners is competent to perform the engagement and has the capabilities, time, and resources to do so. For example, they must make sure that they have audit team members who understand the clothing and footwear business. They also must have enough staff to complete the audit on time. Cloud 9 has a December 31 year end. This means that most of the audit work will be done at a time of year when enough staff may not be available.

In addition, Sharon and Josh must perform and document procedures to show that W&S Partners can comply with all parts of the ethical code, not just those that focus on independence threats and safeguards. Finally, they can draft the engagement letter to cover the contractual relationship between W&S Partners and Cloud 9.

BEFORE YOU GO ON

2.5.1 What will an auditor consider in assessing the integrity of a client's management, board, and other personnel?

2.5.2 What are the key components of an engagement letter?

2.5.3 Why must an auditor seek a client's permission before communicating with its prior auditor or any other relevant third party?

SUMMARY

1 Describe the fundamental principles of professional ethics and list some of the specific rules professional accountants are required to follow.

The fundamental principles of professional ethics include integrity (being straightforward and honest); objectivity (not allowing personal feelings or prejudices to influence professional judgement); professional competence and due care (maintaining knowledge and skill at an appropriate level); confidentiality (not sharing information that is learned at work); and professional behaviour (upholding the reputation of the profession). There are also specific rules that incorporate the guiding ethical principles, and that are enforceable. Some of these rules concern fees and pricing, advertising, contact with predecessor auditors, firm names, and professional contact.

2 Define and explain auditor association and independence.

Association is the term used to indicate a public accountant's involvement with financial information. Public accountants should not be associated with anything false and misleading; therefore, they should take care to communicate the level of their involvement with the information.

Independence is the ability to make a decision that is free from bias, personal beliefs, and client pressures. An external auditor must not only be independent of their client, they must also appear to be independent of their client. Threats to auditor independence include self-interest, self-review, advocacy, familiarity, and intimidation threats. A self-interest threat can occur when an auditor has a financial interest in a client. A self-review threat can occur when an auditor must form an opinion on their own work or work done by others in their firm. An advocacy threat can occur when an auditor acts on behalf of their client. A familiarity threat can occur when there is a close relationship between the auditor and their client. An intimidation threat can occur when an auditor feels threatened by their client. Safeguards to auditor independence include the code of ethics, legislation, the establishment of audit committees by clients, client acceptance, and continuance procedures, partner rotation policies, and education within accounting firms.

3 **Explain the relationship between an auditor and key groups they have a professional link with during the audit engagement.**

Auditors report to their clients' shareholders. These are the owners who rely on the audited financial statements when evaluating the performance of their company. The board of directors represents the shareholders and oversees the activities of the company and its management. It is the directors' responsibility to ensure that the financial statements being audited are fairly presented. The audit committee is responsible for liaising between the external auditor, the internal auditor, and those charged with governance to aid the board of directors in ensuring that the financial statements are fairly presented and that the external auditor has access to all records and other

evidence required to form their opinion. The external auditor may use the work performed by the internal auditors after considering the function's objectivity, technical competence, and due professional care, and the effectiveness of communication between internal and external auditors.

4 **Explain the auditor's legal liability to their client, contributory negligence, and the extent to which an auditor is liable to third parties.**

Contributory negligence is where a client is found to be negligent and to have contributed to the loss suffered by the plaintiff. To successfully sue an auditor, a plaintiff must prove that a duty of care was owed by the auditor, there was a breach of that duty, and a loss was suffered as a result of that breach. Several cases are discussed in the chapter in relation to an auditor's liability to third parties. To establish that an auditor owes them a duty of care, a third party must now establish that the auditor was aware that the third party was going to use the financial statements and that the users relied on the financial statements for the purpose they were prepared.

5 **Identify the factors to consider in the client acceptance or continuance decision.**

Factors to consider include the integrity of a client, such as the client's reputation and attitude to risk, accounting policies, and internal controls. An auditor will gain an understanding of the client through communication with the client's previous auditor (in the case of a client acceptance decision), staff, management, and other relevant parties. The final stage in the client acceptance or continuance decision process involves the preparation of an engagement letter, which sets out the terms of the audit engagement to avoid any misunderstandings between the auditor and their client.

KEY TERMS

Advocacy threat, 43
Association, 41
Audit committee, 50
Board of directors, 41
Confidentiality, 39
Corporate governance, 46
Due care, 39
Engagement letter, 57
Executive director, 49

Familiarity threat, 43
Independence, 41
Independent directors, 46
Integrity, 39
Internal auditors, 50
Intimidation threat, 44
Negligence, 51
Non-executive director, 49
Objectivity, 39

Professional behaviour, 39
Professional competence, 39
Reporting issuer, 44
Self-interest threat, 42
Self-review threat, 43
Shareholders, 49
Technical competence, 51
Third parties, 53

MULTIPLE-CHOICE QUESTIONS

2.1 Professional competence and due care means that members of the professional body must:

(a) maintain their knowledge and skill at the required level.

(b) keep up to date with changes in regulations and standards.

(c) act diligently.

(d) all of the above.

2.2 Professional behaviour means that members of a profession must:

(a) comply with rules and regulations.

(b) claim to possess all qualifications.

(c) question the reputation of accountants who are not members of professional bodies.

(d) provide all services clients request.

2.3 Professional independence for auditors:

(a) detracts from the ability of users to rely on the financial statements to make their decisions.

(b) is the ability to act with integrity, objectivity, and professional scepticism.

(c) is important when the auditor acts independently, and it does not matter what people believe about the auditor's independence.

(d) is only relevant to audits for new clients, not for continuing clients.

2.4 A self-interest threat arises when:

(a) the auditor owns shares in the client's business.

(b) an assurance team member has recently been a director of the client.

(c) the auditor encourages others to buy shares in the client's business.

(d) the client threatens to use a different auditor next year.

2.5 A self-review threat arises when:

(a) the auditor has a loan from the client.

(b) the auditor represents the client in negotiations with a third party.

(c) the auditor performs services for the client that are then assured.

(d) there is a long association between the auditor and its client.

2.6 Safeguards to independence:

(a) minimize the risk that a threat to independence will surface.

(b) deal with a threat when one becomes apparent.

(c) are developed by the accounting profession, legislators, regulators, clients, and accounting firms.

(d) all of the above.

2.7 Safeguards to independence:

(a) are not the responsibility of the client.

(b) are too difficult to implement by audit firms; they must be contained in legislation.

(c) include audit committees.

(d) apply only to business relationships between auditors and clients, not to social relationships.

2.8 Audit committees for listed entities per the CSA:

(a) must include the CFO if he or she is on the board of directors.

(b) can be any size.

(c) have the same chair as the board of directors.

(d) should have a formal charter.

2.9 Generally, the auditor could be legally liable:

(a) under contract law to third parties and to the client.

(b) under contract law and under the tort of negligence to the client.

(c) under contract law but not under the tort of negligence to third parties.

(d) under the tort of negligence but not contract law to the client.

2.10 If a prospective new audit client does not allow the auditor to contact its existing auditor:

(a) the auditor should contact the existing auditor anyway because it is their duty.

(b) the auditor should consider refusing to take on the prospective new client.

(c) the existing auditor should contact the new auditor to tell them all about the client.

(d) the auditor should respect the prospective client's right to privacy.

REVIEW QUESTIONS

2.1 Explain how compliance with each of the five fundamental principles in the code of professional conduct contributes to the ability of the auditor to discharge their duty to act in the public interest.

2.2 Which is more important, independence of mind or independence in appearance? Explain.

2.3 Self-interest, self-review, and familiarity threats all arise from an inappropriate closeness between the auditor and the client. Explain how that closeness is likely to manifest in each case and why it is a problem for the value of the audit.

2.4 Explain the relationship between the auditor and the shareholders of the audited company. How realistic is it to regard the shareholders as the clients of the auditor?

2.5 Why is it so important that an audit committee not have any executive directors as members?

2.6 Some companies outsource their internal audit function to a public accounting firm. Explain how this would affect the external auditor's evaluation of the reliability of the internal audit function.

2.7 What are the three conditions that must be proven for an auditor to be found negligent under tort law? Based on a review of the legal cases discussed in the chapter, which conditions appear to be most difficult to prove?

2.8 Explain how an auditor would use auditing standards to avoid legal liability.

2.9 Why are there procedures governing the client acceptance or continuance decision? Explain why auditors do not accept every client.

2.10 What is the purpose of an engagement letter? Are all engagement letters the same?

PROFESSIONAL APPLICATION QUESTIONS

Basic ★   Moderate ★ ★   Challenging ★ ★ ★

2.1 Ethical principles ★

Charles is at a neighbourhood Christmas party with several of his roommates. Over a few beers, Charles gets into a conversation with a neighbour, William, about mutual acquaintances. Charles is a senior auditor with a large accounting firm (although he tells William that he is a partner at the firm) and William works for a large bank. During the conversation, Charles and William discover that they have both had professional dealings with a particular family-owned manufacturing company. William reveals that the company's line of credit is about to be cancelled because of some irregularities with the security. Charles is concerned to hear this news because he has just participated in the company's financial statement audit and there was no indication of any problems with its borrowings. However, as Charles explains to William, he has his doubts about the patriarch of the family, who Charles believes is having an affair with his personal assistant. Charles also tells William that the family has quietly increased its shareholdings in a listed company that supplies components to the family's manufacturing company. The components manufacturing company is about to announce to the share market that it has just won a very large and very profitable contract with a Chinese company.

Required

Discuss the ethical principles that are potentially breached by Charles's behaviour at the party.

2.2 Receiving shares through inheritance ★ ★

Kerry is a senior auditor and a member of the team auditing a long-standing client, the listed public company Darcy Industries Ltd. Kerry's wife's uncle died recently and his estate is being finalized. Kerry's wife has just received a letter from the executor of her uncle's estate advising her that she will receive a large parcel of shares in Darcy Industries Ltd. from the estate, in addition to cash and other property. Kerry and his wife didn't know that her uncle had included her in the will, and they had not realized that her uncle was a large shareholder in Darcy Industries Ltd. Kerry's wife is very worried because she knows that Kerry must abide by strict rules laid down by his audit firm about holding shares in client companies. She asks him if he will be dismissed because of this.

Required

Advise Kerry's wife of the options available to Kerry to avoid any conflict of interest, and thus avoid being dismissed from the audit firm.

2.3 Provision of non-audit services to audit clients ★ ★

Elise Lauzière is the partner in charge of the audit of Hertenstein Ltd., a large listed public company. Elise took over the audit from Marjorie Szliske, who has recently retired from the audit firm. Marjorie was a very experienced auditor and the author of several reports into ethical standards in business, but Elise did not regard her highly for her ability to grow non-audit service fee revenue. Elise sees an opportunity to increase the provision of non-audit services to Hertenstein Ltd. and thus increase her reputation within the audit firm.

Required

(a) Comment on Elise's belief that increasing non-audit service fee revenue from her audit client would increase her reputation in the audit firm.

(b) Which non-audit services would you advise Elise to avoid trying to sell to Hertenstein Ltd. because of the potential ethical issues for the audit firm?

(c) Would it make any difference to your answers if Hertenstein Ltd. was a private company, not a listed public company? If so, how? If not, why not?

2.4 Unpaid audit fees ★ ★

Linda is the managing partner of Osuji and Associates, a small audit firm. Linda's role includes managing the business affairs of the firm, and she is very worried about the amount of fees outstanding from audit clients. One client, Dreamers Ltd., has not paid its audit fees for two years despite numerous discussions between Linda, the audit partner, Bill, and the management of Dreamers Ltd. Dreamers Ltd.'s management promised the fees would be paid before the audit report for this year was issued. Linda called Bill this morning to ensure that the audit report was not issued because Dreamers Ltd. had paid only 10 percent of the outstanding account. She discovers that Bill is about to sign the audit report.

Required

Explain the ethical problem in this case. Why is it a problem? What can be done about it?

2.5 Using the work of internal auditors ★ ★

Theobald Ltd. has an internal audit department that primarily focuses on audits of the efficiency and effectiveness of its production departments. The other main role of the internal audit department is auditing compliance with various government regulations surrounding correct disposal of waste and storage of raw materials at its five factories. Theobald Ltd.'s internal audit department is run by Harry Giolti, a professional accountant and a member of the Institute of Internal Auditors. There are three other members of the department, all of whom have experience in performance auditing and, in addition, have completed industry-run training courses in waste management and handling dangerous goods. Harry meets regularly with the chief production manager and sends monthly reports to the CEO and the board of directors. Your initial investigations suggest that Harry is highly regarded within Theobald Ltd., and his reports are often discussed at board meetings. In most cases, the board authorizes the actions recommended in Harry's reports with respect to major changes to production and logistics.

Required

Comment on the extent of reliance the external auditor should place on the work of the internal audit department at Theobald Ltd. Explain the likely impact of the internal audit department's work on the audit plan.

2.6 Legal implications of client acceptance ★ ★ ★

Godwin, Key & Associates is a small but rapidly growing audit firm. Their success is largely due to the growth of several clients that have been with the firm for more than five years. One of these clients, Carolina Company Ltd., is now listed on the TSX and must comply with additional reporting regulations. Carolina Company Ltd.'s rapid growth has meant that it is financially stretched and its accounting systems are struggling to keep up with the growth in business. The client continuance decision is about to be made for the next financial year.

The managing partner of Godwin, Key & Associates, Rebecca Haque, has recognized that the audit firm needs to make some changes to deal with the issues created by the changing circumstances of their major client and the audit firm's overall growth. She is particularly concerned that the audit firm could be legally liable if Carolina Company Ltd.'s financial situation worsens and it fails.

Required

(a) Provide guidance to Rebecca about the steps she can take to avoid the threat of litigation if Carolina Company Ltd. fails.

(b) What should Rebecca consider when making the client continuance decision for Carolina Company Ltd. for the next financial year?

2.7 Independence safeguards ★ ★

Stave, Brown and Paul, a three-partner accounting firm, has implemented the following independence safeguards.

1. In the audit report for Weltzin Educational Services Inc., partner Jessica Brown has the CFO of Weltzin sign the following: "I approve the proposed journal entries made by Stave, Brown and Paul."
2. On January 3 of each year, the firm has all of its staff review a client list and sign a disclosure statement indicating whether they hold any shares in any of the clients.
3. Cameron Stave has been the lead engagement partner on the Borba Manufacturing Ltd. audit for the last six years. This year, Jessica Brown will fulfill that role.
4. The firm's policy states it is inappropriate for staff to date client personnel.
5. Every six months, Jessica Brown reviews the proportion of fees per client to total fees.
6. Jake Paul has decided to leave the partnership. He intends to go work for his largest audit client after he travels through Asia over the next year.

Required

For each safeguard above, identify the independence threat the safeguard is designed to prevent.

2.8 Independence threats and safeguards ★ ★

Featherbed Surf & Leisure Holidays Ltd. (Featherbed) is a resort company based on Vancouver Island. Its operations include boating, surfing, fishing, and other leisure activities; a backpackers' hostel; a family hotel; and a five-star resort. Justin and Sarah Morris own the majority of the shares in the Morris Group, which controls Featherbed. Justin is the chairman of the board of directors of both Featherbed and the Morris Group, and Sarah is a director of both companies as well as the CFO of Featherbed.

In February 2016, Justin Morris approached your audit firm, KFP Partners, to carry out the Featherbed audit for the year ended June 30, 2016. Featherbed has not been audited before but this year the audit has been requested by the company's bank and a new private equity investor group that has just acquired a 20 percent share of Featherbed. You know that one of the partners at KFP went to school with Justin and has been friends with both Justin and Sarah for many years.

Source: Adapted from the Institute of Chartered Accountants Australia's CA Program's *Audit and Assurance Exam*, May 2008. Provided courtesy of Chartered Accountants Australia and New Zealand.

Required

(a) Identify and explain the significant threats to independence for KFP Partners in accepting the audit of Featherbed.

(b) Explain any relevant and practical safeguards that KFP could implement to reduce the threats.

2.9 Independence threats and safeguards ★ ★ ★

Securimax Limited has been an audit client of KFP Partners for the past 15 years. Securimax is based in Waterloo, where it manufactures high-tech armour-plated personnel carriers. Securimax often has to go through a competitive market tender process to win large government contracts. Its main product, the small but powerful Terrain Master, is highly specialized and Securimax only does business with nations that have a recognized, democratically elected government. Securimax maintains a highly secure environment, given the sensitive and confidential nature of its vehicle designs and its clients.

Clarke Field has been the engagement partner on the Securimax audit for the last five years. Clarke is a specialist in the defence industry and intends to remain as review partner when the audit is rotated next year to a new partner (Sally Woodrow, who is to be promoted to partner to enable her to sign off on the audit).

In September 2015, Securimax installed an off-the-shelf costing system to support the highly sophisticated and cost-sensitive nature of its product designs. The new system replaced a system that had been developed in-house, as the old system could no longer keep up with the complex and detailed manufacturing costing process that provides tender costings. The old system also had difficulty with the company's broader reporting requirements.

Securimax's information technology (IT) department, together with the consultants from the software company, implemented the new manufacturing costing system. There were no customized modifications. Key operational staff and the internal audit team from Securimax were significantly engaged in the selection, testing, training, and implementation stages.

The manufacturing costing system uses all of the manufacturing unit inputs to calculate and produce a database of all product costs and recommended sales prices. It also integrates with the general ledger each time there are product inventory movements such as purchases, sales, wastage, and damaged inventory losses.

Securimax has a small internal audit department that is headed by an ex-partner of KFP, Rydell Creek. Rydell joined Securimax after leaving KFP six years ago after completing his chartered accountant's qualifications. Rydell is assisted by three junior internal auditors, all of whom are completing bachelor of commerce studies at the University of Waterloo.

Securimax's end of financial year is December 31.

Source: Adapted from the Institute of Chartered Accountants Australia's CA Program's *Audit and Assurance Exam,* May 2008. Provided courtesy of Chartered Accountants Australia and New Zealand.

Required

(a) Are there any threats to independence for KFP in its audit of Securimax?

(b) Can you propose any recommendations to safeguard KFP against the potential independence threats you have identified? Explain.

Questions 2.10 and 2.11 are based on the following case.

Fellowes and Associates Chartered Accountants is a successful mid-tier accounting firm with a large range of clients across Canada. During the 2016 financial year, Fellowes and Associates gained a new client, Health Care Holdings Group (HCHG), which owns 100 percent of the following entities:

- Shady Oaks Centre, a private treatment centre
- Gardens Nursing Home Ltd., a private nursing home
- Total Laser Care Limited (TLCL), a private clinic that specializes in the laser treatment of skin defects
- Year end for all HCHG entities is June 30

TLCL owns two relatively old laser machines used in therapy. Recently, staff using these machines have raised concerns that they have adverse impacts on patients.

The CEO of TCCL, Betty Raman, has approached Tania Fellowes, the audit partner responsible for the financial statement audit, about undertaking an engagement with respect to the laser machines. Betty has asked Tania to provide an opinion that the machines are fit for use. Betty pointed out that the auditor for TLCL has not been appointed for the following year and suggested Fellowes and Associates might like to take on the laser machines engagement without charging a fee as a gesture of goodwill.

Prior to the appointment for the 2016 financial year of Fellowes and Associates as the auditor for HCHG, the group that controls TLCL, some preliminary analysis by Tania Fellowes identified the following situations:

1. One of the accountants who intended to be part of the 2016 audit team owns shares in HCHG. The accountant's interest is not material to him.
2. Fellowes and Associates was previously engaged by HCHG to value its intellectual property. The consolidated balance sheet (statement of financial position) as at June 30, 2016, includes intangible assets of $30 million, which were valued by Fellowes and Associates on March 1, 2016, following HCHG's acquisition of the subsidiary Shady Oaks Centre. The intangibles are considered material to HCHG.

Source: Adapted from the Institute of Chartered Accountants Australia's CA Program's *Audit and Assurance Exam*, December 2008. Provided courtesy of Chartered Accountants Australia and New Zealand.

2.10 Ethics of accepting engagements ★ ★

Required

Explain why Tania Fellowes should have reservations about accepting the HCHG engagement to provide an opinion with respect to the laser machines. Make appropriate reference to fundamental ethical principles in your answer.

2.11 Independence issues in accepting engagements ★ ★ ★

Required

(a) Identify and explain the potential type of threat to Fellowes and Associates' independence in situations (1) and (2) above.
(b) What action should Fellowes and Associates take to eliminate the potential threats to independence in situations (1) and (2) above? What safeguards should be instituted to reduce the risk of similar independence threats occurring in the future?

2.12 Principles and rules of the code of professional conduct ★ ★

Required

Identify and discuss any professional conduct issues in the following independent scenarios.

(a) Adnan is a certified general accountant working for a national firm. He is at his desk when he overhears his colleague Joan having a phone conversation. She is telling the person on the other end of the call that Gupta Co., the firm's largest audit client, is about to release the company's audited annual financial statements and the results are spectacular. Joan says she just bought some shares as she expects that the share price will go up.
(b) John Drake, a partner at Drake and Buetz, is meeting with a potential new client. The client recently saw the firm's TV advertisement claiming that the firm was "the premier accounting firm in western Canada." The client requires a review engagement report with its financial statements to obtain a bank loan. John advises that his fee will be 10 percent of any bank loan granted.
(c) Sue Chen, CPA, is working on the audit engagement for Jones Construction, a reporting issuer. José, the accountant at Jones Construction, is unsure how to calculate the tax provision. Sue has advised José not to worry. She will prepare the tax provision and ensure that the disclosures are in accordance with generally accepted accounting principles (GAAP) so that she can issue a clean audit opinion.
(d) Sue Chen is working on the audit engagement for Jones Construction, a private entity. During the course of the audit, she prepares a number of routine journal entries. She makes the required adjustments before she releases the financial statements.
(e) Sue Chen is working on the compilation engagement for Jones Construction. The book-keeper, Luc, processes the day-to-day transactions, but he does not prepare any closing adjusting entries. Sue prepares the year-end amortization entry and the adjustment to the shareholder account. She then reviews the financial statements with Wade Jones, the owner, and releases the financial statements.

(f) Jack Bond is a partner in a national firm. He is responsible for the audit for Canada Bank. He recently purchased a car for his daughter and took out a car loan with Canada Bank.

(g) Jack Bond is a partner in a national firm. The firm is the auditor for Canada Bank. Jack's father-in-law is the chief operating officer for Canada Bank.

(h) James Lei, CPA is reviewing his firm's accounts receivable. He notices that one of his largest audit clients has not paid its fees for the last two years.

(i) Alison Kotecha, CPA, is meeting with a potential new audit client, Klein Advertising. She paid Johan Smit, a former colleague, $1,000 for the referral. Although she hasn't performed any audit engagements for the last four years, she did recently take a GAAP course. During the meeting, she reads over the prior year's financial statements and tells the client she will accept the engagement. She tells the client that she will do a substantive-based audit; therefore, she is certain that the fee will be less than the fee charged by the previous auditor.

(j) Matt Green is married to Jennifer Green, who owns Muffins to Go, a small private entity. Jennifer is a baker and not an accountant. However, she needs a set of financial statements prepared to attach to her tax return. Her husband Matt tells her that he will prepare them.

2.13 Engagement ethics ★ ★

Jules is a student in the CPA program, and was recently hired as a junior auditor. His employer is conducting an external audit of DDD Ltd.'s 2016 financial statements. DDD is a wholesale distributor of electronic supplies. Jules found a purchase invoice with all required supporting documentation, including a receiving memo attached to a packing slip, showing that DDD had purchased and received 20,000 pieces of a particular item. However, the supplier invoice only listed 2,000 pieces, and the supplier mistakenly billed DDD only for 2,000 pieces. When Jules brought this to his audit manager's attention, he was told not to worry about it. The manager said an audit can never find all mistakes and that sometimes mistakes work in the client's favour, and sometimes work against the client, so they "balance out." The manager told Jules: "If we were to advise the client, we would have to modify our audit opinion if the client refused to notify the supplier, and DDD would lose money." Jules was told that if he wanted to keep his new position, he had better learn how business everywhere really operates. The manager is also a professional accountant.

Required

Identify four unethical issues in the above situation, and explain why they are unethical.

Source: © CGA-Canada, now CPA Canada. Reproduced with permission.

2.14 Auditor legal liability ★ ★

Ahmad & Partners is a public accounting firm in eastern Canada. Last year it audited Chan Corporation, a publicly traded company that manufactures automobile component parts. Although the company has been profitable for many years, Ahmad & Partners was hired by Canada Bank, which was considering extending a large loan to Chan Corp. The bank wanted the audit because Chan's expansion plans would change the company's financial structure significantly from the previous year. Ahmad & Partners conducted the audit and gave an unmodified opinion. Xing Investments Inc. purchased $750,000 of the common stock of Chan, intending to hold the stock as a long-term investment. Unfortunately, Chan went bankrupt shortly after the share purchase and Xing Investments lost all of its $750,000 investment. Canada Bank was unable to recover any of its loan to the company. Xing Investments and Canada Bank subsequently sued Ahmad & Partners to recover their losses.

Required

(a) Did Ahmad & Partners owe a duty of care to Xing Investments?

(b) What are some of the arguments Ahmad & Partners could make in their defence?

Source: © CGA-Canada, now CPA Canada. Reproduced with permission.

2.15 Breaches to the principles and rules of the code of professional conduct ★ ★ ★

Required

Identify and discuss any breaches, if any, to the principles and rules of the code of professional conduct in the following independent scenarios. Explain.

(a) Susanne, a professional accountant, has agreed to audit the financial statements of a newly formed biotechnology company that is publicly traded. The company has an immaterial amount of revenues and mostly incurs research and development costs, which results in a fairly simple set of financial statements. Accordingly, Susanne charges the client a very low audit fee of $7,000 for the first year, since she expects to make a substantial amount of money in preparing the personal tax returns of the company's key executives for 2016.

(b) Aziz, a professional accountant and a partner in a public accounting firm, is discussing the audit plan for his client, a private entity. The company's unaudited financial statements show exceptional revenue growth and earnings this year, and Aziz is concerned that management may be manipulating the financial statements in anticipation of a future public offering. Accordingly, Aziz tells the senior auditor to contact him immediately if she uncovers any evidence of deliberate fraud because Aziz does not want his firm to be associated with clients who lack integrity and he may resign from the engagement.

(c) Mandip, a professional accountant, has been engaged to compile the quarterly financial statements for his new client, a private company that develops and markets computer software. The owners employ a part-time bookkeeper to maintain basic accounting records but rely on Mandip to put all the information in proper form each quarter. The statements consist of a balance sheet, income statement, and statement of cash flows, but no footnotes or other disclosures. The owners use the quarterly statements to help them manage the company. Because the company has limited resources, Mandip's fees for his services are paid in company shares. Mandip has agreed to this unusual arrangement since he knows that the owners plan a public offering of shares within the next few years, and he will then be able to sell the shares. Finally, to obtain a better knowledge of the company's operations and to make sure that the reported dollar amounts are plausible, Mandip performs a thorough ratio analysis of the compiled statements each quarter and discusses any unusual findings with management.

Source: © CGA-Canada, now CPA Canada. Reproduced with permission.

2.16 Auditor legal liability ★ ★

HHH Corporation manufactures automobile engines. In 2014, the treasurer at HHH decided to invest the company's surplus funds in the commodities market. She intended for it to be a short-term investment, as the company had $1 million in extra funds that would not be needed for three months. Unfortunately, the market price of the commodity she purchased declined sharply and in three months the investment was sold for only $500,000. The treasurer prepared documents to make the loss of the investment appear as a sale of excess inventory, so the company showed a lower profit on sales than usual, but no trading loss. The auditor audited the 2014 financial statements and issued an unmodified report, even though the amount in question exceeded the materiality threshold. HHH has always been owned privately. In 2014, all of the shares of the company were purchased by a group of engineers who had retired from the automobile industry. There were no other changes in the shareholders during 2015 or 2016.

Required

Assume that the shareholders of HHH sued the auditors. Explain how the elements of negligence would apply to this case.

Source: © CGA-Canada, now CPA Canada. Reproduced with permission.

2.17 Ethical issues and consequences ★ ★ ★

Roy Dussault is a CPA who started a sports equipment importing business. The business became very successful and he sold it to his neighbour. As part of the sale agreement, Roy agreed to perform an audit of the financial statements for the first year at no charge. Roy told the new owner that there would be no problem in issuing an unqualified opinion if the new owner operated the business without increasing the debt levels and kept inventory low. Roy also has been a partner in an audit firm for several years and to avoid any ethical problems, Roy arranged for other staff to do the audit. Roy only reviewed the work of the other auditors and did not do any of the audit planning or testing himself. The audit for the first year was free, and if the new owner wanted an audit for the second year, Roy's firm would only charge 5 percent of the net income of the company.

Roy's firm found no material misstatements but the audit report noted a going-concern issue. The new owner took on extra debt from a private source, trying to expand the business too quickly. The excess debt caused the company's current ratio to fall below 1.8, which violated a covenant of the company's bank loan agreement. Under the terms of the lending agreement, the bank then called its loan and the new owner went into bankruptcy within 18 months.

The new owner sued Roy's audit firm for negligence, claiming that Roy had issued an audit report that ruined her business.

Required

(a) Identify and explain at least four ethical issues in the above situation.
(b) Explain whether or not Roy's audit firm could be found negligent by issuing the audit report that harmed the client's business.

Source: © CGA-Canada, now CPA Canada. Reproduced with permission.

2.18 Quality assurance ★ ★

Required

You have been working with a national chartered accounting firm for a number of years and you now feel like you are ready to start your own chartered accounting firm.

(a) Given the requirements of the code of professional conduct, what is an acceptable name for your firm?
(b) Given the requirements of the code of professional conduct, how will you market and advertise the services offered by your firm?
(c) As you plan to take on assurance work, you realize that you will need a quality assurance manual. Create the table of contents for your manual.
(d) Describe the requirements of your quality assurance manual with respect to the file quality review and monitoring.

2.19 Professional conduct ★ ★

Required

Identify and discuss any professional conduct issues in the following independent scenarios.

(a) Arun Sidhu was the auditor of Red Brick Ltd. and issued a clean audit opinion despite the fact that the depreciation expense of the client was materially misstated due to a calculation error.
(b) Jason Crane became a CPA in 2015. He is now glad to be finished his education as he does not plan to take any further accounting courses.
(c) Samantha Karadzic received a letter from Malik and Rudolph, another accounting firm, asking if there is any reason they should not accept the audit engagement of her biggest client, Franks Plumbing Inc. Samantha was so upset about losing the client, she threw the letter away and decided not to reply.
(d) Samantha Karadzic received a letter from Malik and Rudolph, another accounting firm, asking if there is any reason they should not accept one of her clients, Vanderkrujk Farm Ltd. Because she had disputes with management of Vanderkrujk, she was glad to see

them go. She called Malik and Rudolph right away and told them about all of the issues she had.

(e) William Aruna decided to start his own CPA firm. In order to attract new clients, he started cold calling businesses in his neighbourhood.

(f) Alan Reed discovered his longtime client, the Daily Diner, was in financial distress. He decided to lend the Diner $20,000 and he had the owner sign a note payable. He informed Canada Bank, primary user of the financial statements of this loan, after the audit report was issued.

CASES

CASE STUDY—CLOUD 9

Sharon Gallagher, Josh Thomas, and Jo Wadley are members of the audit firm W&S Partners. Sharon is the audit manager and Josh is the audit senior assisting the partner, Jo Wadley, evaluate the decision to accept the Cloud 9 Ltd. (Cloud 9) audit engagement for the year ended December 31, 2016.

Background information about the company is presented in Appendix B of this book. In addition, Josh has discovered the following facts and has requested your help to document and assess the factors that affect the client acceptance decision.

- The finance director of Cloud 9, David Collier, is married to a distant relation of P. S. Nethercott, a partner in W&S Partners' consulting department.
- The consulting department at W&S Partners has quoted on an IT installation project at Cloud 9. The fees from this project, if the tender is successful, would be twice the size of the audit fee.
- A survey of audit staff at W&S Partners has revealed that 30 percent have purchased Cloud 9's products (basketball shoes) in the past.
- Four members of the IT department at W&S Partners have shares in retailers that sell Cloud 9's products. In each case, the shareholdings were disclosed on the firm's share register, and the size of the shareholding is deemed material under W&S Partners' ethical guidelines.
- An article in a newspaper published in Canada has claimed that Cloud 9 Inc. (Cloud 9's parent company) was secretly running "third-world sweat shops." The article alleged that shoes made by other wholly owned subsidiaries of Cloud 9 Inc. in China and Brazil were using illegal child labour in factories that did not meet local health and safety rules. Cloud 9 Inc. has vehemently disputed the accuracy of the article, suggesting that it was planted by a rival company. Cloud 9 Inc. has invited international advocacy groups to visit its factories at any time.

Required

Answer the following questions based on the information presented above, in Appendix B of this book, and throughout chapters 1 and 2. Consider your answers to the case study questions in chapter 1 where relevant.

(a) Prepare a document that explains the impact, if any, of each piece of information relevant to your client acceptance decision for Cloud 9.

(b) List and explain any additional actions you would take before making your client acceptance recommendation to the partner, Jo Wadley.

(c) Assume the decision is made to accept Cloud 9 as a client. Prepare the client engagement letter.

RESEARCH QUESTION 2.1

One way of getting accounting expertise onto audit committees is to recruit ex-audit firm partners and/or employees onto the board of directors. However, appointing former audit firm partners to boards and audit committees raises independence concerns, and the Canada Business Corporations Act states that a retired partner must not take on a senior role at an audit client's firm for one year after retiring.

Naiker and Sharma provide evidence that financial statements are of higher quality when former audit partners are on the audit committee, and raise doubts about the benefits of a rule limiting their recruitment.

Required

(a) What are the arguments for and against allowing former audit firm partners and/or employees to join audit committees?

(b) Explain how these accounting experts could help or hinder the audit process and thereby have an impact on the quality of a company's internal controls and financial statements.

FURTHER READING

Certified General Accountants Association of Canada. *Independence Standard* and *Code of Ethical Principles and Rules of Conduct*. 2013, www.cga-canada.org.

Certified Management Accountants of British Columbia. *Rules of Professional Conduct*. September 2013, www.cmabc.com.

Chartered Professional Accountants Ontario, Rules of Professional Conduct, 2014, www.icao.on.ca. *Rules of Professional Conduct*. November 2010, www.icao.on.ca.

SOLUTIONS TO MULTIPLE-CHOICE QUESTIONS

1. d, 2. a, 3. b, 4. a, 5. c, 6. d, 7. c, 8. d, 9. b, 10. b.

NOTES

1. Makkula Ethics Center, Santa Clara University. A Framework for Thinking Ethically, November 2010, www.scu.edu.
2. Canadian Institute of Chartered Accountants, Guide to New Canadian Independence Standards, October 2003, www.icans.ns.ca.
3. The Free Dictionary 2009, www.legal-dictionary.thefreedictionary.com/.
4. Davison, Alan G. "Auditors Liability to Third Parties for Negligence," *Accounting & Business Research*, Autumn 82, Vol. 12, Issue 48, pp. 257–64.
5. Drew Hasselback, "Livent Auditor Ordered to Pay $84.8 million for Failing to Detect Fraud," *Financial Post*, April 6, 2014; Janet McFarland, "Livent Decision Could Pave Way for New Suits Against Auditors," *The Globe and Mail*, April 7, 2014.

CHAPTER 3

Audit planning I

LEARNING OBJECTIVES

After studying this chapter, you should be able to:

1 identify the different stages of an audit

2 explain the process used in gaining an understanding of the client

3 explain how related parties can impact risk

4 define fraud risk and understand audit procedures to reduce this risk

5 explain the going concern assumption

6 describe corporate governance

7 explain how a client's information technology (IT) can affect risk

8 explain how client closing procedures can affect reported results.

AUDITING AND ASSURANCE STANDARDS

CANADIAN	INTERNATIONAL
CAS 240 *The Auditor's Responsibilities Relating to Fraud in an Audit of Financial Statements*	ISA 240 *The Auditor's Responsibilities Relating to Fraud in an Audit of Financial Statements*
CAS 300 *Planning an Audit of Financial Statements*	ISA 300 *Planning an Audit of Financial Statements*
CAS 315 *Identifying and Assessing the Risks of Material Misstatement Through Understanding the Entity and Its Environment*	ISA 315 *Identifying and Assessing the Risks of Material Misstatement Through Understanding the Entity and Its Environment*
CAS 550 *Related Parties*	ISA 550 *Related Parties*
CAS 570 *Going Concern*	ISA 570 *Going Concern*

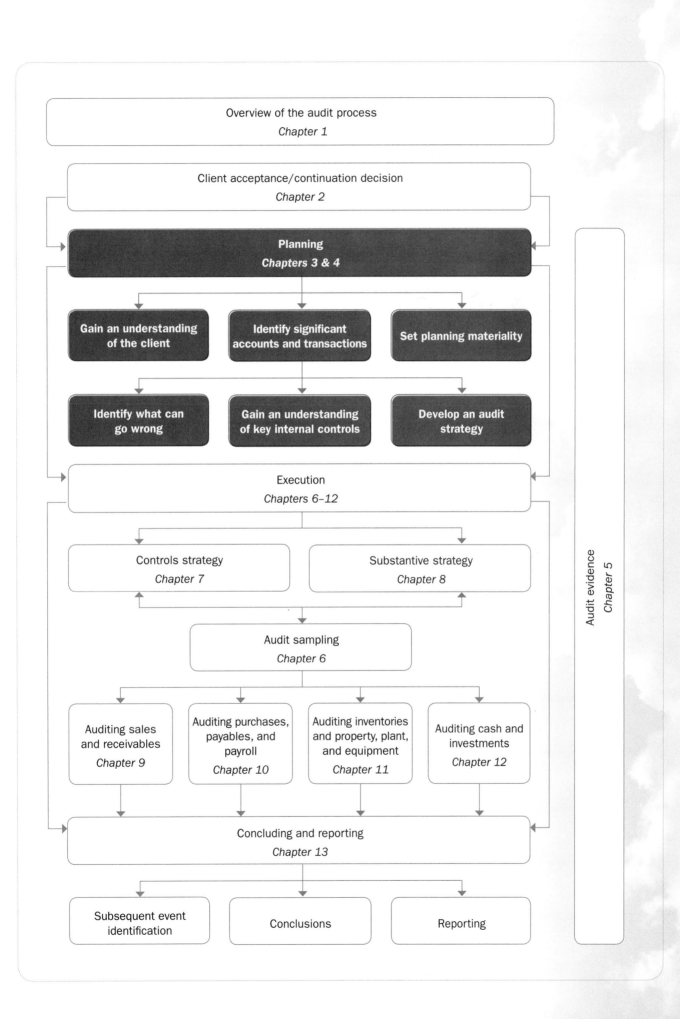

Cloud 9

"*Great news!*" announces Sharon Gallagher at the weekly team meeting. "We have just had word that the audit engagement letter for Cloud 9 Ltd. (Cloud 9) has been signed. We are now officially their financial statement auditors and the planning phase starts now!"

Later, at the first planning meeting, Sharon and Josh Thomas focus on assigning the tasks for gaining an understanding of Cloud 9. Ian Harper, a first-year graduate, is not happy. He grumbles to another new member of the team, Suzie Pickering, as he leaves the room, "This is such a waste of time. Why did we sign an engagement letter if we don't understand the client? Why don't we just get on with the audit? What else is there to know?"

"Oh boy, are you missing the point!" Suzie says. "If you don't spend time planning, where are you going to start 'getting on with it'?"

"The same place you always start," replies Ian. Suzie realizes that she has a big job explaining to Ian, and invites him for a coffee so that they can talk. Although Suzie is new to the team, she has audit experience with other clothing and footwear clients, and will be helping Sharon and Josh manage the Cloud 9 audit. Her first question to Ian at coffee is "What do you think could go wrong with the Cloud 9 audit?"

AUDIT PROCESS IN FOCUS

Audit planning is an important topic that we will cover in this and the next chapter. In this chapter, we begin with a discussion of the different stages (or phases) of the audit: the planning stage, the performing stage (where the detailed work is conducted), and the reporting stage (where the audit opinion is formed). At the planning and reporting stages, the auditor adopts a broad view of the client as a whole and the industry in which it operates. An understanding of the client is gained in the early stages of each audit and that knowledge drives the planning of the audit. It informs the choice of where to focus the most attention throughout the audit. When forming an opinion on the fair presentation of the financial statements, consideration is given to the evidence gathered during the performing stage of the audit, placing that information within the context of the knowledge of the client gained from the planning stage.

During the planning stage, an assessment is made of the risk that a material misstatement (significant error or fraud) could occur in the client's financial statements. By understanding where the risks are most significant, an auditor can plan their audit to spend more time where the risks are greatest. During the planning stage, an auditor will gain an understanding of their client, their client's internal controls, their client's information technology (IT) environment, their client's corporate governance environment, and their client's closing procedures. An auditor will identify any related parties, factors that may affect their client's going concern status, and significant accounts and classes of transactions that will require close audit attention to gauge the risk of material misstatement.

Each of these important elements of the planning stage of the audit is considered in this chapter. The process adopted when gaining an understanding of a client is explained in detail. That explanation is followed by a discussion of the specific audit risks associated with related party transactions and the risk that a client's financial statements are misstated due to fraud. The audit procedures used to assess the risk that a fraud has occurred and common frauds are included in the discussion. That is followed by a discussion of the processes used to assess the going concern assumption.

Corporate governance is the rules, systems, and processes within companies used to guide and control. During the planning stage, an auditor will assess the adequacy of their client's corporate governance structure in assessing the risk that the financial statements are materially misstated.

A client's IT system is used to capture, process, and report on the accounting records. During the planning stage, an auditor will assess the adequacy of their client's IT system. This process is discussed in this chapter.

The final section of this chapter includes a discussion of the procedures used by an auditor to assess their client's closing procedures. Closing procedures aim to ensure that transactions are recorded in the appropriate accounting period. An auditor will assess the adequacy of their client's closing procedures to assess the risk that a material misstatement will occur in the financial statements as a consequence.

3.1 STAGES OF AN AUDIT

Before commencing our discussion of audit planning, we provide an overview of the various stages of the audit, which is represented diagrammatically in figure 3.1. The main stages of an audit are planning, performing, and reporting. Once the client acceptance or continuation decision has been made (described in chapter 2), the first stage is planning the audit. Broadly, the **planning stage** involves gaining an understanding of the client, identifying factors that may impact the risk of a material misstatement in the financial statements, performing a risk and **materiality** assessment, and developing an **audit strategy**. The risk of a material misstatement is the risk that the financial statements include a significant error or fraud. The **execution stage** (or performing stage) of the audit involves the performance of detailed testing of controls and substantive testing of transactions and accounts. The **reporting stage** involves evaluating the results of the detailed testing in light of the auditor's understanding of their client and forming an opinion on the fair presentation of the client's financial statements. An overview of each stage of the audit follows.

FIGURE 3.1 **Overview of the audit**

3.1.1 Planning an audit

CAS 300 *Planning an Audit of Financial Statements* requires that an auditor plan their audit to reduce audit risk to an acceptably low level. Audit risk is the risk that an auditor issues an unmodified or clean audit opinion when the financial statements are in fact materially misstated. The planning stage involves assessing the audit risk and materiality, determining the audit strategy, as well as identifying the nature and the timing of the procedures to be performed. In order to plan an efficient and effective audit, an auditor must understand the entity and its environment to make a reasonable preliminary assessment of audit risk and materiality. This also allows the auditor to identify any significant risks or unique features of the entity or the environment that may impact the audit planning. Efficiency refers to the amount of time spent gathering audit evidence. Effectiveness refers to the minimization of audit risk. A well-planned audit will ensure that **sufficient appropriate evidence** is gathered for those accounts at most risk of material misstatement. Figure 3.2 provides a graphical depiction of the preliminary risk identification process used during the planning stage of each audit.

Each element of figure 3.2 is now discussed in turn, starting with "understand the client" and proceeding clockwise. The process used by an auditor when gaining an understanding of their client is outlined in section 3.2. Part of that process includes the identification of a client's related parties to ensure that they are identified and appropriately disclosed following the relevant accounting standards. CAS 550 *Related Parties* provides audit guidance associated with related party transactions and disclosures. This is further discussed in section 3.3.

When planning an audit, an auditor will assess the risk of material misstatement due to **fraud** (CAS 240 *The Auditor's Responsibilities Relating to Fraud in an Audit of Financial Statements*) and consider whether it is appropriate to assume that their client will remain as a **going concern** (CAS 570 *Going Concern*). Fraud risk is discussed in section 3.4 and going concern is discussed in section 3.5.

1 Identify the different stages of an audit.

planning stage the audit stage involving gaining an understanding of the client, identifying risk factors, developing an audit strategy, and assessing materiality

materiality information that impacts the decision-making process of the users of the financial statements

audit strategy a strategy that sets the scope, timing, and direction of the audit and provides the basis for developing a detailed audit plan

execution stage the audit stage involving detailed testing of controls and substantive testing of transactions and accounts

reporting stage the audit stage involving evaluating the results of the detailed testing in light of the auditor's understanding of their client and forming an opinion on the fair presentation of the client's financial statements

sufficient appropriate evidence the quantity and quality of the evidence that has been gathered

fraud an intentional act through the use of deception to obtain an unjust or illegal advantage

going concern the viability of a company to remain in business for the foreseeable future

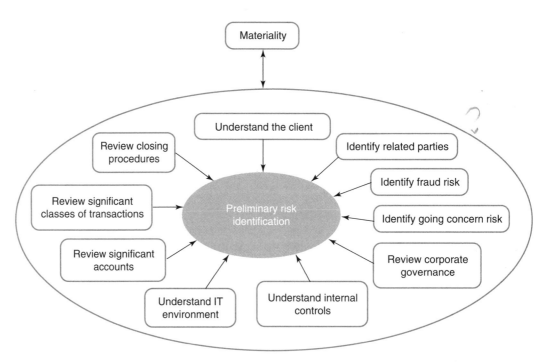

FIGURE 3.2 **Preliminary risk identification**

corporate governance the rules, systems, and processes within companies used to guide and control

A client's **corporate governance** structure is assessed when planning an audit. The Canadian Securities Administrators (CSA) have issued a policy statement for reporting issuers. This policy statement provides guidance on corporate governance practices; however, it does not prescribe any particular practices. The CSA's policy is discussed further in section 3.6.

According to CAS 315 *Identifying and Assessing the Risks of Material Misstatement Through Understanding the Entity and Its Environment,* an auditor must gain an understanding of their client's system of internal controls. Elements of control risk are discussed in chapter 4, and chapter 7 contains a discussion of the procedures used by an auditor in gaining an understanding of a client's system of internal controls. When gaining an understanding of their client's system of internal controls, an auditor will consider the impact of IT (CAS 315). IT is discussed in more detail in section 3.7.

closing procedures processes used by a client when finalizing the books for an accounting period

Significant accounts and classes of transactions are identified when planning so that an auditor can structure their audit testing to ensure that adequate time is spent testing these accounts and classes of transactions. During the planning stage, an auditor will also consider the adequacy of their client's **closing procedures**. An auditor's consideration of their client's closing procedures and the associated risks are discussed in section 3.8. An important task in the early stages of every audit is to set the planning materiality. This important concept is discussed in detail in chapter 4.

Cloud 9

Ian thinks that all audits are pretty much the same and that W&S Partners must have an audit plan that they can use for the Cloud 9 audit. Suzie explains that if they tailor the plan to the client, the audit is far more likely to be efficient and effective. That is, they will get the job done without wasting time and ensure that sufficient appropriate evidence is gathered for the accounts that are most at risk of being misstated. If they can do this, W&S Partners will not only issue the right audit report, but make a profit from the audit as well. In other words, if the plan is good, performing the audit properly will be easier.

3.1.2 Performing an audit

The performance, or execution, stage of the audit involves detailed testing of controls, transactions, and balances. If an auditor plans to rely on their client's system of internal controls, they will conduct tests of control (discussed in chapter 7). An auditor will conduct detailed substantive tests of transactions throughout the year and detailed substantive tests of balances recorded at year end (discussed in chapter 8, 9, 10 and 11). This detailed testing provides the evidence that the auditor requires to determine whether the financial statements are fairly presented (discussed in chapter 13).

3.1.3 Concluding and reporting on an audit

The final stage of the audit involves drawing conclusions based on the evidence gathered and arriving at an opinion regarding the fair presentation of the financial statements. The auditor's opinion is expressed in the audit report (see chapter 13). At this stage of the audit, an auditor will draw on their understanding of the client, their detailed knowledge of the risks faced by the client, and the conclusions drawn when testing the client's controls, transactions, and account balances.

BEFORE YOU GO ON

3.1.1 What are the three main stages of the audit?

3.1.2 List three factors that affect an auditor's preliminary risk identification.

3.1.3 What are related parties?

3.2 GAINING AN UNDERSTANDING OF THE CLIENT

At the outset of every audit, an auditor must gain an understanding of their client. This allows the auditor to make a reasonable preliminary risk assessment and to assess planning materiality. It also allows the auditor to determine the appropriateness of the entity's accounting policies, identify areas where additional audit work may be required (i.e., related parties), and develop expectations for analytics. This ensures the auditor is able to assess the risk that the financial statements contain a material misstatement due to:

2 Explain the process used in gaining an understanding of the client.

- the nature of the client's business
- the industry in which the client operates
- the level of competition within that industry
- the client's customers and suppliers
- the regulatory environment in which the client operates

CAS 315 provides guidance on the steps to take when gaining an understanding of a client. It requires the auditor to do the following:

1. Make inquiries of management and of others within the entity who may have information to help identify the risk of material misstatements. This includes making inquiries of both financial and non-financial staff at all levels of the organization, including those charged with governance, internal audit, sales, and operational personnel.

2. Perform analytical procedures at the planning stage of the audit to identify any unusual or unexpected relationships that may highlight where risks exist. Analytical procedures are a study of plausible relationships between both financial and non-financial data.

3. Perform observation and inspection procedures to corroborate the responses made by management and others within the organization. These procedures also provide information about the entity and its environment. Examples of such audit procedures include observation or inspection of the entity's operations, premises, and facilities; business plans and strategies; internal control manuals; and any reports prepared and reviewed by management (such as management reports, interim financial statements, and minutes of board of directors' meetings).

By performing these activities, the auditor will gain an understanding of the issues at the entity level, the industry level, and the economy level.

Cloud 9

Ian knows that there are many possible problems in an audit that would cause the auditor to issue the wrong type of audit report, but he is struggling to understand why the audit team will be spending time gaining an understanding of a client. How does this help? Why aren't audits all the same?

Suzie explains to Ian that issuing the wrong type of audit report is a risk the auditor always faces, but the risk varies across audits. The variation in the risk is partly related to how well the audit team performs its tasks, which is dependent on the team members' level of skill, effort, supervision, and so on. But the variation in risk is also related to the particular characteristics of the client and its environment. Some clients are more likely than others to have errors or deficiencies in their accounting and financial reporting systems, operations, or underlying data. Even within one client's business, some areas are more likely to have problems than, or will have problems different to, others. Suzie asks Ian to think about what sort of problems Cloud 9's draft financial statements are most likely to have, and why.

3.2.1 Entity level

It is important that an auditor gain a detailed knowledge of their client. Knowledge about the entity is gained through interviews with client personnel, including those charged with governance. The auditor will ask questions about what the client does, how it functions, how its ownership is structured, and what its sources of financing are. For new clients, this process is very detailed and time consuming. For a continuing client, this process is less onerous and involves updating the knowledge gained on previous audits. By gaining an understanding of the client, the auditor is in a stronger position to assess entity-level risks and the financial statement accounts that require closer examination. The following paragraphs outline some of the procedures followed by an auditor when gaining an understanding of their client at the entity level.

Major customers are identified so that the auditor may consider whether those customers have a good reputation, are on good terms with the client (that is, they are likely to remain a customer in future), and are likely to pay the client on a timely basis. Dissatisfied customers may withhold payment, which affects the allowance for doubtful accounts and the client's cash flow, or may decide not to purchase from the client in the future, which can affect the going concern assumption. If a client has only one or a few customers, this risk is increased. The auditor also considers the terms of any long-term contracts between their client and their client's customers.

Major suppliers are identified to determine whether they are reputable and supply quality goods on a timely basis. Consideration is given to whether significant levels of goods are returned to suppliers as faulty, and what the terms of any contracts with suppliers and the terms of payment to suppliers include. The auditor also assesses whether the client pays its suppliers on a timely basis. If the client is having trouble paying its suppliers, it may have trouble sourcing goods because suppliers may refuse to transact with a company that does not pay on time.

Whether the client is an *importer or exporter* of goods is identified. If the client trades internationally, the auditor considers the stability of the country (or countries) the client trades with, the stability of the foreign currency (or currencies) the client trades in, and the effectiveness of any risk management policies the client uses to limit exposure to currency fluctuations (such as hedging policies).

The client's *capacity to adapt to changes in technology and other trends* is assessed. If the client is not well positioned to adjust to such changes, it risks falling behind competitors and losing market share, which in the longer term can affect the going concern assumption. If the client operates in an industry subject to frequent change, it risks significant losses if it doesn't keep abreast of such changes and "move with the times." For example, if a client sells laser printers, the auditor will need to assess whether the client is up to date with changes in technology and customer demands for environmentally friendly printers.

The nature of any *warranties* provided to customers is assessed. If the client provides warranties on products sold, the auditor needs to assess the likelihood that goods will be returned and the risk that the client has underprovided for that rate of return (adequacy of the warranty provision). The auditor will pay particular attention to goods being returned for the same problem, indicating that there may be a systemic fault. For example, say a client sells quality pens and the auditor notices that a number of pens are being returned because the mechanism to twist the pen open is faulty. In this case, the auditor will assess the likelihood that other pens will be returned for the same reason, the steps being taken by the client to rectify the problem, and whether the provision for warranty is adequate in light of this issue.

The terms of *discounts* given by the client to its customers and received by the client from its suppliers are reviewed. An assessment is made of the client's bargaining power with its customers and suppliers to determine whether discounting policies are putting profit margins at risk, which may place the future viability of the client at risk.

An assessment is made of the client's *reputation* with its customers, suppliers, employees, shareholders, and the wider community. A company with a poor reputation places future profits at risk. It is also not in the best interests of the auditor to be associated with a client that has a poor reputation.

An understanding is gained of client *operations.* The auditor will note where the client operates, the number of locations it operates in, and the dispersion of these locations. The more spread out the client's operations are, the harder it is for the client to effectively control and coordinate its operations, increasing the risk of errors in the financial statements. The auditor will need to visit locations where the risk of material misstatement is greatest to assess the processes and procedures at each site. If the client has operations in other provinces or overseas, the auditor may plan for a visit to those sites by staff from affiliated offices at those locations where risk is greatest. For example, an auditor is more likely to visit client operations if the client opens a new, large site, or if the business is located in a country where there is a high rate of inflation or where there is a high risk of theft.

An understanding is gained of the *nature of employment contracts* and the client's *relations with its employees.* The auditor will consider the way employees are paid, the mix of wages and bonuses, the level of unionization among the workforce, and the attitude of staff to their employer. The more complex a payroll system, the more likely that errors can occur. When staff are unhappy, there is greater risk of industrial action, such as strikes, which disrupt client operations.

The client's *sources of financing* are reviewed. An assessment is made of a client's debt sources, the reliability of future sources of financing, the structure of debt, and the reliance on debt versus equity financing. An auditor assesses whether the client is meeting interest payments on funds borrowed and repaying funds raised when they are due. If a client has a covenant with a debt provider, the auditor will need to understand the terms of that covenant and the nature of the restrictions it places on the client. Debt covenants vary. A company may, for example, agree to limit further borrowings. It may agree to maintain a certain debt-to-equity ratio. If the client does not meet the conditions of a debt covenant, the borrower may recall the debt, placing the client's liquidity position at risk, and increasing the risk that the client may not be able to continue as a going concern.

The client's *ownership structure* is assessed. The auditor is interested in the amount of debt funding relative to equity, the use of different forms of shares, and the differing rights of shareholder groups. The client's dividend policy and its ability to meet dividend payments out of operating cash flow are also of interest.

Cloud 9

Ian is starting to think about Cloud 9 more closely. He can remember something being said about Cloud 9 importing the shoes from a production plant in China and then wholesaling them to major department stores.

"OK," says Suzie. "Let's just take that one aspect of the operations and think about the issues that could arise."

Ian realizes that the department stores would be customers of Cloud 9 (although they should check that the stores actually purchase the shoes rather than hold them on consignment). If there was a mistake or a dispute with one of the stores, or if the store was in financial difficulties, the collectability of the accounts receivable would be in doubt, so assets could be overstated. If the store disputed a sale, or a sale return was not recorded correctly, sales (and profit) could be overstated. Is Cloud 9 liable for warranty expenses if the shoes are faulty? Would the auditors need to read the terms of the contract to determine if a warranty liability should be recorded on the balance sheet? What about the balance of inventory? Do the shoes belong to Cloud 9 when they are being shipped from China, or only after they arrive at the warehouse?

Suzie points out that the answer to each of these questions could be different for Cloud 9 than for other clients because of its different circumstances. The auditors need to gain an understanding of these circumstances so that they can assess the risk that accounts receivable, sales, sales returns, inventory, and liabilities are misstated. Once they understand the risks, they are in a position to decide how they will audit Cloud 9.

3.2.2 Industry level

At the industry level, an auditor is interested in their client's position within its industry, the level of competition in that industry, and the client's size relative to competitors. The auditor evaluates the client's reputation among its peers and the level of government support for companies operating in that industry. Another consideration is the level of demand for the products sold or services supplied by companies in that industry and the factors that affect that demand. For example, a soft-drink manufacturer is affected by the weather; that is, revenue is seasonal. Also, competition is generally strong.

A comparison is made between the client and its close competitors nationally and internationally. When an auditor has a number of clients that operate in the one industry, this stage of the audit is more straightforward than if the client operates in an industry that the auditor is not already familiar with. The following paragraphs outline some of the procedures followed by auditors when gaining an understanding of their client at the industry level.

The *level of competition* in the client's industry is assessed. The more competitive the client's industry, the more pressure placed on the client's profits. In an economic downturn, the weakest companies in highly competitive industries face financial hardship and possible liquidation. A key issue for an auditor is their client's position among its competitors and its ability to withstand downturns in the economy.

An auditor also considers their client's *reputation* relative to other companies in the same industry. If the client has a poor reputation, customers and suppliers may shift their business to a competing firm, threatening their client's profits. The auditor can assess their client's reputation by reading articles in the press and industry publications.

Consideration is given to the level of *government support* for the client's industry. This issue is important if the industry faces significant competition internationally or the industry is new and requires time to become established. Support is sometimes provided to industries that produce items in line with government policy, such as manufacturers of water tanks, solar heating, and reduced-flow taps in the context of environmental policies.

An assessment is made of the impact of *government regulation* on the client and the industry in which it operates. Regulations include tariffs on goods, trade restrictions, and foreign exchange policies. Regulations can affect a client's viability and continued profitability. An auditor will consider the level of taxation imposed on companies operating in their client's industry. The auditor assesses the different taxes and charges imposed on their client and the impact these have on profits.

The level of *demand* for the goods sold or services provided by companies in the client's industry is considered. If a client's products or services are seasonal, this will affect revenue flow. If a client is an ice-cream producer, sales would be expected to increase in summer. However, if the weather is unseasonal, profits may suffer. If a client sells swimsuits, sales will fall in a cool summer. If a client sells ski equipment, sales will fall if the winter brings little snow. If a client operates in an industry subject to changing trends, such as fashion, the client risks inventory obsolescence if it does not keep up and move quickly with changing styles. When a product or process is subject to technological change, there is the risk that a client will quickly be left behind by its competitors. Either its products will become obsolete or its outdated processes will mean that it may find it difficult to compete with competitors that stay abreast of technological innovations.

3.2.3 Economy level

Finally, when gaining an understanding of a client, an auditor assesses how economy-level factors affect the client. Economic upturns and downturns, changes in interest rates, and currency fluctuations affect all companies. An auditor is concerned with a client's susceptibility to these changes and its ability to withstand economic pressures.

During an economic upturn, companies are under pressure to perform as well as or better than competitors, and shareholders expect consistent improvements in profits. When conducting the audit in this environment, more focus is given to the risk of overstatement of revenues and understatement of expenses. During an economic downturn, companies may decide to "take a bath." This means that companies may purposefully understate profits. When the economy is poor, there is a tendency to maximize write offs, as a fall in profits can easily be explained to the investment community since most companies experience a decline in earnings. A benefit of "taking a bath" is that it provides a low base from which to demonstrate an improvement in results in the following year. Conducting the audit when the economy is in recession and when clients may be tempted to "take a bath" means the auditor must focus more on the risk of understatement of revenues and overstatement of expenses.

Cloud 9

Suzie explains to Ian that the partner, Jo Wadley, has asked her to join the team for this audit because she has extensive experience in the clothing and footwear industry. Wadley wants to make sure that the team's industry knowledge is very strong. Several other members of the team also have experience in auditing clients in the retail industry, including Jo Wadley and manager Sharon Gallagher. In addition, Josh is highly regarded at W&S Partners for his knowledge of sales and cash receipts systems.

Suzie has the task of assessing the industry-specific economic trends and conditions. The documentation has to include an assessment of the competitive environment, including any effects of technological changes and relevant legislation. So that Ian can appreciate how understanding the client is an important part of planning the audit, Suzie asks him to help research the product and customer and supplier elements. Then, together, they will assess the specific risks arising from the entire report, including risks at the economy level, for the Cloud 9 audit.

BEFORE YOU GO ON

3.2.1 What is the purpose of gaining an understanding of a client?

3.2.2 What will an auditor consider if their client is an importer or exporter?

3.2.3 What does a client risk if it operates in an industry subject to changing trends?

3.3 RELATED PARTIES

As discussed, it is the responsibility of the auditor to ensure that related parties are identified and appropriately disclosed in accordance with relevant accounting standards. Therefore, related party transactions require some specific consideration throughout the audit.

According to the CPA Canada Handbook (IAS 24, *Related Party Disclosures*, and ASPE s. 3840), related parties include parent companies, subsidiaries, joint ventures, associates, company management, and close family members of key management. Since related parties are not independent of each other, these transactions may not be in the normal course of business. Related party transactions not only increase the susceptibility of the financial statements to material misstatement due to fraud and error, they may also impact the overall financial statement results. Therefore, financial statement users need sufficient information to assess the impact of these transactions on the financial statements overall. Some examples of related party transactions that require disclosure are listed below:

- purchase and sales transactions between companies under common control or when one party has significant influence over another
- rent paid from one related party to another
- loans made to shareholders or senior management
- loan guarantees provided by a shareholder of the company

As both the International Financial Reporting Standards (IFRS) and the Accounting Standards for Private Enterprises (ASPE) include specific reporting requirements for related party transactions, the auditor must consider the risk of material misstatement throughout the audit if such

③ Explain how related parties can impact risk.

relationships are not appropriately accounted for or disclosed. Therefore, CAS 550 *Related Parties* requires the auditor to do the following:

- Discuss with the engagement team the susceptibility of the financial statements to material misstatement due to fraud or error that could result from the entity's related party relationships and transactions.
- Ask management to identity all related parties and to provide an explanation as to the nature, type, and purpose of transactions with these entities.
- Obtain an understanding of the processes and procedures management has in place to ensure all related party transactions are identified, authorized, accounted for, and disclosed in accordance with the chosen financial reporting framework.
- Remain alert when inspecting documents such as bank confirmations, unusual sales and purchase invoices, minutes of board of director and shareholder meetings, and contracts for indicators that related party transactions may not have not been identified or disclosed to the auditor.
- Identify and assess the risk that transactions may not be in the normal course of operations. For such transactions, inspect any underlying documents and determine the business rationale for such transactions to ensure that they are not an attempt to fraudulently misstate the financial results.

Figure 3.3 lists risk assessment procedures outlined in the *Canadian Professional Engagement Manual (C·PEM)*.

Preparation

(a) Review the entity's list of directors, managers, key staff, family members, and advisors to identify potential or existing related party transactions.

(b) Obtain or prepare a listing of related party transactions.

(c) Consider history (if any) of not disclosing related parties or transactions.

(d) Inquire of management and document what internal controls (if any) or procedures exist to ensure that related parties are identified, approved (especially those outside the normal course of business), and accounted for in accordance with the applicable financial reporting framework. Assess the control design and implementation of any relevant internal controls.

2. Risk of unidentified transactions

(a) Identify where related party transactions could possibly occur. Consider existence of transactions designed to improve liquidity or profitability, reduce debt to equity leverage, avoid corporate or personal taxes, avoid breach of a bank covenant, shift income/expense to future periods, or conceal other financial statement manipulation or misappropriation of assets.

(b) Inquire of management, key employees, and any component auditors* about the existence of:
- Related parties not already identified and details of such transactions.
- Agreements or loan guarantees not reflected in the financial statements.
- Any payments (kickbacks), preferential terms, or side deals not disclosed.

(c) Review minutes of corporate meetings and other relevant documentation.

*A component auditor is an auditor who, at the request of the audit team, performs work on financial information related to a component for the audit group.

FIGURE 3.3 **Sample risk assessment procedures, *C·PEM*, Form 515**

Source: CPA Canada, "Understanding Related Parties," *C·PEM*, Electronic Templates, Form 515, 2010–2011.

BEFORE YOU GO ON

3.3.1 Define related parties.

3.3.2 How do related parties impact risk? Why?

3.3.3 What are three procedures the auditor should perform regarding related parties?

3.4 FRAUD RISK

As a part of the risk identification process during the planning stage of the audit, an auditor will assess the risk of a material misstatement due to fraud (CAS 240). When assessing fraud risk, an auditor will adopt an attitude of **professional scepticism** to ensure that any indicator of a potential fraud is properly investigated. This means that the auditor must remain independent of their client, maintain a questioning attitude, and search thoroughly for corroborating evidence to validate information provided by the client. The auditor must not assume that their past experience with client management and staff is indicative of the current risk of fraud.

Fraud is an intentional act to obtain an unjust or illegal advantage through the use of deception (CAS 240, para. 11). An auditor can use red flags[1] to alert them to the possibility that a fraud may have occurred. Red flags include:

- key finance personnel refusing to take leave
- overly dominant management
- poor compensation practices
- inadequate training programs
- a complex business structure
- no (or ineffective) internal auditing staff
- a high turnover of auditors
- unusual transactions
- weak internal controls

There are two kinds of fraud. Financial reporting fraud is intentionally misstating items or omitting important facts from the financial statements. Misappropriation of assets generally involves some form of theft. Table 3.1 provides examples of financial reporting and misappropriation of assets frauds.

The responsibility for preventing and detecting fraud rests with those charged with governance at the client. Prevention refers to the use of controls and procedures aimed at avoiding a fraud. Detection refers to the use of controls and procedures aimed at uncovering a fraud should one occur. It is the responsibility of the auditor to assess the risk of fraud and the effectiveness of the client's attempts to prevent and detect fraud through their internal control system. When assessing the risk of fraud, an auditor can consider incentives and pressures to commit a fraud, opportunities to perpetrate a fraud, and attitudes and rationalizations used to justify committing a fraud (CAS 240, App. 1).

4 Define fraud risk and understand audit procedures to reduce this risk.

professional scepticism maintaining an attitude that includes a questioning mind, being alert to conditions that may indicate possible misstatement due to error or fraud, and a critical assessment of audit evidence

FINANCIAL REPORTING FRAUDS	MISAPPROPRIATION OF ASSETS FRAUDS
· Improper asset valuations · Unrecorded liabilities · Timing differences—bringing forward the recognition of revenues and delaying the recognition of expenses · Recording fictitious sales · Understating expenses · Inappropriate application of accounting principles	· Using a company credit card for personal use · Employees remaining on the payroll after ceasing employment · Unauthorized discounts or refunds to customers · Theft of inventory by employees or customers · Using a company car for unauthorized personal use

TABLE 3.1 **Examples of frauds**

3.4.1 Incentives and pressures to commit a fraud

In assessing the risk of fraud, an auditor will consider incentives and pressures faced by their client to commit a fraud. While the examples provided below indicate that a client may be inclined to commit a fraud, they in no way indicate that a fraud has definitely occurred. When an auditor becomes aware of any of these risk factors, in isolation or combination, they will plan their audit to obtain evidence in relation to each risk factor.

Examples of incentives and pressures that increase the risk of a client committing fraud include:

- operation in a highly competitive industry
- a significant decline in demand for products or services
- falling profits
- a threat of takeover
- a threat of bankruptcy
- ongoing losses
- rapid growth
- poor cash flows combined with high earnings
- pressure to meet market expectations
- planning to list on a stock exchange
- planning to raise debt or renegotiate a loan
- about to enter into a significant new contract
- a significant proportion of remuneration tied to earnings (that is, bonuses, options)

3.4.2 Opportunities to perpetrate a fraud

After identifying one or more incentives or pressures to commit a fraud, an auditor will assess whether a client has an opportunity to perpetrate a fraud. An auditor will utilize their knowledge of how other frauds have been perpetrated to assess whether the same opportunities exist at the client. While the examples below of opportunities to commit a fraud suggest that a fraud may have been carried out, their existence does not mean that a fraud has definitely occurred. An auditor must use professional judgement to assess each opportunity in the context of other risk indicators and consider available evidence thoroughly.

Examples of opportunities that increase the risk that a fraud may have been perpetrated include:

- accounts that rely on estimates and judgement
- a high volume of transactions close to year end
- significant adjusting entries and reversals after year end
- significant related party transactions
- poor corporate governance mechanisms
- poor internal controls
- a high turnover of staff
- reliance on complex transactions
- transactions out of character for a business (for example, if a client leases its motor vehicles it should not have car registration expenses)

3.4.3 Attitudes and rationalization to justify a fraud

Together with the identification of incentives or pressures to commit a fraud and opportunities to perpetrate a fraud, an auditor will assess the attitudes and rationalization of client management and staff to fraud. Attitude refers to ethical beliefs about right and wrong, and rationalization refers to an ability to justify an act. While the examples below indicate that a fraud may occur in companies where these characteristics are identified, they do not mean that a fraud has occurred.

Examples of attitudes and rationalizations used to justify a fraud include:

- a poor tone at the top (that is, from senior management)
- the view that implementing an effective internal control structure is not a priority
- an excessive focus on maximization of profits and/or share price
- a poor attitude to compliance with accounting regulations
- rationalization that other companies make the same inappropriate accounting choices

PROFESSIONAL ENVIRONMENT

Application of the fraud triangle

According to Dr. Donald Cressey, a criminologist who has studied fraudsters, three factors need to be present for fraud: incentives and pressures, opportunities, and attitudes and rationalizations. This has become known as the fraud triangle.

All of these factors can be found in Bernie Madoff's $50-billion Ponzi scheme, which has been described as one of the largest frauds in U.S. history.

Incentives and Pressures

Mr. Madoff, as manager of Ascot Investments, became known in the 1980s for producing double-digit returns and creating significant wealth for his clients. However, the 1987 stock market crash and the subsequent slow economic recovery made such returns impossible. His steady 10- to 12-percent investment returns suddenly dropped to 4.5 percent. It was at this time that Mr. Madoff felt the pressure to maintain the returns his firm had become known for. He started taking investors' capital to pay out redeeming investors and falsified results to show big returns to appear more successful.

Opportunities

How was Mr. Madoff able to pull off such a large fraud? Apparently, Mr. Madoff refused to disclose how he was able to earn such significant returns and investors never pressed for more information beyond the falsified return statements

they received. He did admit, however, to turning down potential clients if they asked too many questions about his investment strategies.

Rationalization

Mr. Madoff rationalized his fraudulent scheme as he believed everyone was greedy. He claims he warned potential investors that his investment choices could be risky and lead to losses, and the drive for larger returns simply led them to give him more money.

In 2009, Mr. Madoff pleaded guilty to several U.S. federal felonies and he was sentenced to 150 years in prison. While this does little to rectify the losses of his victims, perhaps the best lesson we can take from this case is that when all elements of the fraud triangle are present, a "potent combination of elements" exists. While it is virtually impossible to prevent all fraud, knowing and understanding the fraud triangle can make a significant difference in reducing one's exposure.

Sources: Ali Velshi, "Ex-Nasdaq Chair Arrested for Securities Fraud," CNN Money, December 12, 2008; Robert Lenzner, "Bernie Madoff's $50 Billion Ponzi Scheme," *Forbes*, December 2008; David Lieberman, Pallavi Gogoi, Theresa Howard, Kevin McCoy, and Matt Krantz, "Investors Remain Amazed over Madoff's Sudden Downfall," *USA Today*, December 15, 2008; "Bernard Madoff Gets 150 Years behind Bars for Fraud Scheme," CBC News, June 29, 2009; Walter Pavlo, "Bernard Madoff Is The Fraud Triangle," *Forbes*, March 2011.

Cloud 9

Suzie explains that fraud risk is always present and that auditors must explicitly consider it as part of their risk assessment. Being aware of the incentives and pressures, opportunities, and attitudes within the client relating to fraud helps the auditor make the assessment. Ian admits that he has a little trouble understanding the difference between incentives and attitudes, but he thinks he understands the concept of opportunity. Suzie explains that incentives relate to what pushes (or pulls) a person to commit a fraud. Examples include a need for money to pay debts or gamble. Attitudes or rationalization relate to the thinking about the act of fraud. For example, a person believes it is acceptable to steal from a nasty boss; that is, the theft is justified by the boss's nastiness.

3.4.4 Audit procedures relating to fraud

Besides assessing the fraud risk factors noted above, the following are some of the specific procedures the auditor should perform to comply with CAS 240:

1. The auditor should ask management and those charged with governance if they are aware of a known fraud or suspect there has been a fraud. If the company being audited has an internal audit department, it should also be asked this question. The results of these enquiries should be documented.

2. All members of the audit team, including the partner, should attend a team planning meeting. During this planning meeting, the significant fraud risk factors and where the financial statements may be particularly susceptible to fraud should be reviewed. This allows the more experienced team members to share their knowledge with the less experienced members.

3. The auditor should perform preliminary analytics (discussed in more detail in chapter 4) to identify any unusual relationships that may indicate fraud and thus require further investigation during the audit.

4. The auditor must consider the risk of management override. As management is in a position to manipulate the accounting records or override the controls designed to prevent such fraud, the auditor should test a sample of journal entries, review accounting estimates for reasonableness, contemplate the risk of earnings management (particularly in the area of revenue recognition), and carefully examine unusual business transactions to ensure that they have business substance.

If during the course of the audit, the auditor finds fraud, then they should contemplate their legal and professional responsibilities. As the auditor remains bound by confidentiality, they should seek legal advice to determine if there is a requirement to report the fraud to an outside third party. The auditor may also consider withdrawing from the engagement. Finally, the auditor must report the fraud to the level of management above that under which the fraud occurred and report the fraud to the audit committee.

BEFORE YOU GO ON

3.4.1 What are the responsibilities of the client and the auditor when it comes to fraud?

3.4.2 List four incentives and pressures that increase the risk of fraud.

3.4.3 What is management override and what procedures should the auditor perform to address it?

3.5 GOING CONCERN

5 Explain the going concern assumption.

When planning an audit, performing an audit, and evaluating the results of an audit, an auditor will consider whether it is appropriate to assume that their client will remain as a going concern (CAS 570). The concept of going concern is introduced here and will appear again at various stages throughout this book. The going concern assumption is made when it is believed that a company will remain in business for the foreseeable future (CAS 570, para. 2). Under this assumption, assets are valued on the basis that they will continue to be used for the purposes of conducting a business, and liabilities are recorded and classified as current and non-current on the basis that the client will pay its debts as they fall due in the years to come. It is the responsibility of management and those charged with governance to assess whether their company is likely to remain a going concern. It is the responsibility of the auditor to obtain sufficient appropriate evidence to assess the validity of the going concern assumption made by their client's management and those charged with governance when preparing the financial statements.

3.5.1 Going concern risk—indicators

For each client, an auditor will use their professional judgement to assess whether the going concern assumption is valid. There are a number of indicators that, alone or combined, can suggest that the going concern assumption may be at risk. A comprehensive list of events and conditions that place doubt on the going concern assumption is provided in CAS 570. Indicators include:

- a significant debt-to-equity ratio
- long-term loans reaching maturity without alternative financing in place
- prolonged losses
- an inability to pay debts when they fall due
- supplier reluctance to provide goods on credit
- the loss of a major market, key customer, franchise, or licence
- overreliance on a few customers or suppliers
- high staff turnover
- staff regularly out on strike
- shortage of a key input or raw material
- rapid growth with insufficient planning
- being under investigation for non-compliance with legislation
- falling behind competitors

If the auditor identifies risk factors that indicate that the going concern assumption is in doubt, they will undertake procedures to gather evidence regarding each risk factor. For example, if a client has a significant debt coming due for payment, the auditor will assess the ability of the entity to settle the debt or to raise the funds to replace it. If the auditor believes that there is an unresolved going concern issue outstanding, an assessment is made of the appropriateness of management disclosures in the notes to the financial statements regarding that issue. An auditor will assess the process used by management to evaluate the extent of the going concern risk. If a company has a history of losses and difficulties, an auditor will expect management to take a great deal of time and care in their going concern assessment. Once the auditor has an under-standing of the process used by management, which may include the careful preparation of detailed cash flow projections and budgets, they will assess the adequacy of that process and conduct additional procedures if necessary.

If the auditor concludes that the going concern assumption is in doubt, further procedures are undertaken. CAS 570 provides a list of appropriate audit procedures. They include:

- assessment of cash flows
- assessment of revenue and expense items
- assessment of interim financial statements
- review of debt contracts
- review of board and other meetings
- discussions with client management and lawyers
- identification and assessment of mitigating factors

3.5.2 Going concern risk—mitigating factors

Mitigating factors reduce the risk that the going concern assumption may be in doubt. For example, if a client is experiencing a severe cash shortage but has a letter from its bank agreeing to provide additional financing, the letter reduces (but does not remove) the risk that the going concern assumption may be invalid. Other mitigating factors include:

- a letter of guarantee from a parent company
- the availability of non-core assets, which can be sold to provide needed cash, without inter-rupting the company's operating capacity
- the ability to raise additional funds through the sale of shares
- the ability to raise additional funds through borrowings
- the ability to sell an unprofitable segment of the business

Cloud 9

Going concern is another type of audit risk. When management adopts the going concern assumption, it records assets and liabilities on the basis that the entity will be able to realize its assets and discharge its liabilities in the normal course of business. If the going concern assumption is not valid, the financial statements should include adjustments to the recoverability and classification of recorded assets and liabilities. If these adjustments are not made, the auditor must express an adverse opinion.

Suzie explains that in most cases the assessment of going concern is not clear-cut. Sometimes there are questions about the going concern assumption and various circumstances that mitigate such questions. The auditor's job is to gather evidence about the issues in order to make a judgement about the nature of the uncertainties surrounding the going concern assumption and decide if, and how, these affect the audit report.

BEFORE YOU GO ON

3.5.1 What is the going concern assumption?

3.5.2 List three factors that indicate that the going concern assumption may be at risk.

3.5.3 List three factors that mitigate the risk that the going concern assumption may be in doubt.

3.6 CORPORATE GOVERNANCE

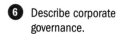 **6** Describe corporate governance.

Corporate governance is the rules, systems, and processes within companies used to guide and control. It includes the processes used to manage the business and the affairs of the entity. As stated in chapter 1, public entities are regulated by legislation and securities regulators. Private entities have essentially the same responsibilities except they are not regulated by securities law and stock exchange requirements.

Governance structures are used to monitor the actions of staff and assess the level of risk faced. Controls are designed to reduce identified risks and ensure the future viability of the company. The CSA published national policy guidelines on corporate governance to help improve performance and enhance accountability to shareholders. Figure 3.4 is an excerpt from those guidelines. While these guidelines do provide a framework for corporate governance practices, they do not dictate any particular requirements. However, reporting issuers must disclose their corporate governance practices and state why they believe these practices are appropriate for the entity.

The CSA guidelines do consider the composition of the board of directors to a degree. While the guidelines do not specifically dictate the size or the specific composition of the board of

---

Board Composition

· The board should have a majority of independent directors.
· The chair of the board should be an independent director.

Meetings of Independent Directors

· The independent directors should hold regularly scheduled meetings at which non-independent directors and members of management are not in attendance.

Board Mandate

· The board should adopt a written mandate in which it acknowledges responsibility for the stewardship of the issuer, including responsibility for:
  (a) satisfying itself as to the integrity of senior management;
  (b) adopting a strategic planning process that takes into account the opportunities and risks of the business;
  (c) identifying the key risks to the business, and ensuring there are appropriate systems in place to manage these risks;
  (d) ensuring succession planning;
  (e) adopting a communication policy;
  (f) overseeing the internal control and management information systems; and
  (g) developing the issuer's approach to corporate governance, including outlining a set of corporate governance principles and guidelines to be followed.

The written mandate of the board should also set out:
  (i) establishing methods for receiving feedback from stakeholders (whistleblowers);
  (ii) setting expectations and responsibilities of directors.

Position Descriptions

· The board should develop job descriptions for the chair of the board and the chair of each board committee.

Orientation and Continuing Education

· The board should ensure all new directors receive a comprehensive orientation so they fully understand their role and the nature and operation of the business.
· The board should provide continuing education opportunities for all directors.

Code of Business Conduct and Ethics

· The board should adopt a written code of business conduct and ethics to address conflicts of interest, protection and proper use of corporate assets, confidentiality of corporate information, fair dealing with investors, customers, suppliers, competitors and employees; compliance with laws, rules and regulations; and reporting of any illegal or unethical behaviour.
· The board should monitor compliance with this code.

FIGURE 3.4 **Excerpt from the CSA's *Corporate Governance Guidelines***

Source: CSA, *National Policy 58-201: Corporate Governance Guidelines,* June 30, 2005.

directors, they do require that there be at least three directors who are independent of the entity. The CSA also recommends, but does not require, that the chair of the board be an independent. Therefore, the CEO of the entity can also be the chair of the board.

The board of directors is not required to participate in the day-to-day decision-making of the entity; however, it is responsible to act in the best interest of the corporation. To help achieve this, the CSA recommends the board of directors develop a written mandate in which it explicitly acknowledges responsibility for the stewardship of the entity. They recommend that this written mandate assure that the entity has systems and practices in place addressing strategic planning, risk identification, risk mitigation, internal control, a code of conduct, succession planning, and the supervision of senior management. It is recommended the board meet regularly and meeting minutes be maintained.

All listed entities must have an audit committee. The audit committee is to consist of independent board members who are financially literate. The audit committee is responsible for appointing the auditor, overseeing the work of the auditor, pre-approving all audit and non- audit services, and ensuring that a process is in place to permit the reporting of weaknesses in internal control. Some boards of directors may also elect to have other committees such as a compensation committee to review the CEO's compensation.

From an auditor's perspective, considering a client's corporate governance principles is an important part of gaining an understanding of that client. A client that does not take its corporate governance obligations seriously may not fulfill its obligation to ensure its financial statements are fairly presented.

BEFORE YOU GO ON

3.6.1 What is corporate governance?

3.6.2 Why is the auditor concerned with an entity's corporate governance?

3.6.3 List three guidelines that should be included in a board of directors' mandate.

3.7 INFORMATION TECHNOLOGY

When gaining an understanding of a client, an auditor will consider the particular risks faced by the client associated with **information technology** (IT). IT is a part of most companies' accounting processes, which include transaction initiation, recording, processing, correction as necessary, transfer to the general ledger, and compilation of the financial report. CAS 315 requires that the auditor gain an understanding of the client's IT system and the associated risks.

Risks associated with IT include unauthorized access to computers, software, and data; errors in programs; lack of backup; and loss of data. Unauthorized access to data can occur when there is insufficient security or poor password protection procedures. Unauthorized access can result in data being lost or distorted. Unauthorized access to computer programs can result in misstatements in the financial statements. Access can be limited in a number of ways, such as through the use of security (such as locked doors) and passwords.

Errors in computer programming can occur if programs are not tested thoroughly. It is important that new programs and changes to programs be tested extensively before being put into operation. Errors can also occur if mistakes are made when writing a program or if programs are deliberately changed to include errors. Deliberate changes may be made by staff or outsiders who gain unauthorized access to a client's IT system. For example, unhappy staff may purposefully change a program, causing errors to embarrass their employer. It is therefore important that access be limited to authorized staff. Errors can also occur if programming changes are not processed on a timely basis. Programs need to be changed from time to time for a variety of reasons, such as to change sales prices, update discounts being offered to customers, and so on. It is important that these changes be made by authorized personnel on a timely basis to avoid errors.

New programs can be purchased "off the shelf" from a software provider or developed internally by a client's staff. When a client purchases a general-purpose program off the shelf, there is a risk that it will require modification to suit the client's operations, which can lead to errors. An advantage of purchasing general-purpose programs from reputable companies is that they will

 Explain how a client's information technology (IT) can affect risk.

---

information technology the use of computers to store and process data and other information

have been tested before being made available for sale. In contrast, when a client's staff develop a program internally, the program is more likely to have the features required, but there is a risk of errors if the program is written by inexperienced staff or the program is not adequately tested before being put into operation.

When a client installs a new IT system, there are a number of risks. There is the risk that the system may not be appropriate for the client and its reporting requirements. After installation, there is the risk that data may be lost or corrupted when transferring information from an existing system to the new system. There is the risk that the new system does not process data appropriately. There is the risk that client staff are not adequately trained to use the new system effectively. It is important that a client has appropriate procedures for selecting new IT systems, changing from an old to a new system, training staff in using the new system, and ensuring that a new system includes embedded controls to minimize the risk of material misstatement.

When a client has an established IT system, an auditor will gain an understanding of the risks posed by that system as part of their assessment of the risk of a material misstatement in the client's financial statements. An auditor will assess whether their client has the processes and procedures in place required to reduce IT risk to an acceptably low level. The two broad categories of controls used to reduce IT risk are general controls and application controls.

general controls controls that apply to a company's IT system as a whole. They include policies and procedures for the purchase, maintenance, and daily operations of an IT system, security, and staff training

General controls are policies and procedures that relate to many applications and support the effective functioning of application controls (CAS 315). They include procedures for purchasing, changing, and maintaining new computers; procedures for purchasing, changing, and maintaining new software; the use of passwords and other security measures to minimize the risk of unauthorized access; and procedures to ensure appropriate segregation of duties between, for example, the staff who amend and maintain the programs and the staff who use the programs.

application controls manual or automated controls that operate at a business process level and apply to the processing of transactions by individual applications

Application controls are manual or automated procedures that typically operate at a business process level and apply to the processing of transactions by individual applications (CAS 315). These controls are designed to prevent and/or detect a material misstatement in the financial statements by ensuring all transactions are recorded only once, and rejected transactions are identified and corrected. Application controls impact procedures used for data entry, data processing and output, or reporting. They include reconciliations between input and output data and automated checks on data entered to ensure accuracy; for example, a check that a customer number entered is valid. A more detailed discussion of general and application controls is included in chapter 7.

When an auditor has identified an IT risk, they will assess the adequacy of their client's general and application controls in mitigating that risk. If an auditor believes that their client's general and application controls appear adequate, their audit strategy is to test those controls with a view to relying on the client's procedures to minimize IT risk exposure. If an auditor believes that a client's general and application controls do not appear to be adequate, their audit strategy is to rely more heavily on their own tests of the transactions and balances produced by the client's IT system.

Cloud 9

Suzie explains to Ian that her experience in the clothing and footwear industry has taught her to be very inquisitive about the systems used to manage orders. She has seen a few clothing businesses fail because they could not get their goods to retail outlets in time. Fashion is such a fickle market that even being a few weeks late means that stores run out of inventory, and, when inventory does arrive, stores have to discount it to sell it. After this situation occurs a couple of times, retailers turn to more reliable suppliers, even if the designs aren't as imaginative.

Suzie has heard that Cloud 9 is very reliant on an inventory management software program developed by their parent company. Because it is not a widely used package, she does not know anything about it and is concerned about its ability to provide reliable data. Suzie and Ian decide to allocate extra time in the audit plan to assessing the reliability of this software.

BEFORE YOU GO ON

3.7.1 What are some of the risks associated with the purchase of a new IT system?

3.7.2 What are two common sources of new computer programs?

3.7.3 What are application controls?

3.8 CLOSING PROCEDURES

When finalizing the financial statements, a client will close its accounts for the financial reporting period. Revenue and expense items must include all transactions that occurred during the period and exclude transactions that relate to other periods. Asset and liability balances must include all relevant items, accruals must be complete, and contingent liabilities must accurately and completely reflect potential future obligations. From an audit perspective, there is a risk that the client's closing procedures are inadequate.

8 Explain how client closing procedures can affect reported results.

An auditor is concerned that transactions and events have been recorded in the correct accounting period. This is the responsibility of those charged with governance. It is the responsibility of the auditor to ensure that their client has applied its closing procedures appropriately.

An auditor will determine the risk associated with their client's closing procedures. In addition to the annual financial statements, clients prepare monthly and quarterly financial statements for internal and/or external purposes. An auditor can check these reports to assess the accuracy of their client's closing procedures when preparing those reports. If there are significant errors, where closing procedures are inadequate and transactions are not always recorded in the appropriate reporting period, an auditor will plan on spending more time conducting detailed testing around year end.

There are a number of ways that an auditor can assess the adequacy of their client's closing procedures. Clients that report monthly are more likely to have in place well-established closing procedures than clients that only report annually. An auditor will check the accuracy of accrual calculations around year end. An auditor can look at earnings trends to assess whether the reported income is in line with similar periods (months or quarters) in prior years. For example, revenues are generally higher for an ice-cream seller in warmer months, and wages are generally higher during the months when a client holds its annual sales and extra staff are hired to help out with the increased activity.

If an auditor believes that their client is under pressure to report strong results, there is a risk that revenues earned after year end will be included in the current year's income and expenses incurred before year end will be excluded. If the auditor believes that their client is under pressure to smooth its income and not report any unexpected increases, there is a risk that revenues earned just before year end will be excluded from current income and expenses incurred after year end will be included. In both cases, the auditor will trace transactions recorded close to year end to source documentation and confirm that all transactions are recorded in the appropriate accounting period.

Figure 3.5 lists additional recommended risk assessment procedures from the *Canadian Professional Engagement Manual (C·PEM)*.

FIGURE 3.5 **Excerpt of risk assessment procedures, *C·PEM*, Form 435**

Source: CPA Canada, "Risk Asessment Procedures—Planning & Execution" *C·PEM*, Form 435, April 2010.

Procedure	WP	Comments	Completed by and date
OBSERVATION AND INSPECTION			
Identify potential risk factors from reading key entity documents such as the following: a) Business plans, budgets and most recent financial results. b) Minutes of directors'/audit committee meetings. c) Reports/letters, etc. from regulators or government agencies. d) Internet/magazine/newspaper articles on the entity or industry. e) Details of actual or threatened litigation including correspondence with external legal counsel. f) Significant contracts and agreements. g) Communications with staff on changes in entity-level control matters. h) Tax assessments and correspondence.			

(continued)

FIGURE 3.5 **Excerpt of risk assessment procedures, *C·PEM*, Form 435** (continued)

Procedure	WP	Comments	Completed by and date
INQUIRY			
Make inquiries of management and those responsible for financial reporting. Who Interviewed By whom Date Ask about: a) Business objectives, industry trends, management's assessment of current and potential risk factors and their planned responses. b) Major events or changes that took place during the period. Consider • economic conditions • changes in products and services • new technologies, contracts • funding • operating results • ownership • organizational structure • key personnel, bonus plans • IT infrastructure or applications • internal control processes and financial reporting. c) Any instances of alleged, suspected or actual fraud (Forms 511 and 512). d) Any performance bonuses or incentive plans. e) The identity of and nature and amount of related party transactions during the period (Form 640). f) Any going-concern events or conditions (complete Form 527 and, if necessary, Form 625). g) Transactions, events and conditions that give rise to accounting estimates (Form 635). h) Nature, extent and status of litigation/claims against the entity or key personnel. i) Whether the entity is in compliance with required filings (tax returns, etc.), declarations and other regulatory requirements.			
Where applicable, make inquiries of members of the governance board (directors and audit committee members, etc.). Who interviewed By whom Date Ask about: a) The composition, mandate and meetings of the board of directors and any audit committee. b) Any knowledge of management override, fraud or suspected fraud. c) Their opinion on: • The effectiveness of management oversight. • The control environment (culture, competence, attitudes, etc.). • What financial statement areas are susceptible to fraud (Form 512).			

PROFESSIONAL ENVIRONMENT

Top management compensation

Just how big are the incentives for good performance by chief executive officers (CEOs) of publicly traded Canadian companies? A survey of Canadian executives shows that they can be very big indeed. The top paid CEO in Canada in 2012, Hunter Harrison, the head of the Canadian Pacific Railway, was paid $49.1 million in salary, stock options, and bonuses.

Second on the list was James Smith of Thomson Reuters Corp., who took home $18.8 million. He was followed by the then-CEO of Talisman Energy Inc., John Manzoni, with $18.1 million. An annual review conducted by the Canadian Centre for Policy Alternatives found that the average compensation for Canada's top 100 CEOs was $7.96 million in 2012. The average Canadian worker's annual salary was $46,634.

Academic research suggests that auditors need to be aware of the potential effects of incentives related to compensation packages. For example, Paul Healy provided evidence that when top executives are paid a bonus according to a formula incorporating minimum and maximum profit levels, profits appear to be "managed" in predictable ways. Healy's evidence suggests that if the minimum profit is not likely to be reached, managers will take action to increase accruals (such as closing entries) to reduce the current year's profit.

When the overaccrual reverses in the next year, there will be a boost to profit, and therefore managers will receive a bonus on the amount that they are able to "shift" into the next year. Managers take the same action to reduce profit if it is likely to be above the required maximum, therefore deferring the profit and bonus to the following year. However, if profit is between the required minimum and maximum, managers will try to increase profit to increase their bonus.

The lesson from the academic research is that if auditors understand how the bonus arrangement works, they will be more alert to the type of profit shifting likely to be attempted by managers.

Sources: Hugh MacKenzie, "All in a Day's Work? CEO Pay in Canada," Canadian Centre for Policy Alternatives, January 2014; Paul Healy, "The Effect of Bonus Schemes on Accounting Decisions," *Journal of Accounting and Economics*, April 1985, pp. 85–107.

Cloud 9

The partner, Jo Wadley, has learned of pressure from the parent company on Cloud 9's management to increase revenue by 3 percent this year. Jo is also aware of cost increases associated with a new store and sponsorship deals. Jo believes that this places additional pressure on Cloud 9's management to meet targets, resulting in additional risks for closing procedures. Jo has instructed Suzie to allocate additional time to auditing closing procedures on the Cloud 9 audit.

BEFORE YOU GO ON

3.8.1 Explain how an auditor can assess the risk associated with their client's closing procedures.

3.8.2 Outline how an auditor can assess the adequacy of their client's closing procedures.

3.8.3 What is the particular risk when an auditor believes that their client is under pressure to report strong results?

SUMMARY

❶ Identify the different stages of an audit.

The stages of an audit include planning, performing, and reporting. During the planning stage, an auditor will gain an understanding of their client in order to make an informed risk assessment, develop an audit strategy, and set their planning materiality. During the performing stage, an auditor will execute their detailed testing of account balances and transactions. The final stage of every audit involves reviewing all of the evidence gathered throughout the audit and arriving at a conclusion regarding the fair presentation of the client's financial statements. The auditor will then write an audit report that reflects their opinion based upon their findings.

❷ Explain the process used in gaining an understanding of the client.

An auditor will gain an understanding of their client to aid in the risk identification process. This process involves consideration of issues at the entity level, the industry level, and the broader economic level. At the entity level, an auditor will identify the client's major customers, suppliers, and stakeholders (that is, banks, shareholders, and employees). The auditor will also determine whether their client is an importer or exporter, who the client's competitors are, what the client's capacity is to adapt to changes in technology, and what the nature of any warranties provided to customers is. At the industry level, an auditor is interested in their client's position within its industry. At the economic level, an auditor will assess how well positioned the client is to cope with current and changing government policy and economic conditions.

❸ Explain how related parties can impact risk.

Related parties include parent companies, subsidiaries, joint ventures, associates, company management, and close family members of key management. Since related parties are not independent of each other, these transactions may not be in the normal course of business. This increases the risk of material misstatement and may impact the overall financial results. Therefore, related party transactions require some specific consideration throughout the audit and specific procedures should be performed and documented.

4 Define fraud risk and understand audit procedures to reduce this risk.

Fraud is an intentional act through the use of deception to obtain an unjust or illegal advantage. The two kinds of fraud are financial reporting fraud and misappropriation of assets fraud. There are a number of techniques the auditor uses to assess the risk of fraud. The audit file must document the fraud risk assessment and procedures performed to support that assessment.

5 Explain the going concern assumption.

The going concern assumption is made when it is believed that a company will remain in business for the foreseeable future. An auditor will consider the appropriateness of this assumption during the planning stage and then throughout the audit.

6 Describe corporate governance.

Corporate governance is the rules, systems, and processes within companies used to guide and control. Among other things, governance structures are used to assess the level of risk faced and to design controls to reduce identified risks.

7 Explain how a client's information technology (IT) can affect risk.

There are a number of risks associated with IT. During the planning stage of the audit, the auditor will assess the likelihood that their client's financial statements are misstated due to limitations in its IT system.

8 Explain how client closing procedures can affect reported results.

There are a number of risks associated with a client's closing procedures. Closing procedures are the processes used by a client at year end to ensure that transactions are recorded in the appropriate accounting period. From an audit perspective, there is a risk that the client's closing procedures are inadequate.

KEY TERMS

Application controls, 90
Audit strategy, 75
Closing procedures, 76
Corporate governance, 76
Execution stage, 75

Fraud, 75
General controls, 90
Going concern, 75
Information technology, 89
Materiality, 75

Planning stage, 75
Professional scepticism, 83
Reporting stage, 75
Sufficient appropriate evidence, 75

MULTIPLE-CHOICE QUESTIONS

3.1 When gaining an understanding of the client, the auditor will identify the geographic location of the client because:
(a) more spread-out clients are harder to control.
(b) the auditor will need to visit the various locations to assess processes and procedures at each site.
(c) the auditor will plan to use staff from affiliated offices to visit overseas locations.
(d) all of the above.

3.2 When gaining an understanding of the client's sources of financing, the auditor:
(a) is not interested in debt covenants because all debt contracts are the same.
(b) will assess if the client is meeting interest payments when they are due.
(c) will ignore the relative reliance on debt versus equity funding because that is a management decision, not an audit issue.
(d) none of the above.

3.3 When gaining an understanding of the client at the industry level, the auditor:
(a) will not ignore information about the client's industry.
(b) will not consider the level of demand for the goods and services provided by other companies in the client's industry.
(c) will not consider government taxes on the industry because they are out of the client's control.
(d) will not listen to bad news reports about the client firm because the client's reputation in the press is not important.

3.4 The CSA's *Corporate Governance Guidelines* are designed to help companies:
(a) improve their corporate structure.
(b) improve performance.
(c) enhance their accountability to shareholders and other interested third parties.
(d) all of the above.

3.5 An attitude of professional scepticism means:
(a) the auditor can rely on past experience to determine current risk of fraud.
(b) any indicator of fraud is properly investigated.
(c) the auditor can rely on management assertions.
(d) all of the above.

3.6 An example of an incentive or pressure that increases the risk of fraud is:
(a) the client operates in a highly competitive industry.
(b) the client has a history of making losses.
(c) a significant percentage of management remuneration is tied to earnings.
(d) all of the above.

3.7 The auditor must consider whether it is appropriate to assume that the client will remain as a going concern:
(a) because this means that assets are valued on the basis that they will continue to be used for the purposes of conducting a business.
(b) only if the client is facing bankruptcy, and long-term debt is likely to be withdrawn.
(c) only if the client is listed on a stock exchange.
(d) because mitigating circumstances are not important.

3.8 The planning stage of an audit does not include:
(a) gaining an understanding of the client.
(b) identifying factors that may affect the risk of a material misstatement in the financial statements.
(c) developing an audit strategy and a risk and materiality assessment.
(d) executing and reporting on an audit.

3.9 When gaining an understanding of the client, the auditor will consider:
(a) related party identification.
(b) the appropriateness of the client's system of internal controls to mitigate identified business risks.
(c) controls over the technology used to process and store data electronically.
(d) all of the above.

3.10 Client closing procedures:
(a) are routine transactions that do not have an impact on audit risk.
(b) are the responsibility of those charged with governance who must ensure that transactions are recorded in the correct accounting period.
(c) affect expense accounts only.
(d) all of the above.

REVIEW QUESTIONS

3.1 Explain the relationship between the planning, executing, and reporting stages of an audit. Why is risk identification in the first stage?

3.2 Explain the importance of the planning stage of a financial statement audit.

3.3 When gaining an understanding of a client, an auditor will be interested in an entity's relationships with both its suppliers and customers. What aspects of these relationships will the auditor be interested in and how would they affect the assessment of audit risk?

3.4 List and briefly explain the key factors that the auditor would consider during preliminary risk identification with respect to related parties.

3.5 In the context of fraud, explain the differences between (1) incentives and pressures, (2) opportunity, and (3) attitudes and rationalization. Why is it important for an auditor to consider client systems relevant to all three concepts?

3.6 What procedures should the auditor perform with respect to fraud?

3.7 What does it mean when we say that a business is a "going concern" or, alternatively, has "going concern issues"? Why must an auditor specifically consider evidence about the going concern assessment for each client?

3.8 What are mitigating factors in the context of the going concern assessment? Give some examples of mitigating factors for a loss-making client.

3.9 Why does an auditor need to understand a client's IT system? Explain how IT affects the financial statements.

3.10 Give an example of a client closing procedure. Using your example, explain the accounts that would be affected if the closing procedure is performed inadequately.

PROFESSIONAL APPLICATION QUESTIONS

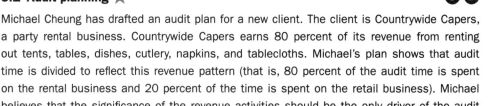

Basic ★   Moderate ★ ★   Challenging ★ ★ ★

3.1 Audit planning ★   ❶❷

Michael Cheung has drafted an audit plan for a new client. The client is Countrywide Capers, a party rental business. Countrywide Capers earns 80 percent of its revenue from renting out tents, tables, dishes, cutlery, napkins, and tablecloths. Michael's plan shows that audit time is divided to reflect this revenue pattern (that is, 80 percent of the audit time is spent on the rental business and 20 percent of the time is spent on the retail business). Michael believes that the significance of the revenue activities should be the only driver of the audit plan because the client has no related parties and has a simple, effective corporate governance structure.

Required

What questions would you have for Michael before accepting his audit plan?

3.2 Understanding the client and its risks—audit planning ★ ★   ❶❷

Ivy Bishnoi is preparing a report for the engagement partner of an existing client, Scooter Ltd., an importer of scooters and other low-powered motorcycles. Ivy has been investigating certain aspects of Scooter Ltd.'s business given the change in economic conditions over the past 12 months. She has found that Scooter Ltd.'s business, which experienced rapid growth over its first five years in operation, has slowed significantly during the last year. Initially, sales of scooters were boosted by good economic conditions and solid employment growth, coupled with rising gas prices. Consumers needed transport to get to work and the high gas prices made the relatively cheap running costs of scooters seem very attractive. In addition, the low purchase price of a small motorcycle or scooter, at between $3,000 and $8,000, meant that almost anyone who had a job could obtain a loan to buy one.

However, Ivy has found that the sales of small motorcycles and scooters have slowed significantly and that all importers of these products, not just Scooter Ltd., are being adversely affected. The onset of an economic recession has restricted employment growth, and those people who still have jobs are less certain of continued employment. In addition, the slowdown in the world economy has caused oil prices to fall, further reducing demand for this type of economical transport. Ivy has also discovered that, due to the global financial crisis, the finance company used by Scooter Ltd.'s customers to finance the purchase of scooters and motorcycles has announced that it will not be continuing to provide loans for any type of vehicle with a purchase price of less than $10,000.

Required

(a) Identify the issues that potentially have an impact on the audit of Scooter Ltd.
(b) Explain how each issue affects the audit plan by identifying the risks and the financial statement accounts that require closer examination.

Questions 3.3 and 3.4 are based on the following case.

Featherbed Surf & Leisure Holidays Ltd. (Featherbed) is a resort company based on Vancouver Island. Its operations include boating, surfing, diving, and other leisure activities; a backpackers' hostel; a family hotel; and a five-star resort. Justin and Sarah Morris own the majority of the shares in the Morris Group, which controls Featherbed. Justin is the chairman of the board of directors of both Featherbed and the Morris Group, and Sarah is a director of both companies as well as the CFO of Featherbed.

In February 2016, Justin Morris approached your audit firm, KFP Partners, to carry out the Featherbed audit for the year ending June 30, 2016. Featherbed has not been audited before but this year the audit has been requested by the company's bank and a new private equity investor group that has just acquired a 20-percent share of Featherbed.

Featherbed employs 30 full-time staff. These workers are employed in administration, accounting, catering, cleaning, and hotel/restaurant duties. During peak periods, Featherbed also uses part-time and casual workers.

Justin and Sarah have a fairly laid-back management style. They trust their workers to work hard for the company and they reward them well. The accounting staff, in particular, are very loyal to the company. Justin tells you that some of the accounting staff enjoy their jobs so much that they have never taken any holidays, and hardly any workers ever take sick leave.

There are three people currently employed as accountants, the most senior of whom is Peter Pinn. Peter heads the accounting department and reports directly to Sarah. He is in his fifties and plans to retire in two or three years. Peter prides himself on his ability to delegate most of his work to his two accounts staff, Kristen and Julie. He claims he has to do this because he is very busy developing a policy and procedures manual for the accounting department. This delegated work includes opening mail, processing payments and receipts, banking funds received, performing reconciliations, posting transactions, and performing the payroll function. Julie is a recently designated chartered accountant. Kristen works part-time—coming into the office on Mondays, Wednesdays, and Fridays. Kristen is responsible for posting all journal entries into the accounting system and the payroll function. Julie does the balance of the work, but they often help each other out in busy periods.

Source: Adapted from the Institute of Chartered Accountants Australia's CA Program's Audit and Assurance Exam, May 2008. Provided courtesy of Chartered Accountants Australia and New Zealand.

3.3 Gaining an understanding of a new client  ②

You have access to the following information for Featherbed:
- prior period financial statements
- anticipated results for the current year
- industry comparisons

Required

Explain how you would use this information to understand your new client.

3.4 Assessing fraud risk ★ ★ ④

Required

(a) Identify and explain any significant fraud risk factors for Featherbed.
(b) For each fraud risk factor you identify, explain how the risk will affect your approach to the audit of Featherbed.

3.5 Fraud risk ★ ★ ④

An airline company has been adversely impacted by the global financial crisis's effect on business travel. In addition to lower overall demand, the airline company faces increased competition from other airlines, which are heavily discounting flights. The airline company policy for revenue is to credit sales to revenue received in advance, and subsequently transfer to revenue when passengers or freight are uplifted or tours and travel air tickets and land transportation are utilized.

In preparing for the 2016 audit, you review the 2015 financial statements and note that revenue from passengers represents 8 percent of total revenue. The interim financial information for the 2016 year shows a 6-percent fall in revenue from passengers, and an 11-percent decrease in revenue from passengers in advance.

You read in the financial press that the global financial crisis has led to an increased incidence of fraud and the majority of these frauds are committed by company directors and senior managers.

Required

Explain why the revenue from passenger accounts in the income statement is at significant risk of fraudulent financial reporting by management.

Source: Adapted from the Institute of Chartered Accountants Australia's CA Program's Audit and Assurance Exam, May 2010. Provided courtesy of Chartered Accountants Australia and New Zealand.

3.6 Financial reporting fraud risk ★★

Vaughan Enterprises Ltd. has grown from its beginnings in the steel fabrication business to become a multinational manufacturer and supplier of all types of packaging, including metal, plastic, and paper-based products. It has also diversified into a range of other businesses, including household appliances in Europe, the United States, and Asia. The growth in the size of the business occurred gradually under the leadership of the last two CEOs, both of whom were promoted from within the business.

At the beginning of last year, the incumbent CEO died of a heart attack and the board took the opportunity to appoint a new CEO from outside the company. Despite the company's growth, returns to shareholders have been stagnant during the last decade. The new CEO has a reputation of turning around struggling businesses by making tough decisions. The new CEO has a five-year contract with generous bonuses for improvements in various performance indicators, including sales to asset ratio, profit from continuing operations to net assets ratio, and share price.

During the first year, the new CEO disposed of several segments of the business that were not profitable. Very large losses on the discontinued operations were recorded and most non-current assets throughout the business were written down to recognize impairment losses. These actions resulted in a large overall loss for the first year, although a profit from continuing operations was recorded. During the second year, recorded sales in the household appliances business in the United States increased dramatically, and, combined with various cost-saving measures, the company made a large profit.

The auditors have been made aware through various conversations with middle management that there is now an extreme focus on maximizing profits through boosting sales and cutting costs. The attitude toward compliance with accounting regulations has changed, with greater emphasis on pleasing the CEO than taking care to avoid breaching either internal policies or external regulations. The message is that the company has considerable ground to make up to catch up with other companies in both methods and results. Meanwhile, the share price over the first year and a half of the CEO's tenure has increased 65 percent, and the board has happily approved payment of the CEO's bonuses and granted the CEO additional options over the company's shares in recognition of the change in the company's results.

Required

(a) Discuss the incentives, pressures, and opportunities to commit financial statement fraud, and the attitudes and rationalizations to justify a fraud in the above case.
(b) What financial statement frauds would you suspect could have occurred at Vaughan?
(c) What are the procedures surrounding the fraud risk assessment that should be performed and documented?

3.7 Fraud risk ★★★

Fellowes and Associates Chartered Accountants is a successful mid-tier accounting firm with a large range of clients across Canada. During 2016, Fellowes and Associates gained a new client, Health Care Holdings Group (HCHG), which owns 100 percent of the following entities:
· Shady Oaks Centre, a private treatment centre
· Gardens Nursing Home Ltd., a private nursing home
· Total Laser Care Limited, a private clinic that specializes in laser treatment of skin defects
  Year end for all HCHG entities is June 30.

The audit partner for the audit of HCHG, Tania Fellowes, has discovered that two months before the end of the financial year, one of the senior nursing officers at Gardens Nursing

Home was dismissed. Her employment was terminated after it was discovered that she had worked in collusion with a number of patients to reduce their fees. The nurse would then take secret payments from the patients.

The nursing officer had access to the patient database. While she was only supposed to update room-located changes for patients, she was able to reduce the patient period of stay and the value of other services provided. The fraud was detected by a fellow employee who overheard the nurse discussing the "scam" with a patient. The employee reported the matter to Gardens Nursing Home's general manager.

Required

(a) Which accounts on the balance sheet and income statement are potentially affected by the fraud?

(b) Describe how Gardens Nursing Home's business could be affected as a result of the fraud.

Source: Adapted from the Institute of Chartered Accountants Australia's CA Program's Audit and Assurance Exam, December 2008. Provided courtesy of Chartered Accountants Australia and New Zealand.

3.8 Motives and opportunities to commit fraud ❹

Required

From the list below, identify what you would consider as

(a) a motive for fraud, and

(b) an opportunity for fraud.

1. college or university tuition
2. gambling debts
3. the fact that nobody counts the inventory, so losses are not known
4. the fact that the petty cash box is often left unattended
5. illegal drugs
6. the finance vice-president having investment authority without any review
7. alimony and child support
8. expensive lifestyle (homes, cars, boats)
9. business or stock speculation losses
10. the fact that upper management considered publishing a written statement of ethics but decided not to
11. taxation on good financial results
12. supervisors setting a bad example by taking supplies home
13. the fact that an employee was caught and fired, but not prosecuted

3.9 The fraud triangle ❹

Francine Rideau, controller of Quatco Company, is reviewing the year-end financial statements with Tonya Kowalski, the company president. The financial statements currently report a net income of $563,480. Tonya is applying for a very substantial bank loan for a plant expansion, and thus would like to report a net income of at least $700,000.

Toward this end, Tonya suggests accruing several sales based on orders received, even though the goods will not be shipped at year end, and thus are technically sales of the following year. She said, "If we record sales revenue for these two large orders, our net income should be more than $700,000. This should not be a problem even next year, as we will never notice the loss of these sales then, since our sales revenue will dramatically increase once the expanded plant is in place."

Required

Identify the incentives or pressures to commit a fraud, the opportunity to perpetrate a fraud, and the rationalizations used to justify committing a fraud.

3.10　Going concern ★ ★

The Wellington Plaza Hotel is located close to the main railway station in a large regional city. Its main client base is business people visiting the city for work-related purposes. The second largest group of clients consists of groups of (mainly) women visiting the city for its great shopping. All major department stores have a presence in the city and there are also lots of specialty shops and factory outlets. Another large group of clients are groups of (mainly) men visiting the city for various sports events, including several important hockey games during the winter.

Occupancy rates have been reasonable but stagnant for several years, providing a steady but unsatisfactory rate of return for the owners of the hotel. Revenues have been sufficient to cover operating costs, but no substantial progress has been made on repaying the large, long-term loans used to finance the hotel. In an effort to increase the hotel's profitability, a major renovation program was undertaken and completed earlier this year. The renovation was predicted to increase the relative attractiveness of the hotel to guests. It was also undertaken to earn additional revenue from the rent of a new coffee shop on the ground floor. The coffee shop is run by a separate company that has purchased a franchise of a major international brand.

The global financial crisis has hit the hotel business very hard this financial year. Business travel is down by 25 percent across the country. Further, discretionary retail spending is down by 40 percent. Several specialty shops in the city have already shut down and others are cutting their opening hours. In addition, the hockey series was won by the local team in four games (instead of the possible seven games). Thousands of visitors left the city early once the game was over. Just before the hockey games began, the coffee-shop owners went bankrupt and closed down, breaking their lease. The hotel owners are seeking legal advice on whether they can claim penalty fees on the broken lease.

Finally, the hotel owners' bank is warning that the short-term financing obtained for the renovations will not be renewed when it is due (one month after year end). The hotel managers had expected to repay the debt from this year's bookings and the coffee-shop lease. The hotel owners are still hopeful that the summer will bring a large lift in occupancy (and revenue) as the weather is expected to be nice. This expected summer trade is essential to meet repayments on the long-term debt and to convince the bank to extend the short-term debt.

Required

(a) Is there a going concern issue in this case? Explain.

(b) Are there mitigating factors? Explain them and how they would affect the auditor's conclusion.

3.11　Risk assessment—going concern financial considerations ★

A new client, an oil and gas explorer in Western Canada, is currently negotiating a loan worth $3 million to avoid defaulting on its long-term debt that is due in three months. Its latest quarterly earnings report indicated the entity has a working capital deficiency of $500,000, while its cash balance fell to $250,000, down from $500,000 a year earlier. There is a 0.5:1 current ratio. With little expectation of improved sales, the entity plans to cut back on production to preserve cash. It has also been paying suppliers late consistently and as a result some suppliers have begun demanding cash on delivery from the client. As a result, the share price has plunged and the entity has lost more than half of its market value in the last week.

Required

Discuss whether there are any events or conditions that may cast doubt on the new client's ability to continue as a going concern.

3.12 Understanding the client and its governance ★

Ajax Ltd. is a listed company and a new client of Delaware Partners, a medium-sized audit firm. Jeffrey Nycz is the engagement partner on the audit and has asked the members of the audit team to start the process of gaining an understanding of the client in accordance with CAS 315. One audit manager is leading the group investigating the industry and economic effects, and another is helping Jeffrey consider issues at the entity level. Jeffrey is holding discussions with members of the audit committee, and his talks will cover a wide range of issues, including the company's corporate governance principles. He has a meeting arranged for next week with the four members of the audit committee, including the chair of the committee, Stella South, who, like the other members of the audit committee, is an independent director.

Required

(a) Make a list of the main factors that will be considered by each audit manager's group.
(b) What are the required disclosures related to Ajax Ltd.'s corporate governance practices?

3.13 Assessing the risks associated with information technology ★ ★

Shane Whitebone is getting to know his new client, Clarrie Potters, a large discount electrical retailer. Ben Brothers has been the engagement partner on the Clarrie Potters' audit for the past five years, but the audit partner rotation rules have meant that the engagement partner has had to change this year. Shane discovers that toward the end of last year, Clarrie Potters installed a new IT system for inventory control. The system was not operating prior to the end of the last financial year, so its testing was not included in the previous audit. The new system was built for Clarrie Potters by a Montreal-based software company, which modified another system it had designed for a furniture manufacturer and retailer.

Required

What audit risks are associated with the installation of the new inventory IT system at Clarrie Potters?

3.14 Audit planning in an EDP environment ★ ★ ★

Farm Fresh Foods Inc. (FFF) is a new food distribution company that has been profitable since the second month of operations. It has arranged with Smith LLP, a certified general accounting firm, to conduct an external audit of its first year of operations. FFF has a large electronic data processing (EDP) installation with six EDP employees, including the EDP manager, a former accountant who is taking courses to upgrade her skills in computer operations and programming. Mary Heston of Smith LLP is in charge of designing an audit plan for the EDP function, and Ahmed Khan is auditing receivables, purchases, and payroll.

Required

What information does Smith LLP need to obtain about the EDP function when developing its audit plan for FFF? State six examples.

Source: Adapted from the Certified General Accountants Association of Canada, Auditing 1 Exam, June 2006.

3.15 IT risk assessment ★ ★

Expansion Aviation has installed a new payroll module to its existing accounting system that integrates with the general ledger application. The new payroll application is more complex than the old system, but its reporting function provides more details. For example, the new application calculates vacation, pension, payroll tax and workers' compensation expenses, as well as the corresponding accounting accruals. There was very little time available to implement the new system, so the old application ceased operation on December 31, 2015 and the new application went live on January 1, 2016. There was no time to run the two systems in parallel and there was limited staff training and testing of the new application.

Required

What concerns would you have about the payroll application's integration with the general ledger application?

Source: Adapted from the Institute of Chartered Accountants Australia's CA Program's Audit and Assurance Exam, July 2010. Provided courtesy of Chartered Accountants Australia and New Zealand.

3.16 Impact of closing procedures on performance ★ ★

Dunks Holdings Ltd. (Dunks) is an importer of hardware goods and distributes the goods to hardware retailers around the country. The growth in the do-it-yourself (DIY) market, which has accompanied the boom in house prices in most capital cities over the past five years, has provided consistent sales growth for both hardware retailers and wholesalers like Dunks. However, the recession that began last year has cast doubt on the ability of this sector to keep growing. Some analysts believe that the DIY market will not be affected by the recession because, in tough economic times, homeowners increase their "nesting" behaviour; that is, they spend even more on improving their homes and retreat from outside activities such as holidays, the theatre, and restaurants. This view is disputed by other analysts who believe that job losses and general pessimism in the economy will impact adversely on all company profits, including Dunks.

Dunks's share price has fallen over the last year as doubt about its ability to grow its profits in the current year spreads. The CEO and other senior management have large bonuses linked to both share prices and company profitability, and there is a mood within the company that achieving sales and profit targets this year is vital to avoid job losses at the company.

You have been brought into the audit team for Dunks this year and given the responsibility for auditing Dunks's closing procedures. Dunks has a monthly reporting system for internal management, but you notice that the reports are being issued later in the following month this year than they were last year.

Required

(a) Explain why and how the circumstances described above could affect your risk assessment.
(b) How do you plan to audit Dunks's closing procedures? What potential errors would you be most interested in?

CASES

3.17 Cool Look Limited—Integrative Case Study ★ ★ ★

Cool Look Limited (CLL) is a high-end clothing design and manufacturing company that has been in business in Canada since 1964. CLL started as an owner-managed enterprise created and run by Hector Gauthier. Its ownership has stayed within the family, and Martin Roy, Hector's grandson, is the newly appointed president, chief executive officer, and chairman of the board of CLL.

You are a chartered accountant and the audit senior on the CLL audit for its fiscal year, which ended November 30, 2016. Today is December 9, 2016, and you are reviewing correspondence from CLL's bank. You come upon a letter dated November 1, 2016, from the bank's credit manager that causes you some concern (Exhibit I). You pull out your notes from your review of the board's minutes (Exhibit II) to clarify your thoughts.

EXHIBIT I

LETTER TO CLL FROM BANK

November 1, 2016

Dear Sir:

We have reviewed CLL's internal third-quarter financial statements, dated August 31, 2016. As a result of this review, we have determined that your financial ratios continue to decline and that you are in default of the covenants in our agreement for the second consecutive quarter.

However, since the bank and CLL have a long history, and because CLL continues to make required debt payments on time, we are willing to extend the $6,000,000 secured operating line of credit until the end of February 2017.

Based on CLL's February 28, 2017, internal financial statements, we will expect CLL to meet the following financial ratios. If this is not done, we reserve the right to call the loan at that time.

Ratios:

Current ratio no less than 1:1

Maximum debt-to-equity ratio (Debt/Debt + Equity) of 80%; debt is defined as total liabilities.

We thank you for your business.

Yours truly,

Mr. Charles Burbery
Credit Manager

EXHIBIT II

EXCERPTS FROM NOTES TAKEN DURING REVIEW OF BOARD MINUTES

- August 7, 2016. Management presented a document discussing the temporary cash crunch at CLL. Management presented options to conserve cash until the Christmas buying season, when a new large contract with a U.S. chain of stores begins. One alternative was to delay remitting HST and employee withholdings. The board passed a resolution to temporarily delay remitting HST and employee withholdings until cash flows improved.
- September 5, 2016. The board received information from management regarding an incident at the factory. Some dirty rags had caught fire in a metal garbage can. The fire was put out quickly and no damage was done. Management and the board were quite relieved that the fire had not spread because CLL has not renewed its fire and theft insurance this year due to the need to conserve cash. For the same reason, CLL has not renewed the directors' liability insurance. The board decided that the renewals would be done immediately after cash flows improved.
- November 10, 2016. The board passed a motion to allow Martin Roy to postpone repayment of his interest-free shareholder loan by another six months to May 31, 2017. He owes CLL $500,000.

Financial facts

- The November 30, 2016, unadjusted financial statements show CLL's current ratio is 1.64:1.
- If the long-term debt is re-classified as a current liability, the current ratio would be 0.42:1.

- The $500,000 shareholder loan to Martin Roy is also classified as long term; however, if it is classified as current, the ratio would decline further.
- The debt-to-equity ratio is 85.8 percent.
- The company has traditionally had a history of positive earnings; however, in the last two years, it has reported a net loss.
- Cash on hand is $1,094,000.
- Accounts payable has increased by more than 100 percent.
- Share capital is reported on the 2016 balance sheet at $10,386, 000.
- CLL's long-term debt includes the $6 million secured operating line of credit. The line of credit is a revolving loan, which the bank can call on three months' notice if certain financial covenants are not met. It had been classified as long-term debt in 2015 because the bank waived its right to call the loan before December 1, 2016.

Required

(a) What facts indicate that CL may not be a going concern? What facts indicate that CL may be a going concern? Make a conclusion on whether you believe it is appropriate to assume the company will remain a going concern.

(b) What are the risks related to the shareholder loan? What are three recommended procedures the auditor should perform related to the shareholder loan?

(c) What type of report should be issued if management refuses to disclose the shareholder loan as required by IFRS and ASPE? Why?

(d) Discuss the decisions made by the board. Are they ethical? Explain. Do they comply with the requirements of CSA's *Corporate Governance Guidelines*?

Source: Adapted from the Uniform Final Exam (UFE), The Institutes of Chartered Accountants in Canada and Bermuda, Paper 3, 2005.

CASE STUDY—CLOUD 9

You are a graduate working for W&S Partners, a Canadian accounting firm with offices located in each of Canada's major cities. W&S Partners has just been awarded the December 31, 2016, statutory audit for Cloud 9 Ltd. (Cloud 9). The audit team assigned to this client is:

- Jo Wadley, partner
- Sharon Gallagher, audit manager
- Josh Thomas and Suzie Pickering, audit seniors
- Mark Batten, IT audit manager
- Ian Harper and you, graduates

As a part of the planning process for the new audit, the audit team needs to gain an understanding of Cloud 9's structure and its business environment. By understanding the client's business, the audit team can identify potential risks that may have a significant effect on the financial statements. This will assist the team in planning and performing the audit.

Required

Answer the following questions based on the additional information about Cloud 9 presented in the appendix to this book and in this and earlier chapters. You should also consider your answer to the case study questions in earlier chapters where relevant.

Your task is to research the retail and wholesale footwear industries and report back to the audit team. Your report will form part of the overall understanding of Cloud 9's structure and its environment.

You should concentrate your research on providing findings from those areas that have a financial reporting impact and are considered probable given Cloud 9's operations. In conducting your research, you should consider the following key market forces as they relate to Cloud 9's operations.

General and industry-specific economic trends and conditions
(a) What is the current condition of the economy?
(b) Is the business affected by developments in other countries, foreign currency fluctuations, or other global forces?
(c) If the industry is labour intensive, are there unusual or unique labour relations issues?
(d) How does the company's growth and overall financial performance compare with the industry, and what are the reasons for any significant differences?
(e) What is the volume and type of transactions in the business?
(f) Are the client's operations centralized or decentralized?
(g) Is the client's business cyclical in nature or influenced by seasonal fluctuations in the market?
(h) What is the susceptibility to fraud and theft? (Is the product something that can easily be stolen and has a sale market?)

Competitive environment
(i) What products does the client sell? Have there been significant changes with respect to:
    i. major products or brands?
    ii. selling strategies?
    iii. sales/gross margin by product?
(j) Who are the client's major competitors, and what share of the market does each hold?
(k) Is there significant differentiation between the client's and competitors' merchandise?
(l) What is the effect on the client of potential new entrants into the market? Are there any significant barriers to entering the market?

Product information
(m) Is there a specific life cycle for the product?
(n) Is the product dependent on trends or styles?

Customer information
(o) Are there specific customers on whom the client is highly dependent?
(p) What is the overall profile of the client's customers? Have there been significant fluctuations in the client's customer base?

Supplier information
(q) Who are the key suppliers?
(r) Are the materials subject to significant price movements or influenced by external market forces?

Technological advances and the effect of the Internet
(s) How does the industry use technology?
(t) What technological trends are impacting the industry?

Laws and regulatory requirements
(u) Are the client's operations affected significantly by local or foreign legislation?
(v) What new laws and regulations recently enacted (or pending) may have significant effects on the company?

RESEARCH QUESTION 3.1

The auditor and the Ponzi scheme

Bernard Madoff was convicted in 2009 of running a Ponzi scheme, the biggest in U.S. history. A Ponzi scheme is essentially the process of taking money from new investors on a regular basis and using the cash to pay promised returns to existing investors. The high and steady returns received by existing investors are the attraction for new investors, but they are not real returns from investments.

As long as new investors keep contributing and existing investors do not seek redemptions, or the return of their money, the scheme continues. However, eventually, as in the Madoff situation, circumstances change, the scheme is discovered, and the remaining investors find that their capital has disappeared.

At age 71, Madoff was sentenced to prison for 150 years and will die in jail. Now that Madoff is behind bars, attention has turned to Madoff's auditor, David G. Friehling. Friehling is accused of creating false and fraudulent audited financial statements for Madoff's firm, Bernard L. Madoff Investment Securities LLC. Prosecutors allege that these fraudulent reports covered the period from the early 1990s to the end of 2008.

Required

(a) Research the progress of the case against David Friehling. Write a report explaining his alleged role in the Madoff Ponzi scheme and the current (at the time you write your report) state of the legal action against him.

(b) Friehling was subject to U.S. auditing standards and legislation. Explain if, and how, Friehling's alleged actions would violate Canadian auditing standards and professional ethics.

Sources: Dionne Searcey and Amir Efrati, "Sins and Admission: Getting into Top Prisons," *The Wall Street Journal: Europe* 17–19, July 2009, p. 29; Chad Bray and Amir Efrati, "Madoff Ex-auditor Set to Waive Indictment," *The Wall Street Journal: Europe* 17–19, July 2009, p. 29.

RESEARCH QUESTION 3.2

Public company financial statements

The financial statements for public companies are available through the website SEDAR (www.sedar.com). This is the official site that provides access to information filed by public companies and investment funds with the CSA. The statutory objective in making public this filed information is to enhance investor awareness of the business and affairs of public companies, and to promote confidence in the transparent operation of capital markets in Canada. Achieving this objective relies heavily on the provision of accurate information on market participants.

Required

Go to www.sedar.com and select the most recent set of audited annual financial statements for a Canadian public company. Using this set of financial statements, answer the following:

(a) When planning the audit, the auditor needs to gain an understanding of the entity's structure and its business environment. To do this, the auditor focuses on identifying potential risks that may have a significant effect on the financial statements. Prepare a memo for the audit planning file and discuss the entity, industry, and economy-level factors that the auditor should consider to plan the audit for this entity.

(b) Review the financial statement notes. Are there any related parties? If so, who are the related parties? Are there many or just a few? What is disclosed in the related party note? What impact will this have on the auditor's preliminary risk assessment?

(c) With the information provided, discuss the entity's ability to continue as a going concern using the going concern indicators discussed in this chapter.

Source: www.sedar.com.

FURTHER READING

Canadian Securities Administrators. (2005). *National Policy 58–201: Corporate Governance Guidelines*. www.osc.gov.on.ca/documents/en/Securities-Category5/rule_20050415_58-201_gov-practices.pdf

Chartered Professional Accountants of Canada. (2013). *Canadian Professional Engagement Manual*. www.castore.ca/product/canadian-professional-engagement-manual-members/5

KnowledgeLeader. www.knowledgeleader.com.

Wilson, J.D., & Root, S.J. (2000). *Internal Auditing Manual*. Warren, Gorham & Lamont Inc.

SOLUTIONS TO MULTIPLE-CHOICE QUESTIONS

1. d, 2. b, 3. a, 4. d, 5. b, 6. d, 7. a, 8. d, 9. d, 10. b.

NOTE

1. Wilson, J.D. & Root, J.J. *Internal Auditing Manual* 2nd ed. (1989), Warren, Gorham & Lamont.

CHAPTER 4

Audit planning II

LEARNING OBJECTIVES

After studying this chapter, you should be able to:

1 define audit risk

2 explain and apply the concept of materiality

3 describe how an auditor determines the audit strategy

4 outline how clients measure performance

5 summarize how an auditor uses analytical procedures when planning an audit.

AUDITING AND ASSURANCE STANDARDS

CANADIAN	INTERNATIONAL
CAS 200 *Overall Objectives of the Independent Auditor and the Conduct of an Audit in Accordance with Canadian Auditing Standards*	ISA 200 *Overall Objectives of the Independent Auditor and the Conduct of an Audit in Accordance with International Standards on Auditing*
CAS 300 *Planning an Audit of Financial Statements*	ISA 300 *Planning an Audit of Financial Statements*
CAS 315 *Identifying and Assessing the Risks of Material Misstatement Through Understanding the Entity and Its Environment*	ISA 315 *Identifying and Assessing the Risks of Material Misstatement Through Understanding the Entity and Its Environment*
CAS 320 *Materiality in Planning and Performing an Audit*	ISA 320 *Materiality in Planning and Performing an Audit*
CAS 520 *Analytical Procedures*	ISA 520 *Analytical Procedures*

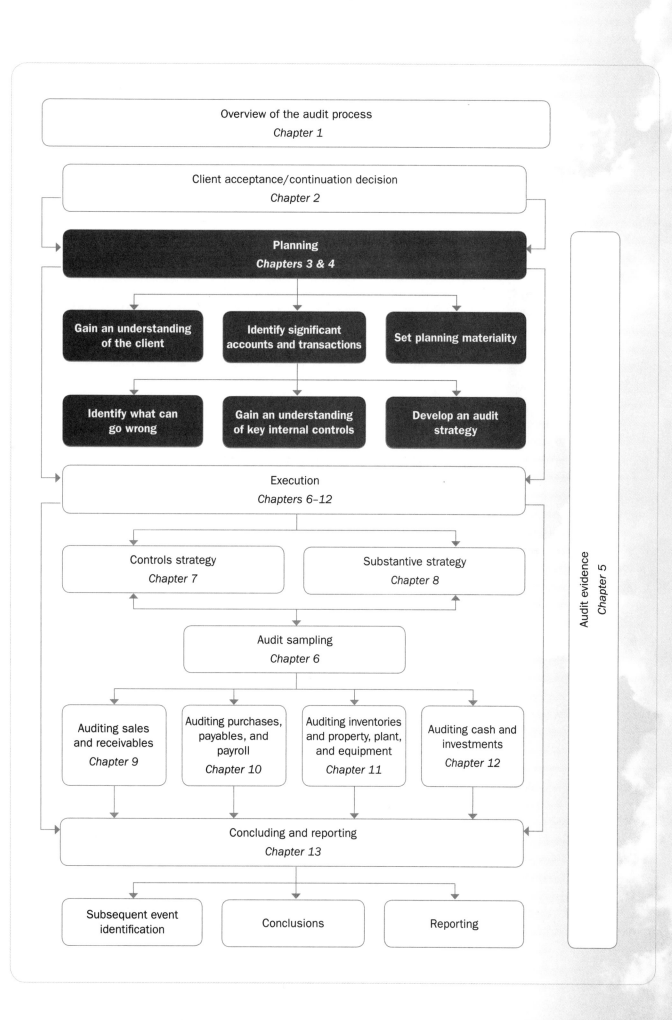

Cloud 9

Ian Harper is still impatient. Despite his lengthy conversation with Suzie Pickering about the importance of gaining an understanding of the client in order to identify and manage audit risk, he is still not convinced that it makes a real difference to the audit. He has been with W&S Partners for only a few months, but every audit seems to him to be the same. Suzie knows that Ian has not yet seen enough audits to be able to understand the different strategies being used for different areas of the audit. How can she explain this to him?

Suzie calls Ian to her office. "I want you to work with me on the draft audit plan for Cloud 9," she tells him. "We have already started, but there is still a lot of work to do. What do you think is already in the plan?"

Ian is a bit surprised by Suzie's question, but he thinks about their previous discussions. "Well, first we have the results of the work done to assess the client before the engagement, followed by the engagement letter that sets out the work we have promised to perform. Then, after the client was accepted, we have the results of the partner's assessment of Cloud 9 Ltd.'s corporate governance. We also have the report on the economy-wide conditions likely to affect firms in the clothing and footwear industry, plus the specific industry reports on competition, technology, and so on. I helped you with the preliminary risk assessments based on those reports, which identify the accounts most at risk. Those risk assessments are not complete, because we haven't yet done a control system evaluation. However, the preliminary risk assessments include some consideration of going concern and fraud risk.'

"That's very good," says Suzie. "So, what do you think we need to do next?"

AUDIT PROCESS IN FOCUS

In chapter 3, we began our discussion of audit planning by considering the audit as a whole. Then we focused on gaining an understanding of the client's business and identifying key risk factors that impact the audit plan. Auditors use this information to develop their audit strategy.

When developing an audit strategy, auditors consider the risks identified when gaining an understanding of their client's business. This helps them assess the risk that their audit procedures will not identify a material misstatement in the client's financial statements should one exist (audit risk). This chapter begins with a discussion of audit risk.

The process of setting planning materiality is then described. Qualitative and quantitative materiality factors are explained, as are performance and specific materiality. We then move on to describe how auditors develop their audit strategy based on their assessment of the risk of material misstatement.

The final sections of this chapter deal with performance measurement and analytical procedures. By understanding how a client assesses its own performance, an auditor gains an insight into which accounts may be at risk of material misstatement. An overview is provided of the performance measurement mechanisms used by companies that an auditor will focus on when planning their audit. The conduct of analytical procedures is a key element of the planning stage of each audit and is explained in detail in this chapter.

4.1 AUDIT RISK

1 ▸ Define audit risk.

audit risk the risk that an auditor expresses an inappropriate audit opinion when the financial statements are materially misstated

inherent risk the susceptibility of the financial statements to a material misstatement without considering internal controls

Audit risk is the risk that an auditor expresses an inappropriate audit opinion when the financial statements are materially misstated (CAS 200 *Overall Objectives of the Independent Auditor, and the Conduct of an Audit in Accordance with Canadian Auditing Standards*). This means that an auditor reports that in their opinion the financial statements are fairly presented when, in fact, they contain a significant error or fraud, and therefore are materially misstated. While it is impossible to eliminate audit risk altogether, an auditor will aim to reduce it to an acceptably low level. Audit risk can be reduced at the planning stage of the audit by identifying the key risks faced by the client and allocating more audit time to gathering sufficient and appropriate evidence where the risk of material misstatement is highest.

The first stage in assessing the risk of material misstatements involves an **inherent risk** assessment, where the auditor considers the risk of material misstatement before consideration of any internal controls. This is done at the financial statement level by considering such things as the nature of the business, the industry, and any previous experience with the client. Inherent risk is also assessed at the assertion level for classes of transactions, account balances, and disclosures. An **assertion** is a statement made by management regarding the recognition, measurement, presentation, and disclosure of items included in the financial statements and notes. Assertions help guide the testing conducted by an auditor. For example, if a client sells valuable goods, such as precious stones, the auditor will consider the risk of overstatement of inventory because goods may be stolen but remain recorded in the client's books. Therefore, there is a high inherent risk regarding the inventory account, as there is a risk that management's assertion about the existence of the recorded inventory may not be valid. In this example, the auditor will spend more time testing for the existence of recorded inventory than in the case of a client that sells lower valued goods.

When identifying accounts and related assertions at risk of material misstatement, some risks are classified as being more significant than others. A **significant risk** is an identified and assessed risk of material misstatement that, in the auditor's judgement, requires special audit consideration (CAS 315 *Identifying and Assessing the Risks of Material Misstatement Through Understanding the Entity and Its Environment*). When classifying risks as being significant, consideration is given to whether the risk:

- involves fraud
- is related to significant economic or accounting developments
- involves complex transactions
- involves significant related party transactions
- involves significant subjectivity in measurement of financial information
- involves significant transactions outside the client's normal course of business

The second stage in the audit risk assessment involves an evaluation of the client's system of internal controls (**control risk**). The auditor is interested in whether the client has controls in place to minimize the risk of material misstatement in the financial statements for each account and related assertion that the auditor has identified as high risk. In the above example, if a client sells valuable goods, an auditor will assess whether the client has controls in place to reduce the risk that inventory may be stolen.

Finally, an auditor will plan to undertake detailed testing of each identified account to the extent determined necessary. This final assessment will depend upon the assessed riskiness of the account and related assertion and the deemed effectiveness of the client's system of internal controls.

assertion statement made by management regarding the recognition, measurement, presentation, and disclosure of items included in the financial statements

significant risk an identified and assessed risk of material misstatement that, in the auditor's judgement, requires special audit consideration

control risk the risk that a client's system of internal controls will not prevent or detect a material misstatement

Cloud 9

Ian is still struggling with the idea of risk. He knows that audit risk is the risk that the auditor issues the wrong audit report, or gives an inappropriate audit opinion, and that this risk is related to the client's circumstances. But how does that actually work in practice? What does an auditor do differently for each audit?

Suzie reminds Ian of how taking just one issue, such as how sales are made to major department stores, helped him to focus on some specific questions about accounts receivable, sales, liabilities, and inventory.

"Let's break this down," she advises. "Auditors face the risk that they issue an unmodified opinion when, in fact, the financial statements are materially misstated. So, how does a material misstatement get into the published financial statements?"

Ian works through the logic. "First, the error has to be created, either by accident or on purpose. Second, the client's control system must fail to either prevent the error from getting into the accounts or detect the error once it is in the system. And, finally, the auditor has to fail to find the error during the audit."

"Correct!" says Suzie. "Now, before we go on, I want to break down the idea of 'financial statements,' too. The financial statements are the balance sheet (statement of financial position), income statement (statement of comprehensive income), cash flow statement

(statement of cash flows), statement of changes in equity, and all the notes. So when we talk of the risk of misstatements, we are referring to the risk of misstatement in every line item in each of these statements. If we focus on just one line in a balance sheet—say, accounts receivable— what are the possible misstatements that could occur?"

Ian tries to work through the logic again. "The amount could be either understated or overstated. I suppose there are lots of errors that could occur. Obviously, basic mathematical mistakes and other clerical errors could affect the total in either direction. In addition, accounts receivable would be understated if management omitted some customer accounts when calculating the total. I think the deliberate 'mistakes' are more likely those that overstate accounts receivable because they make the balance sheet look better, and probably mean that profit is overstated, too. Accounts receivable would be overstated if some of the customer accounts claimed in the total did not exist at year end, did not belong to Cloud 9, or were overvalued because bad debts were not written off, or because sales from the next period were included in the earlier period."

"Very good," says Suzie. "It is the same for every line item. Every time management prepares the financial statements it *asserts* that all of these errors did not occur—that all of the individual items in the statements are not materially misstated. The auditor has to break down the financial statements into accounts and assertions and consider the risk of misstatement for *each* assertion for *each* account. The auditor deals with the risk of material misstatement of all of the financial statements by gathering evidence at the assertion level for each account. Then all the evidence is put together so the auditor can form an overall opinion on all of the financial statements. Now, let's see how this works for Cloud 9."

4.1.1 The audit risk model and its components

Audit risk is a function of the risk of material misstatement and detection risk (CAS 200).

The risk of material misstatement exists at the financial statement level and at the assertion level. At the financial statement level, the risk of material misstatement involves risks that affect the financial statements as a whole. For example, if a client purchases a new computer system and does not adequately train staff in its use, there is a risk of errors when recording transactions used to prepare the financial statements. All accounts are at risk of material misstatement. At the assertion level, the risk of material misstatement involves risks that affect classes of transactions, account balances, and disclosures. For example, if a client sells goods overseas, there is a risk that transactions may not be recorded correctly using appropriate exchange rates at the date of each transaction. The risk of material misstatement at the assertion level comprises inherent risk and control risk (CAS 200, para. 13). Inherent risk is the possibility that a material misstatement could occur before consideration of the internal controls. This is the risk that errors can simply happen. If errors do happen, the next part of the audit risk model is control risk. That is, do the controls implemented by the client prevent or detect a misstatement before the financial statements are prepared? In assessing these risks, the auditor must identify client characteristics that place the financial statements at risk of material misstatement (inherent risk) and determine whether controls designed to limit such a risk are in place and effective (control risk). It is important to note that inherent risk and control risk are the client's risks and exist separately from the financial statement audit. The auditor has no influence on either. However, in response to the assessed client inherent and control risk combined (the risk of material misstatement), the auditor determines the amount of substantive work required to reduce the risk of material misstatement to an acceptable level. This is detection risk: the risk that auditors' procedures will not be effective in detecting a material misstatement should there be one. It is impossible to reduce detection risk to zero. Detection risk is the only element of the audit risk model the auditor can influence by doing more or less substantive audit work.

The audit risk model is illustrated in figure 4.1. The blocks represent material errors that may occur due to the nature of the business (inherent risk). The flattened circles represent "filters," which are the controls and audit procedures that are expected to prevent and detect errors. The first filter is the control of the client. If the auditor believes there are controls in

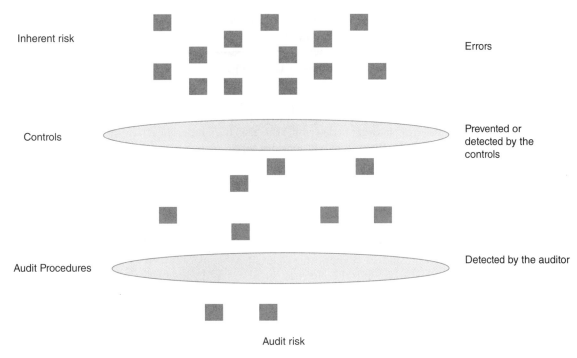

FIGURE 4.1 **Audit risk model**

place and assesses the control risk as low, the auditor believes the controls will be effective in preventing or detecting some of the blocks (errors) from getting through the filter. In this case, the auditor will plan to test these controls. The second filter is the amount of substantive work the auditor plans to perform. The auditor will plan to do enough work to reduce the risk of the blocks (errors) getting through the second filter to an acceptable level. However, there is always some risk some blocks (errors) may get through the filter. This is the audit risk.

The inherent risk assessment is based on the knowledge of the business as discussed in chapter 3, since many of the factors that contribute to business risks may affect inherent risk. The knowledge of the competitive environment, the current economic environment, the risk of technological obsolescence, and the level of government regulation assist in the inherent risk assessment. When assessing inherent risk, it is also important to consider such factors as the type of products and services offered by the entity, the size and complexity of the organization, the experience and knowledge level of employees, the pressures on management to meet earning targets, the extent of errors found in previous audits, and the accounting policies selected.

The factors listed above help the auditor determine whether there may be a management bias or economic pressures that increase the likelihood of a material misstatement. For example, an organization in a highly competitive industry will have a higher inherent risk than an entity in an industry with few competitors, as greater competition usually places pressure on margins. It also may put pressure on management to make the financial results appear more favourable, therefore increasing inherent risk. By understanding the entity, the auditor can also identify the risks that may be related to the business and the business structure. For example, an entity with a significant number of cash transactions or valuable assets on hand may be more susceptible to theft, and therefore will have a higher inherent risk. A geographically dispersed conglomerate will have a higher inherent risk than an organization with a single location, as this usually translates into a greater number of transactions and more complexity. For example, an entity with complex transactions, such as numerous foreign exchange transactions, will have a higher inherent risk than one with transactions only in the local currency. An organization undergoing a first-time audit will also be assessed as having a higher inherent risk than an entity having a repeat audit, as the auditor does not have the benefit of previous experience with the entity. Also, if a client is a repeat client and the auditor has found a significant number of misstatements in the past, the auditor may assess inherent risk as higher as there is a higher likelihood of misstatements recurring. Lastly, an organization with significant staff turnover will have higher inherent risk than one with a stable staff environment, primarily due to the new employees' learning curve with the entity's various business practices and policies.

Control risk is the risk that a client's system of internal controls will not prevent or detect a material misstatement. That is, if a misstatement has been made, will the client's controls prevent or detect this error? In order to determine this risk, the auditor must have an understanding of the controls in place. The auditor will consider, for example, the organization's attitudes toward controls and the control procedures implemented. If the auditor determines the controls are effective, then control risk may be assessed as lower. If control risk is assessed as lower, the auditor will plan to rely on the controls and therefore perform less detailed audit work on year-end balances. If control risk is assessed as high, where the auditor believes the controls are ineffective, the auditor will do the minimum work required on the controls and then perform more detailed work on the year-end balances.

An auditor must identify client characteristics that place the financial statements at risk of material misstatement (inherent risk, the first stage in audit risk assessment) and determine whether controls designed to limit such a risk exist and are effective (control risk, the second stage in audit risk assessment). As a result of this assessment, the auditor will then determine the detection risk required in response to the assessed audit risk and the client's inherent and control risk combined. **Detection risk** is the risk that the auditor's testing procedures fail to detect a material misstatement should there be one. That is, if an error was made by the client, and the controls did not detect it, will the auditor's procedures detect it?

detection risk the risk that the auditor's testing procedures will not be effective in detecting a material misstatement

As noted in CAS 200, para. A36, audit risk can be presented in a mathematical model that indicates the relationship between its components. The model states that audit risk is inherent risk multiplied by control risk multiplied by detection risk, as shown in figure 4.2.

$$AR = IR \times CR \times DR$$

where:

AR = Audit risk

IR = Inherent risk

CR = Control risk

DR = Detection risk

FIGURE 4.2 **Audit risk calculation**

An auditor will plan and perform their audit to hold audit risk to an acceptably low level (CAS 200). The acceptable audit risk for the financial statements overall is set by the auditor at the beginning of the audit. This generally tends to be quite low, and it remains constant throughout the audit. The inherent and control risks are then assessed, and the auditor determines the acceptable level of detection risk. Therefore, there is an inverse relationship between the assessed level of inherent and control risk (the risk of material misstatement) and the acceptable level of detection risk. For example, if inherent and control risk are assessed as high, the resulting detection risk will be assessed as low to bring audit risk down (see table 4.1). This means that the auditor will increase the level of reliance placed on their detailed substantive procedures, which involve intensive testing of year-end account balances and transactions from throughout the year.

TABLE 4.1 **Assessment of detection risk in a high-risk client**

Audit risk =	Inherent risk	Control risk	Detection risk
	High	High	Low

Example

A client sells high-end fashion clothing and has inadequate security. Inherent risk is high for inventory because clothing may be stolen but not removed from the client's books. Control risk is high because there is inadequate security, increasing the risk of theft. The auditor cannot rely on the client's security system to reduce the risk of material misstatement associated with the existence of inventory. The auditor will set detection risk as low and spend more time checking that recorded inventory is actually on hand.

Example

A client is an importer with inexperienced clerical staff. Inherent risk is high for the accuracy of recorded purchases because they involve foreign currency translation. Control risk is high because clerical staff is inexperienced and not accustomed to recording complex foreign currency transactions. Therefore, the auditor will not test the controls. Because detection risk is assessed as low, the auditor will perform more substantive testing, such as checking that purchases are recorded at appropriate amounts.

In contrast, if inherent risk and control risk are assessed as low, the auditor will assess the detection risk as high (see table 4.2). As above, there is an inverse relationship between the assessed level of inherent and control risk (the risk of material misstatement) and the auditor's acceptable level of detection risk. By assessing detection risk as high, an auditor will reduce the level of reliance placed on their detailed substantive procedures. This does not mean that the auditor is eliminating their detailed testing of year-end account balances and transactions from throughout the year. Rather, the auditor is acknowledging that the client is low risk; that is, there is a low risk of material misstatement in the client's financial statements, and extensive substantive testing is not required.

Audit risk =	Inherent risk	Control risk	Detection risk
	Low	Low	High

TABLE 4.2 **Assessment of detection risk in a low-risk client**

The examples provided in this section are extremes. The reality will often fall somewhere in-between, where inherent risk is high, but the client has an effective system of internal controls in place to mitigate that risk. For example, a client sells high-end fashion clothing and has adequate security, so the risk for the existence of inventory is reduced. Alternatively, inherent risk is low

Example

A client sells mud bricks and has a high-voltage fence surrounding the inventory of bricks. Inherent risk is low for the existence of inventory as mud bricks are very heavy and difficult to move; thus, it is unlikely that recorded bricks do not exist. After checking that the security system is working and has been operational throughout the year, the auditor can assess control risk as low. In this case, the auditor will need to spend relatively little time checking that the recorded bricks actually exist.

Example

A client uses a reputable off-the-shelf computer program to record purchases of raw materials. Inherent risk is low for the accuracy of recorded purchases because the program is considered reliable; thus, purchases should be recorded accurately. After checking that the program is working properly and the transactions are recorded correctly, the auditor will verify that access to the program is limited to authorized personnel and that the program has not been tampered with. When the auditor is satisfied that the program is working well and that the client's controls are effective, the auditor can set control risk as low. In this case, the auditor will need to spend relatively little time testing that purchases are recorded accurately.

and the client does not consider it worthwhile investing in sophisticated control procedures. (That is, any benefit is perceived to exceed the cost). For example, a client sells mud bricks and has low security, reasoning that the bricks would be very difficult to steal. In both cases, an auditor will spend a moderate amount of time testing for the existence of inventory.

4.1.2 Quantification of the audit risk model

Another way of viewing audit risk is to highlight the role of detection risk, which is demonstrated in figure 4.3. As previously stated, detection risk is the only element of the audit risk model the auditor can change in response to the client's risk of material misstatement.

$$DR = AR / RMM$$

where:

DR = Detection risk

AR = Audit risk

RMM = Risk of material misstatement (IR × CR)

FIGURE 4.3 **Detection risk calculation**

Audit risk is the risk the auditor will issue the wrong audit opinion. Because audits involve sampling and professional judgement, audit risk can never be zero or eliminated entirely. Therefore, an auditor has to be willing to accept some audit risk. However, because auditors want to minimize the risk of issuing the wrong opinion, their acceptable level of risk is generally low. Most auditors assess an acceptable level of audit risk as no more than 5 percent. This means the auditor is willing to accept a 5 percent likelihood that the financial statements are materially misstated or the auditor is seeking 95 percent assurance that there are no material misstatements.

Once the acceptable audit risk has been determined, the auditor then assesses the risk of material misstatement. They do this by assessing the inherent and control risks, as previously discussed. Based on the auditor's assessment of the audit risk, inherent risk and control risk, the auditor then determines the detection risk required. This establishes the amount of audit evidence required from substantive procedures to obtain the desired level of audit assurance.

For example, assume the auditor of Cloud 9 determines that an acceptable audit risk is 0.05 percent. If the auditor believes there is a high inherent risk, in that there is a high likelihood of errors happening, the auditor assesses inherent risk at maximum or 100 percent. Assuming the auditor believes there are few controls in place that can be relied upon, the auditor then sets control risk at high, again 100 percent. The auditor then determines the required detection risk by solving the following: DR = AR / RMM or 0.05 / 100 = 5 percent. This means the auditor requires 95 percent assurance from substantive procedures that there are no material misstatements.

Using the same example and assuming the auditor determines audit risk is 0.02 percent, the result will be DR = 0.02 / 100. Therefore, the auditor is willing to accept a 2-percent risk of not detecting errors and therefore wants 98 percent assurance from substantive procedures that there are no material misstatements. Comparing the two examples, assuming all things being equal, the higher the level of assurance desired by the auditor, the more audit work the auditor will have to do to achieve the desired level of assurance.

Cloud 9

Cloud 9 sells customized basketball shoes. The shoes are likely to "go out of fashion" reasonably quickly, making obsolescence a big issue. These factors affect the inherent risk of inventory valuation. Based on their brief discussion of the complications surrounding transporting the shoes from the Chinese factory to the department stores in Canada, Ian can see that there is a risk of errors occurring in transactions with suppliers, which will also affect inventory balances. How high is the control risk? Much to Suzie's delight, Ian suggests that they will be able to make better assessments of both inherent and control risk for all assertions now that they have a better understanding of the client.

PROFESSIONAL ENVIRONMENT

A Canadian auditing drama

Auditors played a leading role in the dramatic accounting scandal involving the now-defunct, Toronto-based live theatre company, Livent. In one courtroom, company co-founders Garth Drabinsky and Myron Gottlieb were convicted of fraud for misstating financial results for five years. In a parallel legal drama, the firm's auditors were found guilty of professional misconduct in a case that could rewrite the standards of liability for Canadian auditors.

The Institute of Chartered Accountants of Ontario (ICAO), the self-governing body for the accounting profession in Ontario at the time, found that the auditors failed to meet generally accepted practices of the profession. The ICAO said that the auditors suspected irregularities regarding Livent's accounting practices, even deeming the risk of financial statement error as "sky high," but they still issued a clean audit opinion of its financial statements. These actions "should have caused the (auditors) to increase their level of scepticism in conducting the audit and examining evidence," the ICAO found.

The ICAO found that the auditors questioned an agreement Livent had with a real estate company to refurbish one of its theatres. The real estate firm had the right to pull out of the redevelopment deal ahead of other investors. But Livent managers told the auditors that it cancelled the agreement because it required Livent to hold off on recording revenue from the redevelopment until later. However, the auditors discovered that the agreement was still in place, and when they asked for an explanation, Livent provided letters that were conflicting. In another instance, the auditors requested that Livent write down its production costs, which Gottlieb resisted until just days before the audit was completed when he suggested writing off $27.5 million, more than twice what the auditors were suggesting. These events should have caused the auditors to more closely scrutinize the company's books, the ICAO determined.

The auditors lost their appeal before the ICAO's appeal committee, a divisional court, and the Ontario Court of Appeal. They were slapped with more than $1.5 million in fines—the largest ICAO penalty ever, following the ICAO's longest disciplinary proceedings.

Livent, known for such productions as Phantom of the Opera, went bankrupt in 1998 after the new owners discovered accounting irregularities.

Drabinsky and Gottlieb appealed their criminal convictions in mid-2011 but they were upheld. Gottlieb's lawyer admitted that the two men received kickbacks from suppliers before the company went public in 1993 and that a company employee had counted the revenue as an asset on the financial statements. The lawyer said that neither Drabinsky nor Gottlieb had sophisticated accounting knowledge, and they were unaware that the company's assets were overinflated when Livent became publicly traded. Drabinsky and Gottlieb were granted full parole in early 2014.

Sources: Janet McFarland, "Former Livent CEO Drabinsky Wins Full Parole," *The Globe and Mail,* January 20, 2014; Janet McFarland, "Drabinsky Lawyer Calls for New Livent Trial," *The Globe and Mail,* May 2, 2011; Janet McFarland, "Gottlieb Not Involved in Major Livent Decisions: Lawyer," *The Globe and Mail,* May 3, 2011; "Court Reinstates Ruling Against Livent Auditors," *Toronto Star,* June 6, 2011; "Livent Auditors' Misconduct Appeal Denied," *Canadian Business,* February 18, 2009; Institute of Chartered Accountants of Ontario, Appeal Committee decision, February 13, 2009; Sandra Rubin, "Auditors Take Centre Stage," *Financial Post,* May 29, 2002.

BEFORE YOU GO ON

4.1.1 What are the three components of audit risk?

4.1.2 What is the relationship between audit risk and detection risk?

4.1.3 What are four factors that affect inherent risk?

4.2 MATERIALITY

Materiality is used to guide audit testing and to assess the validity of information contained in the financial statements and their notes. Information is considered material if it impacts the decision-making process of the users of the financial statements. This includes information that is misstated or omitted but should be disclosed. CAS 320 *Materiality in Planning and Performing an Audit* provides guidelines on materiality from an audit perspective.

Materiality is a key auditing concept and is assessed during the planning stage of every audit. This preliminary assessment of materiality guides audit planning and testing. Before explaining how an auditor arrives at their preliminary materiality assessment, it is important to understand the qualitative and quantitative factors to be considered when determining materiality.

 2 Explain and apply the concept of materiality.

materiality information that impacts the decision-making process of users of the financial statements

4.2.1 Qualitative and quantitative factors

When determining materiality, the auditor needs to consider both quantitative and qualitative factors as information can be considered material because of its nature and/or its magnitude.

These concepts are explained below. The auditor should also consider whether performance materiality or specific materiality are necessary. This is also explained below.

Qualitative factors

Information is considered material if it affects a user's decision-making process. This may be due to factors other than the magnitude of misstatements. For example, a misstatement due to fraud is considered to be significant due to its nature. When such a misstatement is uncovered, it is investigated further by an auditor. After gaining an understanding of the client, an auditor will ensure that all disclosures in the financial statements and the notes to the financial statements accurately reflect the auditor's understanding of the client. Therefore, when reading the notes to the financial statements, an auditor will assess accounting disclosure accuracy and compliance with any regulations and legislation, and ensure that any legal matters that should be disclosed are disclosed correctly. If any of these disclosures are inaccurate or omitted in error, an auditor will consider the potential impact on users. If an auditor believes that an inaccurate disclosure or omission will affect a user's decision-making process, the inaccuracy or omission is considered to be material, and the auditor will request that the client amend the disclosure or include any omitted information. Items that should be considered significant due to their nature include a change in an accounting method, related party transactions, a change in operations that affects the level of risk faced, and the danger of breaching a debt covenant.

Quantitative materiality factors

quantitative materiality
information that exceeds an auditor's preliminary materiality assessment

Information is considered **quantitatively material** if it exceeds an auditor's preliminary materiality assessment. An auditor uses their professional judgement to arrive at an appropriate materiality figure for each client. In doing so, they are mindful of the primary users of the financial statements. For listed entities, the primary users are the shareholders. For private companies, the primary users are generally the owners and/or major lenders of funds. Audit firms vary in the method they use to set materiality in the risk assessment phase of the audit. Some will follow the guidelines provided on the *Canadian Professional Engagement Manual (C•PEM)*, which we discuss below. Materiality is a percentage of an appropriate base. An auditor will select an appropriate base and then decide on the percentage to use depending on the client's circumstances.

In selecting an appropriate base, an auditor can choose an item from the balance sheet or income statement. Balance sheet bases are generally total assets or equity. Income statement bases are profit before tax, revenue, expenses, or gross profit. An auditor will select an appropriate base, using their professional judgement based on their knowledge of the client and the needs of financial statement users for decision-making. For example, if a client is publicly listed, net income before tax is likely to be important as it drives dividends and return-on-investment decisions. Therefore, the base selected would be net income before tax. However, if a client is a not-for-profit organization, either assets or expenses are more likely to be chosen as a base.

Net income before tax will not be used as a base when a client is in a loss position. When profits vary significantly from one year to the next, the auditor may use either an average of net income or revenue as a base. For newly established companies with little or no revenue, equity or total assets are generally the preferred base. These choices depend on an auditor's knowledge of their client and on the auditor's professional judgement.

Once a base is selected, consideration should be given to whether there are any unusual or non-recurring items that may need to be "normalized" or adjusted for. Examples of such normalizing items include bonuses paid to owner managers for tax-planning purposes, unusual gains and losses, and significant repair and maintenance expenses that may not be recurrent in nature. Once a selected base is normalized, an appropriate percentage is determined. The *C•PEM* provides guidelines on the percentages to use when calculating materiality (see figure 4.4). Normally, any item that is 10 percent or greater of profit before tax is considered to be material, and any item that is less than 5 percent of profit before tax is considered to be immaterial. The determination of the appropriate percentage to determine materiality of any item is a matter for professional judgement. When using total assets or revenue as a base, the percentages fall to 0.5–2 percent and when equity is the base, the percentages are 1–2 percent. Whichever base is used, there is a percentage above which items are deemed to be clearly material, a percentage below which items are deemed to be immaterial, and a range in the middle that is a matter for an auditor's professional judgement.

- 5–10% of normalized pre-tax profit
- 0.5–2% of total assets
- 0.5–5% of equity
- 0.5–2% of revenues or expenditures

FIGURE 4.4 **Common bases and percentages used for materiality**

When a lower planning materiality level is established, an auditor increases the quality and quantity of evidence that needs to be gathered. When gathering evidence, one of the criteria may be to test material items. The lower the materiality level set, the more items will fall into this definition. For example, if the auditor determines planning materiality to be $10,000, then more work will have to be done to ensure there is no material misstatement than if materiality is set at $100,000. Also, by setting a lower materiality level, an auditor increases their sensitivity to potential misstatements. The lower the materiality, the more likely the auditor will conclude that misstatements are material.

Performance materiality

The auditor may also determine **performance materiality**. This is an amount less than materiality, which is set by the auditor to reduce the likelihood that any uncorrected and undetected misstatements within a class of transactions, account balances, or disclosures, in aggregate, do not exceed overall materiality. For example, if an auditor assesses that there is a risk of recorded inventory not being valued appropriately, materiality when testing for the valuation of inventory may be set lower than it would be when testing for other assertions. The determination of performance materiality is again a matter of professional judgement; however, the *C•PEM* suggests 60–85 percent of overall materiality may be appropriate.

> **performance materiality** an amount less than materiality, which is set to reduce the likelihood that a misstatement in a particular class of transactions, account balances, or disclosures, in aggregate, do not exceed materiality for the financial statements as a whole

Specific materiality

The third level of materiality the auditor may determine is called **specific materiality** for account balances, specific transactions, and disclosures. Specific materiality is relevant when some areas of the financial statements are expected to influence the economic decisions made by users of the financial statements. For example, if an entity has a bank loan, and one of the requirements of the loan agreement is to maintain a particular current ratio, the auditor should consider the need to determine specific materiality for the accounts included in the current ratio calculation. This would be necessary if a material misstatement less than overall financial statement materiality could impact the bank's decision to continue extending the loan. Figure 4.5 shows a sample of materiality calculation.

> **specific materiality** information that is relevant when some areas of the financial statements are expected to influence the economic decisions made by users of the financial statements

4.2.2 Materiality and audit risk

Materiality and audit risk are both considered in identifying and assessing the risk of a material misstatement. They both determine the nature, timing, and extent of the audit work performed, and they are both considered when evaluating the effect of uncorrected misstatements on the financial statements and in forming the opinion in the auditor's report.

However, the auditor should not use audit risk to make the materiality determination. Audit risk is based on factors that relate to the entity, while materiality is based on the needs of the users of the financial statements. In the materiality example in figure 4.5, it is important to note that when calculating materiality for Trudo Inc., audit risk was not considered. This is because regardless of whether the auditor assesses the audit risk as high, moderate, or low, materiality is based on the user needs and users generally do not consider audit risk. For Trudo Inc., the bank is the user. Regardless of the auditor's risk assessment, the bank is still sensitive to any material misstatement of $85,000. This does not change due to audit risk being high or low. If the auditor believes there is a high risk of misstatement, it does not mean materiality should now be lower, say $20,000. If audit risk is high, it simply means the auditor will have to do more substantive work to reduce the likelihood of issuing the wrong audit opinion. Conversely, if the auditor

Trudo Inc. has a December 31 year end. Although Trudo is a private company, its annual financial statements must be audited as a condition of Trudo's long-term debt agreement with Canada Bank. Extracts from the entity's financial statements are as follows:

Revenue	$10,525,000
Pre-tax profit	$1,525,000 (after bonus to owner of $200,000)
Total assets	$15,500,000

To determine materiality, the auditor's first step is to identify the financial statement users. In this example, Trudo is a profit-oriented entity. The primary user of the financial statements is the bank. The bank has requested audited financial statements as it is primarily concerned with Trudo's ability to generate a positive net income, which is the best predictor of its ability to repay the loan in the future. Management is a user and they are interested in net income to assess the entity's overall performance. The tax authorities are also users as they use the financial statements to assess the entity's tax position.

Various materiality bases could be considered, such as total assets or total revenues, but based on the user needs assessment above, the bank is most sensitive to net income. Therefore, this is the most appropriate base. If net income was negative or fluctuated significantly from year to year, the auditor would consider an alternative base, such as total assets, total revenue, or perhaps an average net income.

Before performing any calculations, the auditor considers whether there are any non-recurring items that may need to be normalized. This includes any unusual gains or losses, any discontinued operation, or management bonuses. In this case, there was a $200,000 bonus paid to management that was included in the expenses and that reduced overall net income. This will be added back to get the normalized net income.

Pre-tax profits	$1,525,000
Add: Management bonus deducted from net income:	200,000
Normalized net income	1,725,000

The percentage to be applied in the calculation is a matter of professional judgement. In this case, the auditor applies 5% to normalized pre-tax profit.

Planning materiality calculation:

Normalized pre-tax profits	1,725,000
Percent applied	5%
	86,250

Once a preliminary determination of materiality is made, the auditor then considers whether any qualitative items exist that may suggest the calculated balance is not appropriate. In this case, nothing indicates this is true.

Performance materiality: To reduce the risk of an aggregate material misstatement in account balances and classes of transactions, performance materiality is 60 percent of planning materiality:

60% × $86,250 = $51,750

Specific materiality: As there is no indication that users of the financial statements will be affected by any particular account balance, specific materiality is not required.

Conclusion: Materiality for financial statements overall is $85,000 (rounded). This means total misstatements should be less than $85,000 for the auditor to issue an unmodified opinion.

Performance materiality is $50,000 (rounded). This means any error found in a specific account greater than $50,000 is considered material.

However, if one error is found that exceeds performance materiality, but total errors remain below overall materiality, the auditor can conclude the financial statements are not materially misstated.

FIGURE 4.5 **Example of materiality calculation**

believes it is a lower audit risk, it does not mean materiality should now be assessed as higher, say $100,000. It means the auditor may do less substantive testing to reduce the likelihood of issuing the wrong opinion. Therefore, regardless of audit risk, the bank remains sensitive to a misstatement of $85,000. While both concepts impact the quality and quantity of the audit evidence required, audit risk should not be used to determine materiality.

Cloud 9

Throughout their conversation, Suzie and Ian have been discussing "material" misstatements in financial statements. What is material for Cloud 9? Suzie explains that if they set materiality at a low level in the planning phase, they will have to plan to gather more and better quality evidence to be sure that a mistake of this low magnitude has not occurred. This will give the auditor confidence that the opinion is the appropriate one, but it will also increase the cost of the audit.

Ian is worried about getting the materiality level right. "What if we set it too low or too high?" Suzie explains that all parts of the audit plan, including the materiality decision, will be reviewed throughout the audit and changed if necessary.

BEFORE YOU GO ON

4.2.1 What is qualitative materiality?

4.2.2 What is quantitative materiality?

4.2.3 What is the most appropriate materiality base for a for-profit entity? Why?

4.3 AUDIT STRATEGY

CAS 300 *Planning an Audit of Financial Statements* requires that an auditor establish an overall **audit strategy**, which sets the scope, timing, and direction of the audit and provides the basis for developing a detailed audit plan. The audit strategy chosen depends on the auditor's preliminary inherent and control risk assessment (that is, the auditor's overall assessment of the risk of material misstatement). Tables 4.3 and 4.4 provide examples of audit strategies for two extreme cases: a high-risk client and a low-risk client.

When inherent and control risk are assessed as high (see table 4.3), the risk of material misstatement is assessed as high and, therefore, detection risk will be low to reduce audit risk to an acceptably low level. There is an inverse relationship between audit risk (a client's inherent and control risk combined) and detection risk, as previously stated. By assessing control risk as high, an auditor has determined that the client's system of internal controls is non-existent, very poor, or unlikely to be effective in mitigating the inherent risks identified.

For example, a client sells expensive medical testing equipment and has limited security. Not many of these pieces of equipment have to go missing or be stolen for there to be a material impact on the value of the inventory. No regular inventory counts are performed either. In this case, inherent risk is high for the inventory as it may be recorded but not actually on hand. In this case, control risk is high as there are no controls in place to mitigate (reduce) the identified risk.

By assessing control risk as high (see table 4.3), an auditor will adopt a **substantive audit strategy**. When this audit strategy is adopted, an auditor will gain the minimum necessary knowledge of the client's system of internal controls as required by the auditing standards (CAS 315), but will generally not conduct tests of those controls. If a client's system of internal controls is non-existent,

3 Describe how an auditor determines the audit strategy.

audit strategy strategy that sets the scope, timing, and direction of the audit and provides the basis for developing a detailed audit plan

substantive audit strategy strategy used when the auditor does not plan to rely on the client's controls and increases the reliance on detailed substantive procedures that involve intensive testing of year-end account balances and transactions from throughout the year

TABLE 4.3 **Audit strategy—high-risk client**

Audit risk	Inherent risk	Control risk	Detection risk
	High	High	Low
Audit strategy		No (or very limited) tests of controls	Increased reliance on substantive tests of transactions and account balances

TABLE 4.4 **Audit strategy—low-risk client**

Audit risk	Inherent risk	Control risk	Detection risk
	Low	Low	High
Audit strategy		Increased reliance on tests of controls	Reduced reliance on substantive tests of transactions and account balances

very poor, or unlikely to be effective in mitigating an identified inherent risk, there is generally no point in testing the internal controls because the auditor will not be planning to rely on them. Instead, an auditor will increase their level of reliance on detailed substantive procedures, which involves intensive testing of year-end account balances and transactions from throughout the year. An exception is where an auditor has identified a significant risk. In this case, an auditor will gain an understanding of the client's controls relevant to that risk (CAS 315, para. 29). For example, if a client has significant transactions that involve estimation, an auditor will review the processes used by management to make those estimations. If a client does not have adequate controls to address significant risks, this is considered a significant deficiency in a client's system of internal controls (CAS 315, para. A126).

When assessing control risk as low (see table 4.4), an auditor will generally plan to perform a **combined audit strategy** where the auditor obtains a detailed understanding of the client's system of internal controls and plans to rely on that system to identify, prevent, and detect material misstatements.

combined audit strategy strategy used when the auditor obtains a detailed understanding of their client's system of internal controls and plans to rely on that system to identify, prevent, and detect material misstatements

Once an auditor has gained a detailed understanding of their client's system of internal controls, they will conduct extensive tests of those controls. When the cost of testing controls exceeds the benefit expected, an auditor may decide not to test the client's internal controls. For low-risk clients, if tests of controls are conducted and found to be effective, an auditor will plan on reducing their reliance on detailed substantive testing of transactions and account balances. However, an auditor can never completely rely on a client's system of internal controls and will always conduct some substantive procedures to gather independent evidence regarding the numbers that appear in the client's financial statements. Control risk and testing of controls are discussed further in chapter 7.

For example, a client sells nuts and bolts and conducts regular inventory counts. Inherent risk is low as a significant number of nuts and bolts would have to be stolen before there was a material impact on the amount recorded for inventory. The auditor will plan on testing the effectiveness of the inventory counts and the timeliness with which records are updated for any inventory losses.

The example provided above is for the development of an audit strategy at the financial statement (client) level. In practice, an audit strategy is developed for each identified risk at the assertion level. Figure 4.6 shows the process used when developing an audit strategy for identified risks. Risks are identified when gaining an understanding of the client as described in chapter 3. Part of that process involves conducting a **walkthrough** for each significant class of transactions. This means that each transaction flow is traced from inception to the recording in the general ledger. When conducting a transaction walkthrough, an auditor will identify the risk factors.

walkthrough tracing a transaction through a client's accounting system

For each identified risk, the first step is to assess whether an internal control could reduce the likelihood of a material misstatement occurring as a result of the risk. If the auditor believes one or more internal controls could be designed to mitigate the identified risk, the auditor will assess whether the client has controls in place; that is, do they exist?

If the client has one or more appropriate controls in place, the audit strategy is to test the effectiveness of those controls; that is, do they work? If, after testing the controls, the auditor concludes that they are effective, the auditor plans to rely on those controls and is able to reduce their reliance on detailed substantive procedures. However, if the auditor tests the controls and believes them to be ineffective (that is, the controls do not work), the auditor cannot rely on the controls. In this case, the auditor reports any significant deficiencies to those charged with governance, and identifies other weaknesses to management. The auditor also makes recommendations on improving the controls, and increases the reliance placed on detailed substantive procedures.

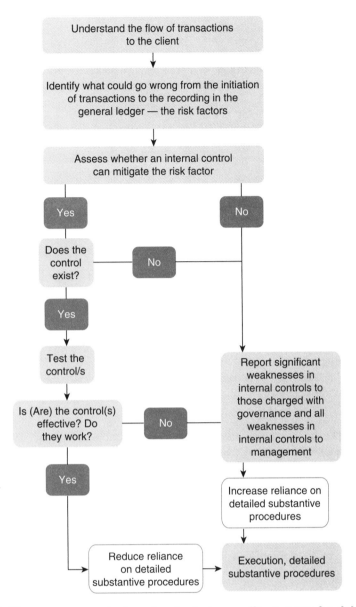

FIGURE 4.6 **The process used when developing an audit strategy for risks identified**

If the client does not have appropriate controls for the identified risk in place, the audit strategy is to conduct few or no tests of controls for the identified risk. In this case as well, the auditor reports the weaknesses identified to those charged with governance, makes recommendations on improving the controls, and increases the reliance placed on detailed substantive procedures.

Cloud 9

Suzie explains that Cloud 9's audit could be planned and conducted in different ways, depending on the audit strategy adopted. In fact, the overall audit strategy sets the scope, timing, and direction of the audit, and guides the development of the detailed audit plan.

"What audit strategy would be suitable for Cloud 9? Start by thinking about the scope of the audit," she prompts Ian. "The scope is about the different types of work we have to do—some audits have extra requirements."

"I suppose we should find out if Cloud 9's parent company has any special requirements. The fact that it is a Canadian public company might mean it has some additional regulations that apply," Ian suggests. "Plus, Cloud 9's statements would have to be consolidated into the parent's accounts. We would have to make sure that we plan to do the work they would need for that."

"That is a good start," says Suzie. "What else?"

"Well, I can think of a number of other things, such as whether any other auditors will be involved (including Cloud 9 Inc.'s internal auditors); whether any foreign currency translation issues exist; whether any industry-specific regulations must be followed (although I don't think this is as big an issue for clothing and footwear as it would be for banks, for example); whether any service organizations are involved, such as payroll services; and whether computer-aided audit technology is to be used."

"Very good," says Suzie. "That will do for now. What about timing issues? Are there any special considerations we should take into account for Cloud 9?"

"What date does the audit have to be finished?" asks Ian.

"Good question," says Suzie. "If we have a deadline, we obviously have to work toward it."

"Also," says Ian, "when are our staff available and when are their key people available to talk to us?"

"Yes," says Suzie. "This is all kind of basic. But if we don't ask these really important questions, we will find ourselves unable to meet the deadlines and perhaps be under pressure to cut corners. We also have to think about the timing of requests to third parties for information and so on. Now, can you think of anything to say about the direction of the audit?"

"I understand about the extra requirements and working out the timing. But I don't really know what you mean by 'direction,'" Ian says, confused.

"We have already discussed it to some extent," Suzie explains. "Remember when we spoke about the risk for Cloud 9 created by complex inventory transactions, and dealing with purchases from international suppliers? 'Direction' is about where we think there should be extra attention because of higher risk, and how we give that extra attention. We could, for example, make sure that we have suitable experts available, if required, to value the inventory. This is also where we bring in our work on materiality, both setting materiality for planning purposes and identifying the material account balances. In our plan, we need to allocate additional time to areas where there may be higher risk of material misstatement. And, one of our biggest tasks will be considering the evidence about the design and operating effectiveness of internal controls at Cloud 9, which we haven't yet considered in detail."

"I see," says Ian. "If we assess the internal controls as being strong, then we plan to do more testing of controls (to confirm our assessment), and less testing of the underlying substance of transactions and account balances. We have to put this in our plan now. But what if our first thoughts about controls are wrong? Our plan will be wrong!"

"That happens," replies Suzie. "That is why a plan is constantly changing as we gather more information about the client. Particularly, as in this case, for a new client that we don't have a lot of detailed information on yet. However, we already know what accounts are important to Cloud 9—its previous years' statements and interim results show us that. We have an understanding of the drivers of its profits and the pressure to increase profits coming from the head office. We also know about its new store opening this year (including the new debt) and the change in marketing strategy. We actually know quite a lot—certainly enough to make a start on a detailed audit plan."

BEFORE YOU GO ON

4.3.1 What is the purpose of developing an overall audit strategy?

4.3.2 What is a substantive audit strategy and when might an auditor adopt this approach?

4.3.3 To whom will an auditor report uncovered deficiencies in a client's system of internal controls?

4.4 CLIENT APPROACHES TO MEASURING PERFORMANCE

Part of the process used when gaining an understanding of a client involves learning how the client measures its own performance. The **key performance indicators (KPIs)** used by a client to monitor and assess its own performance and the performance of its senior staff provide an auditor with insight into the accounts that their client focuses on when compiling its financial statements and indicate which accounts are potentially at risk of material misstatement.

Some KPIs are common to many clients, such as return on assets and return on shareholder funds. Other KPIs will vary from industry to industry and client to client. For example, a client in the airline industry is concerned about revenue per passenger kilometre, a client in the retail industry is concerned about inventory turnover, and a client in the finance industry is concerned about its risk-weighted assets and interest margins. It is very important for an auditor to understand which KPIs a client is most concerned about throughout the year so that the audit can be planned around relevant accounts. It is inappropriate to assume that all clients will use the same KPIs. It is also inappropriate to assume that a client will use the same KPIs every year. Just as businesses change their focus, KPIs change to help businesses achieve new goals.

> **4** Outline how clients measure performance.
>
> **key performance indicators (KPIs)** measurements, agreed to beforehand, that can be quantified and that reflect the success factors of an organization

4.4.1 Profitability

It is common for companies to use **profitability** measures to assess their performance and that of their senior staff. Companies will track their revenue and expenses over time and assess any variability. They will compare their revenue and expenses with close competitors and assess their ability to compete, as well as provide valuable insights to management as to whether results are matching expectations based on known factors such as seasonality or economic downturns. This also provides the auditor with valuable insights into the expectations of management.

> **profitability** the ability of a company to earn a profit

A company will track revenues from month to month to identify and explain trends. Large companies will compare revenues earned across divisions to highlight good and poor performance. Comparisons between divisions may be used to assess how well the managers of those divisions are controlling costs. Changes from one year to the next may reflect an increased cost of doing business or highlight that it may be time to source cheaper suppliers.

Companies are concerned about their shareholders (owners). The **price-earnings (PE) ratio** (market price per share divided by earnings per share) shows how much a shareholder is willing to pay per dollar of earnings. **Earnings per share (EPS)** (profit divided by weighted average ordinary shares issued) reflects the book value of the company. When a client's PE ratio or EPS are in decline, an auditor may be concerned that management may be under pressure to manipulate earnings.

> **price-earnings (PE) ratio** market price per share to earnings per share
>
> **earnings per share (EPS)** profit to weighted average ordinary shares issued

Retailers and manufacturers are generally concerned about their inventory turnover (cost of goods sold divided by inventory). An assessment of this ratio is made within the context of the industry in which a company operates. For example, a company that sells perishable goods, such as ice cream, requires a much higher turnover than a company that sells non-perishable goods, such as furniture. If a client's inventory turnover falls sharply, an auditor may be concerned that stock is overvalued.

4.4.2 Liquidity

Liquidity is the ability of a company to meet its needs for cash in the short and long term. It is vital for a company to have access to cash to pay its debts when they fall due. If it cannot meet these obligations, a company may go into liquidation. Companies require cash to pay their employees' wages, utility bills, supplier bills, interest payments on money lent, dividends to shareholders, and so on. In the longer term, companies need cash to repay long-term debt and undertake capital investment.

> **liquidity** the ability of a company to pay its debts when they fall due

Companies enter into debt covenants with lenders when taking on significant loans. That is, they promise to maintain specified profitability, liquidity, or other financial ratios, or to seek the lender's permission before taking on new borrowings or acquiring other companies. These covenants are written into the borrowing contracts and restrict a company's activities. If a company breaches a debt covenant, it will need to renegotiate or repay the loan.

By understanding how their client measures and assesses its own performance and any restrictions implied by debt covenants, an auditor will gain a deeper understanding of the accounts potentially at risk of material misstatement. An auditor will use their own ratio calculations and trend analyses to identify any unusual fluctuations that warrant further investigation. This analysis is referred to as analytical procedures, which are explained in detail in the next section.

Cloud 9

In her discussions with the partner, Jo Wadley, Suzie learns that the senior people in the Cloud 9 finance section are entitled to participate in the company's employee stock purchase plan and also to receive stock options in the parent company if revenue targets are met. The Canadian parent company is a public company and its share price, which determines the value of the stock options, reflects market expectations about the group's future profits.

Cloud 9 has taken on additional debt this year, and costs are rising because of issues associated with its drive to increase market share. When these results are consolidated into the group, they increase debt/equity ratios and decrease profitability ratios, potentially reducing the value of the stock options. Suzie decides to allocate time in the audit plan to consider whether these pressures could impact any of the senior staff's incentives and increase audit risk.

PROFESSIONAL ENVIRONMENT

Have analytic procedures changed?

Analytic procedures are required in the risk assessment stage of the audit; however, they can also be used as substantive procedures during the execution stage, and as a reasonableness check at the completion stage. In performing analytics, the auditor considers the reasonableness of results based on expectations developed and formed when gaining the knowledge of the client, the industry, and the economy. As a consequence of some past accounting frauds, such as Enron, allegations were made that "had the auditors been aware of the client's industry conditions and conducted appropriate analytical procedures, such frauds would have been detected." This leads to the question: Have firms changed their practices with respect to analytical procedures as a safeguard against future financial reporting failures?

Trompeter and Wright in the United States conducted a study that examined practices of the Big Four accounting firms and their use of analytic procedures. They compared their findings with past research studies and concluded that, on some dimensions, there has been little change. "Data reveal similarities in that auditors still rely a great deal on clients for information, (e.g., inquiry, budgets) to set expectations and evaluate explanations. Also, relatively simple analytical techniques continue to be employed, such as a comparison of the current year to the prior year," the authors state.

Nevertheless, analytic procedures have changed in some ways. Trompeter and Wright found that technology has had a significant impact on the setting of expectations when performing analytical procedures. "Auditors now have access to industry and analyst databases enabling the development of more precise quantitative expectations. Auditors also gather and consider a broader array of industry and company information than in the past, as nonfinancial information is now widely available through the internet." The study also found that while analytic procedures are being conducted by more junior staff, seniors and managers still design the majority of the procedures performed. Also, there is now greater inquiry of non-accounting personnel, because with the shift toward the risk-based audit, "auditors are more knowledgeable about business processes and, thus more comfortable talking with nonfinancial staff." Lastly, they noted a greater willingness to reduce substantive testing, likely because firms put more emphasis on audit planning and risk analysis, which allows them to rely more on analytic procedures.

Source: Greg Trompeter and Arnold Wright, "The World Has Changed—Have Analytical Procedure Practices?" *Contemporary Accounting Research*, June 1, 2010, p. 669. © 2010 Canadian Academic Accounting Association.

BEFORE YOU GO ON

4.4.1 What is a PE ratio?

4.4.2 Explain how internal performance reports may be used.

4.4.3 What is a debt covenant?

4.5 ANALYTICAL PROCEDURES

CAS 520 *Analytical Procedures* defines **analytical procedures** as an evaluation of financial information by studying plausible relationships among both financial and non-financial data. They involve the identification of fluctuations in accounts that are inconsistent with the auditor's expectations based upon their understanding of their client. For example, if an auditor is aware that the client has borrowed a significant amount of money in the previous financial year, a reduction in the client's debt-to-equity ratio would be unusual and would warrant further investigation. It is essential that an auditor have clear expectations about the client's results for the reporting period before conducting analytical procedures, so that unexpected fluctuations can be correctly identified and investigated. An auditor's expectations are based on their understanding of the client, the industry in which it operates, and the economy as a whole.

Analytical procedures are conducted throughout an audit. During the planning stage, analytical procedures are used to aid in the risk identification process. During the **execution stage**, analytical procedures are an efficient method of identifying differences between recorded amounts and the auditor's expected values that require further investigation (CAS 520.5d). At the final review stage, analytical procedures are used to assess whether the financial statements reflect the auditor's knowledge of their client. In this section, we will concentrate on the application of analytical procedures at the planning stage of the audit. The use of analytical procedures when conducting substantive procedures is discussed in chapters 8 to 12.

Analytical procedures are conducted at the planning stage of the audit to:

- highlight unusual fluctuations in accounts
- aid in the identification of risk
- enhance the understanding of a client
- identify the accounts at risk of material misstatement
- reduce audit risk by concentrating audit effort where the risk of material misstatement is greatest

CAS 315 stipulates that an auditor should perform analytical procedures as part of their risk identification process. Analytical procedures include simple comparisons, trend analysis, common-size analysis, and ratio analysis. Each of these forms of analysis is now discussed, followed by a review of factors to consider when undertaking analytical procedures.

 Summarize how an auditor uses analytical procedures when planning an audit.

analytical procedures an evaluation of financial information by studying plausible relationships among both financial and non-financial data

execution stage detailed testing of controls and substantive testing of transactions and accounts

4.5.1 Comparisons

Simple comparisons are made between account balances for the current year and the previous year and for the current year and the budget. When comparing account balances from one year to the next, significant changes can be tracked and investigated further by the auditor. An auditor will assess these changes in light of their expectations based on their understanding of the client and any changes experienced over the past year. For example, if the client has opened a new retail outlet, sales may be expected to have increased since last year. When comparing account balances with budgeted amounts, an auditor is concerned with uncovering variations between actual results and those expected by the client. Significant unexpected variations are discussed with client personnel.

Figure 4.7 illustrates a comparative income statement, which shows how the auditor will calculate the dollar and percentage changes for all line items for both the income statement and the balance sheet. The auditor will identify areas where the calculated results are different from expectations based on the knowledge of the business and the evidence gathered to date, and will highlight the areas that may require further audit work. For example, if the current economy is in a slowdown, is it reasonable for revenues to grow by almost 10 percent? If the auditor determines that this is a mature company in a stable industry and expects that revenues will stay relatively flat, then this is an unexpected result, indicating that more work may be needed in this area. If this is an industry with relatively stable margins, why did the gross margin increase by 4.5 percent? Why did the cost of sales not increase in the same proportion as the revenues? These results may indicate that the company is missing some expenses and this area requires further investigation.

XYZ Company Comparative Income Statement					
	Current year	**Prior year**	**Dollar change**	**% change**	**Explanation**
Revenue	1,790,000	1,630,000	160,000	9.8%	
Cost of goods sold	1,320,000	1,275,000	45,000	3.5%	
Gross margin	470,000	355,000	115,000	32.4%	
Gross margin %	26.26%	21.78%		4.5 percentage points	
Operating expenses:					
Rent	60,000	58,000	2,000	3.4%	
Wages	150,000	145,000	5,000	3.4%	
Interest	75,000	25,000	50,000	200.0%	
Amortization	64,000	64,000	0	0.0%	
	349,000	292,000	57,000	19.5%	
Net income	121,000	63,000	58,000	28.72%	

FIGURE 4.7 **Comparative income statement of XYZ Company**

4.5.2 Trend analysis

trend analysis a comparison of account balances over time

Trend analysis (horizontal analysis) involves a comparison of account balances over time. It is conducted by selecting a base year and then restating all accounts in subsequent years as a percentage of that base. Trend analysis allows the auditor to gain an appreciation of how various accounts have changed over time. When conducting a trend analysis, it is important for an auditor to consider significant changes in economy-wide factors, such as a recession, which may affect their interpretation of the trend. Figure 4.8 provides an example of a trend analysis.

Various accounts can be selected for inclusion in a trend analysis. Accounts that vary from one year to the next are generally the focus. In the trend analysis depicted in figure 4.8, 2013 was selected as the base year. The following years appear as a percentage increase or decrease of the 2013 amount. For example, sales in 2014 were 20 percent lower than sales in 2013; in 2015, sales were only 10 percent lower than the 2013 figure; and in 2016, sales were 20 percent higher than the 2013 amount. A trend analysis allows an auditor to assess movements in the accounts over time and to determine whether the underlying trends discovered through this type of analysis match their understanding of the client and its activities over the period under review.

	2013	2014	2015	2016
	$M	%	%	%
Income statement items				
Sales	250	(20)	(10)	20
Cost of sales	110	(10)	0	10
Interest expense	10	(30)	30	0
Wages expense	70	(20)	30	6
Rent expense	40	0	0	0
Balance sheet items				
Cash	400	20	10	25
Inventory	350	30	20	10
Trade receivables	300	(10)	5	15

FIGURE 4.8 **Trend analysis**

4.5.3 Common-size analysis

common-size analysis a comparison of account balances with a single line item

Common-size analysis (vertical analysis) involves a comparison of account balances with a single line item. In the balance sheet, the line item used is generally total assets. In the income statement,

	2013	2014	2015	2016
	%	%	%	%
Income statement items				
Sales	100	100	100	100
Cost of sales	44	50	48	40
Interest expense	4	4	6	3
Wages expense	28	28	22	25
Rent expense	16	20	18	13
Balance sheet items				
Cash	5	4	4	3
Inventory	20	27	23	23
Trade receivables	18	25	22	18
Payable	15	15	17	16
Total assets	100	100	100	100

FIGURE 4.9 **Common-size analysis**

the line item used is generally sales or revenue. A common-size analysis allows the auditor to gain a deeper appreciation of how much each account contributes to the totals presented in the financial statements. By preparing common-size accounts for a number of years, an auditor can trace the relative contribution of various accounts through time. Figure 4.9 provides an example of a common-size analysis.

The common-size analysis depicted in figure 4.9 shows that the cost of sales grew and then reduced as a proportion of sales. This reduction may reflect a change in prices charged by suppliers, a change in prices charged to customers, or the quantity of goods on hand. In the balance sheet, inventory levels rose and then dropped, which may indicate a buildup of inventory on hand when sales dropped in 2014.

4.5.4 Ratio analysis

Ratio analysis is conducted by an auditor to assess the relationship between various financial statement account balances. An auditor will calculate profitability, liquidity, and solvency ratios.

Profitability ratios

Profitability ratios reflect a company's ability to generate earnings and ultimately the cash flow required to pay debts, meet other obligations, and fund future expansion. Table 4.5 shows the common profitability ratios: gross profit margin, profit margin, return on assets, and return on shareholders' equity.

The gross profit and profit margins indicate the proportion of sales turned into profits. The **gross profit margin** indicates whether a seller of goods has a sufficient markup on goods sold to pay for other expenses. A markup is the difference between the selling price and cost price for goods sold. A decline in this ratio indicates that a client may be paying more for its inventory or charging less to its customers. If the gross profit margin continues to decline, the client may face making an overall loss if it is not able to cover its operating expenses.

gross profit margin gross profit to net sales

RATIO	DEFINITION
Gross profit margin	$\dfrac{\text{Gross profit}}{\text{Net sales}}$
Profit margin	$\dfrac{\text{Profit}}{\text{Net sales}}$
Return on assets	$\dfrac{\text{Profit}}{\text{Average assets}}$
Return on shareholders' equity	$\dfrac{\text{Profit}}{\text{Average equity}}$

TABLE 4.5 **Common profitability ratios**

profit margin profit to net sales

return on assets (ROA) profit to average assets

return on equity (ROE) profit to average equity

The **profit margin** indicates the profitability of a company after taking into account all operating expenses. By looking at the trend in the profit margin over time, the auditor is able to identify variability in the profit-earning capacity of their client. If the profit margin is steadily falling, this may affect the future viability of the client. If the profit margin varies widely from year to year, this indicates volatility and uncertainty, which makes it difficult to assess the fair presentation of the current reported earnings without further investigation.

The **return on assets (ROA)** indicates the ability of a company to generate income from its average investment in total assets. The **return on equity (ROE)** indicates the ability of a company to generate income from the funds invested by its common (ordinary) shareholders. If a company is unable to generate a sufficient return on funds invested, there may be insufficient funds available to pay dividends and invest in future growth. An auditor will calculate these ratios to assess trends in profitability. If the ROA and ROE are falling, they will affect the ability of a client to generate funds to pay dividends and interest and to repay loans.

An auditor will make comparisons between the current year and previous years to identify trends in their client's profitability. Comparisons will also be made with budgeted results and with competitors. When comparing with budget, an auditor will assess how profitable the client is compared with management's expectations. An auditor will discuss any significant variance with management. When comparing the client with competitors, an auditor will assess the client's profitability relative to companies of a similar size operating in the same industry. Any significant trends that appear unusual when compared with previous years, budget, or competitors are investigated further by an auditor as they indicate that there may be a risk of a material misstatement.

Liquidity ratios

Liquidity ratios reflect a company's ability to meet its short-term debt obligations. If a company is unable to pay its debts when they fall due, the company may lose key employees, suppliers may refuse to supply goods, and lenders may recall funds borrowed. An auditor is concerned with the client's liquidity situation and will alert the client to any potential going concern issues. Table 4.6 shows a number of short-term liquidity ratios. These include the current ratio and the asset-test (quick) ratio. The inventory and receivables turnovers are used as liquidity ratios as well as indicators of managerial efficiency and client activity.

current ratio current assets to current liabilities

asset-test (quick) ratio liquid assets to current liabilities

The **current ratio** indicates how well current assets cover current liabilities. A ratio that is greater than one indicates that a company should be able to meet its short-term commitments when they fall due. In reality, this will depend on the ability of a company to convert its inventory and receivables into cash on a timely basis. The **asset-test (quick) ratio** indicates how well liquid (cash or near cash) assets cover current liabilities. Liquid assets include cash, short-term investments, and receivables. Acceptable current and asset-test ratio benchmarks vary from one industry to another. An auditor will compare the trend in both ratios over time to assess whether their client's liquidity situation is improving or deteriorating. An auditor will also compare the client's ratios with the industry average to assess the client's liquidity relative to close competitors. If a client's liquidity situation is deteriorating or is poor when compared with the industry average, an auditor may be concerned about the future viability of the company.

inventory turnover cost of sales to average inventory

Inventory turnover measures how many times a company sells its inventory in a year. An auditor will look at the trend in this ratio to determine whether inventory is being turned over

TABLE 4.6 **Short-term liquidity ratios**

RATIO	DEFINITION
Current ratio	$\dfrac{\text{Current assets}}{\text{Current liabilities}}$
Asset-test (quick) ratio	$\dfrac{\text{Cash + Short-term investments + Receivables (net)}}{\text{Current liabilities}}$
Inventory turnover	$\dfrac{\text{Cost of sales}}{\text{Average inventory}}$
Receivables turnover	$\dfrac{\text{Net credit sales}}{\text{Average net receivables}}$

more or less frequently from year to year. This turnover will vary widely from one industry to another. For example, the turnover for a supermarket would be expected to be much higher than for a luxury boat manufacturer. An auditor will compare the inventory turnover for their client with the industry average to determine whether their client is competitive and has as high a turnover as its rivals. If a client operates in a high-technology industry or the fashion industry, where customer preferences change quickly, a slowing down of inventory turnover may indicate that the client is not keeping up with change. When a client's inventory turnover slows, an auditor will spend more time testing for the valuation of inventory, as stock may need to be written down in response to slowing demand.

Receivables turnover measures how many times a year a company collects cash from its accounts receivable customers. A slowdown in this ratio may indicate that the client is making sales to customers who are unable to pay for their goods on a timely basis or that the client is not efficiently following up on customers who are late in paying. If receivables turnover falls, an auditor will spend more time considering the adequacy of the allowance for doubtful accounts.

receivables turnover net credit sales to average net receivables

Solvency ratios

Solvency ratios are used to assess the long-term viability of a company. Liquidity ratios tend to take a short-term view of a company; solvency ratios have a long-term perspective. Table 4.7 shows common solvency ratios: the debt to equity ratio and times interest earned.

The **debt to equity ratio** indicates the relative proportion of total assets being funded by debt relative to equity. A high debt to equity ratio increases the risk that a client will not be able to meet interest payments to borrowers when they fall due. Companies with long-term debt are more likely to have a debt covenant with a lender, which restricts the company's activities. An auditor will consider the trend in the client's debt to equity ratio over time. An increasing ratio increases the risk that a client will not be able to repay their loans when they fall due, and the risk that a client will breach a debt covenant, as many covenants restrict the raising of additional debt. An auditor will also compare a client's debt to equity ratio with similar companies in the same industry as this ratio tends to vary across industries.

debt to equity ratio liabilities to equity

Times interest earned measures the ability of earnings to cover interest payments. A low ratio indicates that a client will have difficulty meeting its interest payments to lenders. An auditor will consider how this ratio has changed over time. A downward trend is a concern as it indicates that lenders may charge the client a higher rate of interest on future borrowings. At the extreme, lenders may recall monies lent if the client does not meet interest payments.

times interest earned profit before income taxes and interest expense

RATIO	DEFINITION
Debt to equity ratio	$\dfrac{\text{Liabilities}}{\text{Equity}}$
Times interest earned	$\dfrac{\text{Profit before income taxes and interest expense}}{\text{Interest expense}}$

TABLE 4.7 **Common solvency ratios**

4.5.5 Factors to consider when conducting analytical procedures

There are a number of factors to consider when conducting analytical procedures. The first is the reliability of client data. If the auditor believes there is a significant risk that the client's records are unreliable due to, for example, poor internal controls, then the auditor is less likely to rely on analytical procedures. Another issue is the ability to make comparisons over time. If the client has changed accounting methods, this will reduce the comparability of the underlying data. In this case, an auditor will need to restate prior years' financial statements using the current accounting methods before making any comparisons. If past results are unaudited, they are considered less reliable for comparison purposes.

During the planning stage of an audit, an auditor may have access only to the client's interim results. In this case, an auditor will need to annualize revenue and expense items before making comparisons with the prior year. If the client earns revenues evenly throughout the year, it is appropriate to double the half-year revenues. If the client earns more revenues in some months relative to others (for example, an ice seller in warmer months), trends must be considered when annualizing interim results.

When comparing actual financial results with budgeted results, an auditor will consider the reliability of the budget. This can be assessed by comparing budget with actual results for prior years. If the client continually overestimates earnings, for example, an auditor can take this into account when comparing actual and budgeted results for the current period.

When benchmarking a client with industry data, care must be taken. If the client is significantly smaller or larger than most companies in its industry, the comparison may not be valid. If competitors do not use the same accounting methods, the comparison is problematic. If the client has very different results and ratios compared with the industry average, there may be a problem with industry data rather than with client data.

In conducting analytical procedures, the following information sources are generally considered to be reliable:

- information generated by an accounting system that has effective internal controls
- information generated by an independent reputable external source
- audited information
- information generated using consistent accounting methods
- information from a source internal to the client that has proven to be accurate in the past (for example, information used to prepare budgets)

After conducting analytical procedures, an auditor will investigate all significant unexpected fluctuations: the existence of fluctuations where none were expected and the absence of fluctuations where they were expected. An example of the former would be a significant increase in sales for no apparent reason. An example of the latter would be no significant change in inventory turnover when the auditor is aware that sales have fallen significantly.

Cloud 9

Ian volunteers to start the analysis of Cloud 9's interim results and previous period's financial data. He has previously attended a training session on the W&S Partners' software that he will use to produce reports showing unusual relationships and fluctuations. Suzie is grateful for the help but cautions Ian, "You do realize that judging what is 'unusual' is a little more complex than getting a software program to identify a change above a certain percentage? You need considerable industry experience and client knowledge to make sense of the information. For example, no change in a figure can be more suspicious than a large change, depending on the circumstances."

"Yes, I realize that," Ian says, "and I know that I don't have the experience to complete the analysis, but I am hoping that I will learn from you by seeing what you do with the data and reports that I hadn't considered doing."

BEFORE YOU GO ON

4.5.1 Why are liquidity ratios calculated?

4.5.2 Define the gross profit ratio and explain what it indicates.

4.5.3 What is a trend analysis and why might an auditor use this form of analysis?

SUMMARY

❶ Define audit risk.

Audit risk is the risk that an auditor expresses an inappropriate audit opinion when the financial statements are materially misstated. The three components of audit risk are inherent risk, control risk, and detection risk.

❷ Explain and apply the concept of materiality.

Information is considered to be material if it impacts the decision-making process of users of the financial statements.

3 **Describe how an auditor determines the audit strategy.**

The audit strategy is a key component of the planning stage of the audit. It sets the scope, timing, and direction of the audit and provides the basis for developing a detailed audit plan. An audit strategy will depend on the auditor's preliminary inherent and control risk assessment.

4 **Outline how clients measure performance.**

By understanding how a client measures its own performance, an auditor can plan the audit to take into consideration areas where the client may be under pressure to achieve certain outcomes.

5 **Summarize how an auditor uses analytical procedures when planning an audit.**

Analytical procedures are conducted at the planning stage of the audit to identify unusual fluctuations, help identify risks, help when gaining an understanding of a client, identify the accounts at risk of material misstatement, and reduce audit risk by concentrating audit effort where the risk of material misstatement is greatest. There are many processes that can be used when conducting analytical procedures. The processes discussed in this chapter included simple comparisons, trend analysis, common-size analysis, and ratio analysis.

KEY TERMS

Analytical procedures, 127
Assertion, 111
Asset-test (quick) ratio, 130
Audit risk, 110
Audit strategy, 121
Combined audit strategy, 122
Common-size analysis, 128
Control risk, 111
Current ratio, 130
Debt to equity ratio, 131
Detection risk, 114

Earnings per share (EPS), 125
Execution stage, 127
Gross profit margin, 129
Inherent risk, 110
Inventory turnover, 130
Key performance indicators (KPIs), 125
Liquidity, 125
Materiality, 117
Performance materiality, 119
Price-earnings (PE) ratio, 125
Profitability, 125

Profit margin, 130
Quantitative materiality, 118
Receivables turnover, 131
Return on assets (ROA), 130
Return on equity (ROE), 130
Significant risk, 111
Specific materiality, 119
Substantive audit strategy, 121
Times interest earned, 131
Trend analysis, 128
Walkthrough, 122

MULTIPLE-CHOICE QUESTIONS

4.1 A substantive audit strategy:
(a) is appropriate when internal controls are very strong.
(b) means that the auditor will gain the minimum necessary knowledge of the client's system of internal controls.
(c) requires the auditor to conduct extensive control testing.
(d) means that the auditor will conduct some interim testing and minimal year-end account balance testing.

4.2 A combined audit strategy:
(a) is appropriate when internal controls are minimal.
(b) means that the auditor will gain the minimum necessary knowledge of the client's system of internal controls.
(c) requires the auditor to conduct extensive control testing.
(d) means that the auditor will conduct extensive testing of year-end account balances.

4.3 Profitability ratios are used to assess performance and:
(a) companies will be interested in trends in the ratios.
(b) companies will try to have the same ratio in each month of operation.

(c) should be the same for all divisions of the company.
(d) companies will track their revenue and expenses over time and assess any variability.

4.4 Common uses of analytical procedures include:
(a) risk identification during the audit planning stage.
(b) estimation of account balances during the audit execution stage.
(c) overall assessment of the financial statements at the final review stage of the audit.
(d) all of the above.

4.5 An auditor is interested in the client's inventory turnover ratio because it helps the auditor understand:
(a) if the industry is the same as another industry.
(b) if the client is as competitive and has as high a turnover as the industry average.
(c) if the client's accounts receivable customers are paying their accounts on time.
(d) if the client is in the right industry.

4.6 Analytical procedures:
(a) cannot be performed on interim data.
(b) are not affected by different accounting methods between the client and other members of the industry.

(c) must take into account seasonal variation in the client's business.

(d) are only useful if the client's variance from budget is low.

4.7 An auditor will identify accounts and related assertions at risk of material misstatement:

(a) after testing internal controls.

(b) before writing the audit report.

(c) in order to plan the audit to focus on those accounts.

(d) to eliminate audit risk.

4.8 For an audit, the auditor can control:

(a) inherent risk.

(b) control risk.

(c) financial risk.

(d) detection risk.

4.9 An example of an item that is material is:

(a) a theft of $100.

(b) an undisclosed lawsuit for $1 million.

(c) an undisclosed related party.

(d) all of the above.

4.10 Testing controls means that:

(a) the auditor can completely rely on a client's system of internal controls.

(b) no substantive testing is required.

(c) the auditor can plan to reduce their reliance on detailed substantive testing of transactions and account balances.

(d) all of the above.

REVIEW QUESTIONS

4.1 Explain the approach adopted by auditors of identifying accounts and related assertions at risk of material misstatement. How does this approach help reduce audit risk to an acceptably low level?

4.2 How does the auditor's preliminary assessment of materiality affect audit planning? What does an auditor consider when making the preliminary assessment of materiality?

4.3 The materiality of an item is assessed relative to a particular base number. What are some of the choices for this base and what factors guide the auditor in this choice?

4.4 If an auditor adopts a predominantly substantive strategy for the audit, do they have to consider and test the client's internal controls? If an auditor adopts a combined audit strategy, do they have to perform any substantive procedures? Explain.

4.5 A client has physical controls over inventory, including a locked warehouse with access restricted to authorized personnel. Testing of these physical controls over inventory shows that they are very effective. Can the auditor conclude that the valuation assertion for inventory is not at risk? Explain.

4.6 Explain using examples how you could use analytical procedures in assessing the risk of misstatement of sales revenue.

4.7 What are some possible explanations of a change in the gross profit margin? How could the auditor investigate which of these explanations is the most likely cause of the change in the ratio?

4.8 What is the difference between liquidity and solvency? Why does this difference matter to an auditor?

4.9 Consider the following statement: "If inherent and control risk are high, the auditor will set detection risk as low, to bring audit risk down." Explain how setting detection risk as low brings down audit risk.

4.10 What is the relationship between audit risk and materiality, and evidence? Why does setting a lower materiality level affect the number of items that are material and the assessment of the sufficiency and appropriateness of audit evidence?

PROFESSIONAL APPLICATION QUESTIONS

Basic ★	Moderate ★ ★	Challenging ★ ★ ★

4.1 Audit risk and revenue ★

Ajax Finance Ltd. (Ajax) provides small- and medium-sized personal, car, and business loans to clients. It has been operating for more than 10 years and run throughout its life by Bill

Schultz. Bill has been the public face of the finance company, appearing in most of its television and radio advertisements. He has developed a reputation as a friend of the "little person" who has been mistreated by the large finance companies and banks.

Ajax's major revenue stream is generated by obtaining large amounts on the wholesale money market and lending in small amounts to retail customers. Margins are tight, and the business is run as a "no frills" service. Offices are modestly furnished and the mobile lenders drive small, basic cars when visiting clients. Ajax prides itself on full disclosure to its clients, and all fees and services are explained in writing to clients before loans are finalized. However, although full disclosure is made, clients who do not read the documents closely can be surprised by the high exit charges when they wish to make early repayments or transfer their business elsewhere.

Ajax's mobile lenders are paid on a commission basis; they earn more when they write more loans. For example, they are encouraged to sell credit cards to any person seeking a personal loan. Ajax receives a commission payment from the credit card companies when it sells a new card and Ajax also receives a small percentage of the interest charges paid by clients on the credit card.

Required

What are the inherent and control risks for Ajax's revenue? Explain which assertions are most at risk.

4.2 Audit risk and inventory ★

Cheap-as-Chips stocks thousands of items in inventory that range in value from $1 to $100. The inventory on hand represents a material portion of current assets. The merchandise items change according to the season and the promotional theme adopted by the stores' management for the year. Merchandise is ordered up to four months in advance from Chinese and Korean suppliers. These special orders require Cheap-as-Chips to give the suppliers substantial deposits upon placement of the orders.

Required

What are the inherent risks for Cheap-as-Chips' inventory? Discuss the assertions being made by management about the inventory.

Source: Adapted from the Institute of Chartered Accountants Australia's CA Program's *Audit and Assurance Exam*, December 2010. Provided courtesy of Chartered Accountants Australia and New Zealand.

4.3 Control risk ★

Clear Sky Aviation credits prepayments of air travel to a deferred revenue account until the travel service is provided, at which point it transfers the appropriate amount to sales revenue. A problem with its control system means that the proper allocation of revenue between sales revenue recorded in the profit and loss and the deferred revenue account balance in the balance sheet does not always occur. The auditor is considering conducting additional substantive testing to test whether the sales transactions have been properly classified.

Required

Describe how the balance sheet and income statement may be at risk of material misstatement if the controls regarding the proper allocation of revenue are not functioning properly.

Source: Adapted from the Institute of Chartered Accountants Australia's CA *Program's Audit and Assurance Exam*, December 2010. Provided courtesy of Chartered Accountants Australia and New Zealand.

4.4 Risk assessment ★ ★

LLL Avionics Ltd. has contacted your accounting firm to inquire about the cost of an external audit. The company's president explained that he feels that "the previous auditor charged too much and only issued a qualified opinion." Your firm was recommended to LLL by your bank manager. LLL has a large loan request at the bank, and the interest rate of the new loan will depend on the audit opinion. As the partner in charge of this file, you interviewed the president and controller of the company as part of your decision to accept or reject LLL as a client. You have found that the company has a new design for an aircraft and plans to borrow funds from the bank and to issue common shares to finance a prototype plane to test the design. The new funds will also greatly improve the company's balance sheet by providing the funds to bring the company's existing bank loan up to date. If the design is successful, more common shares will be issued for more capital.

The controller was very helpful in your discussions, and you note his high level of enthusiasm for the project as this is his first job at this level. However, the president was not so helpful and seemed annoyed with your questions.

Required

Indicate five factors in the above situation that impact the risk of material misstatement. Explain your answer.

Source: © CGA-Canada, now CPA Canada. Reproduced with permission.

4.5 Audit risk ★ ★

This is the second year that your firm is auditing JJ Company, which is developing a new drug for a rare form of cancer. The company is controlled by Jack Mukash, who purchased the shares from the previous owner this year. You have been informed that the company's bank requires an audit to increase the company's operating line of credit. Jack has also informed you that he would like to convert the company into a public company next year, and sell shares on the stock exchange, as he does not expect that the company will have significant revenues for at least four years. At present, the company has two other drugs under patent, and these products produce sufficient revenues to service the debt load of the company, including anticipated new borrowing this year. However, these patents will expire in five years, so Jack is trying to plan ahead.

Required

Indicate whether you feel the overall audit assurance should be high or low in the audit of JJ. State two reasons to support your answer.

Source: © CGA-Canada, now CPA Canada. Reproduced with permission.

4.6 Audit risk ★ ★

Triple J Movers Ltd. is owned by Jacques Tétreault. The company used to be profitable but several new small companies have started to compete with Triple J, offering very low prices that Triple J cannot match. Jacques thinks he can make his company profitable again if he eliminates his competitors, which will allow him to raise prices.

He therefore decided to purchase one of his competitors each year for the next four years. The first company he bought was a proprietorship called Jerry's Trucking. Jacques has hired your audit firm to review the accounting system and controls at Jerry's Trucking to see what changes are needed before he can integrate it into Triple J Movers. Jacques hopes there are not many problems.

You interviewed the owner of Jerry's Trucking and the company's bank manager and learned the following information:

The company has customers in both Canada and in the United States, and the owner was not very knowledgeable about customs fees that must be paid and regulations that have to be followed when transporting goods across the borders. Also, the owner, Jerry, often simply took any cash that the business earned and spent it on personal items, instead of claiming a wage from the business. There is only one office staff besides Jerry: Jerry's cousin, who does all of the bookkeeping. His cousin is not an accountant but has taken some accounting courses. Jerry explained that controls at Jerry's Trucking are strong because:

- He can trust his cousin completely. (Having honest employees is important for effective control.)
- Jerry personally checks all of the bookkeeping entries, making any corrections he feels are necessary.
- At the year end, Jerry takes the bookkeeping records to a tax preparer who prepares his tax return.

Required

Discuss the inherent risk at Jerry's Trucking based on the above information. Include six observations in your answer.

4.7 Materiality ★ ★ ★

Ana Dinh used 0.5–5 percent of gross profit in determining materiality of $70,000 in her audit of XYZ Inc., a company that builds replacement engines for tractors and combines. She used the $70,000 amount as her planning materiality, identifying account balances and transactions to be tested. She also used materiality as a guide when deciding on the appropriate audit opinion in her report.

Required

(a) Provide three other examples of a base (other than 0.5–5 percent of gross profit) that an auditor could use in determining materiality in a financial statement audit.
(b) Suppose Ana initially reviewed parts inventory account #102641–1 and found that none of the account transactions exceeded $45,000. Does this mean that none of these transactions should be selected for examination, based on her materiality decision of $70,000? Explain your answer.

Source: © CGA-Canada, now CPA Canada. Reproduced with permission.

4.8 Planning, performance, and specific materiality ★ ★ ★

Claytonhill Beverages Ltd. is 100 percent owned by Buzz Bottling. While the company has in the past been profitable, it incurred a loss for the year ended December 31, 2016. The parent company, Buzz Bottling, has indicated that if Claytonhill incurs another loss, it will put the subsidiary up for sale. In response, Claytonhill is looking to expand its market share and therefore its profitability by performing private labelling for a nationwide supermarket chain, ValueFoods Inc. Private labelling involves producing and packaging pop and other non-alcoholic beverages under the ValueFoods label. However, in order to proceed with this endeavour, Claytonhill needs a packaging facility dedicated exclusively to co-packing. To finance this expansion, the company has applied to the Better Business Bank for financing.

The bank has indicated that before it will approve the loan application it would like to see audited financial statements for 2016. It also wants to ensure the entity has a current ratio of 2:1.

Claytonhill Beverages has provided you, their new auditor, with the draft (unaudited) financial statements in Figure 4.10:

Income Statement for the Year Ended December 31, 2016 (partial)

FIGURE 4.10 **Unaudited financial statements for Claytonhill Beverages**

Revenue

Sales	2,057,505
Cost of goods sold	1,445,450
Gross margin	612,055

Less:
General and administration costs
(including bonuses of $100,000)   775,899
Net income before tax   (163,844)

(continued)

FIGURE 4.10 **Unaudited financial statements for Claytonhill Beverages** (continued)

Balance Sheet as at December 31, 2016

Assets

Current assets

Total cash	179,825
Accounts receivable, net	64,475
Prepaid expenses	3,004
Inventory	1,507,413
Total current assets	1,754,717

Capital assets

Office furniture and equipment, net	85,106
Building, net	964,224
Land	2,004,933
Total capital assets	3,054,263

Total assets	4,808,980

Liabilities

Current liabilities

Accounts payable	799,255
Other accrued expenses	44,875
Warranty provision	9,456
Current portion long-term debt	25,000
Total current liabilities	878,586

Long-term liabilities

Bank loans	2,200,000
Total long-term liabilities	2,200,000

Total liabilities	3,078,586

Equity

Common shares	248,000
Retained earnings	1,482,394
Total equity	1,730,394

Liabilities and Equity	4,808,980

Required

(a) Identify the users of the financial statements and their needs.

(b) Given the users' needs, what is the most appropriate base for materiality?

(c) Calculate the three levels of materiality and conclude on each.

(d) What impact did audit risk have on the materiality calculation?

4.9 Audit risk components and materiality ★ ★

Carl's Computers imports computer hardware and accessories from China, Japan, Korea, and the United States. It has branches in every capital city, and the main administration office and central warehouse is in Montreal. There is a branch manager in each store plus a number (depending on the size of the store) of permanent staff. There are also several casual staff who work on weekends—the stores are open both Saturday and Sunday. Either the branch manager or a senior member of the permanent staff is on duty at all times to supervise the casual staff. Both casual and permanent staff members are required to attend periodic company training sessions covering product knowledge and inventory and cash handling requirements.

The inventory is held after its arrival from overseas at the central warehouse and distributed to each branch on receipt of an inventory transfer request authorized by the branch manager. The value of inventory items ranges from a few cents to several thousand dollars. Competition is <u>fierce</u> in the computer hardware industry. New products are continuously coming onto the market, and large furniture and office supply discount retailers are heavy users of advertising and other promotions to win customers from specialists like Carl's Computers. Carl's Computers' management has faced difficulty keeping costs of supply down and has started to use new suppliers for some computer accessories such as printers and ink.

Required

(a) Explain the inherent risks for inventory for Carl's Computers. How would these risks affect the financial statement accounts?

(b) What strengths and weaknesses in the inventory control system can you identify in the above case?

(c) Comment on materiality for inventory at Carl's Computers. Is inventory likely to be a material balance? Would all items of inventory be audited in the same way? Explain how the auditor would deal with these issues.

4.10 Audit risk and materiality ★ ★ ★

Gold Explorers Inc. is a major Canadian gold mining corporation. Gold Explorers has mines and development projects in Canada (Northern Ontario and British Columbia), the United States, and South America. Shares of Gold Explorers trade on three major international stock exchanges—New York, Toronto, and London. Gold Explorers is known as one of the lowest-cost producers of gold worldwide, and in the current fiscal year it achieved record gold production levels. Due to the record levels, revenues increased this year. Revenues grew from $1,357 million last year to $1,432 million in this year's draft financial statements (all dollar figures are U.S. dollars). Corresponding gross profit figures are $642 million for last year and $678 million for the current year.

Terrence, chairman and CEO of Gold Explorers, is known throughout the Canadian mining industry as a man of principle and integrity. He governs Gold Explorers in accordance with three key guiding principles, which he articulated in 1978 when he founded the company. These principles are entrepreneurial management, financial discipline, and corporate responsibility. Adherence to these principles has given Gold Explorers a stable and dedicated work force, and a strong balance sheet that includes $623 million in cash, virtually no net debt, and shareholders' equity of just over $3 billion ($3,023 million). In addition, Gold Explorers boasts an "A" credit rating and has access to a $1-billion line of credit. Gold Explorers' efforts with respect to corporate responsibility have been recognized internationally, and the company was awarded eight major awards for environmental protection in the past four years. In spite of this, however, Gold Explorers has had to expend some money on site restoration in the past in order to meet the requirements of environmental compliance orders.

Your firm has been Gold Explorers' auditors for the past eight years. In that time, there have been very few misstatements discovered during the audits, which have required adjustments to the draft financial statements. In fact, Raj, the partner in charge of the audit, and Margaret, audit manager, have found the audit to be almost routine in the past four years of their involvement with Gold Explorers. However, this year promises to be a little different. Responding to the need for consolidation in the industry, Gold Explorers merged this year in an all-share deal with a major U.S. gold company that had significant mining operations in Canada. Furthermore, immediately prior to year end, Gold Explorers reassessed the carrying value of its capital assets. The reassessment resulted in a $1.1-billion writedown of Gold Explorers' property, plant, and equipment assets to a carrying value of $3,565 million. Even with this writedown, Gold Explorers' total assets remain at a substantial $4,535 million; however, the writedown resulted in a significant net loss before taxes of $944 million in the current year, compared with net incomes before taxes of $441 million and $443 million in the preceding two years.

Required

(a) Identify eight factors that Margaret needs to consider that would affect her assessment of audit risk, inherent risk, and control risk for this year's audit of Gold Explorers. For each factor you identify, indicate which one of the three risks would be affected and state whether the factor is likely to increase or decrease Margaret's assessment of that risk relative to other companies in other industries. In addition, for each factor, explain why the risk will increase or decrease. Set up your answer in the following manner:

FACTOR	TYPE OF RISK	IMPACT (INCREASE/DECREASE)	EXPLANATION

(b) Identify the most appropriate basis for determining materiality for this year. Justify the basis of the materiality you selected and explain why other bases are not appropriate.

Source: © CGA-Canada, now CPA Canada. Reproduced with permission.

4.11 Audit planning ★★

Tom's Trailers Ltd. (TTL), located in London, Ontario, manufactures industrial trailers that are used to ship goods across the country. Originally, Tom Tran owned 60 percent of the common shares of TTL and the other 40 percent was owned equally by Tom's four brothers. Tom's brothers have always been happy with their investment in TTL as they have always received a healthy dividend at the end of each fiscal year from TTL. In a strategic decision last year, Tom sold 9 percent of his shares to Junior Strategic Investments Ltd., a venture capital firm, in exchange for a $30-million investment. This investment has been used to fund the purchase of a new production plant in Burnaby, BC, and to fund the research and development of new technologies that would allow Tom's to produce better trailers that would hold more. The terms of the agreement with Junior Strategic Investments Ltd. require TTL to provide audited financial statements 60 days after its December 31 year end.

The following is select information from the financial statements:

	Dec. 31, 2016 ('000)	Dec. 31, 2015 ('000)
Total assets	$ 46,601	$ 34,268
Total revenues	$160,100	$109,059
Gross profit	$ 30,681	$ 19,306
Earnings before tax	$ 19,212	$ 2,316
Earnings after tax	$ 15,361	$ 1,613

Shane and Wayne Co. has been TTL's accounting firm since its inception; however, they have always performed a review engagement. Based on past engagements, Shane and Wayne Co. is aware that overall, the controls seem strong at TTL, as there is a formal code of conduct, and there appear to be established lines of authority. However, this year Tom has indicated that he is concerned about the gross margin at the new Burnaby plant. It is much lower than the gross margin at the local London plant. The production manager at the Burnaby location is blaming the higher costs on the start-up of the plant.

Tom's Trailers has a large number of foreign sales and Shane and Wayne noted in previous review engagements that several accounting adjustments were required due to foreign exchange translation errors. In discussions with the client, they also determined that the client implemented a new IT system.

Shane and Wayne is starting its audit planning for the upcoming year. The firm uses the CPEM and follows the CPEM guidelines for materiality. The firm assesses performance materiality at 65 percent of planning materiality.

Required

(a) Discuss the risk of material misstatement and conclude on the detection risk.

(b) Assess planning materiality.

4.12 Determining an audit strategy ★ ★ ★

Niagara Dairy is a boutique cheese maker based in the Niagara region of Ontario. Over the years, the business has grown by supplying local retailers and, eventually, by exporting cheese products. In addition, there is a "farm-gate" shop and café located next to the main processing plant in Niagara-on-the-Lake, which serves tourists who also visit other specialist food and wine businesses in the region. Quality control over the cheese manufacturing process and storage of raw materials and finished products at Niagara Dairy is extremely high. The company is committed to high quality control because poor food-handling practices could cause a drop in cheese quality or contamination of cheese products, which would ruin the business very quickly.

The export arm has been built up to become the largest revenue earner for the business by the younger of the two brothers who have run Niagara Dairy since it was established. Jim Bannock has a natural flair for sales and marketing but is not as good at completing the associated detailed paperwork. Some of the export deals have been poorly documented, and Jim often agrees to different prices for different clients without consulting his older brother, Bob, or informing the sales department. Consequently, there are often disputes about invoices, and Jim makes frequent adjustments to accounts receivable using credit notes when clients complain about their statements. Jim sometimes falls behind in responding to customer complaints because he is very busy juggling the demands of making export sales and running his other business, Café Consulting, which provides contract staff for the café business at Niagara Dairy.

Required

(a) Identify the factors that would affect the preliminary assessment of inherent risk and control risk at Niagara Dairy.

(b) Explain how these factors would influence your choice between a predominantly substantive strategy and the combined audit strategy for sales, inventory, and accounts receivable.

4.13 Planning analytical procedures using profitability ratios ★ ★

Li Chen has calculated profitability ratios using data extracted from his client's pre-audit trial balance. He also has the values for the same ratios for the preceding two years (using audited figures). Table 4.8 presents the data for the gross profit and profit margins.

	2016	2015	2014
Gross profit margin	0.45	0.35	0.40
Profit margin	0.09	0.15	0.20

TABLE 4.8 **Gross profit and profit margin**

Li is a little confused because the profit margin shows declining profitability, but the gross profit margin has improved in the current year and is higher in 2016 than in the previous two years.

Required

(a) Make a list of possible explanations for the pattern observed in the gross profit and profit margins.

(b) Which of your explanations suggests additional audit work should be planned? For each, explain the accounts and/or transactions that would need special attention in the audit.

4.14 Analytical procedures for liquidity and solvency issues ★ ★ ★

Bright Spark Fashion has retail outlets in six large regional cities in eastern Canada. The shops are run by local managers but purchasing decisions for all stores are handled by Ray Bright, the owner of the business. Fashion is an extremely competitive business. Bright Spark Fashion sells only for cash and generates sales through a reputation of low prices for quality goods. The winter range is quite slow moving, but summer fashion sells very well, providing a disproportionate amount of the business's sales and profits. Ray is constantly monitoring cash flow, and negotiating with suppliers about payment terms and banks about interest rates and extensions of credit.

Jenna Kowalski has the tasks of assessing the liquidity and solvency of Bright Spark Fashion and identifying the audit risks arising from this aspect of the business. She discovers that a major long-term debt is due for repayment two months after the close of the financial year, but Ray is having difficulty obtaining approval from his current bank for a renewal of the debt for a further two-year term. In addition, interest rates have risen since the last fixed rate was agreed upon two years ago, adding 2 percentage points to the likely rate for the new debt (if it is approved).

The seasonality of the business means that inventory levels fluctuate considerably. At the end of the financial year (December 31), Ray placed pre-paid orders for the summer fashion line, and the goods started arriving in the stores by February.

Required

(a) What liquidity and solvency issues does Bright Spark Fashion face? Explain the likely impact of each issue on the usual liquidity and solvency ratios.

(b) Advise Jenna Kowalski about the audit risks for Bright Spark Fashion and suggest how she could take these into account in the audit plan.

4.15 Risk assessment ★ ★

Featherbed Surf & Leisure Holidays Ltd. is a resort company based on Vancouver Island. Its operations include boating, surfing, diving, and other leisure activities: a backpackers' hostel, a family hotel, and a five-star resort. Justin and Sarah Morris own the majority of the shares in the Morris Group, which controls Featherbed. Justin is the chairman of the board of directors of both Featherbed and the Morris Group, and Sarah is a director of both companies as well as the CFO of Featherbed.

In February 2016, Justin Morris approached your audit firm, KFP Partners, to carry out the Featherbed audit for the year ended June 30, 2016. Featherbed has not been audited before but this year the audit has been requested by the company's bank and a new private equity investor group that has just acquired a 20-percent share of Featherbed.

Featherbed employs 30 full-time staff. These workers are employed in administration, accounting, catering, cleaning, and hotel/restaurant duties. During peak periods, Featherbed also uses part-time and casual workers. These workers tend to be travellers visiting the west coast who are looking for short-term employment to help pay their travelling expenses.

Justin and Sarah have a fairly laid back management style. They trust their workers to work hard for the company and they reward them well. The accounting staff, in particular, are very loyal to the company. Justin tells you that some accounting staff enjoy their jobs so much they have never taken any holidays, and hardly any workers ever take sick leave.

There are three people currently employed as the accountants, the most senior of whom is Peter Pinn. Peter heads the accounting department and reports directly to Sarah. He is in his fifties and plans to retire in two or three years. Peter prides himself on his ability to delegate most of his work to his two accounting staff, Kristen and Julie. He claims he has to do this because he is very busy developing a policy and procedures manual for the accounting department. This delegated work includes opening mail, processing payments and receipts, banking funds received, performing reconciliations, posting journals, and performing the payroll function. Julie is a recently graduated chartered accountant. Kristen works part-time—coming into the office on Mondays, Wednesdays, and Fridays. Kristen is responsible for posting all journal entries into the accounting system and the payroll function. Julie does the balance of the work, but they often help each other out in busy periods.

Required

Using the factors in the above scenario, assess audit risk.

Source: Adapted from the Institute of Chartered Accountants Australia's CA Program's *Audit and Assurance Exam*, May 2008. Provided courtesy of Chartered Accountants Australia and New Zealand.

Questions 4.16 and 4.17 are based on the following case.

Securimax Limited has been an audit client of KFP Partners for the past 15 years. Securimax is based in Waterloo, Ontario, where it manufactures high-tech armour-plated personnel carriers. Securimax often has to go through a competitive market tender process to win large government contracts. Its main product, the small but powerful Terrain Master, is highly specialized and Securimax only does business with nations that have a recognized, democratically elected government. Securimax maintains a highly secure environment, given the sensitive and confidential nature of its vehicle designs and its clients.

In September 2016, Securimax installed an off-the-shelf costing system to support the highly sophisticated and cost-sensitive nature of its product designs. The new system replaced a system that had been developed in-house, as the old system could no longer keep up with the complex and detailed manufacturing costing process that provides tender costings. The old system also had difficulty with the company's broader reporting requirements.

The manufacturing costing system uses all of the manufacturing unit inputs to calculate and produce a database of all product costs and recommended sales prices. It also integrates with the general ledger each time there are product inventory movements such as purchases, sales, wastage, and damaged stock losses.

Securimax's end of financial year is December 31.

Source: Adapted from the Institute of Chartered Accountants Australia's CA Program's *Audit and Assurance Exam*, May 2008. Provided courtesy of Chartered Accountants Australia and New Zealand.

4.16 Assessing inherent risk ★ ★ ★

Required

Based on the background information, what are the major inherent risks in the Securimax audit? Consider both industry and entity risks in your answer.

4.17 Assessing preliminary materiality ★ ★ ★

Required

Discuss the factors to consider when determining preliminary materiality for Securimax.

Questions 4.18 and 4.19 are based on the following case.

Fellowes and Associates is a successful mid-tier accounting firm with a large range of clients across Canada. During the 2016 financial year, Fellowes and Associates gained a new client, Health Care Holdings Group (HCHG), which owns 100 percent of the following entities:

- Shady Oaks Centre, a private treatment facility
- Gardens Nursing Home Ltd., a private nursing home
- Total Laser Care Limited (TLCL), a private clinic that specializes in laser treatment of skin defects

Year end for all HCHG entities is June 30.

On April 1, 2016, Gardens Nursing Home Ltd. switched from its "homegrown" patient revenue system to the HCHG's equivalent system. HCHG is confident that its "off-the-shelf" enterprise system would perform all of the functions that Gardens Nursing Home's homegrown system performed.

Gardens Nursing Home's homegrown patient revenue system comprised the following:

1. Billing system—a system that produced the invoice to charge the patient for services provided, such as accommodation, medications, and medical services. This software included a complex formula to calculate the patient bill allowing for government subsidies, pensioner benefits, and private medical insurance company benefit plans.
2. Patient database—a master file that contained personal details about the patient as well as the period of stay, services provided, and the patient's medical insurance details.
3. Rates database—a master file that showed all accommodation billing rates, rebate discounts, and government assistance benefits.

At the request of the board, the group's internal audit unit was involved throughout the entire conversion process. The objective of its engagement, as the board stated, was to "make sure that the conversion worked without any problems."

As part of the planning arrangement for the 2016 financial statement audit, the audit partner, Tania Fellowes, asked her team to speak with a number of Gardens Nursing Home staff about the impact of the switching to the HCHG patient revenue system. Below is an extract of the staff's comments:

- "There were some occasions where we invoiced people who were past patients. This seems to have happened when they shared the same surname as a current patient."
- "We seem to have some patient fee invoices where, for no reason, we have billed patients at a lower room rate than what we have on the rates database."
- "Lately we've had an unusually high number of complaints from recently discharged patients that the fee invoice we sent them does not line up with the agreed-upon medical fund and government subsidy rates. We then found out that halfway through last month someone from the IT team made a software change to fix a bug in the billing calculation formula."
- "There was some sort of power surge last Friday, and we had to re-enter every patient invoice that we had processed in the last two weeks."

Source: Adapted from the Institute of Chartered Accountants Australia's CA Program's Audit and Assurance Exam, December 2008. Provided courtesy of Chartered Accountants Australia and New Zealand.

4.18 Planning in context of IT system changes ★ ★ ★

Required

Identify the audit risks associated with the installation of the new IT system for patient revenue for Gardens Nursing Home.

4.19 Determining audit strategy ★ ★ ★

Required

Comment on the audit strategy likely to be adopted for the audit of patient revenue for Gardens Nursing Home.

CASES

4.20 Integrative Case Study—AutoCare Ltd. ★ ★ ★

AutoCare Ltd. (ACL) is a federally incorporated public company formed in 2010 to manufacture and sell specialty auto products such as paint protection and rust proofing. By 2014, ACL's board of directors felt that the company's products had fully matured and that it needed to diversify. ACL aggressively sought out new "concepts," and in November 2015, it acquired the formula and patent for a new product—synthetic motor lubricant (Synlube).

Synlube is unlike the synthetic motor oils currently on the market. Its innovative molecular structure accounts for what management believes is its superior performance. Although Synlube is more expensive to produce and, therefore, has a higher selling price than its conventional competitors, management believes that its use will reduce maintenance costs and extend the life of the equipment in which it is used.

ACL's main competitor is a very successful multinational conglomerate that has excellent customer recognition of its products and a large distribution network. To create a market niche for Synlube, management is targeting commercial businesses in western Canada that service vehicle fleets and industrial equipment.

ACL's existing facilities were not adequate to produce Synlube in commercial quantities, so in June 2016 ACL began construction of a new blending plant in a western province. The new facilities became operational on December 1, 2016.

ACL has financed its recent expansion with a term bank loan. Management is considering a share issue later in 2017 to solve the company's cash flow problems. ACL's March 31, 2016, draft balance sheet is provided in Exhibit I.

Although they had been with the company since its inception, ACL's auditors have just resigned. It is now April 22, 2016. You and a partner meet with the CEO to discuss the services your firm can provide to ACL for the year ended March 31, 2016. During your meeting, you collect the following information:

· ACL has started a lawsuit against its major competitor for patent infringement and industrial espionage. Management has evidence that it believes will result in a successful action and wishes to record the estimated gain on settlement of $4 million. Although no court date has been set, legal correspondence shows that the competitor intends "to fight this action to the highest court in the land."

· The CEO, Arif Saleh, contacted your firm after ACL's former auditors resigned. The previous auditors informed Mr. Saleh that they disagreed with ACL's valuation of deferred development costs and believed that the balance should be reduced to a nominal amount of $1.

ACL has incurred substantial losses during the past three fiscal years, but revenue for 2016 was $6.2 million.

EXHIBIT I

AutoCare Ltd.
DRAFT BALANCE SHEET
as at March 31 (in thousands of dollars)

Assets

	2016 (Unaudited)	2015 (Audited)
Current		
Accounts receivable	$ 213	$ 195
Inventories	1,650	615
Prepaid expenses	45	30
	1,908	840
Capital assets	2,120	716
Investment in JDP Ltd.	1	1
Deferred development costs	1,979	686
Patent	835	835
	$6,843	$3,078
Liabilities		
Current		
Bank indebtedness	$1,225	$ 462
Accounts payable	607	476
Current portion of long-term debt	400	98
Advances from shareholders	253	—
	2,485	1,036
Long-term debt	3,114	650
	5,599	1,686
Shareholders' Equity		
Capital stock	2,766	2,766
Deficit	(1,522)	(1,374)
	1,244	1,392
	$6,843	$3,078

Required

(a) List five procedures that the auditor should perform before deciding to accept ACL as a client.

(b) Evaluate four factors that impact the audit risk assessment for the current year and indicate how these factors influence audit risk (that is, increase or decrease audit risk).

(c) Conclude on overall audit risk and indicate how this will impact the audit planning.

(d) Using at least three of your calculations of materiality, calculate the range of materiality for the current year. Conclude on the most appropriate materiality and include a detailed explanation supporting your decision.

(e) Perform planning analytic procedures and identify at least three accounts with unusual fluctuations. For each of the "risky" accounts you identify, indicate a possible client error that may have caused this significant fluctuation as well as a possible business reason for the change.

CASE STUDY—CLOUD 9

PART 1 Materiality

W&S Partners commenced the planning phase of the Cloud 9 audit with procedures to gain an understanding of the client's structure and its business environment. You have completed your research on the key market forces as they relate to Cloud 9's operations. The topics you researched included the general and industry-specific economic trends and conditions; the competitive environment; product, customer, and supplier information; technological advances and the effect of the Internet; and laws and regulatory requirements. The purpose of this research is to identify the inherent risks. The auditor needs to identify which financial statement assertions may be affected by these inherent risks. Identifying the risks will help determine the nature of the audit procedures to be performed.

Management implicitly or explicitly makes assertions regarding the recognition, measurement, presentation, and disclosure of the various elements of the financial statements. Auditors use assertions for account balances to form a basis for the assessment of risks of material misstatement. That is, assertions are used to identify the types of errors that could occur in transactions that result in the account balance. Consequently, further breaking down the account into these assertions will direct the audit effort to those areas of higher risk. The auditors broadly classify assertions as existence or occurrence; completeness; valuation or allocation; rights and obligations; and presentation and disclosure.

An additional task during the planning phase is to consider the concept of materiality as it applies to the client. The auditor will design procedures in order to identify and correct errors or irregularities that would have a material effect on the financial statements and affect the decision-making of the users of the financial statements. Materiality is used in determining audit procedures and sample selections, and in evaluating differences from client records to audit results. It is the maximum amount of misstatement, individually or in aggregate, that can be accepted in the financial statements. In selecting the base figure to be used to calculate materiality, an auditor should consider the key drivers of the business and ask, "What are the end users (that is, shareholders, banks, and so on) of the accounts going to be looking at?" For example, will shareholders be interested in profit figures that can be used to pay dividends and increase share price?

W&S Partners' audit methodology dictates that one planning materiality (PM) amount is to be used for the financial statements as a whole. Further, only one basis should be selected—a blended approach or average should not be used. The basis selected is the one determined to be the key driver of the business.

W&S Partners use the percentages in table 4.9 as starting points for the various bases.

TABLE 4.9 **Starting percentages for materiality bases**

BASE	THRESHOLD (%)
Profit before tax	5.0
Revenues	0.5
Gross profit	2.0
Total assets	0.5
Equity	1.0

These starting points can be increased or decreased by taking into account qualitative client factors, such as:
- the nature of the client's business and industry (for example, rapidly changing through growth or downsizing, or because of an unstable environment)
- the client is a public company (or subsidiary of) that is subject to regulations
- the knowledge of or high risk of fraud

Typically, profit before tax is used; however, it cannot be used if reporting a loss for the year or if profitability is not consistent.

When calculating PM based on interim figures, it may be necessary to annualize the results. This allows the auditor to plan the audit properly based on an approximate projected year-end balance. Then, at year end, the figure is adjusted, if necessary, to reflect the actual results.

Required

Answer the following questions based on the information presented for Cloud 9 in Appendix B to this book and in the current and earlier chapters. You should also consider your answers to the case study questions in earlier chapters.

(a) Using the December 31, 2016 trial balance (in Appendix B), calculate planning materiality and include the justification for the basis that you have used for your calculation.

(b) Based on your results from researching the client and its industry in chapter 1 and chapter 2, discuss the inherent risks in the audit of Cloud 9. Identify the associated financial accounts that would be affected and provide an assessment of "high," "medium," or "low" in relation to the likelihood and materiality of the risk occurring.

PART 2 Analytical procedures

Required

Answer the following questions based on the information presented for Cloud 9 in Appendix B to this book and the current and earlier chapters. You should also consider your answers to the case study questions in earlier chapters.

(a) Using analytical procedures and the information provided in the appendix, perform preliminary analytics of Cloud 9's financial position and its business risks. Discuss the ratios indicating a significant or an unexpected fluctuation.

(b) Which specific areas do you believe should receive special emphasis during your audit? Consider your discussion of the results of analytical procedures as well as your preliminary estimate of materiality. Prepare a memorandum to Suzie Pickering outlining potential problem areas (that is, where possible material misstatements in the financial report exist) and any other special concerns (for example, going concern). Specify the accounts and related assertions that would require particular attention.

RESEARCH QUESTION 4.1

Executive remuneration

Listed companies are required to make certain disclosures in their annual reports about the compensation paid to their top executives. One reason for this is to help interested stakeholders assess the performance of executives. It also helps executives and companies set appropriate compensation levels based on what other companies in the same industry and/or of the same size are paying their executives. These disclosures are audited.

Required

Obtain the annual reports of five listed Canadian companies in the same industry through the website SEDAR (www.sedar.com). You can search by industry and choose the companies whose annual reports you want to review. Extract the information on executive remuneration and describe the data using graphs and tables. Write a report addressing the following questions (justify your responses by referring to the data where appropriate).

- How are the executives paid (cash, bonuses, and so on)?
- Which companies' executives are paid the most and what is the range of pay?
- Which companies' executives' pay is most linked to the company's profit and/or share price performance? (Explain any assumptions you have to make.)
- Overall, what do you conclude about how Canadian company executives are paid and how clearly the compensation data are reported?

RESEARCH QUESTION 4.2

Public company financial statements

The financial statements for public companies are available through SEDAR (www.sedar.com). This is the official site that provides access to information filed by public companies and investment funds with the Canadian Securities Administrators (CSA). The objective in making public this financial information is to enhance investor awareness of the business and affairs of public companies and to promote confidence in the transparent operation of capital markets in Canada. Achieving this objective relies heavily on the provision of accurate information on market participants.

Required

Go to www.sedar.com and select the most recent set of *audited annual* financial statements for a Canadian public company. Using this set of financial statements:

(a) Assess the inherent risk of the company chosen.
(b) Calculate materiality for the engagement.
(c) Perform preliminary analytics and summarize your findings.

FURTHER READING

Chartered Professional Accountants of Canada (2013). *Canadian Professional Engagement Manual*.
www.castore.ca/product/canadian-professional-engagement-manual-members/5

SOLUTIONS TO MULTIPLE-CHOICE QUESTIONS

1. b, 2. c, 3. a, 4. d, 5. b, 6. c, 7. c, 8. d, 9. d, 10. c.

CHAPTER 5

Audit evidence

LEARNING OBJECTIVES

After studying this chapter you should be able to:

1. outline the audit assertions
2. identify and describe different types of audit evidence and define sufficient appropriate audit evidence
3. determine the persuasiveness of audit evidence
4. explain the issues to consider when using the work of an expert
5. explain the issues to consider when using the work of another auditor
6. describe the evidence-gathering procedures most often used by auditors
7. explain how auditors arrive at a conclusion based upon the evidence gathered
8. describe how auditors document the details of evidence gathered in working papers.

AUDITING AND ASSURANCE STANDARDS

CANADIAN	INTERNATIONAL
CAS 230 *Audit Documentation*	ISA 230 *Audit Documentation*
CAS 315 *Identifying and Assessing the Risks of Material Misstatement through Understanding the Entity and Its Environment*	ISA 315 *Identifying and Assessing the Risks of Material Misstatement through Understanding the Entity and Its Environment*
CAS 330 *The Auditor's Responses to Assessed Risks*	ISA 330 *The Auditor's Responses to Assessed Risks*
CAS 500 *Audit Evidence*	ISA 500 *Audit Evidence*
CAS 501 *Audit Evidence—Specific Considerations for Selected Items*	ISA 501 *Audit Evidence—Specific Considerations for Selected Items*
CAS 505 *External Confirmations*	ISA 505 *External Confirmations*
CAS 580 *Written Representations*	ISA 580 *Written Representations*
CAS 600 *Special Considerations—Audits of Group Financial Statements (Including the Work of Component Auditors)*	ISA 600 *Special Considerations—Audits of Group Financial Statements (Including the Work of Component Auditors)*
CAS 620 *Using the Work of an Auditor's Expert*	ISA 620 *Using the Work of an Auditor's Expert*
Rules of *Professional Conduct of each Provincial Institute/Order*	Code of *Ethics for Professional Accountants*
CSQC 1 *Quality Control for Firms that Perform Audits and Reviews of Historical Financial Information, and other Assurance and Related Services Engagements*	ISQC 1 *Quality Control for Firms that Perform Audits and Reviews of Historical Financial Information, and other Assurance and Related Services Engagements*

```
┌─────────────────────────────────────────────────────────────┐
│                  Overview of the audit process                │
│                          Chapter 1                            │
└─────────────────────────────────────────────────────────────┘

┌─────────────────────────────────────────────────────────────┐
│              Client acceptance/continuation decision           │
│                          Chapter 2                            │
└─────────────────────────────────────────────────────────────┘

┌─────────────────────────────────────────────────────────────┐
│                          Planning                             │
│                        Chapters 3 & 4                         │
└─────────────────────────────────────────────────────────────┘
```

Gain an understanding of the client

Identify significant accounts and transactions

Set planning materiality

Identify what can go wrong

Gain an understanding of key internal controls

Develop an audit strategy

```
┌─────────────────────────────────────────────────────────────┐
│                         Execution                             │
│                       Chapters 6–12                           │
└─────────────────────────────────────────────────────────────┘
```

Controls strategy
Chapter 7

Substantive strategy
Chapter 8

Audit sampling
Chapter 6

Auditing sales and receivables
Chapter 9

Auditing purchases, payables, and payroll
Chapter 10

Auditing inventories and property, plant, and equipment
Chapter 11

Auditing cash and investments
Chapter 12

```
┌─────────────────────────────────────────────────────────────┐
│                  Concluding and reporting                     │
│                        Chapter 13                             │
└─────────────────────────────────────────────────────────────┘
```

Subsequent event identification

Conclusions

Reporting

Audit evidence
Chapter 5

Cloud 9

At the next planning meeting for the Cloud 9 Ltd. audit, Suzie Pickering presents the results of the analytical procedures performed so far and the working draft of the audit plan. The audit manager, Sharon Gallagher, and the audit senior, Josh Thomas, are also involved in the planning, with special responsibility for the internal control assessment.

The purpose of the meeting is to discuss the available sources of evidence at Cloud 9 and specify these in the detailed audit program. The team also has to make sure that they have enough evidence to conduct the audit. There are two specific issues worrying members of the team. First, there are three very large asset balances on Cloud 9's trial balance that have particular valuation issues. Suzie suggests that an expert valuator will be required for the derivatives, but they can handle the accounts receivable and inventory themselves. Second, Sharon is worried about the auditors of Cloud 9's parent company, Cloud 9 Inc.—the auditors did some audit work on the relationship between the two companies (Cloud 9 Inc. and Cloud 9 Ltd.) during the year and she hasn't been able to gain access to the confidential report yet.

The questions being considered by the team in the planning meeting include:

- What evidence is available?
- What criteria will the team use to choose between alternative sources of evidence?
- What are the implications of using the work of experts and other auditors?

AUDIT PROCESS IN FOCUS

In this chapter, we look at audit evidence. In the last two chapters, we considered audit risk and planning. A great deal of that discussion considered the importance of risk identification to aid with audit risk minimization. Once an auditor has identified the key risk factors for their client, they will plan their audit to obtain sufficient appropriate audit evidence to ensure that relevant accounts and related note disclosures are reported accurately. In the chapters that follow, we discuss the detailed testing conducted by auditors. In these chapters, the evidence-gathering procedures introduced in this chapter will be explained in more detail.

We start this chapter by defining and describing audit assertions, which are used when designing and conducting testing. We then consider the different types of evidence that an auditor will gather, including evidence gathered through confirmations, documentary evidence, representations, verbal evidence, computational evidence, physical evidence, and electronic evidence. Each form of evidence is used to substantiate the information provided by the client in its trial balance and its preliminary financial statements. Some forms of evidence are more persuasive than others: internally generated evidence is the least persuasive; externally generated evidence sent directly to the auditor is the most persuasive. Examples are provided of different types of evidence and the evidence that auditors tend to rely on most as providing the most dependable, independent proof that the amounts included in the client's financial statements are fairly presented.

After considering the relative persuasiveness of different types of evidence, we consider special types of evidence. In particular we consider evidence provided by experts and evidence provided by other auditors. Using the work of these two groups presents particular challenges for an auditor. These challenges are discussed in this chapter.

We then provide an overview of the evidence-gathering procedures used by auditors. These procedures include inspection of records and physical assets, observation of procedures used by clients where no audit trail is left, inquiry of client management and personnel, confirmation of balances with external parties, recalculation to ensure numerical accuracy, re-performance of procedures used by a client, and analytical procedures.

A discussion follows on how the auditor arrives at a conclusion regarding the fair presentation of the financial statements. This conclusion is based upon an auditor's understanding of their client, the risks identified during the planning stage of the audit, and the evidence gathered throughout the remainder of the audit when conducting detailed testing of controls, transactions, and accounts.

Auditors document the details of evidence gathered in their working papers. An auditor's working papers provide proof of audit work completed, procedures used, and evidence gathered. Each accounting firm has its own working paper format and preferences. In this chapter, we provide some examples of a typical audit file and the types of working papers it may contain.

5.1 ASSERTIONS

It is the responsibility of those charged with governance to ensure that the financial statements are prepared so as to give a fair presentation of the entity and its operations. When preparing the financial statements, management makes **assertions** about each account and related disclosures in the notes. For example, when reporting on inventory, management should ensure that the amount disclosed exists, is owned by the entity, represents a complete list of the inventory owned, and is valued appropriately. When reporting on sales, management should ensure that the amount disclosed represents sales of the entity that occurred during the accounting period. They should also ensure that sales are recorded at the correct amount, represent a complete list of all sales, and are classified correctly.

Auditors use assertions for transactions, account balances, and presentations and disclosures when assessing the risk of material misstatement and when designing their audit procedures. CAS 315 *Identifying and Assessing the Risks of Material Misstatement through Understanding the Entity and Its Environment* provides a summary of the assertions used by auditors. Transaction-based assertions focus on the transactions that took place during the period as opposed to the account balance. For example, when auditing inventory, the auditor will audit a sample of the transactions that impact the inventory account, such as purchases and sales, but they will also conduct procedures on the ending inventory balance (the account balance). Table 5.1 shows the assertions used for transactions and events, including income statement items, for an accounting period.

1 Outline the audit assertions.

assertions statements made by management regarding the recognition, measurement, presentation, and disclosure of items included in the financial statements

Occurrence	Transactions and events that have been recorded have occurred and pertain to the entity.
Completeness	All transactions and events that should have been recorded have been recorded.
Accuracy	Amounts and other data relating to recorded transactions and events have been recorded appropriately.
Cut-off	Transactions and events have been recorded in the correct accounting period.
Classification	Transactions and events have been recorded in the proper accounts.

TABLE 5.1 **Assertions about classes of transactions and events for the period under audit**

When testing for **occurrence**, an auditor searches for evidence to verify that a recorded transaction or event, such as a revenue or an expense item, took place and relates to the entity. This assertion is particularly important when the auditor believes that there is a risk of overstatement and that some transactions or events are recorded but did not actually occur—for example, false sales recorded to overstate revenue and profit.

When testing for **completeness**, an auditor searches for transactions or events and makes sure these have been recorded. This assertion is particularly important when the auditor believes there is a risk of understatement and that some transactions or events that should have been recorded have not been recorded—for example, expenses incurred but not recorded to understate expenses and overstate profit.

When testing for **accuracy**, an auditor searches for evidence that transactions and events have been recorded at appropriate amounts. This assertion is particularly important when the auditor believes there is a risk that the reported amounts are not accurate—for example, when a client has complex discounting systems or foreign exchange calculations where errors can easily occur.

When testing for **cut-off**, an auditor searches for evidence that transactions have been recorded in the correct accounting period. This assertion is particularly important for transactions close to year end. For example, a client may record a sale before year end that occurred after year end. Or, a client may record an expense after year end that was incurred before year end. When testing

occurrence transactions and events that have been recorded have occurred and pertain to the entity

completeness all transactions, events, assets, liabilities, and equity items that should have been recorded have been recorded

accuracy amounts and other data relating to recorded transactions and events have been recorded appropriately

cut-off transactions and events have been recorded in the correct accounting period

TABLE 5.2 **Assertions about account balances at year end**

Existence	Assets, liabilities, and equity interests exist.
Rights and obligations	The entity holds or controls the rights to assets, and liabilities are the obligations of the entity.
Completeness	All assets, liabilities, and equity interests that should have been recorded have been recorded.
Valuation and allocation	Assets, liabilities, and equity interests are included in the financial statements at appropriate amounts and any resulting valuation or allocation adjustments are appropriately recorded.

classification transactions and events have been recorded in the proper accounts

existence recorded assets, liabilities, and equity interests exist

rights and obligations rights to assets held or controlled by the entity, and liabilities (obligations) of the entity

valuation and allocation assets, liabilities, and equity interests are included in the financial statements at appropriate amounts and any resulting valuation or allocation adjustments are appropriately recorded

for **classification**, an auditor ensures that transactions and events have been recorded in the proper accounts.

Table 5.2 shows the assertions used when testing balance sheet items. When testing for **existence**, an auditor searches for evidence to verify that asset, liability, and equity items included in the account balances that appear in the financial statements actually exist. This assertion is particularly important when the auditor believes there is a risk of overstatement.

When testing for **rights and obligations**, an auditor searches for evidence to verify that recorded assets are owned by the entity and that recorded liabilities represent commitments of the entity. This assertion is particularly important when the auditor believes there is a risk that recorded assets or liabilities are not owned by the entity. This assertion is different from existence, as the assets and liabilities may exist but not be owned by the entity. For example, inventory held on consignment (and therefore not owned by the entity) is recorded as an asset of the entity.

When testing for **completeness**, an auditor searches for assets, liabilities, and equity items and ensures that they have been recorded. This assertion is particularly important when the auditor believes there is a risk of understatement and the client has omitted some items from the balance sheet. For example, an auditor will search for unrecorded liabilities.

When testing for **valuation and allocation**, an auditor searches for evidence that assets, liabilities, and equity items have been recorded at appropriate amounts and allocated to the correct general ledger accounts. This assertion is particularly important when the auditor believes there is a risk of over- or undervaluation. For example:

- an auditor checks that inventory has been appropriately recorded at the lower of cost and net realizable value (risk of overstatement),
- an auditor tests for the adequacy of the allowance for doubtful accounts (risk of understatement),
- an auditor checks that transactions are allocated to the correct account when auditing research and development expenditure (risk of understatement of the expense account).

Cloud 9

Ian and Suzie have already talked in general terms about the errors that could occur in Cloud 9's accounts receivable. For example, basic mathematical or other clerical errors could affect the accounts receivable total in either direction. Suzie emphasizes that Cloud 9's management asserts that this error does not exist when they prepare the financial statements—they assert that accounts receivable are valued correctly. The auditor has to gather evidence about each assertion for each transaction class, account, and note in the financial statements. Now that Ian understands this idea better, he is able to identify the assertions that relate to the potential errors in accounts receivable that they discussed earlier:

- There are no mathematical or other clerical errors that could affect the total in either direction—valuation and allocation.
- No accounts receivable were omitted when calculating the total—completeness.
- Accounts receivable represent valid amounts owing for goods sold in the current period—existence.
- All accounts receivable belong to Cloud 9—rights and obligations.

- Bad debts are written off—valuation and allocation. Suzie confirms that there can be more than one instance of a type of assertion for an account.
- Sales from the next period are not included in the earlier period—cut-off. Ian is a bit confused about this one, because cut-off is an assertion for transactions, not assets. Suzie agrees that it is a special sort of assertion that relates to transactions or events but also gives evidence about balance sheet accounts. This is due to double entry accounting, and when auditors test cut-off for sales, they also gather evidence for the balance sheet side of the entry, which is usually accounts receivable.

Table 5.3 shows the assertions used for presentation and disclosure. An auditor ensures that all items included in the financial statements are presented and disclosed appropriately. They check that disclosed items represent events and transactions that occurred for the entity, are recorded at appropriate amounts, and are described accurately. An auditor searches to ensure that all items that should have been disclosed are included in the financial statements.

Occurrence, rights, and obligations	Disclosed events, transactions, and other matters have occurred and pertain to the entity.
Completeness	All disclosures that should have been included in the financial statements have been included.
Classification and understandability	Financial information is appropriately presented and described, and disclosures are clearly expressed.
Accuracy and valuation	Financial and other information is disclosed fairly and at appropriate amounts.

TABLE 5.3 **Assertions about presentation and disclosure**

For example, required presentation and disclosures for inventory include the way inventories are measured, including the cost formula, as well as the carrying amount of inventory in total and by classification. If the cost formula was not disclosed, the inventory note would not be complete and therefore the completeness assertion over presentation and disclosure would not be satisfied. If the entity discloses the first in first out method (FIFO) as its cost method but in fact it uses the weighted average cost formula, then the presentation assertion of accuracy would not be met. Lastly, if the entity does not disclose its raw material and finished goods separately, then the classification and understandability assertion would not be realized.

PROFESSIONAL ENVIRONMENT

Fraud at the audit assertion level

Details of material fraudulent transactions and other illegal acts detected by the corporate regulator in the United States are published periodically in the Securities and Exchange Commission's (SEC) Accounting and Auditing Enforcement Releases (AAERs). The companies identified in the AAERs have been found by the SEC to have misstated their financial statements. The companies, typically relatively large, publicly listed entities, have been ordered to correct their financial statements. In each case, the SEC can take action against the company, its managers, its auditors, or other parties and initiate an investigation based on news reports or anonymous tip-offs.

Wang, Radich, and Fargher investigated the AAERs from 2005 to 2008, with a focus on those that related to accounting manipulations. They sought to determine the role of management override of internal controls relating to the preparation of financial statements. The authors were interested in which audit assertions relating to transactions

tend to be violated when management overrides the internal controls and issues fraudulent financial statements.

The authors examined financial statement fraud at the audit assertion level for 160 companies with 440 transactions alleged to involve accounting manipulations. They report that the assertions most at risk for revenue transactions are *occurrence, accuracy,* and *cut-off,* and the assertion most at risk for expense transactions is *completeness.*

Revenue fraud arose primarily from the creation of fictitious transactions such as "round-trip" and "circular" transactions. The authors provide an example of this type of revenue fraud as the series of transactions reported by a telecom company, Qwest. Qwest swapped with other telecom firms the rights to use fibre-optic strands for no legitimate business reason and immediately recognized revenue, allegedly to meet Wall Street's earnings expectations. Another common revenue fraud was the use of contingent or consignment sales to inflate revenue, where the accounts misrepresented the actual transaction, or where the underlying transaction did not even exist. These transactions violate the occurrence assertion. The cut-off assertion was violated when the companies backdated or misdated contracts to overstate revenue by recording revenue of next-period sales or services into the current year's accounts.

Wang et al. report that the majority of the fraudulent transactions in their study were non-routine transactions, which implies that they would not be detected if auditors focused solely on testing internal controls over routine transactions. They suggest that auditors need to be aware of the assertions at high risk of fraud and consider the need for additional testing to compensate for the risk of control override by management.

Sources: P. M. Dechow, W. Ge, C. R. Larson, & R. G. Sloan, "Predicting Material Accounting Misstatements," unpublished paper, University of California, Berkeley, 2009. I. Wang, R. Radich, & N. Fargher, "An Analysis of Financial Statement Fraud at the Audit Assertion Level," unpublished paper, Macquarie University, 2009.

BEFORE YOU GO ON

5.1.1 List the assertions for classes of transactions and account balances.

5.1.2 What does the accuracy assertion mean?

5.1.3 What is the auditor trying to ensure when conducting cut-off tests?

5.2 TYPES OF AUDIT EVIDENCE

② Identify and describe different types of audit evidence and define sufficient appropriate audit evidence.

evidence information gathered by the auditor that is used when forming an opinion on the fair presentation of a client's financial statements

Audit **evidence** is the information that an auditor uses when arriving at their opinion on the fair presentation of their client's financial statements (CAS 500 *Audit Evidence*). It is the responsibility of management and those charged with governance of a client to ensure that the financial statements are prepared in accordance with Canadian generally accepted accounting principles (GAAP). They are also responsible for ensuring that accurate accounting records are maintained and any potential misstatements are prevented, or detected and corrected. It is the responsibility of the auditor to gather sufficient appropriate evidence to arrive at their opinion. This involves gathering evidence to support the audit assertions for the transactions and account balances. Before considering the different types of evidence that an auditor will use, we start this section with a discussion of what is meant by the term "sufficient appropriate evidence."

5.2.1 Sufficient appropriate audit evidence

sufficient appropriate evidence quantity (sufficiency) and quality (appropriateness) of audit evidence gathered

Sufficient appropriate evidence is a core concept in auditing. Sufficiency relates to the quantity and appropriateness relates to the quality of audit evidence gathered. These concepts are interrelated, as the quality of evidence gathered will affect the quantity required.

Audit risk affects the quantity and quality of evidence gathered by an auditor during the execution stage of the audit. When there is a significant risk that an account will be misstated and the client's system of internal controls is not considered to be effective at reducing that risk, detection risk is set as low and more high-quality evidence is gathered when conducting substantive tests of that account. This relationship is shown in table 5.4.

TABLE 5.4 **High-risk account**

Audit risk	Inherent risk	Control risk	Detection risk	Evidence
	High	High	Low	More

When there is a low risk that an account will be misstated and the client's system of internal controls is considered to be adequate for that account, detection risk is set as high and less high-quality evidence is gathered when conducting substantive tests of that account. This relationship is shown in table 5.5.

TABLE 5.5 **Low-risk account**

Audit risk	Inherent risk	Control risk	Detection risk	Evidence
	Low	Low	High	Less

The risk patterns illustrated in tables 5.4 and 5.5 are extremes. The risk of material misstatement associated with most accounts falls somewhere in between. As such, the sufficiency evidence gathered when conducting substantive procedures is a matter of professional judgement and will vary from account to account and client to client. Nevertheless, there is a direct relationship between the risk of material misstatement (inherent and control risk) and the amount of evidence gathered when testing transactions and balances.

The appropriateness of audit evidence refers to its relevance and reliability. Relevance of information means there is a logical connection to the audit assertions at risk. Therefore, evidence is considered **relevant** if it provides confirmation about an assertion most at risk of material misstatement. For example, if the auditor determines that the primary assertion at risk is the existence of inventory, it would not be appropriate to spend more time gathering evidence in relation to the completeness assertion than the existence assertion. By identifying the key risk areas for the client, an auditor is able to focus on gathering more (sufficient) high-quality (appropriate) evidence where the risk of material misstatement is believed to be most significant.

Reliability refers to whether the evidence reflects the true state of the information. In terms of the reliability of information, the auditor should consider the following:

relevance extent to which information is logically connected to an assertion

reliability extent to which information reflects the true state of the information

- the source of the information—It is important for the evidence to be unbiased. Information from external third parties, such as those provided from banks and other third parties, is generally reliable, because the respondent or the person from whom the information is sought is independent of the organization.

- the expertise of the respondent—If the respondent does not understand what the confirmation letter is asking for, they will not provide a knowledgeable reply. For example, if a customer is asked to confirm their accounts receivable balance as at year end, but they confirm the balance outstanding at another date, the reliability of the confirmation may be in question.

- the consistency of the information—Evidence that is consistent from one source to another is more reliable than evidence that is inconsistent from one source to another. For example, if responses to inquiries of management and internal audit are not consistent, the reliability of the information will be reduced.

- the source of the information and whether it is produced where internal controls operate effectively—For example, if there are good controls over the payroll cycle, then employee time cards, cheque stubs, and journal entries will provide more reliable evidence than if the controls are not effective.

Cloud 9

Ian thinks he finally understands: in order to limit the risk of an inappropriate audit opinion for Cloud 9, the audit team will assess inherent risk and control risk at the assertion level for account balances and transactions. They make these assessments after gaining an understanding of the client because these risks are influenced by the client's circumstances.

If inherent and control risk are assessed as high, then the audit team will set detection risk as low. This means that they will need to gather more, better-quality evidence than if inherent and control risk are assessed as low. In addition, planning materiality is set based on the needs of the users. The lower the materiality level, the more sufficient and appropriate evidence needs to be gathered.

Suzie thinks the money spent on coffee has been well worth it!

The different types of audit evidence described in the remainder of this section are confirmations, documentary evidence, representations, verbal evidence, computational evidence, physical evidence, and electronic evidence.

5.2.2 External confirmations

CAS 505 *External Confirmations* provides guidance on the use of **external confirmations**. An external confirmation is sent directly by an auditor to a third party, who is asked to respond to the auditor on the matter(s) included in the confirmation letter. External confirmations can be sent to the client's bank, lawyers, lenders, and debtors, and third parties holding the client's inventory.

A **bank confirmation** is a request for information about the amount of cash held in the bank or in overdraft, details of any loans with the bank, details of any pledges of assets made to

external confirmation evidence obtained as a direct written response to the auditor from a third party, in paper form, or by electronic or other medium

bank confirmation a letter sent directly by an auditor to their client's bank requesting information such as the amount of cash held in the bank (or overdraft), details of any loans with the bank, and interest rates charged

guarantee loans, and interest rates charged. This information is used to confirm that the asset "cash at bank" is recorded at the appropriate amount (valuation and allocation assertion) and is in the client's name (rights and obligations assertion) and that all loans with the bank are included in the liability section of the balance sheet (completeness assertion). The bank confirmation also requests details of interest rates paid on cash deposits and term deposits, and interest rates charged on bank overdrafts and loans. This information is used when auditing interest income and interest expense items (accuracy assertion). Figure 5.1 shows a sample bank confirmation letter.

An external confirmation may also be sent to a client's suppliers and lenders (**payable confirmation**) to confirm the details of amounts owed to creditors and significant loans. Where payable confirmations are used, vendors provide details of amounts outstanding at year end (completeness and valuation and allocation assertions) and interest rates charged on those amounts (accuracy assertion). They also confirm that the amounts owed are to be paid by the client (rights and obligations assertion). Payable confirmations can only be used if an auditor is certain that the list of vendors supplied by the client is complete, as an incomplete list will not provide evidence regarding the completeness assertion. Also, as the focus is on the completeness assertion, accounts payable confirmations are usually sent to suppliers with small or zero balances (especially if there were significant balances owing in the prior year) to ensure that there are no unrecorded payables.

External confirmations can be sent to customers with credit terms (**receivable confirmation**) to verify the receivables balance. The auditor will select the specific accounts to whom they will send confirmations. Criteria used when selecting the accounts receivable customers to be sent confirmations include materiality (large trade receivables), age (overdue accounts), and location (if customers are dispersed, a selection from various locations). The primary assertion when using receivable confirmations is existence—they provide audit evidence that the credit customers exist. They also provide some evidence on ownership (rights and obligations assertion), as credit customers confirm that they owe money to the client. As they are also asked to confirm that they owe the amount outstanding at year end, very little evidence is provided regarding the valuation and allocation assertion. Credit customers only confirm the amount owing; they do not confirm their intention to pay the amount due. See figures 5.2 and 5.3 for an example accounts receivable confirmation.

External confirmations may be used when a client owns inventory that is held on its behalf in another location; that is, the inventory is held in premises not owned by the client. In this case the auditor may send a confirmation asking the third-party owner of the premises where the inventory is held to verify the description and quantity of inventory held. This type of confirmation provides audit evidence that the inventory recorded by the client exists (existence assertion), is complete (completeness assertion), and is owned by the client (rights and obligations assertion).

There are two broad types of external confirmations: positive and negative confirmations. **Positive confirmations** (figure 5.3) ask the recipient to reply in all circumstances. **Negative confirmations** (figure 5.2) ask the recipient to reply only if they disagree with the information provided. If a recipient does not respond to a negative confirmation, it is assumed that they agree with the information provided. This form of request is of limited benefit when the assertion being tested is existence. A negative confirmation may be used when an auditor has conducted detailed testing for existence using alternative procedures such as inspecting signed receiving reports. In this case, the negative confirmation is used to corroborate other evidence. Positive confirmations provide superior evidence, as a non-response from a negative confirmation request may provide false reassurance. For example, a client may record fake sales to customers that do not exist close to year end to boost revenue. A non-response from a non-existent customer may be interpreted by an auditor as confirmation that the customer agrees with the amount outstanding. In this case the conclusion would be unjustified.

When an auditor sends a receivable confirmation, they ordinarily include the amount recorded in their client's records for each accounts receivable customer to confirm. There is a risk that a customer may sign and return the confirmation to the auditor without checking the balance outstanding. As the primary assertion being tested when using this audit procedure is existence, rather than valuation and allocation, the auditor will perform other procedures to provide evidence on the valuation and allocation of the trade receivables balance. If an auditor were to send a confirmation to credit customers requesting that they provide the balance outstanding, there is a risk that credit customers will not respond, as locating the amount owed takes some effort to find, which would reduce the overall response rate and the amount of evidence available for the existence assertion.

---

payable confirmation a letter sent directly by an auditor to their client's vendor or supplier requesting information about amounts owed by the client to the vendor or supplier

---

receivable confirmation a letter sent directly by an auditor to their client's credit customers requesting information about amounts owed to the client by the debtor

---

positive confirmation a letter sent directly by an auditor to a third party, who is asked to respond to the auditor on the matter(s) included in the letter in all circumstances (that is, whether they agree or disagree with the information included in the auditor's letter)

negative confirmation a letter sent directly by an auditor to a third party, who is asked to respond to the auditor on the matter(s) included in the letter only if they disagree with the information provided

BANK CONFIRMATION

(Areas to be completed by client are marked §, while those to be completed by the financial institutions are marked †)

FINANCIAL INSTITUTION (Name, branch and full mailing address) §	CLIENT (Legal name) §
Regional Bank of Canada 1234 West Street Toronto, Ontario M5J 2X8	ABC Company Ltd. 987 South Road Toronto, Ontario M8G 3R1

The financial institution is authorized to provide the details requested herein to the below-noted firm of accountants

§ _John Smith_
Client's authorized signature

CONFIRMATION DATE § **December 31, 2015**
(All information to be provided as of this date)
(See Bank Confirmation Completion Instructions)

Please supply copy of the most recent credit facility
agreement (initial if required) § _____

1. LOANS AND OTHER DIRECT AND CONTINGENT LIABILITIES (If balances are nil, please state)

NATURE OF LIABILITY/ CONTINGENT LIABILITY †	INTEREST (Note rate per contract) RATE † DATE PAID TO †	DUE DATE †	DATE OF CREDIT FACILITY AGREEMENT †	AMOUNT AND CURRENCY OUTSTANDING †

ADDITIONAL CREDIT FACILITY AGREEMENT(S)

Note the date(s) of any credit facility agreement(s) not drawn upon and not referenced above †

2. DEPOSITS/OVERDRAFTS

TYPE OF ACCOUNT §	ACCOUNT NUMBER §	INTEREST RATE §	ISSUE DATE (If applicable)§	MATURITY DATE (If applicable)§	AMOUNT AND CURRENCY (Brackets if Overdraft) †

EXCEPTIONS AND COMMENTS
(See Bank Confirmation Completion Instructions) †

STATEMENT OF PROCEDURES PERFORMED BY FINANCIAL INSTITUTION †
The above information was completed in accordance with the Bank Confirmation Completion Instructions.

_____   _____
Authorized signature of financial institution   BRANCH CONTACT - Name and telephone number

Please mail this form directly to our chartered accountant in the enclosed addressed envelope.

Name:	Jason Power, Staff Accountant EY
Address:	222 Bay Street Toronto, Ontario M5K 1J7
Telephone:	(416) 864-1234
Fax:	(416) 864-1174

Developed by the Canadian Bankers Association and The Canadian Institute of Chartered Accountants.

FIGURE 5.1 Bank confirmation

Skyward

January 5, 2016

ACT Supply Company
456 North Avenue
Toronto, Ontario
M8G 4C9

Dear Sir or Madam:

Our auditors, EY, are auditing our financial statements and wish to obtain direct confirmation of amounts owed to us as at **December 31, 2015.** If the information is incorrect, please report the details of any discrepancies directly to our auditors in the space provided below. Then sign this request and return it in the enclosed reply envelope directly to our auditors. If no differences are reported to the auditors, this statement will be considered correct.

Our records on December 31, 2015, showed the attached list of invoices totalling $4,790 as receivable from you. Please note that these invoices may not represent the entire balance owed to us as of that date. This is not a request for payment and remittances should not be sent to EY.

Your prompt attention to this request will be appreciated.

Sincerely,

John Smith
Controller

(Please do not detach)
CONFIRMATION

The information as stipulated above by Skyward is correct except as noted below.

Signed: _____   Date: _____
Title: _____   Customer #: ACT-1
Company: _____

FIGURE 5.2 **Accounts receivable—negative confirmation**

Skyward

January 5, 2016

ACT Supply Company
456 North Avenue
Toronto, Ontario
M8G 4C9

Dear Sir or Madam:

Our auditors, EY, are auditing our financial statements and wish to obtain direct confirmation of amounts owed to us as at **December 31, 2015.** Compare the information below with your records on that date and confirm that this information agrees with your records on that date or note the details of any discrepancies in the space provided below. Then please sign this request and return it in the enclosed reply envelope directly to our auditors.

Our records on December 31, 2015, showed $87,425 as receivable from you. This is not a request for payment and remittances should not be sent to EY.

Your prompt attention to this request will be appreciated.

Sincerely,

John Smith
Controller

(Please do not detach)
CONFIRMATION

The information as stipulated above by Skyward is correct except as noted below.

Signed: _____   Date: _____
Title: _____   Customer #: ACT-1
Company: _____

FIGURE 5.3 **Accounts receivable—positive confirmation**

PROFESSIONAL ENVIRONMENT

Updating audit confirmation standards

How has technology influenced audit practice and standards? According to Daniel Goelzer, a member of the Public Company Accounting Oversight Board (PCAOB) in the United States, it has affected practice more than standards. Goelzer believes that changes to the U.S. standard on audit confirmations (AU 330) are necessary to bring it into the 21st century. Goelzer suggests that technological innovations like the Internet and e-mail have changed confirmation practice since AU 330 was written in the early 1990s.

In the U.S., the practice of audit confirmations is essentially mandatory, unlike the situation that typically prevails in the rest of the world, where confirmations are an optional procedure—a tool available for auditors to use as part of a package of audit procedures. The U.S. requirement to use confirmations dates back to a famous fraud case, McKesson Robbins, in the 1930s. More recent scandals, such as the Madoff, Satyam, and Parmalat cases, have meant that the confirmation process is back in the spotlight.

The PCAOB is still debating responses to a concept release on possible revisions to the audit confirmations standard. Public comment has been sought on whether changes are necessary, and, if they are required, how those changes would impact a new standard.

The PCAOB believes that the new confirmation standard should take into account today's sophisticated security and encryption tools for e-mail and online transactions. Specifically, some confirming parties have indicated that instead of responding to confirmation requests, they prefer to allow the auditors to have electronic access to the company's accounts so the auditor may directly check the confirming party's records. PCAOB member Steven Harris

believes that the standard should address the use and reliability of confirmations received electronically: "It should address the authenticity and accuracy of direct access to online account information," he says. In addition, auditors are continually faced with disclaimers—clauses inserted into a client's customer's reply to a confirmation request disclaiming responsibility for any inaccuracy in the information provided. In a litigious society such as that in the U.S., these disclaimers are routinely used to avoid legal liability for statements made. However, the auditor is then faced with a decision: how much weight to place on a statement that is accompanied by a disclaimer? The PCAOB has included this issue in its request for public comment on the new standard.

Following the redrafting of the Canadian Auditing Standards, paragraph A12 of CAS 505 addresses the issue of validating the source of replies received in electronic format, such as e-mail. It may be possible for the auditor to establish a secure environment for electronic responses—for example, by the use of encryption, electronic digital signatures, and procedures to verify website authenticity. However, if this is not possible and the auditor has doubts about the reliability of any form of evidence obtained through the confirmation procedure, CAS 505 requires the auditor to consider alternative procedures—for example, telephone contact with the respondent (CAS 505, para. A14).

Sources: Daniel L. Goelzer, "Statement on Consideration of Concept Release on Possible Revisions to the Standard on Audit Confirmations," Public Company Accounting Oversight Board, April 14, 2009, http://pcaobus.org; WebCPA, "PCAOB Mulls Revising Audit Confirmation Standards," April 14, 2009; S.B. Statement on Proposed Auditing Standard on Confirmation, July 13, 2010, http://pcaobus.org.

Cloud 9

Suzie explains to Ian that they can use external confirmations to gather sufficient and appropriate evidence about Cloud 9's outstanding accounts receivable balances and the existence and rights and obligations assertions. However, the confirmations will not be sufficient for valuation purposes, as a reply from a customer to confirm that the account receivable exists does not mean that the customer is going to be able to pay the balance owing when it is due. They will use other documents to provide evidence about the valuation assertion for accounts receivable.

Suzie also suggests that bank confirmations will be useful on the Cloud 9 audit for the rights and obligations, existence, and valuation assertions for bank accounts. Because they will also ask the banks to supply any information they have about any other bank accounts or loans, bank confirmations will also be useful for gathering evidence about the completeness assertion for these accounts. Suzie suggests that they do not rely on payable confirmations. This is because the biggest issue with these liabilities is discovering any omitted liabilities, not confirming the existence of the liabilities the client has already disclosed to them.

Suzie incorporates her ideas on confirmations into the draft audit plan.

5.2.3 Documentary evidence

Documentary evidence includes invoices, suppliers' statements, bank statements, minutes of meetings, correspondence, and legal agreements. It may be internally generated or externally generated. Internally generated documents are produced by the client. Externally generated

documentary evidence information that provides evidence about details recorded in a client's list of transactions (for example, invoices and bank statements)

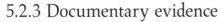

documents are generated by third parties. The persuasiveness of audit evidence varies depending on its source. This issue is explained in detail in section 5.3 of this chapter.

There are a number of ways that documentary evidence can be used during an audit. An auditor can trace details recorded in a client's accounting records to supporting (external) documents to verify the amount recorded. For example, details of the price paid for inventory may be traced to a supplier's invoice to verify the amount recorded. This provides evidence on the accuracy of the purchase price (accuracy assertion). Recorded investments may be traced to share certificates or their electronic equivalent to gain evidence that the investments exist (existence assertion) and that they are owned by the client (rights and obligations assertion).

Documents can be read and details traced to a client's accounting records and financial statements to ensure that items are included correctly (classification and understandability assertion). An auditor may ensure that all inventory confirmed as held by a third party is included in the client's records (completeness assertion). An auditor may ensure that all loans confirmed by external parties are included in the client's records (completeness assertion). Details of lease agreements can be read to ensure that leases are disclosed accurately in the body and the notes to the financial statements (classification and understandability assertion). The minutes of board meetings are read to ensure that relevant issues are adequately disclosed in the notes to the financial statements (classification and understandability assertion).

Cloud 9

An example of documentary evidence that will be useful for auditing Cloud 9's accounts receivable is cash receipts from credit customers after year end. If the customer pays the account owing at year end, there is little doubt about its valuation at year end. However, sales returns or evidence of disputes with customers during the post–year-end period provide evidence that valuation and existence are in doubt.

Also, Suzie recommends in the draft audit plan that the complex inventory transactions (importing from overseas plants with payment in U.S. dollars) can be audited through the relevant documents showing dates of shipping and arrival and details of the goods. She is particularly concerned about auditing the "goods in transit" balance using this evidence. The forward exchange contracts (used because the goods are purchased in U.S. dollars but the accounts are kept in Canadian dollars) are vital pieces of evidence that will be used to establish the correct valuation of the inventory balances, accounts payable, and cost of sales.

Sharon and Josh note in the plan that there are many other documents that will be used as evidence, including the board meeting minutes, lease agreement (for the premises), sponsorship agreements, loan agreements, and other documents supporting the accounting records.

5.2.4 Representations

CAS 501 *Audit Evidence—Specific Considerations for Selected Items* requires an auditor to gather sufficient appropriate audit evidence regarding any legal matters involving their client. Evidence is gathered from board meeting minutes, discussions with client personnel, and representation letters from the client's lawyers and management. When an auditor has reason to believe that there are legal issues that may impact the financial statements, such as the client being sued by a third party, or when a law firm is engaged by the client for the first time, a legal letter is requested from the legal firm(s) that the client deals with. An auditor will come to this conclusion after inquiries of client personnel, reading board meeting minutes, reading other documentation such as contracts and leases, reviewing legal expenses, and reading correspondence between the client and third parties.

A **legal letter** is generally sent by the client to its lawyers asking them to complete the letter and return it directly to the auditor. According to CAS 501 *Audit Evidence—Specific Considerations for Selected Items*, the legal letter can include any legal matters involving the client, and the lawyer's opinion on the client's description of any outstanding legal matters and whether the client's evaluation of those matters appears reasonable. It can include a request to provide details of any legal matters on which the lawyer is in disagreement with the client. Schedule A of CAS 501 contains examples of a request for a legal letter from a client to its lawyer. Figure 5.4 contains an example of a legal (solicitor's) letter where there are claims or possible claims.

legal letter a letter sent to a client's lawyer asking them to confirm the details of legal matters outstanding identified by management

Sandra Carson   January 5, 2016
Jones and Jones LLP
192 Park Avenue
Suite 3500
Toronto, Ontario
MJ7 2K8

Skyward Ltd. (the "Company")

Dear Ms. Carson:

In connection with the preparation and audit of our financial statements as of December 31, 2015, and for the year then ended, we have made the following evaluations of claims and possible claims with respect to which your firm's advice or representation has been sought:

Description	Evaluation
Always Right Inc. vs. Skyward Customer seeking damages of $1,000,000 for product that they claim was defectively manufactured and resulted in lost sales. At this point in time, no proceedings have commenced and Always Right has not been able to provide support that product was not damaged after shipment.	Likelihood that obligation exists is minimal and reliable estimate of any possible obligation or potential settlement cannot be determined.

Would you please advise us, as at February 14, 2016, on the following points:

(a) Are the claims and possible claims properly described?

(b) Do you consider that our evaluations are reasonable?

(c) Are you aware of any claims not listed above which are outstanding? If so, please include in your response letter the names of the parties and the amount claimed.

For your purposes in providing the information requested, your response need not include any matter involving potential losses (or gains) whose expected effects on the financial statements would be less than $25,000, unless the aggregate for all such individual amounts is more than $25,000, (except for (product liability or similar) claims which may be indicative of possible further claims which could in the aggregate exceed $25,000).

We expect to have our audit completed about February 19, 2016, so we would appreciate receiving your reply by February 15, 2016, with a specified effective date no earlier than February 14, 2016.

This inquiry is made in accordance with the Joint Policy Statement of January 1978 approved by The Canadian Bar Association and the Auditing Standards Committee of The Canadian Institute of Chartered Accountants ("CICA") and CPA Canada Auditing Guideline 46. Please address your reply, marked "Privileged and Confidential," to this company and send a signed copy of the reply directly to our auditors, Ernst & Young LLP, 222 Bay Street, Toronto, Ontario M5K 1J7.

Yours truly,

John Smith

c.c.: Ernst & Young LLP

FIGURE 5.4 **Example of a legal letter**
Source: EY, 2014

CAS 580 *Written Representations* requires that an auditor attempt to obtain written representations from their client's management. A **management representation letter** generally includes an acknowledgement that management is responsible for the preparation of the financial statements. Management is responsible for ensuring that the statements give a fair presentation of the company's financial position and comply with Canadian accounting standards. The letter will include written details of any verbal representations made by management during the course of the audit. As verbal evidence is weaker than written evidence, an auditor will seek written confirmation of any significant discussions in the management representation letter.

The management representation letter can also include an undertaking that laws and regulations have been complied with, that there have been no material frauds or errors that would impact the financial statements, and that the internal controls system is effective. The letter can acknowledge that the auditor was provided with access to all documents, records, and other evidence as requested. It can include an undertaking that the financial statements include the required disclosures in relation to related parties, share options, and contingent liabilities and that the company owns all assets listed. Appendix 2 of CAS 580 contains an example of a management representation letter. Figure 5.5 provides another example of a management representation letter.

FIGURE 5.5 **Example of a management representation letter**
Source: C·PEM 350, Completion Documents, Management Representation Letter.

FJR Construction Company

April 30, 2016 (*same date as Auditor's Report*)
To W&S Partners, Chartered Accountants

Dear W&S Partners:

This representation letter is provided in connection with your audit of the financial statements of **FJR Construction Company** for the period ended December 31, 2015, for the purpose of expressing an opinion as to whether the financial statements are presented fairly, in all material respects, in accordance with Canadian accounting standards for private enterprises.

We confirm that (to the best of our knowledge and belief, having made such inquiries as we considered necessary for the purpose of appropriately informing ourselves):

Financial Statements
· We have fulfilled our responsibilities, as set out in the terms of the audit engagement in accordance with Canadian accounting standards for private enterprises; in particular, the financial statements are fairly presented in accordance therewith.
· Significant assumptions used by us in making accounting estimates, including those measured at fair value, are reasonable.
· Related-party relationships and transactions have been appropriately accounted for and disclosed in accordance with the requirements of Canadian accounting standards for private enterprises.
· All events subsequent to the date of the financial statements and for which Canadian accounting standards for private enterprises require adjustment or disclosure have been adjusted or disclosed.
· The effects of uncorrected misstatements are immaterial, both individually and in the aggregate, to the financial statements as a whole.

Information Provided
· We have provided you with:
  – Access to all information of which we are aware that is relevant to the preparation of the financial statements such as records, documentation and other matters;

(continued)

FIGURE 5.5 **Example of a management representation letter** (continued)

Source: C·PEM 350, Completion Documents, Management Representation Letter.

> – Additional information that you have requested from us for the purpose of the audit; and
> – Unrestricted access to persons within the entity from whom you determined it necessary to obtain audit evidence.
>
> All transactions have been recorded in the accounting records and are reflected in the financial statements.
> - We have disclosed to you the results of our assessment of the risk that the financial statements may be materially misstated as a result of fraud.
> - We have disclosed to you all information in relation to fraud or suspected fraud that we are aware of and that affects the entity and involves:
>   – Management;
>   – Employees who have significant roles in internal control; or
>   – Others where the fraud could have a material effect on the financial statements.
> - We have disclosed to you all information in relation to allegations of fraud, or suspected fraud, affecting the entity's financial statements communicated by employees, former employees, analysts, regulators or others.
> - We have disclosed to you all known instances of non-compliance or suspected non-compliance with laws and regulations whose effects should be considered when preparing financial statements.
> - We have disclosed to you the identity of the entity's related parties and all the related-party relationships and transactions of which we are aware.
>
> Yours very truly,
>
> **Jose Parra**
> Chief Financial Officer
>
> **Jack Green**
> Chief Executive Officer

Cloud 9

Sharon notes in the draft audit plan that a management representation letter will be obtained toward the end of the audit to confirm all verbal discussions held up to that point. The legal letter will also be obtained toward the end of the audit to ensure that there are no pending legal cases that would complicate matters.

5.2.5 Verbal evidence

Throughout the audit, an auditor meets with client management and staff to discuss various issues. **Verbal evidence** is used when gaining an understanding of the client and its internal controls system. It can be used to corroborate other forms of evidence. Verbal evidence is documented in the auditor's working papers so that a record is kept of all key discussions with the client.

verbal evidence responses of key client personnel to auditor inquiries throughout the course of the audit

5.2.6 Computational evidence

Computational evidence is gathered when an auditor checks the mathematical accuracy of the numbers that appear in the financial statements (accuracy and valuation and allocation assertions). This involves re-adding the entries included in a client's journals and ledgers. It involves recomputing more complex calculations, such as foreign currency translation, employee benefits, interest of loans outstanding, and fair value modelling. When conducting complex recomputations, an auditor traces the amounts included in the calculations to externally prepared documentary evidence, where available, as well as checking that the formulae used are applied appropriately.

computational evidence evidence gathered by an auditor checking the mathematical accuracy of the numbers that appear in the financial statements

5.2.7 Physical evidence

physical evidence inspection of a client's tangible assets, such as its inventory and fixed assets

inspection an evidence-gathering procedure that involves checking documents and physical assets

An auditor gathers **physical evidence** through **inspection** of a client's tangible assets, such as its inventory and fixed assets. An auditor traces recorded amounts to assets to gain evidence that the assets exist (existence assertion). For example, an auditor will select inventory items from client ledgers for testing and trace the quantities recorded to the physical items, and then count the items on hand to check that the quantities recorded are accurate. This test is done to ascertain whether the quantities recorded are accurate and that assets physically exist.

An auditor also traces details of tangible assets on hand back to the recorded amount (completeness assertion). For example, an auditor selects physical inventory items, counts the number on hand, and traces them back to client records to make sure that the records are complete. This test is done to ascertain whether quantities on hand are accurately included in the client's records.

An auditor inspects a client's physical assets to ascertain whether machinery is functioning, inventory appear to be in good repair, and fixed assets are well looked after. This evidence is used to determine whether assets should be written down below current book value (valuation and allocation assertion). If inventory appears dusty, perhaps the client is having difficulty selling those goods. If machinery is not being used, perhaps it is obsolete or redundant. If the auditor does not have the expertise to ascertain the value of a client's assets, they may ask an independent expert for some help. The process for using the work of an expert is discussed in section 5.4 of this chapter.

Cloud 9

Suzie will head the team gathering evidence about inventory. There are some issues with Cloud 9's inventory controls, including difficulties in delivering merchandise from the warehouse to the store in a timely manner. Suzie is also concerned about the thefts at Cloud 9's retail store. Although Cloud 9's management has been very open in disclosing the thefts, Suzie is concerned about what this means for the quality of the inventory controls. She plans to inspect inventory and gather physical evidence of its existence and quality (because obsolescence is another major concern).

Sharon will also assign a team to inspect the furniture and equipment and the leasehold improvements, as there have been some major additions this year (because of the new store opening).

Ian is a little concerned about being asked to gather physical evidence. "I don't understand how physical evidence can sometimes relate to the existence assertion and at other times relate to the completeness assertion. How do I know when the evidence relates to one assertion and not the other?" he asks Suzie.

Suzie tries to explain that it depends on the process. If you start with the accounting records and then gather physical evidence to support the records, you are gathering evidence about existence. For example, the furniture and equipment ledger account has a record stating that Cloud 9 owns a photocopier. The record contains information about brand, size, and other details. Can you trace the records to the physical item—that is, can you find the photocopier in the office? If so, you have evidence that it exists. (You would also do separate tests for its valuation and rights and obligations.) However, if you start with the photocopier, for example, you see a photocopier in the office, and your question is then whether the item is in the accounting records—that is, are the accounting records complete? In this case you start with the physical item and trace it to the records. If the photocopier is entered in the ledger (furniture and equipment), you have evidence about the completeness of the accounting records.

5.2.8 Electronic evidence

electronic evidence data held on a client's computer, files sent by e-mail to the auditor, and items scanned and faxed

Electronic evidence includes data held on a client's computer, files sent by e-mail to the auditor, and items scanned and faxed. Transactions are commonly initiated and stored electronically. They leave no paper trail. To access the details of these transactions, an auditor must access their client's computer system, where details are kept. It is now common for companies to send their auditors copies of their accounting records and files by e-mail. The auditor then searches for corroborating evidence to verify the amounts included in those files.

If a company initiates and completes a transaction electronically, its auditor will use the electronic evidence to establish that the transaction occurred (occurrence assertion). For example, a client e-mails a supplier placing an order; the supplier replies via e-mail confirming that the order has been received; the supplier provides details regarding the estimated delivery date and the amount to be invoiced upon delivery of the goods; the client's receiving department notifies the accounts department that the goods ordered have been received; finally, the client initiates an electronic transfer of funds from its bank account to its supplier's bank account.

The extent to which an auditor can rely on electronic evidence produced by their client's computer system will depend a great deal on the internal controls in place. As discussed in chapter 3, IT creates risks within a client's accounting system. An auditor must consider those unique risks and assess the effectiveness of their client's internal controls in mitigating those risks. Chapter 7 contains a discussion of the methods used by an auditor when testing their client's internal controls, including those that protect data created and stored electronically.

Cloud 9

Josh is an expert on the computer systems Cloud 9 uses to process transactions, and the audit plan will show him as leading the team assessing the controls and performing the associated tests.

BEFORE YOU GO ON

5.2.1 What is a bank confirmation?

5.2.2 List three things that may be included in a management representation letter.

5.2.3 Which assertion is tested when an auditor traces details of tangible assets on hand back to the recorded amount?

5.3 PERSUASIVENESS OF AUDIT EVIDENCE

As detailed earlier, when an auditor accesses their client's records, they then search for **evidence** to prove that recorded amounts are accurate. Evidence relates to each of the headings used in the previous section of this chapter. Specifically, an auditor verifies amounts recorded in their client's records using confirmations, documentary evidence, representations, verbal evidence, computational evidence, physical evidence, and electronic evidence.

There are three broad categories of corroborating evidence. Each category varies in its persuasiveness. The categories are internally generated evidence, externally generated evidence held by the client, and externally generated evidence sent directly to the auditor. Each category will now be discussed in turn.

 Determine the persuasiveness of audit evidence.

evidence information gathered to confirm amounts recorded in client records

5.3.1 Internally generated evidence

Internally generated evidence held by the client includes records of cheques sent, copies of invoices and statements sent to customers, purchase orders, company documentation regarding policies and procedures, contracts, minutes of meetings, journals, ledgers, trial balances, spreadsheets, worksheets, reconciliations, calculations, and computations. This evidence may be held electronically (soft copy) or in paper form (hard copy). Auditors document in their working papers details of their meetings with client management and staff to gain an understanding of the client's business and system of internal controls. As previously stated, internally generated evidence is the least persuasive, as it can only be used to verify that a client has accurately converted this information into the financial statements. That is, as the client generates and holds this evidence, it is possible that evidence may be manipulated or omitted. Figure 5.6 shows common types of internally generated documents used as evidence by the auditor.

internally generated evidence information created by the client (for example, customer invoices, purchase orders)

The following is a list of internally generated documents frequently used by the auditor as evidence. Sample documents are provided in Appendix A.

Trial balance A listing of the accounts and balances at the end of the accounting period. The balances are used to prepare the financial statements.

General ledger Transaction details are posted to the general ledger, with each general ledger account reflecting the account opening balance, the transactions processed during the period, and the ending balance. The ending balance is reflected in the trial balance.

Sub-ledger Organizes accounting information by characteristic. Sub-ledgers are commonly used for accounts receivable, accounts payable, inventory, and payroll. They sort data by such things as customer, supplier, inventory classification, and employee, making it easier to organize information. For example, an accounts receivable sub-ledger will show the balance outstanding by customer and by days outstanding. The balance in the sub-ledger and the related general ledger control account should agree.

Master files Where the permanent information is maintained. For example, the accounts receivable master file includes customer names, addresses, contact details, and credit limits.

Purchase requisition A request for goods that is prepared and submitted to the purchasing department.

Purchase order Prepared once goods have been sourced, and serves as authorization for the purchase. Indicates the supplier, date, items ordered, quantity, and agreed-upon purchase price.

Receiving report Serves as proof that goods ordered were received, and notes the quantity, date, and receiver.

Invoice Indicates the amount owing for goods received.

Shipping document Sent with goods being shipped, indicating who the receiving company is, what is being shipped, and the shipping terms.

Remittance advice Sent with payment, indicating the invoice being paid.

FIGURE 5.6 **Internally generated evidence commonly used by the auditor**

5.3.2 Externally generated evidence held by the client

externally generated evidence information created by a third party (for example, supplier statements, bank statements)

Externally generated evidence held by the client includes supplier invoices and statements, customer orders, bank statements, contracts, lease agreements, and tax assessments. These sources of evidence are quite persuasive, as they are produced by third parties. It is, however, possible for the client to manipulate these documents, which reduces their reliability to the auditor. Also, if the client provides the auditor with photocopies of information from these external sources, rather than originals, the reliability is reduced.

5.3.3 Externally generated evidence sent directly to the auditor

Externally generated evidence sent directly to the auditor includes bank confirmations, customers' confirmations, correspondence with the client's lawyers, including confirmations and representations, and expert valuations. These sources of evidence are considered to be the most reliable and best quality, as they are independent of the client. As this evidence is generated by third parties and sent directly to the auditor, the client does not have an opportunity to alter it. Further, externally generated evidence is considered the most persuasive when the source of that evidence is considered to be reliable, trustworthy, and independent of the client.

Cloud 9

Whenever Suzie's draft audit plan shows the team using inquiry (or verbal evidence), it also includes additional requirements to obtain evidence from another source. This is because the evidence obtained from the client is less persuasive than evidence gathered directly by an auditor or externally sourced evidence that has passed through the client's hands.

5.3.1 What are the three board categories of corroborating evidence?

5.3.2 What is the risk when using evidence that is held by the client?

5.3.3 Which is the least persuasive evidence?

5.4 USING THE WORK OF AN EXPERT

It may be necessary to engage the services of an **expert** if an auditor does not have the requisite skills and knowledge to assess the validity of an account or a transaction. An expert is someone with the skills, knowledge, and experience required to aid the auditor when gathering evidence. An expert may be a member of the audit firm who is not a member of the audit team, an employee of the client, or a person independent of both the audit firm and its client. Experts commonly used by auditors include valuators for things such as real estate, works of art, collections, and jewellery, and actuaries to calculate liabilities related to employee future benefits and oil and gas reserves.

 Explain the issues to consider when using the work of an expert.

expert someone with the skills, knowledge, and experience required to aid the auditor when gathering sufficient appropriate evidence

CAS 620 *Using the Work of an Auditor's Expert* provides guidelines for auditors when using the work of an expert. An auditor first assesses whether an expert is required. If it is decided that an expert is required, an auditor then determines the scope of work to be carried out. When selecting an expert to complete the work, an auditor assesses the competence and capability of the expert to do so and their objectivity. Once an expert has completed the work, an auditor assesses the work and draws conclusions based on the assessment. The ultimate responsibility for drawing conclusions based on gathered evidence rests with the auditor. Each of the stages in using an expert is now discussed.

5.4.1 Assessing the need to use an expert

When gathering evidence, an auditor may decide that they do not have the expertise necessary to test and evaluate the accuracy of reported information. They may decide that they require assistance in the form of an expert opinion or report to corroborate other evidence obtained. For example, an appraiser may be engaged to provide an opinion on the value of a client's property, a geologist may be engaged to evaluate the quantity and quality of mineral deposits, a vintner may be engaged to assess the quality and value of wine stocks, or an actuary may be engaged to verify insurance premiums.

The need to engage the services of an expert depends on the knowledge of the audit team, the significance and complexity of the item being assessed, and the availability of appropriate alternative corroborating evidence. If the audit team has experience with the item being audited and can draw on their knowledge from previous audits of that client or similar companies in the same industry, there is less need to use an expert. The greater the risk of material misstatement of the item under consideration, the more likely an auditor will turn to an expert for their advice. To summarize, the less knowledge an audit team has of the item under consideration, the greater the risk of material misstatement and the less corroborating evidence available, the more likely an auditor will conclude that an expert opinion is required.

5.4.2 Determining the scope of the work to be carried out

Once it has been determined that an expert opinion is required, the scope of the work to be carried out is determined by the auditor and communicated to the expert. This involves setting the nature, timing, and extent of work to be completed by the expert. It is important for the auditor to be involved in setting the scope of the work required, as the judgement of the expert forms part of the audit evidence upon which the auditor forms their audit opinion.

Written instructions to an expert can cover the issues that the expert is to report upon, such as the market price of properties owned by the client; the details to be included in the report, such as the computations used in arriving at the expert's opinion; the sources of data to be used, such as market interest rates or market prices of shares; clarification of the way that the auditor intends to use the information included in the expert's report; and notice of the requirement that the expert's report and the data used in compiling the report must remain confidential.

5.4.3 Assessing the competence and capability of the expert

Before contacting an expert, an auditor assesses their capacity to complete the work required. This involves an evaluation of the expert's qualifications as a member of a relevant professional (or similar) body. The reputation of the expert within their field and the extent of their experience in providing the type of opinion or report sought by the auditor are also assessed. It is important that the expert's knowledge and experience be appropriate.

5.4.4 Assessing the objectivity of the expert

Objectivity refers to the ability to form an opinion or arrive at a conclusion without the influence of personal preferences. An expert is expected to be more objective if they are not associated with the client. An association will exist when the expert is an employee of the company or is connected with the client in some other way. (For example, the expert is related to one of the key personnel of the client or financially linked with the client.)

When an expert is an employee of the client or is in some other way connected with the client, an auditor assesses the objectivity of the expert with reference to their professional status, their reputation, and the auditor's prior experience with the expert. If an expert's opinion has proven to be accurate in the past, it increases the reliability the auditor may give the expert's opinion in the current audit. Nevertheless, the less independent the expert is from the client, the more corroborating evidence the auditor will require.

5.4.5 Assessing the expert's report

It is important that an expert's report be written in such a way that an auditor, who is not an expert in the field being reported on, can understand the technical content of the report. The report should detail each stage of the process used in arriving at the overall opinion or conclusion of the report. It should include information about the data sources or estimation models used or the calculations conducted. The auditor assesses the appropriateness of the data sources used—it is essential that the expert use data sources that are reputable and reliable. The auditor assesses the consistency of any assumptions made with those made in prior years and with other known information. The auditor assesses the consistency of information included in the expert's report with their understanding of the client. Finally, the auditor assesses the consistency of the conclusions drawn with corroborating evidence gathered by the audit team.

5.4.6 Responsibility for the conclusion

The responsibility for arriving at an overall conclusion regarding the fair presentation of a client's financial statements rests with the auditor. When an auditor decides to use an expert, that responsibility is not reduced in any way. It is the responsibility of the auditor to assess the quality of the evidence provided by an expert and determine whether it is reliable and objective. An auditor does this by following the process outlined above. They will determine the need for an expert, the scope of the expert's work, and the competence and objectivity of the expert. Finally, the auditor will assess the quality of the expert's report and the reliability of the information included in it.

Cloud 9

Suzie will take responsibility for obtaining an expert opinion on the derivatives. She knows that W&S Partners has other staff (who are not part of the audit team) who can provide additional expertise. However, because she believes the accounts are so material to the audit and derivatives have become such a big issue in audits in recent years, she deems that an external expert's opinion is also required. She has some experience using a derivatives expert on prior audits of clients in the footwear and clothing industry, and she also plans to ask Jo Wadley (the partner) to recommend a suitable expert.

Suzie plans to investigate any possible connections between the expert and Cloud 9 that could adversely impact the expert's independence before engaging him or her for this audit.

PROFESSIONAL ENVIRONMENT

Working with IT experts

Specialist IT auditors are often used in audits of clients with complex information technology (IT) environments because the effective audit of the IT systems contributes to overall audit quality. Large audit firms usually have such specialists within the firm, but smaller audit firms could be forced to engage external IT consultants for this part of a financial statement audit. In general, reliance on an IT specialist is appropriate when the financial statement auditor complies with the conditions of CAS 620, *Using the Work of an Auditor's Expert*.

If the IT expert and the financial statement auditor do not work well together, audit quality can be impaired. For this reason, researchers have investigated the factors that affect the way that financial statement auditors work with specialist IT auditors.

Brazel reviewed the research evidence and drew the following conclusions. First, responses from financial statement auditors in the United States who were surveyed about their experiences with IT auditors indicated that they believe IT auditors' competence levels vary in practice. Financial statement auditors also said that IT auditors appear to be overconfident in their abilities in some settings, and questioned the value provided by IT auditors to the financial statement audit.

Second, Brazel suggests that the research shows that both financial statement auditors' IT ability and experience and the IT auditor's competence affect how these two professions interact on an audit engagement. This indicates that audit firms need to ensure that staff training and scheduling produce appropriate combinations of financial statement auditors and IT auditors on an engagement.

Finally, Brazel argues that the research findings mean that auditors need to consider the implications of finding a balance between greater computer-assisted audit technique (CAAT) training for financial statement auditors and greater use of IT specialists for overall audit efficiency and effectiveness.

The role of IT audit specialists could grow to become more than a support function for auditors. Some researchers suggest that in e-businesses, the external financial auditor's authority will be challenged by IT audit specialists because of technological changes and their impact on auditing. In e-businesses, economic transactions are captured, measured, and reported on a real-time basis without either internal human intervention or paper documentation.

Auditing is likely to become more real-time and continuous to reflect the pattern of the transactions and traditional auditors should be willing and able to adapt to the new environment.

Other developments, such as reporting using XBRL (eXtensible Business Reporting Language), provide challenges for auditors as they have to adapt their techniques and approaches to audit financial information that is disaggregated and tagged. Users can extract and analyze XBRL data directly without re-entry and the tag provides additional information about the calculation and source of the data. This means that auditors have to recognize that their clients are reporting financial data with different levels of information and that users might have greater expectations of the data.

Source: J. F. Brazel, "How Do Financial Statement Auditors and IT Auditors Work Together?" *The CPA Journal,* November 2008.

BEFORE YOU GO ON

5.4.1 What factors may influence an auditor's decision on the need to use an expert?

5.4.2 How might an auditor assess the capacity of an expert?

5.4.3 Why is it important that an expert's report include details of data sources used?

5.5 USING THE WORK OF ANOTHER AUDITOR

CAS 600 *Special Considerations—Audits of Group Financial Statements (Including the Work of Component Auditors)* provides guidance when using the work of another audit firm. The auditor who is responsible for signing the audit report (the **group engagement partner**) may need to rely on evidence provided by another auditor for certain components of a client's financial statement. This occurs when a client operates in a number of locations, has divisions or subsidiaries spread around the country or the globe, or has significant assets in other locations.

When making a client acceptance or continuance decision, an auditor will consider their capacity to undertake the audit. They should also consider the proportion of the financial statements for which they will have to rely on another auditor (**component auditor**). The group engagement partner's firm should audit the majority of a client's financial statements and be knowledgeable about the components of the financial statements that they do not audit themselves. If this is not the case, the firm should not accept or continue to audit the client.

When assigning work to a component auditor, the group engagement partner will consider the capacity of the other auditor to undertake the work. The group engagement partner will also

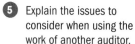 Explain the issues to consider when using the work of another auditor.

group engagement partner the auditor responsible for signing the audit report

component auditor an auditor who, at the request of the group engagement team, performs work on financial information related to a component for the group audit consider the reputation of the component auditor and ensure that they are a member of a reputable professional body. It is the responsibility of the group engagement partner to ensure that the work completed by a component auditor meets the group engagement partner's requirements and standards.

CAS 600 sets out the responsibilities of the group engagement partner when using the work of a component auditor. The group engagement partner determines the work to be conducted by a component auditor. The two auditors may discuss the detailed procedures to be used and the group engagement partner then reviews the main conclusions drawn in the working papers of the component auditor. The extent of review of the component auditor's work depends on a number of factors. The group engagement partner will spend more time if the component of the client's financial statements being audited by a component auditor is material and/or at risk of material misstatement. The group engagement partner will spend less time if the component auditor has a good reputation and/or has done audit work for the group engagement partner in the past.

The group engagement partner uses the evidence provided by a component auditor when drawing a final conclusion on the fair presentation of a client's financial statements. The findings of a component auditor on a component of the financial statements will be placed in the context of the audit as a whole. If the group engagement partner is concerned about the conclusions arrived at by a component auditor, they will discuss the findings with the component auditor. They may also discuss the implications of those findings with those charged with governance at the client to gain a more complete understanding of the component of the financial statements audited by the component auditor. If the group engagement partner decides that the conclusions arrived at by the component auditor indicate a material misstatement in the component audited, and if the impact of the misstatement is material to the financial statements taken as a whole, the group engagement partner will consider issuing a modified audit opinion.

If the group engagement partner is concerned that a component auditor has not been able to gather sufficient appropriate audit evidence regarding the component of the financial statements audited, he or she will ask that further evidence be gathered. If the component auditor cannot access sufficient evidence, the engagement partner will consider issuing a modified audit opinion due to a scope limitation. This will occur when the group engagement partner is unable to obtain additional evidence on the elements of the component audited by a component auditor.

Cloud 9

Sharon knows that Cloud 9 Inc.'s auditor completed some work that was relevant to Cloud 9 before W&S Partners was appointed to the Cloud 9 audit. She has not yet seen these audit findings and does not know whether they will affect their work. She is keen to see them because she believes that some of the findings relate to the inventory management software system (Swift). Because they don't yet have enough information to make a judgement about the usefulness of the other auditor's work, Sharon decides to include in the plan some time for a discussion between the partner (Jo Wadley) and the Cloud 9 management to discuss the other auditor's findings, and whether the audit team can have access to these findings.

BEFORE YOU GO ON

5.5.1   Who is the group engagement partner?

5.5.2   What are some of the factors that a group engagement partner will consider when assigning work to a component auditor?

5.5.3   If the group engagement partner believes that the component auditor has not gathered sufficient appropriate audit evidence, what kind of audit report may be issued?

5.6 EVIDENCE-GATHERING PROCEDURES

The evidence-gathering procedures described in this section are carried out at various stages of the audit, when planning, gaining an understanding of the client, gaining an understanding of a client's system of internal controls, testing those controls, conducting detailed substantive testing, and drawing the final conclusions. CAS 500 provides guidelines, summarized below, on the primary evidence-gathering procedures used by auditors.

Confirmations generally provide evidence that items such as cash and accounts receivable exist (existence assertion). As previously discussed, external confirmations are written inquiries sent by the auditor directly to a third party, who is asked to respond to the auditor on the matter included in the confirmation letter. As confirmations are costly, they will be used when alternative evidence is limited.

Inspection involves examining records and documents and physically examining assets. An auditor will inspect records and documents for a variety of reasons. When testing controls, an auditor will inspect documents for evidence that, for example, calculations have been checked, balances have been reconciled, inputs have been agreed to outputs, and management has authorized significant purchases. Records and documents are inspected when conducting substantive testing to check, for example, the dates of transactions (cut-off assertion), that purchases were made by the client (rights and obligations assertion), and that a transaction occurred (occurrence assertion).

Tangible assets are physically inspected to provide evidence that they exist (existence assertion) and appear to be in good repair or are damaged or past their use-by date (valuation and allocation assertion). When a client conducts an inventory count, the auditor will attend and perform test counts (existence and completeness assertions).

Client staff are observed undertaking various procedures when there is no other way of establishing that a process is being used by the client. For example, an auditor will observe the opening of mail and the conduct of an inventory count to determine whether the appropriate procedures are being followed. Importantly, **observation** only provides evidence of a process at the time the auditor observes it being carried out. An auditor will need to determine whether there is evidence that the procedures observed have been applied consistently throughout the period under audit.

Inquiry is used when gaining an understanding of the client and to corroborate other evidence gathered throughout the audit. The results of inquiries of client personnel and third parties are documented by the auditor. If the evidence is particularly important, an auditor may document that information more formally and ask the other party to the discussion to sign an agreement that the auditor has recorded the discussion accurately.

Recalculations are used to check the mathematical accuracy of client files and records. This will involve checking additions and more complex computations. Simple additions can be checked using CAATs, where client data are copied into an auditor's computer and additions are recalculated using the auditor's software package. More complex calculations will be recalculated individually.

Re-performance means following a process used by a client. When testing controls, client procedures are re-performed to check that controls are effective. When conducting substantive testing, client estimations are re-performed to verify amounts calculated by the client. For example, when testing the allowance for doubtful accounts, an auditor will re-perform the aging of the accounts receivable to arrive at an estimated allowance amount.

Analytical procedures are used to appraise relationships between financial and non-financial information. During the planning stage of the audit, unusual fluctuations are identified. During the execution stage of the audit, analytical procedures are used to evaluate the information included in the financial statements (substantive analytical procedures). For example, hospital ward revenue can be estimated by counting the number of beds in the wards and then multiplying by the average occupancy rate and the amount charged per day. At the final review stage of the audit, analytical procedures are used to assess whether the financial statements reflect the auditor's understanding of the client.

6 Describe the evidence-gathering procedures most often used by auditors.

inspection an evidence-gathering procedure that involves examining records and documents, and physically examining assets

observation an evidence-gathering procedure that involves watching a procedure being carried out by another party

inquiry an evidence-gathering procedure that involves asking questions verbally or in written form to gain an understanding of various matters throughout the audit

recalculation an evidence-gathering procedure that involves checking the mathematical accuracy of client records

re-performance an evidence-gathering procedure that involves redoing processes conducted by the client

analytical procedures an evaluation of financial information by studying plausible relationships among both financial and non-financial data

BEFORE YOU GO ON

5.6.1 Why might an auditor inspect documents when testing controls?

5.6.2 Provide some examples of how an auditor might use observation as part of their evidence-gathering procedures.

5.6.3 At which stage(s) of an audit will an auditor utilize a re-performance procedure? Explain.

5.7 DRAWING CONCLUSIONS

7 Explain how auditors arrive at a conclusion based upon the evidence gathered.

Sufficient appropriate audit evidence must be gathered to enable an auditor to draw a conclusion on which to base their opinion regarding the fair presentation of the client's financial statements (CAS 500). The decision as to what constitutes sufficient appropriate audit evidence is a matter of professional judgement, as it is based upon an auditor's understanding of their client and the significant risks identified when planning the audit and evidence gathered when executing the audit (CAS 315 *Identifying and Assessing the Risks of Material Misstatement through Understanding the Entity and Its Environment*; CAS 330 *The Auditor's Responses to Assessed Risks*).

If an auditor believes that a client has internal controls that can reduce the likelihood of a material misstatement for an identified risk, they will test those controls. This means that evidence will be gathered to establish whether the internal controls are effective. Details of tests of controls will be discussed in chapter 7. Once testing of controls is complete, an auditor will gather further evidence through their substantive testing of transactions and balances.

If an auditor decides that a client does not have in place appropriate controls for the identified risk, an auditor will adopt a substantive approach. The auditor will increase their reliance on evidence gathered through their detailed substantive tests of transactions and account balances. Details of substantive testing will be discussed in chapters 8 to 12.

After gathering all of the required evidence through their tests of controls and substantive testing, an auditor will form an opinion regarding the fair presentation of the client's financial statements. Chapter 13 includes a detailed discussion of the process used when drawing an overall conclusion at the completion of the audit.

Cloud 9

Suzie and Ian have already begun gathering evidence by performing the analytical procedures on Cloud 9's interim results and prior period's statements. Further evidence gathering at the planning stage will be performed by Josh and Sharon when they begin their assessment of the internal controls system by inspecting the relevant documents. They will also gather evidence from observing personnel performing their duties and making inquiries of members of Cloud 9's staff and management. In addition, Jo Wadley held discussions with the previous auditors (Ellis & Associates) before accepting the client. The record of these discussions, plus others that Jo Wadley has held with the Cloud 9 management, are already in the evidence files.

Ian has some questions about the evidence; in particular, why the audit team is bothering to gather verbal evidence, which has low persuasiveness. Suzie explains that all forms of evidence have their limitations. Observation is useful to see how staff perform their tasks (as opposed to what the manuals say they should be doing), but people often "behave" better when they are being watched. Documents can be lost or altered, or misinterpreted, and not everything is written down. Electronic evidence is hard to audit if the system does not have a "hack-proof" audit trail. Signatures on documents do not mean that the author actually read the document properly; people can pre- or post-date documents. The auditor has to judge the appropriateness and sufficiency of the evidence by considering it as a whole and be prepared to follow up any problems or discrepancies until any doubts are satisfactorily resolved.

BEFORE YOU GO ON

5.7.1 How does an auditor decide how much evidence is sufficient?

5.7.2 What will an auditor do if they believe that a client has internal controls that can reduce the likelihood of a material misstatement?

5.7.3 What will an auditor do if they decide that a client does not have in place appropriate controls for the identified risk?

5.8 DOCUMENTATION—AUDIT WORKING PAPERS

CAS 230 *Audit Documentation* requires an auditor to document each stage of the audit in their **working papers** to provide a record of work completed and evidence gathered in forming their audit opinion. The documentation includes the names of the preparers of the documentation, as well as the names of the reviewers of the work performed by the preparers. Documentation is cross-referenced between working papers that summarize the components of an account balance and working papers that provide details of the testing of that balance.

An auditor will document each stage of the audit and the procedures used. During the planning stage of an audit, an auditor will document their understanding of the client, the risks identified, analytical procedures used to aid in risk identification, their materiality assessment, their understanding of the client's system of internal controls, their understanding of the client's information technology, related parties identified, and any going concern matters. During the execution stage of the audit, an auditor will document their audit program, details of tests undertaken, copies of significant documents sighted, correspondence with the client's lawyers and bankers, confirmations received from accounts receivable customers, and inquiries of management.

Documentation will vary from client to client. It will depend upon, for example, the audit procedures used, the risks identified, the extent of judgement used, the persuasiveness of the evidence gathered, the nature and extent of exceptions noted, and the audit methodology utilized (CAS 230, para. A2).

An audit working paper generally includes:

- the client name
- the period under audit
- a title describing the contents of the working paper
- a file reference indicating where the working paper fits in the audit file
- initials identifying the preparer of the working paper together with the date the working paper was prepared
- initials identifying the reviewer(s) of the working paper together with the date(s) the working paper was reviewed
- cross-referencing between working papers indicating where further work and evidence is summarized elsewhere

Working papers are used to document the details of each audit. The two main files held for each client are the permanent file and the current file. The permanent file includes documents that pertain to a client for more than one audit. The current file includes the details of work completed and evidence gathered that relate to the current audit.

5.8.1 Permanent file

The **permanent file** includes client information and documentation that apply to more than one audit. The information included in the permanent file is checked and updated at the beginning of each audit. The permanent file contains the client's head office address, other locations (where relevant), and contact details (telephone, fax, and e-mail). Key personnel are detailed, and an organizational chart will also often be included in the permanent file. A client's organizational chart includes details of key roles within the organization (such as the CEO) and the names of the people who undertake those roles. The file may also include the details of the client's bank(s) and lawyer(s).

The permanent file will include copies of long-term contracts and agreements. These documents will be used to calculate interest payable on outstanding long-term loans, and will enable the assessment of any lease obligations. Debt covenants will be included in the permanent file. An auditor can check the details of these agreements to assess their client's compliance with covenants. If a client has long-term commitments with customers and suppliers, an auditor will include the relevant documentation in the permanent file. Key long-term investments will be described, including the details of the broker used for these transactions.

The permanent file will include details of the client's board directors and its subcommittees (such as the audit committee). It will include the minutes of significant meetings held by the client, such as its board of directors meetings. It may include details of bonus and option schemes for senior client staff.

 8 Describe how auditors document the details of evidence gathered in working papers.

working papers paper or electronic documentation of the audit created by the audit team as evidence of the work completed

permanent file file that contains client information that is relevant for more than one audit

The permanent file will detail a client's principal accounting policies and methodologies. Prior financial statements and audit reports will be included. Details of prior analytical procedures will be included and added to so that the auditor can observe changing trends. Flowcharts and narratives detailing a client's system of internal controls will be included and amended as required during the planning stage of each audit.

Reports sent to the client during previous audits will be included in the permanent file. For example, management letters that detail deficiencies in internal controls identified by the auditor in previous years will be included and referred to by the auditor. An auditor will read these reports and discuss their contents with the client's management.

Cloud 9

Cloud 9 Ltd.'s permanent file contains the basic information about the company (that is, address and key senior staff and their employment contracts) plus the copy of the engagement letter appointing W&S Partners and stating the scope of the audit. Sharon and Suzie have gathered copies of some of the relevant agreements and will add these and more (that is, those relating to leases, sponsorship, and loans) to the permanent file.

5.8.2 Current file

current file file that contains client information that is relevant for the duration of one audit

The **current file** includes client information and documentation that apply to the current audit. Contents of the current file will vary from client to client, depending on the accounts in the client's financial statements and the client's activities. The current file will include the details of all testing and evidence gathered in preparing the audit report.

The current file will also include correspondence between the auditor and the client and the client's bankers and lawyers that pertain to the current audit period. Correspondence with other auditors, experts, and relevant third parties will be included. The engagement letter will be included in the current file, along with the management letter, detailing any deficiencies uncovered in the client's system of internal controls. Representation letters and confirmation letters may also be included in the current file.

The current file will include extracts from the minutes of meetings, such as the board of directors meetings that pertain to the current audit. The file will include details of the audit planning process and the audit program, as well as detailed descriptions of evidence gathered, testing conducted, and audit procedures performed. It will detail the analytical procedures, tests of controls, and detailed substantive testing undertaken, as well as the conclusions drawn at the completion of testing. The current file includes testing of any subsequent events and a copy of the final audit opinion.

Overview of working papers

There are many different ways of preparing working papers, although most have common elements. The working papers that follow are prepared by W&S Partners using common auditing conventions and referencing. Table 5.6 lists common notations found in audit working papers.

Working papers are prepared and stored electronically. Once the audit is concluded, any hard copy working papers are archived in a hard copy file (in the filing room) and soft copy files and working papers are archived in a location that keeps them secure for the required record-keeping period (up to 10 years).

Each audit will have a unique title for ease of identification, which will include the client name and the year end of the financial statements being audited. Each current file created for an audit will be divided into unique sections with each section representing a different element of the audit, typically a group of similar accounts. Each section comprises a series of working papers that provide evidence of the work conducted on the audit. Working papers generally include details such as the client name, the period under audit, a file reference, cross-references to other parts of the audit file, details of the testing conducted, comments and conclusions drawn, and details of the preparer (generally a junior member of the audit team for routine audit tasks or a senior for complex audit tasks) and reviewers (senior members, managers, and partners).

COMMON WORKING PAPER NOTATIONS	MEANING
PY	Agreed to prior year working paper file
∧	Footed, summed down a column
⋏	Crossfooted, summed across a row
TB	Agreed to trial balance
G/L	Agreed to general ledger
e	Recalculated
CK	Agreed to cheque
I	Agreed to invoice
m	Not material
NFWCN	No further work considered necessary
PBC	Prepared by client

TABLE 5.6 **Common working paper notations**

Examples of working papers

The following are a series of fictional working papers prepared by W&S Partners for a client, New Millennium Ecoproducts. The working paper examples are for the audit period ending December 31, 2015. New Millennium Ecoproducts was created by its founders, brothers Tomas and Charles Tyshynski, avid environmentalists. The company's vision is to produce everyday products in a sustainable way, providing an affordable alternative for environmentally conscientious customers. New Millennium operates from three locations and produces a wide range of household products, which it sells to supermarkets and specialty stores.

At the front of every audit file is a copy of the client's trial balance. The trial balance is referenced into the appropriate lead schedule throughout the audit file. Every balance sheet account will have a lead schedule that includes the summary of the account balance and typically also includes a summary of the work performed, any material issues or audit adjustments identified, and the overall conclusion relating to that account balance. Every audit section is assigned a title. Section titles vary between firms; however, most firms use letters and/or numbers to denote different sections. For example, for W&S Partners, accounts receivable is labelled the C section, inventory accounts is labelled the F section, property, plant, and equipment is labelled the U section; accounts payable is labelled the BB section BB-Lead schedule; and so on.

The first working paper example is the accounts receivable C-Lead schedule in figure 5.7.

In the top left corner of the lead schedule is the client name, period end, and working paper title. The reference for this working paper is provided in the top right-hand corner (C-Lead) along with details of the working paper preparer and reviewer(s) with the dates prepared and reviewed.

Details of the accounts receivable follow. The lead schedule notes the following for each item listed:

- account number, per the client records
- account name, per the client records
- preadjusted (preliminary) balance per the client's trial balance (TB), any adjustments, and the adjusted current year balance
- the prior year balance, per the prior year audit file (PY)
- variance and percentage change: the calculated difference between the prior year and current year balances
- the cross-reference to the working paper where supporting evidence is kept for each balance

The detailed audit work on the accounts receivable accounts is documented on subsequent working papers and referenced to the lead schedule. For example, the audit work on the accounts receivable account number 1050 is documented on working paper C-10. It is referenced on the lead schedule to make it easy to refer from one working paper to another. The work performed on the allowance for doubtful accounts appears on working paper C-11. The final section of the lead schedule includes an overall conclusion on the account balances and whether any adjustments were found.

The second working paper example is the confirmations and related alternative procedures working paper from the accounts receivable (C) section of the audit file (figure 5.8).

FIGURE 5.7 **Accounts receivable lead schedule**

	A	B	C	D	E	F	G	H	I	J	K	L	M
1	New Millennium Ecoproducts												
2	Year End: December 31, 2015							Prepared by		Reviewed by		**C-Lead**	
3	Accounts Receivable Lead Schedule							OV		*VW*			
4								03-04-2016		17-04-2016			
5													
6	Account		Prelim	Adj's		Dec. 31, 2015 Yr Adjusted		Dec. 31, 2014		$ Change		% Change	
7													
8	1050 Accounts Receivable	TB	761,513.07	0.00	C.10	761,513.07		981,977.51 PY		-2 20,464.44	*^1	-22	⊕
9	1056 Employee Receivable		433.94	0.00	₥	433.94		0.00		433.94		0	
10			761,947.01	0.00		761,947.01		981,977.51		-2 20,030.50		-22	
11						^				^			
12	1066 Allowance: Doubtful Accounts		-17,791.20	0.00	C.11	-17,791.20		-22,598.00		4,806.80	m	-51	₥
13			-17,791.20	0.00		-17,791.20		-22,598.00		4,806.80		-51	
14						^							
15	Accounts Receivable		744,155.81	0.00		744,155.81 FS		959,379.51		-215,223.70		-29	
16			^			^		^					
17													
18	Conclusion: Based on the work performed, the balance appears reasonable as at December 31, 2015.												
19													
20	1 Accounts receivables decreased compared to the prior year due to increased efforts to collect at year end. In particular, New Millennium collected $160K from ABC Company on December 20, 2015 and 60K from XYZ Company on December 23, 2015.												
21													
22	Legend												
23													
24	₥ Not material												
25	PY Agreed to prior year working paper file												
26	*^Cross-footed												
27	⊕ Calculated												
28													
29													

FIGURE 5.8 **Accounts receivable confirmations and other procedures**

	A	B	C	D	E	F	G	H	I	J	K	L	M
1	New Millennium Ecoproducts						C-10						
2	Year End: December 31, 2015				Prepared by		Reviewed by						
3	Accounts Receivable Confirms and Other Procedures				OV		*VW*						
4					03-04-2016		17-04-2016						
5	Confirmation date:	Dec. 31, 2015											
6	Date sent:	Jan. 15, 2016											
7	First follow-up:	Feb. 28, 2016											
8													
9	Account Number	Customer Name	Amount Owing as of Confirm Date		Date Received		Balance Confirmed	Variance	Subsequent Cash Receipts		Agreed to Invoice and Shipping Documents		
10			⊢ SL ⊣										
11	123456	Cleaner King	198,258		Mar. 28, 2016	C-11	178,362	19,896	19,896	¦γ			
12	678900	Fresh and Clean	259,983		Feb. 15, 2016	C-12	259,983	-					
13	234987	Swept Away	56,925		Jan. 27, 2016	C-13	56,925	-					
14	654098	EcoCarpetCare	69,532				-	69,532	64,921	¦γ	2,500	√	
15	1248098	Pete's Cleaning	89,411		Mar. 2, 2016	C-14	89,411	-					
16													
17	Total		674,109				584,681	89,428	84,817		2,500		
18													
19	Dollar coverage										671,998		
20	Total AR										761,947	C-10	
21	Percent coverage										**88%**		
22													
23	1- Not an error, this is a timing difference. A payment made by the customer before the confirmation date was received by the client just after the confirmation date												
24	Legend												
25	SL Agreed to AR subledger												
26	γ Agreed to cheque copy, admittance advice, bank deposit, and bank statement												
27	√ Agreed to shipping report signed by external carrier that goods were shipped before year end												
28													

The top left-hand corner notes the engagement client name, period end, and working paper title (confirmations and other procedures). In the top right of the working paper is the working paper reference (C-10) along with details of the working paper preparer and reviewer. Next the date of the confirmation is noted. In this case, the confirmation was conducted for the balance at year end. The date is then noted when the confirmations were sent to New Millennium customers to confirm their accounts receivable. The first request was sent on January 15, 2016. A second request was sent on February 28, 2016, to customers that did not reply to the first request.

The balance in the accounts receivable accounts confirmed on that date is noted by the customer and cross-referenced to the accounts receivable subsidiary ledger (SL).

The table contains details of the customers that were sent confirmation requests:

- account or invoice number, per the accounts receivable subsidiary ledger (SL)
- customer name, per the accounts receivable subsidiary ledger (SL)
- balance owing at confirmation date, per the accounts receivable subsidiary ledger (SL)
- the date the auditor received a response from the customer
- the balance outstanding at the confirmation date according to the customer correspondence (filed and cross-referenced to working papers C-11, C-12, C-13, and C-14)
- any variance between the client records and the customer correspondence, which is calculated by the auditor
- documented alternative procedures performed where a customer has not responded or there is a variance, which involve the following:
  - The auditor searches the cash receipts journal for evidence that the customer has paid the amount outstanding, which provides evidence that the amount existed at the confirmation date. The auditor notes the amount received by the client, the date the cash was received, and whether the amount agrees to a copy of the cheque or remittance advice, as well as the bank deposit slip and the subsequent bank statement, which indicates that the invoice was paid by the customer subsequent to the confirmation date.
  - When the customer has not paid the amount outstanding at the date of confirmation, the auditor searches for evidence that the sale occurred. In this case the auditor agrees the amount to shipping reports signed by external carriers, which indicates that the item was shipped prior to the confirmation date.

The working paper then indicates the dollar value of the total accounts receivable that was confirmed, the total verified by subsequent receipts, and the amount vouched to invoices and shipping documents. These are totalled and used to determine the amount of work (or coverage) performed on the accounts receivable (AR) balance. This will help to determine if still more work is required on the existence assertion for the accounts receivable.

The bottom part of the working paper includes the auditor's comments on any unresolved items after the testing is completed. In this case the auditor concludes that a payment made by the customer before the confirmation date was received by the client just after the confirmation date. This timing difference does not affect the existence of a receivable as of the end of December. A legend is also included so any reviewer can understand the symbols and the actual work performed.

The third working paper example is the observation of physical inventory counts working paper from the inventory (F) section of the audit file (figure 5.9). In the top left-hand corner is the client name, period end, and working paper title (observation of inventory count). In the top right of the working paper is the working paper reference (F-10) and details of the working paper preparer and reviewers.

The next section of the working paper notes the location of the inventory count, the date of the inventory count, and the inventory balance on the date of the count. The inventory balance on the date of the count is cross-referenced to another part of the audit file (the inventory lead schedule F-4 Lead).

Ahead of attending the inventory count, the audit team will review and comment on the client's procedures for conducting their count. The details of that review are cross-referenced in the working paper to the location of that documentation in the audit file (F-9).

Next are the details of the items among New Millennium's varied inventory that were selected for testing by the auditor. The number of items selected and the nature of the items selected will depend upon the audit strategy.

FIGURE 5.9 **Observation of inventory count**

The working paper example includes details of five inventory items selected for testing of existence (count sheets to floor) and five items selected for testing of completeness (floor to count sheets). The extent of testing will depend on the risk assessment and other audit procedures included in the audit plan for inventory. For each inventory item selected, the auditor notes in the working paper the following:

- item number,
- mode of measurement (in this case units, cases, or kilograms, but it could be any other weight or length depending on the nature of the inventory being counted),
- quantity counted by the auditor (W&S Partners),
- quantity counted by the client per the client count sheet,
- any variance in the counts,
- final quantity per the inventory compilation at the conclusion of the count agreed by the auditor to the client inventory compilation,
- any variance between the quantity per the compilation and the quantity per the final verified amount, and
- comments by the auditor on the variances.

See Appendix A for further completed audit working papers.

The final working paper we illustrate here is figure 5.10 on the auditor's testing of New Millennium's controls set up by the Tyshynski brothers. Like the previous examples, the working paper includes in the top left corner the name of the client, the client year end, and the working paper reference. The right-hand corner includes the working paper reference number (Control-BB) and the sign-off of the preparer and the reviewer.

The next portion of the controls testing working paper lists the procedures to be performed. This is followed by a table itemizing the details of the items included in the sample, such as the invoice number, the purchase order number, the invoice amount before and after taxes, and the results of the procedures performed. The details of the procedures are indicated by a series of letters (S, T, U, V, W, and X) and tick marks (✓) explained in the legend created by the preparer. A column is provided to allow for comments for any exceptions found. The extent of testing would be determined by the audit team. The example shows a test of 5 for simplicity. This is followed by an overall conclusion as to whether the control is effective.

FIGURE 5.10 **Controls testing: Purchases and payables**

Cheque #	Expense Type	Invoice #	PO #	Supplier Name	Supplier #	Work Order #	Subtotal Amount	GST/HST	Total Amount	S	T	U	V	W	X	Notes
10156	a	560916		Telus	1500		202.54									
10836	m	66953	11788	Braid EcoSystems	1810	22666	690.04	82.80	772.84	√	√	√	√	√	√	
15386	m	TL-075284	11449	Armstrong Electric	2012011	22625	788.75	94.65	883.40	√	√	√	√	√	√	
18888	m	3102650	16754	Parkhill Repairs	2210	22698	10,591.55	1,270.99	11,862.54	√	√	√	√	√	√	
21098	a	12673	19823	Dhaliwal Cleaning	2600	22901	1,425.20	171.02	1,596.22	√	√	√	√	√	√	

New Millennium Ecoproducts
Year End: December 31, 2015
Control Testing: Purchases and Payables

Control-BB F-10
Prepared by Reviewed by
OV *(initials)*
03-04-2016 17-04-2016

Procedures:

1 Obtained a sample of invoices.
2 Agreed the selected cheque numbers to the cheque stub attached to each Invoice bundle to ensure that correct sample was pulled.
3 Agreed invoice PO number, supplier name, selling price, quantity purchased, and total price to information in PO system (payables CEVA); (purchase existence, completeness).
4 Agreed the sales price of purchased units in PO with the invoice from supplier (purchases valuation, accuracy).
5 Vouched invoice details to GL detail.

Conclusion: Based on the work performed, the controls over the purchases and payables can be relied upon.

Annotation

√	=	Completed with **NO** exception
m	=	Materials purchase
a	=	Administrative expenses
e	=	Expense report

Legend

S	Agreed invoice's stamped PO# with PO# in system
T	Agreed purchased units # from PO to packing slip and invoice; recalculated
U	Agreed purchase price in PO system to selling price on invoice
V	Checked invoice stamp for sign-off
W	Vouched through to G/L
X	Traced the account coding to verify it was correct

Cloud 9

The first major item in the current file for Cloud 9 is the audit plan. In addition, every task that is performed during the audit will be documented. Ian and the other junior staff are still struggling with how to correctly complete the papers. They often forget to complete all the relevant fields and Sharon, Suzie, and Josh are continually sending papers back to them with requests to clarify some of their comments. However, embedding the working papers in Excel has made life easier than in the past, when everything was paper-based, because an error message will be generated if certain key fields are not completed.

BEFORE YOU GO ON

5.8.1 What is a current file?

5.8.2 What is a permanent file?

5.8.3 What will an auditor document during the planning stage of the audit?

SUMMARY

1 Outline the audit assertions.

When preparing the financial statements, management will make assertions about each account and related disclosures in the notes. Auditors use these assertions to assess the risk of material misstatement and design audit procedures. The assertions used when testing transactions and events, including income statement items, are occurrence, completeness, accuracy, cut-off, and classification. The assertions used when testing balance sheet items are existence, rights and obligations, completeness, and valuation and allocation.

2 Identify and describe different types of audit evidence and define sufficient appropriate audit evidence.

The different types of audit evidence include external confirmations, documentary evidence, representations, verbal evidence, computational evidence, physical evidence, and electronic evidence. External confirmations are sent directly by an auditor to a third party. Documentary evidence may be generated internally by the client or externally by third parties. Representation letters are requested from a client's lawyers or management. Verbal evidence is the discussions between the auditor and client personnel or third parties. Computational evidence is gathered when an auditor checks the mathematical accuracy of figures included in the financial statements. Physical evidence involves the inspection of tangible assets. Electronic evidence includes data held on a client's computer, files sent by e-mail to the auditor, and items scanned and faxed.

Sufficiency refers to the quantity of evidence gathered. Appropriateness refers to the relevance and reliability of audit evidence gathered.

❸ Determine the persuasiveness of audit evidence.

The persuasiveness of evidence used to corroborate the details included in a client's accounts varies. Internally generated evidence held by the client is the least persuasive, as the client can alter or hide this evidence. Externally generated evidence held by the client is more persuasive, as it is created by an independent third party. Externally generated evidence sent directly to the auditor is the most persuasive, as the client does not handle this evidence.

❹ Explain the issues to consider when using the work of an expert.

When an auditor decides to use the work of an expert, the report produced by the expert forms part of the evidence used by an auditor when forming their audit opinion. An expert is someone with the skills, knowledge, and experience required to help an auditor. The auditor determines the scope of the work to be carried out, and assesses the capability of the expert, the objectivity of the expert, and the expert's report.

❺ Explain the issues to consider when using the work of another auditor.

An auditor may need to use the work of another auditor when their client operates in a number of locations, has divisions or subsidiaries spread around the country or the globe, or has significant assets in other places. When this is the case, the principal auditor may need to rely on evidence provided by another auditor for certain components of the client's financial statements.

❻ Describe the evidence-gathering procedures most often used by auditors.

An auditor will inspect records, documentation, and tangible assets. They will observe client staff undertaking various procedures. An auditor will make inquiries of client personnel and third parties. Confirmations are sent to third parties, including banks, lawyers, lenders, and debtors. An auditor will recalculate numbers appearing in client files and records to check mathematical accuracy. They will re-perform some processes used by the client to check the effectiveness of internal controls and the validity of amounts estimated by client personnel. Analytical procedures are used throughout the audit to appraise the relationships between financial and non-financial information.

❼ Explain how auditors arrive at a conclusion based upon the evidence gathered.

The final audit procedure is to assess the evidence gathered throughout the audit and draw a conclusion on the fair presentation of a client's financial statements.

❽ Describe how auditors document the details of evidence gathered in working papers.

Audit evidence is documented in an auditor's working papers. Audit working papers include the client's name, the period under audit, a title describing the contents of the working paper, a file reference indicating where the working paper fits in the audit file, the initials of the preparer of the working paper together with the date the working paper was prepared, the initials of the reviewer(s) of the working paper together with the date(s) the working paper was reviewed, and cross-referencing between working papers indicating where further work and evidence are summarized elsewhere. Working papers are stored in either the permanent file or the current file. The permanent file includes client information and documentation that apply to more than one audit. The current file includes client information and documentation that apply to the current audit.

KEY TERMS

Accuracy, 153
Analytical procedures, 173
Assertions, 153
Bank confirmation, 157
Classification, 154
Completeness, 153
Component auditor, 171
Computational evidence, 165
Current file, 176

Cut-off, 153
Documentary evidence, 161
Electronic evidence, 166
Evidence, 156, 167
Existence, 154
Expert, 169
External confirmation, 157
Externally generated evidence, 168
Group engagement partner, 171

Inquiry, 173
Inspection, 166, 173
Internally generated evidence, 167
Legal letter, 162
Management representation letter, 164
Negative confirmation, 158
Observation, 173
Occurrence, 153
Payable confirmation, 158

MULTIPLE-CHOICE QUESTIONS

5.1 The auditor is responsible for:
- (a) ensuring that the financial statements are prepared in accordance with accounting standards and the law.
- (b) ensuring that accurate accounting records are maintained.
- (c) ensuring that any potential misstatements are prevented or detected and corrected.
- (d) gathering sufficient appropriate evidence to support an opinion regarding the fair presentation of the client's financial statements.

5.2 The quantity of evidence that an auditor will gather:
- (a) varies with audit risk.
- (b) is the same for all audits because it has to be appropriate.
- (c) depends on the size of the audit team.
- (d) all of the above.

5.3 An external confirmation sent to a bank:
- (a) requests information about the bank balances and loan amounts.
- (b) requests information about interest rates paid on deposits and charged on loans.
- (c) is relevant to the audit of interest revenue and expense.
- (d) all of the above.

5.4 When an auditor gathers documentary evidence or physical evidence to support an entry in the client's records, the auditor is gathering evidence to support the:
- (a) completeness assertion.
- (b) existence assertion.
- (c) both (a) and (b).
- (d) neither (a) nor (b).

5.5 When an auditor inspects tangible assets on hand and traces the details to the details recorded in the client's records, the auditor is gathering evidence to support the:
- (a) completeness assertion.
- (b) existence assertion.
- (c) both (a) and (b).
- (d) neither (a) nor (b).

5.6 Generally the most persuasive form of evidence is:
- (a) internally generated evidence.
- (b) externally generated evidence held by the client.
- (c) externally generated evidence sent directly to the auditor.
- (d) none of the above; they are equally persuasive.

5.7 If an expert is engaged to assist with the audit:
- (a) it means the auditor does not have the requisite skill and knowledge to assess the item.
- (b) it means the auditor should not have taken on the audit because they are not qualified.
- (c) CPA Canada must be contacted and permission obtained before the expert starts work.
- (d) the auditor does not have to take responsibility for the fair presentation of the item in the financial statements.

5.8 Inspecting documents, such as an invoice for the purchase of fixed assets, provides the auditor with evidence relevant to the:
- (a) rights and obligations assertion, because the document will show the client's name as the purchaser.
- (b) occurrence assertion, because the document will show that the transaction took place on the specified date.
- (c) accuracy assertion, because the document will show the purchase amounts.
- (d) all of the above.

5.9 Analytical procedures are used to gather evidence:
- (a) at the planning stage to gain an understanding of a client.
- (b) at the execution stage to evaluate information included in the financial statements.
- (c) at the final review stage to assess whether the financial statements reflect the auditor's understanding of their client.
- (d) all of the above.

5.10 The working papers for a client contain both a permanent and a current file. The difference between the two files is that:
- (a) the permanent file is kept by the audit partner in charge and cannot be altered after the first audit engagement is completed, but the current file can be updated.
- (b) the permanent file is provided to the client and the current file is not.
- (c) the permanent file includes documents that relate to the client and are relevant for more than one audit, and the current file includes the details of work completed and evidence gathered that relate to the current audit.
- (d) all of the above.

REVIEW QUESTIONS

5.1 Explain why the quality of audit evidence is determined by the choice of the audit procedure and the assertion at risk of material misstatement.

5.2 What is a legal letter? What external parties could an auditor send a confirmation to? What other parties provide representation letters to an auditor?

5.3 Explain how gathering physical evidence by inspecting a client's tangible assets assists in the audit of the completeness and existence assertions.

5.4 Discuss the impact of electronic processing of transactions on the audit.

5.5 Why does an auditor have to consider the persuasiveness of corroborating evidence?

5.6 If an auditor does not have sufficient knowledge and skill in an area, the auditor can ask for the assistance of an expert. This creates a problem—how does an auditor know if the expert's work is correct if the auditor is not also an expert? Explain.

5.7 Under what circumstances does an auditor use the work of a component auditor? Why doesn't the group engagement partner do all of the work?

5.8 What are the evidence-gathering procedures an auditor might use? At which stages of the audit are these procedures appropriate? How do the procedures relate to the types of evidence an auditor can rely upon?

5.9 What is the difference between recalculation and re-performance? Explain using examples.

5.10 Review the examples of working papers provided in the chapter. List *six* things that should be included in every working paper.

PROFESSIONAL APPLICATION QUESTIONS

Basic ★   Moderate ★★   Challenging ★★★

5.1 Identifying audit assertions ★   ❶

Required

For each of the following items, identify the related assertion:

(a) Inventory is recorded at the lower of cost and net realizable value.

(b) All delivery vans recorded in the accounting records are owned by the entity.

(c) All payroll-related accruals at year end are recorded.

(d) The accounts receivable sub-ledger agrees to the general ledger control account.

(e) All sales were recorded in the correct period.

(f) There is no inventory on consignment.

(g) Purchases made after year end were recorded in the prior year.

(h) There is no impairment of goodwill.

(i) There are 10 delivery vans in the parking lot.

(j) There are no undisclosed contingent liabilities.

5.2 Audit assertions ★   ❶

Required

State the assertion that is violated in the following sentences:

(a) The client fails to accrue management bonuses in the current year.

(b) The client does not adjust its inventory to the lower of cost or market.

(c) The client books revenue in the current year when it has not yet been earned.

(d) The client issues a payroll cheque to an employee who no longer works for the entity.

(e) The client forgets to include goods on consignment in its inventory count at year end.

(f) The client fails to disclose its related-party payables separately.

(g) The client records its depreciation expense in its rent expense account.

(h) The client forgets to record its allowance for doubtful accounts.

(i) The client forgets to count inventory that is recorded in its books.

(j) The client accidently records its telephone bill twice for the month of November.

5.3 Account balances at risk ★★

Tropical Cruises is a new client of MMM Partners. Tropical Cruises is a low-cost cruise ship operator, travelling between Canada and the United States. The planning for the first audit is underway. The auditors have become aware that police in two countries are investigating several Tropical Cruises employees for stealing food and other supplies from the ships' kitchens and selling it at local markets. The police have charged 10 cabin stewards of Tropical Cruises with theft and fraud.

Required

(a) What account balances are at risk? Explain.
(b) What key assertions for the above accounts are likely to be affected?

Source: Adapted from the Institute of Chartered Accountants Australia's CA Program's Audit and Assurance exam, May 2010. Provided courtesy of Chartered Accountants Australia and New Zealand.

5.4 Assertions ★

A client has a material balance in property, plant, and equipment. The discussions with management indicate that there is a risk the client will capitalize all repair costs to minimize the impact on expenses. Repairs are likely to be material because of the extreme weather conditions affecting operations and machinery operating conditions. Extensive repairs were due to be commenced in the month prior to year end, with completion around two months later.

Required

Based on the above information, what accounts and assertions are likely to be affected? Explain.

Source: Adapted from the Institute of Chartered Accountants Australia's CA Program's Audit and Assurance exam, December 2010. Provided courtesy of Chartered Accountants Australia and New Zealand.

5.5 Confirmations ★★

The following are *independent* questions.

Required

(a) List *four* factors that make audit evidence more reliable.
(b) Explain the difference between positive and negative confirmations for accounts receivable.

Source: © CGA-Canada, now CPA Canada. Reproduced with permission.

5.6 Types and persuasiveness of audit evidence ★

Jenna is working on the audit of a client's accounts receivable. During the last few weeks she has conducted interviews with the accounts receivable manager, the CFO, and staff working in the accounts receivable department. She has also overseen the external confirmations of accounts receivable, 30 percent of which required the recipient to respond as to whether or not the amount stated was correct. Jenna also conducted a review of subsequent cash receipts from the client's customers. She vouched a sample of accounts receivable balances back to the underlying invoices, cash receipts, and sales returns, and traced a sample of these documents to the accounts receivable ledger.

Required

(a) List the types of audit evidence gathered by Jenna and comment on the persuasiveness of each type.
(b) Link each type of evidence to the relevant accounts receivable assertions.

5.7 Identifying assertions and supporting evidence ★★

You are engaged to examine the financial statements of Lauzon Inc. for the year ended December 31.

On October 1, Lauzon Inc. borrowed $250,000 from a local bank to finance a plant expansion. The loan agreement provided for the annual payment of principal and interest over three years. Lauzon's existing plant was pledged as security for the loan.

Unfortunately, Lauzon ran into some difficulties in acquiring the new plant site. Thus, the plant expansion was delayed. Lauzon then proceeded to "plan B," which was to invest the borrowed funds in stocks and bonds. As a result, on October 20, the entire amount borrowed was invested in securities.

Required

Identify the assertions applicable to the above, and describe the relevant evidence that needs to be obtained to support them for the audit of investments in securities at December 31.

5.8 Identifying types of audit evidence ★ ★

Required

Identify the type of audit evidence being used in each situation described below:

(a) The auditor tests cash remittance advices to ensure that allowances and discounts are appropriate and that receipts are posted to the correct customer accounts in the right amounts. In addition, the auditor reviews the documents supporting unusual discounts and allowances.

(b) The auditor examines vehicle insurance policies and checks insurance expense for the year. In addition, the auditor reviews the expense with respect to changes and ending balances in capital asset accounts.

(c) The auditor observes the auditee taking a physical inventory count. In addition, a letter is received from a public storage facility stating the amounts of the auditee's inventory stored in it. The company uses a weighted average cost flow assumption, which is tested by the auditor's computer software program.

(d) Using audit software, an auditor selects vendors' accounts payable with debit balances from the client's computer screen and compares these amounts and their calculation with cash disbursements and vendor credit memos.

5.9 Assertions and evidence ★

The auditor is planning for the audit of a specialty retail store. Inventory is material, and items range in value from $1 to over $500. The nature of the store means that the type of merchandise changes every season, and many items are specially ordered with special branding and promotional packaging. Orders are placed six months in advance from overseas suppliers. Large deposits are required to be paid when orders are placed. The auditor believes that the account balances for inventory and prepayments are at risk of material misstatement.

Required

(a) Identify the key assertions at risk in relation to inventory and prepayments.

(b) For each assertion in (a), identify a type of evidence that would be persuasive.

Source: Adapted from the Institute of Chartered Accountants Australia's CA Program's Audit and Assurance exam, December 2010. Provided courtesy of Chartered Accountants Australia and New Zealand.

5.10 Misstatement risk for depreciation ★ ★

Yellow Aviation is an existing client of PPP Partners. The auditors are aware that the impact of the global financial crisis on airlines has been severe, with predictions of a prolonged downturn. Also, as a result of the crisis along with the entry of new competitors in the domestic and international markets, airlines have been heavily discounting flights. The client's policies include the following:

Aircraft maintenance costs policy
The standard cost of major airframe and engine maintenance checks is capitalized and depreciated over the shorter of the scheduled usage period to the next major inspection or the remaining life of the aircraft.

Yellow Aviation's latest financial data show the aircraft and engines at cost (including major maintenance costs) to be at a similar level as last year while depreciation costs have decreased by 7 percent.

Required

(a) What key assertions for the above accounts are likely to be affected?

(b) Explain what evidence would be persuasive in this case.

Source: Adapted from the Institute of Chartered Accountants Australia's CA Program's Audit and Assurance exam, May 2010. Provided courtesy of Chartered Accountants Australia and New Zealand.

5.11 Revenue assertions ★ ★

The audit program for the Revenue account for a client has been drafted. The following item appears:

ITEM	ASSERTION	DETAILED AUDIT PROCEDURE
1	Completeness	Select a sample of sales from the sales journal and ensure each sales invoice is supported by an authorized delivery slip and approved customer order.

Required

(a) Does the procedure address the stated assertion? Explain.

(b) If your answer to (a) is no, provide the correct assertion or explain what work would be required to address the assertion.

(c) Explain what type of evidence is obtained by performing the stated procedure. How persuasive is it?

Source: Adapted from the Institute of Chartered Accountants Australia's CA Program's Audit and Assurance exam, July 2010. Provided courtesy of Chartered Accountants Australia and New Zealand.

5.12 Revenue assertions ★ ★

The audit program for the Revenue account for a client has been drafted. The following item appears:

ITEM	ASSERTION	DETAILED AUDIT PROCEDURE
2	Cut-off	Select a sample of sales invoices recorded a few days prior to the year end and then agree dates on the invoices to the dates on the delivery documents signed by the customer.

Required

(a) Does the procedure address the stated assertion? Explain.

(b) If your answer to (a) is no, provide the correct assertion or explain what work would be required to address the assertion.

(c) Explain what type of evidence is obtained by performing the stated procedure. How persuasive is it?

Source: Adapted from the CA Program's Audit and Assurance Exam, July 2010.

5.13 Revenue assertions ★ ★

The audit program for the Revenue account for a client has been drafted. The following item appears:

ITEM	ASSERTION	DETAILED AUDIT PROCEDURE
3	Accuracy	Select a sample of sales from the sales journal and agree the sale price to the authorized price list.

Required

(a) Does the procedure address the stated assertion? Explain.

(b) If your answer to (a) is no, provide the correct assertion or suggest additional work.

(c) Explain what type of evidence is obtained by performing the stated procedure. How persuasive is it?

Source: Adapted from the Institute of Chartered Accountants Australia's CA Program's Audit and Assurance Exam, July 2010. Provided courtesy of Chartered Accountants Australia and New Zealand.

5.14 Communication with lawyers ★

Conversations between the board of directors of Acme Ltd. and the engagement partner of the financial audit, Angelo Del Santo, have revealed that Acme uses three legal firms. Ball and Partners performs all legal work related to property transfers, mortgages, and planning applications. Brond Associates handle all employment matters, such as claims for unfair dismissal and complex employment contracts. Zimmerman and Co. are retained for all other matters, such as agreements relating to products and suppliers and any international matters.

Required

(a) What type of communication should Angelo and his audit team have with each legal firm? Explain.
(b) What procedures could Angelo perform to find out whether any other legal firms have performed work for Acme during the financial year?

5.15 Bank reconciliations ★

Mohammad Amed is responsible for preparing bank reconciliation statements at Ajax Ltd. Ajax Ltd. has many bank accounts, including separate accounts for each major branch, imprest accounts for salaries and dividends, and accounts kept in foreign currency for overseas divisions. Mohammad maintains records including bank statements and weekly bank reconciliations for each account. In addition, there are files containing correspondence with banks about disputed transactions, dishonoured cheques from Ajax Ltd.'s customers, and other bank-initiated transactions such as fees and interest.

Required

(a) Comment on the persuasiveness of the evidence in Mohammad's files for Ajax Ltd.'s financial statement audit.
(b) Explain how an auditor would obtain more persuasive evidence for the relevant assertions for the bank accounts at Ajax Ltd.

5.16 Using an expert ★ ★

SolarTubeGen is a start-up company in the renewable energy sector. The founder, Fritz Herzberg, has developed cutting-edge technology to convert the energy in the sun's rays to electricity via a novel system of mirrors designed to focus the sun's rays onto tubes containing a patented type of gas, which then heats and expands to drive turbines. KenKen Partners has won the contract for the first statutory audit of SolarTubeGen on the basis of its expertise in the energy sector. However, the lead partner, Ken Kennedy, recognizes that the success of the audit is dependent on the correct assessment of the technology being used at SolarTubeGen. Ken specified in the successful tender documents that the audit will use an external expert to help with valuation of the company's assets.

Fritz Herzberg is very protective of his company's intellectual property and is resistant to Ken's first suggested expert, Manfred Hamburg. Fritz believes that Manfred Hamburg is hostile toward him because they clashed when they both worked for a German company making photovoltaic cells in the 1990s. Fritz has suggested another expert, Lily Beilherz, with whom he has had good working relations over the last 20 years.

Required

Advise Ken Kennedy about the choice of an expert for the audit of SolarTubeGen. What must he consider when making his choice?

5.17 Considering the work of other auditors ★ ★ ★

Securimax Limited has been an audit client of KFP Partners for the past 15 years. Securimax is based in Waterloo, Ontario, where it manufactures high-tech armour-plated personnel carriers. Securimax often has to go through a competitive market tender process to win large government contracts. Its main product, the small but powerful Terrain Master, is highly specialized and Securimax only does business with nations that have a recognized, democratically elected government. Securimax maintains a highly secure environment, given the sensitive and confidential nature of its vehicle designs and its clients.

Clarke Field has been the engagement partner on the Securimax audit for the last five years. Clarke is a specialist in the defence industry and intends to remain as review partner when the audit is rotated next year to a new partner (Sally Woodrow, who is to be promoted to partner to enable her to sign off on the audit).

Securimax has a small internal audit department that is headed by an ex-partner of KFP, Rydell Crow. Rydell joined Securimax six years ago, after leaving KFP and completing his accountant qualifications. Rydell is assisted by three junior internal auditors, all of whom are completing Bachelor of Accounting and Financial Management studies at the University of Waterloo.

Securimax's fiscal year end is December 31.

Required

Discuss the effect, if any, of CAS 600 on Clarke Field's consideration of Securimax's internal audit department for the financial statement audit.

Source: Adapted from the Institute of Chartered Accountants Australia's CA Program's Audit and Assurance Exam, May 2008. Provided courtesy of Chartered Accountants Australia and New Zealand.

5.18 Gathering evidence ★ ★

Max Crowe is a junior auditor who has just started with the team conducting the audit of a new client in the construction industry. Max is "shadowing" Susan Wong, an experienced auditor. Susan is showing Max how to be a member of an audit team and is trying to teach Max about the benefits of getting to know the client. Susan is also trying to help Max develop experience in picking up subtle signals about the client's problems and what the client might be trying to hide from the auditor.

Max is getting a little frustrated with the "shadowing" assignment. He can't understand why Susan is spending so much time talking to the client's staff and touring the various construction sites and offices. When Susan is not doing this, she is working on a spreadsheet of the client's previous financial statements and unaudited interim data. Max wants to know when they are going to do some "real" work and start gathering audit evidence. Susan tells Max that they have already started.

Required

(a) Discuss Susan's comment that they have already started the audit. What evidence have they gathered so far?
(b) Explain what work is being done with the spreadsheets of financial data. Give some specific examples for this client. How is this type of work relevant to all stages of the audit?

5.19 Documentation ★ ★

Jennifer Daoust is reading the documents prepared by the members of the team working on the audit of receivables for a large client. Jennifer is the senior manager assisting the engagement partner, Ruby Rogers. Jennifer and Ruby have worked together on many audits and Jennifer knows the types of questions that Ruby will ask about the working papers if they are not up to the standard required by CAS 230. Jennifer is trying to make sure that all documents are up to the required standard before Ruby sees them tomorrow.

Jennifer is particularly concerned about the documents relating to the receivable confirmations. This is because the audit assistant who wrote up the confirmation results said that no further work was required. On review of the results, Jennifer discovered that the audit assistant had incorrectly treated "no reply" results as acceptable for a positive confirmation, when they are acceptable only for a negative confirmation. Jennifer had ordered further work be done to follow up these "no reply" results.

Required

(a) What is the minimum standard that the audit documentation must meet?

(b) How would you treat the corrections made to the audit assistant's recommendations and the additional work on receivable confirmations in the working papers? Explain. Refer to both CAS 505 and CAS 230 in your answer.

5.20 Documenting the audit ★★

Featherbed Surf & Leisure Holidays Ltd. is a resort company based on Vancouver Island. Its operations include boating, surfing, diving, and other leisure activities; a backpackers' hostel; a family hotel; and a five-star resort. Justin and Sarah Morris own the majority of the shares in the Morris Group, which controls Featherbed. Justin is the chairman of the board of directors of both Featherbed and the Morris Group, and Sarah is a director of both companies as well as the CFO of Featherbed.

While performing the Featherbed audit you discover that the Wave Travel Agency, which specializes in group travel to Vancouver Island, has an account with Featherbed. The review of the aging of the accounts receivable balance shows that Wave Travel Agency's balance is large and material and is now more than 60 days overdue. However, no allowance has been made for the outstanding debt. You consult Featherbed's accounting staff, Julie and Kristen, about the account and they mention that there are rumours that the Wave Travel Agency is suffering financial difficulties.

You are aware that CAS 230 has specific requirements about documenting audit work. In particular, paragraph 9 states:

In documenting the nature, timing and extent of audit procedures performed, the auditor shall record:

(a) The identifying characteristics of the specific items or matters tested;

(b) Who performed the audit work and the date such work was completed

(c) Who reviewed the audit work performed and the date and extent of such review.

In addition, paragraph 10 states:

The auditor shall document discussions of significant matters with management, those charged with governance, and others, including the nature of the significant matters discussed and when and with whom the discussions took place.

Required

Explain how you would apply the mandatory requirements of the above paragraphs of CAS 230 in relation to the potential bad debt.

Source: Adapted from the Institute of Chartered Accountants Australia's CA Program's Audit and Assurance Exam, May 2008. Provided courtesy of Chartered Accountants Australia and New Zealand.

Questions 5.21 and 5.22 are based on the following case.

Fellowes and Associates Chartered Accountants is a successful mid-tier accounting firm with a large range of clients across Canada. In 2016, Fellowes and Associates gained a new client, Health Care Holdings Group (HCHG), which owns 100 percent of the following entities:

- Shady Oaks Centre, a private treatment centre
- Gardens Nursing Home Ltd., a private nursing home
- Total Laser Care Limited (TLCL), a private clinic that specializes in the laser treatment of skin defects

Year end for all HCHG entities is June 30.

You are performing the audit field work for the 2016 year for Shady Oaks Centre. The field work must be completed in time for the audit report to be signed on August 21, 2016. You have been asked to circulate the receivable confirmations. Shady Oaks Centre's trade receivables arise from the use of clinic facilities (including the provision of medical professionals, treatment rooms, and supplies) by medical practitioners in private practice. The trade receivables balance was $3,974,569 as at June 30, 2016, and was considered material.

The centre's payment terms are 14 days from the date of the invoice. Sixty percent of the balance is represented by invoices outstanding from five different medical practitioners. The remaining 40 percent is made up of numerous smaller amounts, most of which have been outstanding for more than 60 days. Any allowance for doubtful accounts is taken directly against the trade receivables account and not shown separately.

Source: Adapted from the Institute of Chartered Accountants Australia's CA Program's Audit and Assurance Exam, December 2008. Provided courtesy of Chartered Accountants Australia and New Zealand.

5.21 Confirmation evidence ★ ★

Required

Discuss the strengths and weaknesses of accounts receivable confirmations as audit evidence for HCHG.

5.22 Adequacy of documentation and audit evidence ★ ★ ★

Required

Is it possible for Fellowes and Associates to use accounts receivable confirmations only as audit evidence and adhere to the mandatory requirements in CAS 230? Explain.

5.23 Location of file documentation ★

For each of the following documents, state whether it would be located in the auditors' permanent file or the current file.

(a) Articles of incorporation
(b) Bank confirmation for the current year
(c) Management representation letter for the current year
(d) Long-term debt agreement
(e) Organization chart
(f) Process documentation for payroll
(g) Details of employment contracts regarding stock options
(h) Engagement letter
(i) Board of director minutes for the current year
(j) Audit program for cash

5.24 Working paper errors and omissions ★

Required

The working paper in figure 5.11 was prepared by James Parkhill, a first year accountant. Find *seven* errors that James made while completing this working paper.

	A	B	C	D	E	F	G
1	**New Millennium Ecoproducts**						
2	Year End: December 31, 2016						
3	Cash						
4							
5							
6							
7							
8	Account	Prelim	Adj's	Rep	Ann.	Rep 12/16	% Chg
9							
10							
11	1004 CIBC - C$ 0910934	501,631.48	0.00	501,631.48	A.10	207,013.35	142
12	1005 CIBC - U.S.$ 0981298	47,803.91	0.00	47,803.91	A.12	128,193.65	-63
13	1006 CIBC Bank - C$ savings	163,173.08	0.00	163,173.08	A.14	162,497.05	0
14	1060 Petty Cash	500.00	0.00	500.00		400.00	-100
15		**713,108.47**	**0.00**	**713,108.47**		**498,104.05**	**43**
17							
18	Comment: The controller reconciles the bank on a monthly basis.						

FIGURE 5.11 **Working paper**

CASES

5.25 IndaCar—Integrative Case Study ★ ★ ★

IndaCar Inc. (IC) operates a high-end car rental agency that specializes in the rental of unique vehicles and is located next to Lester B. Pearson International Airport in Toronto. IC is a private Canadian company that is wholly owned by Jake Bouvier.

Daytona Lemans LLP, Chartered Professional Accountants (DL), has reviewed IC's annual financial statements since IC was founded five years ago and has experienced no significant problems when performing the previous review engagements. You just found out you are the manager on the job for this year.

As a result of IC's success in Toronto, Jake is exploring the possibility of expanding IC's operations to include the Vancouver and Calgary airports. Jake expects that he will be using IC's fiscal 2016 financial statements to attract equity investors to partially finance this expansion.

To maximize IC's share value attractiveness to potential investors, Jake is wondering if he should have the financial statements audited.

Jake commented that he received a tip from one of the employees at the Pearson location that the manager is stealing cash. He wants to know if the regular audit engagement is likely to identify whether cash is being stolen and what procedures the auditor is likely to perform in this risk area.

You have reviewed the fiscal 2015 engagement file in order to familiarize yourself with the client and to review the planning documentation prepared for the previous year's engagement.

IndaCar Inc.
As at December 31
(in thousands of dollars)

	2016 (unaudited)	2015 (reviewed)
Assets		
Cash	$ 1,453	$ 162
Accounts receivable	1,142	130
Inventory	1,270	1,140
Prepaid expenses	112	3
	3,977	1,435
Property, plant, and equipment (net)	20,657	14,465
Investments	2,000	
	22,657	14,465
	$26,634	$15,900
Liabilities		
Bank operating loan	$ 90	$ 100
Accounts payable and accrued liabilities	1,225	166
	1,315	266
Long-term debt	1,260	200
	2,575	466
Shareholders' Equity		
Common shares	100	100
Retained earnings	23,959	15,334
	24,059	15,434
	$26,634	$15,900

EXCERPTS FROM THE INCOME STATEMENT
For the years ended December 31
(in thousands of dollars)

	2016 (unaudited)	2015 (reviewed)
Revenues		
Car rentals	$22,710	$14,300
Investment income	6,085	4,485
	28,795	18,785
Expenses		
Vehicle operations, including amortization	10,670	8,870
Rent and administration	995	810
Wages and salaries	7,200	6,675
Total expenses	18,865	16,355
Income before income tax	9,930	2,430
Income tax	1,305	780
Net income	$ 8,625	$ 1,650

Required

(a) Advise Jake on the costs and benefits of upgrading from a review engagement to an audit engagement.

(b) In planning the audit, the auditor must consider audit risk. Using the above case facts, make an inherent risk assessment.

(c) If the auditor decides that control risk is high, what type of audit will DL perform? How will this impact the amount of audit work?

(d) Calculate and conclude on the most appropriate planning materiality, and include a detailed explanation supporting your decision.

(e) For the following accounts, what assertions will the auditor be most concerned with? What evidence should the auditor gather to verify the management assertions?

1. Accounts receivable
2. Property, plant, and equipment
3. Accounts payable
4. Long-term debt
5. Car rental sales

Source: (Adapted and) reprinted with the permission of CPA Ontario. Copyright © Chartered Professional Accountants of Ontario (The Institute of Chartered Accountants of Ontario). Any changes to the original material are the sole responsibility of the author (and or the publisher) and have not been reviewed or endorsed by CPA Ontario.

CASE STUDY—CLOUD 9

W&S Partners will need the assistance of auditors in China and the United States and derivatives experts to complete the Cloud 9 audit.

The other auditors will be asked to provide evidence about the inventory shipped to Canada from the production plants in these countries. Although the inventory is shipped FOB (free on board), there have been several occasions where the shipping agent was unable to place the inventory on a ship. In these cases, the inventory is stored in the shipping agent's warehouse until a vessel is made available. Suzie has some concerns about the quality of the warehouses, because if the goods are damaged they could become worthless and the value of "goods in transit" will be overstated.

In addition, Suzie has asked Jo Wadley for help in choosing an expert to help with valuation aspects of the audit of the derivatives. Jo has provided her with three names of experts in the field, but she has had no personal experience with any of them. Suzie must make a choice and engage the expert soon in order to be sure that the expert opinion will be received in time to complete the audit.

Answer the following questions based on the information presented for Cloud 9 in Appendix B at the end of this book and the current and earlier chapters. You should also consider your answers to the case study questions in earlier chapters.

Required

(a) Explain the procedures for engaging component auditors to perform the work on the inventory in China and the United States.

(b) Advise Suzie on engaging the derivatives expert. Discuss the qualities the expert must possess. What procedures must Suzie perform? What should she tell the expert about the engagement? What must the expert give to Suzie so that she can be sure she has sufficient appropriate evidence about the derivatives? Can the expert do all the work on derivatives, or must Suzie perform any other procedures?

(c) Assume you are engaging the component auditors and the derivatives expert. Create a working paper for each task.

RESEARCH QUESTION 5.1

Obtain the latest annual report of a large multinational Canadian company (for example, one of the large banks or mining companies).

Required

(a) What information is given in the annual report about the use of any component auditors, other than the Canadian audit firm issuing the audit report? If any other auditors are mentioned, what work do you think these auditors performed?

(b) Is there any information given in the annual report about the auditor's use of an expert? What sort of work would an expert have performed for the audit of your chosen company?

SOLUTIONS TO MULTIPLE-CHOICE QUESTIONS

1. d, 2. a, 3. d, 4. b, 5. a, 6. c, 7. a, 8. d, 9. d, 10. c.

CHAPTER 6

Sampling and overview of the risk response phase of the audit

LEARNING OBJECTIVES

After studying this chapter, you should be able to:

1 explain how audit sampling is used in an audit

2 understand the difference between sampling and non-sampling risk

3 differentiate between statistical and non-statistical sampling

4 describe sampling methods and the factors to be considered when choosing a sample

5 determine the factors that influence the sample size when testing controls

6 determine the factors that influence the sample size when substantive testing and consider techniques used to perform substantive tests

7 outline how to evaluate the results of tests conducted on a sample

8 understand the difference between tests of controls and substantive tests

9 explain the factors that impact the nature, timing, and extent of audit testing.

AUDITING AND ASSURANCE STANDARDS

CANADIAN	INTERNATIONAL
CAS 200 *Overall Objectives of the Independent Auditor and the Conduct of an Audit in Accordance with Canadian Auditing Standards*	ISA 200 *Overall Objectives of the Independent Auditor and the Conduct of an Audit in Accordance with International Standards on Auditing*
CAS 300 *Planning an Audit of Financial Statements*	ISA 300 *Planning an Audit of Financial Statements*
CAS 330 *The Auditor's Responses to Assessed Risks*	ISA 330 *The Auditor's Responses to Assessed Risks*
CAS 530 *Audit Sampling*	ISA 530 *Audit Sampling*

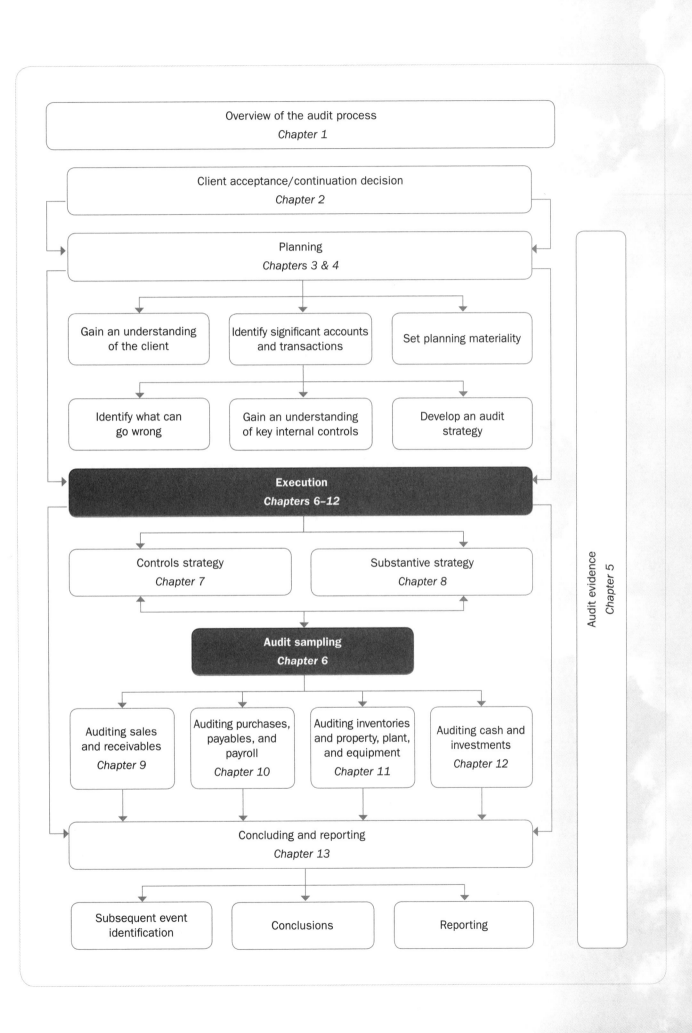

Cloud 9

Another issue that arises at the Cloud 9 Ltd. audit planning meeting is the appropriate scheduling of the control and substantive tests and the sampling criteria. After the meeting finishes, Ian Harper asks Suzie Pickering to coffee again. He wants her to explain how they can plan these tests and write a detailed audit program, including instructions on how to select the sample.

Suzie is happy to drink more coffee and meets Ian that afternoon at their local café. "The sort of tests we have to do, and when and how we do them, depends on the quality of the client's accounting records. However, before we talk about that, we should probably talk about how we use sampling. In most cases, we don't test every transaction or control. We use sampling, conduct the tests on the sample, and then project the results back to the population." Ian indicates he understands the idea of sampling—it saves a lot of time and money. "But do you understand the risks involved in sampling?" Suzie asks.

AUDIT PROCESS IN FOCUS

The purpose of this chapter is to provide an overview of audit sampling and to introduce, compare, and contrast tests of controls and substantive testing.

Audit sampling involves the selection of transactions or accounts within a balance for testing. It is used when the auditor plans on testing less than the entire population of transactions or accounts in a balance available for testing. When selecting a sample, it is important that the items chosen for testing are representative of the entire population of transactions and accounts available for testing. Sampling risk is the risk that the sample chosen is unsuitable and, as a consequence, the auditor arrives at an inappropriate conclusion after testing the sample. Non-sampling risk refers to other factors that result in an auditor arriving at an inappropriate conclusion. Both sampling and non-sampling risk are explained in this chapter.

Sampling can be conducted using statistical or non-statistical methods. These terms are explained and the benefits and drawbacks of each group of techniques are discussed in this chapter. We then provide an overview of different techniques that are used to select a sample during an audit.

The sample size chosen will be affected by a range of factors. Those factors will be different if the sample is selected for tests of controls or for substantive procedures. The factors that influence the final sample size when testing controls or conducting substantive tests are explained in this chapter. Finally, we explain how the results of testing are evaluated when a sample is used. It is vital that an appropriate assessment method is used to generalize the findings for a sample to the entire population. The next section of this chapter provides an overview of the risk response phase of the audit. This phase involves the testing of controls and conducting substantive procedures in line with the auditors' strategy.

6.1 AUDIT SAMPLING

 Explain how audit sampling is used in an audit.

audit sampling the application of audit procedures to less than 100 percent of items within a population

audit plan details of the audit procedures to be used when testing controls and when conducting detailed substantive procedures

CAS 530 *Audit Sampling* provides guidance on **audit sampling**. When creating an **audit plan** and designing audit procedures, an auditor also decides how to select appropriate items for testing. When an audit procedure is tested on an entire group of transactions (for example, the purchase of machinery) or all items within an account balance (for example, motor vehicles), sampling is not required. However, when there are numerous transactions or items within an account balance available for testing, an auditor must decide how best to select a sample that is representative of the entire population of items available for testing.

As defined previously, audit risk is the risk that an auditor expresses an inappropriate opinion when the financial statements are materially misstated. There are two elements to that risk: the risk associated with using sampling for testing, known as sampling risk, and other risks, known as non-sampling risks.

BEFORE YOU GO ON

6.1.1 What is audit sampling?

6.1.2 When is it appropriate to use audit sampling?

6.1.3 How does audit sampling relate to audit risk?

6.2 SAMPLING AND NON-SAMPLING RISK

Sampling risk is the risk that the sample chosen by the auditor is not representative of the population of transactions or items within an account balance available for testing and, as a consequence, the auditor arrives at an inappropriate conclusion (CAS 530). There are two consequences of sampling risk: the risk that the audit will be ineffective and the risk that the audit will be inefficient.

6.2.1 Sampling risk and tests of controls

When testing controls, sampling risk is the risk that an auditor relies on their client's system of internal controls when they should not do so (that is, the auditor concludes that the client's internal controls are effective when they are ineffective), and the risk that an auditor concludes that the client's internal controls are less reliable than they really are (that is, the auditor concludes that the client's internal controls are ineffective when they are effective). Table 6.1 provides details of sampling risk when testing controls and the implications of that risk for the audit.

In the top section of table 6.1, the auditor has tested their client's system of internal controls and concluded that the system is effective when it is ineffective at preventing and detecting potential material misstatements. Another way of stating this risk is that an auditor has concluded that the client's system of internal controls is *more* effective than it is. As a consequence, the auditor places too much reliance on the client's system of internal controls to identify and rectify material misstatements. This can happen when the items selected for testing the effectiveness of the internal controls are not representative of all items available for testing. For example, a manager is away on vacation for two weeks during the year and another member of the client's personnel acts as manager during their absence. The auditor selects items for testing throughout the year, but the sample does not include transactions processed while the manager was on vacation. There is a risk that the auditor concludes that the controls that involve the manager's supervision and authorization are effective throughout the year, when they may not have worked effectively during the two-week vacation period.

From the audit risk model discussed in chapter 4, we know that when an auditor concludes that their client's system of internal controls is effective at preventing and detecting material misstatements, control risk will be assessed as low and the audit strategy will be to reduce reliance on detailed substantive testing of transactions and balances. By conducting fewer substantive procedures, there is an increased risk that the auditor's detailed substantive procedures will not detect a material misstatement (that is, there is a risk that the audit will be ineffective if the auditor's original risk assessment was wrong).

In the bottom section of table 6.1, the auditor has tested their client's system of internal controls and concluded that the system is ineffective when it is, in fact, effective at preventing and detecting potential material misstatements. Another way of stating this risk is that an auditor has concluded that the client's system of internal controls is *less* effective than it is. As a consequence, the auditor does not place sufficient reliance on the client's system of internal controls. This can happen when

 2 Understand the difference between sampling and non-sampling risk.

sampling risk the risk that the sample chosen by the auditor is not representative of the population available for testing and, as a consequence, the auditor arrives at an inappropriate conclusion

SAMPLING RISK	IMPLICATIONS FOR THE AUDIT
The risk that the auditor concludes that the client's system of internal controls is effective when it is ineffective	An increased audit risk (that is, the risk that the auditor will issue an inappropriate audit conclusion)
The risk that the auditor concludes that the client's system of internal controls is ineffective when it is effective	An increase in audit effort when not required (that is, there is a risk that the audit will be inefficient)

TABLE 6.1 **Sampling risk when testing controls**

the items selected for testing the effectiveness of the internal controls is not representative of all items available for testing. For example, a client has a control procedure requiring authorization of purchases in excess of $200,000. The auditor selected purchase orders from one division of the company. The auditor has found the control to be ineffective because the manager has not signed all purchase orders selected. In this example, the auditor runs the risk of placing less reliance on this control than strictly necessary because they did not select the sample from across all divisions, where the control may be working more effectively.

From the audit risk model, we know that when an auditor concludes that their client's system of internal controls is ineffective at preventing and detecting potential material misstatements, control risk will be assessed as high and the audit strategy will be to increase reliance on detailed substantive testing of transactions and balances. By conducting more substantive procedures when control risk is lower than assessed, the audit will be inefficient as the auditor will spend more time conducting substantive procedures than is necessary.

6.2.2 Sampling risk and substantive procedures

When conducting substantive tests, sampling risk is the risk that an auditor concludes that a material misstatement does not exist when it does or an auditor concludes that a material misstatement exists when it does not. Table 6.2 provides details of sampling risk when conducting substantive tests and the implications of that risk for the audit.

TABLE 6.2 Sampling risk when conducting substantive tests

SAMPLING RISK	IMPLICATIONS FOR THE AUDIT
The risk that the auditor concludes that a material misstatement does not exist when it does	An increased audit risk (that is, the risk that the auditor will issue an inappropriate audit conclusion)
The risk that the auditor concludes that a material misstatement exists when it does not	An increase in audit effort when not required (that is, there is a risk that the audit will be inefficient)

In the top section of table 6.2, the auditor has conducted substantive procedures on a sample and concluded that there is no material misstatement when there is a material misstatement. As a consequence, the auditor will conclude that the financial statements are fairly presented when they contain a material misstatement (that is, the audit is ineffective). For example, a client has warehouses in four major cities. The auditor has selected a sample of inventory items for testing. The entire sample of inventory selected for testing is located in the one warehouse near the client's head office. The auditor has not tested material inventory items held at the other three warehouses. As a consequence, the auditor has not detected a significant error in valuing inventory at one of the warehouses. If the auditor had selected a sample for testing from each warehouse, the risk of arriving at an incorrect conclusion would have been reduced, though not eliminated (that is, sampling risk can be reduced though it can never be removed).

In the bottom section of table 6.2, the auditor has conducted substantive procedures on a sample and concluded that there is a material misstatement when there is no material misstatement. As a consequence, the auditor will conduct more extensive testing believing that there is a material misstatement reducing audit efficiency. For example, an error occurred when processing credit sales and a customer was charged twice for the same item by mistake. The auditor detects this error and concludes that if this error was to be repeated throughout the remainder of the population of credit sales, trade receivables would be materially misstated. As a consequence, the auditor increases testing to uncover the cause of the error. If the error is an anomaly and not repeated throughout the population, the audit will be inefficient.

6.2.3 Non-sampling risk

Non-sampling risk is the risk that an auditor arrives at an inappropriate conclusion for a reason unrelated to sampling issues. This can occur when an auditor uses an inappropriate audit procedure, relies too heavily on unreliable evidence, or spends too little time testing the accounts most at risk of material misstatement.

When testing controls, non-sampling risk is the risk that an auditor designs tests that are ineffective and do not provide evidence that a control is operating properly. For example, a client

non-sampling risk the risk that the auditor reaches an inappropriate conclusion for any reason not related to sampling risk

uses passwords to restrict access to its computer programs. To test that the passwords are operating effectively, an auditor observes client personnel accessing programs using their passwords. This test is not effective in assessing whether the client's programs prevent access to users with invalid passwords, since the test is focused on users with valid passwords. An effective test would be to enter invalid passwords to see if access is denied. In another example, an auditor is aware that the client has a new credit policy, which places more restrictions on sales to credit customers with amounts overdue. To test the new policy, the auditor reads the client's policy manual, finds the details of the policy change, and concludes that the internal control procedure is effective. Reading the policy manual is not a test of the control. The auditor would need to select some overdue accounts receivable and check that the new policy had been enforced.

When conducting substantive procedures, there are a number of non-sampling risks. One non-sampling risk is the risk that an auditor relies too heavily on less persuasive evidence. For example, an auditor may rely too heavily on management representations without gathering independent corroborating evidence. Non-sampling risk is also the risk that an auditor spends most of their time testing assertions where the risk of material misstatement is low and ignores or spends insufficient time testing assertions most at risk of material misstatement. For example, a client sells pearls. There is a significant risk that recorded inventory does not exist, yet the auditor spends more time testing for completeness.

Cloud 9

Ian is a bit disappointed. "I thought that if you took a random sample and did not find any errors, you could conclude that there was definitely no error in the overall population. But you are saying that there is still a risk that the population has errors."

"That's right," says Suzie."'Unless you test every item in the population, you will still have a statistical chance of making the wrong conclusion simply because you took a sample. Also, if you take a sample in a way that is biased, it is difficult to conclude that the sample results say anything at all about the population. That's why it is so important that junior staff don't just take the nearest, or most convenient, box of documents to test. Another big trap is that some part of the accounting period has different conditions, such as that a key member of the client's staff is on holidays. The auditor has to recognize this and make sure that the relevant period is included in the sample. We know that Cloud 9 opened its new Toronto store on the first of June. Obviously, inventory levels will be different around this time, so we have to plan to handle these different conditions with our sampling."

BEFORE YOU GO ON

6.2.1 What is sampling risk?

6.2.2 How does sampling risk relate to tests of controls and substantive testing?

6.2.3 What is non-sampling risk?

6.3 STATISTICAL AND NON-STATISTICAL SAMPLING

 **3** Differentiate between statistical and non-statistical sampling.

According to CAS 530, **statistical sampling** involves random selection and probability theory to determine the sample size and evaluate the results, including sampling risk. Any sample selection method that does not incorporate random selection and probability theory is not statistical sampling; for example, when an auditor uses judgement alone to select the sample size and the items to include in the sample for testing. An advantage of statistical sampling is that it allows an auditor to measure sampling risk; that is, the risk that the sample chosen by the auditor is not representative. Sometimes a disadvantage of statistical sampling is the cost involved in using this technique.

Non-statistical sampling is easier to use than statistical sampling, is lower cost, and allows an auditor to select a sample that they believe is appropriate. Most audit firms use a combination of statistical and non-statistical sampling as both methods provide appropriate audit evidence

statistical sampling an approach to sampling where random selection is used to select a sample and probability theory is used to evaluate the sample results

non-statistical sampling any sample selection method that does not have the characteristics of statistical sampling

and allow the auditor to form a conclusion on the items being tested. The next section of this chapter includes a discussion of various statistical and non-statistical sampling techniques.

BEFORE YOU GO ON

6.3.1 What is statistical sampling?

6.3.2 What is non-statistical sampling?

6.3.3 What are the advantages and disadvantages of statistical and non-statistical sampling?

6.4 SAMPLING TECHNIQUES AND FACTORS AFFECTING SAMPLING

④ Describe sampling methods and the factors to be considered when choosing a sample.

In this section, we discuss a range of sampling techniques available to auditors. They include random selection, systematic selection, haphazard selection, block selection, and judgement selection.

6.4.1 Sampling techniques

Random selection

random selection process whereby a sample is selected free from bias and each item in a population has an equal chance of selection

As explained earlier, statistical sampling requires that a sample be selected randomly and the results of the test be evaluated using probability theory. **Random selection** requires that the person selecting the sample does not influence the choice of items selected. The resulting sample is then free from bias and each item within the population has an equal chance of being selected for testing. Random number generators can be used to select a sample (see figure 6.1).

stratification the process of dividing a population into groups of sampling units with similar characteristics

Stratification can be used ahead of random selection to improve audit efficiency. This means that an auditor partitions a population ahead of sampling by identifying sub populations with similar characteristics. For example, for accounts receivable, the auditor may stratify high-dollar items or balances that are overdue. After stratifying a population, items can be randomly selected within each stratum. Thus, stratification can be used to ensure that the sample includes items that have the characteristics required by the auditor, such as material or risky items, and remain a statistical sampling technique when items are randomly selected.

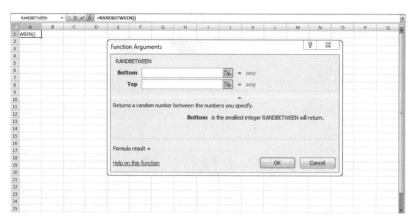

FIGURE 6.1 **Random number generator**

Systematic selection

systematic selection the selection of a sample for testing by dividing the number of items in a population by the sample size, giving the sampling interval (n) and then selecting every nth item in the population

Systematic selection involves the selection of a sample for testing by dividing the number of items in a population by the sample size, resulting in the sampling interval (n). Once the sampling interval has been determined, a starting point is selected, which is an item in the population below the sampling interval. Then the sample is selected by selecting the first item and then every nth item after that.

For example, a client has 600 creditors. The auditor has decided that the sample size when testing creditors is 20. To determine the sampling interval, the following formula is used.

$$\text{Sampling interval} = \frac{\text{Population size}}{\text{Sample size}}$$
$$= \frac{600}{20}$$
$$= 30$$

This means that every 30th item will be selected for testing. An item within the first 30 in the list of creditors is selected as the starting point. From then on, every 30th item is selected for testing. If the first item selected is 15, then the following items will be tested: 15, 45, 75, 105, 135, 165, 195, 225, 255, 285, 315, 345, 375, 405, 435, 465, 495, 525, 555, and 585. If the starting item is selected randomly and the population is not arranged in any particular order, systematic selection can be considered a statistical sampling technique.

The risk in using systematic selection is that items will be listed in such a way that by selecting every *n*th item, the auditor is selecting items that are related in some way. For example, if the sampling interval is 7 and items in the population represent the daily sales of a particular product, then the auditor will select sales made on the same day each week. This risk can be reduced by reviewing the items in a population before calculating the sampling interval.

Haphazard selection

Haphazard selection involves the selection of a sample by an auditor without using a methodical technique. While this technique appears to have much in common with random selection, there is a risk that an auditor will avoid selecting some items or ensure other items are included in the sample. For example, an item that is going to be difficult to test because the documentation is held in another location may be purposefully omitted by the auditor, while an item that looks large or unusual and catches the auditor's eye may be purposefully included. This is a non-statistical technique as human bias may impact the sample selected, and therefore prevent the sample from being a true random sample.

> **haphazard selection** the selection of a sample without use of a methodical technique

Cloud 9

"We are going to use random selection for sales invoices and cash receipts at Cloud 9," Suzie tells Ian. "This way we will be sure we do not influence the items selected in any way. We will be sure the sample will be free from bias and each item within the population has an equal chance of being selected. We will use firm software to generate the sample size require and the items to be tested."

Block selection

Block selection involves the selection of items that are grouped together within the population of items available. This is a non-statistical technique as many populations of items are sorted in a sequence, which makes the selection of groups of items in a block inappropriate. For example, transactions are generally grouped in date order. By using block selection, the items selected will not be representative of transactions made throughout the year.

> **block selection** the selection of items that are grouped together within the population of items available

For example, a client has 600 creditors. They are listed alphabetically. The auditor has decided that the sample size when testing creditors is 20. Using block selection, the auditor selects the first creditor starting with D and includes the next 20 creditors in the sample.

Judgemental selection

Judgemental selection involves the selection of items that an auditor believes should be included in the sample for testing. When testing controls, judgement may be used to ensure that transactions processed when a new computer is installed are included in the sample. When conducting

> **judgemental selection** the selection of items that an auditor believes should be included in the sample for testing

substantive testing, judgement may be used to include in the sample large or unusual items. This is a non-statistical sampling technique.

PROFESSIONAL ENVIRONMENT

Sampling in practice

How do auditors use sampling in practice? Hall et al. conducted a survey of U.S. accountants in public practice, industry, and government to find the answer to this question. Although their study was conducted in 1997 and the results are not necessarily representative of today's practices, their discussion on the advantages and disadvantages of statistical and non-statistical sampling and their impact on the risk of an inappropriate audit opinion still applies.

The researchers asked auditors how they determined sample sizes, selected samples, and evaluated these samples. The auditors were asked if they used statistical selection techniques (such as simple random, stratified, and systematic dollar-unit as described below) and non-statistical selection techniques (such as haphazard, block, and systematic).

The results showed that auditors use non-statistical selection methods 85 percent of the time and only 15 percent of the selections were made using statistical methods. The most common non-statistical sample selection method was haphazard selection. This is a technique where the sample is selected without a method. The choice of items is not supposed to be based on its characteristics, such as colour, size, or convenience of location. However, very few of the auditors reported receiving any training in methods to counter the bias introduced by non-statistical sampling and none reported using any bias-reducing techniques. The results suggest that auditors might not fully understand the influence of sample selection bias on their audit conclusions.

The most common statistical sample selection method according to the study is dollar-unit sampling. This is an approach where the unit sampled is not the transaction or document but the individual dollars making up the transaction or balance. The dollar-unit sampling method means that the auditor samples the dollars in the transactions rather than the transactions themselves. Dollar-unit sampling gives large transactions a greater chance of being sampled than small transactions.

Consider the following example of sales transactions reported by a client:

#1	$2
#2	$2,000
#3	$20,000

The auditor wants to take a random sample and inspect the underlying documents. If the unit of sampling is the sales transaction, the $20,000 transaction has the same chance of being selected as the $2 transaction. However, if dollar-unit sampling is used, then every sales dollar has the same chance of being selected. The chance of the $20,000 transaction being selected is 10,000 times greater than the $2 transaction. Given that auditors are typically concerned about overstatement of sales, dollar-unit sampling has the advantage of being more likely to select potentially overstated transactions.

Source: T.W. Hall, J.E. Hunton, and B.J. Pierce, 2002, "Sampling Practices of Auditors in Public Accounting, Industry, and Government," *Accounting Horizons*, vol. 16, no. 2, June 2002, pp. 125–36.

6.4.2 Factors to consider when selecting a sample

There are a number of factors to consider when selecting a sample. The factors discussed in this section are common to all sampling methods. When selecting a sample, an auditor will use their judgement and knowledge of the client to determine control risk, detection risk, and planning materiality, all of which impact the sample size. The lower the control risk, the smaller the sample size when testing controls. The lower the detection risk, the larger the sample size when conducting detailed substantive procedures. The sample size must be large enough to reduce the sampling risk to an acceptable level. The sample size is determined either using professional judgement or by applying a statistical formula based on tolerable error, the expected error, and the required confidence level. These concepts will be discussed below.

An auditor uses their professional judgement when selecting the population from which a sample is drawn. This decision is determined by the audit procedure undertaken, which, in turn, is determined by the assertion being tested. When testing the existence of inventory, it is appropriate to select a sample from the client's inventory listing (that is, the population from which a sample is selected is the client's complete list of inventory), whereas when testing the completeness of inventory, it is appropriate to select a sample of physical inventory (that is, the population from which a sample is selected is the client's physical inventory).

An auditor may decide to stratify the population before selecting a sample from it. Stratification improves audit efficiency by dividing the population into groups and then selecting items from each group. For example, a population may be divided into months of the year. When testing controls, it is important to ensure effectiveness throughout the year. By dividing items into months of the year and selecting from each month, an auditor can efficiently ensure that the whole year is covered by their test. If stratification were not used in this example, the sample chosen would likely be much larger to ensure each month is included in the sample. In another example, a population may be divided into different characteristics so that riskier items have an appropriate chance of being selected for testing. Credit sales are riskier than cash sales, so sales may be divided into credit and cash before a sample is selected.

An auditor will also use their professional judgement when considering what would be considered an error within the population tested. When testing controls, an auditor will define what represents a deviation from a prescribed control procedure. For example, if a client has a control procedure that requires a manager to authorize purchases greater than $20,000, a deviation will be evidence of unauthorized purchases greater than $20,000. When conducting substantive procedures, an auditor will define what represents a misstatement in transactions or account balances. For example, if an auditor conducts receivable confirmations to test the existence of accounts receivable, a non-reply would be considered a potential error and would require further audit work. If an auditor conducts a test of the accuracy of the depreciation expense by recalculating selected items, and some items are significantly different from the client's depreciation amounts, those differences would be considered potential errors that would require further audit testing.

An auditor will use their professional judgement to determine the **tolerable error** or **misstatement** and required level of confidence. The tolerable misstatement is the maximum error an auditor is willing to accept within the population tested (CAS 530). When testing controls, this is the tolerable rate of deviation that an auditor is willing to accept before concluding that a control is ineffective. When conducting substantive procedures, tolerable error relates to auditor-assessed materiality. If an error is considered material, an auditor will conclude that the account is materially misstated.

> **tolerable error** or **misstatement**
> the maximum error an auditor is willing to accept within the population tested

The required level of confidence is a function of control risk when testing controls and of detection risk when conducting substantive procedures. When control risk is initially assessed as low, based on an auditor's understanding of the client's system of internal controls, an auditor will require a high level of confidence that the controls are effective before concluding that control risk is low. In this situation, an auditor will increase the sample size when testing controls to reduce the risk that the client's system of internal controls is believed to be effective when it is ineffective. (Refer to the top section of table 6.1.)

When detection risk is determined to be low, an auditor will require a high level of confidence that the transactions and accounts are not materially misstated. Recall that by determining a low detection risk, the auditor believes that inherent risk and control risk are high; that is, the transactions and accounts are at risk of material misstatement and the client's internal controls are believed to be ineffective. In this situation, the auditor will increase the sample size when conducting substantive tests of transactions and balances to reduce the risk that the auditor concludes that a material misstatement does not exist when it does. (Refer to the top section of table 6.2.)

To summarize, before selecting a sample, an auditor will use their professional judgement to assess control and detection risk, set planning materiality, select an appropriate population for testing, define what is to be considered to be an error within the population to be tested, set the tolerable error rate, and set the required level of confidence. Once these parameters are set, an auditor will select the sample using a statistical or non-statistical sampling technique.

BEFORE YOU GO ON

6.4.1 What is the difference between random and haphazard sample selection?

6.4.2 What is the risk in using systematic sample selection?

6.4.3 What factors should be considered when selecting a sample?

6.5 FACTORS THAT INFLUENCE THE SAMPLE SIZE—TESTING CONTROLS

There are a number of factors that will influence the sample size when testing controls. These are summarized in table 6.3, which comes from CAS 530.

 Determine the factors that influence the sample size when testing controls.

TABLE 6.3 **Factors that influence the sample size when testing controls**

FACTOR	EFFECT ON SAMPLE SIZE
1. An increase in the extent to which the auditor's risk assessment takes into account relevant controls	Increase
2. An increase in the tolerable rate of deviation	Decrease
3. An increase in the expected rate of deviation of the population to be tested	Increase
4. An increase in the auditor's desired level of assurance that the tolerable rate of deviation is not exceeded by the actual rate of deviation in the population	Increase
5. An increase in the number of sampling units in the population	Negligible

Source: Auditing and Assurance Standards Board 2010, CAS 530 *Audit Sampling*, App. 2, pp. 21–2.

The first factor listed in table 6.3 is an increase in the extent to which the risk of material misstatement is reduced by the operating effectiveness of controls. If an auditor believes that a control will be effective in reducing an identified risk of material misstatement, their audit strategy will be to increase testing of that control to ensure it is effective. When concluding that a control is effective, an auditor will rely on that control to prevent and detect a material misstatement, and reduce their detailed substantive procedures.

The second factor listed in table 6.3 is an increase in the **rate of deviation** from the prescribed control activity that the auditor is willing to accept. As described previously, an auditor will use their professional judgement to determine the tolerable rate of deviation that is acceptable. There is an inverse relationship between the tolerable rate of deviation and sample size. If an auditor intends to rely on a control to prevent and detect a material misstatement, a lower tolerable error rate will be set, and the sample size will be increased to provide the auditor with the evidence required to demonstrate that the control is effective. If an auditor expects to place relatively more reliance on their substantive procedures and reduce their reliance on an internal control, they will increase the tolerable rate of deviation and reduce the sample size when testing the control.

The third factor listed in table 6.3 is an increase in the rate of deviation from the prescribed control activity that the auditor expects to find in the population. If an auditor believes that the rate of deviation has increased when compared to prior audits, they will increase the sample size to accurately evaluate the impact of the changed circumstances. For example, the rate of deviation could increase if the client has new staff, if the client has significantly changed a computer program, or if the client has changed its internal control procedures.

The fourth factor listed in table 6.3 is an increase in the auditor's required confidence level. When control risk is assessed as low for a risk factor, an auditor's required level of confidence in the effectiveness of their client's internal control is higher than when control risk is assessed as medium to high. If an auditor is to rely on the client's internal control procedures to prevent or detect an identified material misstatement, their required confidence level in that control increases and they will increase the sample size when testing that control.

The fifth and final factor listed in table 6.3 is an increase in the number of sampling units in the population. When a population is large and fairly homogenous, there is little benefit from continuing to increase the sample size as the results from continued testing should confirm early findings. For example, an auditor may test control procedures surrounding the processing of sales. When all sales are processed using the same procedure, there will be little difference in the sample size if the population of sales was to vary from one year to the next.

rate of deviation when testing controls, the proportion of items tested that did not conform to the client's prescribed control procedure

---

BEFORE YOU GO ON

6.5.1 What are the factors that influence sample size when testing controls?

6.5.2 What is the relationship between the tolerable rate of deviation and sample size?

6.5.3 How is the auditor's required confidence level influenced by control risk?

6.6 FACTORS THAT INFLUENCE THE SAMPLE SIZE—SUBSTANTIVE TESTING

6.6.1 Factors that influence sample size when performing substantive tests

There are a number of factors that will influence the sample size when testing transactions and balances. These are summarized in table 6.4, which comes from CAS 530.

The first factor listed in table 6.4 is an increase in the auditor's assessment of the risk of material misstatement. This risk is influenced by the auditor's assessment of inherent and control risk. The higher the inherent and control risk, the greater the risk that a material misstatement exists in a client's financial statements, and the more an auditor must rely on their substantive tests of transactions and balances to identify potential material misstatements. When an auditor decides to increase their reliance on their substantive procedures, they will increase the substantive testing sample size.

The second factor listed in table 6.4 is an increase in the use of other substantive procedures directed toward the same assertion. When testing transactions and balances, an auditor will use a number of audit procedures. The more procedures that are directed to the same audit assertion, the less an auditor will need to rely on the evidence provided by one test alone and the smaller the sample size required. For example, when testing the valuation of inventory, a number of procedures can be used. They include inspecting inventory on hand for evidence of damage, recalculating cost multiplied by quantity on hand, tracing of cost to supplier invoices, and testing for the lower of cost and net realizable value.

The third factor listed in table 6.4 is an increase in the auditor's required confidence level. This factor is also related to the level of inherent and control risk. The greater the inherent and control risk, the lower the detection risk established by the auditor, and the greater the confidence level required when conducting substantive tests of transactions and balances. When an auditor requires more confidence from the results of their testing, they will increase the sample size.

The fourth factor listed in table 6.4 is an increase in the total error that the auditor is willing to accept. When an auditor increases the tolerable error, they are indicating that they are not relying on that particular test to provide all of the evidence required for a particular assertion. In that case, the auditor will reduce the sample size. The tolerable error is equal to or less than the materiality level set for the class of transactions or balances being tested.

The fifth factor listed in table 6.4 is an increase in the amount of error the auditor expects to find in the population. When an auditor believes that there is likely to be a material misstatement in the population of transactions or amounts making up an account balance, they will increase the sample size to gain a better estimate of the actual misstatement in the population. This will occur when an account is at risk of material misstatement, such as when it requires estimation (for example, the allowance for doubtful accounts); when it requires complex calculations

6 Determine the factors that influence the sample size when substantive testing and consider techniques used to perform substantive tests.

FACTOR	EFFECT ON SAMPLE SIZE
1. An increase in the auditor's assessment of the risk of material misstatement	Increase
2. An increase in the use of other substantive procedures directed at the same assertion	Decrease
3. An increase in the auditor's desired level of assurance that tolerable misstatement is not exceeded by actual misstatement in the population	Increase
4. An increase in tolerable misstatement	Decrease
5. An increase in the amount of misstatement the auditor expects to find in the population	Increase
6. Stratification of the population when appropriate	Decrease
7. The number of sampling units in the population	Negligible

TABLE 6.4 **Factors that influence the sample size when testing transactions and balances**

Source: Auditing and Assurance Standards Board 2010, CAS 530 *Audit Sampling*, App. 3, pp. 23–5.

(for example, foreign exchange translations); or when it requires difficult valuation techniques (for example, fair values). This will also occur when the auditor has assessed that control risk is high and the client's control procedures are inadequate.

The sixth factor listed in table 6.4 is stratification of the population. As described previously, stratification of the population will result in more efficient sampling and reduce the sample required. The seventh and final factor listed in table 6.4 is the number of sampling units in the population. As described previously for tests of controls, when a population is large and fairly homogenous, there is little benefit from continuing to increase the sample size, as the results from continued testing should confirm early findings.

6.6.2 Techniques for performing substantive tests

There are two main techniques applied when the auditor is performing substantive tests and deciding how much of a balance to test. These are (1) key item testing and (2) representative sampling.

Both of these is now discussed further.

Key item testing

When conducting substantive testing, the auditor uses either a statistical basis or professional judgement to identify and test key items within a balance. Their focus is on selecting the largest transactions (or other individually significant items) within a balance to obtain "coverage" over the total. That is, by selecting the largest transactions to test, the auditor is able to conclude over the entire balance based on the conclusions they reached by testing the largest transactions within a balance.

For example, say an auditor is testing accounts receivable existence using accounts receivable confirmations. The total receivables are $3 million, with two key item trade receivables due from customers totalling $2.75 million of the balance. By selecting these two accounts and sending confirmation requests to them, assuming they reply, the auditor is able to conclude that because 91.7 percent of accounts receivable exist as at the confirmation date ($2.75 million / $3 million), it is reasonable that total accounts receivable of $3 million exist as at the confirmation date.

Some audit firms have software that assists in determining whether key items selected will provide enough of a basis to conclude that the audit assertion being tested has been met (within the confines of materiality). These software tools use a variety of methods to assess the approach planned and ordinarily take into consideration the total population (the account balance being audited), the materiality for the audit, and the other procedures that might be planned that will provide evidence to the auditor about the assertion being tested. The more persuasive the evidence from other procedures, the less coverage these key items need to address. The less persuasive the evidence from other audit procedures, the more coverage is generally necessary from these key items.

Representative sampling

After key items have been segregated, there may remain a large population of items that are individually unimportant but significant in total. These populations can consist of either transactions through a point in time (for example, sales) or items within an account balance at a point in time (for example, year-end finished goods inventory on hand). If risk assessments indicate the results of key item testing do not provide sufficient evidence to conclude that the population is free from material errors, the auditor obtains additional required evidence by sampling from the remainder of the population (after excluding the key items). When sampling from the remainder of the population, the sample items are selected, either statistically or non-statistically, in such a way that the sample is expected to be representative of that remaining population. This is referred to as representative sampling. When a representative sampling approach is appropriate, the sample should be large enough to achieve the audit objective. The auditor also attempts to ensure that every item in the population has an equal chance of selection and that there is no conscious or inappropriate bias in the selection of items.

When the auditor uses representative sampling, there are three common sampling strategies applied, depending on the auditor's expectations of error and their overall audit objective (that is, identifying overstatement or understatement of the amount being audited).

The following are the three sampling strategies.

1. *Representative sampling using audit risk tables.* The auditor uses this technique when they do not expect errors or they expect a low number of errors; that is, the risk of material misstatement has been assessed as low, and their primary concern is with the overstatement in an account balance. This is a common technique used to obtain "coverage" of a total balance as at year end and can be used to calculate errors that can then be extrapolated across a total balance. Many firms have software tools that assist in the calculation of representative samples; the audit risk tables are embedded within the tool and will calculate the sample size, depending on the input of other considerations, such as materiality, total key items already tested, and audit evidence obtained from other substantive procedures. The technique is generally not used for accounts where the key concern is understatement, as the technique will sample (and therefore test) items that are in the balance. It will not, however, select a sample of items that may be missing from the balance. In these cases, the auditor may supplement the testing of the balance with extensive cut-off and completeness substantive tests (for example, testing a sample of transactions after year end to determine if any of the transactions should have been recorded in the period subject to audit).

2. *Variables estimation sampling.* The auditor uses this technique if they expect more than a few errors in an account balance. This technique differs from representative sampling in that it can be used when the concern is both understatement and overstatement. Variables estimation sampling is usually applied to detect misstatements of the book values (carrying amounts or recorded values) of populations. The sample items selected are examined to determine their audited value (that is, the true or estimated amounts at which they should be carried). The differences between the book and audited values are then projected to estimate the error in the population. This technique evaluates selected characteristics of a population on the basis of a sample of the items constituting the population. The design of a variables estimation sampling approach involves mathematical calculations that tend to be complex and difficult to apply manually. Because of this, most audit firms use a specialized tool as well as a sampling specialist to assist them in applying this technique.

3. *Attribute sampling.* The auditor uses this technique to supplement other substantive procedures to obtain audit assurance related to tests of transactions when they do not expect errors (or when they expect a low number of errors). Attribute sampling is used to obtain a level of confidence, based on a statistically valid sample of transactions, that key attributes in existence for the sample tested can be inferred to be in existence for the entire population. Attribute sampling does not ordinarily lend itself to calculating a precise error that can be extrapolated across the entire balance.

Sampling is a complex area that requires the use of mathematically relevant, statistically valid techniques as well as a high degree of professional judgement to determine the nature, timing, and extent of testing.

BEFORE YOU GO ON

6.6.1 What are the factors that influence sample size when conducting substantive procedures?

6.6.2 What influences an increase in the auditor's assessment of the risk of material misstatement?

6.6.3 Describe variables estimation sampling.

6.7 EVALUATING SAMPLE TEST RESULTS

After an auditor has completed their audit testing, the next stage is to evaluate the results. When testing controls, an auditor will consider whether the results of the tests applied to a sample provide evidence that the control tested is effective within the entire population. When testing transactions and balances, an auditor will consider whether the results of the tests applied to a

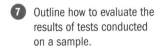 **7** Outline how to evaluate the results of tests conducted on a sample.

sample provide evidence that the class of transactions or account balance tested is fairly stated (that is, does not contain a material misstatement).

If an auditor discovers departures from prescribed controls when testing controls, they will calculate a deviation rate. The deviation rate is the proportion of departures within the sample. For example, if an auditor finds three departures from a prescribed control when testing a sample of 30 items, the deviation rate is 10 percent (3/30). If the sample is representative of the population, the auditor will compare this deviation rate with their tolerable rate of deviation. If the rate of deviation exceeds the tolerable rate, the auditor will extend their testing (particularly when the auditor is concerned that their sample may not be representative) and gather further evidence of other controls that may be aimed at reducing the identified risk of material misstatement. If, after conducting more testing, the auditor finds that the rate of deviation remains consistent with their initial findings and other controls are similarly ineffective, the auditor will conclude that the client's system of internal controls cannot be relied on to prevent or detect a potential material misstatement and the auditor will increase their reliance on their substantive tests of the account tested.

If an auditor discovers errors when testing transactions or account balances, the auditor will need to project the error to the population being tested provided that the sample is representative of the population (CAS 530). First, an auditor will consider whether an error is considered to be an anomaly and not likely to be repeated throughout the population being tested. If an error is considered to be an anomaly, it will be removed before projecting remaining errors to the population. Second, an auditor will consider whether the population was stratified before being sampled. If so, errors are projected within each stratum and then totalled together with any unique errors identified. An auditor will consider the impact of **projected errors** on the class of transactions or account balance being tested to determine whether a material misstatement has occurred.

projected error extrapolation of the errors detected when testing a sample to the population from which the sample was drawn

For example, an auditor has conducted substantive testing on an account balance, which has been split into three strata. The results of that test are summarized in table 6.5. The first column contains the stratum number, the second column the error found for each stratum, the third column the dollar value of the sample tested, the fourth column the dollar value of the entire stratum available for testing, and the final column the calculation of the projected error for each stratum.

TABLE 6.5 **Evaluation of results of substantive testing**

STRATUM (1)	ERROR (2)	SAMPLE (3)	STRATUM (4)	PROJECTED ERROR (2)/(3) × (4)
1	$1,586	$20,235	$25,732	$ 2,017
2	$ (658)	$ 8,398	$15,367	$ (1,204)
3	$1,721	$12,568	$32,456	$ 4,444
Total	$2,649	$41,201	$73,555	$ 5,257

The net total error for the sample is $2,649. It would be incorrect to compare that amount to the tolerable error rate as the error in the sample underestimates the error in the entire population. The errors found are projected to the population in the final column in table 6.5, providing a total net error of $5,257. That error is compared to the tolerable error rate for that account balance. If the tolerable error rate was set conservatively at $3,500, the auditor would conclude that the errors uncovered are material and further work is required. This may involve increasing the sample size and/or conducting other tests aimed at the assertion being tested. If the tolerable error rate was set at $7,500, the auditor would conclude that the errors uncovered are not material. As the total net error is close to the tolerable error rate, some additional testing within the sample may be considered to confirm that conclusion.

While the techniques to project errors can be more sophisticated than noted here, they all have in common a need to consider the sampling technique used, the level of precision required, and the extent of evidence provided by other audit procedures. As described in the professional environment vignette entitled "Sampling in Practice" appearing earlier in this chapter, audit forms tend to use non-statistical sampling techniques, which require less sophisticated interpretation of the results.

Cloud 9

Suzie concludes the discussion of sampling by assuring Ian that it will not be his task to determine sample sizes and apply judgement to consider the results of the tests — that is a job for the other senior people on the team. It will, however, be Ian's task to carry out the instructions very carefully so that he does not inadvertently introduce any bias into the tests.

Suzie returns to Ian's earlier problem. He is confused about how they can proceed with substantive tests and control tests when they seem to be interrelated. How can they determine the appropriate scheduling of control and substantive tests? She starts by asking him a question. "How likely do you think it is that Cloud 9's trial balance contains errors?" she asks Ian. "Well that depends," replies Ian. "On what?" asks Suzie. "On whether they made any mistakes, I suppose." "Well, how likely is that?" persists Suzie.

Ian is even more confused now. He wants to know about control and substantive tests, and Suzie is not telling him. Suzie tries another approach. "What can the client do to prevent mistakes getting into their accounts, or detect and correct mistakes that do enter the records?"

BEFORE YOU GO ON

6.7.1 What will an auditor consider when evaluating test results?

6.7.2 What is the rate of deviation and when will an auditor calculate this?

6.7.3 What will an auditor do if the rate of deviation exceeds the tolerable rate?

6.8 TESTS OF CONTROLS AND SUBSTANTIVE PROCEDURES

 8 Understand the difference between tests of controls and substantive tests.

audit strategy strategy that sets the scope, timing, and direction of the audit and provides the basis for developing a detailed audit plan

audit plan plan that details the audit procedures to be used when testing controls and when conducting detailed substantive audit procedures

substantive audit procedures procedures used when the auditor plans to get a minimum knowledge of the client's controls and conducts extensive substantive procedures that involve intensive testing of year-end account balances and transactions from throughout the year

A key task during the planning stage of every audit involves the development of an **audit strategy**. CAS 300 *Planning an Audit of Financial Statements* requires that an auditor establish an overall audit strategy, as described in chapter 4. The audit strategy provides the basis for a detailed **audit plan**. An audit plan includes the audit procedures to be used when testing controls and when conducting detailed **substantive audit procedures**.

An audit strategy is developed after gaining an understanding of a client's business and its internal control structure. Once an auditor has a thorough knowledge of their client's business, they can determine the overall level of **inherent risk** (the risk that a material misstatement could occur without considering any internal controls). Once an auditor has a thorough understanding of the client's controls, they can assess the **control risk** (the risk that a client's system of internal controls will not prevent or detect a material misstatement), which affect **audit risk** (the risk that an auditor expresses an inappropriate audit opinion when the financial statements are materially misstated). Table 6.6 contains an overview of the link between audit risk and audit strategy. When control risk is assessed as being high (top section of table 6.6), an auditor will adopt a predominantly substantive approach. This means that the audit strategy is to gain a minimum knowledge of the client's system of internal controls, conduct limited or no **tests of controls** (or **controls testing**), and conduct extensive detailed substantive procedures.

When control risk is assessed as low (bottom section of table 6.6), an auditor may adopt a combined audit strategy. This means that the audit strategy is to gain a detailed understanding of the client's system of internal controls, conduct extensive tests of controls, and, if those controls prove effective, conduct less detailed substantive procedures.

TABLE 6.6 **Audit risk and audit strategy**

AUDIT RISK =	INHERENT RISK	CONTROL RISK	DETECTION RISK	AUDIT STRATEGY
High	High	High	Low	
		No tests of controls	Increased reliance on substantive tests of transactions and account balances	Substantive strategy
Low	Low	Low	High	
		Increased reliance on tests of controls	Reduced reliance on substantive tests of transactions and account balances	Combined strategy

Cloud 9

Ian is starting to understand. Suzie has already explained the idea of inherent, control, and detection risk to him, but until now he did not realize the practical implications. He can now answer Suzie's question: he is able to explain that the client is responsible for creating a system of internal controls to stop or detect mistakes entering the accounts. A strong system of internal controls means lower control risk. Tests of controls are designed to gather evidence about the strength of the system of internal controls and to justify the auditor's decision about how much reliance to place on the system. Greater reliance on a strong system of internal controls will allow the auditor to rely less on substantive procedures. This is the combined audit strategy. The other strategy, a predominantly substantive audit strategy, means low (or no) reliance on the system of internal controls and greater reliance on substantive procedures. But Ian is still worried—how do you actually make these assessments?

inherent risk the susceptibility of the financial statements to a material misstatement without considering internal controls

control risk the risk that a client's system of internal controls will not prevent or detect a material misstatement

audit risk the risk that an auditor expresses an inappropriate audit opinion when the financial statements are materially misstated

tests of controls (controls testing) the audit procedures designed to evaluate the operating effectiveness of controls in preventing or detecting and correcting material misstatements at the assertion level

6.8.1 Tests of controls

Later in this book, we will provide a detailed overview of tests of controls (see chapter 7). The purpose of this brief discussion is to introduce those tests and highlight how they differ from substantive tests. When testing controls, an auditor is interested in assessing the effectiveness of internal controls identified when gaining an understanding of their client's system of internal controls during the planning stage of the audit. When making a preliminary assessment that control risk is medium or low (bottom section of table 6.6), an auditor is basing that assessment on their knowledge of the significant risks faced by the client and the suitability of the client's internal controls to mitigate those risks.

Before an auditor can conclude that control risk is medium or low, they test the controls to check their effectiveness. If the controls prove effective, the auditor can reduce their reliance on detailed substantive procedures. If the controls prove ineffective, the auditor reassesses control risk as higher than before and increases their reliance on detailed substantive procedures (that is, moves toward the top section of table 6.6).

Tests of controls are conducted to establish that controls:

- operate effectively, meaning that the rate of deviation from prescribed control procedures are minimized and controls effectively prevent and detect material misstatements, and

- operate consistently throughout the accounting period.

From chapter 5, we know that the main evidence-gathering procedures used by an auditor include inspection, observation, enquiry, confirmation, recalculation, re-performance, and analytical procedures. When testing controls, the procedures commonly used include:

- inspection of documents for evidence of authorization

- inspection of documents for evidence that details included have been checked by appropriate client personnel

- observation of client personnel performing various tasks, such as preparing bank deposits and conducting an inventory count
- enquiry of client personnel about how they perform their tasks
- re-performing control procedures to test their effectiveness

Cloud 9

Suzie explains that control testing means, for example, that the auditor inspects documents, observes personnel, makes enquiries, re-performs certain controls, or conducts other tests that suit that particular client's systems. Suzie gives examples of the control tests that they intend to perform for Cloud 9: read the policies and procedures manuals, check for evidence of supervisors' reviews of cash receipts, observe staff in the shipping department handling dispatches, talk to the financial controller about the inventory management system, and re-perform a sample of bank reconciliations.

All of these control tests (plus others) have to be scheduled in the audit plan. Ian is still confused about how they can schedule substantive tests before they do the control tests. "What if the test results reveal poor controls?" he asks. Suzie explains that they have an initial assessment of control system strength and plan their substantive tests based on that assessment. "Remember," she adds, "we have already done some enquiries at a high level, plus we have the results of the analytical procedures. We have a pretty good idea of where the problems will arise. However, if our expectations are not met, we simply adjust the plan as we go along."

6.8.2 Substantive procedures

Later in this book, we will provide a detailed overview of substantive testing procedures (see chapters 8 to 12). The purpose of this brief discussion is to introduce those tests and highlight how they differ from tests of controls. The three types of substantive procedures include substantive tests of transactions, substantive tests of balances, and analytical procedures.

When an auditor assesses inherent and control risk as low for a client and tests of controls confirm their effectiveness (bottom section of table 6.6), an auditor will reduce the amount of planned detailed substantive procedures. This means that an auditor will rely to some extent on the client's internal control procedures to prevent and detect material misstatements. As a consequence, an auditor can rely more on their analytical procedures, which are more efficient than substantive testing of details, and place greater reliance on the client's accounting records.

When an auditor assesses inherent and control risk as high for a client and decides that the client's internal controls are unlikely to effectively reduce identified inherent risks (top section of table 6.6), an auditor will adopt a predominantly substantive approach to their testing. This means that an auditor will not place too much reliance on the client's system of internal controls to prevent and detect material misstatements and will instead conduct detailed substantive procedures of their own to reduce audit risk to an acceptably low level. Recall that audit risk is the risk that an auditor expresses an inappropriate audit opinion when the financial statements are materially misstated (CAS 200 *Overall Objectives of the Independent Auditor and the Conduct of an Audit in Accordance with Canadian Auditing Standards*). When control risk is high, an auditor will not rely too heavily on their analytical procedures and will instead conduct more time-consuming and costly substantive testing of transactions and balances.

When conducting detailed **substantive procedures** (also called **substantive testing** or **tests of details**), an auditor searches for evidence that recorded transactions occurred and relate to the client (**occurrence** assertion), that all transactions have been recorded (**completeness** assertion), that all transactions have been recorded at appropriate carrying amounts (**accuracy** assertion), that all transactions have been recorded in the correct accounting period (**cut-off** assertion), and that all transactions have been recorded in the correct accounts (**classification** assertion). When gathering this evidence, an auditor uses a variety of audit procedures. Here are a few examples:

- receiving confirmation from the client's bank regarding interest rates charged on amounts borrowed by the client during the accounting period (accuracy assertion)

substantive procedures (substantive testing or tests of details) audit procedures designed to detect material misstatements at the assertion level

occurrence assertion that transactions and events that have been recorded have occurred and pertain to the entity

completeness assertion that all transactions, events assets, liabilities, and equity items that should have been recorded have been recorded

accuracy assertion that amounts and other data relating to recorded transactions and events have been recorded appropriately

cut-off assertion that transactions and events have been recorded in the correct accounting period

classification assertion that transactions and events have been recorded in the proper accounts

- recalculating an interest expense using the confirmed interest rates (accuracy assertion)
- inspecting documents to verify the date of transactions around year end (cut-off assertion)
- inspecting suppliers' invoices to verify amounts purchased (completeness assertion)

When conducting detailed substantive procedures, an auditor searches for evidence that recorded accounts such as assets, liabilities, and equity accounts exist (**existence** assertion), that all accounts that should have been recorded have been recorded (completeness assertion), that recorded accounts represent items owned by the client or amounts owed by the client to third parties (**rights and obligations** assertion), and that recorded accounts appear at appropriate carrying amounts (**valuation and allocation** assertion). When gathering this evidence, an auditor uses a variety of audit procedures. Here are a few examples:

- receiving confirmation from a selection of accounts receivable accounts of amounts owed to the client (existence assertion)
- recalculating the wages payable amount (valuation and allocation assertion)
- inspecting inventory and counting amounts on hand (existence and completeness assertions)
- inspecting supplier statements for amounts outstanding at year end (completeness and valuation and allocation assertions)
- inspecting title deeds to verify that property is owned by the client (rights and obligations assertion)

An auditor can use analytical procedures when testing transactions and account balances. Analytical procedures can be used to:

- estimate depreciation expense by multiplying the average depreciation rate on a class of assets by the balance at the beginning of the year (accuracy assertion)
- compare the wages expense month by month for this year and last year (completeness and occurrence assertions)
- compare inventory balances for this year and last year (existence, completeness, and valuation and allocation assertions)
- compare accounts payable balances for last year and this year (completeness, existence, and valuation and allocation assertions)
- discuss unusual fluctuations with client personnel (occurrence, completeness, and valuation and allocation assertions)
- estimate revenue for a movie theatre, for example, by multiplying the average price of a ticket by the number of seats in the theatre, by the average proportion of seats sold per session, by the average number of sessions per week, by the number of weeks per year (occurrence and accuracy assertions)

existence assertion that recorded assets, liabilities, and equity interests exist

rights and obligations assertion that the entity holds or controls the rights to assets, and liabilities are the obligations of the entity

valuation and allocation assertion that assets, liabilities, and equity interests are included in the financial statements at appropriate amounts and any resulting valuation or allocation adjustments are appropriately recorded

Cloud 9

Ian confesses to Suzie that he has a problem understanding the difference between control and substantive tests. "For example, at Cloud 9, a supervisor is supposed to check and authorize cash receipts deposited to the bank account. Suppose I find that the amount of the bank deposit is correct but that the supervisor forgot to sign the authorization. Is that an error?"

Suzie replies, "Remember, tests of controls are performed to assess whether the controls are working and therefore can be relied upon. Substantive tests are performed to detect misstatements in an account balance. You performed a test of the control that the supervisor authorizes the transaction and found an error or a deviation from the correct performance of the control. However, you then performed an alternate substantive test and found that there was no error in the actual deposit. You have found evidence to substantiate the accuracy and occurrence assertions for that transaction. We would then consider all the other relevant evidence we have gathered about the controls over cash receipts. For example, how often do we find this type of control deviation for cash deposits? If we find significant problems with the controls, we could adjust our control risk assessment for cash receipts."

PROFESSIONAL ENVIRONMENT

Assessing materiality of errors

When auditors detect an omission or misstatement as a result of their substantive testing, they must decide whether or not the error is material, both as an individual error and in aggregate with all other errors. Auditors must take both the size of the error (its quantity) and its qualitative characteristics into account when making the materiality decision. Their final conclusion is that the error is either material or not material.

Researchers Rosner, Comunale, and Sexton argue that the binary choice (material or not) oversimplifies the situation and leads to auditors focusing only on the size of the misstatement, ignoring its qualitative characteristics. While not used in practice, the researchers propose that a "fuzzy logic" approach could be useful in materiality assessments. Fuzzy logic allows "omissions and misstatement to possess a degree of value—that is, each omission or misstatement is material to a greater or lesser degree, measured on a scale from 0 to 1."

The concept of fuzzy logic can be used to construct a rule-based expert system. An initial materiality assessment is made for each aspect of materiality, quantitative and qualitative, for the relevant omission or misstatement. The initial assessment is a number between 0 and 1, with 1 meaning the omission or misstatement is material on that attribute, and 0 meaning that it is not material. A validity value must then be assigned for each rule, where more important attributes of materiality are assigned greater validity values. The authors give the example of a modest 0.35 validity value for the rule relating to the size of the misstatement, with a greater 0.85 validity value for the rule relating to whether the misstatement increases management compensation.

The authors suggest that the final materiality value could be the highest value for the product of the initial materiality assessment value and the validity value across the materiality attributes. Alternatively, the auditor could determine the misstatement is material if any one of the materiality assessments indicated that the misstatement was material (for example, above 0.5). Finally, an auditor could create their own policy for converting the fuzzy materiality values into rules for further audit action. Whichever decision rule is adopted, the authors argue that using a formal model structure requires that the auditor evaluate each quantitative and qualitative factor explicitly. This will encourage better communication between the audit team and the client and will enhance consistency across auditors, engagements, and years.

Source: R.L. Rosner, C.L. Comunale, and T.R. Sexton, "Assessing Materiality: A New 'Fuzzy Logic' Approach," *The CPA Journal* (June 2006), pp. 26–28.

BEFORE YOU GO ON

6.8.1 What will be an auditor's strategy when control risk is assessed as high?

6.8.2 What are the two broad purposes of tests of controls?

6.8.3 What are the main objectives when conducting substantive tests of account balances?

6.9 NATURE, TIMING, AND EXTENT OF AUDIT TESTING

The nature, timing, and extent of audit testing are crucial factors in every audit. An auditor uses their professional judgement when determining the nature, timing, and extent of audit procedures to use for each client. The audit plan details the procedures to be completed by the audit team. The nature, timing, and extent of audit procedures used on each audit varies depending on the audit strategy adopted and the type of testing relied on; that is, tests of controls or detailed substantive procedures (CAS 330 *The Auditor's Responses to Assessed Risks*).

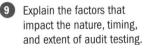 **9** Explain the factors that impact the nature, timing, and extent of audit testing.

6.9.1 Nature of audit testing

The **nature of audit testing** refers to the purpose of the test (that is, to test controls, transactions, or account balances) and the procedure used (that is, inspection, observation, enquiry, confirmation, recalculation, re-performance, or analytical procedures). The nature of an audit procedure will also depend on the assertion being tested. The higher the risk of material misstatement, the greater the use of audit procedures that access the most persuasive audit evidence.

nature of audit testing the purpose of the test and the procedure used

As described above, tests of controls are quite different from substantive procedures. Tests of controls are concerned with providing evidence that an internal control procedure exists and is effective. The nature of these controls tests is to re-perform certain procedures, inspect documents for evidence of procedures carried out by client personnel, and observe client personnel performing control procedures. Controls can also be tested by purposefully trying to trip them up. For example, transactions can be created by an auditor to test controls embedded in the client's computer programs, also referred to as application controls. Such transactions (referred to as test data) can include valid and invalid items. Valid data are traced to ensure that appropriate accounts are updated when the transactions are processed. If a client's internal controls are effective, invalid data should be identified and rejected by the program. For example, if a sales program includes a procedure to check the customer number against an approved customer listing before processing a credit sale, an auditor could include a sale to a fictitious credit customer to test that the control is working. If the program processes the sale to a fictitious customer created by the auditor, the control procedure cannot be relied on as it has not operated effectively during this instance and there is a risk that some sales have been processed by the client that did not occur (occurrence assertion).

As described above, substantive procedures include detailed tests of transactions, balances, and analytical procedures. The lower the risk of material misstatement and the more effective the controls, the more reliance is placed on more efficient, less costly, analytical procedures. For these tests to be effective, it is important that an auditor plan to spend time testing all the assertions but more persuasive evidence is required for the assertions most at risk of material misstatement for each transaction class and account balance. For assertions most at risk, an auditor endeavours to gather the most persuasive evidence.

6.9.2 Timing of audit testing

timing of audit testing the stage of the audit when procedures are performed and the date, such as within or outside the accounting period, that audit evidence relates to

Timing of audit testing is the stage of the audit when procedures are performed and the date, such as within or outside the accounting period, that audit evidence relates to. Tests of controls are designed to provide evidence that a control was effective throughout the accounting period. As such, tests of controls can be conducted during the interim stage of the audit and then extended to the end of the year when conducting the year-end audit. The interim stage of the audit is the initial visit to a client, before year end, where planning takes place. It is common for audit planning to begin before year end to aid in efficiency and to free up time at year end. After gaining an understanding of the client and its internal controls, an auditor can begin tests of controls during the interim period. Substantive testing of transactions, which also occur throughout the year, can also begin during the interim audit.

For low-risk accounts, it is common to conduct more work during the interim audit, including testing controls and conducting substantive tests of transactions. If, after conducting these preliminary tests, the auditor concludes that the risk of material misstatements matches their initial low- to moderate-level assessment, detection risk will be set as high to medium and less reliance will be placed on detailed substantive testing at year end. If, after conducting preliminary tests of controls, the auditor concludes that control risk is higher than initially estimated because, for example, the rate of deviation in controls from the client's prescribed procedures is above the expected rate for a low-risk account, the auditor will increase their reliance on detailed substantive testing at year end.

For high-risk accounts, the timing of most audit procedures will be at, or after, year end. When there is a high risk of material misstatement in the amounts appearing in the financial statements, an auditor will spend most time conducting detailed substantive tests of those account balances. Analytical procedures may be used to aid in the identification of those accounts most at risk of material misstatement, but these procedures will not be relied on as the only audit evidence obtained.

Some assertions, such as cut-off, can only be conducted on transactions around year end. For example, as inventory counts are generally conducted on, or close to, year end, audit procedures used to assess the effectiveness of the count can only be conducted around year end. Some audit procedures are conducted throughout an accounting period (tests of controls and substantive tests of transactions), while others are predominantly conducted at year end (substantive tests of account balances). The higher the risk of material misstatement, the greater the reliance on testing conducted close to year end.

6.9.3 Extent of audit testing

The **extent of audit testing** refers to the amount (quantity) of audit evidence gathered when testing controls and conducting detailed substantive procedures. When control risk is low (bottom section of table 6.6), the audit strategy is to increase reliance on tests of controls and reduce reliance on substantive testing of transactions and account balances. This means that the auditor will increase the extent of their testing of controls to gain evidence that their client's system of internal controls is effective in preventing and detecting material misstatements. If that extensive testing confirms the auditor's belief that their client's system of internal controls is indeed effective, the auditor will reduce the extent of substantive testing of transactions and balances and increase the extent of their reliance on more efficient analytical procedures.

extent of audit testing the amount of audit evidence gathered when testing controls and conducting detailed substantive procedures

When control risk is high (top section of table 6.6), the audit strategy is to do little or no tests of controls and to increase reliance on substantive testing of transactions and account balances. This means that the auditor will not rely on their client's system of internal controls to prevent and detect material misstatements. Instead, the auditor must rely on their own extensive substantive procedures to uncover any material misstatements. In the next section of this chapter, we will discuss how an auditor selects an appropriate sample for testing controls and conducting substantive procedures.

Cloud 9

Suzie emphasizes to Ian that the detailed audit program section of the audit plan must specify three things about every test—nature, timing, and extent. That is, which tests will be performed, when they will be performed and to which period the data belong to, and how many times the tests will be performed. The "how many" part relates to the size of the sample. The population from which a sample is drawn could be documents, inventory items, people (to talk to or observe), and so on.

Because W&S Partners has been appointed before year end, it can test interim data and spread the testing over the available time before the audit report deadline. However, timing is not just about convenience. If controls are weak, more tests have to be scheduled around year end. Control risk has a very pervasive effect on testing because weaker controls mean that the auditor must perform tests that will produce more persuasive evidence and select larger samples.

BEFORE YOU GO ON

6.9.1 What are the three main categories of substantive procedures?

6.9.2 What are the two most common types of testing that can be started during the interim audit?

6.9.3 What does the extent of audit testing refer to?

SUMMARY

❶ Explain how audit sampling is used in an audit.

When creating an audit plan and designing audit procedures, an auditor also decides how to select appropriate items for testing. When there are numerous transactions or items within an account balance available for testing, an auditor must decide how best to select a sample that is representative of the entire population of items available for testing.

❷ Understand the difference between sampling and non-sampling risk.

Sampling risk is the risk that the sample chosen by the auditor is not representative of the population of transactions or items within an account balance available for testing and, as a consequence, the auditor arrives at an inappropriate conclusion. Non-sampling risk is the risk that an auditor arrives at an inappropriate conclusion for a reason unrelated to sampling issues, such as an auditor using an inappropriate audit procedure.

❸ Differentiate between statistical and non-statistical sampling.

Statistical sampling involves random selection and probability theory to evaluate the results. Non-statistical sampling is any sample selection method that does not have these characteristics.

4 **Describe sampling methods and the factors to be considered when choosing a sample.**

Sampling methods include random selection, systematic selection, haphazard selection, block selection, and judgemental selection. Before selecting a sample, an auditor will set parameters pertaining to control and detection risk, planning materiality, population, tolerable error rate, and the required level of confidence. Once these parameters are set, an auditor may select a sample using a statistical or non-statistical sampling technique.

5 **Determine the factors that influence the sample size when testing controls.**

When testing controls, the factors that influence the sample size include the extent to which the risk of material misstatement is reduced by the operating effectiveness of controls, the rate of deviation from the prescribed control activity that the auditor is willing to accept, the rate of deviation from the prescribed control activity that the auditor expects to find in the population, the auditor's required confidence level, and the number of sampling units in the population.

6 **Determine the factors that influence the sample size when substantive testing and consider techniques used to perform substantive tests.**

When conducting substantive testing of transactions and balances, the factors that influence the sample size include the auditor's assessment of the risk of material misstatement, the use of other substantive procedures directed at the same assertion, the auditor's required confidence level, the tolerable error, the amount of error the auditor expects to find in the population, the stratification of the population, and the number of sampling units in the population.

Three main techniques are applied when the auditor is performing substantive tests and deciding how much of a balance to test. These are (1) key item testing, (2) representative sampling, and (3) other tests of transactions/underlying data.

7 **Outline how to evaluate the results of tests conducted on a sample.**

When testing controls, the auditor will compare the rate of deviation with the tolerable rate of deviation and determine whether they believe that the control tested is effective in preventing and/or detecting a material misstatement. When testing transactions and balances, the error in the sample will be projected onto the population and then compared to the tolerable error rate. The auditor will then determine whether the class of transactions or account balance being tested appears to be materially misstated.

8 **Understand the difference between tests of controls and substantive tests.**

The purpose of tests of controls is to assess the effectiveness of a client's system of internal controls throughout the accounting period being audited. The purpose of substantive testing is to gather direct evidence that the financial statements are free from material misstatement.

9 **Explain the factors that impact the nature, timing, and extent of audit testing.**

The nature of audit testing refers to the purpose of the test and the procedure used. The timing of audit testing refers to the stage of the audit when procedures are performed and the date, such as within or outside the accounting period, that audit evidence relates to. The extent of audit testing refers to the amount of audit evidence gathered when testing controls and conducting detailed substantive procedures.

KEY TERMS

MULTIPLE-CHOICE QUESTIONS

6.1 A detailed audit plan:
   (a) is based on the overall audit strategy.
   (b) contains a description of the control testing procedures.
   (c) lists the audit procedures to be used in substantive testing.
   ✓ (d) all of the above.

6.2 When testing controls the auditor:
   ✓ (a) is interested in assessing the effectiveness of controls.
   (b) gathers evidence about the balances of the main accounts.
   (c) does not have to have any prior knowledge of the client's inherent risks and how the controls address those risks.
   (d) all of the above.

6.3 Deviations:
   (a) are errors that affect account balances by a material amount.
   ✓ (b) occur when controls do not operate as intended.
   (c) are relevant only when they occur consistently throughout the accounting period.
   (d) are caused by auditors choosing incorrect audit procedures.

6.4 Analytical procedures:
   (a) are less efficient than substantive testing of details.
   (b) place less reliance on the client's accounting records than substantive testing of details.
   ✓ (c) are relied on to a greater extent when a client's internal controls are effective.
   (d) are most useful when inherent and control risk are high.

6.5 The relationship between audit risk, reliance on substantive testing, and evidence persuasiveness is:
   (a) high audit risk, low reliance on substantive testing, low evidence persuasiveness required.
   (b) low audit risk, high reliance on substantive testing, low evidence persuasiveness required.
   ✓ (c) high audit risk, high reliance on substantive testing, high evidence persuasiveness required.
   (d) low audit risk, low reliance on substantive testing, high evidence persuasiveness required.

6.6 If preliminary testing of controls reveals that the rate of deviation in controls is above the expected rate, the auditor will:
   ✓ (a) reduce detection risk and increase reliance on detailed substantive testing at year end.
   (b) increase detection risk and increase reliance on detailed substantive testing at year end.
   (c) reduce detection risk and decrease reliance on detailed substantive testing at year end.
   (d) increase detection risk and decrease reliance on detailed substantive testing at year end.

6.7 Sampling risk:
   (a) is the risk that the results of the test will be misinterpreted by the auditor.
   ✓ (b) is the risk that the sample chosen by the auditor is not representative of the population of transactions.
   (c) can be eliminated by taking a random sample.
   (d) applies only to samples for substantive testing.

6.8 Non-sampling risk:
   (a) occurs only if you test every member of the population.
   (b) applies only to samples taken for the purposes of control testing.
   ✓ (c) is the risk that an auditor arrives at an inappropriate conclusion for a reason unrelated to sampling issues.
   (d) does not occur if an auditor relies on unreliable evidence.

6.9 Tolerable error:
   ✓ (a) is the maximum error an auditor is willing to accept within the population.
   (b) is positively related to sample size.
   (c) relates only to control testing.
   (d) is an amount prescribed by CAS 530.

6.10 The auditor has discovered errors when conducting substantive testing on a sample of invoices. If the total error discovered is $3,442, the dollar value of the sample is $25,136, and the population dollar value is $64,912, then the projected error is:
   (a) $3,442.   ✓ (b) $8,889.   (3442/25,136)(64912)
   (c) $1,885.   (d) $1,369.

REVIEW QUESTIONS

6.1 Explain the difference between the two types of sampling risk for controls: overreliance on an ineffective system of internal controls, and underreliance on an effective system of internal controls. What are the errors' different implications for the audit? Which is the more serious risk? Explain.

6.2 Why does non-sampling risk exist for all types of tests in all audits? Explain.

6.3 Describe the main non-statistical sampling methods. What are the advantages of non-statistical sampling?

6.4 Explain the relationship between the sample size for controls testing and each of the following factors: (1) the likely effectiveness of a control; (2) the acceptable rate of deviation; (3) the expected rate of deviation; (4) the required level of confidence in the effectiveness of the client's system of internal controls; and (5) the number of units in the population.

6.5 Give an example of substantive testing where stratification would be appropriate.

6.6 Assume an auditor finds total errors of $25,300 in a sample of sales invoices. Why is it not appropriate to conclude that sales are misstated by $25,300? How would you determine the estimate of misstatement in sales?

6.7 Explain the difference between tests of controls and substantive procedures. How are the results of tests of controls related to decisions about the nature, timing, and extent of substantive procedures?

6.8 Explain how analytical procedures could be used for control testing and substantive testing. Give examples of each.

6.9 How is test data used to gather evidence about the effectiveness of controls? Why is using test data likely to be a more effective audit test than reading client procedure manuals?

6.10 Why are audit tests more likely to be conducted at or after year end for high-risk clients than for low-risk clients? Explain.

PROFESSIONAL APPLICATION QUESTIONS

Basic ★	Moderate ★★	Challenging ★★★

6.1 Sampling methods ★★

Bob Downe is auditing Red Gum Home Furniture (RGHF), a manufacturer and retailer of boutique home furniture. RGHF was founded 25 years ago by a husband and wife team and has grown rapidly in the last five years as solid, environmentally friendly, wooden furniture has grown in popularity. However, although RGHF's owners have attempted to expand the administration department to keep pace with the growth in sales, some systems are not operating as effectively as they should. This is partly due to difficulty in attracting and retaining accounting staff with appropriate experience and skills.

RGHF's owners have recently realized that they need to increase pay and improve conditions for the accounting staff to avoid having periods with unqualified staff, particularly for sales invoice processing. The staff shortages have resulted in sluggish performance in processing invoices, sending out customer statements, and collecting cash from account customers. In addition, there have been numerous mistakes in processing sales invoices, some of which have been discovered after customer complaints.

Bob is selecting a sample of sales invoices for substantive testing. All documents relating to sales invoices for the last five years are stored in boxes in the shed behind the office. The shed is very small and the boxes are stacked on top of each other because the shelves are full. Due to the damp conditions, some labels have peeled from the boxes, so it is not clear which boxes relate to the current year.

Required

(a) Describe the population(s) that would be relevant to Bob's sample selection.

(b) Which sample selection methods would be appropriate for choosing sales invoices for substantive testing at RGHF? Explain the factors that would influence your choice.

6.2 Types of audit sampling and sampling risk ★

Required

Match the numbered situations below with one of the following types of audit sampling or sampling risk:

(a) Statistical sampling
(b) Non-statistical sampling
(c) Sampling risk
(d) Non-sampling risk

1. Rather than looking only for authorized signatures, an auditor checked to see if there were any signatures in the credit approval box on a sample of sales orders.

2. An auditor concluded that, based on a statistical sample, the client's control system was working acceptably when, in fact, the population deviation rate was unacceptable.

3. Using the laws of probability, an auditor selected a sample and evaluated the results of her sample.

6.3 Benefits of statistical sampling ❸

You are an audit senior, and your manager, Monique Lauzon, feels that non-statistical sampling is the best method to use on the audit of Konway Corporation. However, you believe that statistical sampling is much superior, and you have a great deal of training in the proper use of sampling techniques.

Required

Which arguments could you use to convince Monique that statistical sampling should be used?

6.4 Sample selection in practice ❹

Rahim, a first-year auditor, is asked to select a sample of invoices to audit the utility expense account. Below is the account detail.
The audit program asks to select a sample of four items.

Month	Balance
January	15,245
February	12,973
March	11,359
April	9,326
May	6,380
June	4,558
July	2,901
August	2,837
September	3,690
October	5,890
November	9,823
December	14,906

Required
(a) Using systematic selection, determine which four months will be selected.
(b) Using haphazard selection, determine which four months will be selected.
(c) Using block selection, determine which four months will be selected.

6.5 Potential impact of sampling risk ❷❹

Your friend, Alexei Antropov, has recently began working for an auditing firm and he wants your advice regarding some tests of sales transactions that he is currently undertaking with respect to one of his clients. He has been careful not to disclose to you the name of his client so as not to breach confidentiality.

Alexei selected a haphazard sample of 30 sales with a total book value of $150,000. In his sample, he found a total of $1,000 in net overstatement errors. The total sales balance per books is $20 million. Overall materiality for the engagement is $600,000. Tolerable error for sales is $140,000. The sample results indicate that Alexei's best estimate of total misstatement in sales is $70,000.

Required

Could Alexei safely conclude that no additional audit work is needed in this area? Support your answer.

6.6 Sample size selection ★   5

Patrizia Montani is considering the sample size needed for a selection of sales invoices relating to the test of internal controls of the Caistor Company. She is determining the acceptable risk and deviation rates, and is considering two possible scenarios as shown in table 6.7.

TABLE 6.7 **Risk or deviation rate for sample scenarios**

RISK OR DEVIATION RATE	CASE A	CASE B
Acceptable risk of underreliance	High	Low
Acceptable risk of overreliance	High	Low
Tolerable deviation rate	High	Low
Expected population deviation rate	Low	High

Required

In which of the two cases should Patrizia select a larger sample size?

6.7 Sampling and non-sampling risk for control testing ★ ★

Fred Saros is auditing cash payments for OGA, a large supermarket. OGA deals with several very large corporate suppliers who expect payment by electronic funds transfer within three business days of delivery. Other large suppliers will accept cheques or electronic funds transfer on terms of 14 days, and small suppliers receive cheques with payment terms of 30 days. Other regular, large cash payments include wages (paid weekly by electronic funds transfer from a wages imprest account), utilities (electricity accounts are paid monthly by cheque), cleaning (paid monthly by cheque), and rent (paid monthly by electronic funds transfer). In addition, there are irregular payments for items such as maintenance, fixtures purchase and lease, and vehicle running costs.

All cash payments are processed in the central office after the required set of documents has been assembled and checked by two junior accounts staff. Payments are authorized by a senior accountant, and electronic funds transfer authorities and cheques are countersigned by the chief accountant (except if he is on leave, when another member of the accounting staff performs this task). Journals and ledgers are maintained by staff not involved in cash payment processing.

Fred needs to test controls over cash payments and has planned to make extensive use of sampling.

Required

(a) What population(s) would be relevant to Fred's control testing?
(b) Explain the potential implications of sampling risk for the audit of cash payments.
(c) What possible non-sampling risks exist in this case?

6.8 Determining sample size for control testing ★ ★

Alice Pang is planning the control testing of the accounts payable function in the hardware retailer Bunns and Major. Alice is attempting to determine the appropriate sample size for her tests and is writing a report to the engagement partner of the audit justifying her choices. She has had the opportunity to talk to management at Bunns and Major and tour the facilities. She has also reviewed the working papers from the previous audits and identified factors that have changed from previous years. She notes that the number of accounts payable has increased by 50 percent since last year because Bunns and Major has changed some of its suppliers from large corporate wholesalers to dealing directly with manufacturers.

Overall, Alice believes that the controls in accounts payable are likely to be operating more effectively than in previous years, and she expects a reduction in control deviations. This situation is likely because of the appointment of an additional staff member in the accounts payable department three months after the start of the fiscal year. However, she is recommending that a lower rate of deviation would be acceptable this year because of the increased importance of accounts payable to Bunns and Major's solvency situation in the current economic climate. In addition, she is recommending that substantive testing of accounts payable be less extensive than in past years.

Required

Explain how the factors mentioned above would impact the sample size for control testing of accounts payable.

6.9 Evaluating substantive testing results ★★★

The results of substantive testing of sales invoices at City Electronics are shown in table 6.8. The three strata correspond to different departments and the overall tolerable error is set at $40,000.

STRATUM	ERROR FOUND	SAMPLE TOTAL VALUE	STRATUM TOTAL VALUE	PROJECTED ERROR
1	$ 7,930	$101,170	$128,660	
2	$ 3,290	$ 41,990	$ 76,830	
3	$ 8,600	$ 62,840	$162,280	
Total	$19,820	$206,000	$367,770	

TABLE 6.8 **Substantive testing results of City Electronics' sales invoices**

Required

(a) Project the errors for each stratum and calculate the total projected error. Is the projected error material? What difference would it make if the tolerable error was set at $30,000? Explain.
(b) Discuss the implications for the substantive testing if it was discovered that the permanent staff member in the department corresponding to stratum 3 was on long-term leave for three months of the fiscal year.

6.10 Interpreting sampling documentation ★★★

Min-Li is auditing RRR Services Inc. and has designed the following tests:

Test A
1. Select 150 cancelled cheques (8 percent of the total number of cheques) at random from the purchases journal for the year.
2. Ignore any cheques with a recorded value of less than $1,000.
3. Examine the cancelled cheques to verify if they have been approved by the accounting supervisor (indicated by her initials on the cheque).
4. Compare the percentage of cheques (of the sample) that lacks the accounting supervisor's initials to a pre-determined percentage of 5 percent.

Test B
1. Select 150 cancelled cheques (8 percent of the total number of cheques) at random from the purchases journal for the year.
2. Compare the amount of each cheque to the amount recorded in the purchases journal.

3. Total the net overstatement or understatement for all cheques examined and project this amount to obtain an estimate for the population.
4. Compare the population estimate from step 3 to a predetermined amount of $8,000.

Required

(a) Identify the attribute being tested in the test of controls.
(b) Can the results in Test B be used to project a value for the population? Explain your answer.
(c) Can the results in Test A be used to project a value for the population of cancelled cheques for the year? Explain your answer.
(d) Explain sampling risk in substantive testing (in one or two sentences).

Source: © CGA-Canada, now CPA Canada. Reproduced with permission.

6.11 Results of control testing 1 ⭐

The controls at a retail store were assessed by the lead auditor as being effective and the auditor intended to rely on the operative effectiveness of controls around payroll in determining the nature, timing, and extent of substantive procedures. There is no evidence of fraud.

The control activities include controls that ensure that part-time staff are paid at the correct rate. The results of testing the relevant control are: sample size 40; tolerable deviation rate 5 percent; exceptions noted: one instance of part-time staff paid an incorrect hourly rate.

Required

(a) What is a tolerable deviation rate?
(b) Explain why the exceptions are evidence that the control did not work effectively in these cases.
(c) Explain in general terms what impact the control test results would have on the nature, timing, and extent of substantive testing.

Source: Adapted from the Institute of Chartered Accountants Australia's CA Program's *Audit and Assurance Exam*, December 2010. Provided courtesy of Chartered Accountants Australia and New Zealand.

Questions 6.12 and 6.13 are based on the following case.

Fabrication Holdings Ltd. (FH) has been a client of KFP Partners for many years. You are an audit senior and have been assigned to the FH audit for the first time for the fiscal year ended December 31, 2016. You are completing the audit planning for the property, plant, and equipment (PPE) account class, which is one of FH's most material balances. You are also aware that FH has made a large investment in a new manufacturing process to place itself in a more competitive position. Your analytical procedures indicate an increase in acquisitions of PPE.

You are testing the appropriateness of the depreciation rate assigned to PPE, and whether it is consistent with the present condition and expected use of the assets over their remaining life. You have sampled 35 PPE items, with a total dollar value of $1,145,000. The results show that for the sample items, some depreciation rates were too low and/or the remaining useful life of the equipment was overstated by management. Together, these issues produce an error in the sample of $48,500. FH has a profit before tax for the current year of $1,875,000, and a PPE account balance at the end of the year of $11,345,000.

Source: Adapted from the Institute of Chartered Accountants Australia's CA Program's *Audit and Assurance Exam*, May 2008. Provided courtesy of Chartered Accountants Australia and New Zealand.

6.12 Sampling methods and risk ⭐ ⭐

Required

Discuss the appropriate method of sampling FH's PPE for the planned tests of depreciation. Define the population. What assertions are most at risk?

6.13 Projecting errors for property, plant, and equipment ★ ★

Required

What conclusion would you draw about "valuation and allocation" of PPE from the above information? Justify your conclusion.

Questions 6.14 and 6.15 are based on the following case.

Fellowes and Associates Chartered Accountants is a successful mid-tier accounting firm with a large range of clients across Canada. During the financial year 2016, Fellowes and Associates gained a new client, Health Care Holdings Group (HCHG), which owns 100 percent of the following entities:

- Shady Oaks Centre, a private treatment centre
- Gardens Nursing Home Ltd., a private nursing home
- Total Laser Care Limited (TLCL), a private clinic that specializes in the laser treatment of skin defects

Year end for all HCHG entities is June 30.

During the 2016 financial year, Shady Oaks released its own line of treatment supplies, such as orthotics, massage oils, and exercise discs and balls, which are sold by direct marketing by a sales team employed by the centre. The sales team receives a base salary and a bonus component, which is based on the dollar value of sales it generates. You recognize that the team's main motivation is to maximize its bonuses. You select a sample of payments received by the centre post year end and trace the payments back to the general ledger and customer account balance.

In addition, you are reviewing the results of a number of tests in relation to accounts payable at Gardens Nursing Home as shown in table 6.9.

Source: Adapted from the Institute of Chartered Accountants Australia's CA Program's *Audit and Assurance Exam,* December 2008. Provided courtesy of Chartered Accountants Australia and New Zealand.

TABLE 6.9 Testing results of Gardens Nursing Home's accounts payable

TEST	RESULT	CONCLUSION
1	A number of suppliers were selected from the list of trade creditors at year end and balances traced to supplier invoices and goods received notes to ensure that goods were received prior to the year end. For two creditors out of 15 tested, the balance was only marginally overstated.	Accepted as no material errors were found
2	A number of suppliers' invoices were selected and checked to ensure that the pricing and discount terms were reviewed and authorized by the purchase manager. Three out of 20 invoices tested had not been authorized and incorrect discounts were recorded for these invoices. A follow-up of the three samples with deviations did not highlight a pattern or specific reason for the errors.	Accepted as the errors in discounts taken were immaterial

6.14 Substantive testing and assertions ★ ★

Required

(a) Identify the key account balance at risk because of the remuneration of the sales team at Shady Oaks. Identify and explain the key assertion at risk.
(b) Identify the key account balance and key assertion being tested using the substantive procedure. Given the bonus structure in place for the sales team, justify your answer.

6.15 Substantive testing versus control testing ★ ★ ★

Required

For each of the test results for Gardens Nursing Home:

(a) Identify whether this is a test of controls or a substantive test of detail.
(b) Determine the key assertion addressed by the test procedure.

(c) Explain why the conclusion reached is appropriate or inappropriate.

(d) Outline the key additional procedure that you believe needs to be performed.

6.16 Control testing in previous year ★

BBB auditors have been the auditor on the Wild Ride Theme Park for the past two years. They have completed both the financial audit and the audit for the Department of Sport and Leisure, stating that the business has adhered to the Theme Park Regulations. Wild Ride Theme Park has requested that BBB undertake both the financial statement audit and the compliance audit engagement for the current year. In each of the previous two years, BBB has tested all of Wild Ride Theme Park's internal controls relevant to ensuring compliance with the Regulations. There have been no exceptions detected in this testing of controls in the past two years. A combined approach is also planned for the current year.

Required

The junior auditor on the engagement has suggested that, since there were no exceptions detected in previous years, no work on internal controls is required because last year's evidence will be sufficient. Explain why the junior auditor's suggestion is not appropriate.

Source: Adapted from the Institute of Chartered Accountants Australia's CA Program's *Audit and Assurance Exam*, March 2011. Provided courtesy of Chartered Accountants Australia and New Zealand.

6.17 Auditing low-value assets ★ ★

MICA is a regional credit union with 10 branches across the province. MICA leases its premises and buys furniture, such as waiting-area chairs and back-office desks, through a central asset purchasing department. All computer assets are acquired on finance leases. The furniture in the waiting area has a life of four years and repairs are common because of constant use. Back-office furniture items have a life of seven years and are often relocated as branches are refurbished or relocated at the expiration of the premises' lease. MICA has adopted a "green" office policy over the last three years and refurbishment and recycling of furniture is encouraged. Where furniture is replaced, suppliers with "green" credentials are preferred. In these cases, old furniture is returned to the supplier as a trade-in on new furniture, even when the market value of these items is virtually zero.

Required

Make a list of audit procedures that could be used for substantive testing of furniture at MICA. Explain which assertion each procedure is testing.

6.18 Testing accounts receivable ★

Emma Maltz has been appointed as audit senior of the accounts receivable area in the audit of Fantastic Cruises, a company operating leisure cruises from ports in eastern Canada. Fantastic Cruises sells cruises to individuals (via its website) and to travel agents for resale to customers. All cruises are paid in advance, with a 10-percent deposit on booking, and the remainder collected at least four weeks prior to sailing. Travel agents collect money from their customers, deduct their commission, and forward the remainder to the cruise company before the deadline. Emma has made a preliminary assessment that the client is a low control risk and plans to conduct extensive testing of controls in the accounts receivable area to support her assessment.

Required

(a) What is Emma's objective in testing of controls over accounts receivable?

(b) Assuming Emma achieves her objective, discuss the implications for the nature, timing, and extent of substantive testing of accounts receivable.

CASE

CASE STUDY—CLOUD 9

Answer the following questions based on the information for Cloud 9 presented in Appendix B of this book and in the current and earlier chapters. You should also consider your answers to the case study questions in earlier chapters.

Required

(a) Consider and explain the effects that the opening of Cloud 9's first retail store would have on its accounting.

(b) Describe how this business change would affect the components of audit risk.

(c) What changes would you expect to see in inventory transactions and balances as Cloud 9 changes from a wholesale-only business to a retail and wholesale business? Be specific in your answer.

(d) Which inventory balance and transaction assertions would be most affected? Explain.

(e) Describe the population(s) and suggest a sampling approach for controls and substantive testing for inventory.

RESEARCH QUESTION 6.1

McKesson & Robbins was a company at the centre of a famous fraud in the United States in the 1930s.

Required

(a) Research the facts of the McKesson & Robbins fraud and write a short description of the case.

(b) Make a list of the defects in the company's system of internal controls that are relevant to the fraud and suggest audit tests that would have revealed these problems.

SOLUTIONS TO MULTIPLE-CHOICE QUESTIONS

1. d, 2. a, 3. b, 4. c, 5. c, 6. a, 7. b, 8. c, 9. a, 10. b.

CHAPTER 7

Understanding and testing the client's system of internal controls

LEARNING OBJECTIVES

After studying this chapter, you should be able to:

1 define internal control

2 state the seven generally accepted objectives of internal control activities

3 understand and describe the elements of internal control at the entity level

4 identify the different types of controls

5 explain how to select and design tests of controls

6 explain the different techniques used to document and test internal controls

7 understand how to interpret the results of testing of controls

8 explain how to document tests of controls

9 describe the importance of identifying strengths and weaknesses in a system of internal controls

10 explain how to communicate internal control strengths and weaknesses to those charged with governance.

AUDITING AND ASSURANCE STANDARDS

CANADIAN	INTERNATIONAL
CAS 230 *Audit Documentation*	ISA 230 *Audit Documentation*
CAS 260 *Communication with Those Charged with Governance*	ISA 260 *Communication with Those Charged with Governance*
CAS 265 *Communicating Deficiencies in Internal Control to Those Charged with Governance and Management*	ISA 265 *Communicating Deficiencies in Internal Control to Those Charged with Governance and Management*
CAS 315 *Identifying and Assessing the Risks of Material Misstatement Through Understanding the Entity and its Environment*	ISA 315 *Identifying and Assessing the Risks of Material Misstatement Through Understanding the Entity and its Environment*

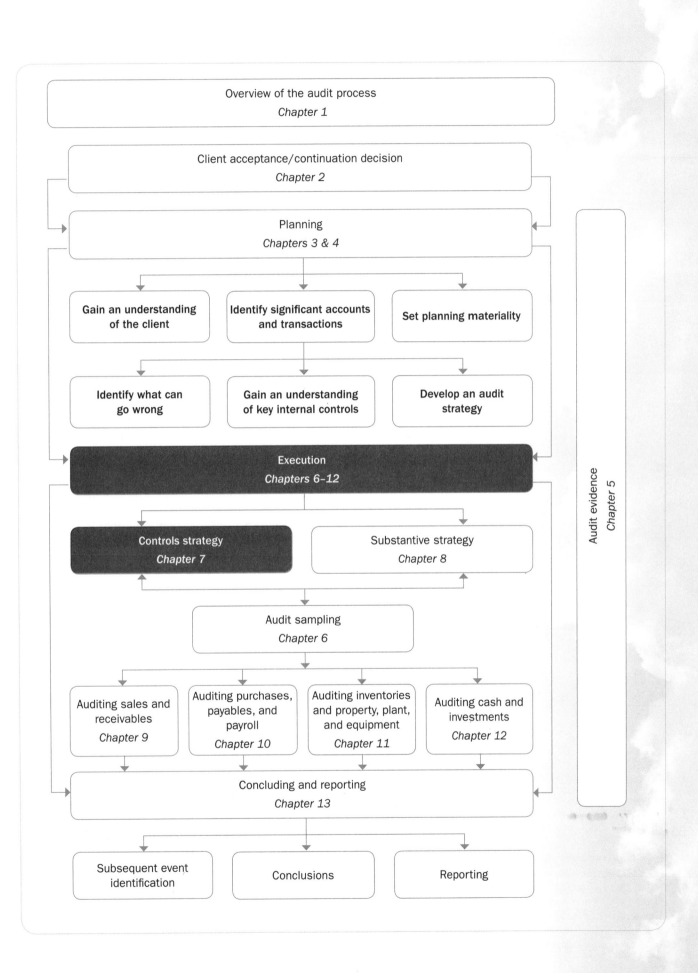

Overview of the audit process
Chapter 1

Client acceptance/continuation decision
Chapter 2

Planning
Chapters 3 & 4

Gain an understanding of the client

Identify significant accounts and transactions

Set planning materiality

Identify what can go wrong

Gain an understanding of key internal controls

Develop an audit strategy

Execution
Chapters 6–12

Controls strategy
Chapter 7

Substantive strategy
Chapter 8

Audit sampling
Chapter 6

Auditing sales and receivables
Chapter 9

Auditing purchases, payables, and payroll
Chapter 10

Auditing inventories and property, plant, and equipment
Chapter 11

Auditing cash and investments
Chapter 12

Concluding and reporting
Chapter 13

Subsequent event identification

Conclusions

Reporting

Audit evidence
Chapter 5

Cloud 9

Sharon Gallagher and Josh Thomas are working on the draft of their internal control assessment report for Cloud 9 Ltd. They met with the Cloud 9 finance director, David Collier, to gain an understanding of the internal controls at the entity level. The interview covered issues such as management integrity, policies and procedures, and monitoring of control activities. Sharon asks Josh to write up the results of the interview and make an assessment about the effectiveness of entity-level controls. Does the company demonstrate an environment where potential material misstatements are prevented or detected?

AUDIT PROCESS IN FOCUS

The purpose of this chapter is to assist in understanding the client's system of internal controls as it relates to the audit of the financial statements. This involves understanding the term "internal control," being aware of the objectives of the internal controls put in place by management and the components of these controls (particularly at the entity level), and understanding a client's system of internal controls.

This chapter will also consider the importance of evaluating how the design and implementation of controls will prevent material misstatements from occurring, or how they will detect and correct material misstatements after they have occurred.

When the auditor decides to include controls testing in their audit strategy, they select those controls that will provide the most efficient and effective audit evidence. Also, the auditor will test only those controls they believe are critical to their opinion and are likely to be working effectively. That is, they select those controls that are likely to be working effectively and are extensive and sensitive enough to cover of the WCGWs. Deciding which controls to test will be influenced by the type of control, the frequency with which the control is performed, and the level of assurance the auditor wants to gain from the control being designed and implemented effectively.

There are many techniques available to test and document the controls identified when planning the audit, and in this chapter we will provide an overview of several of the more typical testing techniques. This overview will include examples of the extent of controls testing to perform and how this extent of testing will influence the level of assurance we obtain toward the overall audit conclusion or opinion. We will discuss what the auditor's response should be to any exceptions or errors found in their testing of controls, as well as how the auditor should document the results of their testing. In the discussion of the results we will also include examples of how these affect the overall risk assessment and the resulting substantive audit procedures performed. Finally, we will also discuss the implications of an absence of internal controls and provide a description of how strengths and weaknesses in a system of internal controls are communicated to both management and those charged with governance.

7.1 INTERNAL CONTROL DEFINED

1 Define internal control.

internal control the process designed, implemented, and maintained by those charged with governance, management, and other personnel to provide reasonable assurance about the achievement of the entity's objectives with regard to reliability of financial reporting, effectiveness and efficiency of operations, and compliance with applicable laws and regulations

Why is understanding the internal controls of an organization important? Because when controls are effective, the organization is more likely to achieve its strategic and operating objectives. Internal control is a very broad concept and encompasses all of the elements of an organization—its resources, systems, processes, culture, structure, and tasks. When these elements are taken together, they support the organization to achieve its objectives. For the purposes of this chapter, we will focus on the components of internal control that have a direct impact on the financial reporting. We will consider the safeguards put in place by management to prevent and detect errors including misappropriation of assets and human errors. **Internal control** is defined in the auditing standards as:

> The process designed, implemented and maintained by those charged with governance, management and other personnel to provide reasonable assurance about the achievement

of the entity's objectives with regard to reliability of its financial reporting, effectiveness and efficiency of operations, and compliance with applicable laws and regulations. The term "controls" refers to any aspect of one or more of the components of internal control. (CAS 315)

Understanding internal control is a key component of the overall **audit risk** assessment and provides evidence that influences the resulting strategy developed by the auditor. Also, CAS 315 *Identifying and Assessing the Risks of Material Misstatement Through Understanding the Entity and its Environment* requires the auditor to obtain an understanding of internal control on all audit engagements.

audit risk the risk that an auditor expresses an inappropriate audit opinion when the financial statements are materially misstated

Frameworks for internal controls have been developed such as the *Internal Control—Integrated Framework* developed by the Committee of Sponsoring Organizations of the Treadway Commission (COSO) and the *Guidance on Controls* issued by the Criteria of Control Board of CPA Canada. These frameworks provide a structure that allows the auditor to assess the internal controls of an organization as compared with a theoretical model. Therefore, where internal controls put in place by management agree closely with the theoretical framework, the internal controls may be described as strong. However, where internal controls do not agree closely with the theoretical framework, they may be described as weak.

While we will not discuss these frameworks specifically, the general principles are consistent with the objectives and components of internal control discussed in more detail in this chapter and included in CAS 315.

BEFORE YOU GO ON

7.1.1 What is an internal control?

7.1.2 Why is it important to understand (and assess) internal controls?

7.1.3 Name a generally accepted framework used to describe internal controls.

7.2 OBJECTIVES OF INTERNAL CONTROLS

It is important for the auditor to understand the objectives of internal controls. While the auditor links controls to audit assertions and account balances, the objectives of controls is to connect the auditor's understanding of why the controls are important with the issues they are designed to prevent. The reason an organization puts controls in place is to ensure errors in the processing of transactions do not occur, and if they do, that these errors are identified and rectified quickly. Without understanding the intention of management in implementing these controls, it is harder to connect them to our understanding of what can go wrong with the process and how to prevent it from happening.

2 State the seven generally accepted objectives of internal control activities.

There are seven generally accepted objectives of internal controls. Internal controls are designed and implemented to ensure that transactions are real, recorded, correctly valued, classified, summarized, and posted on a timely basis. When the system of internal controls meets its objectives as these relate to the recording of transactions and balances, management assertions are also likely to be valid. The internal control objectives are matched with the relevant assertions as follows:

1. Real—there are controls in place to ensure that fictitious or duplicate transactions are not included in the books and records of the organization (occurrence, rights and obligations, and existence assertions).

2. Recorded—there are controls in place that will prevent or detect the omission of transactions from the books and records of the organization (accuracy, completeness, and valuation and allocation assertions).

3. Valued—there are controls in place to ensure that the correct amounts are assigned to the transactions (accuracy, and valuation and allocation assertions).

4. Classified—there are controls in place to ensure that transactions are charged and allocated to the correct general ledger account (accuracy, classification, and valuation and allocation assertions).

5. Summarized—there are controls in place to ensure that the transactions in the books and records are summarized and totalled correctly (accuracy and valuation and allocation assertions).

6. Posted—there are controls in place to ensure that the accumulated totals in the transaction file are correctly transferred to the general ledger and subsidiary ledgers (accuracy, classification, and valuation and allocation assertions).

7. Timely—there are controls in place to ensure that transactions are recorded in the correct accounting period (cut-off and completeness assertions).

The assertion relating to classification and understandability, which is a presentation and disclosure assertion, is not specifically addressed by these internal control objectives. An entity may still design controls over this assertion. The auditor performs procedures based on the controls the entity has in place. The auditor usually ensures this assertion is met by substantively testing the draft financial statements. An example of how this is often done is by using a disclosure checklist. These checklists typically include all of the disclosures required by the accounting standards. They assist the auditor in ensuring that all of the required material disclosures have been made.

When the auditor gains an understanding of the client's system of internal controls and how the client uses internal controls to manage risks in the business, it is important for the auditor to remember each of these objectives. By focusing on each of these objectives, the auditor will be able to select the appropriate controls to test to gain the greatest level of assurance possible that the client's system of internal controls is operating effectively.

The concept of testing and assessing controls is discussed in more detail later in this chapter. It is worth mentioning here that when the objectives of internal controls are not met, it is considered to be a deficiency in internal control. The auditor then considers whether the weakness has a significant impact on their risk assessment for the relevant account balances and transactions. This is also discussed in further detail later in this chapter.

Internal control, no matter how effective, can only provide an entity with reasonable assurance in achieving its financial reporting objectives. There are inherent limitations of internal control. These include:

- human error that results in a breakdown in internal control
- ineffective understanding of the purpose of a control
- collusion by two or more individuals to circumvent a control
- a control within a software program being overridden or disabled.

An example of a limitation is an internal control that may be designed appropriately but never implemented by management. The control, therefore, has no ability to mitigate risks. These limitations of internal controls are often mitigated by other controls (often referred to as compensating controls). If there are no other controls mitigating the weaknesses or limitations, the risks are addressed by the auditor performing extensive substantive procedures.

Cloud 9

Josh knows that as he writes his report he has to think about the whole system of internal controls at Cloud 9 and how effective it is in helping the company achieve its objectives. However, as the auditor, he has to focus mostly on the controls that relate to the integrity of the company's financial statements. Which controls are keeping transactions real, recorded, correctly valued, classified, summarized, and posted on a timely basis? Also, which controls are protecting assets and ensuring that the company complies with relevant laws and regulations? The better these controls, the more likely W&S Partners can adopt a combined audit approach strategy.

BEFORE YOU GO ON

7.2.1 What are the seven generally accepted objectives of internal controls as related to the recording of transactions?

7.2.2 Why are internal controls important to an organization?

7.2.3 Why are internal controls important to an auditor?

7.3 ENTITY-LEVEL INTERNAL CONTROLS

As set out in CAS 315, internal control consists of five components:

1. the control environment
2. the entity's risk assessment process
3. the information system, including the related business processes, relevant to financial reporting, and communication
4. control activities
5. monitoring of controls

3 Understand and describe the elements of internal control at the entity level.

These internal control components, when collectively assessed, are often referred to as **entity-level controls** because each exists at an organizational or entity level rather than at a more detailed transactional level. For example, a control ensuring that sales are recorded in the sales ledger is a transaction-level control. A control such as the internal audit function of a company is an entity-level control.

Gaining an understanding of the entity-level internal control components helps in establishing the appropriate level of professional scepticism, gaining an understanding of the client's business and financial statement risks, and making assessments of inherent risk, control risk, and the combined risk of material misstatement, which, in turn, determines the nature, timing, and extent of audit procedures (as discussed in chapters 4, 6, and 8).

entity-level controls the collective assessment of the client's control environment, risk assessment process, information system, control activities, and monitoring of controls

7.3.1 The control environment

The control environment sets the tone of an entity and influences the control consciousness of its people. It is the foundation for all other components of internal control and is often thought of as a combination of the culture, structure, and discipline of an organization. It reflects the overall attitude, awareness, and actions of management, the board of directors, others charged with governance, and the owners concerning the importance of controls and the emphasis given to controls in determining the organization's policies, processes, and organizational structure. Therefore, the control environment is sometimes referred to as the "tone at the top."

The **control environment** also sets the foundation for effective internal control, providing discipline and structure, and includes the following elements.

control environment the attitudes, awareness, and actions of management and those charged with governance concerning the entity's internal control and its importance in the entity

- *Communication and enforcement of integrity and ethical values.* Integrity and ethical values are essential elements of the control environment, affecting the design, administration, and monitoring of key processes. Integrity and ethical behaviour are the products of the organization's ethical and behavioural standards, how they are communicated, and how they are monitored and enforced in its business activities. Control activities include management's actions to remove or reduce incentives, pressures, and opportunities that might prompt personnel to engage in dishonest, illegal, or unethical acts. Other control activities also include the communication of the organization's values and behavioural standards to personnel through policy statements and codes of conduct, and the examples set by management.

  For example, management may state in its code of conduct that employees are not allowed to accept gifts from suppliers valued above a certain price and that all offers of gifts (whether accepted or not) are to be reported in a gift register (or something similar). Although a code of conduct does not guarantee that employees will act ethically regarding gifts, it does indicate that management communicates standards of behaviour that it expects employees to adhere to. Coupled with other procedures, such actions may demonstrate an effective control environment. It is also important that management is seen to comply with its own policies.

- *Commitment to competence.* Management's commitment to competence refers to considering the skill levels required for particular positions within the organization and making sure that staff with the required skills are hired and matched to the right jobs. Among the factors that management may consider are the nature and degree of judgement to be applied to a specific job and the extent of supervision required. Auditors use professional judgement to determine whether they believe management and employees appear to be competent to carry out their assigned roles and receive adequate supervision where required.

    For example, do employees have the knowledge and expertise necessary to understand and execute the requirements of the generally accepted reporting framework, the International Financial Reporting Standards (IFRS), or the Canadian Accounting Standards for Private Enterprises (ASPE)?

- *Participation by those charged with governance.* The organization's control environment is influenced significantly by its board of directors and others charged with governance of the entity: for example, by the audit committee members or the executive members of the board of directors if they are charged with responsibility for governance and are members of management. Those charged with governance are responsible for overseeing the entity's accounting and financial reporting policies and procedures. As a result, those charged with governance have an obligation to be concerned with the entity's financial reporting to shareholders and the investing public, and to monitor the entity's accounting policies and the internal and independent (external) audit processes.

    In determining the effectiveness of the participation of those charged with governance, in particular the board of directors, auditors consider the board's independence from management, the experience of its members, the extent of its involvement and scrutiny of management's day-to-day activities, and its interactions with the internal and/or external auditors. For example, if the board has regular and open communications with its auditors, management may be more willing to inform the board of issues arising in the business on a timely basis (to avoid "surprises").

- *Management's philosophy and operating style.* Obtaining an understanding of management's philosophy and operating style is necessary to identify the factors that influence management's attitudes toward internal control. This understanding affects the auditor's assessment of how management makes judgements and accounting estimates, and provides an insight into the competence and motivations of management. The more confidence an auditor gains regarding management's abilities and integrity, the more reliance the auditor can place on the information, explanations, and representations provided by management. Alternatively, doubts about management's ability and integrity will increase the level of corroborating evidence required for representations made by management. An understanding of management's operating style is therefore a fundamental input into assessing audit risk.

- *Organizational structure.* The client's organizational structure provides the framework within which its activities for achieving entity-wide objectives are planned, executed, controlled, and monitored. Establishing an organizational structure includes considering the key areas of authority and responsibility as well as the appropriateness of the lines of reporting.

    The size and complexity of the organization together with management's business and operating philosophies significantly affect the organizational structure and the need for formal organization charts, job descriptions, and policy statements. In addition to the formal organizational structure, an informal structure may also exist that affects the control environment. An auditor will gain an understanding of their client's organizational structure and the suitability of its policies and procedures in light of its size and complexity.

    The information technology (IT) environment is also an important aspect of the auditor's review of the organizational structure. Consideration needs to be given to whether the IT deployed by the entity allows clear assignment of responsibilities. This should include the assignment of authorization to initiate and/or change transactions and programs as well as efforts to ensure that there is appropriate segregation of duties related to the programming, administration, operation, and use of IT. Segregation of duties is explained further in section 7.3.4.

- *Assignment of authority and responsibility.* Assignment of authority and responsibility includes how authority and responsibility for operating activities are assigned, and how reporting relationships and authorization hierarchies are established. It includes policies relating to appropriate business practices, knowledge, experience of key personnel, and resources provided for carrying out duties. Assignment of authority and responsibility also includes policies and communications directed toward ensuring that all employees understand the organization's objectives, know how their individual roles and actions contribute to those objectives, and recognize how they will be held accountable for their actions.

- *Human resource policies and practices.* Human resource policies and practices relate to hiring, inducting, training, evaluating, counselling, promoting, and compensating employees. As discussed above, the competence and integrity of an entity's employees are essential elements of its control environment. The organization's ability to recruit and retain competent and responsible employees is therefore dependent to a large extent on its human resource policies and practices.

For example, standards are often set for hiring qualified individuals, focusing on educational background, prior work experience, past accomplishments, and evidence of a cultural fit with the employer organization (values and ethics). These standards show the organization's commitment to employing only competent and trustworthy people. Often job descriptions illustrate the expected levels of performance and behaviour.

When gaining an understanding of the control environment, the auditor considers each of the above elements and their interrelationships. In particular, the auditor needs to understand whether there are any significant deficiencies in any one element, as these deficiencies may have an impact on the effectiveness of the other elements. For example, management may establish a formal code of conduct but then act in a manner that condones breaches of that code.

The assessment of internal controls, as well as the impact of weaknesses in or exceptions to internal controls, is discussed in more detail later in this chapter. Figure 7.1 shows how the tone at the top affects the control environment.

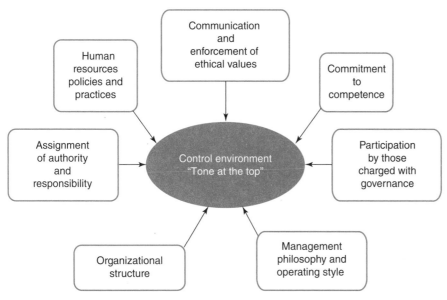

FIGURE 7.1 **Control environment**

Cloud 9

During the interview Josh and Sharon held with David Collier, they learned a lot about the tone at the top at Cloud 9. Top-level management at the company is bound by a code of conduct based on a similar document adopted by the parent company, Cloud 9 Inc. The parent company has adopted a very strict approach to management integrity. Cloud 9's board members and senior managers attend training and awareness sessions on the code at least annually. In addition, there has been a rigorous process of embedding the code's main points throughout the company's policies and procedures, most of which have been rewritten in the previous two years.

A copy of the company's code of conduct and the policies and procedures are included in the audit working papers. Josh also writes a description of the company's efforts to communicate its approach to management integrity in the report. He assesses the control environment at Cloud 9 as effective.

Human risks

What are the big risks for businesses? According to a report published by EY, human resource (HR) issues rank among the top five business issues impacting a company's results. Human resource issues are perennial because they are among the most difficult to define, control, and manage.

The EY report contains the results from surveying senior finance, accounting, risk, and HR executives at 150 Fortune 1000 companies. The executives were asked to rank the HR issues that they perceive as having a high impact and likelihood of occurrence within a global organization. The top five HR issues were:

1. talent management and succession planning
2. ethics/tone at the top
3. regulatory compliance
4. pay and performance alignment
5. employee training and development

The executives were also asked about the methods used to monitor these risks. The results show that 41 percent of executives surveyed admit to reviewing these risks on an ad hoc basis or never. This result reinforces the view that HR issues are not managed effectively enough in many organizations.

One aspect of HR risk that is closely related to financial statement auditing is the effect of HR policies on promoting and communicating ethical values throughout the organization and ensuring that the appropriate "tone at the top" trickles down through the organization. The EY survey revealed that these issues have become more visible and significant in recent years, possibly as a result of adverse publicity about corporate ethics. However, although ethics is becoming more significant as an HR risk, the executives responding to the survey rated the likelihood of ethical problems arising throughout the organization as low. The survey's authors suggest HR executives should pay more attention to the alignment between values espoused by company management in public arenas and actual practices by employees at all levels within the organization.

Sources: EY, 2008 Global Human Resources (HR) Risk: From the Danger Zone to the Value Zone: Accelerating Business Improvement by Navigating HR Risk, 2008, www.ey.com; S. Steffee, "HR Risks Are Largely Ignored," Internal Auditor, 65, no. 6 (December 2008): pp. 14–5.

7.3.2 The entity's risk assessment process

All entities, regardless of their size, structure, nature, or industry, encounter risks at all levels within the organization. Risks will affect the entity's ability to survive, compete, grow, and improve the quality of its products, services, and people. It is not possible to reduce these risks to zero; however, management (in conjunction with those charged with governance) needs to determine how much risk is acceptable to the organization. Some organizations have a risk committee, which is responsible for ensuring that all of these risks are identified, managed, and reported to the board of directors.

The entity's risk assessment process is its method for identifying and responding to business risks. For financial reporting purposes, the entity's **risk assessment process** includes how management identifies risks relevant to the preparation of the financial statements to ensure a fair presentation in accordance with the entity's applicable financial reporting framework. For identified risks, management estimates their significance, assesses the likelihood of their occurrence, and decides upon actions to manage them.

Risks relevant to financial reporting include external and internal events and circumstances that may occur and adversely affect an entity's ability to initiate, record, process, and report financial data consistent with the assertions of management in the financial statements. For example, new accounting pronouncements and significant changes to the financial reporting standards (such as the change from local accounting standards to IFRS) are externally created risks relevant to the entity's financial reporting. Corporate restructurings that result in reduced employee levels may weaken the segregation of duties, and the internal control structure is an internally generated risk relevant to an entity's financial reporting. An organization's risk assessment process is different from the auditor's consideration of risk. The purpose of the entity's risk assessment process is to identify, analyze, and manage the risks that affect its ability to achieve its operational effectiveness. In an audit, the purpose is to assess the combined **inherent**, **control**, and **detection risks** to evaluate the likelihood that material misstatements could occur in the financial statements.

An entity's risk assessment for financial reporting purposes is its identification, analysis, and management of the risks relevant to the preparation of the financial statements that are fairly presented in compliance with the accounting framework (for example, IFRS or ASPE). Once risks are identified, management will ordinarily initiate plans, programs, or other actions to address the risks. Alternatively, management may decide to accept the risk without addressing it. Usually, this decision is made on the basis of the cost versus the benefit of managing the risk.

risk assessment process the entity's process for identifying and responding to business risks

inherent risk the susceptibility of the financial statements to a material misstatement without considering the internal controls

control risk the risk that a client's system of internal controls will not prevent or detect a material misstatement

detection risk the risk that the auditor's testing procedures will not be effective in detecting a material misstatement

Risks can arise or be transformed as a result of changes to the organization and the environment it operates within. These include changes in the operating environment, new personnel, new technology, rapid growth, business restructuring, and new accounting pronouncements as discussed above. It is important for the auditor to understand the risks identified by the entity as this will assist the auditor in considering where (and if) a material misstatement in the financial statements might exist. The overall potential for risks to have a material impact on the financial statements is increased when management appears willing to accept unusually high risks when making business decisions, when entering into major commitments without sufficient consideration of the risks, and when failing to closely monitor and control the risks associated with commitments entered into.

Cloud 9

In their interview, Josh and Sharon ask David Collier about Cloud 9's risk assessment process. They want to know which risks management has identified so that they can consider whether those risks could cause a material misstatement in the financial statements. They also want to know about the company's methods of responding to the identified risks. David Collier tells them that Cloud 9's management continually monitors its competitors' activities. It also considers the risk of interruption to supplies because of shipping problems and labour disputes at production plants or transport companies.

Another example of risks that could have a major impact on the financial statements is the use of forward exchange contracts to control the risks caused by purchasing in foreign currencies. Management is also very aware of risks associated with the just-in-time inventory system, which has had some problems lately, and has planned some changes to deal with those problems.

Management is monitoring the risks of using a hockey player as a spokesman for the brand, plus the broader risks arising from sponsorship of the hockey team because there has been a lot of adverse publicity about hockey players' behaviour over the past year. Such adverse publicity could impact negatively on sales. Cloud 9's management ensures that the hockey team's management keeps the company's management informed of players' activities, where appropriate.

Josh concludes from the interview that Cloud 9 has an effective system of risk assessment because it actively searches out and considers potential risks to the business and has developed action plans to deal with each risk, depending on its likely occurrence.

7.3.3 Information systems and communication

The role of information systems is to capture and exchange the information needed to conduct, manage, and control an entity's operations. The quality of information and communication affects management's ability to make appropriate decisions in controlling the organization's activities and to prepare reliable financial statements. Information and communication involves capturing and providing information to management and employees so that they can carry out their responsibilities, including providing an understanding of individual roles and responsibilities as they relate to internal controls over financial reporting.

Information is needed at all levels of the entity to run the business and to assist in the achievement of financial reporting, operating, and compliance objectives. An array of information is used. Financial information, for instance, is used not only in developing financial statements for external dissemination; it may also be used for operational decisions, such as monitoring performance and allocating resources. Similarly, operating information (for example, airborne particle emissions and personnel data) may be needed to achieve compliance and financial reporting objectives as well as operating objectives. However, certain operating information (for example, purchases and sales data) is essential for developing the financial statements. As such, information developed from internal and external sources, both financial and non-financial, is relevant to all three objectives.

Information is identified, captured, processed, and reported by information systems. Information systems may be computerized, manual, or a combination thereof. The term "information systems" is frequently used in the context of processing internally generated data relating to transactions (for example, sales) and internal operating activities (for example, production processes). However, information systems as they relate to internal controls are much broader. That is, information systems also deal with information about external events, activities, and conditions.

Auditors are most interested in the information systems that are relevant to the financial reporting objective; that is, the systems responsible for initiating and recording transactions, balances, and events that will ultimately be reflected in the financial statements. These systems consist of the procedures, whether automated or manual, and records established to initiate, authorize, record, process, and report transactions (as well as events and conditions) and to maintain accountability for the related assets, liabilities, and equity. They include the client's asset safeguarding controls and the process for authorizing transactions, including adequate segregation of incompatible duties. The quality of system-generated information affects management's ability to make appropriate decisions in managing and controlling the entity's activities and to prepare reliable financial statements.

The information systems that are relevant to the financial reporting objective encompass methods that ensure transactions and disclosures are real, recorded, valued, classified, summarized, and posted on a timely basis. (Refer to section 7.2 for discussion of the seven generally accepted objectives of internal controls.)

Communication is the process by which information is provided to those who need it on a timely basis. For example, a monthly management reporting package contains information about the company's financial performance and is used by many companies as the major way of communicating this information to executives and directors.

Cloud 9

Josh is an expert on information systems and based on the interview with David Collier, which covered the information systems at a high level, he can conclude that the entity-level controls in this area are effective. Josh will gather further information in an interview with Cloud 9's financial controller, Carla Johnson. Based on this second interview and a review of the company's documents, he will write a description of his understanding of the processes used in each of the major transaction cycles.

7.3.4 Control activities

control activities policies and procedures that help ensure that management directives are carried out. Control activities are a component of internal control

Control activities are policies and procedures that help ensure that management's directives are carried out. They help guarantee that necessary actions are taken to address risks affecting the achievement of the organization's objectives. Control activities, whether automated or manual, have various objectives and are applied at various organizational and functional levels. Generally, control activities that may be relevant to an audit may be categorized as policies and procedures pertaining to the following:

- *Performance reviews.* These control activities include reviews of actual performance versus budgets, forecasts, and prior-period performance. Performance reviews compare different sets of data (operating or financial), analyzing these relationships and investigative and corrective actions. They also include reviews of functional or activity performance, such as, at a bank, a consumer loan manager's review of reports by branch, region, and loan type for loan approvals and collections. By investigating unexpected results or unusual trends, management identifies circumstances where the underlying activity objectives are in danger of not being achieved.

- *Information processing.* A variety of controls are performed to check accuracy, completeness, and authorization of transactions within information processing environments. Information processing controls can be manual controls; automated controls (that is, application dependent); manual controls dependent on an automated process (that is, IT dependent); or IT general controls (ITGCs). These concepts are discussed further in this chapter.

- *Authorization controls.* These control activities define who can approve the various transactions within the organization. There is typically an approval hierarchy indicating authorization levels within the organization. The approval level generally increases as management responsibility increases. Approval should be required before any expenditure is made, including the hiring of employees, the ordering of goods and services, and the ability to extend credit.

- *Account reconciliations.* Reconciliations involve the preparation and review of account reconciliations on a timely basis. Bank accounts, intercompany accounts, and any clearing and suspense accounts should be reconciled on a regular basis. Sub-ledgers should be reconciled to the general ledger accounts. Reconciling items should be investigated and corrected promptly.

- *Physical controls.* These control activities encompass the physical security of assets, including adequate safeguards over access to assets and records (such as secured facilities and authorization for access to computer programs and data files) and periodic counting and comparison with amounts shown on control records. The extent to which physical controls intended to prevent theft of assets are relevant to the success of the business and the reliability of the financial statement preparation and, therefore, the audit, depends on the circumstances, such as if assets are highly susceptible to misappropriation.

- *Segregation of incompatible duties.* This control activity encompasses the concept that no one employee or group of employees should be in a position to both perpetrate and hide errors or fraud in the normal course of their duties. In general, the principal duties that are incompatible and should be segregated are:
  - custody of assets
  - authorization or approval of transactions affecting assets
  - recording or reporting of transactions.

In addition, a control over the processing of a transaction should not be performed by the same person who is responsible for actually recording or reporting the transaction.

Assigning different people the responsibilities of authorizing transactions, recording transactions, and maintaining custody of assets reduces the opportunity for an individual to both carry out and hide errors (whether intentional or not) or commit fraud in the normal course of his or her duties. Adequate segregation of duties is an important consideration in determining whether a client's controls are effective, as it reduces the likelihood that errors (intentional or not) will remain undetected. When IT is used in an information system, segregation of incompatible duties is often achieved by implementing system-based controls (referred to as logical access controls).

In understanding the client's control activities at the entity level, consideration is given to factors such as:

- the extent to which performance of control activities relies on IT
- whether the necessary policies and procedures exist with respect to each of the entity's activities, including IT security and system development
- the extent to which controls included in the organization's policies are being applied
- whether management has clear objectives in terms of budget, profit, and other financial and operating goals, and whether these objectives are clearly written, communicated throughout the entity, and actively monitored
- whether planning and reporting systems are in place to identify variances from planned performance and communicate such variances to the appropriate level of management
- whether the appropriate level of management investigates variances and takes appropriate and timely corrective actions
- to what extent duties are divided or segregated among different people to reduce the risk of errors, fraud, or manipulation of results
- whether software is used to control access to data and programs and, if so, the extent to which segregation of incompatible duties is achieved by implementing these software controls
- whether periodic comparisons are made of amounts recorded in the accounting system with physical assets
- whether adequate safeguards are in place to prevent unauthorized access to or destruction of documents, records, and assets.

The auditor finds these controls the easiest to test when compared with other types of entity-level controls as their operation is readily verifiable. For example, the controls surrounding the segregation of duties can be observed, while management integrity is not observable or easily verified.

7.3.5 Monitoring of controls

After establishing and maintaining internal controls, another important responsibility of management is to monitor the controls to assess whether they are operating as intended and are modified for changes in conditions on a timely basis. Over time, systems of internal controls change and the way controls are applied may evolve. Also, the circumstances for which the system of internal controls was originally designed may change, causing it to be less effective in warning management of risks brought about by new conditions. Accordingly, management needs to determine whether its internal controls continue to be relevant and able to address new risks.

Monitoring is a process of assessing the quality of internal control performance over time, considering whether controls are operating as intended, and making sure controls are modified as appropriate for changes in conditions. It involves assessing the design and implementation of controls on a regular basis and taking necessary corrective actions. This process is accomplished through ongoing activities and separate evaluations, or through a combination of the two.

Ongoing monitoring procedures are built into the normal recurring activities of the entity and include regular management and supervisory activities. For example, managers of sales, purchasing, and production at divisional and corporate levels should understand the entity's operations and question the accuracy of reports that differ significantly from their knowledge of operations. Monitoring activities may include using information obtained from communications with external parties. For example, customers ordinarily verify and corroborate a client's billing data by paying their invoices or by complaining about overcharging.

Much of the information used in monitoring is produced by the entity's information systems. If management assumes that data used for monitoring is accurate without having a basis for the assumption, errors may exist in the information, potentially leading management to incorrect conclusions from its monitoring activities.

One of the most common monitoring activities is the internal audit function. In many organizations, internal auditors (or personnel performing similar functions) contribute to the monitoring of the client's activities through separate evaluations. They regularly provide information about the functioning of internal controls, focusing considerable attention on the evaluation of the design and implementation of controls. They communicate information about strengths and weaknesses and make recommendations for improving internal control. The importance that a company places on its internal audit function also provides evidence about its overall commitment to internal control.

As discussed in chapter 2 when evaluating the effectiveness of the internal audit function, factors to consider include independence, reporting lines, adequacy of staffing, adherence to applicable professional standards, scope of activities, adequacy of work performed, and conclusions reached.

The internal audit activities most relevant to the audit include those that provide evidence about the design and effectiveness of internal controls or that provide substantive evidence about potential material misstatements in the financial statements.

Finally, when gaining an understanding of the client's monitoring processes at the entity level, factors such as the following are ordinarily considered:

- whether periodic evaluations of internal control are made
- the extent to which personnel, in carrying out their regular duties, obtain evidence as to whether the system of internal controls continues to function
- the extent to which communications from external parties corroborate internally generated information, or indicate problems
- whether management implements internal control recommendations made by internal and external auditors
- whether management's approach to correcting known significant deficiencies is on a timely basis
- whether management's approach to dealing with reports and recommendations from regulators is effective
- whether an internal audit function exists that management uses to assist in its monitoring activities
- whether evaluations or observations are made by the external auditors.

Cloud 9

In the interview with David Collier, Sharon and Josh ask about both the control activities and the monitoring of those activities at Cloud 9. Sharon and Josh are particularly interested in the systems used at the company to make sure that information about management's plans and orders is transmitted throughout the organization and that there are policies and procedures to ensure that the appropriate actions are taken and reviewed.

In addition to asking David Collier about these matters, Josh reads the policy and procedures manuals and he and Sharon tour the offices and other facilities. For example, Cloud 9 has a tightly structured system of performance reviews. Managers at each level must report financial and operating performance against budget at regular intervals. Higher-level managers are able to access information about activities within their area of responsibility for monitoring purposes through the information system. Although there have been some issues with theft of goods from the retail store, the losses have been contained following the installation of additional security, including cameras. Josh and Sharon are particularly impressed with the thorough approach to segregation of incompatible duties.

Josh is able to conclude that at an entity level, there is sufficient evidence that these controls are effective. He plans to review the specific controls that affect transaction cycles in more detail so that he can document his understanding of these processes.

7.3.6 Concluding on entity-level controls

Having gained an understanding of each of the components of internal control at the entity level, tested them to ensure they are designed effectively and implemented properly, and ensured that there are no factors relating to the five components of entity-level control that indicate ineffective controls, the conclusion is made that the client's internal control environment at the entity level is considered to be supportive of the prevention or detection and correction of material misstatements whether due to fraud or error. If one or more factors exist that indicate poor internal control, this does not automatically mean that internal control at the entity level is ineffective. The evaluation of the factors is often highly subjective and requires considerable professional judgement. There are no formulas or other explicit indicators that tell us when internal control at the entity level is ineffective. This means that it is critical that the more experienced audit personnel (including the engagement partner) make this overall assessment. In reaching their conclusion, they will consider the size, complexity, and ownership of the client. This is because the importance of many of the factors considered in reaching the conclusion is affected by these three characteristics (size, complexity, and ownership). For example, a small company may not have a written code of conduct but through the active involvement of management in the day-to-day activities of the business, it may have cultivated a culture that emphasizes the importance of integrity and ethical behaviour. That is, the lack of a formal document may not be a concern. However, for a larger more complex group of companies with multiple overseas locations, a similar lack of documentation may indicate an area for concern.

Cloud 9

Cloud 9 Ltd. has effective internal controls at the entity level. Sharon Gallagher, the audit manager, believes that when considered at a high level, the company has an environment where potential misstatements are preventive or detective. Sharon has instructed the audit team to turn its attention to considering the transaction-level controls. Josh has asked Weijing Fei, a new member of his group, to identify the controls that Cloud 9 uses to either prevent or detect misstatements. Weijing needs some help with this because she does not understand the difference between preventive and detective controls.

BEFORE YOU GO ON

7.3.1 What are the five components of internal control?

7.3.2 Why is segregation of duties important when understanding internal control?

7.3.3 How does management's attitude and control consciousness affect the internal control environment of an organization?

7.4 TYPES OF CONTROLS

4 Identify the different types of controls.

transaction-level controls controls that affect a particular transaction or group of transactions

Transaction-level controls relate to one of the five components of entity-level internal control as set out in CAS 315 *Identifying and Assessing the Risks of Material Misstatement Through Understanding the Entity and Its Environment.* (The five components are the control environment, the client's risk assessment process, information and communication, control activities, and monitoring.) Transaction-level controls are controls that affect a particular transaction or group of transactions. Transactions in this sense refer to transactions that are ordinarily recorded in the general ledger. Transaction-level controls respond to things that can go wrong with transactions. They must be sensitive enough to either prevent an error from occurring or to detect the error, report it, and have it rectified on a timely basis. Transaction-level controls over specific accounts will be discussed in greater detail in subsequent chapters. Transaction-level controls are implemented by businesses to reduce the risk of misstatement due to error or fraud as well as to ensure that processes are operating effectively. Controls can include any procedure the client uses and relies on to prevent errors from occurring during the processing of transactions, or to detect and correct errors that may occur in these transactions.

Controls have two main objectives: to prevent or detect misstatements in the financial statements, or to support the automated parts of the business in the functioning of the controls in place. Preventive controls are those applied to each transaction that prevent fraud or errors from occurring. Detective controls are those applied after transactions have been processed to identify whether fraud or errors have occurred. These concepts will be explained in more detail in section 7.4.1.

Controls are classified as one of four types:

1. manual

2. automated (otherwise known as application controls)

3. information technology (IT) general controls (ITGCs) (the overall controls put in place to manage changes to applications and programs, as well as to limit access to appropriate users of those IT applications only)

4. a combination of control types referred to as IT-dependent manual controls

Figure 7.2 illustrates the types of controls and how they interrelate. As the figure also shows, each type of control has the potential to be a preventive or a detective control. Each of these control types is discussed in more detail in section 7.4.1.

The reason controls are classified is to assist the auditor in understanding the type of risks each control addresses, how the control addresses those risks, and the potential audit evidence that a control provides. Also, the classification assists in considering the nature, timing, and extent of the tests of controls and in determining the skills needed to perform the tests. It is not important what these controls are labelled; what is important is whether the control can be tested, is effective, and can be relied on to provide audit evidence.

tests of controls (controls testing) the audit procedures designed to evaluate the operating effectiveness of controls in preventing, or detecting and correcting, material misstatements at the assertion level

7.4.1 Preventive and detective controls

Tests of controls (or **controls testing**) are the audit procedures performed to test the operating effectiveness of controls in preventing, or detecting and correcting, material misstatements at the assertion level. The controls are tested to determine if they are properly applied throughout the entire period. Remember, this testing is required if the auditor plans to rely on the controls to reduce the amount of substantive work to be performed.

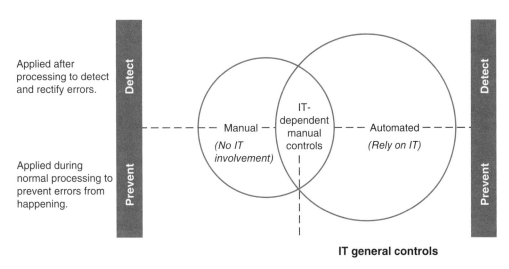

FIGURE 7.2 **Types of controls**

Preventive controls

Preventive controls can be applied to each transaction during normal processing to avoid errors occurring. Preventing errors during processing is an important objective of every accounting system. To be effective, controls over transactions should ideally include both preventive and detective controls. This is because without the underlying preventive controls, detective controls may not be sufficiently sensitive to identify and correct misstatements. This concept is discussed further in the detective controls section below.

When designing controls, consider what can go wrong with the transaction (that is, what is the risk of material misstatement) that would result in an error. These are sometimes referred to as **WCGWs** (what can go wrongs). Effective preventive controls should prevent the WCGWs from occurring. If they do occur, detective controls should ensure that the errors are detected and corrected as quickly as possible.

Table 7.1 shows examples of preventive controls and some of the WCGWs each control is designed to prevent.

Preventive controls do not always produce physical evidence indicating whether the control was performed, who performed it, or how well it was performed. In other cases, there may be evidence that the control was performed, but evidence as to the effectiveness of the control may not be available. For example, the signature of the warehouse receiver on a receiving report or a bill of lading indicates that the receiver agreed that goods were physically received into the warehouse, but it does not guarantee that the person carefully reviewed the shipment or checked that the quantities of each item matched the quantities on the bill of lading. The documentation may have been signed based on a quick glance or without any review at all. Thus, goods may be recorded that do not exist, excess goods may have been received but not recorded, or the goods received may not match the goods ordered and recorded. Therefore, in this example, the quality of the evidence that the control will prevent one of these errors from occurring is not persuasive enough for the auditor to conclude that the control operated effectively throughout the reporting period.

WCGWs areas where material misstatements due to error or fraud could occur in a flow of transactions or in the sourcing and preparation of information that affects a relevant financial statement assertion

TABLE 7.1 **Examples of preventive controls**

WCGW	PREVENTIVE CONTROL
Sales occur that are not collectible.	The computerized accounting program will not allow a sale to be processed if a customer has exceeded its credit limit.
Fictitious employees are paid.	Amounts cannot be paid to employees without first matching a valid social insurance number to the employee master file.
Sales are recorded at the wrong amount.	Sales invoices are automatically priced using a master pricing file.
Transactions are classified and coded to incorrect accounts.	The account coding on each purchase order is checked by the computer using a table of valid account numbers, and then various logic tests are performed by the computer.

A lack of effective preventive controls increases the risk that errors will occur or that fraud may occur and therefore increases the need for controls that are sensitive enough to detect these errors should they occur.

Detective controls

The purpose of detective controls is to discover fraud or errors that may have occurred during transaction processing (in spite of any preventive controls) and to rectify those errors. As discussed earlier, companies put detective controls in place to help management ensure that WCGWs do not occur and that the business is functioning as planned through the design and implementation of its business processes.

Generally, detective controls are not applied to each transaction during the normal flow of processing. Instead, they are applied outside the normal flow of individual transactions to groups of transactions that have been fully or partially processed. For example, often when payables are paid, a cheque run is processed to print the cheques, but the transaction is not completed: the debit is not recorded to the payables account and credit is not recorded to the cash account. Instead, the transaction is only partially processed and then "held" by the system. Once the cheques have been signed as approved for payment, the payables clerk will process the rest of the transaction by "releasing" the payments and recognizing the debit to payables and credit to cash.

Detective controls vary from client to client to a greater extent than preventive controls. Detective controls can depend on the nature of the client's business and on the competence, preferences, and imagination of the people who perform the controls. Detective controls may be formally established procedures, such as the preparation of a monthly reconciliation and the subsequent follow-up of reconciling or unusual items. Or they may be procedures that employees regularly perform and typically document, even though they are not formally required to do so by the company. For example, the financial accountant may keep a list of standard month-end journal entries to use as the basis for checking the entries each month as they are made, following up on any exceptions. Detective controls are often "unofficial" procedures similar to this example, which client personnel perform to make sure that the information they are responsible for is accurate.

It is important that detective controls:

1. completely and accurately capture all relevant data
2. identify all potentially significant errors
3. are performed consistently and regularly
4. include timely follow-up and correction for any misstatements or issues detected.

There are many examples of detective controls, including the following:

- Management-level reviews are made of actual performance versus budgets, forecasts, prior periods, competitors (if available), and industry averages (if available). Management's actions in analyzing and following up on unexpected variances is a detective control. For example, the financial controller may review the monthly results and compare the number of days' sales outstanding to previous periods to ensure any allowance for doubtful accounts is reasonable.

- Reconciliations are prepared, reconciling or unusual items are then investigated, and issues are resolved or corrections made, if necessary. The performance of reconciliations without following up on reconciling or unusual items is not a control. The control is the follow-up. Typical reconciliations are performed between the general ledger and some other form of external evidence or a subsidiary ledger. For example, the bank reconciliation reconciles the bank statement to the cash recorded in the general ledger. The accounts receivable reconciliation reconciles sales recorded in the trade receivables subsidiary ledger (via the sales ledger) to the trade receivables recorded in the general ledger.

- Reports are automatically produced showing transactions/groups of transactions that fall outside a set of parameters selected by the client. These exception reports are then reviewed and followed up (if necessary). For example, a report may be produced that shows all sales made to a customer that has exceeded its credit limit. The credit manager then follows up these sales with the salesperson to ensure no further sales are made until the balance is brought below the credit limit. Alternatively, if necessary, a re-evaluation of the customer's credit limit is performed and the limit is increased (if appropriate).

WCGW	DETECTIVE CONTROL
Cash is received but not recorded in the general ledger, payments are made but not recorded, cash receipts or cash payments are not real or not recorded on a timely basis.	Bank reconciliation and follow-up of unexpected outstanding items (for example, unexpected or large deposits not yet cleared by the bank, cheques presented by the bank but not recorded in the general ledger).
Shipments are not billed and recorded, or billings are not related to actual shipments of product.	The computer performs a daily comparison of quantities shipped to quantities billed. If differences are revealed, a report is generated for review and follow-up by the billing supervisor.
Unrecorded billings and errors in classifying sales or cash receipts.	Quarterly reviews of credit balances in accounts receivable to determine their causes.
Errors in the number of units or unit prices being calculated or applied incorrectly.	The sales manager reviews daily shipments, total sales, and sales per unit shipped.

TABLE 7.2 Examples of detective controls

Table 7.2 shows examples of detective controls and some of the WCGWs each control is designed to prevent.

As illustrated in this section, detective controls are often accompanied by physical evidence, such as a monthly reconciliation. This is in direct contrast to preventive controls, which are often driven by the programming of the particular software used by the company, and therefore produce no physical evidence of the control.

When assessing detective controls, it is not necessary for the auditor to re-perform all of the steps in, for example, preparing a reconciliation to gain sufficient evidence that the control is operating effectively. It is normally enough to examine evidence that the reconciliation was properly completed and that the appropriate reviews and follow-ups were carried out by the client in a timely manner.

Preventive and detective controls compared

Preventive controls may be dependent on IT (that is, they are IT-dependent manual controls). Specialist IT skills are required to audit IT-dependent manual controls, depending on how sophisticated the client's IT system is. It is important to note, however, that detective controls are only effective, and therefore only provide audit assurance, when the underlying data and transactions (and therefore preventive controls) can be relied on. Therefore, it is important to gain an understanding of (and possibly test) the preventive controls in addition to the detective controls to which they relate.

For example, the review and follow-up of a monthly management report that compares actual results to budget results would be ineffective if there is no evidence available to show that the budgeted amounts are the approved amounts and the actual amounts are the total of the transactions recorded in the general ledger. In addition, the auditor needs to obtain evidence that the underlying transactions are captured and recorded properly. This is ordinarily done via the identification and testing of the underlying preventive controls. Also, the monthly comparison needs to be at an information level that is detailed enough to identify material misstatements, and the review and follow-up need to be timely.

Because detective controls can be applied to groups of transactions rather than on a transaction-by-transaction basis, they are ordinarily performed less frequently than preventive controls. Therefore, if detective controls operate effectively throughout the period, a high degree of reliance can be obtained by examining a relatively small amount of evidence.

As noted earlier, this does not mean that the auditor will forego tests of controls over individual transactions. Performing tests of transactions allows the auditor to satisfy themselves that a preventive control was in use and functioned as intended. The auditor also performs tests of transactions to confirm that their understanding of the flow of transactions from initiation to reporting is correct (as described in chapter 4). In computerized environments, preventive controls can often be tested just as effectively and efficiently as detective controls. This is because preventive controls are accompanied by direct evidence (for example, review and follow-up of exception reports) as to the effectiveness of their operation. As well, the auditor is able to re-perform the control to ensure it is operating effectively. This is discussed in more detail in the section on automated controls.

Cloud 9

Weijing asks Josh about the types of controls that are normally used in a company like Cloud 9. Josh explains that it is useful to start by classifying controls as automated, manual, IT-dependent manual, or IT general controls. However, he says that Weijing's focus should be on considering whether each of these controls prevents an error occurring in the first place, or whether each is designed to detect an error that has already occurred so it can be brought to someone's attention.

Josh gives Weijing an example of a preventive control at Cloud 9. Based on his conversation with Carla Johnson, the financial controller, he has discovered that the computerized credit checking system at Cloud 9 will not allow a sale to be processed if a customer has exceeded its credit limit. This control prevents a customer order becoming a sale unless the client has been assessed as being able to pay the amount. It also helps prevent some clerical errors, such as 10 units being entered incorrectly as 1,000 units (because this would usually take a customer's order over the customer's credit limit). This control is designed to operate for every order, but there does not seem to be anything in Cloud 9's system to show if and when it is done, so it is not easy to know if the control is operating effectively.

Josh also gives Weijing an example of a detective control at Cloud 9. Carla Johnson performs a monthly bank reconciliation that is reviewed and approved by David Collier, the financial director. However, Josh explains to Weijing that he does not know yet if there is any follow-up on unusual items discovered during the reconciliation and review. If this follow-up is being done, then the control should detect errors in the bank account.

7.4.2 Manual and automated controls

In this section we consider manual and automated controls, as well as ITGCs and application controls and IT-dependent manual controls (which combine the characteristics of manual and automated controls).

Manual controls

Purely manual controls are those that do not rely on the client's IT environment for their operation. An example is a locked safe for cash to which only a few authorized staff have access. However, manual controls may use IT-produced information from third parties. For example, a client may reconcile the amount of consignment inventory that was manually counted during its inventory count to the amounts listed in the third party's computer-generated consignment inventory listing.

There are very few, if any, companies that do not use some form of IT to assist in transaction processing, and most controls rely on IT in some way. (Refer to the section on IT-dependent manual controls.)

Automated controls

Controls generally rely on the client's IT applications (or software) in some way. It is important to identify how much a control is automated in order to determine how IT will affect the evaluation of controls. The key consideration is to determine whether or not the client has effective ITGCs.

IT general controls (ITGCs)

ITGCs are the client's controls over the hardware and software it uses, including acquisition and maintenance of equipment, backup and recovery procedures, and the organization of the IT department to ensure the appropriate segregation of duties.

These ITGCs support the ongoing functioning of the automated (that is, programmed) aspects of preventive and detective controls and also provide the auditor with a basis for relying on electronic audit evidence. The auditor needs to identify, understand, walk through, test, and evaluate the ITGCs that have been implemented for computer applications they plan to rely on, as they do for any other type of control.

Ordinarily, an entity has three types of ITGCs in place:

1. program change controls—only appropriately authorized, tested, and approved changes are made to applications, interfaces, databases, and operating systems. All changes are documented so systems documentation is up to date.

2. logical access controls—only authorized personnel have access to IT equipment, data files, programs, and applications, and these personnel can perform only authorized tasks and functions. For example, the accounts receivable clerk does not have access to or authorization to use the cash payments application; the payroll manager may have access to the electronic funds transfer application but is unable to process any pay runs without the additional approval (and use of passwords) of the financial controller.

3. other ITGCs (including IT operations)—often difficult to identify in smaller organizations, these include controls such as ensuring regular and timely backups of data, following up and resolving program faults and errors regularly, following up any deviations from scheduled processing on a timely basis, and planning regular upgrades to programs and applications, as well as ensuring the existence of a disaster recovery plan.

Table 7.3 provides a more complete list of common IT general controls.

TABLE 7.3 Common IT general controls

Source: Based on CICA C·PEM form 530 "General IT controls," in C·PEM Forms—Audits, August 2013.

CONTROLS TO ENSURE THE EFFECTIVE MANAGEMENT OF THE IT DEPARTMENT

- Specific job descriptions exist for the IT manager and support staff (or person(s) assigned IT responsibilities).
- The data access and span of control exercised by IT staff is limited, where possible, through access cards, passwords, and segregation of duties.
- Contracts are signed with qualified third-party service providers that address the expectations, risks, security controls, and procedures/controls for information processing (for example, payroll).
- Job performance of IT staff is periodically evaluated and reviewed with the employee, and appropriate action is taken.

CONTROLS TO ENSURE THE ACCURATE PROCESSING OF DATA

- Entity uses mainstream accounting and other software packages with no modification.
- Access to applications is restricted by passwords, etc., to authorized personnel.
- Staff that uses or enters data into software applications has been suitably trained.
- Only authorized software is permitted for use by employees.
- Custom software is subject to an appropriate level of testing before being implemented.
- Program changes are subject to formal change management procedures.

CONTROLS TO PREVENT UNAUTHORIZED ACCESS TO DATA (including destruction of data, improper changes, unauthorized or non-existent transactions, or inaccurate recording of transactions)

- Networks, servers, firewalls, routers, and switches are properly configured to prevent unauthorized access.
- Management protects data in storage and during transmission against unauthorized access or modification.
- Data files and critical applications are regularly backed up and stored in offsite locations.
- Access to IT facilities, equipment, and applications (including remote access) is restricted to authorized personnel.
- Passwords are changed regularly.
- Policies exist to ensure departing employees are denied access to software programs and databases.
- Procedures exist to protect against computer viruses.

ITGCs are important because they impact the effectiveness of both application controls and IT-dependent manual controls, as well as potentially affecting the reliability of electronic audit evidence the auditor may wish to rely on during the audit. For example, if a client relies on an application that records a sale and then automatically records and updates the accounts receivable ledger for that particular customer, the client also relies on its IT program change procedures and security to verify that the program and this specific control are not changed without appropriate approval and testing.

Examples of tests of controls over program changes and access to data files include:

- program change controls—examine documentation for evidence (for example, signatures on the program change forms) that the changes were authorized, tested, documented, and approved by appropriate personnel (for example, users, programmers, the IT manager)
- access controls—check whether the access control software options in effect are properly approved and whether the options selected are reasonable; test or observe attempts to log on to terminals and access files using unauthorized user IDs; review the related access violation or exception reports to determine whether all of the attempts are properly recorded.

Application controls

Application controls are the fully automated controls that apply to the processing of individual transactions. They are the controls that are driven by the particular software application being used, hence the name "application" controls. These are the controls that ensure transactions are processed correctly. There are generally three categories of application controls:

1. Input controls are the controls designed to detect and prevent errors during the data input stage. Examples of input controls include:
   - verification controls to check input to previously entered data such as the master file
   - missing data checks to ensure all required data have been input and no data are missing
   - check digits to prevent input errors by applying a mathematical formula.

2. Processing controls are the controls in place to ensure the data are processed as intended and no data are lost, added, duplicated, or altered during processing. Examples of processing controls include:
   - control totals ensure that input totals are balanced and reconciled
   - reasonable checks compare actual data to expected data and ensure they are reasonable
   - sequence tests review sequential data and produce exception reports for missing numbers.

3. Output controls ensure that the processed results are correct and that only authorized personnel have access to the output. Examples of output controls include:
   - reconciling totals to ensure that input totals agree with the output totals
   - uploading output to a secure server location in read-only format
   - printing output on a secure printer with limited access.

Application controls may also be important in enforcing the segregation of incompatible duties, particularly in large organizations.

It is usually difficult for smaller organizations to implement effective application controls unless there are enough employees to make sure that the physical segregation of duties is mirrored by appropriate access restrictions for particular applications.

IT-dependent manual controls

In many situations, the auditor identifies preventive or detective controls that have both manual and automated aspects. These are referred to as IT-dependent manual controls, and consideration must be given to both their manual and automated aspects. For example, suppose management reviews a monthly variance report and follows up on significant variances. Because management relies on the computer-generated report to identify the variances, the auditor also needs to check that there are controls in place to ensure that the variance report is complete and accurate.

When evaluating the completeness and accuracy of computer-produced information, before the auditor can rely on the information, they need to identify the source and the controls that ensure the information is complete and accurate. As illustrated earlier, the client often relies on both application and IT general controls to make sure that any computer-produced information is complete and accurate. If the auditor does not test both the application controls and the ITGCs and determine that the controls are effective (as they relate to particular reports or data), they run the risk of placing undue reliance on reports or data produced by the client's IT system. Auditors need to ensure any evidence they plan to rely on (even if it is in the form of an internal system-generated report) is accurate, complete, and can be relied on. This testing can either be performed directly on the report in question or, alternatively, can be performed on the overall application that produces the report and the relevant ITGCs, which then removes the need to test the actual report.

PROFESSIONAL ENVIRONMENT

COSO internal control framework

All companies benefit from an effective system of internal controls because it helps organizations achieve their goals. In addition, companies subject to an external financial statement audit can benefit from a more effective system of internal controls because it means financial statement audits are more efficient and effective.

The Committee of Sponsoring Organizations (COSO) of the Treadway Commission produced an integrated framework on internal control in 1992 following the release of the Treadway Commission's recommendations. The framework provides principles-based guidance for designing and implementing effective internal controls. It is now the most widely used internal control framework in the United States and is widely used around the world. COSO provided an updated *Internal Control-Integrated Framework* in 2013. COSO expects the guidance to help organizations adapt to changing business conditions, including greater complexity, and to mitigate the risks of operation as well as to increase the quality of decision-making.

An example of rapid change in business is the practice of keeping data and files stored on the Internet, also known as cloud computing. A recent COSO project developed guidance

for organizations using cloud computing to meet their technology needs. The focus is to consider the risks and benefits of using cloud computing, and to help management and boards integrate risk management of cloud computing with the organization's other risk management practices. Among the risks of using cloud computing is the reliance of the organization on the technical competence and financial viability of the cloud service provider (CSP). That is, the organization owning the data becomes more reliant on an external party, potentially reducing costs but increasing risk. The risk is greater if the CSP is in another legal jurisdiction. The external auditor is obliged to consider the nature of controls over the integrity of the data stored via cloud computing as part of the audit (CAS 402) *Audit Considerations Relating to an Entity Using a Service Organization*.

Sources: Committee of Sponsoring Organizations of the Treadway Commission website, www.coso.org; "COSO Issues Updated *Internal Control-Integrated Framework* and Related Illustrative Documents," COSO news release, May 14, 2013; Crowe Horwath LLP, W. Chang, E. Leung, and H. Pili, "Enterprise Risk Management for Cloud Computing," COSO, June 2012.

BEFORE YOU GO ON

7.4.1 What are the different types of controls?

7.4.2 What is the difference between an application control and an IT general control?

7.4.3 Which type of control, preventive or detective, is usually a more efficient control type to test?

7.5 SELECTING AND DESIGNING TESTS OF CONTROLS

The auditor must decide which controls should be selected for testing and how much audit testing must be performed. Both decisions require the auditor to apply a large degree of professional judgement, and the considerations that must be taken into account are explained in the following sections.

5 Explain how to select and design tests of controls.

7.5.1 Which controls should be selected for testing?

As explained above, controls are put in place to prevent or detect errors occurring (or a WCGW from actually going wrong). When the auditor decides to include controls testing in the audit approach, they select those controls that will provide the most efficient and effective audit evidence (that is, evidence that will provide the assurance required that the controls are working). To improve efficiency, the auditor will test only those controls that they believe are critical or key to their opinion. These may also be referred to as key controls. In other words, they must decide which controls identified for each assertion are likely to be most effective at preventing the WCGWs from occurring or detecting them if they do occur. The auditor also considers which controls provide reasonable assurance that the controls operated effectively throughout the period of reliance. Deciding which controls to test will be influenced by the types of controls, the frequency at which the controls are performed, and the level of assurance the auditor wants to gain from the controls being designed and implemented effectively. As a general rule, the best controls to test are those that address the WCGWs most effectively with the least amount of testing required (this is an efficient testing strategy). If one control addresses multiple WCGWs, it stands to reason that this control would be selected instead of testing several different controls that each address one of the WCGWs to obtain the same level of assurance that a WCGW had not occurred.

7.5.2 How much testing does the auditor need to do?

Once the controls have been selected for testing, the auditor must decide how much testing is to be performed, a decision that is driven by the frequency of the control in question. For example, is the control operating daily, weekly, monthly, or for every transaction processed?

When testing controls, either statistically based sampling techniques (as described in chapter 6) or professional judgement can be used to determine the extent of testing. There are a number of factors to consider. The more assurance the auditor wants from the performance of the controls, the more testing they need to do. That is, if they are intending to reduce control risk to the lowest level possible, they perform more testing than if they are planning to obtain only limited assurance from their testing (and reducing control risk by only a limited amount). The factors to consider when deciding the extent of testing include the following:

- How often the control is performed. The less frequently a control is performed (for example, a control applied monthly compared to a control applied daily), the fewer instances of the control there are to test and therefore the less testing the auditor needs to perform to be satisfied the control is operating effectively.

- The degree to which the auditor intends to rely on the control as a basis for limiting their substantive tests. The greater the degree of intended reliance (that is, the more they intend to rely on the particular control and thereby limit their substantive procedures), the more they test that control to provide the required assurance.

- The persuasiveness of the evidence produced by the control. As discussed earlier, if the performance of a control results in little or no direct evidence that the control operated effectively, the tests of that control—no matter how extensive—may not provide the necessary assurance required. Conversely, if direct evidence of the effective operation of a control is available, the auditor might decide that they need to examine a limited amount of that evidence to be satisfied that it is operating effectively.

- The need to be satisfied that the control operated as intended throughout the period of reliance. When planning audit procedures to test the effective operation of a control, the auditor must consider whether they need evidence from different times during the period of reliance. For some controls they may need evidence only at year end, whereas for most controls they need evidence that the control operated throughout the year.

- The existence of a combination of controls that may reduce the level of assurance needed from any one of the controls. When other controls related to a particular objective or WCGW are also in place and are tested, the level of assurance that might be needed from any one control is not as high as it would be if the auditors were relying solely on a single control.

- The relative importance of the "what could go wrong" questions or statements being considered. Considering the WCGWs and the level of assurance needed to address the WCGWs is a matter of professional judgement and requires the consideration of a number of issues. These include the inherent risk of the transactions or account, the audit assertion being addressed, the volume of transactions subject to the control, the complexity of the transactions, and the materiality of the transactions being processed.

- Other factors that relate to the likelihood that a control operated as intended. In determining the extent of tests of a control, the auditor considers several other factors that affect the auditor's perception of the likelihood that a control operated as intended throughout the period of reliance, including:
  - The competence and integrity of the employee performing the control, the employee's independence from the related processing procedures, the degree to which the employee is supervised, and the extent of employee turnover all contribute to the perception of whether the control operated as intended.
  - The quality of the control environment. The extent of testing is affected by the quality of the control environment, with consideration being given to:
    - the likelihood that a control is bypassed during peak processing periods
    - the potential for management to override a control
    - the extent to which the internal auditors have performed similar or related tests during the year
    - the likelihood in a good control environment that a control will continue to operate as intended throughout the period of reliance.
  - Changes in the accounting system. Where there have been changes in the accounting system, the auditor considers whether a control may have been less effective during the period when the changes were being implemented, and whether the control is still applicable to the new accounting system.
  - Unexplained changes in related account balances. When the client cannot provide satisfactory explanations for fluctuations (or for the absence of expected fluctuations) in the related account balances, the auditor considers whether they need to revise the extent of their tests of controls.
  - The auditor's prior-period experiences with the engagement. The results of the tests in prior audits and the current audit to date affect the perception of risk. If tests in prior audits indicated that a particular control was ineffective, and if there have been no improvements in the control, tests of that control in the current audit are not likely to be useful. Similarly, if in prior audits the tests showed that the control was effective, the expectation of errors would be reduced and, therefore, the tests of controls might be less extensive. The auditor also considers whether the changes in the types or volume of transactions could affect the auditor's expectations.

Even though the factors listed above may reduce the expectation of errors, the auditor's tests of a control need to be sufficiently extensive to provide reasonable assurance that the control operated effectively throughout the period of reliance.

When the control is applied every month, the auditor may decide to test the application of the control in detail for two months and review the remaining 10 months for unusual items. If the control is applied more frequently (say, weekly or daily), the auditor might test more than one application of the control in detail and review a sample of the remaining applications for unusual items.

Tests of preventive controls that are accompanied only by inferential (rather than physical) evidence of their effective operation include, for example, reviewing documents for an initial or signature and re-performing the checking routine itself. (For example, if the signature signifies that the price, extensions, and additions have been checked, the auditor checks the price, extensions, and additions.) The extent of such tests is a matter of professional judgement, but, generally speaking, large sample sizes are not necessary. Under normal circumstances, a random sample of, say, 25 to 30 items, assuming no control exceptions (that is, deviations) are observed, when combined with the evidence obtained from other audit procedures performed on the related accounts, provides evidence that controls operated as intended (that is, the control was effective). This sample size has been calculated using audit risk tables and a technique called **attribute sampling**, a sampling technique used to reach a conclusion about a population in terms of a rate (frequency) of occurrence. For instance, a sample of cash payments can be examined for signatures that are required as evidence of proper approvals. The number of missing signatures (that is, exceptions) is then used to estimate the overall rate of exceptions for the entire file of payments. Each sample item provides one of only two possible outcomes: the attribute being tested (for example, a signature, price, or recorded balance) is either correct or incorrect, present or absent, valid or not valid.

attribute sampling a sampling technique used to reach a conclusion about a population in terms of a rate (frequency) of occurrence

Normally, attribute sampling by itself does not provide a direct estimate of dollar values, such as the dollar amounts of exceptions. That is why attribute sampling is most often used for tests of controls (rather than as a substantive test of account balances). However, by using this sampling technique, the auditor is able to determine with a certain level of confidence (90 percent or more) that the error rate for **control exceptions** is acceptably low; that is, they may not need to perform additional controls testing to reduce control risk further. If the audit objective is to obtain evidence directly about a dollar amount being examined, the auditor generally uses a different sampling technique (such as systematic selection).

There may be circumstances where more or less testing is carried out. Regardless of the size of the sample, all control exceptions (deviations) (including those that are accompanied by errors) are investigated by the auditor. The auditor is careful not to dismiss an observed control exception as a random, non-systematic occurrence. Therefore, the detection of one control exception results in the auditor extending the sample size (when the auditor anticipates no further control exceptions will be found), amending the decision to rely on that control, and/or considering whether another control is available that can be substituted for the control being tested (often referred to as a compensating control).

control exception an observed condition that provides evidence that the control being tested did not operate as intended

Cloud 9

Talking with Josh about the factors that have to be considered when deciding how much control testing to do helps Weijing appreciate her task. She realizes that her previous understanding of a combined audit strategy was too simple. Gathering evidence about the effectiveness of controls in order to reduce the reliance on substantive testing does not mean that the auditor has to test every control in the same way.

Weijing realizes that if the evidence that would be produced from testing a control is not very persuasive, there is little point in devoting a lot of effort to testing that control. For example, a preventive control that requires a supervisor to authorize a transaction only produces evidence of the presence or absence of a signature, not evidence of whether the supervisor was performing the task of reviewing the transaction effectively. Obtaining plenty of evidence that the supervisor's signature was on the appropriate form will not provide much assurance by itself about the effectiveness of the control.

Also, Weijing is now starting to understand what Josh means by "key or critical controls." Josh wants to know which of the controls identified for each assertion are likely to be the most effective at preventing the WCGWs from occurring or detecting them if they do occur. Josh would like to focus testing on these controls and gather sufficient, appropriate evidence to justify reduced substantive testing.

For example, there are usually several controls designed to prevent or detect errors and misstatements in inventory and sales. In the wholesale sales area at Cloud 9, these controls include signed delivery receipts, policies requiring undelivered goods to be returned to the warehouse at night, and use of a locked shipping cage. Other controls include the use of electronic scanners and matching and authorizing documents in the shipping and invoicing process. However, despite all these controls, Josh has also identified from his conversation with Carla Johnson that unless the controls over the inventory management software system are tested thoroughly, they will not be able to justify reduced substantive testing. This is because so much of the document matching and authorization depends on the correct operation of the programs.

Application controls

The auditor may decide to rely on application controls identified and evaluated earlier in the audit. The functioning of the application control is tested to determine whether it can be relied on as an effective control. The auditor also tests the operating effectiveness of the control over the period of reliance by one or both of the following methods.

1. Focusing on manual follow-up procedures that support the application control. For example, if the computer prices the invoices using data in the price master file, the application control is a computer-generated exception report listing all sales orders entered for which there are no

prices on the master file. The auditor may choose to focus on how the client follows up on these exceptions.

2. Testing controls over program changes and/or access to data files. Here the auditor is testing the ITGCs (as discussed previously). Using the example in (1) above, the auditor may choose to test controls to ensure that all additions, deletions, and changes to the pricing master file are approved.

If these testing strategies are not feasible, the auditor can still rely on application controls by testing them throughout the period of reliance. Using the price master file example above, the auditor may choose to select a sample of invoices from throughout the period and compare the prices to the approved price list instead of just testing at a single point in time.

When the client relies on controls over program changes and/or access to data files (ITGCs), it is efficient for the auditor to test these controls, as they may support reliance on several other application controls. For example, the auditor may decide to do a system-wide test of access to data files for controls that apply to more than one control objective or application.

Regardless of which testing strategy is selected, the auditor establishes a basis for concluding that the underlying processing of data is complete and accurate. The techniques to test controls over program changes and/or access to data files are similar to those used to test manual controls. They usually involve enquiry, observation, and examination of physical evidence. The testing applies to the specific applications of interest (for example, a test of program changes is limited to changes to the sales application only) if it is possible and efficient to do so.

Recognizing that application controls operate in a systematic manner, the auditor may be able to limit their testing of those controls to the significant transaction types. For example, a computerized interest calculation may consistently use the same formula (principal multiplied by an interest rate from a rate master file). Or a computerized edit check will not allow the finalization of payments greater than $100,000 without appropriate authorization. In these examples, the auditor could limit their testing to a "test of one" per transaction type (that is, test one interest calculation or attempt to process a cheque request in excess of $100,000) rather than testing a sample using audit risk tables. This test of one may have been performed as part of the walk-through, which took place when the auditor gained an understanding of the transaction, the WCGWs, and the controls.

Timing of tests of controls

Tests of controls will usually be carried out at an interim date (that is, before year end). It is preferable to test entity-level controls and ITGCs early in the audit process because the results of this testing could affect the nature and extent of other procedures the auditor plans to perform. For example, if it is found that the ITGCs are not effective and cannot, therefore, be relied on, more extensive testing of application controls will need to be performed if the auditor is planning to rely on applications and computer-generated audit evidence.

The auditor updates their evaluation of controls from the time of their interim procedures through to the year-end date. They update their evaluation by identifying changes, if any, in the control environment and in the controls themselves. If changes are identified, consideration is given to the effect of such changes on their evaluation of the controls. This update is often done via enquiry, observation, and, in some cases, testing the control again at year end. In most cases, a client will not have made significant changes in the control environment or controls between completion of the interim work and year end. When this is the case, and the auditor has noted an effective control environment, they satisfy themselves by enquiry and observation that controls continued to function throughout the remainder of the period without the need for additional detailed tests of controls.

Summary of extent of testing

Table 7.4 suggests how many tests of each control might be performed depending on the frequency of use for the control in question. For example, if it is a monthly control and the auditor wants to obtain a reasonable level of assurance from the controls testing, two controls (for example, a monthly bank reconciliation) would be tested from throughout the year. If, however, only a limited level of assurance from the controls testing is required, only one control would be tested from throughout the year.

TABLE 7.4 **Suggested extent of testing**

FREQUENCY	REASONABLE ASSURANCE FROM TESTS OF CONTROLS	LIMITED ASSURANCE FROM TESTS OF CONTROLS
> 1,000 instances	25–30	10–15
Daily	25–30	10–15
Weekly	5	2
Monthly	2	1
Quarterly	2	1
Annually	1	1
Other	Professional judgement	Professional judgement
Application control (effective ITGCs)	1	1

substantive procedures (substantive testing or **tests of details)** audit procedures designed to detect material misstatements at the assertion level

A limited level of assurance may be planned for when additional evidence from other testing is already available to the auditor (such as evidence from substantive procedures—also called **substantive testing** or **tests of details**—which are audit procedures performed to detect material misstatements at the assertion level), or where it may be an efficient strategy to test some controls and to perform some additional substantive procedures. Reasonable assurance may be planned for when there is no additional audit evidence available from other testing, or when it is more efficient to test and rely on controls without performing a significant amount of substantive testing. This is an area that requires a significant level of professional judgement. However, the limited approach is rarely used in practice. Many auditors feel if you are going to perform some tests of controls, you should test as many as necessary to reduce control risk to the lowest level. If the auditor is testing controls, they will want to get as much benefit from it as possible.

Cloud 9

Making sure that testing covers the critical or key controls and provides sufficient, appropriate evidence of the effectiveness of the controls allows the auditor to reduce the control risk of the related financial statement assertion. Josh and Weijing have a discussion about how they can design their control tests so that they can conclude that each control:
- operated as it was understood to operate
- was applied throughout the period of intended reliance
- was applied on a timely basis
- encompassed all applicable transactions
- was based on reliable information
- resulted in timely correction of any errors that were identified.

Josh explains that if they can satisfy the above objectives in their design, and no exceptions are found when they perform their tests, the control will be deemed to be effective. If any exceptions are found, they need to perform additional procedures to obtain sufficient assurance, or reduce their reliance on the control. This latter action might require additional testing of another compensating control or increased substantive testing.

BEFORE YOU GO ON

7.5.1 Name three factors to consider when deciding the extent of testing to be performed.

7.5.2 When would testing application controls warrant performing a test of more than one?

7.5.3 Why does the auditor update the interim evaluation of controls at year end?

7.6 DOCUMENTING AND TESTING INTERNAL CONTROLS

7.6.1 Documenting internal controls

Before the auditor tests the internal controls, they need to document their understanding of them. The most common forms of documentation include the following:

- *Narratives*—this is the most common form of documentation, particularly in smaller environments where accounting and internal control activities are simple or where a particular flow of a transaction is relatively simple and straightforward. It involves the auditor describing (in words) each step of the flow of transaction from start to finish (that is, from initiation to reporting in the financial statements). Refer to figure 7.3 for an example.

- *Flowcharts*—this form of documentation is used in larger and more complex environments. It involves the auditor summarizing (in flowcharts/boxes) each step of the flow of a transaction from start to finish (that is, from initiation to reporting in the general ledger). While a flowchart may take longer to prepare, it provides a visual representation of the flow of the transaction and the key controls throughout the flow that is often simpler for the reader or reviewer to understand. The key to a good flowchart is to keep it as simple as possible, with as few words as possible so as not to overload the reader with information. Refer to figure 7.4 for an example.

- *Combinations of narratives and flowcharts*—this form of documenting internal controls is typically a page divided into two sections with the process flowchart on the left-hand side (or the top side) and the narrative describing each step in the flow on the right-hand side (or the bottom half of the page). The flowchart side highlights the key activities from initiation to reporting, while the narrative column contains the details about what happens in the flow of the transaction. Refer to figure 7.5 for an example.

- *Checklists and preformatted questionnaires*—an internal control checklist or questionnaire is another technique used to systematically identify the most common types of internal control procedures that should be present. This is particularly helpful in industries that the auditor may not personally be familiar with auditing, or when less experienced auditors find it difficult to identify which are the critical controls (for example, when documenting entity-level controls). Refer to figure 7.6 for an example.

6 Explain the different techniques used to document and test internal controls.

Sales order is received by fax or e-mail. Check customer details against customer account balance to see if the customer has exceeded its credit limit. If the customer has exceeded its limit, refer the sales order to the credit manager (S. Fitzpatrick) for approval. If approval is denied, refer the order back to the sales manager to notify or discuss with the customer and notify customer. If customer has not exceeded its credit limit or the credit manager (S. Fitzpatrick) has provided an approval to exceed the limit, process the sale in the sales ledger.

FIGURE 7.3 **Example narrative for documenting credit sales process**

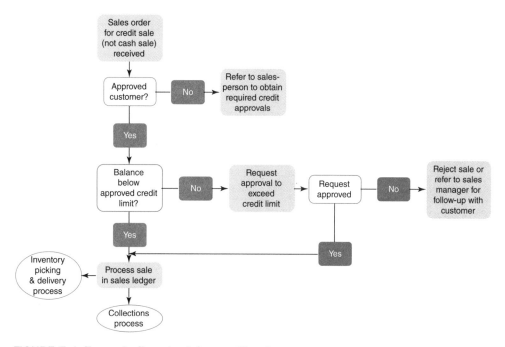

FIGURE 7.4 **Example flowchart for credit sales process**

- Sales order is received by fax or e-mail.
- Check customer details against customer account balance to see if the customer has exceeded its credit limit.
- If customer has exceeded its limit, refer the sales order to the credit manager (S. Fitzpatrick) for approval. If approval is denied, refer the order back to the sales manager to notify or discuss with the customer.
- If customer has not exceeded its credit limit or the credit manager (S. Fitzpatrick) has provided an approval to exceed the limit, process the sale in the sales ledger.

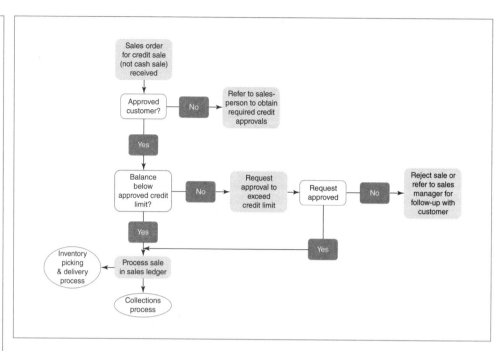

FIGURE 7.5 **Example combination documentation for credit sales process**

Process step	Performed by	IT/reliance on electronic data Yes/No?
Customer places sales order and order is input into sales order program		
Credit and/or credit terms approved		
Order filled and prepared for shipment		
Shipping/delivery documents prepared		
Order shipped/delivered to or picked up by customer		
Sales invoice prepared		
Prices (or deviations from standard prices) approved		
Invoice reviewed for accuracy and mailed/delivered to customer		
Sales journal produced		
Sales journal summarized and posted to general ledger and trade receivables detail		
Provide any other details that are necessary to understand the initiation, processing, recording, and reporting of the transactions:		
Briefly describe the client's **revenue recognition policy**, *including* **standard billing** *and* **collection terms**:		
Briefly describe the client's **credit terms** *and* **credit authorization procedures**:		
Briefly describe the client's procedures for **sales returns and allowances** *and the issuance of* **credit memos**:		

FIGURE 7.6 **Example checklist for documenting a credit sales process**
Source: EY, 2015.

7.6.2 Testing internal controls

Once the controls are documented, the auditor may decide to test the controls. Techniques used to test controls include enquiry, observation, inspection of physical evidence, and re-performance. Ordinarily, a combination of these testing techniques provides the evidence that the control operated as intended throughout the period in which the auditor wishes to place reliance on it.

Enquiry

This technique involves the auditor asking questions to determine how the control is performed and whether it appears to have been carried out properly and on a timely basis. For example, the auditor may ask the employees who prepare the sales invoices how they determine when to prepare the invoice and how they ensure that the revenue is recorded on a timely basis. They may also ask management how it makes sure revenue is reported correctly and completely at year end.

Observation

This technique involves the auditor observing the actual control being performed. For example, they may observe the preparation of an invoice to determine if the related shipping report has been received. The limitation with this technique is that employees may perform the procedures more diligently when they know they are being observed. Therefore, the evidence gathered applies only to the point of time of the observation.

Inspection of physical evidence

This technique relies on the auditor testing the physical evidence to verify that a control has been performed properly. For example, the auditor may select a sample of invoices to determine if the related shipping document is attached. Also, they may review a sequential listing of invoices and shipping documents issued during the period to determine whether the control routinely detected missing invoices and whether explanations were documented to ensure the exceptions were dealt with appropriately.

Re-performance

This technique involves the auditor re-performing the control to test its effectiveness. For example, the auditor may test the application controls for accessing the billing module to ensure an unauthorized employee is unable to generate invoices (and that an unauthorized attempt to do so is recorded on an exception report).

Regardless of which of the above approaches is used to document and test internal controls, the extent of the documentation and testing will increase as the complexity of the client, its systems, and its internal controls increases.

Cloud 9

Josh will prepare a flowchart or narrative to document his understanding of the different transaction cycles. This will help him understand the stages at which the errors can occur. He will include the entire process from the initiation of the transaction through to recording in the general ledger. Where appropriate, he will link several accounting processes together into one seamless flow of transactions. For example, he has made a simple diagram of the flow of transactions from initiation of a purchase order through to the cash payment to the supplier (see figure 7.7). The process comprises three smaller processes: Initiating a purchase order through to receipting the goods as they arrive, receiving the purchase invoice from the supplier through to entering the invoice in the general ledger, and requesting cash payment and recording the payment to the supplier. Once the transaction cycles are documented, Josh will perform walk-throughs. That is, he will walk one transaction from its inception to when it is recorded in the books to ensure his understanding of the processes are correct.

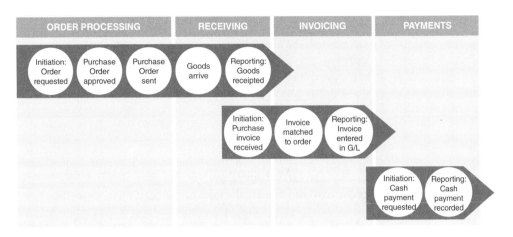

FIGURE 7.7 **Cloud 9 flow of transactions—order to payment**

BEFORE YOU GO ON

7.6.1 Explain the different techniques used to document internal controls.

7.6.2 When would it be more appropriate to use a flowchart instead of a narrative to document internal controls?

7.6.3 Name the four different techniques for testing controls.

7.7 RESULTS OF THE AUDITOR'S TESTING

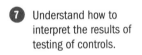

Understand how to interpret the results of testing of controls.

Before the auditor tests the controls, they should review the internal control documentation. This will ordinarily be in the form of narratives, flowcharts, checklists, a questionnaire, or a combination of these. This review should be used to validate the controls testing strategy.

If the tests of controls confirm the auditor's preliminary evaluation of controls (and control risk), the planned substantive audit procedures are not modified. If the test results do not confirm their preliminary evaluation of controls (and control risk), the auditor revises the overall audit risk assessment for the related account and the planned audit strategy (that is, they increase the level of substantive procedures). For example, if the tests of controls indicate that certain controls are not as effective as originally believed or have not functioned as prescribed, and if mitigative (compensating) controls are not available or were not effective, the auditor revises their audit risk assessment (increases control risk), reduces or eliminates the intended reliance, and reduces detection risk by designing more extensive substantive audit procedures (which are intended to detect and estimate the effect of errors in the related significant account balances). As mentioned previously, when a control has not been performed as it was intended, it is referred to as a control exception (deviation).

Figure 7.8 illustrates the decision tree or thought process an auditor goes through when assessing the results of their controls testing.

The auditor needs to investigate any control exceptions (deviations) they identify during their testing to find out, to the extent practical, the causes (for example, whether the exceptions may be indicative of a pattern of similar exceptions), the amounts involved, the financial statement accounts affected, and the potential effect on other audit procedures. The auditor is required to document the resolution of any control exceptions (including the impact on the remaining audit approach) and report the control exceptions in a management letter to those charged with governance, as they are considered matters of governance interest in accordance with CAS 260 *Communication with Those Charged with Governance* and CAS 265 *Communicating Deficiencies in Internal Control to Those Charged with Governance and Management.*

If the auditor extends their testing and another control exception is identified, they should change their decision to rely on that control. If another (compensating) control is not available to be substituted for the control being tested, or if it is not considered efficient to continue testing

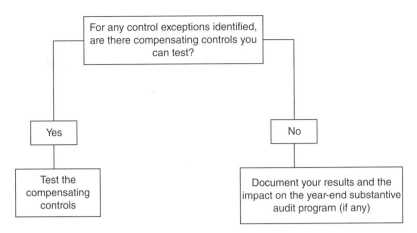

FIGURE 7.8 **Results of testing**

controls, the auditor should update (and potentially increase) the nature, timing, and extent of the planned substantive procedures. That is, the audit strategy is altered and detection risk is reduced. Therefore, if tests of controls indicate the controls are not operating effectively, then control risk must be assessed as high for that assertion. It is not possible to moderate control risk if the controls are only effective some of the time.

In trying to determine whether there is a need for additional detailed tests of controls, the following factors are considered.

- *Results of enquiries and observations.* If, during their enquiries or observations later in the audit process, the auditor identifies that significant changes to processes and controls have occurred, their previous tests of controls may no longer provide a basis for relying on those controls. Therefore, they may need to identify and test other controls, perform additional tests of controls, or increase the level of substantive testing performed at year end. Changes to processes or controls are only significant if they have implications for the continued functioning and effectiveness of controls on which the auditor is relying in the first place.

- *Evidence provided by other tests.* Tests of account balances (substantive testing) can often provide evidence about the continued functioning of controls. For example, when the auditor examines vendors' invoices in support of year-end creditors and expense account balances, they learn whether controls relating to the recording of these transactions continue to function. To the extent that their other audit procedures provide evidence of the effectiveness of controls from the date of interim work to the end of the period under audit, additional tests that otherwise might be necessary can be reduced.

- *Changes in the overall control environment.* An effective entity-level control environment may allow the auditor to limit their tests of controls to enquiry and observation during the period between when they tested the controls (interim) and year end. If they become aware of adverse changes in the overall control environment of the entity, such as a loss of employees and key management who perform key controls and who provide evidence as to the effectiveness of the overall entity control environment, additional tests of controls may be necessary.

BEFORE YOU GO ON

7.7.1 What does the auditor do when they identify control exceptions?

7.7.2 Why does the auditor consider the entity's overall control environment when performing controls testing?

7.7.3 Why does the auditor always investigate control exceptions?

7.8 DOCUMENTING CONCLUSIONS

8 Explain how to document tests of controls.

Once controls have been tested, the auditor documents their work in a working paper. In this working paper, the auditor would ordinarily set out the purpose of the tests of the controls identified. This assists in carrying out the testing by reminding the auditor of their overall purpose in testing the controls. If the auditor identifies any exceptions or issues, they are able to decide if there is an impact on their testing strategy by considering whether the control exception means that the control no longer meets the objective of the test. For example, assume that the control selected for testing is a bank reconciliation, and the objective of the test is to verify that a review by the financial controller occurred on a timely basis. When performing the testing, however, it was noted that while there was evidence of the review (a signature), there was no date, so timeliness could not be verified. Therefore, the auditor is able to conclude that the control operated, but they are not able to conclude that it operated on a timely basis. The

EXAMPLE TEST OF CONTROL WORKING PAPER							
Client name: Aubergine Ltd.				Year end: December 31, 2016			
Working paper: Cash controls testing							

Purpose of test:
The purpose of this test is to verify that the bank reconciliation control was adequately designed and implemented for the 12 months ending December 31, 2016.

Work performed:
Selected two bank reconciliations from different months, tied the balance as per the bank statement to the bank statement and bank confirmation, tied the balance as per the general ledger to the trial balance, and vouched all reconciling items between the bank statement and the trial balance greater than $50,000 to supporting documentation to ensure valid reconciling items and that the reconciliation had been performed correctly. Ensured the reconciliation had been prepared and reviewed on a timely basis.

Findings/results of testing:
Selected bank reconciliations for the months of April and September 2016. No errors noted in the preparation of the reconciliation. Both were prepared and reviewed within four days of month end. Considered this to be on a timely basis.

Month tested	Balance agreed to bank statement and bank confirmation	Balance agreed to general ledger and trial balance	Vouched deposits >$50,000 to stamped deposit slips and cut-off bank statement	Vouched outstanding cheques >$50,000 to cheque register, cancelled cheque, and cut-off bank statement	Vouched all other outstanding items >$50,000 to supporting documentation	Verified mathematical accuracy	Date prepared and reviewed
April	Y	Y	Y	Y	NA	Y	Prepared May 2, reviewed May 4
September	Y	Y	Y	Y	NA	Y	Prepared October 3, reviewed October 4

Conclusion:
Based on testing performed, the bank reconciliation appears to have been designed, implemented, and operating effectively for the 12 months ended December 31, 2016.

	Prepared by: SEF	Reviewed by: FMC	Index: CI:I

FIGURE 7.9 **Example test of control working paper**

auditor would need to determine whether a compensating control should be tested, or whether the timeliness of the review is not critical to the auditor's ability to rely on the bank reconciliation as audit evidence.

The auditor also documents the test performed, the actual controls selected for testing, and the results of the testing. There must be enough detail regarding the controls selected to allow another auditor to review the working paper, re-perform the steps (if necessary), and reach the same conclusion as the auditor who prepared the working paper. The results are often set out in a table to make it easier to review and identify quickly what (if any) exceptions were identified during the testing. Before an overall conclusion is reached for each section of work performed, the results table also assists the person reviewing the working paper to determine if enough work has been performed and if the right conclusion regarding the controls testing has been reached. The working paper should also include a conclusion specific to whether the test results support the overall purpose of the test. This is the documentation standard that is required by CAS 230 *Audit Documentation*.

Regardless of how they prepare their working papers and document their results, the extent of the auditor's documentation will increase as the complexity of the client's operations, systems, and controls increases. Also, the more complex the client's operations and its internal controls, the more experienced the auditor who performs the work needs to be.

Figure 7.9 is an example of a working paper relating to controls testing.

The first part of figure 7.10 illustrates in a table format the impact of controls testing on the subsequent amount of substantive testing required to be performed. For example, if inherent risk is low and a reasonable level of assurance has been gained from controls testing (that is, controls are operating effectively), the auditor can rely on his or her original control risk assessment and continue to perform a combined audit. This means that the controls tested can be relied on, and less substantive work is required. Therefore, potentially only overall analytical review procedures would need to be performed to reduce detection risk (and audit risk) to an acceptable level to be able to make a conclusion about the significant account assertion. If, however, the auditor has found control deviations, the cause of the deviations and the number need to be assessed. If the number of deviations exceeds a predetermined tolerable rate, the auditor may conclude that no assurance has been obtained from the controls

Inherent risk assessment		Reasonable level of assurance from controls testing	Limited level of assurance from controls testing	No assurance obtained from controls testing
	Low	Overall analytical review	Some substantive procedures	Considerable testing
	High	Some substantive procedures	Considerable testing	Extensive procedures focused on estimating errors in the balance

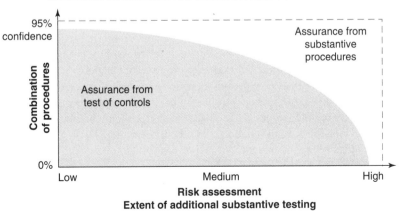

FIGURE 7.10 **Impact of controls testing on level of substantive testing**

testing. In this case, control risk will be assessed as higher than originally planned and the audit strategy may be revised to a substantive approach. This means extensive substantive procedures designed to estimate the dollar value of any error in the balance would need to be performed. The second part of figure 7.10 illustrates the same information in a graph format. That is, the higher the level of confidence gained from controls testing, the lower the level of assurance required to be obtained from the substantive procedures in order to form conclusions (a combined audit strategy).

Cloud 9

Josh has been busy over the last few days answering questions from Sharon and the partner about particular aspects of the controls testing performed to date. He is looking forward to continuing this work as they continue the documentation of controls over the various financial statement accounts.

BEFORE YOU GO ON

7.8.1 What level of detail does the auditor need to include in the audit working papers when documenting the results of their controls testing?

7.8.2 Which auditing standard sets the minimum level of documentation required in the working papers stored in the audit files?

7.8.3 What is the impact on the extent of required substantive testing if inherent risk is high and no assurance has been obtained from controls testing?

7.9 IDENTIFYING STRENGTHS AND WEAKNESSES IN A SYSTEM OF INTERNAL CONTROLS

9 Describe the importance of identifying strengths and weaknesses in a system of internal controls.

Strengths and weaknesses in internal control are usually noted by the auditor when performing tests of controls as part of the control risk assessment. An internal control strength is when a control is in place and working as intended; therefore, it is effective in preventing and detecting a material misstatement in the financial statements. Weaknesses in internal controls exist when an internal control is unable to prevent, detect, and correct material misstatements. While clients will often be interested in obtaining feedback from external auditors as to the relative strengths of their internal controls, focus is ordinarily on the areas of weakness identified. This is because it is the weaknesses that increase the risk of material misstatements being undetected by management's processes and controls, and, thus, it is on the areas of weakness that the auditor typically performs additional substantive testing to quantify the (potential) material misstatements.

Some observations made by the auditor will relate to controls that are not directly relevant to the audit. As discussed previously, some controls within the system of internal controls have a financial reporting impact, whereas other controls are implemented to assist the entity in meeting its organizational and compliance objectives. For example, a bank reconciliation is a control that has a financial reporting impact, whereas an approved supplier list is a control that ensures inventory is only purchased from reputable sources but has no direct financial reporting impact. Significant levels of professional judgement are required when deciding whether an internal control observation (individually or in combination with other observations) is, in fact, relevant to the audit and should be tested.

CAS 260 *Communication with Those Charged with Governance* and CAS 265 *Communicating Deficiencies in Internal Control to Those Charged with Governance and Management* require the auditor to provide those charged with governance with timely observations arising from the audit that are significant and relevant to their responsibility to oversee the financial reporting process, and to promote effective two-way communication between the auditor and those charged with governance. The auditor should communicate matters of governance interest to management, such as significant (or material) weaknesses in the design or implementation of internal control, as soon as practicable, and at an appropriate level of responsibility. Examples of significant deficiencies include the following:

- evidence of an ineffective control environment, such as identification of management fraud
- absence of a risk assessment process within the entity
- evidence of an ineffective entity risk assessment process
- evidence of an ineffective response to identified significant risks
- misstatements that were not prevented or detected by the entity's internal control
- evidence of management's inability to oversee the preparation of the financial statements.

It is for these key reasons that the auditor prepares what is often called a management letter.

BEFORE YOU GO ON

7.9.1 Why is it important to identify both the strengths and weaknesses in a system of internal controls?

7.9.2 Does the auditor provide feedback on strengths in internal controls or just weaknesses? Explain.

7.9.3 What obligations does the auditor have regarding communicating strengths or weaknesses in internal controls?

7.10 MANAGEMENT LETTERS

A **management letter** is a deliverable prepared by the audit team and provided to management and those charged with governance. The management letter discusses internal control weaknesses and other matters discovered during the course of the audit. The purpose of the management letter is to inform the client of the auditor's recommendations for improving its internal controls.

The example management letter shown in figure 7.11 demonstrates that the combination of the auditor's experience in auditing various businesses, and the thorough understanding they gain while conducting an audit, places them in a unique position for communicating insights about the system of internal controls designed and monitored by those charged with governance. The management letter also enables the auditor to provide timely feedback to management on the implementation of internal controls.

Significant **professional judgement** is necessary in deciding whether a weakness identified is significant enough to warrant communicating to management and to those charged with governance. When the auditor identifies risks of material misstatement that the entity has not controlled (or has not adequately controlled), or if in the auditor's judgement there is a significant deficiency in the entity's design or implementation of internal control, the auditor is required to communicate these deficiencies as soon as practicable to those charged with governance. Deciding whether an observation should be reported to those charged with governance is often a matter of consultation and discussion among the audit team. As discussed in chapter 2, various cases have demonstrated that in the past some auditors have observed significant deficiencies but failed to communicate them. As a result of these cases, auditors often report all matters observed, irrespective of whether they are considered material or not. Some of the most recent and high-profile corporate collapses globally led to the creation of the U.S. Public Company Accounting Oversight Board (PCAOB) by the U.S. Securities and Exchange Commission and to the Sarbanes-Oxley Act (2002), which contains explicit provisions for internal control reporting.

The auditor may also identify and communicate internal control deficiencies not considered significant but still worthy of management's attention. While it is not mandatory to provide this feedback in writing, the auditor ordinarily prefers to provide their recommendations in the form of a letter or report to avoid any ambiguity or confusion as to what

 10 Explain how to communicate internal control strengths and weaknesses to those charged with governance.

management letter a document prepared by the audit team and provided to the client that discusses internal control weaknesses and other matters discovered during the course of the audit

professional judgement the exercise of the auditor's professional characteristics such as their expertise, experience, knowledge, and training

observations, conclusions, and recommendations they have made. Responding to a management letter also provides a simple way for management to document the actions they have taken in response to the issues raised and to share these actions (and the progress toward the resolution of the issues) with those charged with governance. Such a response also provides the auditor with valuable insights into management's attitude toward the importance of internal controls by being able to evaluate what management has done in response to the recommendations made in the previous year at the start of each audit. Depending on the size of the engagement and the timing of when control weaknesses are identified relative to the final audit visit, teams will sometimes prepare an interim management letter at the end of planning and interim procedures, with a final management letter issued at the completion of the audit.

FIGURE 7.11 **Example management letter**

Ernst & Young LLP
Ernst & Young Tower
222 Bay Street, PO Box 251
Toronto, ON M5K 1J7

Tel: +1 416 864 1234
Fax: +1 416 864 1174
ey.com

To the Management Team of Skyward Ltd.:   15 March 2016

Our audit of the financial statements as at and for the year ended 31 December 2015 has been completed. In performing our audit procedures at Skyward, we noted certain items that may be of interest to you and your team.

Our procedures were designed to express an opinion on the financial statements of Skyward Ltd. and were not designed to evaluate the adequacy of individual internal controls. Accordingly our audit would not necessarily discover all conditions requiring your attention or all opportunities to improve internal controls. Furthermore, the observations below should not be considered to be the sole matters to be addressed by management.

Our observations are as follows:

A. Internal Controls over Cash Disbursements

Observation - We noted that user access to the online banking system was granted to many individuals and certain of these individuals did not require such access for their day-to-day activities.

Implication - Without proper controls over cash disbursements, fictitious payments may be issued without detection from management.

Recommendation - Management should adopt a formalized review process for access to the online banking system. Stronger controls in this area can prevent any potential loss arising from inappropriate access to Skyward's online banking portal. In particular, management should consider those parties who require access to the online bank account, including which users require the ability to execute transactions versus read-only access. Access for personnel not requiring access should be removed.

(continued)

FIGURE 7.11 **Example management letter** (continued)

EY
Building a better
working world

Ernst & Young LLP
Ernst & Young Tower
222 Bay Street, PO Box 251
Toronto, ON M5K 1J7

Tel: +1 416 864 1234
Fax: +1 416 864 1174
ey.com

B. Review of Bank Reconciliation

Observation – While executing our testing of controls over the cash disbursement and cash receipts processes, we noted some instances where there was a lack of documentation of the review process for bank reconciliations by appropriate individuals.

Implication - The lack of formalized review and approval of bank reconciliations could lead to undetected misappropriation of cash or unreconciled items that are not resolved on a timely basis. Timely preparation and review of bank reconciliations is a critical control activity, that when properly conducted, can lead to the detection and correction of errors in account balances or improvements in other related processes.

Recommendations - We recommend that management ensure that a timely and thorough review and approval process for bank reconciliations is adhered to on a monthly basis.

C. No Formal Analysis of Leases

Observation - We noted that management does not perform a formal analysis of new lease agreements as they are entered into.

Implication - Without a formalized process for analyzing new leases on a timely basis, the accounting for leases could be materially misstated.

Recommendations - Management should establish a formalized process by which all new leases are analyzed based on the finance lease criteria. This analysis should be maintained for all leases that are in use at the current time and the conclusions reached should be supported by the contracts associated with the lease.

We would like to take this opportunity to thank the employees and management of Skyward for the excellent cooperation given to us throughout the audit.

This letter is intended solely for the information and use of Skyward's Management and its Audit Committee and Board of Directors and is not intended to be and should not be used by anyone other than these specified parties.

Sincerely,

Audit Partner, Ernst and Young LLP

Source: EY, 2015.

Cloud 9

Josh provides his documented understanding of Cloud 9's system of internal controls and his preliminary assessment of the system's strengths and weaknesses to Jo Wadley, the engagement partner of the audit. The audit team will gather additional evidence about the system of internal controls during the audit, and at the completion of the audit the senior members of the audit team will make a final assessment of Cloud 9's internal controls and write a management letter. Providing a management letter, including recommendations for future changes to the system of internal controls, is an important part of the auditor's role. The management letter not only discharges the audit team's responsibilities to the client, but helps the client improve its systems. In turn, this will likely increase the quality of the client's financial reporting in the future and improve the efficiency and effectiveness of future financial statement audits.

BEFORE YOU GO ON

7.10.1 Do we always communicate weaknesses in internal controls to those charged with governance? Explain your answer.

7.10.2 Can the content ordinarily included in a management letter be delivered verbally to those charged with governance? Explain your answer.

7.10.3 Why is it preferred that most communications with those charged with governance be done in writing?

SUMMARY

❶ Define internal control.

Internal control is the process designed, implemented, and maintained by those charged with governance, management, and other personnel to provide reasonable assurance about the achievement of the entity's objectives with regard to reliability of financial reporting, effectiveness and efficiency of operations, and compliance with applicable laws and regulations. The term "controls" refers to any aspects of one or more of the components of internal control. Controls include entity-level controls and transaction-level controls.

❷ State the seven generally accepted objectives of internal control activities.

Internal controls are designed and implemented to ensure that transactions are real; recorded; correctly valued, classified, summarized, and posted; and timely.

❸ Understand and describe the elements of internal control at the entity level.

The elements of internal control at the entity level are the control environment, the entity's risk assessment process, the entity's information system and communications, control activities, and monitoring. Internal control also includes how the controls are implemented, such as through appropriate segregation of duties.

❹ Identify the different types of controls.

There are four different types of controls: manual, automated (otherwise known as application controls), IT general controls (ITGCs), or a combination of control types referred to as IT-dependent manual controls. Each of these types can be described as either a preventive control or a detective control. Preventive controls, as the name suggests, prevent errors from occurring. Detective controls detect the error after it has occurred and rectify the error on a timely basis.

❺ Explain how to select and design tests of controls.

The selection of which controls to test is a matter of professional judgement. Deciding which controls to test will be influenced by the control objective, the type of control, the frequency at which the control is performed, and the level of assurance the auditor plans to gain from determining whether the control is designed and implemented effectively. As a general rule, the best controls to test are those that address the WCGWs most effectively with the least amount of testing required. The extent of testing of controls (that is, deciding how many to test) is also a matter of professional judgement, although there are sampling techniques available (discussed in chapter 6). The extent of testing is affected by many factors, including how often the control is performed, the degree to which reliance will be placed on the control as part of the audit, the persuasiveness of the evidence produced by the control, the need to be satisfied that the control operated as intended throughout the period of reliance, the existence of a combination of controls that may reduce the level of assurance that might be needed from any one control, the relative importance of the WCGW questions or statements being considered, and any other factors such as the competence of the person carrying out the control, the quality of the control environment, and any changes in the accounting system.

6 **Explain the different techniques used to document and test internal controls.**

The most common forms of documentation are narratives, flowcharts, combinations of narratives and flowcharts, and checklists and preformatted questionnaires. There are four key techniques used for testing controls: enquiry (questions are asked regarding the operation of the control), observation (the operation of the control is observed to be occurring), inspection (physical evidence resulting from the performance of the control is examined), and re-performance (the control is re-performed to test its effectiveness).

7 **Understand how to interpret the results of testing of controls.**

If the controls tested are considered to be effective and can be relied on for the purposes of reducing overall audit risk for a particular significant account and assertion, the level of additional substantive testing required is reduced. If the controls tested are considered to be ineffective and are not able to provide any audit evidence

that reduces overall audit risk for a particular significant account and assertion, the level of additional substantive testing that is required is increased.

8 **Explain how to document tests of controls.**

The purpose of the test of controls, the selection of controls to test, the results of the controls testing performed, and the conclusion regarding the design and implementation of the controls are all documented in the audit working papers. The working papers are then reviewed by more experienced auditors to determine if sufficient work was performed and if the appropriate conclusion was reached.

9 **Describe the importance of identifying strengths and weaknesses in a system of internal controls.**

An important outcome of understanding a client's system of internal controls is the ability to make observations, draw conclusions, and offer recommendations regarding the strengths and weaknesses observed. CAS 260 and CAS 265 require auditors to provide those charged with governance with timely observations arising from the audit. This is generally done through a management letter.

10 **Explain how to communicate internal control strengths and weaknesses to those charged with governance.**

A management letter (sometimes also referred to as a letter of recommendations) is a deliverable prepared by the audit team and provided to the client (including those charged with governance). It informs the client of the auditor's recommendations for improving its internal controls.

KEY TERMS

Attribute sampling, 251
Audit risk, 231
Control activities, 238
Control environment, 233
Control exception, 252
Control risk, 236

Detection risk, 236
Entity-level controls, 233
Inherent risk, 236
Internal control, 230
Management letter, 263
Professional judgement, 263

Risk assessment process, 236
Substantive procedures (substantive testing or tests of details), 254
Tests of controls (controls testing), 242
Transaction-level controls, 242
WCGWs, 243

MULTIPLE-CHOICE QUESTIONS

7.1 Internal control is a process:
   (a) designed to provide reasonable assurance about the achievement of the entity's objectives with regard to reliability of financial reporting, effectiveness and efficiency of operations, and compliance with applicable laws and regulations.
   (b) that is the responsibility of those charged with governance.
   (c) that is designed and implemented to address identified business risks that threaten the achievement of the entity's objectives.
   (d) All of the above.

7.2 The objectives of internal controls include:
   (a) that fictitious transactions are not included in the organization's records.
   (b) that correct amounts are assigned to transactions.
   (c) that transactions are recorded in the correct accounting period.
   (d) All of the above.

7.3 The control environment:
   (a) is the economic environment in which the organization operates.
   (b) is the combination of the culture, structure, and discipline of an organization.

(c) applies only to listed companies.

(d) All of the above.

7.4 The following is not a type of control:

(a) automated controls.

(b) substantive controls.

(c) manual controls.

(d) IT-dependent manual controls.

7.5 The auditor decides which controls to test by considering:

(a) the type of control.

(b) the frequency of the control being performed.

(c) the level of assurance the auditor wishes to gain.

(d) All of the above.

7.6 Inspection of physical evidence is a control test used by auditors. It:

(a) relies on questioning skills.

(b) is subject to a limitation because employees may be more diligent when they know they are being observed.

(c) relies on testing the physical evidence.

(d) requires the auditor to re-perform the control.

7.7 A major change in the accounting system has taken place during the year. The effect on control testing is that:

(a) the auditor should ensure controls testing is performed for periods both before and after the accounting change became effective.

(b) the auditor can assume the accounting system change was necessary and has improved the client's controls, so should only test the period following the change.

(c) the auditor can assume the accounting system change was necessary and has improved the client's controls, so should only test the period before the change.

(d) the auditor will not conduct controls testing because obviously the client has thought about making sure the accounting system works well.

7.8 Working papers:

(a) document the purpose of the test of the control identified and the results of the test, including a specific conclusion about whether the test results supported the overall purpose of the test.

(b) are necessary for the junior auditor to keep track of the daily work but are not important to the overall audit.

(c) document the results of the tests but not the purpose of the control selected for testing.

(d) document the purpose of the control selected for testing and the conclusion made by the auditor but not the results of the test.

7.9 Documenting internal controls:

(a) is always handled through the use of checklists and preformatted questionnaires.

(b) is done after internal controls are tested so that the results can be included in the documentation.

(c) can be handled with a combination of narratives and flowcharts.

(d) is not done for smaller clients because of the risk of management override.

7.10 A management letter:

(a) contains recommendations for improving internal control and discusses other issues discovered during the course of the audit.

(b) is written by management to the auditor at the start of the audit.

(c) lists only the significant deficiencies discovered during the audit.

(d) All of the above.

REVIEW QUESTIONS

7.1 If an auditor does not intend to rely on internal controls in the audit, does the auditor need to obtain an understanding of internal control? Explain.

7.2 Explain the difference between entity-level controls and transaction-level controls. Is an auditor interested in both?

7.3 Discuss the contention that the control environment is the most important part of a system of internal controls because it provides the foundation.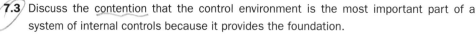

7.4 Explain the purpose of (a) preventive controls and (b) detective controls. Why would it be important for an entity to have both types of controls?

7.5 Explain the importance of segregation of incompatible duties. What sorts of duties would be segregated within the sales process? Why?

7.6 What are the four types of tests of controls? Explain them and comment on the reliability of the evidence obtained from each.

7.7 What factors do auditors consider when deciding how much control testing to do?

7.8 Discuss the concepts of nature, timing, and extent as they relate to controls testing.

7.9 Four approaches to internal control documentation are discussed in the chapter. Assess the advantages and disadvantages of each. How would documentation assist the auditor to identify strengths and weaknesses of an entity's system of internal controls?

7.10 Why do auditors prepare management letters?

PROFESSIONAL APPLICATION QUESTIONS

 Basic ★   Moderate ★ ★   Challenging ★ ★ ★

7.1 Importance of internal control ★

Powersys is an electricity distribution company based in a large capital city. Its business is to manage the electricity assets, including poles, wires, and other equipment, that are used to deliver electricity to more than 500,000 retail and business customers in the city. Pole, wire, and substation maintenance and improvements are a large part of the company's operations, and teams of highly trained technicians are used for both planned work and emergency response activities. Emergency response is required when storms or fires bring down power lines, the power must be turned off at the direction of police, or the electricity supply fails for any reason.

Each team has several vehicles (vans and trucks) and uses additional heavy equipment, such as cherry pickers, cranes, and diggers, as required. Each vehicle carries a core set of specialized parts and tools, and additional items are obtained as required from the stores, which are located in a large warehouse in the northern suburbs. The warehouse is staffed on a 24-hour basis to assist night maintenance (designed to minimize disruption to business customers) and emergency response.

Required

(a) Make a list of the potential problems that could occur in Powersys's maintenance and improvements program.

(b) Suggest ways that good internal control over parts, equipment, and labour could help Powersys avoid these problems.

7.2 Objectives of internal control ★ ★

Carmel Harrison runs Emerald Spa, a business providing women-only hairdressing, beauty, relaxation massage, and counselling services in a small tourist town. Ninety percent of the clients using the beauty and massage services at Emerald Spa are weekend visitors to the town, but 80 percent of the hairdressing and counselling clients are locals. The masseuse and counsellor have formal qualifications and are registered with the medical authorities, allowing clients to claim the cost of the service with their private health insurer if an appropriate receipt is provided when the client pays.

Emerald Spa has just opened another branch of the business in a town 100 kilometres away, and there are plans for a third branch to be opened next year. Carmel has been very busy establishing each new branch and relies on staff in each office to run the day-to-day operations, including ordering supplies and banking receipts. In addition, the branch manager organizes the staff and authorizes their time sheets. Carmel makes the payments for rent, power, salaries, and large items of expenditure, such as furniture purchases.

Required

(a) Give examples of transactions that would occur at Emerald Spa.

(b) Explain what could go wrong with these transactions if the system of internal controls could not meet any of the seven generally accepted objectives of internal controls.

7.3 Control environment at a large company ★ ★

International Bank is experiencing bad publicity surrounding huge fraud losses in its foreign currency department. Accusations are being made in the press that the rogue trader blamed for the losses was operating outside the official guidelines with the tacit approval of senior management in the department because of the large profits made by this trader in previous years. The press claims that it was common knowledge in the foreign currency department that strict policies and procedures surrounding the size of trades and the processes for balancing out trades at the end of each day were not to be followed if the trader had verbally informed his supervisor of the trade. The press is also suggesting that the problems are not confined to the foreign currency department, and that poor attitudes are prevalent throughout all commercial departments at International Bank.

Required

Discuss the control environment at International Bank, assuming the press reports are correct. Which parts appear to be most deficient?

7.4 Segregation of duties in a small business ⭐

Big Town Computers has premises in the main street of a large regional city. The business is owned by Max and Betty Waldup, who purchased it three years ago. Betty has an extensive background in IT and has a talent for diagnosing and solving problems with computers that are brought in for repair. Max also has an IT background and oversees the sales and administration staff. There are three staff in the business: a computer technician who assists Betty; a part-timer who helps with sales; and a junior trainee, Sally, who does other tasks, such as banking. Sally is also responsible for issuing invoices and statements to clients who have a service contract with the business. These clients are generally other businesses who ask Betty to visit their premises for routine and emergency repairs, and who purchase software and hardware from the business.

   Max and Betty have worked very hard over the last three years, but they have cash flow problems. Their bank manager has requested a meeting to discuss the business's growing overdraft. The bank manager asks Max and Betty to prepare for the meeting by analyzing their accounts receivable and customer receipts. Max and Betty review the accounts receivable ledger and find that it is not up to date. They also discover that client statements have not been issued for four months. They are also unable to identify from the cash receipts journal which clients have paid their accounts.

Required

(a) Discuss the attitude and control consciousness of Big Town Computers' management.
(b) Which duties should be segregated in this business? Recommend an appropriate allocation of duties for the staff at Big Town Computers.

7.5 Categories of controls ⭐

There are several categories of control activities listed in this chapter. They include performance reviews, authorization controls, account reconciliations, physical controls, and segregation of duties.

Required

For each of the following, identify the type of control:
(a) Petty cash is kept in a safe.
(b) All invoices are stamped "paid" after processing.
(c) Cheques received are pre-listed by the receptionist and recorded in the books by the accounts receivable clerk.
(d) Accounts receivable sub-ledger is agreed to the general ledger at each month end.
(e) Passwords are required before journal entries may be posted.
(f) Monthly results are compared with budget, and unexpected results are investigated.
(g) Overtime must be approved by a supervisor.
(h) Pre-numbered purchase orders are required before an invoice will be paid.
(i) Employee payroll records are kept in a locked filing cabinet.
(j) The person responsible for shipping and receiving goods does not perform the related billing.
(k) Monthly results are sent to divisional managers for review.

7.6 Preventive controls ★ ★

Alabama Industries manufactures and wholesales small tools. It sells the tools to a large group of regular customers and makes most sales by telephone to this group. Additionally, it receives orders online from its sales team, who sign up new customers within the sales area. In the past, Alabama Industries has had trouble with customers who do not pay their accounts on time. Despite instructing the sales team not to make sales to customers before their credit-worthiness has been assessed, sales are still being made to new customers before their limits have been set and to existing customers beyond their credit limit. Also, the economic situation has started to impact Alabama's customers, and management is concerned about the possibility of increasing bad debts.

Required

(a) What sort of preventive control could be used to deal with the problems faced by Alabama Industries? Explain how the control would work.
(b) Assume the preventive control is implemented, and during this year there have been no sales to customers that have taken any customer beyond its credit limit. What are two possible explanations for this that the auditor must consider?
(c) If an auditor finds two sales transactions during the year that are in excess of a customer's credit limit at the time of the sale, what conclusion would the auditor draw from this evidence? What other evidence could the auditor consider before concluding that the preventive control has failed?

7.7 Controls at a small start-up company ★ ★

Two of your friends from high school will soon realize their lifetime dream of opening an English-style pub. They recently spoke with their accountant who indicated that they should ensure that they implement some strong controls. They have no idea what the accountant was talking about. They know you are studying accounting and they have come to you for advice about what their accountant meant.

Required

(a) Explain the concept of internal controls.
(b) List four things your friends should do to ensure that they create a strong control environment.
(c) List eight control activities they should have in place. Describe how each activity is relevant to their business.

Source: © CGA-Canada. Reproduced with permission.

7.8 Testing bank reconciliation controls ★ ★

You are testing the controls over bank accounts for your audit client, Manitoba Ltd. You note that the responsibility for bank reconciliations has changed due to a corporate reorganization halfway through the current financial year. Both the staff member performing the bank reconciliations and the supervisor have changed. You are only able to talk to the current staff member and supervisor because the other staff took voluntary retirement and left the client's employment three months ago.

Required

(a) What techniques are available to you to gather evidence about the bank reconciliations? Explain how you would use each technique and comment on the quality of the evidence obtained from each.
(b) When you ask the employees responsible for bank reconciliations about how they perform the reconciliations, there is a possibility that they will not tell the whole truth about their performance of the reconciliations. Given this, will you bother to ask them? Explain.
(c) Explain the impact of the staff changes on your controls testing program.

7.9 Inventory program controls ★ ★

Ontario Drapers supplies custom-fitted curtains and blinds to retail customers. It has recently expanded to offer a wide variety of home decorating products through its six stores across the province. After some initial problems with inventory control, it installed a new automated inventory system in April this year. The system replaced another automated system that had been modified so often over the years that the auditor had advised Ontario's management that they did not regard it as reliable. That is, the auditor was unable to rely on the old system sufficiently to assess control risk for inventory as anything less than high.

Required

(a) Explain the normal process an auditor would expect to find in the client's systems governing changes to computer programs. Why is an auditor concerned about program changes?

(b) Ontario Drapers' financial year end is December 31. Does the auditor need to obtain evidence about the performance of the inventory control system from every month in the year or from a sample of months? Explain.

(c) If the auditor conducts tests of the inventory controls at an interim date, is it appropriate to conclude that the controls are still in place at the end-of-period date? Why or why not?

Questions 7.10 and 7.11 are based on the following case.

Featherbed Surf & Leisure Holidays Ltd. is a resort company based on Vancouver Island. Its operations include boating, surfing, diving, and other leisure activities; a backpackers' hostel; a family hotel; and a five-star resort. Justin and Sarah Morris own the majority of the shares in the Morris Group, which controls Featherbed. Justin is the chair of the board of directors of both Featherbed and the Morris Group, and Sarah is a director of both companies as well as the CFO of Featherbed.

Justin and Sarah have a fairly laid-back management style. They trust their workers to work hard for the company and they reward them well. The accounting staff, in particular, are very loyal to the company. Justin tells you that some accounting staff enjoy their jobs so much they have never taken holidays, and they rarely take sick leave. Justin and Sarah have not bothered much in the past with formal procedures and policies, but they have requested that the accounting staff start documenting the more common procedures. Justin and Sarah do not conduct formal performance reviews; they rely on their staff to tell them when there is a problem.

There are three people currently employed in the accounting department, the most senior of whom is Peter Pinn. Peter heads the accounts department and reports directly to Sarah. He is in his fifties and plans to retire in two or three years. Peter prides himself on his ability to delegate most of his work to his two staff members, Kristen and Julie. He claims he has to do this because he is very busy developing the policy and procedures manual for the accounting department. The delegated work includes opening mail, processing payments and receipts, banking funds received, performing reconciliations, posting journals, and performing the payroll function. Julie is a recently graduated chartered accountant. Kristen works part-time—coming into the office on Mondays, Wednesdays, and Fridays. Kristen is responsible for posting all journal entries into the accounting system and the payroll function. Julie does the balance of the work, but they often help each other out in busy periods. Kristen authorizes Julie's transactions, and Julie returns the favour by authorizing Kristen's transactions. Together, they usually make the accounts balance.

Source: Adapted from the Institute of Chartered Accountants Australia's CA Program's *Audit and Assurance Exam,* May 2008.

7.10 Internal control components ★ ★ ★

Required

Assess the internal controls at Featherbed. What changes would you recommend?

7.11 Communication with management ★ ★

Required

Write a management letter to Justin and Sarah Morris.

Questions 7.12 and 7.13 are based on the following case.

Securimax Limited has been an audit client of KFP Partners for the past 15 years. Securimax is based in Waterloo, Ontario, where it manufactures high-tech armour-plated personnel carriers. Securimax often has to go through a competitive market tender process to win large government contracts. Its main product, the small but powerful Terrain Master, is highly specialized and Securimax only does business with nations that have a recognized, democratically elected government. Securimax maintains a highly secure environment, given the sensitive and confidential nature of its vehicle designs and its clients.

In September 2016, Securimax installed an off-the-shelf costing system to support the highly sophisticated and cost-sensitive nature of its product designs. The new system replaced a system that had been developed in-house, as the old system could no longer keep up with the complex and detailed manufacturing costing process that provides tender costings. The old system also had difficulty with the company's broader reporting requirements.

Securimax's IT department, together with the consultants from the software company, implemented the new manufacturing costing system. There were no customized modifications. Key operational staff and the internal audit team from Securimax were significantly engaged in the selection, testing, training, and implementation stages.

The manufacturing costing system uses all of the manufacturing unit inputs to calculate and produce a database of all product costs and recommended sales prices. It also integrates with the general ledger each time there are product inventory movements such as purchases, sales, wastage, and damaged inventory losses.

It is now October 2016 and you are beginning the audit planning for the December 31, 2016 annual financial statement audit. You are assigned to assess Securimax's IT controls with particular emphasis on the recent implementation of the new manufacturing costing system.

Source: Adapted from the Institute of Chartered Accountants Australia's CA Program's *Audit and Assurance Exam*, May 2008.

7.12 Components of internal control ★ ★ ★

Required

Select two components of internal control. Explain how the roles of the internal and external audits would differ when assessing these components in relation to the new manufacturing costing system.

7.13 Understanding types of controls ★ ★

Required

In relation to the new manufacturing costing system, describe two automated application controls that you would expect to find.

Questions 7.14 and 7.15 are based on the following case.

Fellowes and Associates Chartered Professional Accountants is a successful mid-tier accounting firm with a large range of clients across Canada. During the financial year 2016, Fellowes and Associates gained a new client, Health Care Holdings Group (HCHG), which owns 100 percent of the following entities:

- Shady Oaks Centre, a private treatment centre
- Gardens Nursing Home Ltd., a private nursing home
- Total Laser Care Limited (TLCL), a private clinic that specializes in the laser treatment of skin defects

  Year end for all HCHG entities is June 30.

During the financial year 2016, HCHG released its own line of treatment supplies, such as orthotics, weights, and other equipment, which are sold by direct marketing by a sales team employed by the centre. The sales team receives a base salary and a bonus component, which is based on the dollar value of sales it generates. You recognize that the team's main motivation is to maximize its bonuses.

On April 1, 2016, Gardens Nursing Home Ltd. switched from its "homegrown" patient revenue system to HCHG's equivalent system. HCHG is confident that its "off-the-shelf" enterprise system would perform all of the functions that Gardens Nursing Home's homegrown system performed.

Gardens Nursing Home's homegrown patient revenue system comprised the following:

1. **Billing system**—a system that produced the invoice to charge the patient for services provided, such as accommodation, medications, and medical services. This software included a complex formula to calculate the patient bill allowing for government subsidies, pensioner benefits, and benefits from private medical insurance benefit plans.
2. **Patient database**—a master file that contained personal details about the patient as well as the period of stay, services provided, and the patient's medical insurance details.
3. **Rates database**—a master file that showed all accommodation billing rates, rebate discounts, and government assistance benefits.

At the request of the board, the group's internal audit unit was involved throughout the entire system conversion process. The objective of its engagement, as the board stated, was to "make sure that the conversion worked without any problems."

Source: Adapted from the Institute of Chartered Accountants Australia's CA Program's *Audit and Assurance Exam,* March 2009.

7.14 Control environment ★ ★ ★

Required

Discuss the implications of the sales bonus system for the control environment within HCHG. What special factors would management have to consider?

7.15 Control risks in new IT systems ★ ★ ★

Required

With reference to the control activities component of internal control, formulate one question that the internal audit team and the external audit team will ask regarding the conversion of the patient revenue systems by Gardens Nursing Home.

7.16 Control testing results and documentation ★ ★ ★

Arne Eklund, the audit senior, is reviewing the working papers written by the audit assistant on the audit of Quebec Creepers, a nursery and retailer of garden accessories. Arne reads the following description of the results of testing of inventory controls written by the audit assistant:

> The Inventory Manager advises that no changes have been made to the inventory programs during the current financial year. There are no documents on file authorizing program changes, so I conclude the Inventory Manager's statement is true. The Inventory Manager also advises that management did not attempt to override any controls relating to inventory. There are no memoranda or e-mails from management on file instructing the Inventory Manager to go against procedures, so I conclude the Inventory Manager's statement is true.

The audit assistant concludes that the inventory controls have not been changed or overridden during the financial year, so the results of the interim testing of controls can be relied on.

Required

(a) Examine the statements by the audit assistant. What deficiencies in the testing can you identify?
(b) If the results of testing one control show that the control is not effective, does the auditor have to increase substantive testing? What other options are available to the auditor?
(c) Explain why it is important for the working papers to be completed with sufficient detail for another auditor to understand what has been done. Make a list of the parties who might review the documents.

7.17 Techniques for testing computerized controls ★ ★ ★

The sales transactions at Alberta Park, a new audit client, are handled by a software application that is not supported by very detailed documentation. The audit partner requests that the team re-perform some controls to ensure that the software application controls are working as described by Alberta Park's management. The audit software used by the audit team can access the data on the client's files, allowing the use of standard audit procedures.

Required

Provide a list of possible audit procedures that could be used by the audit team to test the controls in the client's sales software application.

7.18 Control Objectives ★

The following errors due to sloppy paperwork and poor controls were found during an audit.
1. A customer's order was shipped without credit approval.
2. Some sales made in January were recorded as being made in December. The company has a December 31 fiscal year end.
3. Duplicate sales were recorded.
4. Sales to a subsidiary were recorded as sales to outsiders instead of as intercompany sales.
5. Some shipments of goods to customers were not recorded.

Required

Identify which internal control objective applies in each case.

CASES

7.19 Integrative Case Study—Armstrong, Aldrin & Collins Professional Corporation

Armstrong, Aldrin & Collins Professional Corporation (AAC) operates a public accounting practice that is located in Woodstock, Ontario. AAC's common shares are owned equally by its three shareholders, who are Chartered Professional Accountants (CPAs). A plan to open an office in Stratford, Ontario, on November 1, 2016, has been developed. Financing has been arranged with the bank subject to AAC providing the bank with its audited financial statements prepared in accordance with Accounting Standards for Private Enterprises for the fiscal year ending September 30, 2016, and for subsequent fiscal years.

AAC has engaged Smithee & Co., CPAs, to perform the audit of AAC's financial statements for the year ending September 30, 2016. You, CPA, have been assigned the role of audit senior on this engagement. It is July 25, 2016, and Gus Grissom, the engagement partner, calls you into his office and says: "I want you to prepare the audit engagement planning memo for the AAC audit. Please consider the risk and appropriate audit strategy. You should note that AAC's financial statements have not been previously independently audited or reviewed." The partner continues: "AAC has implemented a new working paper preparation and maintenance system and the shareholders have asked us to identify any weaknesses in the system and to provide recommendations for improving the system. The shareholders want the new system to provide proper quality control for AAC. I want you to prepare a draft report that addresses this client request."

Background Information

AAC was formed seven years ago and has experienced rapid growth. AAC has hired three university graduates who will start work in September 2016. Gus says that Wally Cunningham, AAC's controller, is responsible for setting accounting policies because the shareholders are "too busy growing the business to spend time on internal accounting matters, and Wally has a university accounting degree and knows what he is doing." However, Wally has recently found it difficult to keep up to date with the auditing and accounting standards due to the rapid pace of change with the transition to IFRS and ASPE.

NOTES PREPARED BY THE PARTNER ABOUT THE NEW WORKING PAPER PREPARATION AND MAINTENANCE SYSTEM

Background Information

A new working paper preparation and maintenance system was developed during the three months from November 2015 to January 2016. The new system, which became effective on February 1, 2016, allows for the storage of all working paper files on a secure website from which a client's information can be accessed, worked on, and reviewed from any place having an Internet connection (e.g., the AAC office, client offices, residences of staff members, and hotel rooms).

Passwords

The website is a secure site that uses 128-bit encryption for any interaction with remote computers. Each authorized AAC staff member is assigned a personal password that allows access to the system and records who uses the system and the names of the files opened. These specific passwords are stored on each staff member's computer, which allows for quick and automatic login once the site is connected by the Internet browser. After login has been achieved, the staff member starts the working paper preparation software, "ClientPrep," and can use any element of this program.

Software

The ClientPrep software includes audit and review engagement assurance planning templates, standard audit program forms and working paper templates, and standard correspondence forms. When the ClientPrep working papers are completed, the software produces financial statements using standard templates, with standard note disclosures. An AAC partner can assess and review any portion of a working paper file on which a staff member is still working.

Updates

ClientPrep is updated annually; however, revisions are made immediately for any income tax changes or programming errors that are identified. The annual update (or any other revision) of ClientPrep is sent directly to the website host, which makes the necessary changes to the ClientPrep program stored on the server and sends notification of the change to AAC.

When AAC wants to change the graphics or the links on the website, Michelle Collins (an AAC partner and the designated information technology officer) sends an e-mail to the website host requesting that the desired changes be made.

Backup and Security

Each week the entire population of working paper files is copied from the server to CD-ROMs which are sent by courier to AAC's office for storage. The website host prepares a report indicating those AAC staff members who have accessed files during the week and the time of each access. The AAC shareholders are concerned about the possibility of the website being infected with a virus, which could not only destroy client documentation but also prevent staff from viewing and working on client files. To address this concern, the website host scans the client data and other files used by AAC consistently using a well-respected anti-virus program.

Required

(a) Prepare an audit planning memo considering the audit risk and audit approach.
(b) Prepare a draft report that addresses the control weaknesses of the new system. For each item, address the implication and make a recommendation.

CASE STUDY—CLOUD 9

Answer the following questions based on the information presented for Cloud 9 in Appendix B to this book and in the current and earlier chapters. You should also consider your answers to the case study questions in earlier chapters.

Sharon Gallagher and Josh Thomas have assessed the internal controls at Cloud 9 as being effective at an entity level. This means that, at a high level, the company demonstrates an environment where potential material misstatements are prevented or detected.

PART A
Required

You have been assigned the task of documenting the understanding of the process for recording sales, trade receivables, and cash receipt transactions for wholesale customers. In your absence, Josh met with the Cloud 9 financial controller, Carla Johnson, and received permission to tape the interview, which is provided as a transcript (see Appendix B to this book). Using this interview transcript and other information presented in the case, you are asked to:

(a) Prepare a flowchart or narrative documenting your understanding of the sales to cash receipts process for wholesale sales.

(b) Identify any follow-up questions you would like to ask the client if aspects of the process are not adequately explained. You could address such questions to Carla Johnson or any other employee you deem appropriate.

(c) Identify the potential material misstatement that could occur in the sales to cash receipts process for wholesale sales.

(d) Identify, for the material misstatements in part (c), the financial statement assertion that is affected.

To answer parts (c) and (d), draw up a worksheet using the following format. Use as many rows as you need. Use the first three columns to present your findings. (You will complete the fourth column in Part B of this question.)

SIGNIFICANT PROCESS	POTENTIAL MATERIAL MISSTATEMENT	ASSERTIONS	TRANSACTION-LEVEL CONTROLS

PART B
Required

(a) Use your worksheet from Part A to complete this part of the assignment. In column four, include the transaction-level internal controls Cloud 9 has implemented to prevent and/or detect potential errors.

(b) In designing the audit strategy, auditors should consider the effectiveness of the client's internal control structure, thereby determining the control risk. An auditor should perform a preliminary assessment of control risk in order to be confident that they can use a controls-based approach to the audit strategy. A controls-based strategy is one in which the internal controls of a significant process are tested and proven to be effective, which means they can be relied on to reduce the level of substantive testing needed.

If internal controls are tested and proven to be operating effectively, the auditor can reduce the control risk of the related financial statement assertion. This method of testing controls can reduce the number of substantive procedures to be performed or can allow substantive testing to be performed prior to year end.

When designing control tests, consider whether there will be sufficient evidence that the control:

- operated as it was understood to operate
- was applied throughout the period of intended reliance
- was applied on a timely basis
- encompassed all applicable transactions
- was based on reliable information
- resulted in timely correction of any errors that were identified

Based on the preliminary assessment of Cloud 9's control environment obtained in earlier procedures, the audit team has decided to test controls over the sales to cash receipts process. It is expected that there will be no deficiencies in the transaction-level internal controls.

Josh has partially completed the testing for selected controls over the sales/receivables and cash receipts processes. He has asked you to complete the testing for him. All information has been provided by the client (refer to Appendix B of this book). Document your findings on the workpapers Josh has started (see tables 7.5 and 7.6), and then conclude with your assessment on the overall effectiveness of the controls tested.

TABLE 7.5 **Cloud 9 controls testing—sales/receivables process as at December 31, 2016**

	SALES INVOICE #	DATE	CUSTOMER NAME	SALE AMOUNT (EXCL. HST)	INVOICE MATCHES SHIPPING NOTE (A)	SHIPPING NOTE #	SHIPPING SUPERVISOR AUTHORIZATION (B)
1	124874	1/14/2016	David Jones— Moose Jaw	645.87	✔	D00124874	✔
2	125048	1/23/2016	Foot Locker— Ottawa	745.21	✔	D00125048	✔
3	125324	2/7/2016	Rebel Sport— Vancouver Island	905.46	✔	D00125324	✔
4	125542	2/16/2016	Rebel Sport— Sunshine Coast	517.32	✔	D00125542	✔
5	125987	3/2/2016	Myer— Moncton	675.28	✔	D00125987	✔
6	126067	3/10/2016	Dick's Sports— St. John's	367.96	✔	D00126067	✔
7	126845	4/8/2016	Foot Locker— Regina	781.62	✔	D00126845	✔
8	127111	4/27/2016	Running Shop— Calgary	457.24	✔	D00127111	✔
20							
21							
22							
23							
24							
25							

Note: For the purposes of this case study, sample tests 9 to 19 have been removed. There were no exceptions noted in the results.

Aim: To test selected controls over the sales and receivables process.

Sample: We randomly selected 25 sales invoices from the entire year.

(a) To complete this test, we matched the sales invoice to the shipping note, ensuring it was signed by the customer.

(b) We used the shipping note reference number in order to recall the online authorization screen. We noted the passcode entered by the shipping supervisors, which agreed with the passcode listings obtained by the IT manager.

TABLE 7.6 **Cloud 9 controls testing—cash receipts process as at December 31, 2016**

	DATE	TOTAL POSTED TO TRADE RECEIVABLES	TOTAL BANK DEPOSIT	EVIDENCE OF REVIEW
1	1/8/2016	10,548.45	10,548.45	✔
2	1/18/2016	9,587.37	9,587.37	✔
3	2/15/2016	11,486.82	11,486.82	✔
4	2/27/2016	7,456.24	7,456.24	✔
5	3/11/2016	5,836.08	5,836.08	✔
6	3/19/2016	8,012.74	8,012.74	✔
7	4/4/2016	8,753.91	8,753.91	✔
8	4/22/2016	9,687.45	9,687.45	✔
20				
21				
22				
23				
24				
25				

Note: For the purposes of this case study, sample tests 9 to 19 have been removed. There were no exceptions noted in the results.

Aim: To test selected controls over the cash receipts process.

Sample: We randomly selected 25 working days from the entire year in order to test the reconciliation of daily bank receipts to trade receivables.

Document the conclusion of the controls testing.

Using the results of your controls testing, assess the control risk for the following assertions and write your conclusions in the worksheet in table 7.7. Use the information you provided in the worksheet completed for part (a) to focus your controls testing on the significant assertions.

TABLE 7.7 **Cloud 9 controls testing conclusions**

ACCOUNT ASSERTION	CONTROL RISK	EXPLANATION
Sales—occurrence		
Sales—completeness		
Sales—measurement		
Trade receivables—existence		
Trade receivables—completeness		
Trade receivables—valuation		
Cash—existence		
Cash—completeness		

RESEARCH QUESTION 7.1

Concerns have been raised over how quickly the Alberta oil sands are being developed. Amid the international concern of global warming, the oil sands have emerged as Canada's fastest growing source of greenhouse gas pollution. Other ecosystem impacts include toxic waste, strip mining, and species loss. Assume you are a member of senior management at a large company that wants to develop property in the oil sands.

Required

Write a report identifying the main risks to your company that you believe should be considered at the next meeting of the risk assessment committee. Include risks to the company's operations and assets, finances, and personnel.

Source: Environmental Defence, The Pembina Institute, and Equiterre. *Duty Calls: Federal Responsibility in Canada's Oil Sands,* 2010, www.pembina.org.

SOLUTIONS TO MULTIPLE-CHOICE QUESTIONS

1. d, 2. d, 3. b, 4. b, 5. d, 6. c, 7. a, 8. a, 9. c, 10. a.

CHAPTER 8

Execution of the audit— performing substantive procedures

LEARNING OBJECTIVES

After studying this chapter you should be able to:

1 define substantive audit procedures

2 understand the link between the audit risk model and the nature, timing, and extent of substantive procedures

3 provide examples of different substantive audit procedures

4 explain the different levels of audit evidence obtained when performing substantive procedures

5 describe the documentation of the conclusions reached as a result of performing substantive procedures.

AUDITING AND ASSURANCE STANDARDS

CANADIAN	INTERNATIONAL
CAS 200 *Overall Objectives of the Independent Auditor and the Conduct of an Audit in Accordance with Canadian Auditing Standards*	ISA 200 *Overall Objectives of the Independent Auditor and the Conduct of an Audit in Accordance with International Standards on Auditing*
CAS 240 *The Auditor's Responsibilities Relating to Fraud in an Audit of Financial Statements*	ISA 240 *The Auditor's Responsibilities Relating to Fraud in an Audit of Financial Statements*
CAS 315 *Identifying and Assessing the Risks of Material Misstatement Through Understanding the Entity and Its Environment*	ISA 315 *Identifying and Assessing the Risks of Material Misstatement Through Understanding the Entity and Its Environment*
CAS 500 *Audit Evidence*	ISA 500 *Audit Evidence*
CAS 501 *Audit Evidence—Specific Consideration for Selected Items*	ISA 501 *Audit Evidence—Specific Considerations for Selected Items*
CAS 505 *External Confirmations*	ISA 505 *External Confirmations*
CAS 520 *Analytical Procedures*	ISA 520 *Analytical Procedures*
CAS 530 *Audit Sampling*	ISA 530 *Audit Sampling*

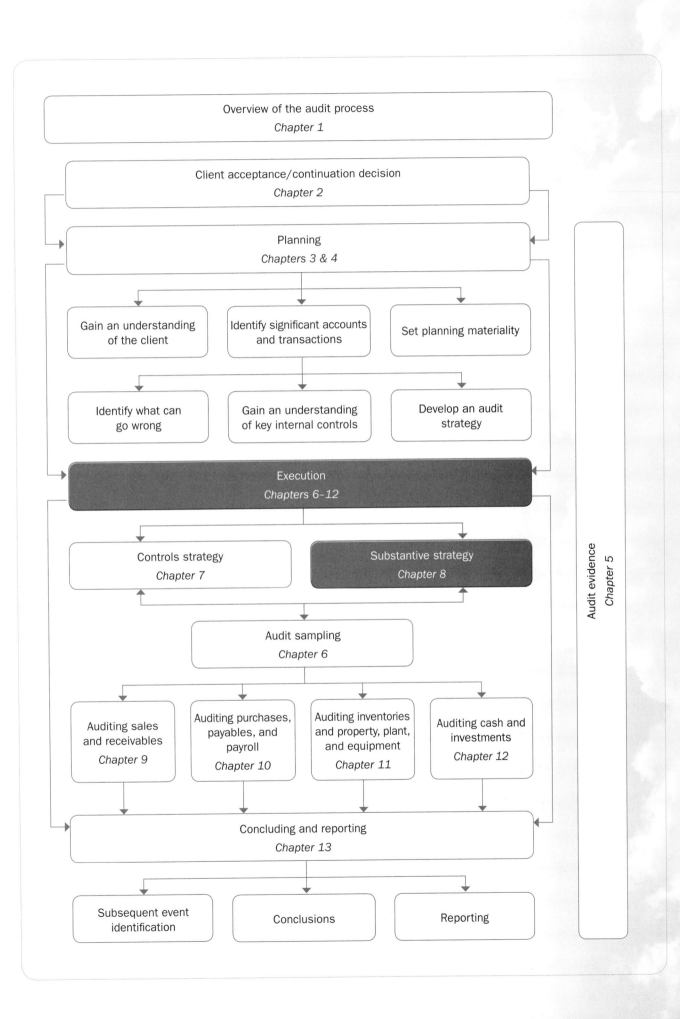

Cloud 9

Suzie Pickering is the clothing and retail industry specialist on the Cloud 9 Ltd. (Cloud 9) audit. Suzie is mentoring Ian Harper, a junior member of the audit team, and they are working together on the detailed substantive audit program.

Ian remembers that Suzie used analytical procedures in the early planning phase and that she explained to him how useful they could also be in the testing phase. Ian suggests that they plan to rely extensively on analytical procedures for Cloud 9's substantive tests. He is very enthusiastic and wants to put analytical procedures in the plan for all transaction cycles and major balances because he believes that analytical procedures will help keep the cost down and help the team bring the audit in on budget. Suzie is more cautious. Although she definitely plans to use some analytical procedures, she knows they will also need other types of tests.

"Why?" asks Ian. "How will I know when to use only analytical procedures? What other tests do we need?"

AUDIT PROCESS IN FOCUS

Finding an appropriate combination of audit procedures to minimize an engagement's audit risk at an acceptable cost to the auditor is a constant challenge. The purpose of this chapter is to describe the audit execution process, often referred to as "performing substantive procedures." The overall objective of substantive procedures is to supplement controls testing the auditor may have performed in order to determine that the underlying accounting records are materially correct and reconcile to the financial statements on which the auditor will ultimately form an opinion. (Further discussion on the overall conclusion of the audit is in chapter 13.)

The types of substantive procedures discussed in this chapter include analytical procedures, tests of underlying transactions and data, and the use of computers to assist in performing substantive procedures.

We will explain the link between the audit risk model and the nature, timing, and extent of substantive procedures. This link helps in the preparation of the audit program. We will also describe the levels of audit evidence the auditor can obtain from the various substantive procedures they have available to select from, and we will explain how to conclude that the overall account balance or disclosure being audited is not materially misstated.

8.1 OVERVIEW OF SUBSTANTIVE PROCEDURES

1 Define substantive audit procedures.

In this section we discuss the link between audit risk, assertions, and substantive procedures, and we define substantive procedures in detail.

8.1.1 Substantive procedures and assertions

significant account an account or group of accounts that could contain material misstatements based on their materiality and/or relationship to identified inherent and financial statement risks

As discussed in previous chapters, the nature, timing, and extent of audit procedures are determined in response to the risk assessment for each **significant account** and assertion using the formula for **audit risk** (that is, the risk that an auditor expresses an inappropriate audit opinion when the financial statements are materially misstated). This determination requires the use of **professional judgement**. Figure 8.1 contains the audit risk model introduced in chapter 4.

audit risk the risk that an auditor expresses an inappropriate audit opinion when the financial statements are materially misstated

Inherent risk is the risk of a misstatement occurring irrespective of any controls management may put in place. These risks tend to be driven by the nature of the significant account or business that the client is in. There is no way for the auditor to influence the inherent risk of an account or assertion.

professional judgement the auditor's exercise of professional characteristics such as expertise, experience, knowledge, and training

Control risk is assessed as high when there are no internal controls that the auditor can test or rely on (or when there are internal controls but they cannot be tested and relied on). Control risk is assessed as low when there are good internal controls in place that have been designed and implemented effectively to reduce an identified risk, and when the auditor has been able to

$$AR = IR \times CR \times DR$$

where:

AR = Audit risk

IR = Inherent risk

CR = Control risk

DR = Detection risk

FIGURE 8.1 **Audit risk model**

test the controls and verify their operating effectiveness throughout the period subject to audit. (Control risk and controls testing were discussed in detail in chapter 7.)

The combination of inherent risk and control risk (the risk of material misstatement as described in CAS 200 *Overall Objectives of the Independent Auditor and the Conduct of an Audit in Accordance with Canadian Auditing Standards*) determines the level of **detection risk** (that is, the risk that the auditor's testing procedures will not detect a material misstatement) that the auditor is willing to accept to be able to conclude that the financial statements are not materially misstated. There is an inverse relation between the auditor's assessed risk of material misstatement and detection risk. Detection risk is reduced or increased in direct proportion to the amount of substantive testing performed. For example, if the combined inherent risk and control risk is high (that is, the client is in a high-risk industry and a particular assertion of a significant account has a higher chance of being materially misstated because there are no controls in place and no controls have been tested), the amount of detection risk the auditor is likely to accept will be low, so significant substantive procedures will be necessary to reduce the detection risk. If the combined inherent risk and control risk are low (that is, the client is in a low-risk industry and a particular assertion of a significant account has a lower chance of being materially misstated because there are controls in place), the auditor will likely accept a higher amount of detection risk, and only a small number of substantive procedures will be necessary to reduce the detection risk.

Figure 8.2 shows how the assessment of inherent risk and control risk affects the amount of substantive testing required to reduce detection risk to an acceptable level.

As discussed in previous chapters, the risk assessments discussed in this section must be performed at the assertion level as well as at the financial statement level. Figure 8.3 gives an example of this risk assessment by assertion using accounts receivable. Chapter 5 introduced and defined each of the audit assertions, as outlined in CAS 315 *Identifying and Assessing the Risks of Material Misstatement Through Understanding the Entity and Its Environment*. They are reproduced in table 8.1 and grouped to show the assertions that have common objectives.

inherent risk the susceptibility of the financial statements to a material misstatement without considering the internal controls

control risk the risk that a client's system of internal controls will not prevent or detect a material misstatement

detection risk the risk that the auditor's testing procedures will not be effective in detecting a material misstatement

Control risk assessment

		Low	Medium	High
		Controls tested extensively and able to be relied on	Limited controls testing, and they are not to be relied on	No controls tested and no assurance from controls
Inherent risk assessment — Low	Lower risk of material errors if no controls in place	Few substantive procedures required	Some substantive procedures required	Considerable substantive procedures required
Inherent risk assessment — High	Higher risk of material errors if no controls in place	Some substantive procedures required	Considerable substantive procedures required	Extensive substantive procedures required

FIGURE 8.2 **Linkage between inherent risk, control risk, and detection risk**

ACCOUNT ASSERTION	INHERENT RISK	CONTROL RISK	OVERALL RISK ASSESSMENT	DETECTION RISK	AUDIT APPROACH
Accounts receivable— valuation	High	High	High	Low	Substantive approach
Accounts receivable— rights and obligations	Low	Low	Low	High	Combined audit approach
Accounts receivable— completeness	Low	Low	Low	High	Combined audit approach

FIGURE 8.3 **Example of accounts receivable risk assessment**

Table 8.1 illustrates how the objective of each assertion relates to the particular type of account or disclosure. For example, the auditor needs to verify that sales transactions recorded in the income statement occurred and relate to the entity (the occurrence assertion). Those same sales transactions flow through to the trade receivables balance in the balance sheet, and the auditor needs to verify that the balance of trade receivables as at year end exists and that the client holds the rights to those receivables (the existence assertion, and the rights and obligations assertion). The auditor then needs to verify that the balances disclosed in the financial statements as sales revenue and trade receivables occurred and relate to the entity (the occurrence assertion, and the rights and obligations assertion).

It is clear from table 8.1 that testing performed on sales revenue transactions will also provide evidence on trade receivables in the balance sheet and in the financial statement disclosures; however, additional testing will still be needed on the trade receivables balance regarding the other assertions not addressed by this example (such as testing the valuation assertion).

Do not assume that audit assertions across all three categories are the same. For example, "classification" in the income statement is not exactly the same as "classification and understandability" in the financial statements. Classification as it relates to transactions requires verification that transactions and events have been recorded in the proper accounts (that is, within the general ledger). Classification and understandability as they relate to the financial statement disclosures require verification that financial information included in the financial statements is appropriately presented and described, and that disclosures are clearly expressed. This is slightly different from

TABLE 8.1 **Audit assertions**

ASSERTIONS ABOUT CLASSES OF TRANSACTIONS AND EVENTS	ASSERTIONS ABOUT ACCOUNT BALANCES AT YEAR END	ASSERTIONS ABOUT PRESENTATION AND DISCLOSURE
Typically income statement accounts	*Typically balance sheet accounts*	*Disclosures made in the financial statements*
Occurrence	Existence	Occurrence
	Rights and obligations	Rights and obligations
Completeness	Completeness	Completeness
Cut-off		
Accuracy	Valuation and allocation	Accuracy and valuation
Classification		Classification and understandability

the first audit assertion discussed, as the first assertion is focused on the transaction being captured in the correct general ledger account. The second assertion discussed focused on the information being presented, described in the notes, and disclosed correctly and clearly. To ensure that this audit assertion is met, the auditor must ensure that the right account(s) in the general ledger are summarized, presented, described in the notes to the accounts, and disclosed in the financial statements in accordance with an applicable accounting framework (such as International Financial Reporting Standards or ASPE).

It is also important to note that when determining the substantive procedures to be performed, the auditor will consider the nature of the account, and the key assertions at risk. For example, usually the auditor is concerned with an overstatement of the asset accounts; therefore, the procedures performed will generally focus on whether the assets exist and if they are appropriately valued. Conversely, for liability accounts, the auditor is most concerned with an understatement, so the auditor focuses on the completeness assertion, to ensure that all liabilities have been recorded.

Cloud 9

Suzie emphasizes to Ian that their testing must respond to the risk of material misstatement at the assertion level. For each assertion, the audit team determines the level of detection risk, which is based on the inherent risk assessment and the results of the control testing, which is used to establish the level of control risk. The auditors also have to consider a range of practical factors, such as constraints on timing and the complexity of the client's systems.

"Analytical procedures are always useful, but the decision to use analytical procedures and/or other substantive procedures must consider risk and practical factors," she says. "We have to decide what an acceptable level of detection risk is, and how to achieve it, for every assertion about transactions, account balances, and disclosures."

8.1.2 Definition of substantive procedures

Substantive procedures are designed to obtain direct evidence of the completeness, accuracy, and validity of data, and the reasonableness of the estimates and other information contained in the financial statements. Substantive procedures include inspection, observation, enquiry, confirmation, recalculation, re-performance, and analytical reviews. These procedures were introduced in chapter 5. They are also referred to as **substantive testing** or **tests of details**.

The number of substantive tests performed, and their timing, are influenced by several factors. The most important factor, described in section 8.1.1, is the overall risk assessment for the item being tested. Before making this assessment, the auditor will have performed planning procedures and controls testing (including testing of any controls that the auditor has identified and intends to rely on). The results of these planning and interim procedures allow the auditor to make an overall assessment as to how much detection risk still exists before any substantive testing is performed. The auditor then designs what they believe are appropriate substantive audit procedures that will allow material errors and exceptions to be identified and rectified before an overall conclusion is made. These procedures are documented in what is usually referred to as the **audit program**. The audit program typically includes a detailed listing of the audit procedures to be performed during the planning, interim, and year-end stages. The program should include enough detail to enable the auditor to understand the nature, timing, and extent (or scope) of testing required. It describes the controls testing (as detailed in chapter 7) as well as the resulting substantive procedures (as detailed in this chapter). Examples of typical substantive procedures for common significant accounts are included in chapters 9 to 12.

There are several other factors (over and above the audit risk assessment) that influence how much (extent) and when (timing) substantive procedures are performed. These include the following.

- The nature of the test. Some tests lend themselves more easily to testing during the year-end visit as opposed to during the interim audit visit(s). For example, it is easy to verify prepayment amounts with their supporting documentation (that is, the invoices that were paid

substantive procedures (substantive testing or tests of details) audit procedures designed to detect material misstatements at the assertion level

audit program a detailed listing of the audit procedures to be performed, with enough detail to enable the auditor to understand the nature, timing, and extent of testing required

during the year) before year end. In contrast, verifying the calculation of the split between the amount to be recognized as a prepayment and the amount to be expensed in the income statement is easier to do at or after year end.

- The level of assurance necessary. If you want reasonable assurance, rather than just moderate assurance, you will have to obtain more evidence from substantive procedures in order to reach a conclusion.

- The type of evidence required. For example, are the procedures designed to provide persuasive, corroborative, or minimal audit evidence? (These concepts are discussed further in section 8.4).

- The complexity of the client's data-capturing systems. The more complex the systems, the more complex and sophisticated the substantive audit procedures need to be.

It is ordinarily more efficient to test and rely on controls than to carry out substantive procedures; however, there are situations when this may not be possible or practicable. In these situations, the auditor will need to perform extensive substantive procedures to provide sufficient audit evidence to reach a conclusion. This is often the case when auditing smaller businesses that do not have appropriate segregation of duties, or that may not have internal controls in place for the entire period of reliance.

The types of procedures used to reduce detection risk to an acceptable level consist of tests of details and analytical procedures. These are described in more detail in section 8.3.1. When controls are tested and determined to be effective, the auditor may address any residual detection risk by using substantive analytical procedures. These are described in more detail in section 8.3.2.

The auditor must use professional judgement to decide whether the substantive audit procedures start with analytical procedures and are then supplemented with additional procedures as necessary, or whether to begin with tests of details, including key item testing, and to use analytical procedures after enough other substantive procedures have been performed.

By using a combination of techniques, the auditor is able to perform substantive procedures that, when coupled with any other audit evidence obtained during the planning and interim phases of the audit, will provide sufficient and appropriate audit evidence to enable the auditor to conclude both at the significant account level and overall at the financial statement level.

It is worth noting that there are certain substantive procedures that are normally performed. These include sending bank confirmations, observing inventory counts (CAS 501 *Audit Evidence— Specific Consideration for Selected Items*), confirming receivables balances (CAS 505 *External Confirmations*), and examining material journal entries and other adjustments of audit importance during the course of preparing the financial statements (CAS 240 *Auditor's Responsibilities Relating to Fraud in an Audit of Financial Statements*).

Cloud 9

Ian is starting to realize that the standards of professional practice would not allow him to rely exclusively on analytical procedures. Cloud 9 has significant inventory balances (around 25 percent of total assets) and receivables (more than 40 percent of total assets), so the auditors will need to gather persuasive evidence about the existence, valuation, and rights and obligations assertions for these accounts. Procedures such as confirming receivables balances and observing inventory counts are definitely going to be included in the detailed audit program.

Suzie warns Ian that it is not always the size of the account that determines the use of analytical procedures or other procedures. For example, in Cloud 9's trial balance there is a liability called "Loans with directors." The balance of this account at September 30 is $149,354, less than 1 percent of total assets, but the accounting standard covering related party transactions (IAS 24 *Related Party Transactions*) creates additional disclosure requirements for these accounts, increasing the significance of the account and the amount of testing required.

"Auditors also have to be particularly careful in assessing the materiality of any liability balance," Suzie explains. "This is because we are usually more worried about understatement than overstatement of liabilities, so the assertion most at risk is completeness, not existence."

BEFORE YOU GO ON

8.1.1 Describe why audit assertions are important in the determination of audit risk.

8.1.2 Define substantive procedures.

8.1.3 Are there any audits where the auditor would perform no substantive audit procedures? Explain your answer.

8.2 RELATIONSHIP BETWEEN RISK ASSESSMENT AND THE NATURE, TIMING, AND EXTENT OF SUBSTANTIVE PROCEDURES

The nature of substantive procedures varies from account to account and ordinarily consists of one or a combination of the following techniques:

- tests of transactions/underlying data
- analytical procedures

These techniques are described in more detail in section 8.3.

The appropriate mix of substantive procedures depends on factors such as the nature of the account balance (that is, balance sheet versus income statement account) and the risk assessment for both the specific account and the client overall (that is, at the account level and at the financial statement level).

The nature, timing, and extent of substantive procedures are responsively related to the risk assessments for each of the relevant sources of information affecting a significant account. In the case of an accounting estimate, the auditor may conclude, for example, that the likelihood of material misstatement is lower in measuring the provision for warranty claims, but there is a risk that not all such claims are identified, as there may be a management bias to minimize warranty expense. In this case, extensive tests are directed at determining whether all claims have been identified (completeness assertion), while less extensive tests are directed at determining whether the amounts already recognized as claims are appropriate (existence assertion, valuation and allocation assertions). Risk assessments not only affect the extent of the tests but can also affect the nature and timing. For example, in the situation described above, the auditor would likely test the completeness of claims at or near year end; however, the tests of the valuation for individual claims by product type could be carried out before year end.

Similarly, the auditor may have agreed with the client that, based on the risk assessment, it is appropriate for the client to carry out a physical inventory count prior to year end (existence assertion). However, it is not appropriate for the auditor to test the client's valuation (pricing) of its inventory at that date. Rather, the auditor would perform tests of inventory pricing at a date nearer to or at year end.

Significant professional judgement is therefore required in relating the risk assessment to the nature, timing, and extent of the tests in order to hold overall audit risk to an acceptable level.

As can be seen from figure 8.4, the timing of substantive procedures is directly influenced by the level of control risk (that is, how much assurance has already been gained from the controls testing performed). Typically, substantive testing tends to be performed at or near year end, with controls testing performed during visits before year end (interim).

For accounts that accumulate transactions that, for the most part, will remain in the account balance at year end, the auditor can normally perform effective procedures before year end. For example, they could test additions and disposals to the fixed asset register or vouching of individually material expense items, such as severance expenses. Since these transactions accumulate during the year and, for the most part, remain in the account balance at the end of the year, the auditor's decision to perform procedures prior to year end does not generally depend on the effectiveness of controls or the likelihood of material misstatement. Rather, the timing of

2 Understand the link between the audit risk model and the nature, timing, and extent of substantive procedures.

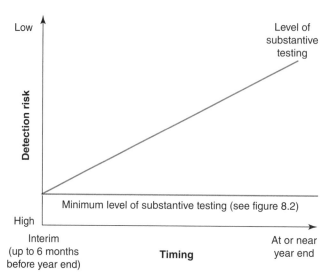

FIGURE 8.4 **Timing of substantive procedures**

such procedures is a matter of convenience and whether it is expected to contribute to audit efficiencies. It is normal for an auditor to perform as much audit testing as possible before the client's year end due to the large number of clients needing their audits completed by the same date. The more work the auditor performs prior to the year-end visit, the less year-end work they will need to perform during the audit firm's "busy season," which will allow more flexibility when performing audits.

For other accounts, the auditor's ability to perform substantive audit procedures at an interim date generally depends on the existence of an effective control environment and the effectiveness of controls. When the control environment is ineffective or there are specific ineffective controls, the auditor considers whether or not it is appropriate to perform substantive procedures at an interim date.

The timing of the substantive procedures is most flexible when controls have been assessed as effective and tested to confirm this assessment. In these circumstances, the substantive procedures may be performed earlier in the year (for example, six months before year end). When controls are assessed as effective but not tested, the substantive procedures may still be performed at an interim date (for example, two or three months before year end).

Whenever substantive procedures are performed prior to year end, the auditor performs **roll-forward procedures** to update their audit findings from the time of the interim procedures through to year end. The nature and extent of these roll-forward procedures are matters of judgement and are responsive to the risk assessment. For example, when the entity's control environment has been assessed as effective, controls have been tested, and no significant changes in the control environment and controls have occurred, limited roll-forward procedures such as analytical procedures or limited testing of intervening transactions may be all that is necessary.

The auditor might also perform substantive procedures prior to year end because of a client reporting requirement. For example, the auditor may be requested to confirm receivables and observe the counting of inventory before year end so the client is able to close its books promptly.

In the absence of specific effective controls, it may be acceptable for the auditor to perform substantive procedures prior to year end when they are able to conclude overall that the client's control environment is effective and the likelihood of errors is not high, or when they can perform sufficient procedures both at an interim date and during the intervening period (often referred to as the "roll-forward period"). The nature of the roll-forward procedures performed is responsive to the risk associated with the absence of controls and the timing of substantive procedures.

roll-forward procedures procedures performed during the period between an interim date and year end (the roll-forward period) to provide sufficient and appropriate audit evidence to base conclusions on as at year end when substantive procedures are performed at an interim date

Cloud 9

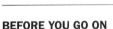

Suzie asks Ian to consider Cloud 9's warranty provision. Cloud 9 has a provision at September 30 of $91,456, which is slightly higher than the provision for the previous financial year of $85,597. What is the likelihood that the provision is understated? Are there any reasons to believe there are unidentified claims, and how would the auditors detect such claims?

Ian does not know of any change in manufacturing conditions that would affect the quality of Cloud 9's product and, by extension, the obligation under the warranty program. However, there was a new product introduced at the start of the previous year. "Because sales of the new 'Heavenly 456' walking shoe are now 20 percent of total sales," he notes, "we should consider any possible effects on the warranty provision. I recommend specific work be done to assess the claims from this product.

"However, if we remove this product from the analysis, the relationship between the warranty provision and sales is likely to be similar to past years. Because warranties apply to products, the amount of the warranty liability is determined by sales volume and product quality. Therefore, if conditions affecting product quality have not changed, and there is no change to the warranty program, analytical procedures are a useful way of testing the reasonableness of the provision.

"Finally," Ian concludes, "relying on analytical procedures to test the warranty provision is more justified if control testing suggests that Cloud 9 has effective controls over warranty claim identification and processing."

BEFORE YOU GO ON

8.2.1 Name the four different types of substantive procedures discussed.

8.2.2 Describe the relationship between the amount of substantive testing to be performed and the timing of the testing.

8.2.3 When is the timing of substantive procedures most flexible? When are substantive procedures performed in these circumstances?

8.3 SUBSTANTIVE AUDIT PROCEDURES

In this section we explore the types of substantive procedures, including tests of details and analytical procedures. We also consider using computer-assisted audit techniques in performing substantive testing.

 Provide examples of different substantive audit procedures.

8.3.1 Tests of details

Substantive procedures that are not analytical procedures are referred to as "tests of details"; they may include tests of details of transactions or tests of details of account balances. **Tests of details of transactions** are predominantly designed to verify a balance or a transaction back to supporting documentation (called "vouching" or "tracing").

Vouching is when a balance or transaction is taken from the underlying accounting records and verified by agreeing the details to supporting evidence outside the accounting records of the company. (Typically, the details are agreed to external third-party information such as a supplier invoice or delivery documentation.) Because vouching involves testing and verifying information already recorded in the accounting records, the primary purpose of the testing is to ensure that the balances or transactions are not overstated (for example, existence and occurrence assertions). **Tracing** is when a source document is traced back to the underlying accounting records. Because tracing involves testing and verifying information outside the accounting records that is not necessarily recorded (for instance, it does not appear on a source document such as an invoice), the primary purpose of the testing is to ensure that the balances are not understated (for example, completeness assertion).

Sometimes, tests of details of transactions are **dual purpose tests** in that the procedures performed provide evidence of a control's effectiveness (test of controls) and also indicate if an item is being recorded properly (substantive test). An example of a dual purpose test is when the

tests of details of transactions tests predominantly designed to verify a balance or a transaction back to supporting documentation; therefore, they usually include vouching and tracing

vouching taking a balance or transaction from the underlying accounting records and verifying it by agreeing the details to supporting evidence outside the accounting records of the company

tracing tracking a source document back to the underlying accounting records

dual purpose tests procedures that provide evidence for both tests of controls and substantive procedures

auditor tests the postings of the totals in the sales ledger to the general ledger and the sub-ledger. This is a test of control in that it provides evidence there are controls in place to ensure that totals are transferred correctly from the general ledger to the subsidiary ledger. It is also a substantive procedure that provides evidence for the completeness audit assertion because if the balances do not agree, it indicates something is missing.

tests of details of balances tests that support the correctness of an account ending balance

Tests of details of balances are tests that support the ending general ledger balance of an account. An example of this type of test is when the auditor sends out accounts receivable confirmations, as this provides evidence that the accounts receivable ending balance exists.

When agreeing a balance or transaction to supporting documentation, the auditor must consider the type of evidence that is available. As noted in CAS 500 *Audit Evidence*, evidence that is external to the client is ordinarily considered more relevant and reliable audit evidence than evidence generated internally by the client. For this reason, appropriate external evidence (or "third-party" evidence), when it is available, is preferred when performing these types of tests.

Auditors do not ordinarily audit an entire balance or class of transactions. Auditing requires that professional judgement be applied when determining how much testing to apply to a balance. For this reason, an auditor uses audit sampling (CAS 530 *Audit Sampling*). Audit sampling was defined and described in detail in chapter 6 and is a valid way of performing audit procedures. The auditor is not required (nor are they able) to perform audit procedures on 100 percent of the balances and disclosures within the financial statements. Instead, they select transactions, balances, and disclosures that are more likely to contain material errors. Further, the nature, timing, and extent of testing are based on the application of professional judgement in assessing the risks of material misstatement in the financial statements.

Another key factor impacting the nature, timing, and extent of testing is the auditor's ability (or inability) to rely on computer-generated data or reports. When the auditor is unable to rely on the IT general controls or application controls of a client, control risk is assessed as high; in this case, the sample size when conducting substantive testing is likely to be larger and will be subject to a higher level of precision or confidence in the test results. When the client has strong controls and these have been tested to provide a basis for reliance, control risk is assessed as low, the sample size when conducting substantive testing is likely to be smaller, and the auditor would ordinarily accept a lower level of precision or confidence in the test results.

The auditor often performs other tests of transactions or underlying data. Some common examples of these other tests are:

- tests of client-prepared schedules for mathematical accuracy
- tests using confirmations for such things as bank balances, accounts receivable, accounts payable, and various types of debt and share capital
- tests that inspect the physical existence of items such as inventory and capital assets
- tests to agree sub-ledger balances to general ledger balances for completeness
- tests to agree individual customer account balances to control account balances for completeness
- tests to confirm items are recorded in the correct period to ensure cut-off
- tests performed at an interim date and then roll-forward procedures performed on the intervening period between the interim date and year end
- tests of underlying data to be used as part of the analytical procedures (refer to section 8.3.2)
- tests of income statement accounts for account classification
- tests of individual transactions by vouching/agreeing to supporting documentation

A decision on the amount of testing to perform (the extent of testing) is a matter of professional judgement. Testing needs to be sufficient to allow the auditor to conclude that the underlying data are free from material misstatement (material error).

If the auditor identifies errors when performing these tests, they request the client to investigate the reason for the errors. The reason the client provides will help the auditor determine the impact these errors may have on their risk assessment and the resultant change to the auditor's planned audit approach. (This change is ordinarily to perform additional audit work.)

Cloud 9

During their conversation about Cloud 9's warranty provision, Suzie asks Ian how they would use other substantive procedures to obtain evidence about the completeness assertion for the liability balance. "For example," Suzie asks, "would vouching and tracing be useful and, if so, how would you use them?" Ian is still keen on using analytical procedures, but he considers the question carefully. "I think we would use vouching to get evidence about transactions or balances that are recorded as warranty claims by Cloud 9. However, it might be more useful to consider tracing, because this would allow us to start with the documents and get evidence about how and whether the transactions are recorded in the accounts. If we find a warranty claim has been incorrectly recorded as another type of expense, we would be concerned that the liability is understated, or not complete. Additionally, we would like to examine transactions around the balance sheet date and make sure they are recorded in the correct accounting period. This evidence relates to the cut-off assertion, and is part of considering completeness."

8.3.2 Analytical procedures

The fourth type of substantive procedures, **analytical procedures**, may be used:

- as primary (persuasive) tests of a balance
- as corroborative tests in combination with other procedures
- to provide at least some minimal level of support for the conclusion

As outlined in CAS 520 *Analytical Procedures*, properly designed and executed analytical procedures provide an efficient alternative to tests of details of account balances and, in some cases, may provide the most effective test of the appropriateness of account balances (for example, management's estimate of the allowance for doubtful accounts or accrual for warranty costs). In other cases, analytical procedures may provide the only method of testing. For example, if the client does not maintain an effective costing system, overheads in the closing inventory might be estimated by relating actual overheads for the year to actual direct labour (assuming reliable direct labour reporting and reliable overhead expense records). It is expected that overall analytical procedures at the financial statement level will be performed on every audit engagement, irrespective of the audit approach planned for a client.

Therefore, when planning the audit approach, the auditor should consider what analytical procedures are available. The extent to which analytical procedures can reduce the extent of, or eliminate, other substantive procedures will depend on the risk assessment and the level of assurance provided by the analytical procedures.

analytical procedures evaluations of financial information made by a study of plausible relationships among both financial and non-financial data. Analytical procedures also encompass the investigation of identified fluctuations and relationships that are inconsistent with other relevant information or deviate significantly from predicted amounts.

Types of analytical procedures

There are a number of techniques that can be used to perform analytical procedures as a substantive test. As discussed in chapter 4, the objective is to select the most appropriate technique (or combination of techniques) to provide the necessary levels of assurance and precision. The techniques or types of analytical procedures include:

- absolute data comparisons (comparing current year to previous year, budgets, and forecasts)
- ratio analysis (activity, liquidity, profitability, and leverage ratios)
- trend analysis (comparing certain data for several accounting periods)
- preparation of common-size financial statements
- break-even analysis
- pattern analysis and regression analysis (sophisticated techniques not often used on audits)

Testing the reliability of underlying data

The biggest risk when performing analytical procedures is that the results will lead the auditor to accept an account balance as materially correct when, in fact, it contains material misstatements. The key way to minimize this risk is to evaluate the relevance of the information used in the analytical procedure and to ensure that the financial and non-financial data used in the analytical procedure are reliable.

The following are examples of points the auditor should consider when evaluating the relevance of the information used in the analytical procedure:

- Analytical procedures may not be useful when they are used on a company with significantly diverse operations and geographical segments. In order to be useful, consolidated balances need to be broken down by geography, nature, etc. to facilitate a meaningful analysis.
- The analytical procedure is adversely affected if the industry data are unreliable or are not comparable to the client's data. Industry ratios that are no longer meaningful because of rapidly changing economic conditions may be misleading.
- For entities with operations in inflationary economies, the extent to which increases in, say, costs or prices have been affected by inflation should be considered before performing analytical procedures and relying on the results.
- The comparison of budget to actual results is meaningful only if the client's budget process is well controlled. In some cases it may be necessary to expand the understanding of the process beyond that obtained during the planning phase of the audit (as described earlier).

The auditor also needs to be satisfied, when using an analytical procedure, that the financial and non-financial data used are reliable, especially when the analytical procedure is used as a persuasive substantive procedure. When using analytical procedures as part of an overall financial statements analysis, it is not necessary to test the underlying data, because an overall financial statements analysis is performed to increase the understanding of the client's business, provide a basis for developing the scope of the audit, and identify areas requiring further investigation. However, when the analytical procedures are to be persuasive and the primary (and potentially only) substantive test of a balance, it is necessary to test the reliability of the data being used. For example, if the auditor uses an aging report to support the reasonableness of the allowance for doubtful accounts, they ordinarily first test the accuracy of the aging.

The extent to which the auditor needs to test the underlying data is driven by the extent to which they have been able to test and form a basis for reliance on the controls surrounding the data. Primarily, this means assessing the overall control environment at the company (is it effective?), the IT general controls (are they effective?), and the application controls (have they been tested and can they be relied on?). The more effective the controls over the data that the auditor intends to use in an analytical procedure, the more the analytical procedure can be relied on as a substantive procedure. Conversely, the less effective the client's controls over the data, the less reliable the analytical procedure is likely to be, although it still may be useful in identifying areas for further investigation.

Another factor to consider is that often client-produced non-financial data used in analytical procedures (such as the tonnage of product produced in a particular location) are not subject to the same type of controls as the client's financial data. As a result, the auditor may not be able to draw a conclusion about the reliability of the non-financial data without performing tests of that data. On the other hand, if such data are used as a key indicator of performance in running the business, the auditor may take comfort in the fact (in the absence of evidence to the contrary) that the client finds the data reliable for such purposes.

In summary, the auditor tests the reliability of underlying data when the analytical procedure is to provide persuasive assurance; they use judgement to determine the need for, and extent of, tests of underlying data when the analytical procedure provides corroborative assurance; and they need not test underlying data when the analytical procedure provides minimal assurance. (Refer to section 8.4 for a discussion of each of these levels of assurance or evidence.)

Substantive analytical procedures—summary

When the auditor performs analytical procedures, the steps they take can be summarized as follows:

1. Identify the computation, comparison, or relationship to be made or to be investigated.
2. Assess the reliability of any data to be used.
3. Estimate the probable balance in the account or the probable outcome of the computation.
4. Make whatever computations are needed using data in the client's records or data from reliable outside sources.

5. Compare the estimated amount with the computed or recorded amount and evaluate whether the difference, if any, is significant.

6. Determine appropriate procedures for investigating the reasons for the difference if it is significant.

7. Perform the procedures.

8. Draw conclusions.

Let us look at an example of how and when a substantive analytical procedure can be used.

Step 1: Identify the computation, comparison, or relationship to be made or to be investigated.

Ian Harper of W&S Partners is currently auditing the payroll expense of a cycling shop. The audit program indicates he should apply substantive analytic procedures to determine the reasonableness of the payroll expense. The audit program specifically requires Ian to determine the average salary per employee and then extrapolate this over the year to determine the reasonableness of the total payroll expense.

Step 2: Assess the reliability of any data to be used.

Before proceeding any further, Ian assesses the reliability of the payroll data to be used in this test. He reviews the file documentation regarding the payroll processes and any significant control weaknesses. He is glad to see that other members of the W&S audit team have tested the controls over adding and removing personnel on the payroll and that the testing indicates the controls are effective. Ian concludes the information he is using for this test is reliable, and proceeds to perform the calculations.

Steps 3 and 4: Estimate the probable outcome of the computation and make necessary computations using data in the client's records.

Ian documents the work performed as follows:

Randomly selecting two pay periods ("PP"), Ian calculates the average gross salary per employee. These averages are then used to assess the reasonableness of the total payroll expense.

		NUMBER OF STAFF	TOTAL PAYROLL	AVERAGE PAY PER EMPLOYEE
PP 2	Jan. 15, 2016	20	42,000.00	2,100.00
PP 17	Aug. 15, 2016	30	62,000.00	2,066.67
		25	52,000.00	2,083.33

Given that Ian has determined the average number of staff during the year is 25 and the average gross pay per employee is $2,083.33, he then calculates an expected total payroll of $2,708,333.33 (below).

Step 5: Compare the estimated amount with the computed or recorded amount and evaluate whether the difference, if any, is significant.

He then compares this with the actual payroll expense recorded in the general ledger, which is $2,700,500.88. This results in a difference of $7,832.45, which Ian concludes is below performance materiality.

Annualize:

Average Number of Employees	× Average Pay per Employee	× No. of Pay Periods
25	2,083.33	52

Total average annualized salary per W&S	2,708,333.33
Total salaries per general ledger	2,700,500.88
Difference	(7,832.45)

As this difference is not material, Ian will skip steps 6 and 7 (determine and perform procedures to investigate the reasons for the difference if significant) and will go directly to step 8.

Step 8: Draw conclusions.

Ian concludes that based on the work performed, the payroll expense appears reasonable as at December 31, 2016. If a significant difference was identified, further work would have to be done to audit this difference.

8.3.3 Performing substantive testing using computers

As clients have become more sophisticated and complex over time, the auditor's audit procedures and techniques have needed to respond to these complexities and have also become more sophisticated. One such development is the use of computers to assist the auditor with their testing. This is often referred to as "computer-assisted audit techniques" (CAATs).

There are two main categories of CAATs. The first type is software used to interrogate and examine client data files. Whenever computers are used to maintain or process accounting data, CAAT software can be used to perform procedures such as calculations (for example, the re-adding of a report) and logic tests (for example, sorting or comparing current year amounts with those from the previous year), and to select and print key items and representative samples for testing.

Using CAAT software makes the audit (1) more comprehensive, because each item in a file can be examined and subjected to a variety of tests; and (2) more efficient, because the computer can handle large volumes of data, thereby reducing time-consuming clerical tasks. Using software will also allow the auditor to concentrate on designing the test criteria and on evaluating and interpreting the results, rather than on performing the detailed audit procedures. Available software ranges from large, highly sophisticated products through to basic electronic spreadsheets and financial statement packages. Software does not necessarily have to be designed specifically for audit purposes.

The second type of CAAT is software that individual firms have either purchased or developed that is designed to plan, perform, and evaluate audit procedures, regardless of whether the client is automated or not.

The main considerations in deciding whether to use CAATs are the completeness of the records and the reliability of the data. As with any audit procedure, the nature and extent of the procedures performed with a CAAT will largely depend on the evaluation of the effectiveness of the client's control environment, IT general controls, and application controls.

Cloud 9

Ian and Suzie continue their discussion about using analytical procedures. Ian is starting to feel more confident and suggests that there are some factors to consider about the Cloud 9 audit that would affect the use of the various procedures. "We could use all of the usual techniques in the Cloud 9 audit, although we have to be careful in making comparisons across years for a couple of reasons. We have only just taken over the audit, so although prior-year data was audited, we are still building up our level of familiarity with the data and don't really understand all the conditions that applied to the previous years. Also, the changes at Cloud 9, in particular the opening of the retail store and the additional borrowing to finance the purchase of the delivery trucks that we discovered during our preliminary work, will impact the data, and we will have to think through these impacts before using the data in our tests."

BEFORE YOU GO ON

8.3.1 Name two common sampling techniques.

8.3.2 How do the control environment and results of control testing influence the timing of the substantive audit procedures?

8.3.3 Why is it important to test the reliability of the underlying data used in analytical procedures?

8.4 LEVELS OF EVIDENCE

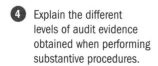

4 Explain the different levels of audit evidence obtained when performing substantive procedures.

Several different levels of evidence can be obtained when performing substantive procedures, depending on the type of substantive procedure performed. Evidence can be persuasive, corroborative, minimal, or general. Each of these levels is described below, illustrated by an example of substantive analytical procedures. Examples of the different types of evidence show that analytical procedures performed for planning purposes (as outlined in chapter 4) are quite different from those used for substantive testing purposes.

8.4.1 Persuasive

Analytical procedures can be the primary test of a balance (that is, the primary basis for the conclusion) if they provide persuasive evidence. This would be the case when the procedures generate an amount that the auditor believes is a reasonable estimate of what the balance should be, thus enabling them to conclude that the account balance is free from material errors. If an analytical review procedure is classified as persuasive, it means that no further substantive procedures need to be performed on the related account balance, even in moderate risk situations. Accordingly, the auditor must give careful consideration to the quality of evidence provided by the particular analytical procedure before they conclude that the analytical procedure is persuasive. Table 8.2 includes examples of analytical procedures that may provide persuasive evidence.

TABLE 8.2 **Examples of analytical procedures that provide persuasive evidence**

EVIDENCE	ANALYTICAL PROCEDURE
Material content of work in progress and finished goods	Relate raw materials put into production and quantities sold to normal yield factors
Overheads in closing inventory	Relate actual overheads for the period to actual direct labour, production volumes, or another appropriate measure
Finished goods pricing	Refer to selling prices less selling costs and "normal" gross margin
Charges for depreciation	Refer to asset balance, effect of additions and disposals, and average depreciation rate
Payroll expense	Refer to days accrued and average daily payroll or subsequent period's gross payroll
Commission expense	Refer to commission rates and related sales
Accruals for commissions or royalties	Refer to terms of agreements and payment dates
Accrued warranty costs for established products	Refer to applicable payroll and previous year's contribution rate
Scrap income	Relate standard cost scrap factor to weight of material processed and apply the result to published scrap prices
Interest expense and related accrual	Refer to the average debt outstanding, weighted average interest rate, and payment dates
Investment income	Relate average amounts invested to an average interest rate or yield
Total revenue for a private school	Relate school fee per each grade by number of students in the respective grade

8.4.2 Corroborative

An analytical procedure provides corroborative evidence if it (1) confirms audit findings from other procedures and (2) supports management representations or otherwise decreases the level of audit scepticism. For example, year-to-year detailed comparisons by product line of inventory levels and other key relationships such as turnover, gross margin, percentage composition of materials, labour, and overheads provide some evidence of the reasonableness of the inventory balance, but do not provide sufficient evidence by themselves to allow us to conclude that the account is free from material misstatement.

A corroborative analytical procedure includes comparisons of account balances to expectations developed and documented earlier in the audit. These comparisons generally provide corroborative evidence about an account balance and enable the auditor to limit the extent of other procedures in that area. In these cases, the auditor's understanding of the client's business should help confirm the reasonableness of a balance. For example, an auditor expects general administrative expense for the year to be approximately $10 million based on their review of the client's budget and the trend in the relationship of those expenses to sales. If actual general and administrative expenses fall within a reasonable range of the expected balance, a comparison of the recorded balance with the expected balance would provide corroborative evidence about the reasonableness of the balance. In addition, this supports the auditor's plan to reduce the extent of or eliminate other substantive testing of general administrative expenses. However, if an unexpected fluctuation is noted (for example, if general administrative expenses are less than, or exceed, the auditor's expectation by a significant amount), the auditor would expand other substantive audit procedures to obtain an explanation for the fluctuation and to provide additional evidence that would allow them to conclude that the balance was free from material misstatement. For example, they may review a listing of accounts comprising general and administrative expenses for individual account balance fluctuations, and investigate those with significant or unexpected fluctuations. Table 8.3 includes examples of analytical procedures that may provide corroborative evidence.

TABLE 8.3 **Examples of analytical procedures that provide corroborative evidence**

EVIDENCE	ANALYTICAL PROCEDURE
Trade receivables, sales, going concern	Review the volatility of the customer base (for example, new customers as a percentage of existing customers) and compare with expectations
Trade receivables	Compare the current period's receivables as a percentage of net sales with prior periods' percentages, and consider the reasonableness of the current period's percentage in relation to current economic conditions, credit policies, and collectibility
Prepayments	Compare the prepayment account balances with those of prior periods and investigate any unexpected changes (or the absence of expected changes)
Property, plant, and equipment	Review the reasonableness of the depreciation expense by referring to the previous year's balance and the effects of acquisitions and disposals
Sales, commissions expense	Compare sales commissions or bonuses with related sales
Payroll expense	Compare payroll tax expenses with the annual payroll times the statutory tax rates

8.4.3 Minimal

Analytical procedures that do not provide persuasive or corroborative evidence contribute minimal support for the conclusion. In deciding whether a particular analytical procedure or combination of procedures provides corroborative evidence or only minimal support for the conclusion, the auditor evaluates both the extent of their analytical procedures and the quality of the evidence they expect to obtain. For example, they may simply compare a current-year overall balance (for example, inventory) with the prior-year balance to help identify potential problems or trends, and not to reduce the extent of other substantive procedures. If they do not supplement that comparison with any other analytical procedures (for example, product-line comparisons of turnover, gross margin, or percentage composition of materials, labour, and overhead), they obtain only minimal support for the conclusion. Table 8.4 includes examples of analytical procedures that provide minimal evidence.

TABLE 8.4 **Examples of analytical procedures that provide minimal evidence**

EVIDENCE	ANALYTICAL PROCEDURE
Trade receivables	Understand the reason for any large credit transactions/balances on the ledger
Trade receivables	Compare the number and amounts of credit notes issued with those of prior periods

(continued)

EVIDENCE	ANALYTICAL PROCEDURE
Property, plant, and equipment	Review the property, plant, and equipment and related accounts in the general ledger for unusual items
Trade payables	Compare the number of days purchases in trade payables with those of prior years
Equity	Compare the equity account balance with that of prior years and investigate any unexpected changes (or the absence of expected changes)
Payroll expense, cost of sales	Compare the relationship between direct labour costs and number of employees with those of prior periods

TABLE 8.4 **Examples of analytical procedures that provide minimal evidence** (continued)

8.4.4 General

Analytical procedures might provide persuasive evidence in one circumstance but not in another. To illustrate, the risk assessment related to investments might indicate a low likelihood of material misstatement related to recording investment income. If a client has a relatively stable investment portfolio, a comparison of the average amount invested with an average market rate of interest or yield may provide the auditor with persuasive evidence to conclude that the amount of investment income recorded for the year is free from material misstatement. On the other hand, another client's portfolio might be more diversified, with rapid turnover. In that case, the auditor may need to expand the analytical review by segmenting the client's portfolio and applying the average yield test to the various segments. If that is not feasible, they may find it necessary to perform a test of details of investment income.

Cloud 9

Suzie agrees with Ian's assessment of the usefulness of analytical procedures and the possibility of using other techniques for testing the warranty provision at Cloud 9. "Using analytical procedures as the only substantive procedure is appropriate if we can find a close relationship between the underlying activity data and the account balance," she says. "The weaker or less consistent the relationship between the account balance and the other data, the more likely it is that we will have to perform other substantive procedures in order to obtain sufficient and appropriate evidence."

Ian suddenly has a thought. "I have just realized that when we are using prior-year data, we know it is audited, but the trial balance is unaudited. This means that we need to recognize that there could be errors in those figures. Also, as we do the audit and we find and correct misstatements, we should have another look at our analytical procedures—the change in the underlying data might change our conclusions."

"That's right," says Suzie. "We might also discover a change in conditions, such as operational changes, that could affect our interpretation of the data. We have to be aware of how everything is connected and review our conclusions and decisions as we go through the audit.

"If we can get persuasive evidence from using analytical procedures," Suzie concludes, "we can reduce the reliance on the other substantive tests."

BEFORE YOU GO ON

8.4.1 What is persuasive audit evidence? Give an example.

8.4.2 When does an analytical procedure provide corroborative audit evidence?

8.4.3 When does an analytical procedure provide minimal audit evidence?

8.5 EVALUATING AND DOCUMENTING SUBSTANTIVE ANALYTICAL PROCEDURES' RESULTS

5 Describe the documentation of the conclusions reached as a result of performing substantive procedures.

The auditor's understanding of the client's business and industry alerts the auditor to likely fluctuations in the financial data when they are planning the audit. These fluctuations may be caused by trends, seasonal patterns, cyclical patterns, dependent relationships, specific business decisions taken, or external decisions directly impacting the business. For example, if management and the union representing the workforce have negotiated a 3-percent pay raise over the next two years, the auditor would expect the analytical procedures performed on average wages and salaries per employee to confirm this increase. Also, if the federal government enacted a law to collect an additional 1 percent in payroll tax, the auditor would expect the analytical procedure to confirm this increase in payroll tax expense.

The lack of a significant change from one year to the next does not necessarily mean that the auditor can assume that the balance is reasonable. Whether and to what extent they investigate the lack of change in a balance depends on the auditor's understanding of the client's business, the relevant controls, and the industry in which the client operates.

PROFESSIONAL ENVIRONMENT

Interpreting the results of analytical procedures

Before they can complete an audit, auditors need to evaluate the causes of any unexpected fluctuations in a client's financial statements detected by the use of analytical procedures. Auditors have to consider possible causes of the fluctuation, search for additional information about these possible causes, evaluate the alternatives, and decide which possible cause of the fluctuation is the correct one. As part of this process, auditors can make inquiries of management to obtain their explanations of the fluctuation's cause. Management could provide the correct explanation because of their superior knowledge of the situation. However, it is possible that management will give the auditor an incorrect explanation, deliberately or not.

Wendy Green conducted an experiment to investigate whether receiving an incorrect management explanation affected auditors' performance in determining the correct explanation for financial data fluctuations. The subjects in the experiment were 61 auditors from one large accounting firm, with an average of almost four years' experience. The subjects were required to complete a computerized experimental task involving analytical procedures relating to an error in cost of sales. The subjects in a control group did not receive a management explanation while the other auditors received a management explanation either before or after considering their own alternative explanations.

Green found that only 15 of the 61 auditors selected the correct cause of the data fluctuation, with the remainder selecting either management's explanation or another cause considered a possibility by the auditor. Although 47 of the auditors actually considered the correct cause, 32 dismissed it in favour of another alternative. The data showed that 14 auditors never even considered the correct cause as a possibility during their investigations.

Overall, Green concluded that receiving an incorrect explanation from management affected the auditors' performance by influencing them to judge it as the correct cause. None of the auditors in the control group, who did not receive the management explanation, judged that explanation to be the correct one. Green suggests that audit firms could consider offering more guidance to auditors to prompt their consideration of more alternatives. In addition, auditor training could focus more on the evaluation of evidence, particularly in relation to management explanations. However, it is possible that, in practice, more experienced auditors, such as partners, would not be so easily distracted by management's explanations.

Source: Wendy Green, "Are Auditors' Analytical Procedures Judgements Affected by Receiving Management Explanations?" *Australian Accounting Review* 15, no. 3 (2005), pp. 67–74. © 2005 CPA Australia.

Cloud 9

Ian and Suzie have decided that analytical procedures will not be sufficient for all accounts. For each major transaction cycle and account balance, they will also conduct tests of details. For the vouching tests, the auditors will sample transactions and balances in the accounting records and go to the underlying documentation (or physical assets) to confirm the recorded details. For example, for sales recorded as being made prior to the financial year end, they will examine the invoices and shipping documents to gather evidence on the date, amount, and other details of the transactions. If they find a sales invoice with a January date has been included in the sales for the year ended December 31, they will have evidence of a misstatement in the occurrence and cut-off assertions for sales.

They will also trace the details in a sample of documents through to Cloud 9's accounting records. This means that they will start with the documents and then test how that transaction (or asset or liability) is recorded in the client's accounts. For example, if they find a sales invoice with a December date that is *not* included in the sales for the year, they will have evidence of a misstatement in the completeness and cut-off assertions for sales. Suzie advises Ian that the sample sizes and approach to sampling are determined by the results of the controls testing and the resulting expectations for errors.

Suzie also asks Ian to include tests of schedules, such as trade receivables and property, plant, and equipment (PPE), in the detailed audit plan. Where the risk is low, such as PPE, they will perform these tests at an interim date.

Finally, Suzie informs Ian that the IT audit manager, Mark Batten, is writing a CAAT program.

8.5.1 Evaluating errors identified in testing

As the auditor executes their substantive procedures, they may identify misstatements or errors. When they identify differences they did not expect, they reconsider their evaluation of the effectiveness of controls and overall risk assessments made in planning to determine whether additional procedures need to be performed. When a **misstatement** (either an error—including fraud—or a difference between the auditor's professional judgement and the client's as to whether a balance is correct) is identified, it is captured centrally in the audit working papers. This will allow the auditor to assess the overall impact of all misstatements at the financial statements level during the completion phase of the audit.

As mentioned, there are two key types of misstatements ordinarily identified during the audit procedures: errors (including fraud) and judgemental misstatements. Errors may arise from a one-off event or may systematically arise as the result of a breakdown in controls. The auditor may have identified these errors as part of controls testing or as part of their substantive testing. They may have been specifically identified as a result of the testing performed, or they may have been extrapolated from a statistically valid sample. Errors do not ordinarily have any element of judgement to them and are often considered by those charged with governance as just wrong; they may therefore be corrected by management irrespective of their size or potential effect on the financial statements.

Judgemental misstatements, however, often arise due to a difference between the auditor's and management's interpretation or application of an accounting policy or standard. These differences tend to be the focus of discussions held with those charged with governance and are often round numbers or a possible error "range" rather than an exact number.

The identification and resolution of misstatements is one of the auditor's most important responsibilities in an audit and is a critical step in the formulation of their opinion on the fairness of the client's financial statements. This is discussed in greater detail in chapter 13.

misstatement a difference between the amount, classification, presentation, or disclosure of a reported financial statement item and the amount, classification, presentation, or disclosure that is required for the item to be in accordance with the applicable financial reporting framework. Misstatements can arise from error or fraud.

8.5.2 Concluding and documenting the results of substantive procedures

As discussed earlier, the nature, timing, and extent of the audit procedures are influenced by a range of factors, including the type of balance or disclosure being tested, the level of detection risk remaining after the planning procedures and controls testing is complete, and the audit assertion addressed by the test. Once the auditor has determined the nature, timing, and extent of the substantive procedures, these are documented in the audit program. This program then serves as the instructions for the audit team members to complete the required testing.

When reaching their conclusion on the results of substantive procedures, the auditor considers the results of all of their testing related to the account balance or disclosure being audited, the responses to inquiries made during the performance of the procedures, and the resolution of any misstatements identified during the audit testing. With respect to all substantive procedures, the auditor documents the conclusion statement for each significant account (including the execution of the relevant audit program steps), the results, and any significant findings, including any misstatements. They also document that the financial statements reconcile to the underlying accounting records.

Overall conclusion statements are usually prepared for each audit program step completed, as well as for each significant account and significant assertion. These overall significant account conclusion statements are captured on what are often referred to as "lead sheets."

Cloud 9

Suzie asks Ian to set up the working papers for the tests they will perform. The priorities for Ian are to ensure that each test is described in sufficient detail in the audit program so the audit staff can perform the test correctly and identify any misstatements. The working papers also have to provide for comments to be included as the work is completed and by senior staff when they review the test results and form their conclusions on each account's assertions.

BEFORE YOU GO ON

8.5.1 What is a misstatement?

8.5.2 What is the difference between an error and a judgemental misstatement?

8.5.3 What is an audit program?

SUMMARY

❶ Define substantive audit procedures.

Substantive audit procedures are procedures designed to obtain direct evidence of the completeness, accuracy, and validity of data, and the reasonableness of the estimates and other information contained in the financial statements. Substantive procedures include inspection, observation, enquiry, confirmation, recalculation, re-performance, analyses of many types, and analytical reviews.

❷ Understand the link between the audit risk model and the nature, timing, and extent of substantive procedures.

The combination of inherent risk and control risk determines the level of detection risk the auditor is willing to accept that will still allow them to conclude that the financial statements are not materially misstated. Detection risk is reduced or increased in direct proportion to the amount of substantive testing performed. There are several factors that influence how much substantive testing must be performed, including the nature of the test, the level of assurance necessary, the type of evidence required, and the complexity of the client's data-capturing systems. The timing of substantive procedures is most flexible when controls have been tested and assessed as effective. In that case, the procedures can be performed up to six months before year end. When controls are not tested or are not assessed as effective, the timing of substantive procedures is at or near year end.

❸ Provide examples of different substantive audit procedures.

The different types of substantive procedures are tests of transactions/underlying data, and analytical procedures. Different analytical procedures include absolute data comparisons, ratio analysis, trend analysis, common-size financial statements, break-even analysis, and pattern and regression analysis. Substantive analytical procedures are different from those analytical procedures used during the planning phase of the audit.

❹ Explain the different levels of audit evidence obtained when performing substantive procedures.

The different levels of audit evidence obtained when performing substantive procedures include persuasive, corroborative, minimal, and general audit evidence.

❺ Describe the documentation of the conclusions reached as a result of performing substantive procedures.

Conclusion statements are documented for each significant account (including the execution of the relevant audit program steps), the results, and any significant findings, including any misstatements. The auditor also documents that the financial statements reconcile to the underlying accounting records. Overall conclusions are usually prepared for each audit program step completed, as well as for each significant account and significant assertion.

KEY TERMS

MULTIPLE-CHOICE QUESTIONS

8.1 Designing substantive procedures responds to:

  (a) the risk of material misstatement at the entity level.

  ✓(b) the risk of material misstatement at the assertion level.

  (c) the risk of all types of misstatements at the assertion level.

  (d) the risk of all types of misstatements at the entity level.

8.2 The following factor(s) influences how much and when substantive procedures are performed:

  (a) the nature of the test.

  (b) the level of assurance necessary.

  (c) the type of evidence required.

  ✓(d) All of the above.✓

8.3 Analytical procedures:

  (a) are used to test controls and are not substantive procedures.

  (b) are substantive procedures and cannot be used at any other stage of the audit.

  ✓(c) are used at planning and substantive testing stages of the audit.

  (d) can be used as substantive tests but cannot be used as primary tests of a balance.

8.4 We can conclude that analytical procedures provide persuasive evidence:

  (a) always.

  (b) never.

  (c) if they do not provide sufficient evidence by themselves to allow us to conclude that the account is free of material errors.

  ✓(d) if we are able to conclude that no further substantive tests need to be performed on the related account balance.

8.5 The following conditions make absolute data comparisons relatively less useful:

  (a) multiple years of financial data available.

  (b) single-location clients.

  ✓(c) changes in production methods.

  (d) budgets that are carefully prepared.

8.6 The reliability of data used for analytical procedures:

  ✓(a) affects the persuasiveness of the evidence from analytical procedures.

  (b) is more useful on a consolidated basis than an individual business segment basis.

  (c) is unaffected by inflation.

  (d) is never affected by the strength of controls over the client's budgetary processes.

8.7 Vouching is:

  (a) not a useful audit procedure.

  ✓(b) agreeing a balance or transaction to supporting documentation.

  (c) the main audit procedure used to gather evidence on the completeness assertion.

  (d) not designed to be used as a substantive audit procedure.

8.8 The primary advantage of selecting the largest transactions within a balance to test is:

  (a) it is an example of random sampling.

  (b) it is more interesting for the auditor because they see the most important transactions in detail.

  ✓(c) that the auditor is able to draw a conclusion about the entire balance based on the conclusions they reached by testing the largest transactions.

  (d) all of the above.

8.9 Roll-forward procedures:

  ✓(a) need to be responsive to the control risk assessment.

  (b) are procedures done during the month after year end.

  (c) have no effect on audit efficiency.

  (d) none of the above.

8.10 Misstatements:

  (a) are documented in the audit working papers.

  (b) can be categorized as errors or judgemental misstatements.

  (c) must be considered for their effect on the financial statements both individually and in aggregate.

  ✓(d) all of the above.

REVIEW QUESTIONS

8.1 Explain how the nature of a substantive test could affect decisions about when and how much substantive testing is performed. How do these decisions relate to the overall risk assessment for the item being tested?

8.2 What are substantive procedures designed to obtain evidence about? What are the main types of substantive procedures?

8.3 What are analytical procedures? Describe how they can be used as substantive tests in an audit.

8.4 What conditions must be satisfied before we can regard evidence from analytical procedures as persuasive rather than corroborative or minimal? Why are these conditions important?

8.5 Why is it important to consider the quality of the data used in analytical procedures? How important to this question are client controls over financial data?

8.6 Vouching transactions and balances back to supporting documentation would ordinarily provide evidence about which assertions? Which assertions would vouching be least likely to provide evidence about?

8.7 Explain the differences between key items testing and representative sampling using audit risk tables. How would software to select each type of sample be used?

8.8 Explain the two main types of CAATs. What are the advantages of using software to interrogate and examine client data files? Does using CAATs remove the need to test client control systems? Why or why not?

8.9 Which accounts and/or clients are more suitable for interim substantive testing?

8.10 Provide an example of (1) an error and (2) a judgemental misstatement that could affect the balance of property, plant, and equipment.

PROFESSIONAL APPLICATION QUESTIONS

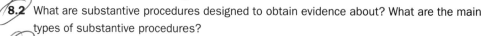

Basic ★   Moderate ★★   Challenging ★★★

8.1 Designing substantive procedures ★

Carla DaCosta been asked to join the team responsible for designing the audit program for a new client, Gaskin Industries Ltd., a manufacturing and wholesaling firm. Gaskin recently went public and is now listed on the Toronto Stock Exchange. Carla has worked for the audit firm for a year and received a very high performance rating from her supervisors on the previous year's audit of Bryson Ltd., a firm that provides marketing and other consulting services. Gaskin and Bryson have total revenue of approximately the same amount, so Carla feels confident that she can apply her knowledge to the new audit. She takes a copy of the audit program for Bryson to the first meeting, intending to suggest they use it as the basis for the audit program for Gaskin. Carla thinks that the Gaskin audit program could use the same substantive procedures they used on the Bryson audit.

Required

List some of the problems with Carla's idea of using Bryson's audit program as a basis for designing substantive procedures for Gaskin.

8.2 Sales cut-off ★

Boris Shonkoff suggests the following audit procedure should be included in the audit program to gather evidence on the cut-off assertion for the revenue account:

Select a sample of sales from the sales journal and agree the dates on the invoices to the dates on the delivery documents signed by the customer.

Required

Explain how the procedure addresses the assertion. What does it mean if (a) the dates agree, or (b) the dates do not agree?

Source: Adapted from the Institute of Chartered Accountants Australia's CA Program's *Audit and Assurance Exam*, July 2010. Provided courtesy of Chartered Accountants Australia and New Zealand.

8.3 Sales journal and invoices ★

Boris Shonkoff has another suggestion for the audit program for the revenue account. This time he suggests:

Select a sample of sales from the sales journal and agree the details in the journal to the sales invoices, delivery slips, and customer orders.

occurrence

Required

Explain which assertion for the revenue account would be addressed by this test.

Source: Adapted from the Institute of Chartered Accountants Australia's CA Program's *Audit and Assurance Exam*, July 2010. Provided courtesy of Chartered Accountants Australia and New Zealand.

8.4 Sales invoices and journal ★

Seb Lee and Boris Shonkoff are discussing the audit program for the revenue account. Seb and Boris disagree about whether they should use procedure A or B below to test the occurrence assertion for the revenue account:

A. *Select a sample of sales from the sales journal and agree the details in the journal to the sales invoices, delivery slips, and customer orders.*

B. *Select a sample of sales invoices, delivery slips, and customer orders and agree the details to the details recorded in the sales journal.*

completeness

Required

Which test provides evidence about the occurrence assertion? Why? Which assertion does the other test provide evidence about?

Source: Adapted from the Institute of Chartered Accountants Australia's CA Program's *Audit and Assurance Exam*, July 2010. Provided courtesy of Chartered Accountants Australia and New Zealand.

8.5 Payroll testing ★

Anna Mourani has the task of designing the audit program for the payroll area. There have been no recent changes to the payroll system, or its interface with the general ledger. Among other tests, Anna is considering using the following analytical procedures to gather evidence:
1. Compare payroll tax expenses with the annual payroll times the statutory tax rates.
2. Compare the relationship between direct labour costs and number of employees with prior periods.

Required

Discuss the type of evidence that would be obtained from each of the procedures.

8.6 Data for analytical procedures ★ ★

North West Paper Ltd. provides cardboard, paper, and plastic packaging materials to a large number of manufacturers and distributors in all provinces. The cardboard and paper division is a well-established business, but North West has been providing plastic products only since it took over Plastic Products Ltd. 18 months ago. The takeover doubled North West's revenue and caused changes in its management structure, adding another two divisional managers. These new divisional managers are in charge of plastic product sales to different areas of the country—Plastic (Eastern) and Plastic (Western)—and they join the Paper (Eastern) and Paper (Western) division managers in reporting directly to the CEO.

All internal operating reports are now structured along the four divisional reporting lines, although external financial statements continue to be produced for the whole business. All purchasing and billing systems are fully integrated, although it is possible to extract data along divisional lines and by province (as before). North West purchases bulk supplies of raw plastic and paper and makes boxes, rolls, and sheets of these materials to fill customer orders. Production processes in the paper divisions have not changed, and North West has made minimal changes to the production processes used by Plastic Products Ltd.

Required

List and discuss the factors that would increase or decrease the reliability of data used in analytical procedures at North West.

8.7 Persuasiveness of evidence from analytical procedures ★ ★

Mathieu Lapointe has the task of reviewing the evidence from analytical procedures conducted by the audit juniors on the audit of Soleil Services Ltd. The audit juniors have reported the results of these analytical procedures:

1. Comparison of depreciation expense with the closing balance of each depreciable asset class in property, plant, and equipment.
2. Recalculation of sales commission expenses using the standard sales commission rate and total sales.
3. Comparison of payroll expense with previous year payroll.

Required

(a) What questions would Mathieu ask about each analytical procedure?
(b) If all questions could be answered satisfactorily, explain whether the evidence from each analytical procedure would be persuasive, corroborative, minimal, or general. What are the implications of this judgement for further substantive testing?

8.8 Tests of details ★ ★

Marty Novakowski has to audit the sales transactions of Okawa Ltd., which supplies tools to the mining industry. Okawa Ltd. carries a large number of different makes and models of standard mining tools. It also designs and manufactures tools for special purposes and for miners operating in difficult conditions. The custom-designed tools are made only after a contract has been signed and a deposit received, while standard tools are supplied to regular customers on receipt of a telephone order. Okawa Ltd.'s sales transactions vary from a few dollars to millions of dollars depending on the number of items sold, whether the individual items are large or small tools, and whether the tools are standard items or custom designed.

   Marty is instructed to gather evidence about the sales transactions using sampling and vouching. This is explained in detail in the audit program.

Required

(a) What would you expect to see in the audit program given to Marty about (1) the sample selection and (2) the vouching procedures? Explain.
(b) How could Marty use CAATs to help gather the evidence?

8.9 Timing of substantive tests ★ ★ ★

Connie Cyr is the recently appointed engagement partner of the audit of Camel Ltd. She has just taken over the audit from Kar-Ming Leo, who rotated off the audit after a seven-year period as the engagement partner. Kar-Ming had a small portfolio of clients and was able to complete most substantive testing for Camel at year end. Connie is unable to do this because she is facing difficulties with two of her other large clients. These clients have just been advised that their financing arrangements with U.S.-based banks may not be renewed, raising doubts about their ability to continue as going concerns. The U.S. banks will make their financing decisions very close to the clients' year ends, forcing Connie to spend considerable time in this period with these clients.

   The financing problems of Connie's existing clients have created demands on her audit team that she must resolve. The audit firm cannot provide her with the additional staff she has requested for the year-end period because the clients of several other partners are also facing financing difficulties due to the credit crisis in the United States.

The audit firm's ethical rules do not allow Kar-Ming to remain as the auditor of Camel, and it is too late to find new partners for any of her other clients, so Connie must find a way to continue with the audit and still meet all professional and legal standards. So far, the audit team has conducted the preliminary risk assessment for Camel, and the results of early control testing confirm that Camel has excellent controls.

Connie calls a meeting with her senior audit team members to discuss the issue.

Required

Explain how Connie could vary the timing of the substantive testing at Camel to help her meet her audit obligations. Specifically:

(a) Give examples of substantive procedures that could be performed prior to year end.
(b) Explain how Connie will use roll-forward procedures to complete the audit.
(c) Explain any other considerations that would affect the timing of substantive procedures for Camel.

Questions 8.10 and 8.11 are based on the following case.

Fellowes and Associates Chartered Accountants is a successful mid-tier accounting firm with a large range of clients across Canada. During 2016, Fellowes and Associates gained a new client, Health Care Holdings Group (HCHG), which owns 100 percent of the following entities:

· Shady Oaks Centre, a private treatment centre
· Gardens Nursing Home Ltd., a private nursing home
· Total Laser Care Ltd. (TLCL), a private clinic that specializes in the laser treatment of skin defects
  Year end for all HCHG entities is June 30.

You are a senior auditor working on the Shady Oaks Centre engagement for 2016 and are currently in the planning stage of the audit. In discussions with management, you discover that Shady Oaks has recently acquired two new full-body scanning machines. These machines use the latest technology and cost the company more than $10 million each. Although they are more than 50 percent more likely to detect abnormalities, new academic studies suggest there may be potential long-term side effects for patients scanned by these machines. However, because the machines are new, the evidence about long-term effects will not be known for many more years. Despite this, there has been some bad press for Shady Oaks highlighting the potential risks to patients.

Shady Oaks charges a premium price for patients using the scanning machines, and there is extremely high demand. To manage the demand, Shady Oaks requires that all patients pay for their scans in full at the time of booking, and the payments are immediately recognized as revenue by the centre. Shady Oaks has taken bookings for four months in advance—although it is only April 2016, the centre has bookings for July and August 2016.

The Canadian Medical Association is currently reviewing the use of the scanning machines and is considering banning their use within Canada until the issue is resolved. A decision is expected on August 1, 2016, and managers tell you that they believe there is an 80 percent chance the scanners will be approved.

Source: Adapted from the Institute of Chartered Accountants Australia's CA Program's Audit and Assurance Exam, December 2008 and March 2009. Provided courtesy of Chartered Accountants Australia and New Zealand.

8.10 Substantive testing for specific assertions at risk ★ ★ ★

Required

(a) Identify two key account balances likely to be affected by the above information.
(b) For each account balance identified in part (a), identify and explain the key assertions most at risk.
(c) For each assertion identified in part (b), identify specific substantive tests of detail that would be responsive to the identified risk.

8.11 Using analytical procedures ★ ★

Your assurance services manager has requested you use substantive analytical procedures to calculate Shady Oaks' estimated revenue for patients staying in the centre, excluding medical procedures and ancillary costs such as medication.

Required

Based on the background provided, describe all the key information required to estimate Shady Oaks' revenue for patients staying in the centre.

8.12 Planning substantive tests ★ ★ ★

Inventory of various medical supplies and drugs is a material account on the Shady Oaks Centre audit engagement. You are planning to adopt a combined audit approach for existence of inventory and rely heavily on preventive control procedures (for example, access to the dispensary and the store room being limited to a few authorized staff) to ensure the physical security of inventory.

You have just completed your tests of controls in relation to physical security procedures. Your projected error rate, based on the results of your already large sample size, is higher than the tolerable error. You are satisfied that the sample is representative and the errors occurred throughout the period audited.

Required

(a) Briefly outline the impact of the projected error rate on your planned substantive audit procedures.

(b) Assume that all of the deviations from the internal control procedures tested (that is, all the errors in the sample) relate to a three-week period when a senior staff member was on annual vacation. Discuss how this would affect your planned substantive tests of detail.

8.13 Persuasiveness of evidence ★ ★

Required

Review your answers to the previous questions. Comment on the persuasiveness of evidence from each test. Explain any factors that would affect your assessment.

8.14 Analytical procedures ★ ★

Analysis is a substantive audit procedure that auditors use when they are performing financial statement audits.

Required

(a) Distinguish between analysis and analytical procedures.

(b) Identify the three stages in the audit process at which analysis can be performed.

(c) For each stage identified in part (b), state the auditor's objective in using analysis.

(d) Briefly describe three ways in which auditors can ensure that the data they use in their analytical procedures are reliable.

Source: © CGA-Canada, now CPA Canada. Reproduced with permission.

8.15 Evaluating substantive testing results ★ ★

The following items are documented in the audit working papers:

1. Sales transaction included in the year ended December 31, 2016, but evidence from the cut-off procedure suggests that the sale should be dated January 2, 2017 ($1,250,000).

2. Warranty expenses in the trial balance for the year to December 31, 2016, total $150,000; the provision for warranty claims as at December 31, 2015, was $100,000. Evaluation of correspondence suggests that an additional $200,000 in warranty claims could result from ongoing disputes with customers. No provision for these claims has been made. Management has made a warranty provision for 2016 of $120,000.

3. Severance expenses related to reorganization of head office administration were incorrectly charged to rental expenses ($578,920).

4. Management has not recorded an impairment for assets. A drought-induced recession has hurt property values in regional cities where seven branch offices are located. (Head office and two branch offices are located in the capital city.) Total land and buildings in the trial balance is $5.5 million.

Required

(a) Evaluate each item above and explain whether it is an error or a judgemental misstatement. What action do you recommend for each?

(b) Which accounts would be affected, and how, if an adjustment is made for each item?

CASE STUDY—CLOUD 9

Answer the following questions based on the information presented for Cloud 9 in Appendix B and in the current and earlier chapters. You should also consider your answers to the case study questions in earlier chapters.

Required

Based on your conclusions from the case study questions in previous chapters, complete the following worksheet to determine the overall risk assessment (ORA) and the acceptable detection risk (DR).

ACCOUNT ASSERTION	INHERENT RISK	CONTROL RISK	OVERALL RISK ASSESSMENT	DETECTION RISK
Sales—occurrence				
Sales—completeness				
Trade receivables—existence				
Trade receivables—completeness				
Cash—existence				

RESEARCH QUESTION 8.1

Economic conditions and financial markets have been significantly affected by the global financial crisis that swept around the world in 2008. Love and Lawson identified a series of specific issues flowing from the crisis that must be considered by financial statement auditors and that may affect the procedures used in conducting an audit.

Required

Explain the impact of the global financial crisis on decisions about the nature, timing, and extent of substantive testing. Give some specific examples of impact on analytical procedures. Explain how auditors would adjust their audit programs to ensure that overall audit risk remains acceptable.

Source: V.J. Love and C. Lawson, "Auditing in Turbulent Economic Times," *The CPA Journal* (May 2009), pp. 30–35.

SOLUTIONS TO MULTIPLE-CHOICE QUESTIONS

1. b, 2. d, 3. c, 4. d, 5. c, 6. a, 7. b, 8. c, 9. a, 10. d.

CHAPTER 9

Auditing sales and receivables

LEARNING OBJECTIVES

After studying this chapter, you should be able to:

1 identify the audit objectives applicable to sales and receivables

2 describe the functions and control procedures normally found in information systems for processing sales, cash receipts, and sales adjustment transactions

3 outline audit strategy considerations including the risk of material misstatement and tests of controls for sales, cash receipts, and sales adjustments transactions

4 indicate the factors relevant to determining an acceptable level of detection risk for the audit of sales and receivables

5 design a substantive audit program for sales and receivables.

AUDITING AND ASSURANCE STANDARDS

CANADIAN	INTERNATIONAL
Framework for Assurance Engagements	*International Framework for Assurance Engagements*
CAS 315 *Identifying and Assessing the Risks of Material Misstatement through Understanding the Entity and Its Environment*	ISA 315 *Identifying and Assessing the Risks of Material Misstatement through Understanding the Entity and Its Environment*
CAS 500 *Audit Evidence*	ISA 500 *Audit Evidence*
CAS 505 *External Confirmations*	ISA 505 *External Confirmations*
CAS 530 *Audit Sampling*	ISA 530 *Audit Sampling*
CAS 540 *Auditing Accounting Estimates, Including Fair Value Accounting Estimates, and Related Disclosures*	ISA 540 *Audit of Accounting Estimates, Including Fair Value Accounting Estimates, and Related Disclosures*

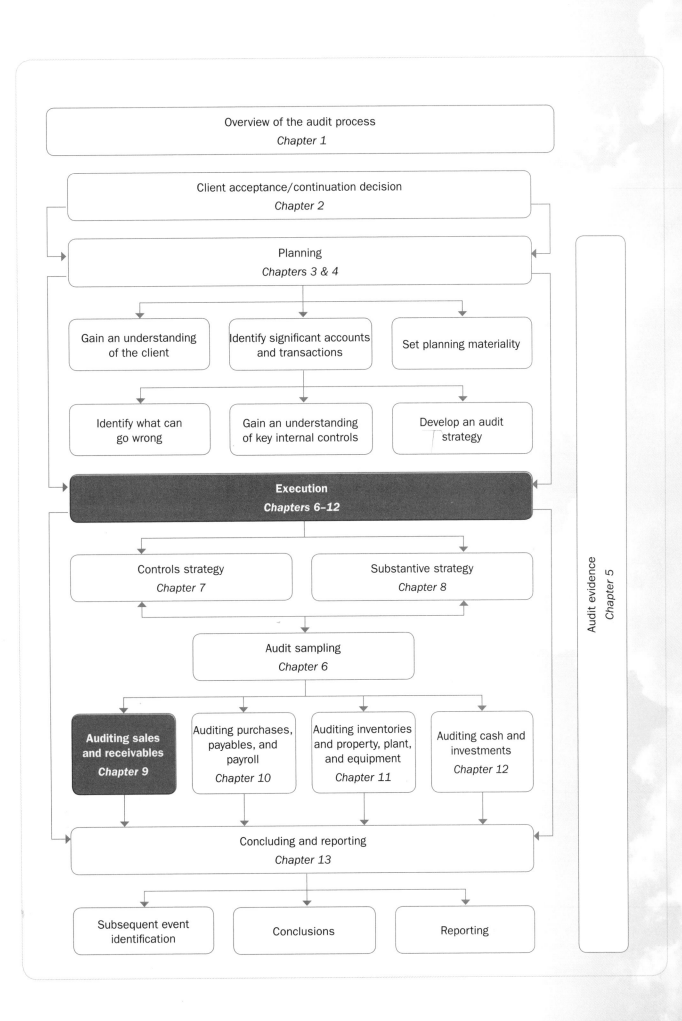

Overview of the audit process
Chapter 1

Client acceptance/continuation decision
Chapter 2

Planning
Chapters 3 & 4

Gain an understanding
of the client

Identify significant accounts
and transactions

Set planning materiality

Identify what can
go wrong

Gain an understanding
of key internal controls

Develop an audit
strategy

Execution
Chapters 6–12

Controls strategy
Chapter 7

Substantive strategy
Chapter 8

Audit sampling
Chapter 6

**Auditing sales
and receivables**
Chapter 9

Auditing purchases,
payables, and
payroll
Chapter 10

Auditing inventories
and property, plant,
and equipment
Chapter 11

Auditing cash and
investments
Chapter 12

Concluding and reporting
Chapter 13

Subsequent event
identification

Conclusions

Reporting

Audit evidence
Chapter 5

Cloud 9

Now that Josh Thomas has concluded on the entity-level controls at Cloud 9, it is time for the audit team to focus on the transaction cycles. Sharon Gallagher, the audit manager, has asked Josh and his team to start documenting an understanding of the controls at the transaction level for the accounts receivable and sales cycle. Sharon explains that this documentation should include details on the procedures and controls in place that Cloud 9 incorporates when processing sales, receivables, cash receipts, and sales allowances. Josh wonders why this level of detail is necessary. Sharon explains the documentation will allow the audit team to identify the points within the accounting process where errors or fraud can occur. These points are more likely where information is changed, there is significant human involvement, or access to systems is not restricted. In essence, it is where something in the process can go wrong. The audit team will then concentrate on those points that have a financial statement impact. This documentation will support their assessment of the system's strengths and weaknesses, which will influence the remainder of the planning process.

AUDIT PROCESS IN FOCUS

The purpose of this chapter is to examine the audit of the sales cycle, which includes accounts receivable, sales, cash receipts, and sales adjustment accounts. This involves the identification of the audit objectives that apply to the relevant classes of transactions and the account balances for each of the financial statement assertions.

We begin this chapter by describing (1) the audit objectives for sales and receivables; (2) procedures involved in sales, cash receipts, and sales adjustment transactions; and (3) the accounting system and control procedures commonly associated with these accounts. We consider factors relevant to developing the audit plan, including assessing the inherent and control risks, determining the appropriate audit strategy, and, where appropriate, including the use of tests of controls.

Lastly, we discuss the design of substantive procedures, including analytical procedures and tests of details of transactions and balances for these accounts.

9.1 AUDIT OBJECTIVES

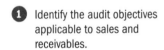

Identify the audit objectives applicable to sales and receivables.

In the auditing of sales and receivables, the key issues are to ensure the following:

- The receivables do actually exist and are collectible, and adequate allowances have been made for balances where collectibility is doubtful. (These are related to the financial statement assertions of existence and valuation and allocation.)
- The sales are genuine and are neither understated nor overstated. (These are related to the financial statement assertions of completeness and occurrence, respectively, and also accuracy and cut-off.)

It is essential to understand the systems and controls in place for processing transactions that result in sales and, when sales are made on credit, the resulting receivables. Sales can be made either for cash, such as when customers pay for goods with cash in a department store, or on credit, such as when a large footwear wholesaler buys running shoes from a footwear manufacturer. In the latter case, a sale (revenue) has occurred and a receivable (asset) has to be collected.

When auditing sales and receivables, the auditor's objective is to obtain sufficient appropriate evidence about each significant assertion for the applicable classes of transactions and balances. The main audit objectives for these transaction classes and account balances are shown in table 9.1. These objectives are those that would apply to most merchandising entities selling on credit; they are not intended to apply to all entities.

To achieve each of these specific audit objectives, the auditor may use a combination of tests of controls and substantive procedures as determined by the audit strategy adopted. Each audit objective is numbered (OE1, OE2, C1, AV42, and so on) in table 9.1. Using this numbering system, we can reference specific controls and audit procedures described in this chapter to the applicable audit objective. Some of the assertions for classes of transactions are combined with assertions for account balances in the numbering system: occurrence and existence (**OE**), completeness for transactions and completeness for balances (**C**), accuracy and valuation and allocation (**AV**), and classification with presentation and disclosure assertions (**PD**). These combinations reflect the fact that audit evidence obtained to support an assertion for transactions will also give some comfort for a balance assertion. For example, an audit test that gives some comfort to the auditor that a sales transaction has occurred will also give some comfort that a valid receivable exists; hence, occurrence and existence are combined.

Table 9.1 summarizes assertions for both classes of transactions and account balance audit objectives.

TABLE 9.1 **Selected specific audit objectives for sales and receivables**

CLASSES OF TRANSACTION OBJECTIVES	
Occurrence (**OE**)	Sales recorded represent goods that were shipped to customers during the period (**OE1**).
	Cash receipts represent cash received from customers during the period (**OE2**).
	Sales adjustment transactions represent authorized discounts, returns and allowances, and bad debts applicable to the period (**OE3**).
Completeness (**C**)	All goods shipped to customers during the period are recorded (**C1**).
	All cash received from customers during the period is recorded as cash receipts (**C2**).
	All discounts, returns and allowances, and bad debts arising during the period are recorded as sales adjustments (**C3**).
Accuracy (**AV**)	All sales, cash receipts, and sales adjustment transactions are properly (accurately) recorded (**AV1**).
Cut-off (**CO**)	Particularly relevant to transactions around the year end; all sales, cash receipts, and sales adjustment transactions arising before the period end are recorded in the current period and those arising after the period end are included in the next accounting period (**CO1**).
Classification (**PD**)	All sales (**PD1**), cash receipts (**PD2**), and sales adjustment transactions are recorded in the correct accounts (**PD3**).
ACCOUNT BALANCE OBJECTIVES	
Existence (**OE**)	Accounts receivable represent amounts owed by customers at the end of the reporting period (**OE4**).
Rights and obligations (**RO**)	Accounts receivable at the end of the reporting with respect to sales period represent legal claims of the entity on customers for payment (**RO1**).
Completeness (**C**)	All amounts owed by customers at the end of the reporting period are included in accounts receivable (**C4**).
Valuation and allocation (**AV**)	Accounts receivable represent gross claims on customers at the end of the reporting period and agree with the sum of the accounts receivable subsidiary ledger (**AV2**).
	The allowance for doubtful accounts represents a reasonable estimate of the difference between gross accounts receivable and their net realizable value (**AV3**).
PRESENTATION AND DISCLOSURE OBJECTIVES (PD)	
Occurrence and rights and obligations	Disclosed revenue events have occurred and pertain to the entity (**PD4**).
Completeness	All revenue cycle disclosures that should have been included in the financial statements have been included (**PD5**).
Classification and understandability	Sales cycle information is appropriately presented and information disclosed is clearly expressed (**PD6**).
Accuracy and valuation	Sales cycle information is disclosed accurately and at appropriate amounts (**PD7**).

Cloud 9

Josh has prepared a diagram documenting his understanding of Cloud 9's sales and receivables cycle. This diagram documents his understanding of how a sales order is initiated through to when the cash is deposited in the bank (see figure 9.1). He has included initiating a sales order from the customer through to shipping the goods; invoicing the customer through to posting the transaction in the general ledger; and receiving the payment and recording the payment from the customer. Based on this diagram, Josh is preparing to write a narrative of the process.

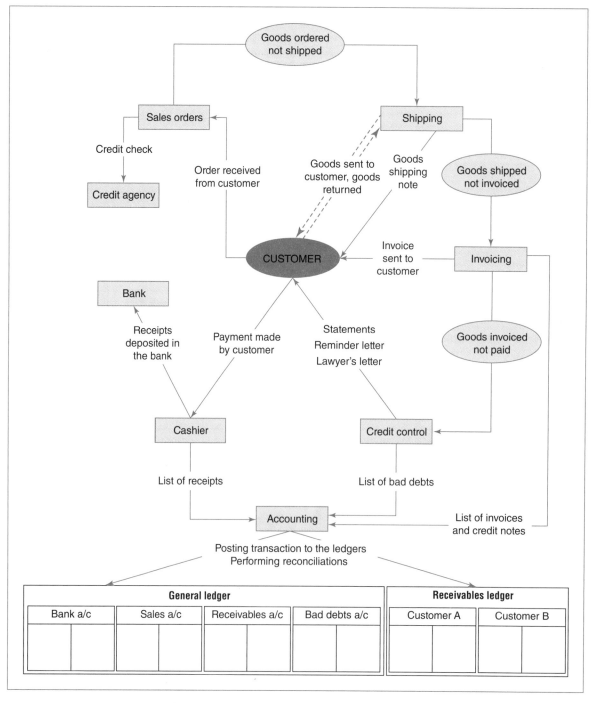

FIGURE 9.1 **Credit sales cycle**

9.2 THE PROCESS FOR CREDIT SALES TRANSACTIONS

The sale process starts when a customer places an order for goods with the company. Sales orders may be taken over the counter, via the telephone, by mail order, through sales representatives, by facsimile, or via the Internet. The goods may be picked up by the customer or shipped by the seller. The accounting for sales transactions may be done manually or with a computer, in real-time or batch processing mode. We begin by identifying the separate functions involved in making sales transactions, the documents and records used in processing the transactions, and the control procedures interwoven into each to reduce the risk of misstatements in the financial statements. As we explained in chapter 7, control procedures include information processing controls, physical controls, the segregation of duties, authorization controls, account reconciliations, and performance reviews. Information processing controls specific to credit sales transactions include authorization and independent checks.

2 Describe the functions and control procedures normally found in information systems for processing sales, cash receipts, and sales adjustment transactions.

9.2.1 Credit sales transactions

The processing of credit sales transactions involves the following:

- accepting customer orders
- approving credit
- filling and shipping sales orders
- invoicing customers
- recording the sales

These functions and the applicable control procedures are explained in the following sections.

Accepting customer orders

The first step in the sales cycle is the acceptance of a sales order. The acceptance of sales orders is normally performed by the sales department. When sales orders are received, they need to be checked for their authenticity, the acceptability of terms and conditions, and the availability of inventory. Orders submitted in writing or electronically on a **customer order** provide ready evidence of legitimacy in that they indicate goods were ordered by an actual customer, which supports the occurrence (**OE1**) assertion.

customer order a document indicating the goods requested by a customer that provides evidence of authenticity

Telephone or e-mail orders from businesses are sometimes authenticated by requiring a purchase order number from the customer. Specification of a purchase order number provides reasonable assurance that the order has been issued in accordance with the customer's purchasing procedures. Terms and conditions relate to matters such as prices, delivery dates, and modifications. Sales clerks accept only orders that meet the entity's normal terms. In some businesses, it is necessary to check the availability of the goods in inventory before accepting an order. Any orders not meeting the above checks need to be referred to a manager with the authority to accept orders that depart from normal entity policy.

Once accepted, the order is recorded on a multi-copy **sales order**, which is a form showing the description of the goods, the quantity ordered, and other relevant data. It is signed by the clerk accepting the order and serves as the basis for internal processing of the customer order. Sales orders are commonly pre-numbered in case they are misplaced and business is lost as a result. This supports the completeness (**C1**) assertion for sales. It also represents the start of the transaction trail of documentary evidence and confirms the existence of a valid order. It thus relates to the audit objective occurrence (**OE1**) in table 9.1.

sales order a form showing the description of the goods, the quantity ordered, and other relevant data, which serves as the basis for the internal processing of the customer order

Approving credit

Before a customer order is forwarded to the warehouse, a credit check should be performed. This should be required for both new customers and existing customers. New customers should complete a credit application and a credit report should be obtained from a credit rating agency. If the credit rating is acceptable, the credit manager determines an appropriate credit limit and creates a new record in the **accounts receivable master file** (see Appendix A, figure 9A). For existing customers, a credit department employee compares the amount of the order with the customer's authorized credit limit and the current balance owing by the customer. This comparison may also be done electronically through the entity's computerized information system. Credit approval may be refused if the order would take the balance over the customer's credit limit or if the account is overdue. To indicate approval (or non-approval) of credit, an authorized credit department employee signs or initials the sales order form and returns it to the sales order department, or does so electronically, following prescribed procedures.

For an auditor, controls over credit approval reduce the risk of a sales transaction being initially recorded in an amount in excess of the amount of cash expected to be realized, and thus contributes to the audit objective of accuracy (**AV1**). The expectations of realizing some of these amounts will change over time, resulting in the need for an allowance for doubtful accounts, as generally the longer an amount remains unpaid, the less likely it will be collected. Controls over credit approval enable management to make a more reliable estimate of the size of the allowance needed. Strong controls over extending credit reduce the likelihood of sales being made on credit to customers unable to pay in the future (valuation and allocation **AV3**).

Filling and shipping sales orders

Once the credit check has been completed, a copy of the approved sales order form (or an electronic notification) is sent to the warehouse as authorization to fill the order and release the goods to the shipping department (or the shipping area). This approved sales order form should be required before goods are removed from the warehouse, and the inventory account is relieved. This ensures goods removed by warehouse personnel without appropriate authorization will appear as an inventory shortage for which they are held accountable. To reduce the likelihood of such inventory shortages, there should be a segregation of the following duties: the custody of inventory, the maintenance of the inventory records, and the physical check of goods on hand.

Segregating responsibility for shipping from the responsibility for approving and filling orders prevents shipping clerks from making unauthorized shipments (**OE1**). In addition, shipping clerks are normally required to make independent checks to determine that goods received from the warehouse are accompanied by an approved sales order form or an electronic authorization.

The shipping function involves preparing multi-copy **shipping documents** (see Appendix A, figure 12A).

Shipping documents on pre-numbered forms are usually produced by the computer information system using order information already logged into the system with appropriate delivery data added (such as quantities shipped, carrier details, and freight charges). Subsequent checks of the numerical continuity of the shipping documents invoiced ensure completeness (**C1**) of recorded sales transactions. Pre-numbering shipping documents also helps in establishing cut-off at year end (**CO**) as the auditor can ensure that the last goods shipped out are the last goods invoiced, and that orders shipped after year end are invoiced after year end. Gatekeepers are sometimes required to check that drivers of all vehicles leaving the premises possess shipping documents for the goods in their vehicle, as a double-check against failure to record deliveries.

Shipping documents provide evidence that goods were shipped and thus of the occurrence (**OE1**) of the credit sale, giving rise to a claim against the customer within accounts receivable. Some entities obtain a copy of the shipping document signed by the customer on receipt of the goods, as evidence of the claim on the customer.

Invoicing customers

The invoicing function involves preparing and sending **sales invoices** (see Appendix A, figure 13A) to customers. Applicable control objectives for invoicing are:

- All deliveries are invoiced to customers.
- Only actual deliveries are invoiced (and there should be no duplicate invoices or fictitious transactions).

---

accounts receivable master file a computer file containing customer details in terms of contact information, address, and approved credit limit

shipping document a form authorizing the release of goods from inventory and the delivery of the goods to the customer

sales invoice a form detailing the goods or services supplied to a customer and the amount owing

- Deliveries are invoiced at authorized prices and the invoice amount is accurately calculated.

Control procedures designed to achieve these objectives are likely to include the following:

- segregating invoicing from the foregoing functions (**OE1, C1**)
- checking the existence of a shipping document and matching it to the approved sales order before each invoice is prepared (**OE1**)
- using an **authorized price list** in preparing the sales invoices (**AV1**)
- performing independent checks on the pricing and mathematical accuracy of sales invoices (**AV1**)
- comparing control totals for shipping documents with corresponding totals for sales invoices (**OE1, C1**)

File copies of the sales invoices are usually maintained in the invoicing department.

> **authorized price list** a list of selling prices for each product

Recording the sales

The main control objective is to ensure that sales invoices are recorded accurately and in the proper period, which is usually when the goods are shipped.

The recording process involves entering sales invoices in a **sales journal**, posting the invoices to the **accounts receivable subsidiary ledger** (see Appendix A, figure 8A), and posting the sales journal totals to the general ledger. It is common practice for invoices to be entered separately in the sales journal and the accounts receivable sub-ledger. The accounts receivable sub-ledger balance is periodically compared with the general ledger control account (**AV2**). Failure of the balances in the accounts receivable sub-ledger to agree in total with the control account in the general ledger indicates that an error has been made. A further control is the use of prelists, whereby the total of invoices entered in the sales journal is checked against the total of sales invoices posted to the accounts receivable ledger (**AV1**). Sales invoices should also be entered in numerical sequence and a check should be made on missing numbers (**C1**). A **monthly customer statement** should be sent to each customer to give the customer an opportunity to alert a designated accounting supervisor (who is not otherwise involved in the execution or recording of sales transactions) if the balance does not agree with the customer's records (**OE1**).

> **sales journal** a journal listing completed sales transactions

> **accounts receivable subsidiary ledger** a ledger recording the details of transactions by customer and balances owing by invoice

> **monthly customer statement** a listing sent to each customer of transactions with that customer that have occurred since the date of the previous statement, which shows the closing balance due

As indicated previously, balances in the accounts receivable sub-ledger should be regularly and independently checked against the balance in the control account in the general ledger. Periodic performance reviews by sales executives of sales analyzed by product, division, salesperson, or region—along with comparisons with budgets—contribute to controls over sales transactions.

Many entities now use online systems, and once an order has been entered into the computer information system, the computer can be programmed to validate the customer credit, check inventory availability, and issue the necessary instructions to the shipping department. On delivery of the order, the shipping department enters the necessary shipping details and the computer automatically produces the invoice and updates the accounts receivable master file (see Appendix A, figure 9A), as well as the related inventory and general ledger files. Additionally, the computer information system maintains a **sales transactions file** or equivalent data within a database system. Important controls in such a system include access controls, programmed application controls, and controls over standing data files.

> **sales transactions file** a computer file listing details of all sales transactions

Access controls should permit read-only access to transaction and master files except for authorized individuals. Those people with authority should have prescribed limits to that authority; for example, the credit manager may have the right to override rejections of orders when an order marginally breaches a customer's credit limit; and similarly the sales manager may have the right to amend price or discount rates for individual customers or sales transactions.

Programmed application controls should include checks to ensure the following:

- Only orders from customers on the accounts receivable master file are accepted.
- Only orders for goods in the entity's product range are accepted.
- The numerical continuity of documents is assured.
- Transactions are chased at regular intervals.
- Duplicate document numbers are rejected.
- Unreasonable quantities, amounts, and dates are questioned.

The correctness of master file data is of particular significance in a computer information system. Master file data in a sales system include authorized customers, their credit limits, and product sales prices. Access controls should ensure that only authorized managers can amend master file data; for example, only the credit manager should be able to add new customers and vary the credit limits of existing customers, and only the sales manager should be able to amend selling prices. As an added precaution, master file data should be periodically printed out for review and approval.

9.2.2 Cash receipts transactions

The processing of receipts from cash and credit sales involves the following cash receipts functions:

- receiving cash
- depositing cash in the bank
- recording the receipts

Receiving cash

A significant risk over cash receipts is that cash paid by customers is stolen before it is recorded. For control purposes, accountability measures must be in place from the moment cash is received, and the cash must be safeguarded. A second risk is the possibility of errors occurring in the subsequent processing of the receipts.

For over-the-counter receipts, a cash register or point-of-sale terminal is normally used. These devices provide:

- immediate visual display for the customer of the amount of the cash sale and the cash tendered
- a printed receipt for the customer and an internal record of the transaction on a computer file or a tape locked inside the register
- printed control totals of the day's receipts

The customer's expectation of a printed receipt and supervisory surveillance of over-the-counter sales transactions helps to ensure that all cash sales are processed through the cash registers or terminals (**C2**). In addition, there should be an independent check of the agreement of cash on hand with the totals printed by the register or terminal (**OE2, C2, AV1**). The cash is then forwarded to the cashier's department for deposit in the bank, together with the register or terminal-printed totals.

Many customers pay by credit or debit cards. These payments are processed via online terminals linked to the bank or other card issuer that validates the transaction. Staff need to be properly trained in the use of such terminals and in procedures to be followed where the transaction is refused. Procedures must be in place for reconciling card sales with cash register totals as part of the daily agreement of cash on hand. Amounts due from card issuers also need to be recorded and checked against subsequent payments. The use of credit and debit cards also facilitates the acceptance of mail or telephone orders from customers without the need for creditworthiness checks once the card transaction has been validated. Because no cash handling is involved, such transactions reduce the risks of misappropriations, and are often preferred despite the commission payable to the card issuer.

There should always be at least two clerks responsible for opening mail so they would need to be in collusion in order to misappropriate cash receipts from the mail. If cheques are received, they should be immediately restrictively endorsed for deposit only. This is done by impressing a rubber stamp imprinted with the words "for deposit to the account of . . . " on the face of the cheques. If they fall into the wrong hands, such cheques cannot subsequently be endorsed for payment to the person acting fraudulently. All these procedures ensure that mail receipts are not misappropriated (**C2**).

Most cash receipts are attached to or accompanied by a **remittance advice** (see Appendix A, figure 14A) indicating the payer and the particulars of the payment. The cheques are forwarded to the cashier's department for banking with a copy of the listing made (which is referred to as a prelist). Remittance advices (or other details of the payment enclosed with the cash receipt) are forwarded to the accounts receivable department for posting to the accounts receivable sub-ledger.

remittance advice a form accompanying cash or cheques paid by a customer, indicating the customer's details and the items being paid

However, the use of cheques for payment is a diminishing practice and most major customers now pay by bank credit transfer. Such payments may be identified as part of the bank reconciliation process (see chapter 12). Because this can lead to delays in recording receipts, entities receiving payments this way usually have online access to their bank account (which may be linked to the accounts receivable master file), which automatically detects credit transfers and updates the accounts receivable records.

Depositing cash in the bank

All cash receipts must be deposited intact daily. Intact means all receipts should be deposited, not used to make payments. This reduces the risk that cash receipts will not be recorded (**C2**). The resulting bank deposit record establishes the occurrence of the transactions (**OE2**).

When cashiers receive over-the-counter and mail receipts, they should check that the cash agrees with both the accompanying register total and the prelist (**OE2, C2, AV1**). Details of cash receipts are then entered on a daily cash summary and the bank **deposit slip** is prepared in duplicate. The cash is deposited in the bank and the copy of the deposit slip is receipted by the bank and retained by the cashier. The daily cash summary is forwarded to the general accounting department.

deposit slip a listing of cash, coins, and individual cheques for deposit with the bank, endorsed by the bank teller, a copy of which is retained by the entity

Recording the receipts

To ensure that only valid transactions are entered, access to the accounting records or computer programs should be restricted to authorized personnel (**OE2**). In manual or partly computerized systems, the duties of journalizing the cash receipts and of posting the receipts to customer accounts should be segregated. The daily cash summary is used to enter the **cash receipts journal**, distinguishing between receipts from cash sales and from credit sale customers. Posting the receipts to the accounts receivable sub-ledger may be done based on the remittance advices received from the mailroom (**AV2**). It is common for accounts receivable clerks to use a terminal to enter mail receipts into a cash receipts transactions file, which is subsequently used in updating both the accounts receivable sub-ledger and general ledger master files.

cash receipts journal a journal recording cash receipt transactions for posting to the ledgers

To ensure the completeness and accuracy of recording mail receipts, independent checks are made of:

- the agreement of the amounts journalized and posted with the amounts shown in the record kept by the mailroom (the prelist)
- the agreement of total amounts journalized and posted for over-the-counter and mail receipts with the daily cash summary and deposit slips retained by the cashier (completeness, accuracy)

In addition, an employee not otherwise involved in executing or recording cash transactions should perform periodic bank reconciliations. These bank reconciliations should be regularly reviewed by a manager on a timely basis.

Opportunities for automating accounting for cash receipts involving currency and cheques are limited, which is why many companies now use online banking and direct debit and credit transfer systems. However, the use of point-of-sale cash register terminals provides controls over the pricing of goods sold and over inventory management.

PROFESSIONAL ENVIRONMENT

Possible point-of-sale frauds

Frauds are committed more often, with greater financial losses, by employees than by customers, suppliers, or other third parties. One common type of employee fraud is point-of-sale fraud, where staff steal money when a sale is made. This is particularly problematic in businesses where there are a lot of low-value transactions and a large number of cashiers, such as in retail or fast food, which makes the fraud easier to conceal.

Fraud is different from theft. Fraud involves employees trying to hide the crime, whereas theft is done without any attempt to hide it, in the hopes the business won't notice the missing money.

Types of point-of-sale frauds

The two most common types of point-of-sale frauds are those where customers pay money to the business, and those where the business pays money to customers, usually by refunding money for returned goods.

In the first type, the most common fraud technique is using void sales. An actual sales transaction must take place, so that the customer hands over the money that the employee steals. However, the employee does not record the sale, so the business doesn't know the money is missing. The employee will either not ring up the sale or will ring up the sale but then void it. Usually the customer will not receive a receipt or else the receipt will not be a normal one. The customer takes the goods but it may be a while before the business notices that the inventory is missing. The cashier will have to alter the inventory records to try to hide the transaction. Another fraud technique is "under-ringing," where the cashier rings in less than the full amount of the transaction, such as charging a customer for a large coffee but only ringing up a small. The cashier then pockets the difference.

In the second type, the most common fraud technique is using a false return. An actual return of goods cannot take place, because the customer would want their money back and that amount would have to be recorded. Instead, the cashier records a false return, falsifying that a customer returned goods and was given a refund. The false return will update the business's bank records to show the false refund to the false customer, so the amount doesn't need to be hidden. However, there was no real return of goods, so the employee will need to falsify the inventory somehow. They may use another inventory item as the returned item, and may even damage an item as a reason for return.

Preventing and detecting point-of-sale frauds
Businesses can implement the following basic controls to help prevent and detect point-of-sale frauds.

- Installing "smart" cash registers that link sales with real-time inventory records.
- Requiring a supervisor or two designated employees to process and approve all returns.
- Examining all returns without the physical goods attached or identified.
- Requiring all returns to scan the item and therefore record the actual return of items, at their actual sales price.
- Requiring a receipt to be issued for each sale and encouraging customers to ensure they receive a receipt for each sale.
- Requiring cashiers to sign in to the register with a unique ID and password for every transaction so each transaction can be traced back to a particular employee.
- Monitoring credit card numbers that are used to process numerous refunds.
- Reviewing daily transactions for suspicious activity, such as a large number of voided sales or returns.

Sources: "Point of Sale Fraud—Stealing Cash Receipts," Association of Certified Fraud Examiners, Brisbane Chapter, http://brisbaneacfe.org/library/occupational-fraud/point-of-sale-fraud-stealing-cash-recipts/; "POS Fraud," PCMS Group, http://www.pcmsgroup.com/retail_systems/pos_fraud.jsp; Oliver Menzel, "How to Tackle Employee Theft," *Hotelier Middle East*, April 2012.

9.2.3 Sales adjustment transactions

Sales adjustment transactions involve the following functions:

- granting cash discounts
- allowing sales returns and allowances
- determining bad debts

The number and dollar value of these transactions vary significantly among entities. However, material misstatements resulting from errors and irregularities in the processing of these transactions are considerable. Of main concern is the possibility of fictitious sales adjustments being recorded to conceal misappropriations of cash receipts. An employee may, for example, conceal stealing cash received from a customer by writing the customer's account off against the allowance for doubtful accounts, or by overstating cash discounts or sales returns and allowances. Controls useful in reducing the risk of such frauds focus on establishing the validity of such transactions (**OE3**).

Such controls include:

- proper authorization of all sales adjustment transactions, such as requiring a senior manager to approve the write off of bad debts (**OE3**)
- use of appropriate documents and records, in particular, an approved credit memo for granting credit for returned or damaged goods, and an approved write off authorization memo for writing off bad debts
- segregation of the duties of authorizing sales adjustment transactions and of handling and recording cash receipts

Cloud 9

While documenting his understanding of the sales and receivables process at Cloud 9, Josh has identified the controls in place along the way. He will next perform a walk-through of one transaction to ensure his documentation reflects what Cloud 9 is doing in practice.

Sharon indicates that once the walk-through is complete, the audit team will need to assess the inherent and control risks at the assertion level for each account. Based on this assessment, they will then design a detailed audit program to address those risks.

BEFORE YOU GO ON

9.2.1 List and briefly describe the five steps involved in processing credit sales.

9.2.2 What is the most significant risk over cash receipts?

9.2.3 What are three controls an entity should enforce to reduce the risk of fraud over sales adjustment transactions?

9.3 AUDIT STRATEGY

As previously discussed, audit strategy refers to the mix of tests of controls and substantive procedures to be applied in the audit. The main determinants of the mix are the assessed inherent risks and control risks. If the auditor believes controls are effective and it is efficient to do so, a combined audit may be planned. This involves conducting tests of controls and assessing their effectiveness. We elaborate on these concepts in this section.

③ Outline audit strategy considerations including the risk of material misstatement and tests of controls for sales, cash receipts, and sales adjustments transactions.

9.3.1 Inherent risk assessment

Sales transactions are the main source of operating revenue for most business enterprises. The accounts receivable produced by credit sales transactions are material to the balance sheet for all businesses except where cash receipts are predominant. While the cash balance reported on the balance sheet may not be material, the flow of cash associated with sales transactions is nearly always material. The significance of sales adjustment transactions varies considerably from one entity to another. However, the bad debts expense is often significant to the profit and loss of entities that sell to customers on credit. Because sales and receivables are material for most businesses, the auditor must assess the risk of material misstatement for these transactions. This begins with an assessment of the inherent risk.

In assessing inherent risk for financial statement assertions, the auditor should consider pervasive factors that may affect assertions in many transaction classes and account balances, as well as factors that may relate only to specific assertions affecting sales and receivables. These factors include:

- pressure to overstate sales, so as to report that announced sales or profitability targets were achieved when they were not; such reporting includes:
  - recording fictitious sales
  - holding the books open to record sales in the next period in the current year (improper cut-off)
  - shipping unordered goods to customers near the year end and recording them as sales in the current period only to have them returned in the next period
- pressure to overstate cash and accounts receivable or understate the allowance for doubtful accounts in order to report a higher level of working capital in the face of liquidity problems or going-concern doubts

good Example

Other inherent risk factors that could contribute to the possibility of misstatements in sales and receivables assertions include:

- the volume of sales, cash receipts, and sales adjustment transactions, resulting in numerous opportunities for errors to occur
- contentious issues relating to the timing of revenue recognition, such as the effect of purchasers' rights of return
- susceptibility to misappropriation of liquid assets generated by cash receipts
- the use of sales adjustment transactions to conceal the theft of cash received from customers by overstating discounts, recording fictitious sales returns, or writing off customers' balances as uncollectible

The auditor needs to consider such inherent risks in deciding on the appropriate audit strategy for sales and receivables assertions.

The main inherent risk is usually that of an overstatement of sales revenue and accounts receivable balances. In the audit of classes of transactions, this relates to the occurrence and the measurement assertions for sales, and to the completeness assertion for cash receipts and sales adjustments.

Internal controls in relation to the sales cycle are discussed in more detail below. In most entities, controls relative to these assertions for sales and cash receipts are effective and therefore the auditor is able to adopt a combined audit strategy for these transaction classes.

Cloud 9

Josh knows that the sales transactions are the main source of revenue for Cloud 9; therefore, the sales and related accounts are material. Furthermore, Josh believes there is a high volume of sales and cash receipts at Cloud 9, which increases the likelihood of errors simply happening. He also thinks the addition of the retail store in the current year increases the likelihood of theft as the stores will have cash and inventory on hand. As most retail customers pay with cash or credit cards, he determines that for these sales, there should be little collection risk. However, as the wholesale sales are primarily on credit, collectibility may be an issue.

PROFESSIONAL ENVIRONMENT

Adjustments cause for concern about control environment

Last year, your firm audited a privately owned electrical wholesaler with about $120 million in sales. The client had two locations in Quebec: Montreal and Quebec City. You stayed in Montreal to do the audit at the main location and sent a staff assistant to the Quebec City branch for accounts receivable audit work. When the assistant returned a few days later, you were relieved when she said she had not found anything, because the audit was over budget and the audit team was under time pressure.

As you reviewed the customer accounts the assistant had selected for testing, you noticed an unusual one: a $120,000 credit to the accounts receivable control account, with an offset to the allowance for doubtful accounts. The explanation for the adjustment was noted as "to adjust the general ledger to the accounts receivable trial balance at the branch." You asked the assistant why an adjustment that significant was necessary and she repeated the branch manager's explanation that the branch office had some collection problems with several long-term customers as it had relaxed credit terms and criteria to increase sales.

When planning the audit, you recognized that the manager dominated the branch and could probably override any controls. Later, as you were reviewing the analytical procedures, you noticed that the accounts receivable write off percentages at the branch in Quebec City were much higher than those of the main store in Montreal. The explanation in the working papers was that "according to the branch manager, write off and return policies were liberalized at the branch in order to attract customers in response to increased competition from a new electrical wholesaler that had recently opened nearby."

However, you began to sense something was not right. While talking to the financial controller at the main store in Montreal, you referred to the problems at Quebec City and said that they were working out "because it appears that those credit policy changes you implemented earlier this year helped to attract new customers." The controller responded, "Credit policy changes? What are you talking about? The company is a wholesale distributor—it doesn't have the kind of customers you find in a retail store. Most of our customers are major electrical contractors. We have been very sensitive to the economic indicators in that industry and the financial health of our customers. If anything, we have tightened credit." You now realize that the Quebec City branch manager's explanation had no basis in fact.

You remembered auditing standard CAS 315 *Identifying and Assessing the Risks of Material Misstatement through Understanding the Entity and Its Environment* and are now convinced something is wrong. What would you do about it?

9.3.2 Control risk assessment

The procedures described in this section are followed only where the process of obtaining the understanding of the internal control structure leads the auditor to believe that it is both possible and cost-effective to assess control risk as being less than high. Where this is not the case, the auditor notes this conclusion in the working papers and obtains the required audit evidence through performing primarily substantive procedures. This decision is made separately for each financial statement assertion, although the same conclusion tends to apply to most, if not all, assertions.

Credit sales transactions

Table 9.2 contains a partial listing of possible "what can go wrongs," necessary controls, potential tests of the operating effectiveness of controls, and the specific transaction class audit objectives for credit sales to which each relates. Using the understanding of the information system, the auditor identifies the presence of necessary controls and makes a preliminary assessment of control risk.

TABLE 9.2 Control risk assessment procedures—credit sales transactions

FUNCTION	WHAT CAN GO WRONG	NECESSARY CONTROL	POSSIBLE TEST OF OPERATING EFFECTIVENESS	RELEVANT CLASS OF TRANSACTIONS AUDIT OBJECTIVE (FROM TABLE 9.1)				
				OE1	C1	AV1	CO	PD1
Accepting customer orders	Sales may be made to unauthorized customers.	Determination that the customer is on the approved customer list	Observe procedure; re-perform.	✓				
		Approved sales order form for each sale	Examine approved sales order forms.	✓				
Approving credit	Sales may be made without credit approval.	Credit department performs a credit check on all new customers	Inquire about procedures for checking credit on new customers.			✓		
		Customer's credit limit checked before each sale	Examine evidence of credit limit check before each sale.			✓		
Filling sales orders	Goods may be released from the warehouse for unauthorized orders.	Approved sales order is required for all goods released to shipping	Observe warehouse personnel filling orders.	✓				
Shipping	Goods shipped may not agree with goods ordered.	Independent check by shipping clerk to agree goods shipped from warehouse with approved sales order	Examine evidence of performance of independent check.	✓	✓			
	Unauthorized shipments may be made.	Segregation of duties for filling and shipping orders	Observe the segregation of duties.	✓				
		Preparation of shipping document for each shipment	Inspect shipping document.	✓				
Invoicing customers	Invoices may be made for fictitious sales or duplicate invoices may be made.	Matching of shipping document and approved sales order for each invoice	Vouch invoices to shipping document and approved sales orders.*	✓				
	Some shipments may not be invoiced.	Matching of sales invoice with each shipping document	Trace shipping document to sales invoices.*		✓		✓	
		Periodic accounting for all shipping documents	Observe procedure; re-perform.		✓		✓	
	Sales invoices may have incorrect prices.	Independent check on pricing of invoices	Inspect copy of invoice for evidence of performance.				✓	
			Re-perform the check on the accuracy of pricing.*				✓	

(continued)

FUNCTION	WHAT CAN GO WRONG	NECESSARY CONTROL	POSSIBLE TEST OF OPERATING EFFECTIVENESS	RELEVANT CLASS OF TRANSACTIONS AUDIT OBJECTIVE (FROM TABLE 9.1)				
				OE1	C1	AV1	CO	PD1
Recording the sales	Fictitious sales transactions may be recorded.	Requirement of sales invoice and matching documents for all entries	Vouch recorded sales to supporting documents.*	✓		✓	✓	
	Invoices may not be journalized or posted to customer accounts.	Independent check of agreement of sales journal entries and amounts posted to customer accounts with control totals of invoices	Review evidence of independent check; re-perform check; trace sales invoices to sales journal and customer accounts.*		✓	✓	✓	
		Periodic accounting for all sales invoices	Observe procedures; re-perform.*		✓		✓	
		Chart of accounts and supervisory review	Observe procedures; re-perform.*					✓
	Invoices may be posted to the wrong customer account.	Mailing of monthly statements to customers, with independent follow-up of customer complaints	Observe mailing and follow-up procedures.*		✓			

Note: * Sometimes performed as part of dual-purpose tests.

TABLE 9.2 **Control risk assessment procedures—credit sales transactions** (continued)

Tests of operating effectiveness

Tests of controls designed to provide evidence of operating effectiveness involve a variety of procedures, including re-performance of certain control procedures by the auditor. Statistical or non-statistical sampling procedures (see chapter 6) may be applied in the performance of some tests. The auditor needs to remember that the direction of testing should be backwards (vouching) along the audit trail when the objective is to test controls over the occurrence assertion, and forwards (tracing) along the audit trail when the objective is to test controls over the completeness assertion. As an example, a sample of invoices from the sales journal would be vouched back to sales orders or shipping documents to test occurrence; to test completeness, a sample of sales orders or shipping documents would be traced to the sales journal to determine that all the transactions were recorded. The auditor must document the tests of controls performed, the evidence obtained, and the conclusions reached. A formal audit program that incorporates several of the tests from table 9.2 is presented in figure 9.2.

Sometimes, control testing also provides substantive evidence as to the correctness of recorded amounts, and these are known as dual-purpose tests. The auditor must be particularly careful in drawing conclusions from such tests. From substantive tests, it may be concluded that misstatements are significant only if material. However, all misstatements suggest that control procedures have not been properly performed. These deviations from prescribed procedures could have caused misstatements in transactions of any size. Therefore, as a test of controls, it is the number of misstatements that is important, not their size. Detections of misstatements of any size, therefore, may require the assessment of control risk to be revised.

Computer information systems

Tests of the operating effectiveness of controls over a computer information system are usually undertaken by computer-assisted audit techniques (CAATs). The two main categories of CAATs are (1) those that test the operation of programs and related programmed application controls directly and (2) those that test data held on computer files.

ASSERTION/TEST OF CONTROLS	W/P REF.	AUDITOR	DATE
Prepared by: _____ **Date:** _____ **Reviewed by:** _____ **Date:** _____ **Cloud 9** **Planned tests of controls — Credit sales transactions** **Year ending December 31, 2016**			
Occurrence			
1. Observe procedures, including segregation of duties, for: • approving sales orders • filling sales orders • shipping sales orders • invoicing customers • mailing monthly statements to customers and following up on customer complaints 2. Select a sample of sales transactions from the sales journal and verify transaction dates, customer names, and amounts by vouching entries to the following matching supporting documents: • sales invoices • shipping documents • approved sales orders			
Completeness			
3. Examine evidence of the use of and accounting for pre-numbered sales orders, shipping documents, and sales invoices. Scan the sequence of sales invoice numbers in the sales journal. 4. Select a sample of approved sales orders and trace to matching: • shipping documents • sales invoices • entries in the sales journal			
Accuracy			
5. For the sample in step 2 above, examine evidence of: • proper credit approval for each transaction • an independent check on proper pricing of invoices • an independent check on the mathematical accuracy of invoices 6. For sales invoices processed in batches, examine evidence of an independent check on the agreement of totals for sales journal entries and amounts posted to customer accounts with batch totals.			
Cut-off			
7. Obtain the number of the last goods shipped at year end, select a sample of shipping documents before this number, and agree: • to sales invoices dated in the current period • entries in sales journal before the period end 8. Following on from step 7, select a sample of the first shipping after this number and agree: • to sales invoices dated in the next accounting period • sales are not recorded in the sales journal until the following accounting period			

FIGURE 9.2 **Partial audit program for tests of controls—credit sales**

In the first category, the most common techniques used for testing controls over the processing of sales transactions are the **test data approach** and the use of embedded audit facilities. Test data are composed of simulated transactions. One batch of data consists of transactions replicating the normal types of transactions processed by the system. A second batch consists of transactions that should activate those programmed application controls of significance to the audit, such as orders exceeding credit limits. Both batches are processed by a copy of the program, and the results are compared with expected results determined manually. Test data are best suited to batch processing systems where the relevant program can be isolated and a copy can be taken

test data approach a method of testing controls in a computerized information system environment, where the auditor prepares fictitious transactions and tests the fictitious data using the entity's software. The output is then compared with the expected output.

embedded audit facility
procedures written directly into the program of a specific computer application allowing the auditor intervention to capture or process data for audit purposes

integrated test facility a type of test of controls that requires using a fictitious entity and entering fictitious transactions for that entity with the regular transactions, and then comparing the result with the expected output

systems control audit review file an embedded audit facility that enables auditors to specify parameters of interest, such as transactions meeting specified criteria, which are then recorded on a special audit file for subsequent review by the auditors

generalized audit software software auditors use under a variety of data organization and processing methods

for audit purposes. With real-time processing, it is less satisfactory and most such systems incorporate embedded audit facilities. One kind of **embedded audit facility** is the **integrated test facility** (ITF) based on dummy accounts to which test data can be processed on a real-time basis. Another is a **systems control audit review file** (SCARF). This facility enables auditors to specify items of interest, such as orders where credit limits are overridden by the credit controller. The facility will then log all such transactions and record them on a special audit file for subsequent review by the auditors.

For tests applied to sales transactions held on computer files, the auditor can use **generalized audit software** for large computer systems and proprietary database packages for smaller, PC-based systems. Both techniques can be used to access data on computer files according to criteria specified by the auditor and to perform a wide range of mathematical functions on that data. For tests involving the inspection of documents, the software can be programmed to select a sample of documents. If statistical sampling techniques are being used (as described in chapter 6), the software can be programmed with the sampling elements, such as the preliminary assessment of inherent and control risk and the tolerable deviation rate. The software selects a suitably random sample and, after testing by the auditor, calculates the achieved deviation rate. For re-performance, the software can be programmed to perform the entire test. In re-performing invoice pricing, for example, the auditor can program the software to select a sample of invoices and compare unit sales prices on those invoices with sales prices held on the master file, and to report differences.

Cash receipts

Table 9.3 illustrates a partial listing of potential misstatements, necessary controls, possible tests of the operating effectiveness of controls, and related classes of transaction audit objectives for cash receipt transactions. The particulars of the items listed in the table vary among entities, based on such factors as the method of data processing used. As we explained for credit sales, the potential misstatements and necessary controls would be the basis of a checklist used to assess design effectiveness. Similarly, an audit program for tests of the operating effectiveness of controls for cash receipts transactions can be prepared based on the potential tests of controls shown in table 9.3.

TABLE 9.3 **Control risk assessment considerations—cash receipts**

FUNCTION	POTENTIAL MISSTATEMENT	NECESSARY CONTROL	POSSIBLE TEST OF OPERATING EFFECTIVENESS	RELEVANT CLASSES OF TRANSACTIONS AUDIT OBJECTIVE (FROM TABLE 9.1)				
				OE2	C2	AV1	CO	PD2
Receiving cash receipts	Cash sales may not be recorded.	Use of cash registers or point-of-sale devices	Observe cash sales procedures.		✓			
		Periodic surveillance of cash sales procedures	Inquire of supervisors about the results of surveillance.		✓			
	Mail receipts may be lost or misappropriated after receipt.	Restrictive endorsement of cheques immediately on receipt	Observe mail opening, including the endorsement of cheques.		✓			
		Immediate preparation of prelist of mail receipts	Observe the preparation of records.	✓	✓	✓		
Depositing cash in the bank	Cash and cheques received for deposit may not agree with the cash count list and prelist.	Independent check of agreement of cash and cheques with register totals and prelist	Examine evidence of independent check.*	✓	✓	✓		

(continued)

FUNCTION	POTENTIAL MISSTATEMENT	NECESSARY CONTROL	POSSIBLE TEST OF OPERATING EFFECTIVENESS	RELEVANT CLASSES OF TRANSACTIONS AUDIT OBJECTIVE (FROM TABLE 9.1)				
				OE2	C2	AV1	CO	PD2
	Cash may not be deposited intact daily.	Independent check of agreement of validated deposit slip with daily cash summary	Re-perform independent check.*	✓	✓		✓	
Recording cash receipts	Some cash receipts may not be recorded.	Independent check of agreement of amounts journalized and posted with daily cash summary	Re-perform independent check.*		✓		✓	
	Errors may be made in journalizing cash receipts.	Preparation of periodic independent bank reconciliations	Examine bank reconciliations.*	✓	✓	✓	✓	
	Cash receipts may be posted to the wrong customer account.	Mailing of monthly statements to customers	Observe mailing of monthly statements.	✓	✓	✓		✓

* Sometimes performed as part of dual-purpose tests.

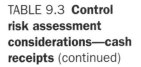

TABLE 9.3 **Control risk assessment considerations—cash receipts** (continued)

Sales adjustments

Sales adjustment information systems are more diverse than sales and cash receipt systems, so it is not practicable to illustrate typical potential misstatements and necessary controls. However, tests of controls that are likely to be appropriate include:

- recalculating cash discounts and determining that the payments were received within the discount period
- inspecting credit memoranda for sales returns for indication of proper approval and accompanying receiving reports for evidence of the actual return of goods
- inspecting written authorizations and supporting documentation (i.e., correspondence with the customer or collection agencies) for the write off of bad debts

9.3.3 Final assessment

Based on the evidence obtained from the procedures performed to obtain an understanding of the internal control structure and the related tests of controls, the auditor can make a final assessment of inherent risks and control risk. For each significant audit objective where the assessment of control risk is less than high and a combined audit strategy is being selected, reasons for this assessment must be documented.

This assessment of inherent and control risk enables the auditor to plan the level of substantive procedures to be performed. Because many tests of controls are dual-purpose tests, they provide evidence of errors in amounts as well as deviations from controls. Therefore, the auditor usually draws up the detailed audit program based on the preliminary assessment of control risk. This improves audit efficiency in that tests of the operating effectiveness of controls that use sources of evidence on which the substantive tests of details are also based are performed simultaneously with those substantive procedures. The auditor must ensure that control deviations are properly identified and that their implications for the assessment of control risk are properly considered in terms of whether further substantive procedures need to be performed.

Cloud 9

After Josh completed his assessment of the inherent and control risks over the sales and receivable cycle, he submitted his assessment to Sharon for review. Sharon agreed that the inherent risks were high; however, the documentation indicated that there were effective controls in place that could be tested and perhaps relied upon. The initial audit strategy over the sales and receivable cycle was to perform a combined audit.

The audit team went to the Cloud 9 office and performed tests of controls. The controls testing involved observing various staff members perform their duties, inspecting assorted documents, and re-performing procedures related to the sales and receivables cycle.

After a week at the client's office, Josh and the rest of the audit team finished testing and assessing the controls at Cloud 9. Again, the audit team sent their completed working papers to Sharon and to Jo Wadley for review. At this stage of the audit, it is important for the more senior members of the audit team to review the results of the controls testing and judge whether there is sufficient and appropriate evidence to support the decision to continue to use a combined audit strategy.

With the controls now tested, it is time to plan the substantive testing, as the audit team's attention turns to this phase of the audit.

BEFORE YOU GO ON

9.3.1 List four inherent risks over the sales and receivable cycle.

9.3.2 What is a dual-purpose test?

9.3.3 What are three possible tests of controls over the operating effectiveness of cash receipts?

9.4 DETERMINING AN ACCEPTABLE LEVEL OF DETECTION RISK

4 Indicate the factors relevant to determining an acceptable level of detection risk for the audit of sales and receivables.

In terms of the accounts receivable, the main consideration is the gross amount due from customers on credit sales and the related allowance for doubtful accounts. To design substantive procedures for these accounts, the auditor must first determine the acceptable level of detection risk for each significant related assertion. Given that the verification of accounts receivable requires consideration of sales, sales adjustment, and cash receipts transactions, the procedures also provide evidence for the income statement balance of sales, and the balance of cash in the balance sheet.

As we explained in chapter 4, for a specified level of audit risk, detection risk is inversely related to the assessed levels of inherent risk and control risk. Thus, the auditor must consider these assessments when determining the acceptable level of detection risk for each accounts receivable assertion. Several pervasive inherent risks that affect sales and receivables transactions and balances were discussed earlier. The combined effects of these factors (especially those contributing to the risk of credit sales being overstated) may result in assessments of inherent risk as being high for:

- the existence and valuation and allocation assertions for accounts receivable
- the valuation and allocation assertion for the related allowance account. Assessments of inherent risk as being lower may be appropriate for the other assertions

The control risk assessment for accounts receivable assertions depends on the control risk assessments for the related classes of transactions, credit sales, cash receipts, and sales adjustments, with the following exception: when transactions decrease the transaction class, the control risk assessment for occurrence and completeness will impact the assessment of the account balance assertion in the opposite direction. Thus, because both cash receipts and sales adjustment transactions decrease the accounts receivable balance, the assessment for the occurrence assertions will impact the assessment for the completeness assertion for the accounts receivable balance. Similarly, the assessment for the completeness assertion for these transaction classes affects the assessment for the existence assertion for the accounts receivable balance.

The audit program will be based on the original assessment of control risk. If tests of controls subsequently lead to a revised assessment of control risk, then the design of substantive procedures in terms of their nature, timing, or extent will also need to be revised. Some auditors use

RISK COMPONENT	EXISTENCE OR OCCURRENCE	COMPLETENESS	RIGHTS AND OBLIGATIONS	ACCURACY OR VALUATION AND ALLOCATION	PRESENTATION AND DISCLOSURE
Audit risk	Low	Low	Low	Low	Low
Inherent risk	High	Moderate	Low	High	Moderate
Control risk—sales transactions	Low	Low	Moderate	Moderate	Moderate
Control risk—cash receipts	Low	Low	Low	Low	Low
Control risk—sales adjustments	Moderate	Low	Moderate	High	Moderate
Combined control risk[1]	Low	Moderate	Moderate	High	Moderate
Acceptable detection risk[2]	Moderate	Moderate	High	Low	Moderate

[1] This is the most conservative (highest) of transaction class control risk assessments used as the combined risk assessment.

[2] Based on the levels of audit risk, inherent risk and combined control risk indicated above for each assertion category.

TABLE 9.4 Correlation of risk components— accounts receivable

a matrix similar to the one illustrated in table 9.4 to document and correlate the various risk components that must be considered in the design of substantive procedures for each account balance assertion.

The risk levels specified in this matrix are illustrative only and vary based on the entity's circumstances.

Consider the following with regard to the existence and occurrence assertions.

- Overall audit risk needs to be low to ensure there is a low risk of giving the wrong audit opinion in relation to existence and occurrence.
- The inherent risk has been assessed as high. The auditor understands the entity and its environment and has concluded that there is a high likelihood that existence or occurrence errors will arise (i.e., there is a high risk that transactions are recorded that do not relate to sales transactions that actually occurred or balances are included for which no receivable actually exists).
- The combined control risk is low, indicating that the auditor has obtained an understanding of the internal controls related to existence and occurrence and performed tests of controls on their effectiveness and has concluded that there is a low risk that any errors that do arise (and this is likely given the high inherent risk identified above) will not be detected and corrected by the internal controls.
- The combined control risk for existence and occurrence is made up of the existence and occurrence control risk for sales transactions and the completeness control risk for cash receipts and sales adjustments, all of which are low. The logic for this is as follows (notice all of the following lead to potential existence problems in the balances):
  - An *occurrence* problem with sales transactions (a sale has been included in the accounts but no valid sale was made) leads to an *existence* problem in the receivables balance (the non-existent sale was recorded so a receivable was created that is not valid).
  - For cash receipts, a *completeness* problem (cash has been received but not recorded) leads to an *existence* problem in receivables balance (the receivable does not exist because it has been paid).
  - For sales adjustments, such as bad debts, a *completeness* problem with bad debts (a receivable has gone bad but is not recorded) leads to an *existence* problem in the receivables balance (the receivable does not exist because the account has gone bad).

- Having assessed inherent risk and control risk, the auditor will now determine the acceptable level of detection risk that will allow the overall audit risk for existence and occurrence to be low. Given that inherent risk is high and control risk is low, the auditor has determined that a moderate level of detection risk is appropriate to achieve the required audit risk. This level of detection risk will be used by the auditor to determine the nature, timing, and extent of substantive procedures that need to be performed. The level and detail of substantive procedures performed is a matter of professional judgement. The auditor will be performing more than the minimum level of testing (detection risk has not been set high) but the auditor will not be performing the maximum level of testing, either (this would be relevant if detection risk was set low).

BEFORE YOU GO ON

9.4.1 What income statement accounts impact accounts receivable? Why?

9.4.2 If tests of controls subsequently lead to a revised assessment of control risk, how will this impact the audit?

9.4.3 Explain how the assessment of the assertions for credit sales, cash receipts, and sales adjustments affects the assessment of the assertions over accounts receivable.

9.5 DESIGNING SUBSTANTIVE PROCEDURES

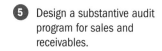 Design a substantive audit program for sales and receivables.

The next step is to finalize the audit program to achieve the specific audit objectives for each account balance assertion. The specific audit objectives covered here are the ones listed in the "Account Balance Objectives" section of table 9.1.

Table 9.5 lists possible substantive procedures to be included in an audit program. This table does not represent a formal audit program because it is not tailored to any specific information system, there is no working paper heading, and there are no columns for supporting working paper references, initials, and dates. Instead, for instructional purposes, there are columns to indicate the categories of substantive procedure and the specific account balance audit objectives from table 9.1 to which each procedure applies. Several of the procedures apply to more than one audit objective, and each objective is covered by multiple possible procedures. The procedures are explained in the sections that follow, including comments on how some procedures can be tailored, based on the planned level of detection risk to be achieved.

TABLE 9.5 **Possible substantive procedures for accounts receivable assertions**

| CATEGORY | SUBSTANTIVE PROCEDURE | ACCOUNT BALANCE AUDIT OBJECTIVE (FROM TABLE 9.1) | | | | |
		OE4	RO1	C4	AV NO.	PD NO.
Initial procedures	1. Perform initial procedures on accounts receivable balances and records that will be subjected to further testing. (a) Trace the opening balances for accounts receivable and related allowance to the previous year's working papers. (b) Review activity in general ledger accounts for accounts receivable and related allowance, and investigate entries that appear unusual in amount or source. (c) Obtain the accounts receivable trial balance and determine that it accurately represents the underlying accounting records by: · adding the trial balance and determining agreement with the total of the subsidiary ledger or accounts receivable master file and the general ledger balance · testing the agreement of customers and balances listed on the trial balance with those included on the subsidiary ledger or master file				✓2, 3	

(continued)

TABLE 9.5 **Possible substantive procedures for accounts receivable assertions** (continued)

CATEGORY	SUBSTANTIVE PROCEDURE	ACCOUNT BALANCE AUDIT OBJECTIVE (FROM TABLE 9.1)				
		OE4	RO1	C4	AV NO.	PD NO.

Analytical procedures	2. Perform analytical procedures.
	(a) Determine expectations.
	(b) Compare current and previous year balances.
	(c) Calculate significant ratios such as:
	  • gross profit
	  • days sales in accounts receivable
	(d) Obtain explanations for unexpected changes.
	(e) Corroborate explanations.
		✓		✓	✓2, 3	

Tests of details of transactions	3. Vouch a sample of recorded accounts receivable transactions to supporting documentation (see also step 6(c)). (a) Vouch debits to supporting sales invoices, shipping documents, and sales orders. (b) Vouch credits to remittance advices or sales adjustment authorizations for sales returns and allowances or bad debt write offs. 4. Perform cut-off tests for sales and sales returns. (a) Select a sample of recorded sales transactions from several days before and after year end, and examine supporting sales invoices and shipping documents to determine that the sales were recorded in the proper period. (b) Select a sample of credit memos issued after the year end, examine supporting documentation, and determine that the returns were recorded in the proper period. Also, consider whether the volume of sales returns after the year end suggests the possibility of unauthorized shipments before year end. 5. Perform cash receipts cut-off test. (a) Observe that all cash received before the close of business on the last day of the fiscal year is included in cash on hand or deposits in transit, and that no receipts of the subsequent period are included. (b) Review documentation such as daily cash summaries, duplicate deposit slips, and bank statements covering several days before and after the year-end date to determine the proper cut-off.	✓ ✓ ✓	✓	✓ ✓ ✓	✓2	

Tests of details of balances	6. Confirm accounts receivable.
	(a) Determine the form, timing, and extent of confirmation requests.
	(b) Select and execute a sample and investigate exceptions.
	(c) For positive confirmation requests for which no reply was received, perform alternative follow-up procedures.
	  • Vouch subsequent receipts identifiable with items constituting the account balance at the confirmation date to supporting documentation, as in step 3(b).
	  • Vouch items constituting the balance at confirmation date to documentary support, as in step 3(a).
	(d) Summarize the results of confirmation and alternative follow-up procedures.
	7. Evaluate the adequacy of the allowance for doubtful accounts.
	(a) Add and cross-add the aged trial balance of accounts receivable and agree the total with the general ledger.
	(b) Test aging by vouching amounts in aging categories for sample of accounts to supporting documentation.
	(c) For past-due accounts:
	  • Examine evidence of collectibility, such as correspondence with customers and outside collection agencies, credit reports, and customers' financial statements.
		✓	✓		✓2
					
					✓3	

(continued)

CATEGORY	SUBSTANTIVE PROCEDURE	ACCOUNT BALANCE AUDIT OBJECTIVE (FROM TABLE 9.1)				
		OE4	RO1	C4	AV NO.	PD NO.
	· Discuss the collectibility of accounts with appropriate management personnel. (d) Evaluate the adequacy of the allowance component for each aging category and in total.					
Presentation and disclosure	8. Compare the presentation of the financial statements with applicable accounting standards. (a) Determine that accounts receivable are properly classified as to type and expected period of realization. (b) Determine whether there are credit balances that are significant in the aggregate and should be reclassified as liabilities. (c) Determine the appropriateness of presentation and disclosure and accounting for related party or factored accounts receivable.				✓2	✓4, 5

TABLE 9.5 **Possible substantive procedures for accounts receivable assertions** (continued)

accounts receivable trial balance a listing of individual customer balances at a particular date on the accounts receivable master file or accounts receivable sub-ledger

aged trial balance an accounts receivable trial balance in which customer balances are analyzed by the period since each sales transaction was entered

9.5.1 Initial procedures

The starting point for verifying accounts receivable and the related allowance account is to trace the current period's opening balances to the closing audited balances in the previous year's working papers (when applicable). Next, the auditor should review the current period's activity in the general ledger control account and related allowance account for significant entries that are unusual in nature or amount and require special investigation.

An **accounts receivable trial balance** (listing all customer balances) is obtained, usually from the entity. To determine that it is an accurate and complete representation of the underlying accounting records, the auditor should add this listing and compare the total with both the total of the subsidiary ledger from which it was prepared and the general ledger control account balance. The auditor should also compare a sample of the customer details and balances shown on the trial balance with those in the subsidiary ledger, and vice versa. The sample can then serve as the physical representation of the population of accounts receivable to be subjected to further substantive procedures.

An example of an **aged trial balance** of an accounts receivable working paper is presented in figure 9.3. This working paper not only provides evidence of performance of the initial procedures just described, but of several of the other substantive procedures discussed in subsequent sections. The initial procedures in verifying the accuracy of the trial balance and determining its agreement with the control account in the general ledger relate mainly to the clerical and mathematical accuracy component of the valuation and allocation assertion.

The auditor can use computer-assisted audit techniques to perform substantive procedures on information stored on computer files through the use of computer audit software. Both generalized audit software and database packages can be used to print a trial balance directly from the accounts receivable master file, test the aging of a sample of accounts, and verify the total and its agreement with the control account in the general ledger.

9.5.2 Analytical procedures

Tests of details are usually planned on the basis that the analytical procedures confirm expectations. It is preferable to perform analytical procedures early in the final audit, so any necessary changes to tests of details can be determined before the start of that part of the audit.

The first stage in applying analytical procedures is to review the understanding of the entity, obtained during the planning phase, as to whether any changes to sales and receivables balances are to be expected.

The second stage is to identify absolute changes in amounts between this year and previous years. This is normally done in the course of preparing the lead sheet for sales and accounts

Bates Ltd. Aged trial balance—Accounts receivable—Trade December 31, 2016 (PBC)						W/P ref. B-1		
						Prepared by: A.C.E		Date: 2/13/17
						Reviewed by: P.A.R		Date: 2/20/17
		Account no. 120						
		Past Due						
	Over 90 days	Over 60 days	Over 30 days		Balance per books 12/31/16		Balance per audit 12/31/16	
Account name				Current		Adjustments		
Ace Engineering		2,529.04	2,016.14	11,875.90	16,421.08 ✓		16,421.08	
⌀ Applied Devices			15,938.89 ⌒	27,901.11 ⌒	43,840.00 ✓		43,840.00	C1
⌀ Barry Manufacturing	1,088.92 ⌒	743.12 ⌒	3,176.22 ⌒	8,993.01 ⌒	14,001.27 ✓		14,001.27	C2
⌀ Brandt Electronics	501.10 ⌒	7,309.50 ⌒	30,948.01 ⌒	24,441.25 ⌒	63,199.86 ✓		63,199.86	C3
Cermetrics Ltd.			3,813.76	8,617.30	12,431.06 ✓		12,431.06	
⌀ Columbia Components				4,321.18 ⌒	4,321.18 ✓		4,321.18	
Drake Manufacturing			739.57	2,953.88	3,693.45 ✓		3,693.45	
EMC		1,261.01	1,048.23	16,194.76	18,504.00 ✓		18,504.00	
⌀ Groton Electric		7,799.36 ⌒	20,006.63 ⌒	89,017.15 ⌒	116,823.14 ✓		116,823.14	C4
Harvey Industries		1,709.16	6,111.25	18,247.31	26,067.72 ✓		26,067.72	
⌀ Jed Ltd.	2,615.87 ⌒	12,098.00 ⌒	15,434.46 ⌒	56,536.88 ⌒	86,685.21 ✓	(9,416.96)	77,268.25	C5
Jericho Electric		1,198.72	13,123.14		14,321.86 ✓		14,321.86	
–	–	–	–	–	–	–	–	
–	–	–	–	–	–	–	–	
–	–	–	–	–	–	–	–	
W & M Manufacturing Ltd.		1,904.65 ⌒	2,166.78 ⌒	28,389.69	32,461.12		32,461.12	C60
Yancey Ltd.	814.98	2,861.05	9,874.13	13,561.80	27,111.96		27,111.96	
	10,157.46	56,705.59	160,537.28	392,136.41	619,536.74	(9,416.96)	610,119.78	
	✓	✓	✓	✓	✓	✓	✓	
					B	B	B	

✓ Added or cross-added

⌀ Customer name and balance per books checked against subsidiary ledger

⌒ Aging verified by examining transaction dates of related unpaid sales invoices in subsidiary ledger

C Account selected for confirmation—see W/P B–2

FIGURE 9.3 **Aged trial balance working paper**

receivable. On this schedule, previous and current year ledger balances making up the financial statement disclosures are recorded side by side, making any differences readily apparent.

The third stage involves the use of more sophisticated relationships such as ratios and trends. This procedure can be performed on accounting data held on computer files, using computer audit software. Significant ratios are gross profit and average collection period. If gross profit is higher than expected, it could be that sales have been overstated to boost revenue, such as by a deliberate cut-off error. An increase in average collection period indicates potential problems in collecting receivables, with the consequent need for a greater allowance. Wherever a change in relationships cannot be readily explained, the auditor must seek an explanation from management and corroborate that explanation, usually by performing more tests of details. For accounts receivable and sales, analytical procedures can provide evidence relating to the existence or occurrence, completeness, and accuracy or valuation and allocation assertions.

9.5.3 Tests of details of transactions

Where balances result from the effects of numerous transactions, it is normally more efficient to concentrate substantive procedures on tests of details of balances, and not tests of details of transactions. The latter are not unimportant, but serve to corroborate tests of details of balances. Often tests of transactions will be performed during the interim audit, commonly in the form of dual-purpose tests. The cut-off tests described in later sections are always performed as part of year-end work and, although they are tests of transactions, serve to verify the recorded balance at the end of the reporting period.

Vouching recorded accounts receivable to supporting transactions

This procedure involves vouching a sample of debits in customers' accounts to supporting sales invoices, and matching documents to provide evidence relevant to the existence, rights and obligations, and accuracy of valuation and allocation assertions. It also involves vouching a sample of credits to remittance advices and sales adjustment authorizations to provide evidence relevant to the completeness assertion for accounts receivable that reductions in customer balances are legitimate.

Performing sales cut-off test

sales cut-off test a substantive procedure designed to obtain reasonable assurance that sales and accounts receivable are recorded in the accounting period in which the transactions occurred, and that the corresponding entries for inventories and cost of sales are made in the same period

The **sales cut-off test** is designed to obtain reasonable assurance that:

- sales and accounts receivable are recorded in the accounting period in which the transactions occurred
- the corresponding entries for inventories and cost of sales are made in the same period.

The sales cut-off test is made as at the end of the reporting period. Given the greater risk of overstatement, the emphasis is on verifying the occurrence of recorded sales before the year end. The auditor usually records the number of the last issued shipping document during attendance at the inventory count and compares it with the cut-off established for inventory purposes. For sales of goods from inventory, the procedure involves comparing a sample of recorded sales from the last few days of the current period with shipping documents numbered before the cut-off number to determine that the transactions occurred before the end of the reporting period. A smaller number of sales recorded after the end of the reporting period are vouched to shipping documents numbered after the cut-off, to ensure that none were delivered before the end of the reporting period.

sales return cut-off test a substantive procedure designed to obtain reasonable assurance that sales returns are accounted for in the period in which the original sales transactions took place

The **sales return cut-off test** is similar and particularly directed toward the possibility that returns made before year end are not recorded until after year end, resulting in the overstatement of accounts receivable and sales. The auditor can determine the correct cut-off by examining dated receiving reports for returned merchandise and correspondence with customers. The auditor should also be alert to the possibility that an unusually heavy volume of sales returns shortly after the year end could signal unauthorized shipments before year end to inflate recorded sales and accounts receivable.

Performing cash receipts cut-off test

cash receipts cut-off test a substantive procedure designed to obtain reasonable assurance that cash receipts are recorded in the accounting period in which they are received

The **cash receipts cut-off test** is designed to obtain reasonable assurance that cash receipts are recorded in the accounting period in which they are received. A proper cut-off at the end of the reporting period is essential to the correct presentation of both cash and accounts receivable. If present at the year-end date, the auditor can observe that all collections received before close of business are included in cash on hand or in deposits in transit, and are credited to accounts receivable. An alternative to personal observation is to review supporting documentation such as the daily cash summary and a validated deposit slip for the last day of the fiscal year. The objective of the review is to determine that the deposit slip total agrees with the receipts shown on the daily cash summary. In addition, the auditor should determine that the receipts were recorded on the closing date.

9.5.4 Tests of details of balances

As explained above, most of the audit effort on receivables is obtained through tests of details of balances, of which the most important is the confirmation of accounts receivable and related follow-up procedures. As discussed in chapter 5, confirmation provides evidence as to existence and rights. It does not provide evidence of completeness, because customers are unlikely to admit to owing more than their recorded balance. The other major test of details of balances is an evaluation of the adequacy of the allowance for doubtful accounts.

Cloud 9

One of the substantive procedures selected and assigned to Josh is preparing the accounts receivable confirmations. As required by the audit program, Josh selected a stratified sample whereby clients with material account balances are selected for confirmation. Of the remaining accounts, a random sample is to be selected. Josh has given the confirmation list to Carla, the controller of Cloud 9, so she can have the confirmations prepared on the Cloud 9 letterhead. While he is waiting for the letters to be returned to him, he prepares a confirmation control working paper listing the customer accounts selected for confirmation. He knows he will need this list to follow up with customers who may not reply right away. He hopes to get a strong response rate, as it will reduce the need to perform alternative procedures over the existence of the accounts receivable.

Confirmation of accounts receivable involves direct written communication by the auditor with individual customers. The test is often referred to as an accounts receivable circularization. The confirmation of accounts receivable is a common audit procedure when they are material and it is reasonable to presume the accounts receivable customers will respond (CAS 505 *External Confirmations*). Confirmation is usually the most efficient procedure for gaining sufficient appropriate audit evidence to support the existence and rights assertions of accounts receivable. There are circumstances, however, in which the auditor concludes that confirmation is unlikely to be effective and that sufficient appropriate audit evidence can be achieved through the performance of alternative audit procedures. Based on the previous year's audit experience on that engagement, the auditor might expect, for example, that responses will be unreliable in the current year or that the response rates will be inadequate. Also, in some cases, customers may be unable to confirm balances if they use voucher systems that show the amount owed on individual transactions, but not the total amount owed to one creditor. The auditor may be able to overcome this problem by confirming individual transactions rather than balances.

As written evidence from third parties, responses to confirmation requests constitute highly reliable evidence. Against this, the following must be remembered:

- Because a customer agrees to owing a balance (existence), it does not mean they will have the cash on hand to settle the receivable when it is due (valuation).

- Some customers may not maintain adequate accounts payable records to provide a reliable response.

- Customers are unlikely to admit to owing more than is shown on the monthly statement, limiting the evidence to that of existence and rights.

- Many trivial differences are likely to be reported as a result of goods and cash in transit.

- The non-response rate may be high, resulting in the performance of alternative procedures.

Given that dealings between the entity and its customers are confidential, the entity must authorize its customers to disclose details of the outstanding balance to its auditors. Occasionally, entities have prohibited auditors from confirming certain accounts receivable. The effect of prohibition should be evaluated on the basis of management's reasons, with the auditor determining whether sufficient evidence from other auditing procedures can be obtained. If the auditor regards management's reasons as unacceptable, then there is a limitation on the scope of the audit that might result in a modified auditor's report.

Form of confirmation

As discussed previously, there are two forms of confirmation request:

1. the positive form, which requires the customer to respond that the balance shown is correct or incorrect
2. the negative form, which requires the customer to respond only when the amount shown is incorrect

Examples of these were provided in chapter 5. The positive form generally produces statistically valid evidence, providing that non-responses are verified by other means. With the negative form, it is impossible to determine whether a lack of response indicates agreement with the balance or simply a failure to reply. The positive form is used when detection risk is low or individual customer balances are relatively large. The negative form should be used only when the following conditions apply:

- detection risk is moderate or high
- there is a large number of small balances in the population
- the auditor has no reason to believe that the respondents are unlikely to give the request due consideration

Timing and extent of requests

When the acceptable level of detection risk is low, the auditor ordinarily confirms receivables as at the end of the reporting period. Otherwise, the confirmation date may be one or two months earlier. In such cases, the auditor must:

- perform analytical procedures on entries in the accounts receivable control account in the period between the date of confirmation and the end of the reporting period, and obtain a satisfactory explanation for any unexpected changes
- perform tests of controls in the intervening period to ensure that the assessment of control risk leading to a decision to accept a high level of detection risk continues to apply

The extent of requests or sample size is determined by the criteria that were described in chapter 6 on audit sampling. Accounts receivable may be divided into distinct populations for sampling. For example, different categories of accounts receivable, such as wholesale and retail, may be subject to different information systems and control procedures and, thus, different control risks. Also, individually material balances are often confirmed directly and the remainder are subdivided into either overdue accounts or other, with a proportionately larger number of the former selected for confirmation as presenting a greater risk of misstatement. Sample size may be determined judgementally or with the aid of a statistical sampling plan. Apart from the exceptions noted, selection of accounts for confirmation should be effectively random.

Control of the requests

The auditor must control every step in the confirmation process. This means:

- before selecting the sample for confirmation, performing the initial procedures described above to ensure the list of balances is complete and accurate
- drawing up a list of selected accounts and verifying that confirmation requests, prepared and signed by entity management at the auditor's request, are in complete agreement with that list
- ascertaining that the amount, name, and address on the confirmation agree with the corresponding data in the customer's account
- maintaining custody of the confirmations until they are mailed
- using the audit firm's own return address envelopes for the confirmations
- personally mailing the confirmation letters
- requiring that the replies be sent directly to the auditor

A working paper should list each account selected for confirmation and the results obtained from each request, cross-referenced to the actual confirmation response (which should also

Cloud 9 Accounts receivable confirmation control						W/P ref. B-2

Cloud 9 Accounts receivable confirmation control
December 31, 2016

	Prepared by: A.C.E	Date: 2/14/17
	Reviewed by: P.A.R	Date: 2/18/17

Account no. 120

Conf. no.	Customer	Book value	Confirmed value	Audited value	(Over)Under statement	Subsequent collections examined to 7/28/16
1	Applied Devices	43,480.00	43,480.00 ⌀	43,480.00		14,001.27 ✓
2	Barry Manufacturing	14,001.27	NR	14,001.27		
3	Brandt Electronics	63,199.86	63,199.86 ⌀	63,199.86		
4	Groton Electric	116,823.14	116,823.14 ⌀	116,823.14		
5	Jed Ltd.	86,685.21	77,268.25 ⌀	77,268.25	(9,416.96)	
60	W & M Manufacturing Ltd.	32,461.12	NR	32,461.12		4,071.43 ✓
	Totals	470,847.92	414,968.57	461,430.96	(9,416.96)	

Response recap:	No. of Items					
Value of confirmations mailed	60	$470,847.92				
Value of confirmations received	58	$414,968.57				
	97%	88%				

Summary of results:	No. of Items					
Value of account total	300	$619,536.74				
Book value of confirmation sample	60	$470,847.92				
Coverage of book value		76%				
Audited value of sample	60	$461,430.96				
Ratio of audited value to book value of sample		98%				

⌀ Signed confirmation response attached for confirmed values

NR No response—alternative procedures performed

✓ Examined entries in cash receipts journal and related remittance advices for total collections indicated

⌐ Examined supporting documentation for portion of book value remaining uncollected as at 7/28/16

Credit memo issued 7/12/16 for merchandise returned 6/28/16. Adjusting entry:

Dr Sales Returns   9,416.96   See W/P B–1 and AE–1

Cr Accounts Receivable   9,416.96

FIGURE 9.4 **Confirmation control working paper**

be filed with the working papers). A confirmation control working paper is illustrated in figure 9.4.

Disposition of exceptions

Confirmation responses will inevitably contain some exceptions. Exceptions may be attributable to goods in transit from the entity to the customer, returned goods or payments in transit from the customer to the entity, items in dispute, or errors and irregularities. The auditor should investigate all exceptions and record their resolution in the working papers (as illustrated in figure 9.4).

Computer information systems

Computer audit software assists the auditor in confirming receivables held on an accounts receivable master file. As explained in our discussion of initial procedures, the software can be programmed to test the completeness and accuracy of receivables listed on the master file. Software can also be used to select accounts on bases as previously discussed, print the letters for circularization, and prepare a working paper for recording responses.

Alternative procedures for dealing with non-responses

When no response has been received after the second (or third) positive confirmation request to a customer, the auditor should perform alternative procedures. The two main alternative procedures are examining subsequent receipts and vouching unpaid invoices and supporting documentation constituting customer balances.

The best evidence of existence and collectibility is the receipt of payment from the customer. Before the conclusion of the auditor's examination, the entity will receive payments from many customers on amounts owed at the confirmation date. The matching of such cash receipts to unpaid invoices at the confirmation date, substantiated by the remittance advice accompanying the cash receipt, establishes the existence and collectibility of the accounts.

Vouching open invoices constituting balances is a variation of step 3(a) in table 9.5. Preferably, the unpaid item should be traced to a shipping document signed by the customer acknowledging receipt of the goods, or to a written order from the customer.

Summary and evaluation of the results

The auditor's working papers should contain a summary of the results of confirming accounts receivable. (The lower part of figure 9.4 illustrates how such data may be presented.) The auditor may use statistical or non-statistical procedures to project misstatements found in the sample to the population. Note though, for a sample test, that it is not sufficient merely to correct errors detected by the confirmation, but that the implications for the entire population of accounts receivable must also be considered.

The auditor evaluates evidence from the confirmations, alternative procedures performed on non-responses, and other tests of details and analytical procedures to determine whether there is sufficient evidence to support management's assertions about accounts receivable.

9.5.5 Evaluating adequacy of the allowance for doubtful accounts

Most entities determine the allowance for doubtful accounts by:

- making a general allowance, such as a percentage of balances overdue by more than a specified period
- making a specific allowance, by identifying customers who are known to be in financial difficulty or who are disputing payment

The allowance is an estimate that the auditor will verify in accordance with CAS 540 *Auditing Accounting Estimates, Including Fair Value Accounting Estimates, and Related Disclosures*. The auditor will review and test the processes used by management, which involves:

- ascertaining management's procedures, including any internal controls, for determining the estimate and considering their reliability
- ensuring that the procedures have been properly followed and that the estimate has been approved
- identifying the assumptions underlying the estimate and considering their reasonableness
- verifying the reliability of the data (such as the aged analysis of accounts receivable) on which the estimate is based
- checking the calculations (such as the percentages applied to each overdue category) in determining the general allowance
- considering the reliability of previous year's allowances

When considering the specific allowances, the auditor might obtain an independent estimate or review subsequent events for confirmation of the estimate. In arriving at an independent estimate, the auditor examines correspondence with customers and outside collection agencies, reviews customers' credit reports and financial statements, and discusses the collectibility of the account with appropriate management personnel. This review includes a consideration of subsequent events, such as news of a customer's financial difficulties or payment of a disputed amount.

9.5.6 Disclosure

The auditor must be knowledgeable about the disclosure requirements for accounts receivable and sales. A review of the accounts receivable trial balance may indicate amounts due from employees, officers, other group entities, and related parties that should be specifically identified if material. The same source may reveal credit balances in customer accounts that may warrant classification as current liabilities. There should also be disclosure of the pledging, assigning, or factoring of accounts receivable. The auditor should be able to obtain evidence of such activities from a review of the minutes of board meetings and from inquiry of management. As one of the final steps in the audit, the auditor should obtain management's representations on these matters in writing in a representation letter (see chapter 13).

Cloud 9

Josh is now happy to be completing his work on the accounts receivable and the sales cycle. He just finished following up on the accounts receivable confirmation requests, and overall he is pleased with the response rate. However, he still needs to perform subsequent receipts testing and vouch unpaid invoices and shipping documents for those accounts that did not send back confirmations. He knows he has to complete these procedures before he can conclude on the existence assertion for the accounts receivable.

In terms of valuation, he did discuss the adequacy of the allowance for doubtful accounts with Carla. His discussions focused on the balances that were over 90 days old and he is overall satisfied with the allowance for doubtful accounts recorded by Cloud 9.

With the substantive procedures almost completed, Josh is hoping to sign off on the accounts receivable procedures by the end of the day, as he is quite anxious to see what is next.

BEFORE YOU GO ON

9.5.1 What is the purpose of vouching recorded accounts receivable to supporting transactions?

9.5.2 What is the purpose of sales cut-off testing?

9.5.3 What are four reasons why accounts receivable confirmations may not provide reliable evidence?

SUMMARY

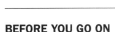 **Identify the audit objectives applicable to sales and receivables.**

When auditing sales and receivables, the auditor's objective is to obtain sufficient appropriate evidence about each significant assertion for the applicable classes of transactions and balances. Significant assertions for sales, cash receipts, and sales adjustments include occurrence, completeness, accuracy, and presentation and disclosure. Significant assertions for accounts receivable and allowance for doubtful accounts include existence, completeness, valuation, and presentation and disclosure.

Evidence may be obtained by tests of controls or substantive testing depending on the audit strategy chosen.

❷ **Describe the functions and control procedures normally found in information systems for processing sales, cash receipts, and sales adjustment transactions.**

The sales cycle includes processing credit sales, cash receipts, and sales adjustment transactions. A typical sales process for credit sales includes accepting customer orders, approving credit, filling and shipping sales orders, invoicing customers, and recording sales transactions. The cash receipts process includes receiving, depositing, and recording cash receipts, while sales adjustments include granting cash discounts, processing sales returns and allowances, and determining bad debts. Control procedures such as appropriate segregation of duties, authorizations, and use of documents and records should be interwoven into each process to reduce the risk of misstatement in the financial statements.

3 **Outline audit strategy considerations including the risk of material misstatement and tests of controls for sales, cash receipts, and sales adjustments transactions.**

To determine the appropriate audit strategy, the auditor starts with obtaining an understanding of the entity. This is necessary for the auditor to assess the inherent and control risks. For audit purposes, the most significant inherent risk is that of overstatement of sales transactions and receivables balances to boost reported profits and assets. For the entity, the greatest inherent risk is that of misappropriation of cash arising from sales transactions. The auditor assesses control risk by evaluating the design effectiveness of internal controls. The auditor drafts the audit program based on the preliminary assessment of control risk, identifying both tests of the operating effectiveness of controls and the reduced level of substantive procedures relevant to the control risk assessment. The

auditor confirms the control risk assessment on completion of the tests of operating effectiveness.

4 **Indicate the factors relevant to determining an acceptable level of detection risk for the audit of sales and receivables.**

Before designing substantive procedures, the auditor must determine the acceptable level of detection risk for each significant related assertion. This level of detection risk will be used by the auditor to determine the nature, timing, and extent of substantive procedures that need to be performed.

5 **Design a substantive audit program for sales and receivables.**

It is usually cost-effective to perform substantive tests on the balance of receivables rather than the transactions making up that balance. The most important test of transactions is that of cut-off at the year end. The major test of balances is the confirmation of accounts receivable. Given that customers are third parties, such evidence is highly reliable. If no response is received, the auditor performs alternative procedures, such as examining subsequent collections and vouching unpaid invoices and supporting documentation constituting customer balances. The auditor must also verify the estimate of the allowance for doubtful accounts.

KEY TERMS

Accounts receivable master file, p. 316
Accounts receivable subsidiary
   ledger, p. 317
Accounts receivable trial balance, p. 332
Aged trial balance, p. 332
Authorized price list, p. 317
Cash receipts cut-off test, p. 334
Cash receipts journal, p. 319

Customer order, p. 315
Deposit slip, p. 319
Embedded audit facility, p. 326
Generalized audit software, p. 326
Integrated test facility, p. 326
Monthly customer statement, p. 317
Remittance advice, p. 318
Sales cut-off test, p. 334

Sales invoice, p. 316
Sales journal, p. 317
Sales order, p. 315
Sales return cut-off test, p. 334
Sales transactions file, p. 317
Shipping document, p. 316
Systems control audit review file, p. 326
Test data approach, p. 325

MULTIPLE-CHOICE QUESTIONS

9.1 **In a credit sales organization, the best place to assign credit approval is in:**
   (a) accounts receivable.
   (b) the sales department.
   (c) the cashier area where receipts will eventually be sent.
   √ (d) a completely separate department.   *Credit dept*

9.2 **Controls over approving credit relate to:**
   (a) the existence or occurrence assertion.
   (b) the completeness assertion.

   √ (c) the accuracy or valuation and allocation assertion.
   (d) the rights and obligations assertion.

9.3 **To enhance controls in the credit sales area, the warehouse should be instructed not to release goods until:**
   (a) a faxed copy of the sales requisition is received.
   (b) a completed sales invoice is received.
   √ (c) an approved sales order is received.
   (d) the shipping department requests the goods.

9.4 An example of a programmed application control is:

(i) numerical sequence (continuity) of documents is assured.

(ii) unreasonable quantities, amounts, and dates are queried.

(iii) only orders for goods in the entity's product range are accepted.

    (a) (i) and (ii) only.

    (b) (ii) and (iii) only.

    (c) (i) and (iii) only.

    √ (d) (i), (ii), and (iii).

9.5 In most audits, the auditor is concerned about sales adjustment transactions because of:

(a) the sheer number and value of these transactions.

(b) the lack of proper authorization for these transactions.

√ (c) the potential use of these transactions to conceal a theft of cash.

(d) poor controls normally found over these transactions and the inherent lack of documentation.

9.6 In relation to materiality, the following statement is most accurate:

(a) accounts receivable produced by credit sales transactions are material to the balance sheet for all businesses except those with cash sales.

(b) cash balances at the end of a particular reporting period will always be material.

(c) the significance of sales adjustment transactions is consistent across entities.

(d) bad debts expense is sometimes material to the profit and loss of entities that sell on credit.

9.7 Control risk assessments for accounts receivable assertions depend on the related control risk assessments for the class of transactions. The classes of transactions that do not relate to the accounts receivable balance are:

(a) credit sales.

(b) cash sales.

(c) sales adjustments.

(d) cash receipts.

9.8 When examining sales transactions, the following is not possible using generalized audit software:

(a) inquiring about segregation of duties for invoicing customers.

(b) selecting a sample of invoices for inspection.

(c) re-performing invoice pricing and reporting differences.

(d) ensuring the sales journal is correctly totalled.

9.9 The following is a cut-off test:

(a) selecting a sample of shipping documents around the year end and agreeing to sales invoice to ensure it is included in the appropriate period.

(b) selecting a sample of receivables balances outstanding at the year end and agreeing to cash received after the year end.

(c) selecting a sample of bad debts written off after the year end and agreeing to sales invoice dated before the year end.

(d) selecting a sample of receivables balances from the list of receivables and agreeing the build-up of the balance to sales invoices.

9.10 Confirming accounts receivable is required whenever:

(a) they are material in amount.

(b) it is reasonable to presume accounts receivable customers will respond.

(c) they are material and it is reasonable to presume accounts receivable customers will respond.

(d) a large number of small balances is involved.

REVIEW QUESTIONS

9.1 Describe the inherent risks specific to sales and receivables the auditor needs to consider.

9.2 Why is the control risk assessment of the completeness of cash receipts and sales adjustment transactions associated with the control risk over the existence of the accounts receivable balance?

9.3 Why is the auditor likely to adopt a combined audit approach to accounts receivable wherever practicable? Why are substantive procedures more likely to be based on the accounts receivable balance than on sales, cash receipts, and sales adjustment transactions?

9.4 Outline the procedures involved in performing accounts receivable confirmations.

9.5 If the auditor does not receive a response after sending a letter to confirm a customer's account balance, what alternative audit procedures may be performed?

9.6 Discuss situations in which sales adjustments may be necessary. Identify necessary controls to ensure that the accounting system recognizes only genuine adjustments.

9.7 Identify situations leading to an inherent risk that an entity may wish to (a) overstate sales revenue and (b) understate sales revenue.

9.8   Explain the kinds of fraud that could be expected in sales, cash receipts, and sales adjustment transactions in the absence of adequate internal control procedures. Consider the importance of the segregation of duties in preventing such frauds.

9.9   Explain what is meant by "cut-off" and why it is important to auditors in establishing the fairness of the financial statements.

9.10 CAS 530 *Audit Sampling* distinguishes between sampling and other selective testing procedures. Explain the application of the requirements of this standard to the selection of accounts receivable confirmations.

PROFESSIONAL APPLICATION QUESTIONS

Basic ★   Moderate ★ ★   Challenging ★ ★ ★

9.1 Cash sales system controls ★

As the internal auditor of the Sellanything Group of companies, you have been asked to investigate the cash sales system of Stationery Ltd., one of the subsidiaries. Stationery sells office supplies in the Halifax area. Its prices are highly competitive and it offers a same-day delivery service for orders telephoned before noon. Costs are kept down by requiring cash on delivery. Sales are made in the following way:

1. The customer phones through an order to the sales department, which raises a pre-numbered multi-copy sales order, two of which (the invoice copies) are priced and totalled.
2. The shipping department makes up the order and gives the goods to the driver with the invoice copies of the order.
3. The driver delivers the goods, collects the cash, and receipts the customer's copy of the invoice.
4. The driver returns and hands over the cash and the second copy of the invoice to the cashier.
5. The cashier records and deposits the cash.

Required

(a) State any weaknesses in the cash sales system.
(b) Describe any audit tests you would perform to ensure that there was no material error or fraud within the system.

9.2 Tests of controls—sales transactions ★ ★

You have been assigned to perform tests of controls on the sales system at EDB Ltd. as part of the December 31, 2016, audit. EDB is a wholesaler of bathroom supplies such as vanity units, toilets, taps, and sinks. During testing, you noted the following errors:

1. Invoice no. 54922 issued on January 12, 2016, was entered twice. The error was discovered when the customer phoned to complain about being charged double the agreed amount.
2. Invoice no. 51839 issued on March 25, 2016, contained incorrect prices. Three vanity units were charged at $453 each instead of $543, and five sinks were charged at $231 each instead of $321. The error was discovered when the salesperson complained about not receiving the full commission for the month.
3. No prices were entered on invoice no. 56329 issued on April 24, 2016, resulting in a zero dollar invoice being issued. The error was discovered when accounts receivable staff noticed the zero amount appearing on the accounts receivable ledger.
4. Invoice no. 59328 issued on July 18, 2016, matched the customer's order. However, the order was only partially filled because of a lack of inventory in the warehouse, meaning items that were never delivered were included in the invoice. The error was discovered when the customer phoned to complain about being overcharged.
5. Invoice no. 61348 issued on August 7, 2016, was sent to the wrong address. Apparently, the invoice had the correct address on it, but a typing error occurred on the envelope. The

error was discovered when the customer phoned to complain about the overdue notice received, stating that the invoice had never been received in the first place.

6. Invoice no. 62875 issued on November 29, 2016, was not processed through the usual channels. The details were correct but certain procedures, such as a formal credit check, were not documented. The invoice was a special order for a large building project and amounted to around 10 times the value of EDB's average invoices. The sale was personally handled by one of the directors and the invoice was prepared by his assistant.

Required

Treating each of the listed errors independently:

(a) Describe application controls (both manual and via the computer information system) that would have prevented or detected the error.

(b) Describe further work you would perform in relation to each of the errors.

(c) Explain the implications of the errors for your substantive testing of accounts receivable.

9.3 Computerized sales system—controls ★ ★

Bestwood Ltd. is planning to replace its computerized sales accounting system. The managing director has asked for your advice on certain matters relating to the new system.

The existing system uses the computer to produce sales invoices from handwritten shipping documents, posts them to the accounts receivable ledger, records cash received, and produces an aged analysis of receivables. The main weaknesses of the existing system are that many documents are still handwritten or typed and it is possible to deliver goods to customers with poor credit ratings, thus creating excessive collection costs and a high level of bad debts.

The managing director suggests that the new system should:

1. produce the order confirmation
2. produce the shipping note when the goods are ready for delivery
3. produce the sales invoice at the same time as the shipping document, using information from the shipping document and prices from a master price list, and post the invoice to the accounts receivable ledger
4. record receipts of cash from customers on the accounts receivable ledger and in the cash book

Access to the system will be from terminals and controlled by the use of passwords and by restrictions on the tasks that can be performed from specific terminals.

In view of the large number of orders, the managing director wants the computer to perform credit checks on customers with minimum intervention by the credit manager. The credit checks by the computer will use data input into the system by the credit manager and information on the customer master file. When the programmed criteria decide that goods should not be sent to a particular customer, the credit manager may override the computer.

Required

(a) Describe the controls the computer system should exercise before:
   (i) confirming a customer's order
   (ii) creating a shipping document authorizing the delivery of goods to the customer

(b) Describe the controls that should be exercised over:
   (i) changing customer details, including adding new customers, amending details of existing customers, and deleting customers
   (ii) changing customer credit limits
   (iii) changing selling prices of goods

(c) Describe:
   (i) the credit criteria that the computer system should use to authorize delivery of goods to customers
   (ii) the manual procedures the credit manager should undertake when overriding the computer

Source: Adapted from ACCA Audit Framework, Paper 6, June 1996.

9.4 Substantive procedures for allowance for doubtful accounts ★ ★

It is common practice for companies to make two allowances for doubtful accounts:

1. The specific allowance is based on accounts the company has reason to suspect may not be paid.
2. The general allowance relates to accounts as yet unknown but that experience suggests may not be paid. The likelihood of a receivable account being unpaid is usually assumed to increase the longer it remains unpaid, and many companies determine a general allowance as a percentage of overdue receivables, with an increasing percentage being applied against the longest overdue accounts.

You are aware that CAS 540 *Auditing Accounting Estimates, Including Fair Value Accounting Estimates, and Related Disclosures* is likely to be relevant to the audit of the allowance for doubtful accounts.

Required

Describe the procedures you would adopt in verifying:

(a) a general allowance for doubtful accounts
(b) a specific allowance for doubtful accounts

9.5 Accounts receivable confirmations ★

Your firm is the external auditor of Southwood Trading Ltd. and you are auditing the financial statements for the year ended June 30, 2016. Southwood Trading has sales of $25 million and the accounts receivable at June 30, 2016, were $5.2 million.

The engagement partner has asked you to consider the relative reliability of evidence from third parties and certain matters relating to an accounts receivable confirmation.

Required

(a) Consider the relative reliability of third party evidence in the form of accounts receivable confirmations for trade receivable balances.
(b) Describe the audit work you would carry out in following up the responses to the accounts receivable confirmations where:
   (i) the customer disputes the balance and provides a different balance
   (ii) no reply to the confirmation has been received from the customer, and all attempts at obtaining a reply have failed

Source: Adapted from ACCA Audit Framework, Paper 6, December 1998.

9.6 Computer-assisted substantive testing for accounts receivable ★

Ally Bobyk is conducting the audit of a wholesale electrical goods distributor, Electra Ltd. Electra supplies appliances to hundreds of individual customers in the metropolitan area of Toronto. It maintains detailed accounts receivable records on a computer system. The customer account master file is updated at the end of each business day. Each customer record in the master file contains the following data:

- customer account number
- customer address
- open (unpaid) invoices at the beginning of the month, by invoice number and date
- sales during the current month, by invoice number and date
- individual cash receipts during the current month
- date of last sale
- date of last cash receipt

Ally is planning to confirm selected accounts receivable as at the end of the current month. She will have available a computer file of the data on the accounts receivable master file on the date on which the company sends monthly statements to its customers. Ally has a generalized software package to help her in this task.

Required

Detail how Ally will be able to use the computer software package and accounts receivable master file to help her in the audit of accounts receivable.

Source: Adapted from an AICPA Audit Framework paper.

9.7 Audit of sales and accounts receivable ★ ★ ★

You have been assigned to audit the sales and accounts receivable balances of Coppero Engineering Ltd. for the year ended September 30, 2016. Coppero Engineering is a major manufacturer of steel parts and fixtures for other manufacturers in the engineering field. The interim work was undertaken in June 2016 and tests indicated that internal controls over sales and accounts receivable are effective and that therefore control risks are acceptable.

You observe that credit sales are made to a group of 2,500 active customers, located in Canada and the United States. Approximately 30 percent of the customers represent 70 percent of the balances, and although most of these customers are in Canada, a number are also based in the United States, England, and Ireland. The sales made into the United States are invoiced in Canadian dollars and you note that the value of the Canadian dollar has escalated by 30 percent in recent months. The total of the accounts receivable balances at September 30 is $95 million and the current allowance for doubtful accounts is $500,000.

Sales and receipts are recorded on the company's computerized accounting system, which simultaneously updates the accounts receivable balances and sales and cash receipts transactions journals on a daily basis. On a weekly basis, an aged trial balance is generated, which is reviewed by the credit manager for slow-paying accounts. Follow-up action is then taken as necessary. Sales returns and bad debt write offs are processed and summarized weekly and any write offs have to be approved by the chief financial officer, based on the recommendations of the credit manager. Documents to support these write offs are kept on file.

After the end of the reporting period, the rising Canadian dollar and a financial crisis in two of the major American markets have caused some concern for the credit manager, who has recently joined the client after a number of years in the retailing industry. Also, rising interest rates in Canada and a slowing economy have affected sales growth in the Canadian market.

Required

You are asked to prepare an audit program to test Coppero Engineering's year-end accounts receivable. You are required to include in your program specific audit objectives you can test using the audit firm's new generalized audit software package. Your manager is particularly worried about the possible negative effects on the collectibility of accounts receivable because of the American financial crisis, the rising dollar, and the slowing Canadian economy.

9.8 Controls over cash receipts ★ ★ ★

The head office of Lighttime Ltd., wholesalers of electrical equipment, has asked you to review the system of control over cash collection at the Edmonton branch because it suspects that irregularities are taking place. The branch is the largest single outlet of the company and has substantial annual sales invoiced by the branch.

Inquiries reveal the following procedures for invoicing sales and collecting cash. (Cash refers to currency and cheques.)

1. There are two sets of invoices, one for cash sales and the other for credit sales.
2. When payment for cash sales is received by the cashier, one copy of the invoice is stamped as paid and filed alphabetically, and the other is given to the customer.
3. Credit sales invoices are sent to the customers.
4. Mail is opened by the secretary, who passes any cheques to the credit manager for his review, without recording the amounts received.
5. The credit manager gives the cheques to the cashier by depositing them in a tray on the cashier's desk.
6. The cashier then makes a listing of the cheques, which is used by the credit controller for posting to the accounts receivable ledger.

7. The cheques from credit customers and receipts from cash sales are banked daily by the cashier, except for once a week when sufficient currency is retained to reimburse petty cash.

8. The credit controller posts remittances to accounts receivable using a computerized accounting system and verifies the cash discount allowable.

9. The credit manager obtains approval from head office to write off bad debts. Any subsequent remittances received in respect of these accounts are credited to "sundry income."

Required

(a) Describe control weaknesses in the accounting for cash receipts.

(b) Suggest improvements in internal control to prevent irregularities in the collection of cash.

(c) Explain substantive audit procedures necessary to determine whether any irregularities have taken place.

9.9 Control weaknesses ★ ★ ★

Namini Corp. sells its products to clients ranging from proprietorships to medium-sized entities. Namini is controlled by two family members, and most of the employees are casual staff employed during the busy seasons (November 1 through January 15, and May 1 to July 15). The company's managers feel that on-the-job training is adequate for their needs and that the labour savings from using temporary staff are reflected in the profits that Namini has earned for the family each year.

The company has made a niche in its market by guaranteeing excellent and quick customer service. When a customer order is received, either by phone or by fax, the customer service clerk (CSC) who takes the order checks that Namini has the goods in stock and the correct price by checking an online database of inventory on hand. If the goods are available, the clerk then personally phones the customer back to verify the order, including both quantity and price for each item and then calculates the extended prices for the entire order. The clerk then prepares a sales invoice and faxes a copy to the customer. Namini's policy is for the sales invoice to show a shipping date of one day from the order date. The clerk then walks to the warehouse (adjacent to the sales office), selects the goods, and takes them to shipping.

The company has a shipping staff of four people, and the shipping department will not ship any goods without a sales invoice initialled by the CSC. The shipping department is determined to reduce the number of shipping errors. This year, only nine shipments have occurred in which there was no sales invoice initialled and attached to the shipping bill. One of these turned out to be an urgent shipment to a long-time customer, sent on the manager's verbal instructions. In that case, the shipping clerk noted that the manager provided a sales invoice within one day for the shipping records. Another shipment resulted in the CSC being fired for fraud when it was discovered that he had sent a shipment of goods to a friend at below cost. Therefore, only the other seven shipments were considered to be true errors.

If the sales invoice does not indicate who is to pay the shipping costs, then Namini sends the goods FOB shipping point. When a shipment is occasionally delivered to an incorrect address, it is the CSC's job to contact the customer and obtain the correct information. If the account is unpaid after the due date (30 days), the receptionist mails a reminder invoice to the customer. If the account remains unpaid after 60 days, the receptionist pulls the sales invoice and gives it to the CSC who made the sale. The CSC is then responsible for contacting the customer by phone to determine if there is a problem.

Required

Identify *five* different types of weaknesses in Namini's internal controls.

Source: © CGA-Canada, now CPA Canada. Reproduced with permission.

9.10 Internal controls over sales ★

Required

For each of the following statements of possible things that can go wrong, identify the audit objective and an internal control that should be implemented to prevent the "WCGW."

(a) Sales are made to customers that do not have approved credit.

(b) Goods not ordered by the customer are shipped.

(c) Unit prices on customer invoices are incorrect.

(d) Invoices are not posted to customer accounts.

(e) Goods are shipped but not invoiced.

9.11 Control strengths and weaknesses ★ ★ ★

Soak City Waterpark is a family-owned business just outside of Winnipeg. The waterpark is only open for business from May to September. During the winter months, the waterpark undergoes repairs and maintenance upgrades.

The capital assets for Soak City are significant and the waterpark recently completed an expansion project, where additional fencing, a restaurant, and a POS system were installed and three additional slides were constructed.

The following are Soak City's accounting procedures for revenue, receivables, and receipts. This is strictly a cash business. Revenues consist primarily of admission fees, but other revenues include restaurant sales and locker rentals. There are six cash registers open at peak times, and each starts with a daily float of $200. When the park is closed, the cash tills are kept in a vault.

At the end of each day, each cashier counts out the float and places the remaining cash in an envelope and gives it to the admissions manager. The admissions manager counts the cash and prepares the bank deposit. The admissions manager also completes a sales summary report, which summarizes the cash sales. This report is forwarded to the accounting department and the sales are recorded in the general ledger based on this report. When completing this report, she calculates and compares the admission revenues recorded in the tills with the cash collected. This information is forwarded to the general manager, who compares the sales with the bank statements.

Required

(a) Identify the control strengths at Soak City Waterpark.

(b) Identify the control weaknesses at Soak City Waterpark. For each weakness, state the implication (the WCGW) of the weakness and make a recommendation to correct it.

9.12 Revenue cycle strengths and weaknesses ★ ★ ★

Venture Volunteers for Troubled Teens (VVTT) is a not-for-profit entity that provides counselling services to troubled teens and adolescents. While the majority of its funding comes from the government, the group also participates in a variety of fundraising activities. To manage the fundraising activities and administer the various programs, there is an executive director, a receptionist, two accounting staff, and several youth counsellors.

The mail is opened by the receptionist. The receptionist photocopies any cheques and then passes them on to Andrea, a member of the accounting staff. When Andrea receives the cheques, she prepares the bank deposit and gives it to Ling for review (which is denoted by an initial on the bank deposit). It is then placed in the safe until Friday, as deposits are made once a week.

Ling then enters the information provided by Andrea into the general ledger based on the cheques received. Andrea subsequently matches the general ledger journal entries to the bank deposit and they are filed by date. The bank reconciliation is performed by Andrea when time allows. The executive director reviews the bank reconciliation when it is complete.

When significant government funds are received in advance, Ling records the cash with the credit to deferred revenue. As the revenue is earned, Ling posts an additional entry recognizing the revenue as earned. This is reviewed by the executive director on a monthly basis.

Once a year, the entity runs a door-to-door canvass to collect donations from the general public. Volunteers knock on people's doors and ask for funds. Each canvasser is provided with a pre-numbered sequential receipt book and duplicate receipts are to be given to all donors for tax purposes. All funds collected are to be remitted to the receptionist with the accompanying receipt book and a summary worksheet of donations collected. The amount collected is counted by the receptionist and forwarded to Andrea. Andrea prepares the deposit and records the cash donations. The deposit runs are done more frequently while this program is running to reduce the amount of cash on hand.

Required

(a) Identify the control strengths of the revenue process at VVTT.

(b) Identify the control weaknesses of the revenue process at VVTT. For each weakness, identify the implication of the weakness and recommend how to improve it.

9.13 Assessing confirmations ★ ★ ★

James Bach is a CPA student working on the confirmations working paper from one of his clients, Dunstan Electric Co. He has so far summarized the results of his testing as shown on page 349.

Required

Help James complete the working paper.

(a) Calculate any differences between the general ledger balance and the confirmed balance.

(b) For any balance determined in part (a), determine what would be considered an audit error.

(c) For the differences determined in part (a), identify the additional audit procedures that James should perform.

(d) Complete the response recap and determine any extrapolated error. For any error, propose an audit adjustment.

CASES

9.14 Integrative Case Study—Harlan Venture

Harlan Venture Inc. (HV) operates a restaurant named Harlan's in Toronto. The shareholder, Stephen Painter, is concerned whether the system and controls in place at the restaurant are appropriate to monitor and control the operations of the restaurant and to make sure that employees don't steal. He provides the following information:

Restaurant Operations

The restaurant manager's duties include looking after reservations, seating customers, and managing the restaurant's operations.

Servers take the customer orders and enter them into a system that uses off-the-shelf restaurant software that HV purchased. Each order is temporarily stored in the "orders placed file" and is transmitted to the kitchen staff, who receive a printed order. This order is the basis for preparing the meal. The kitchen staff throws out the order forms when the meals are picked up by the servers.

The server instructs the system to prepare the customer bill. The customers pay by cash or by credit card (HV accepts Visa, MasterCard, American Express, and Diners Club). The server is to enter the payment amount and method of payment into the system. The amount of the tip is to be entered as a separate item for both cash payments and credit card payments. The order in the "orders placed file" is transferred to the "orders completed file" only when the server enters the customer payment information.

At the end of the day, the restaurant manager prepares cash envelopes, which contain the tips for the servers and kitchen staff based on the amount of the tips recorded in the system. The cash in the tip envelopes is taken from the cash payments made by customers. He then clears the system for any orders that remain in the "orders placed file."

The system generates a daily report of revenue recorded by method of payment, and HST collected. This report is used by the part-time accountant to make the entries in the general ledger.

The restaurant manager prepares the daily bank deposit, which includes the credit card vouchers and the cash to be deposited. A cash float of $250 is maintained in the sales register. He takes the deposit home and makes the bank deposit first thing the next morning.

HV receives monthly statements from the credit card entities that report the amount of the credit card sales processed by the entity and the fee charged by the entity. The bookkeeper enters these expenses in the general ledger.

Accounts receivable confirmation
Dunstan Electric Co.
Dec. 31, 2016

Conf. no.	Customer	Balance per GL	Balance Confirmed	(a) Difference	Customer Response	Explanation	(b) Error	(c) Additional Procedures Required
1.	Applied Devices	117,383	117,383		Sent cheque for $15,000 December 29	Timing difference		
2.	Barry Manufacturing	107,084	92,084					
3.	Brandt Electronics	401,500	401,500					
4.	Groton Electric	227,047	227,047					
5.	Jed Ltd.	58,650	53,000		Returned damaged goods December 30 for $5,650	Discussed with client, credit note processed Jan. 2, so cut-off issue.		
6.	W & M Manufacturing	199,996	178,920		Overcharged for several items based on selling price agreed with sales	Examined invoice pricing to master price list, recalculated the invoices and pricing extensions, determined there was an invoice pricing error.		
	Totals	1,111,660	1,069,934					

Response recap:

	No. of Items	$ Amt.
Value of confirmations mailed		
Value of confirmations received		

Summary of results:

	No. of Items	
Value of account total	10	1,300,000
Book value of confirmation sample		
Total representative errors		
Total representative sample		
Error percent		
Total population		1,300,000
Proposed adjustment:		

The bartender is responsible for all sales of wine and liquor. He provides wine (by the glass or bottle) and drinks to the servers, who are not allowed access to these items. The on-site wine is stored behind the bar and, for expensive wines, in the basement wine cellar. He takes inventory of the wines and liquor weekly and places the appropriate purchase orders.

Catering Services

HV provides both in-restaurant special function catering and out-of-restaurant special function catering (for example, at a private residence). The price of the function is based on the menu cost plus a markup of 60 percent.

The customer is billed in full for the function after it is completed and when the customer indicates satisfaction with HV's performance by sending in the "customer satisfaction form." Revenue is recognized at the time of billing. Discounts are authorized by the restaurant manager if the customer deems HV's performance to be less than satisfactory. The amount of discounts given to date has been minimal. Billings are often made as much as 60 days after the date of the function. As at May 31, 2016, 10 functions with a contract value of $50,000 have been completed and as yet not billed. Forty functions have been billed.

Required

Based in the above, identify *five* control weaknesses. For each weakness, state the implication and make an appropriate recommendation to improve the control weakness.

Source: Adapted from ICAO 2008 Final Exam.

Source: (Adapted and) reprinted with the permission of CPA Ontario. Copyright © Chartered Professional Accountants of Ontario (The Institute of Chartered Accountants of Ontario). Any changes to the original material are the sole responsibility of the author (and/or the publisher) and have not been reviewed or endorsed by CPA Ontario.

9.15 Integrative Case Study—Tinkerbell Toys Co.

Tinkerbell Toys Co. (Tinkerbell) is a manufacturer of children's building block toys. It has been in business for more than 35 years and it sells to a wide variety of customers including large and small toy retailers across the country. The company's year end is May 31, 2016.

The company has a large manufacturing plant, four large warehouses, and a head office. Upon manufacture, the toys are stored in one of the warehouses until they are shipped to customers. The company does not have an internal audit department.

Sales ordering, goods shipped, and invoicing

Each customer has a unique customer account number and this is used to enter sales orders when they are received in writing from customers. The orders are entered by an order clerk and the system automatically checks that the goods are available and that the order will not take the customer over their credit limit. For new customers, a sales manager completes a credit application; this is checked through a credit agency and a credit limit is entered into the system by the credit controller. The company has a price list, which is updated twice a year. Larger customers are entitled to a discount; this is agreed to by the sales director and set up within the customer master file.

Once the order is entered, an acceptance is automatically sent to the customer by e-mail confirming the goods ordered and a likely ship date. The order is then sorted by customer address. The warehouse closest to the customer receives the order electronically and a shipping list and sequentially numbered goods shipped report (GSR) are automatically generated. The warehouse team packs the goods from the shipping list and, before they are sent out, a second member of the team double-checks the shipping list to the GSR, which accompanies the goods.

Once shipped, a copy of the GSR is sent to the accounting team at head office and a sequentially numbered sales invoice is raised and compared to the GSR. Periodically, a computer sequence check is performed for any missing sales invoice numbers.

Fraud

During the year, a material fraud was uncovered. It involved cash/cheque receipts from customers being diverted into employees' personal accounts. In order to cover up the fraud, receipts from subsequent unrelated customers were then recorded against the earlier out-standing receivable balances and this cycle of fraud would continue.

The fraud occurred because two members of staff who were related colluded. One processed cash receipts and prepared the weekly bank reconciliation; the other employee recorded customer receipts in the sales ledger. An unrelated sales ledger clerk was supposed to send out monthly customer statements but this was not performed. The bank reconciliations each had a small unreconciled amount but no one reviewed the reconciliations after they were prepared. The fraud was only uncovered when the two employees went on holiday at the same time and it was discovered that cash receipts from different customers were being applied to older receivable balances to hide the earlier sums stolen.

Required

(a) Recommend six tests of controls the auditor would normally carry out on the sales system of Tinkerbell, and explain the objective for each test.

(b) Describe substantive procedures the auditor should perform to confirm Tinkerbell's year-end receivables balance.

(c) Identify and explain controls Tinkerbell should implement to reduce the risk of fraud occurring again and, for each control, describe how it would mitigate the risk.

(d) Describe substantive procedures the auditor should perform to confirm Tinkerbell's revenue.

Source: Adapted from ACCA Audit and Assurance (International), Paper F8, June 2011.

CASE STUDY—CLOUD 9

Answer the following questions based on the information presented for Cloud 9 in Appendix B of this book and in the current and earlier chapters. You should also consider your answers to the case study questions in earlier chapters.

The worksheet you completed for the case study question in chapter 8 includes your estimates of the overall risk assessment (ORA) and the acceptable detection risk (DR) in the sales to cash receipts process.

Required

Based on your ORA and DR estimates, design substantive audit procedures for Cloud 9 that would address the DR for the accounts recceivable and sales accounts.

RESEARCH QUESTION 9.1

Irregularities in accounting

In the early 2000s, several large corporations such as Enron, WorldCom, and Nortel collapsed because of corporate greed, bad business practices, and accounting irregularities. Others, such as Bristol-Myers Squibb, Xerox, and Harris Scarfe, were forced to restate their earnings, in some cases over a number of years, because of inflation of sales and other accounting irregularities.

Required

Investigate two of the above companies in depth and determine how the irregularities were perpetrated and the reasons behind them. Also determine, to the extent possible, why these irregularities were not found by the auditors during their audits of sales revenue and receivables, and other related areas of the audit.

SOLUTIONS TO MULTIPLE-CHOICE QUESTIONS

1. d, 2. c, 3. c, 4. d, 5. c, 6. a, 7. b, 8. a, 9. a, 10. c.

CHAPTER 10

Auditing purchases, payables, and payroll

LEARNING OBJECTIVES

After studying this chapter, you should be able to:

1 identify the audit objectives applicable to purchases, payables, and payroll

2 describe the functions and control procedures normally found in information systems for processing purchase, payment, and purchase adjustment transactions

3 describe the functions and control procedures normally found in information systems for payroll transactions

4 discuss considerations relevant to determining the audit strategy for purchases, payables, and payroll

5 indicate the factors relevant to determining an acceptable level of detection risk for the audit of purchases, payables, and payroll

6 design a substantive audit program for purchases, payables, and payroll.

AUDITING AND ASSURANCE STANDARDS

CANADIAN	INTERNATIONAL
	International Framework for Assurance Engagements
CAS 315 *Identifying and Assessing the Risks of Material Misstatement through Understanding the Entity and Its Environment*	ISA 315 *Identifying and Assessing the Risks of Material Misstatement through Understanding the Entity and Its Environment*
CAS 500 *Audit Evidence*	ISA 500 *Audit Evidence*

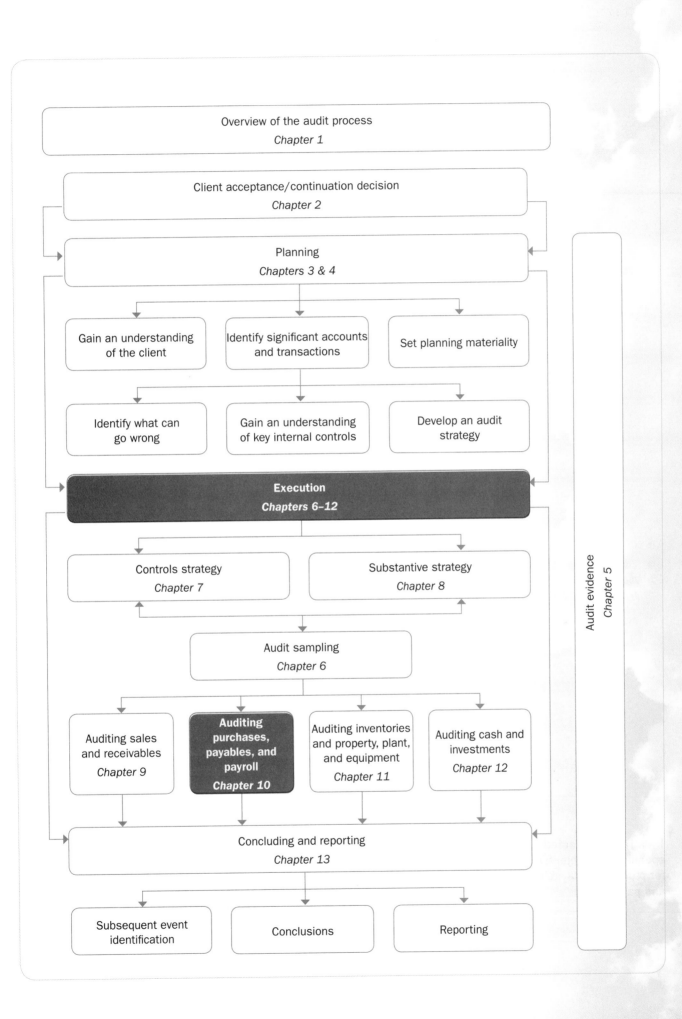

Overview of the audit process
Chapter 1

Client acceptance/continuation decision
Chapter 2

Planning
Chapters 3 & 4

Gain an understanding of the client

Identify significant accounts and transactions

Set planning materiality

Identify what can go wrong

Gain an understanding of key internal controls

Develop an audit strategy

Execution
Chapters 6–12

Controls strategy
Chapter 7

Substantive strategy
Chapter 8

Audit sampling
Chapter 6

Auditing sales and receivables
Chapter 9

Auditing purchases, payables, and payroll
Chapter 10

Auditing inventories and property, plant, and equipment
Chapter 11

Auditing cash and investments
Chapter 12

Concluding and reporting
Chapter 13

Subsequent event identification

Conclusions

Reporting

Audit evidence
Chapter 5

Cloud 9

When Sharon Gallagher, the manager of the audit team, next meets with Josh Thomas, she explains that the audit team will now focus on the purchases, payables, and payroll cycles. These are significant cycles as they relate to the purchases and payments for the acquisition of goods and services from outside suppliers, and the payroll that relates to the acquisition of and payment for labour services from employees. Together, they represent the major expenditures of most entities and this holds true for Cloud 9. Sharon continues to explain that there are similarities between accounts payable and payroll in that both involve the acquisition of resources and payment to the suppliers. However, the nature of the employment contract between the entity and its employees is such that payroll transactions are processed separately, including the payment of salaries and wages.

AUDIT PROCESS IN FOCUS

The purpose of this chapter is to examine the audit of:

- the account balances of accounts payable and of accruals related to payroll
- the classes of transactions of purchases, payments, and payroll

This chapter follows a similar structure to that of the previous chapter on auditing sales and receivables. It begins with the identification of the audit objectives for each of the financial statement assertions that apply to purchases, payments, and payroll and to the accounts payable and accrued payroll liability balances. In the rest of the chapter, the focus is on the audit process—from obtaining an understanding of the internal control structure, through the assessment of the inherent risks and control risks to the design and execution of substantive procedures for the purchases, payables, and payroll processes.

10.1 AUDIT OBJECTIVES

① Identify the audit objectives applicable to purchases, payables, and payroll.

In the auditing of purchases, payables, and payroll, the key issues are to ensure the following:

- The purchases are all recorded and are not understated. (This is related to the financial statement assertions of completeness and also accuracy and cut-off.)
- The payables that are derived from the purchases are all fully recorded in the accounts as a liability. (This is related to the financial statement assertions of completeness and also valuation and allocation.)
- The payroll expense has been properly recorded and the associated deductions for income tax, employee benefits, and related liabilities are properly recorded as liabilities. (These are related to the financial statement assertions related to transactions of completeness, occurrence, and accuracy as well as assertions related to balances of completeness, existence, and valuation and allocation.)

The audit objectives for purchases, payables, and payroll relate to obtaining sufficient appropriate evidence about each significant financial statement assertion for the applicable transactions and balances.

Table 10.1 lists the main objectives for each assertion that apply in most audits of these transactions and balances.

TABLE 10.1 **Selected specific audit objectives for purchases, payables, and payroll**

CLASSES OF TRANSACTION OBJECTIVES	
Occurrence (**OE**)	Recorded purchase transactions represent goods and services received during the period under audit (**OE1**).
	Recorded payment transactions represent payments made during the period to suppliers and creditors (**OE2**).
	Recorded payroll expenses relate to employee services received in the period (**OE3**).

(continued)

TABLE 10.1 **Selected specific audit objectives for purchases, payables, and payroll** (continued)

Completeness (**C**)	All purchase transactions that occurred during the period and that should have been recorded have been recorded (**C1**).
	All payments that occurred during the period and that should have been recorded have been recorded (**C2**).
	Recorded payroll expenses include all such expenses incurred during the year (**C3**).
Accuracy (**AV**)	Purchase, payment, and payroll transactions are properly (accurately) recorded (**AV1**).
Cut-off (**CO**)	Particularly relevant to transactions around the year end; all purchases, cash payments, purchase adjustments, and payroll transactions arising before the period end are recorded in the current period and those arising after the period end are included in the next accounting period (**CO1**).
Classification (**PD**)	All purchases (**PD1**), payments (**PD2**), and payroll transactions (**PD3**) are recorded in the correct accounts.
ACCOUNT BALANCE OBJECTIVES	
Existence (**OE**)	Recorded accounts payable represent amounts owed by the entity at the end of the reporting period (**OE4**).
	Accrued payroll liability balances represent amounts owed at the end of the reporting period (**OE5**).
Rights and obligations (**RO**)	Accounts payable (**RO1**) and accrued payroll liabilities (**RO2**) are liabilities of the entity at the end of the reporting period.
Completeness (**C**)	Accounts payable include all amounts owed by the entity to suppliers of goods and services at the end of the reporting period (**C4**).
	Accrued payroll liabilities include all amounts owed in respect of payroll and deductions at the end of the reporting period (**C5**).
Valuation and allocation (**AV**)	Accounts payable represent gross amounts due to suppliers and agree with the sum of the accounts payable in the accounts payable subsidiary ledger (**AV2**).
	Accrued payroll liabilities are stated at the appropriate amounts (**AV3**).
	Related expense balances conform to applicable accounting standards (**AV4**).
PRESENTATION AND DISCLOSURE OBJECTIVES (PD)	
Occurrence and rights and obligations	Disclosed purchase and payroll events have occurred and pertain to the entity (**PD4**).
Completeness	Accounts payable, accrued payroll liabilities, and related expenses are properly identified and included in the financial statements (**PD5**).
	Disclosures pertaining to commitments, contingent liabilities, and related party creditors are adequate (**PD6**).
Classification and understandability	Purchase cycle and payroll information is appropriately presented and information disclosed is clearly expressed (**PD7**).
Accuracy and valuation	Purchase cycle and payroll information is disclosed accurately and at appropriate amounts (**PD8**).

To achieve each audit objective, the auditor uses a combination of tests of controls and substantive procedures (as determined by the audit strategy adopted). The procedures are much the same as those illustrated for sales and receivables in chapter 9.

Each audit objective is numbered (**OE1**, **OE2**, **C1**, **AV4**, and so on) in table 10.1. Using this numbering system, we can reference specific controls and audit procedures described in this chapter to the applicable audit objective. Some of the assertions for the classes of transactions are combined with account balance assertions in the numbering system: occurrence and exist-ence (**OE**), completeness for transactions and completeness for balances (**C**), accuracy and valu-ation and allocation (**AV**), and classification with presentation and disclosure assertions (**PD**). These combinations reflect the fact that audit evidence obtained in relation to an assertion for transactions will also give some comfort for account balance assertions. For example, an audit test that gives some comfort to the auditor that a sales transaction has occurred will also give some comfort that a valid receivable exists, hence occurrence and existence are combined.

Note that table 10.1 summarizes assertions for both classes of transactions audit objectives and account balance audit objectives. Greater detail regarding assertions is provided in paragraph A111 of CAS 315 *Identifying and Assessing the Risks of Material Misstatement through Understanding the Entity and Its Environment*.

Cloud 9

During Josh's discussion with Sharon, he was surprised to learn that the assertions most at risk for the purchase and payable cycles are completeness and cut-off. He thought the audit team would perform procedures that would focus on the existence and occurrence assertions as they did for the revenue and receivables cycle. He thought that because both cycles are significant, they would have the same audit focus. Sharon explained the most significant risk with the payables and purchases at Cloud 9 is an understatement of these accounts, so the audit team will concentrate their audit work on what may be missing altogether or recorded in the next accounting period in error, therefore focusing on completeness and cut-off.

Not only is Josh surprised, he wonders how he will look for something that may be missing.

BEFORE YOU GO ON

10.1.1   What are three key issues auditors face when auditing the purchases and payables cycle?

10.1.2   What risk is of particular concern when auditing payroll?

10.1.3   Define the audit objective of cut-off with respect to purchases and payables.

10.2 THE PROCESS FOR PURCHASE TRANSACTIONS

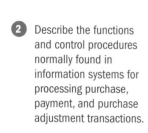

2   Describe the functions and control procedures normally found in information systems for processing purchase, payment, and purchase adjustment transactions.

The following sections look at purchase and payment transactions in detail, including the related information systems and control procedures. Where purchases are made on credit, the informa-tion system needs to maintain records of the accounts payable. The discussions here are designed to give an understanding of the purchasing system; in the later sections of this chapter, we consider how this affects the audit approach. The discussion in this section is based on a company buying goods; however, much of the commentary can easily be adapted to purchases of services.

10.2.1 Purchase transactions

As illustrated in figure 10.1, the processing of purchase transactions involves the following func-tions, a number of which are done electronically:

- requisitioning goods and services
- preparing purchase orders
- receiving the goods
- storing goods received in inventory

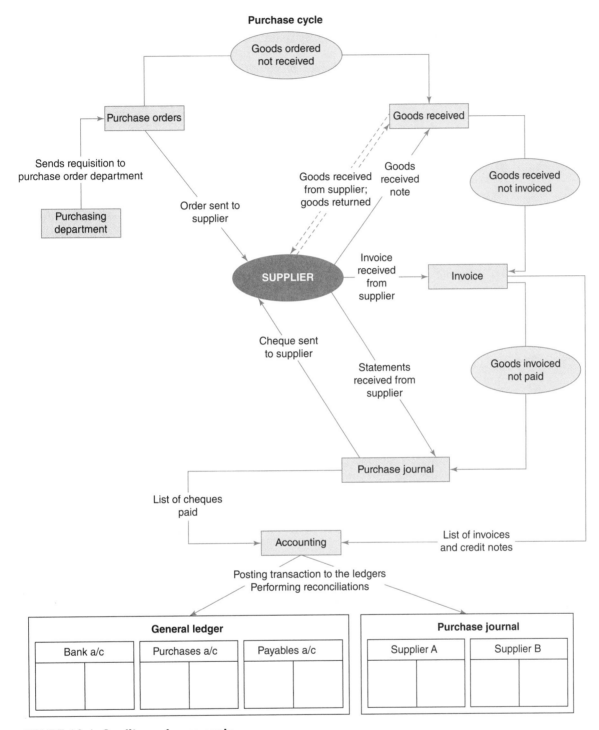

FIGURE 10.1 **Credit purchases cycle**

- checking and approving the supplier's invoice
- recording the liability

When practicable, each of these functions should be assigned to a different individual or department for an appropriate segregation of duties. In such cases, the work of one employee or department can provide an independent check on the accuracy of the work of another.

Requisitioning goods and services

Purchase requisitions (see Appendix A, figure 10A) may originate from the warehouse for inventory or from any department for other items. For inventory items, computerized inventory

purchase order

purchase requisition a form issued by authorized personnel detailing the goods and services required

records are often programmed to issue requisitions automatically when predetermined reorder levels are reached. Where this is the case, controls should be in place to restrict access and adjustments to the reorder point. For purchases other than inventory replenishment, requisitioning authority is granted to specific people. This authority is usually restricted to the value and types of goods and services applicable to the person's function and level of authority. A stationery clerk may requisition sundry stationery supplies, for example, but only the office manager may requisition a photocopier service contract. Special procedures usually apply for requisitioning plant and equipment or for entering into lease contracts. Purchase requisition forms may be prepared manually but are normally generated electronically by authorized employees, or triggered by predetermined criteria programmed into an entity's computer system. The requisition normally indicates the general ledger account coding for the purchase, which the person making the requisition has budgetary responsibility over.

Purchase requisitions are usually pre-numbered within each originating department as a control over outstanding requisitions to ensure that goods requisitioned are duly ordered and received. The purchase requisition represents the start of the transaction trail of documentary evidence in support of management's assertion as to the occurrence of purchase transactions. Thus, it provides evidence that relates to the specific audit objective of occurrence (**OE1**) in table 10.1.

Preparing purchase orders

purchase order a form showing the description of the goods, the quantity ordered, and other relevant data. This is signed by the purchasing officer as evidence of the approval of the purchase.

The purchasing department should issue **purchase orders** (see Appendix A, figure 11A) only on the receipt of requisitions properly approved by an employee who has appropriate requisitioning authority (except for programmed inventory replenishment). Before placing an order, purchasing department personnel should find the best source of supply and, for major items, obtain competitive bids.

Separating requisitioning from ordering achieves two controls. It restricts the opportunity for those making requisitions to issue fraudulent orders, such as for goods for their own use. Purchasing department personnel are less likely to issue improper orders because they do not normally have access to goods delivered. The second control is improved efficiency through the centralization of purchasing in a specialized department. The purchasing department is better able to negotiate more favourable terms and prices and, by amalgamating orders, can obtain better volume discounts.

Purchase orders should contain a precise description of the goods and services required, quantities, price, delivery instructions, and the supplier's name and address. Purchase orders should be pre-numbered and signed or electronically approved by an authorized purchasing officer. The original is sent to the supplier and copies are distributed internally to the receiving department, the accounting department, and the requisitioner.

The purchase orders also become part of the transaction trail of documentary evidence that supports the occurrence assertion for purchase transactions (**OE1**). A file of unfilled purchase orders is generally maintained on the computer or as hard copy. A subsequent independent check on the disposition of purchase orders to determine that the goods and services were received and recorded relates to the completeness assertion for purchase transactions (**C1**).

Receiving the goods

A valid purchase order represents the authorization for the receiving department to accept goods delivered by suppliers. The quantity ordered is sometimes not displayed to ensure that receiving clerks will make careful counts when the goods are received. Receiving department personnel should compare the goods received with the description of the goods on the purchase order, count the goods, and inspect them for damage. Deliveries of unordered goods should be refused.

The segregation of receiving from requisitioning and purchasing prevents those making requisitions from ordering goods directly from suppliers. It also prevents the purchasing department from gaining access to goods improperly ordered.

receiving report a form issued by the receiving department detailing the description and quantity of the goods delivered by the supplier

A pre-numbered **receiving report** should be prepared for each delivery. The receiving report (manual or electronic) is an important document in supporting the occurrence assertion for purchase transactions (**OE1**) because it provides evidence that the goods have been received. A copy of the receiving report is forwarded to the accounts payable. A subsequent periodic independent check on the sequence of pre-numbered receiving reports (to determine that a supplier's invoice has been recorded for each) relates to the completeness assertion (**C1**).

Storing goods received in inventory

On delivery of the goods, the receiving clerks should obtain a signed copy of the **packing slip** (see Appendix A, figure 12A) and keep a copy in the receiving department. This provides further evidence for the occurrence assertion for the purchase transaction (**OE1**). The signed receipt also establishes subsequent accountability for the purchased goods. The physical safekeeping of inventory and the maintenance of records of inventory quantities are considered in chapter 11.

packing slip a form that details the quantity of goods delivered to the entity. This is signed by the receiver as evidence that the goods were actually received.

Checking and approving the supplier's invoice

For goods and services supplied on credit, the supplier is usually instructed by the purchase order to send the invoice directly to the entity's accounting department. Before recording **suppliers' invoices** (see Appendix A, figure 13A), the department checks and approves them. Procedures applicable to this function include:

suppliers' invoice a form issued by the supplier detailing the goods or services supplied and the amount owing

- numbering suppliers' invoices on receipt so that subsequent checks of numerical continuity can confirm that all invoices are recorded (**C1**)
- establishing the three-way match of the details of suppliers' invoices with the related receiving reports and purchase orders to ensure that all invoices relate to valid purchase transactions (**OE1**)
- determining the mathematical accuracy of the suppliers' invoices (**AV1**)
- coding the account distributions on the suppliers' invoices (i.e., indicating the asset and expense accounts to be debited) (**AV1, PD1**)
- approving invoices for payment by having an authorized person sign the invoices (**OE1**)
- preparing a daily prelist of suppliers' invoices approved for payment (**OE1, C1, AV1**)

A common practice is to stamp a grid on the supplier's invoice. The grid has boxes in which to record the serial numbers of purchase orders and receiving reports, the account codes, and the initials of the clerk performing the various checks. Details of the supplier's invoice and subsequent checks for accuracy and validity can all be processed electronically.

Other kinds of supporting documentation (such as copies of contracts) may be required when the invoice relates to certain types of services or to leased assets. In other cases, such as for monthly electricity bills, the supplier's invoice alone may suffice because there is no purchase order and receiving report. Other forms of verification will be required, such as a check of the reasonableness of electricity bills against previous charges.

Unpaid suppliers' invoices and supporting documentation are held in a file in the accounts payable department pending their subsequent payment. Properly approved suppliers' invoices provide the basis for recording purchase transactions.

Recording the liability

Personnel in the accounts payable department either send approved suppliers' invoices in batches to the accounting department or enter the data directly via terminals. Programmed edit checks are made for such matters as valid suppliers and the reasonableness of amounts. When the data for a supplier's invoice are accepted by the computer system, the **accounts payable master file** for that supplier is updated and the invoice is added to the **purchase journal**. Additional controls over the accuracy of the data entry process may include the use of batch totals and exception reports (**OE1, C1, AV1**). The purchase journal is used to update the inventory and general ledger accounts. The update program produces printouts, if required, of the purchase journal and a general ledger summary showing the amounts posted to general ledger accounts.

accounts payable master file a computer file containing details of suppliers, transactions with suppliers, and the balance owing

purchase journal a computer file listing details of all purchase transactions

In the online systems most entities now use, the invoice is entered immediately on receipt, automatically approved by reference to the purchase order and receiving report details, and coded by reference to information recorded on the order. The accounts payable, inventory, and general ledger files are immediately updated. Manual verification is required only if programmed application controls reject the invoice.

Monthly statements received from suppliers should be reconciled with recorded supplier balances. Periodic performance reviews by management—in the form of comparisons of asset, liability, and expense balances with budgeted amounts—can provide a means of both controlling expenditures and detecting misstatements in recorded purchase transactions. For very small purchases, authorized requisitions may be paid out of petty cash or with company-issued credit cards. Limits placed on such cards provide a sufficient safeguard against material loss.

PROFESSIONAL ENVIRONMENT

Be wary of fake invoice fraud

A business receives an invoice that looks genuine. A couple of days later the "supplier" follows up with a phone call for payment. Is it real or fraudulent?

Smaller enterprises are at the greatest risk from fraud. They're the least likely businesses to have dedicated security personnel, and the most likely to lack adequate internal systems and controls to prevent fraud. This makes them the target of scammers around the world, and one of the most common scams is fake invoice fraud.

But even large companies are at risk of invoice fraud. Financial services firm Citigroup announced that it paid $400 million in fake invoices over several years from a supplier to its Mexican subsidiary.

It is recommended that businesses take these measures to prevent fake invoice fraud:

· If a fraudulent invoice is received, do not pay it.
· Check all paperwork closely, watching especially for invoices and cheques from unusual places.
· Scrutinize any solicitation that attempts to collect on products or services outside the scope of the normal routine.
· Confirm orders with the firm and/or with whoever authorized the purchase.

· Avoid payment until it is confirmed that the goods and/or services were ordered and/or received.
· If a cheque is payable to the organization, read and understand all of the terms listed on the back of the cheque before cashing it.
· Contact the relevant governmental authorities and the local Better Business Bureau to check out a suspicious company, invoice, or cheque.

The best defence against fake invoice fraud for any business is to institute strict purchasing and accounting controls. Document every purchase by issuing a signed purchase order to the supplier. The handling of invoices should be centralized and payment authorizations checked carefully before any payments are made. Businesses must protect themselves against scammers; once invoice fraudsters get their hands on a company's money, it's usually gone forever.

Source: Matt Levine, "Citi Paid $400 Million in Fake Invoices," BloombergView, February 28, 2014; "Be Wary of Fake Invoice Fraud," www.suite101.com, viewed December 17, 2010; "Fraud: Fake Invoices Targeted at Businesses," Office of the Minnesota Attorney General, www.ag.state.mn.us.

10.2.2 Payment transactions

In this section, we consider the common documents and records, functions, and control procedures for payment transactions.

The two payment functions are:

- paying the liability
- recording the payments

The same department or individual should not perform both these functions.

Paying the liability

The accounts payable department is responsible for ensuring that suppliers' invoices are processed for payment on their due dates. Payment is normally required within 30 days. Where early payment discounts are available, relevant invoices should be paid within the discount period.

Payments are usually by cheque, or by electronic funds transfer for regular suppliers. The computer system can be programmed to extract the payments due from the accounts payable master file, produce the cheques and a **cheque register**, and update the accounts payable master file. Before being sent, the cheques are reviewed by the accounts payable department, and they are matched with the supporting documents before being forwarded for signing. This may now be done electronically; however, controls must be adequate. The signatory should maintain password control over the electronic signature and scrutinize the list of cheques to be signed. In such systems, cheques must be mailed directly from the computer department and not returned to the accounts payable department. With online banking, electronic funds transfer details may be electronically transmitted to the bank. Access controls should restrict this function to approved signatories.

cheque register a listing of all cheques issued

Controls over the preparation and signing of cheques and electronic fund transfers and related specific audit objectives include the following:

- Authorized personnel in the finance department who otherwise have no responsibility for initiating or processing purchase transactions should be responsible for signing the cheques or controlling the use of electronic signatures (**OE2**) (see table 10.1).

- Authorized cheque signers should determine that each cheque or bank transfer is accompanied by properly approved suppliers' invoices, and that the name of the payee and amount on the payment agree with details on the invoice (**OE2**, **AV1**).

- The suppliers' invoices and supporting documents should be cancelled to prevent resubmission for duplicate payment (**OE2**).

- The cheque signer should control the mailing of the cheques or initiation of the bank transfers to reduce the risk of theft or alterations (**OE2**).

- Where cheques are used, none should be made payable to "cash" or "bearer" and no blank cheques should be issued (**OE2**).

- Pre-numbered cheques should be used (**C2**).

- Access to blank cheques and to electronic signatures should be limited to authorized personnel (**C2**).

Cheques generally include a perforated attachment known as a **remittance advice** (see Appendix A, figure 14A), which identifies the serial numbers of the invoice(s) being paid. Alternatively, copies of the supplier's statement or remittance advice can be enclosed with the cheques mailed to suppliers, or other identifying details can be used where electronic funds transfers are made.

remittance advice a form accompanying cash or cheques paid by a customer, indicating the customer's details and the items being paid

Recording the payments

The cheque register in a computer system is created when cheques or electronic transfers are prepared. When updated, the program produces the cash payments journal and a general ledger summary, and also updates the master files.

Controls over the recording of payments include:

- an independent check by an accounting supervisor of the agreement of the amounts journalized and posted to the accounts payable ledger with the cheque register received from the treasurer (**OE2**, **C2**, **AV1**)

- independently prepared bank reconciliations (**OE2**, **C2**, **AV1**)

Cloud 9

Josh has completed his interview with Carla and he feels he understands the purchasing and payables process at Cloud 9. Carla explained that at Cloud 9, the purchasing process starts when goods or services are needed and a purchase requisition is prepared by the manager of the department requesting the goods. The approved purchase requisition is sent to the purchaser, who must contact at least three different approved suppliers for price quotes, as it is the purchaser's job to secure the best possible quality of goods for the best price. Once the best price is secured and the order placed, the system creates a sequential pre-numbered purchase order, where the quantity ordered and the agreed-upon price is entered. A copy of this purchase order is automatically sent to an open purchase order folder, which the accounts payable department has access to. This provides confirmation that the goods were approved for purchase.

When the goods are delivered to Cloud 9, the receiver counts and records the quantity of goods actually received on a pre-numbered sequential receiving report created by the system. Once the receiving report is completed, the system "attaches" a copy of it to the purchase order. This signals to the accounts payable department that Cloud 9 now has a liability that needs to get recorded in the books.

All supplier invoices are sent directly to the accounts payable department. The invoice must refer to the pre-numbered purchase order, which allows the accounts payable department to easily make the three-way match between the purchase order (indicates authorization), the receiving report (indicates the quantity of goods received), and the invoice details. If there is a three-way match, the invoice is posted to the general ledger and accounts payable sub-ledger.

At the end of each month, Cloud 9 asks each of its suppliers to send monthly statements highlighting any overdue or unpaid invoices. The suppliers' statements are then reconciled to the accounts payable sub-ledger and any discrepancies are followed up. Once such discrepancies are resolved, Cloud 9 prepares the cheques and the payment is processed and recorded.

Josh is in the middle of documenting this process, when he receives a call from Sharon. Sharon tells him they now have an appointment with Carla and Cloud 9's Human Resources Manager, Lorraine Murray, for 4 p.m. today. They need to meet to discuss the processes Cloud 9 has in place over its payroll, including the hiring of employees, the authorizing of payroll changes, and the timekeeping, preparing, recording, and processing of the payroll. Josh sighs, as he foresees this will be a late night.

BEFORE YOU GO ON

10.2.1 List the six steps involved in the purchasing and accounts payable cycle.

10.2.2 What is a packing slip?

10.2.3 What are three controls an entity should have in place over the preparation and signing of cheques and electronic funds transfers?

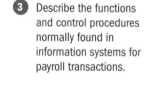

3 Describe the functions and control procedures normally found in information systems for payroll transactions.

10.3 THE PROCESS FOR PAYROLL TRANSACTIONS

Payroll relates to payment for the services of employees. An entity's payroll transactions include salaries and hourly wages, commissions, bonuses, and employee benefits (e.g., paid holidays, sick leave). In this section, we focus on employees paid hourly. Most entities have a detailed information system and related internal control procedures for recording labour services (typically in the form of hours worked) and ensuring that payment is made only to current employees in respect of labour services actually provided. Figure 10.2 gives an outline of the process, which will be discussed in detail below.

The relevant functions for payroll transactions are those of:

- hiring employees
- authorizing payroll changes
- preparing attendance and timekeeping data
- preparing the payroll
- recording the payroll
- paying the payroll

Each function is explained below.

10.3.1 Hiring employees

Employees are hired by the human resources department. All approved positions are documented on a **personnel authorization form**, which should indicate the job classification and the starting wage rate for all positions. In the system, data on new employees are entered in the **personnel master file**. Access to data entry to this file is restricted by password to authorized individuals in the personnel department. Periodically, a computer-generated log of all changes to the master file is printed and independently checked by a personnel manager not involved in entering the data into the computer. One copy of the personnel authorization form is placed in the employee's **personnel file** in the personnel department. Another copy is sent to the payroll department.

Segregating the functions of personnel and payroll reduces the risk of payments to fictitious employees because only the personnel department may add new employees to the personnel

personnel authorization form a form issued by the personnel department indicating the job classification and wage rate for all approved positions

personnel master file a computer file containing details of employees, such as approved wage rate and date of hiring

personnel file a file maintained by the personnel department recording details of individual employees, such as the job classification, wage rate, and date of hiring

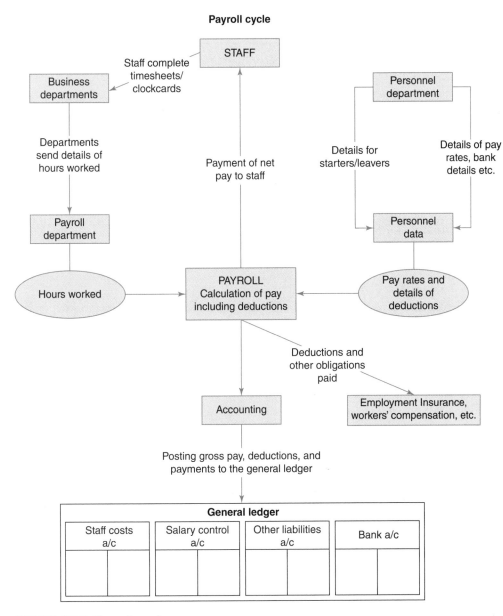

FIGURE 10.2 **Payroll cycle**

master file and only the payroll department may process the payment of wages (**OE3, RO1**). This segregation of functions is also an important control in the next function—authorizing payroll changes. Thus, personnel department employees cannot benefit from falsifying personnel records, and payroll department employees can process payroll only for employees listed in the personnel records and at the wage rates specified therein.

10.3.2 Authorizing payroll changes

An employee's supervisor may initiate the request for a change in job classification (or a wage rate increase). However, all changes should be authorized in writing by the personnel department before being entered in the personnel data master file. Other controls over entering the changes in the computer and distributing the change forms are the same as those for new employees. These controls over payroll changes help to ensure the accuracy of the payroll (**RO1, AV1**).

The personnel department should also issue a **termination notice** on completion of an individual's employment. It is vital that the payroll department be promptly notified of such terminations to prevent payment continuing to be made to employees after they have left (**OE3**).

termination notice a form issued by the personnel department to document the termination of an employee

10.3.3 Preparing attendance and timekeeping data

In most organizations, each employee signs in for the purpose of recording hours of attendance at work by electronic means, where such recording is necessary. Other organizations employ things such as punch clocks, card swipes, or finger scans. These controls ensure that payments are made only for hours worked (**OE3, RO1**).

10.3.4 Preparing the payroll

Time-recording details are manually or electronically entered into the payroll file from approved employee time records, which may be online or manually compiled. The resulting payroll data are then used in preparing the payroll.

The payroll transactions are subjected to supervisory review and approval, which includes a check for a valid employee number and a limit or reasonableness check on the hours worked. The calculation of the payroll is performed and recorded in the **payroll transaction file**, which details the wage payments to employees.

payroll transaction file a file recording details of hours worked, wage rates, and wages paid per employee

10.3.5 Recording the payroll

Using the calculated gross pay, deductions, and net pay for each employee, the data are used to update the employee payroll records and accumulate totals for the payroll journal entry that is generated and entered in the general ledger master file at the end of the run. A **payroll register** is also produced, which contains details of wages paid, withholding taxes, and a cumulative record of wages paid. The following printed outputs of this run can be produced if required for control purposes:

payroll register a document that contains details of wages paid, withholding taxes, and a cumulative record of wages paid per employee, per department, and in total

- an exceptions report
- a copy of the payroll register that is returned to the payroll department
- a second copy of the payroll register and pre-numbered payroll cheques or details of electronic direct bank transfers that are sent to the finance office (or pay slips and a cheque for total net pay if wages are paid in cash)
- a general ledger summary that is sent to accounting, showing the payroll entry generated by the payroll program

Proper review of each of these outputs by the appropriate personnel contributes to control over misstatements (**OE3, C3, AV1**).

It is common practice for a senior accounting officer to approve the payroll details before payroll cheques or bank transfers are prepared. In smaller entities, the authorizing officer could verify payroll by reconciling it with the previous period's payroll, allowing for hirings, terminations, or changes in hours worked. In any event, the payroll should be independently checked against personnel records at regular intervals.

10.3.6 Paying the payroll and protecting unclaimed wages

In the preceding section, we explained that the payroll cheques and a copy of the payroll register are sent to the treasurer's or chief accountant's office where these functions are commonly performed. Applicable controls include the following:

- Finance office personnel should check the agreement of the names and amounts on cheques or bank transfers with payroll register entries (**OE3, C3, AV1**).
- Payroll cheques and bank transfers should be signed or authorized by finance office personnel not involved in preparing or recording the payroll.
- Payroll cheques, where used, should be distributed to employees by finance office personnel not involved in preparing or recording the payroll, who should require proper identification of employees (**OE3, AV1**).
- Any unclaimed payroll cheques should be stored in a safe or vault in the finance office (**OE3, C3**). Another important control over paying the payroll in many large entities is the use of an imprest payroll bank account on which all payroll cheques or electronic transfers are drawn. This account is funded with the amount of net pay. Any errors in preparing payroll cheques or electronic direct bank transfers or deliberate falsification would soon be detected because the amount paid in would exceed the account balance, causing the bank to

refuse acceptance (**OE3**, **AV3**). It is now common practice for entities to pay wages by direct deposit to employee bank accounts, eliminating the need for cheques and the associated risks of their misuse.

PROFESSIONAL ENVIRONMENT

Employee fraud: How you can avoid getting stung?

In Australia, millions of dollars disappeared from the books of electrical goods retailer Clive Peeters. The "accounting discrepancies" mystery was solved when a female payroll officer allegedly admitted to defrauding the company of around AUS$20 million.

The employee falsified entries in the company's payroll accounts, transferred cash from Clive Peeters' bank accounts to her own account, and used the money to buy real estate worth just under AUS$20 million. The legal action came just days after Clive Peeters suspended its shares from trade on the Australian Stock Exchange after warning it had discovered discrepancies in its payroll accounts.

You don't have to go as far as Australia, because similar frauds can be found here in Canada. For example, Adelle Sharpe, a payroll manager at a medium-sized manufacturing firm near Winnipeg, was accused of defrauding her employer of $750,000, to pay off her gambling losses. Ms. Sharpe, a decade-long employee, was described as hardworking, reliable, and loyal in her performance reviews. However perceived by her employer, Ms. Sharpe set up two fictitious employees in the company's payroll system, and deposited the paycheques into a bank account near her home. This scheme went undetected because she was responsible for both processing and receiving the employee payroll without effective oversight. As the fraud went on undetected, Ms. Sharpe also began paying herself unauthorized overtime to the tune of 1,500 hours, as opposed to the 50 hours of overtime she actually did work. It was this excessive claim to overtime that eventually led to her being caught.

How can a company prevent and detect such frauds?

- Ensure an adequate segregation of duties. Payroll preparation, authorization, and distribution should be performed by different individuals.
- Regularly monitor payroll records for unusual "accounting" adjustments.
- Increase the use of direct deposit.
- Review the payroll records for duplicate names or incorrect or invalid social insurance numbers.
- Conduct surprise payroll audits to ensure all employees exist and have a payroll file.
- Perform analytics on payroll expenses including month-to-month, quarter-to-quarter, and year-to-year variances.
- Limit changes to payroll master file data to only authorized personnel.
- Reconcile payroll expenses to the payroll records and the authorized amounts on a regular basis and follow up on any identified discrepancies.

Source: "Risk Spotlight: How to Detect and Prevent Employee Fraud," Marsh USA, February 4, 2013; Edward Nagel, "Padding the Payroll: How to Detect and Prevent Fraud," *Dialogue*, July/August 2010, www.payroll.ca; James Thomson, "Clive Peeters Hit by $20 Million Employee Fraud—How You Can Avoid Getting Stung," SmartCompany.com.au, August 12, 2009; Edward Nagel, "The Payroll Payoff" *CA Magazine*, May 2004.

Cloud 9

After a late night the previous evening, Josh arrives at Cloud 9 ready to start documenting the payroll process. Now that he understands the processes over the purchases, payables, and payroll at Cloud 9, he is ready to assess the inherent risks and control risks and design the auditing procedures to address those risks.

BEFORE YOU GO ON

10.3.1 List the six steps involved in the payroll cycle.

10.3.2 What is a payroll register?

10.3.3 What are four controls over paying the payroll?

10.4 AUDIT STRATEGY

The auditor must obtain an understanding of the entity and its environment to assess the inherent and control risks in order to determine the appropriate level of detection risk. This risk assessment will drive the development of the audit strategy, which will direct audit attention to significant risks through a mix of tests of controls and substantive procedures.

 Discuss considerations relevant to determining the audit strategy for purchases, payables, and payroll.

10.4.1 Inherent risk assessment

Purchase and payroll transactions account for the major expenses incurred by a business, and so are a major component in the determination of profit. They also relate to the acquisition of major classes of assets (notably, inventories and plant and equipment). Moreover, the balance in the accounts payable produced by credit purchase transactions as well as the payroll expenses are nearly always material to the balance sheet. Because purchases, payables, and payroll are material for most businesses, the auditor assesses the risk of material misstatement relating to these transactions. This begins with the assessment of the inherent risk.

In assessing inherent risk for purchase and payroll assertions, the auditor should consider factors that could motivate management to misstate expenditure. These may include:

- pressures to understate expenses in order to falsely report the achievement of announced profitability targets or industry norms
- pressures to understate payables in order to report a higher level of working capital in the face of liquidity problems or going-concern doubts

These factors affect mainly the completeness assertion and reduce the acceptable detection risk, particularly in testing for understatement of liabilities. Other factors that may contribute to misstatements include:

- the high volume of transactions, which affects all assertions
- temptations for employees to make unauthorized purchases and payments, or to misappropriate purchased assets, which relate to the occurrence assertion
- contentious accounting issues such as whether a cost should be capitalized or expensed (such as the treatment of repairs and maintenance costs or the classification of a lease as an operating or finance lease), which relate to the valuation assertion
- the complexity of payroll calculations for factory workers whose gross earnings may be based on time and/or productivity, affecting the accuracy of payroll costs

Payroll fraud is a major concern for the auditor. Employees involved in preparing and paying the payroll may process data for fictitious employees or for employees whose services have already been terminated, and then divert the wages for their own use. This affects the auditor's assessment of risk for the occurrence assertion for payroll.

The high volume of transactions, combined with the likely existence of effective control procedures over these transactions, means that it is normally appropriate to adopt a combined audit, particularly in respect to the occurrence and accuracy assertions. For other assertions, the audit strategy may vary with the preliminary assessment of control risk. The volume of transactions, however, means that a combined audit is preferred wherever the assessment of risk can support such a strategy.

Cloud 9

Josh knows that the purchases, payables, and payroll transactions are material in terms of both volume transactions and dollar amounts. Because of the large number of transactions processed during the year, he believes there is a high risk of errors simply happening. Therefore, he assesses the inherent risk for purchases, payables, and payroll as high for Cloud 9. He contemplates what the control risk assessment will be.

10.4.2 Control risk assessment

Assessment of control risk is normally done in two phases. On obtaining an understanding of the internal control structure, the auditor forms a preliminary assessment of control risk.

Where the design effectiveness of control risk is assessed as low, tests of the operating effectiveness of controls are included in the audit program to confirm the preliminary assessment. Tests of controls for each of the three transaction classes are described in the following paragraphs.

Purchase transactions

Table 10.2 contains a partial listing of potential misstatements, necessary controls, potential tests of the operating effectiveness of those controls, and the specific transaction class audit objective for purchases to which each belongs.

Tests of operating effectiveness

The extent of tests of the operating effectiveness of controls will vary inversely with the auditor's preliminary assessment of control risk. Statistical or non-statistical attribute sampling procedures

TABLE 10.2 **Control risk assessment considerations—purchase transactions**

FUNCTION	WHAT CAN GO WRONG	NECESSARY CONTROL	POSSIBLE TEST OF OPERATING EFFECTIVENESS	RELEVANT CLASS OF TRANSACTIONS AUDIT OBJECTIVE (FROM TABLE 10.1)				
				OE1	C1	AV1	CO	PD1
Requisitioning goods and services	Goods may be requisitioned for unauthorized purposes.	General and specific authorization procedures	Inquire about procedures. Review documents for evidence of approvals.	✓				
Preparing purchase orders	Purchases may be made for unauthorized purposes.	Approved purchase requisition for each order	Examine purchase orders for approved requisitions.	✓				
Receiving goods	Goods received may not have been ordered.	Approved purchase order for each shipment	Examine receiving report for matching purchase order.	✓				
	Incorrect quantities, damaged goods, or incorrect items may be received.	Receiving clerks to count, inspect, and compare goods received with purchase order	Observe the performance by receiving clerks.	✓				
Storing goods received for inventory	Inventory clerks may deny taking custody of purchased goods.	Signed receipt to be obtained on delivery of goods from receiving to inventory	Inspect signed receipts.	✓				
Approving the invoice	Invoices may be recorded for goods not ordered or received.	Matching of purchase order and receiving report with the supplier's invoice	Examine supporting documentation for invoices.*	✓	✓	✓		✓
Recording the liability	Invoices may be recorded incorrectly or not recorded.	Independent check of agreement of prelist with amounts recorded in purchase journal	Examine evidence of independent check; re-perform independent check.*	✓	✓	✓		✓
		Periodic accounting for pre-numbered receiving reports and purchase orders	Observe procedure; re-perform.		✓		✓	
		Periodic performance reviews by management of reports, comparing actual asset, payable, and expense balances with budgeted amounts	Inquire of management about results of performance reviews; inspect reports.*	✓	✓	✓	✓	✓

*Sometimes performed as a part of dual-purpose tests.

(see chapter 6) may be applicable to certain tests. Note that the direction of testing must be compatible with the specific audit objective to which the test relates—vouching for occurrence and tracing for completeness. Also, recall that some tests, particularly those pertaining to checking and approving suppliers' invoices and recording the liability, may be performed as dual-purpose tests. In these tests (marked with an asterisk in table 10.2), evidence is obtained about the effects (measured in dollars) of processing errors on account balances, as well as about the frequency of deviations from controls. Based on the evidence obtained from procedures to obtain an understanding of the internal control structure and related tests of controls, the auditor makes a final assessment of control risk for each significant assertion related to purchase transactions.

A formal audit program that incorporates several of the tests from table 10.2 is presented in figure 10.3.

The auditor normally uses the computer in performing tests of controls, using techniques similar to those described for sales transactions in chapter 9. In particular, tests of effectiveness must be performed for any controls that serve as the basis for a control risk assessment at a reduced level. This includes making inquiries and inspecting documentation concerning general controls over changes to programs and master files used in processing purchase transactions.

Tests of application controls may include the use of test data to determine whether expected results are produced by the entity's program for accepting and recording data for unpaid suppliers' invoices in circumstances such as the following:

- a missing or invalid supplier number
- a missing or invalid account classification code number
- a missing or unreasonable amount
- a missing due date or payment terms
- alphabetical characters in a numerical field

Examples of other possible computer-assisted audit tests are:

- using generalized audit software or a database program to perform sequence checks and print lists of purchase orders, receiving reports, or invoices whose numbers are missing in designated computer files
- designing, selecting, and evaluating a sample of receiving reports or unpaid invoices

FIGURE 10.3 **Partial audit program for tests of controls—credit purchases**

| Prepared by: _____ Date: _____ |
| Reviewed by: _____ Date: _____ |

Cloud 9 Ltd.
Planned tests of controls — Credit purchases transactions
Year ending December 31, 2016

ASSERTION/TEST OF CONTROLS	W/P REF.	AUDITOR	DATE

Occurrence
1. Observe procedures, including segregation of duties, for:
  · completing purchase orders from requisitions
  · receipt of goods
  · receipt of invoices
  · reconciliation of supplier statements
2. Select a sample of purchase transactions from the purchase journal and verify transaction dates, supplier names, and amounts by vouching entries to the following matching supporting documents:
  · purchase invoices
  · receiving reports
  · approved purchase orders
  · approved purchase requisition			

Completeness			
3. Examine evidence of the use of and accounting for pre-numbered purchase requisitions, purchase orders, receiving reports, and sales invoices. Scan the sequence of sales invoice numbers in the sales journal.			
4. Select a sample of approved purchase requisitions and trace to matching: • approved purchase orders • receiving reports • purchase invoices • entries in the purchase journal			
Accuracy			
5. For the sample in step 2 above, examine evidence of: • an independent check on proper pricing of invoices • an independent check on the trade discounts received • an independent check on the mathematical accuracy of invoices			
6. For purchase invoices processed in batches, examine evidence of an independent check on the agreement of totals for purchase journal entries and amounts posted to supplier accounts with batch totals.			
Cut-off			
7. Obtain the number of the last receiving report for the last goods received for the year, select a sample of receiving reports before this number, and agree: • to purchase invoices dated in the current period • entries in purchase journal before the period end			
8. Following on from step 7, select a sample of the receiving reports for the first goods received in the new fiscal period and agree: • to purchase invoices dated in the next accounting period • the purchase is not recorded in the purchase journal until the following accounting period			

Payment transactions

Table 10.3 contains a partial listing of potential misstatements, necessary controls, possible tests of the operating effectiveness of those controls, and the specific classes of transactions audit objectives for payments to which each belongs. As explained for purchases, the potential misstatements and necessary controls are the basis of a checklist used to assess design effectiveness. Similarly, an audit program for tests of the operating effectiveness of controls for payment transactions can be prepared, based on the potential tests of controls in table 10.3. Possible computer-assisted tests of controls are also similar to those for purchase transactions. Thus, for example, test data can be used to test programmed controls relating to the preparation and recording of cheques or electronic bank transfers to suppliers in payment of liabilities. Computer programs can also be used to design, select, and evaluate an attribute sample for payments.

FUNCTION	WHAT CAN GO WRONG	NECESSARY CONTROL	POSSIBLE TEST OF OPERATING EFFECTIVENESS	RELEVANT CLASS OF TRANSACTIONS AUDIT OBJECTIVE (FROM TABLE 10.1)				
				OE2	C2	AV1	CO	PD2
Paying the liability	Cheques may be issued for unauthorized purchases.	Cheque signers to review supporting documentation for completeness and approval	Observe cheque signers performing independent check of supporting documentation.	✓				
	An invoice may be paid twice.	"Paid" stamp to be placed on the invoice and supporting documents when a cheque is issued	Examine paid invoices for "paid" stamp.	✓				
	A cheque may be altered after being signed.	Cheque signers to mail cheques	Inquire about mailing procedures; observe mailing.			✓		
Recording the payment	A cheque may not be recorded.	Use of, and accounting for, pre-numbered cheques	Examine evidence of use of and accounting for pre-numbered cheques.		✓	✓		
	Errors may be made in recording cheques.	Independent check of agreement of amounts journalized and posted with the cheque register	Observe procedure; re-perform.*	✓	✓	✓	✓	✓
	Cheques may not be recorded promptly.	Periodic independent bank reconciliations	Examine bank reconciliations.*	✓	✓	✓	✓	
		Independent check of dates on cheques with dates recorded	Re-perform independent check.	✓	✓		✓	

*Sometimes performed as a part of dual-purpose tests.

TABLE 10.3 **Control risk assessment considerations—payment transactions**

Payroll transactions

The process of assessing the control risk for payroll transactions begins, as for purchases and payments, with identifying potential misstatements and necessary controls (shown in the second and third columns of table 10.4). Possible tests of controls are shown in the fourth column.

In computer information systems, access controls over changes to personnel data are important. In the testing of controls, test data can be used to test programmed controls relating to the preparation and recording of payroll. Where time recording is computerized, test data can also be used in testing programmed controls over timekeeping.

The auditor knows that misstatements in payroll may result from unintentional errors or fraud. Of particular concern is the risk of overstatement of payroll through:

- payments to fictitious employees
- payments to actual employees for hours not worked
- payments to actual employees at higher than authorized rates

The first two risks relate to the occurrence assertion. The third risk relates to the accuracy assertion.

The risk of understatement (the completeness assertion) is of minimal concern because employees will complain when they are underpaid. Accordingly, many tests of payroll controls are directed at controls that prevent or detect overstatements. The direction of testing for these controls is from the recorded payroll data to source documents; for example, the auditor may

FUNCTION	WHAT CAN GO WRONG	NECESSARY CONTROL	POSSIBLE TEST OF OPERATING EFFECTIVENESS	RELEVANT CLASS OF TRANSACTIONS AUDIT OBJECTIVE (FROM TABLE 10.1)				
				OE3	C3	AV1	CO	PD3
Hiring employees	Fictitious employees may be added to the payroll.	Personnel department authorization for all hiring of new employees	Examine authorization forms for hiring of new employees.	✓				
Authorizing payroll changes	Employees may receive unauthorized rate increases.	Personnel department authorization for all rate changes	Inquire about procedures for authorizing rate changes.			✓		
	Terminated employees may remain on the payroll.	Personnel department notification to payroll department of all terminations	Examine termination notices in payroll department.	✓				
Preparing attendance and timekeeping data	Employees may be paid for hours not worked.	Use of time clock or electronic recording procedures and supervisory approval of time recorded	Observe time-recording procedures; examine supervisory approval procedures.	✓	✓	✓		✓
Preparing the payroll	Payroll data may be lost during submission to computer department.	Batch totals of hours worked prepared by payroll department and verified by data control	Examine evidence of the preparation and use of batch totals.		✓			
	Payroll transactions file may include incorrectly keyed or invalid data.	Edit checks of data on payroll transactions file	Observe data entry procedures; examine the exceptions and control report.*	✓	✓	✓		✓
Recording the payroll	Processing errors may occur in recording the payroll.	Exceptions and control report to be reviewed by data control	Inquire about the preparation and use of the exceptions and control report.*	✓	✓	✓	✓	✓
	Unauthorized changes may be made to payroll data in computer department.	Payroll department comparison of payroll register with original batch transmittal data	Re-perform comparison.*	✓	✓	✓		✓
Paying the payroll and protecting unclaimed wages	Payroll cheques may be distributed to unauthorized recipients.	Employee identification on distribution	Witness distribution of payroll.	✓	✓	✓		✓

*Sometimes performed as a part of dual-purpose tests.

TABLE 10.4 Control risk assessment considerations—payroll transactions

vouch data for a sample of employees in a payroll register to approved clock card data and authorized pay rates and deductions.

Two tests of controls relating to the control risk for the occurrence assertion are the test for terminated employees and witnessing a payroll distribution. The former represents an exception to the normal direction of testing for payroll, in that the auditor selects a sample of termination notices and scans subsequent payroll registers to determine that the terminated employees did not continue to receive paycheques. In witnessing the distribution of payroll cheques or envelopes, the auditor observes that:

- segregation of duties exists between the preparation and payment of the payroll
- each employee is identified by a badge or employee identification card

- each employee receives only one cheque or pay envelope
- there is proper control and disposal of unclaimed wages

Such witnessing of payroll distribution is becoming less common as entities increasingly pay by electronic bank transfers.

10.4.3 Final assessment

Based on the evidence obtained from the procedures to gain an understanding of the internal control structure and related tests of controls, the auditor makes a final assessment of inherent risk and control risk. For each significant audit objective where the assessment of risk is less than high, and this assessment is the basis for adopting a combined audit approach, the auditor must document reasons for this assessment. This assessment enables the auditor to confirm the level of substantive procedures to be performed. The auditor must ensure that control deviations are properly identified and that their implications for the assessment of control risk are properly considered in deciding whether further substantive procedures need to be performed.

Cloud 9

Josh has completed the purchase, payables, and payroll cycle documentation and his risk assessment by assertion and account. He has determined that the inherent risk for the completeness assertion over purchases and payables is high, while the control risk is low. This means Josh believes there is a high risk of misstatement in the purchases and payables accounts but he believes there are controls in place that are effective in preventing and detecting such misstatements. Therefore, he is planning a combined audit, in that he is planning to test the controls over these transactions to confirm his original risk assessment.

He has also considered the risks over the payroll transactions. He has concluded the risk of completeness is low, as employees will generally complain if they are underpaid. However, he is not sure if the same holds true for any employees who are overpaid. Therefore, he has assessed the risk of the occurrence assertion as high. While he fears payments may be made to fictitious employees or actual employees may be paid for hours not worked, he believes there are controls in place that prevent this from happening. Therefore, he again suggests a combined audit approach for the payroll cycle.

He documents his conclusion and wonders if Sharon, the audit manager, will agree with him. He decides to confirm his assessment with her and the audit partner before continuing to plan any substantive work.

BEFORE YOU GO ON

10.4.1 List four inherent risks over the purchases and payables cycle.

10.4.2 What are three controls that should be in place over payment transactions?

10.4.3 What are three possible tests of controls over the payroll cycle?

10.5 DETERMINING AN ACCEPTABLE LEVEL OF DETECTION RISK

5 Indicate the factors relevant to determining an acceptable level of detection risk for the audit of purchases, payables, and payroll.

Accounts payable is usually the largest current liability in a balance sheet and a significant factor in the evaluation of an entity's short-term solvency. Like receivables, it is affected by a high volume of transactions and thus is susceptible to misstatements. However, whereas with receivables the auditor is usually concerned with overstatement, understatement is generally the greatest risk with payables. The reason is that management, if motivated to misrepresent payables, is likely to understate them in order to report a more favourable financial position. Compared with the audit of asset balances, the audit of payables places more emphasis on gathering evidence about the completeness assertion than about the existence assertion. This section focuses on accounts payable arising from purchase transactions and payroll liabilities arising from payroll transactions.

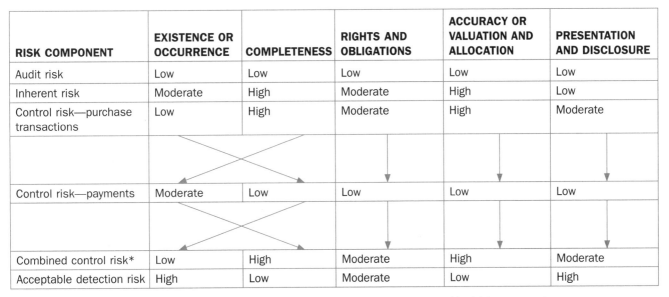

RISK COMPONENT	EXISTENCE OR OCCURRENCE	COMPLETENESS	RIGHTS AND OBLIGATIONS	ACCURACY OR VALUATION AND ALLOCATION	PRESENTATION AND DISCLOSURE
Audit risk	Low	Low	Low	Low	Low
Inherent risk	Moderate	High	Moderate	High	Low
Control risk—purchase transactions	Low	High	Moderate	High	Moderate
Control risk—payments	Moderate	Low	Low	Low	Low
Combined control risk*	Low	High	Moderate	High	Moderate
Acceptable detection risk	High	Low	Moderate	Low	High

*This is the most conservative (highest) of transaction class control risk assessments used as the combined risk assessment.

TABLE 10.5 Correlation of risk components— accounts payable

Accounts payable is affected by purchase transactions that increase the account balance and payment transactions that decrease the balance. Thus, detection risk for payables assertions is affected by the inherent and control risk factors related to both these transaction classes. The auditor considers the audit risk model or a risk matrix, to determine the acceptable level of detection risk in planning the audit. The application of this process for accounts payable is summarized in table 10.5. The risk levels specified in this matrix are illustrative only and would vary based on the entity's circumstances. Furthermore, note that the acceptable detection risk levels shown in table 10.5 indicate the need for more persuasive evidence for the completeness assertion and the accuracy or valuation and allocation assertion than for the other assertions.

Consider the completeness assertions:

- Overall audit risk needs to be low to ensure there is a low risk of giving the wrong audit opinion in relation to completeness.
- The inherent risk has been assessed as high. The auditor understands the entity and its environment and has concluded that there is a high likelihood that completeness errors will arise. (That is, there is a high risk that purchase transactions that actually occurred have been omitted or there are payable balances that exist that have been omitted.)
- The control risk is high, indicating that the auditor has obtained an understanding of the internal controls related to completeness and performed tests of controls on their effectiveness and has concluded that there is a high risk that any errors that do arise (and this is likely, given the high inherent risk identified above) will not be detected and corrected by the internal controls.
- The control risk for completeness is made up of the completeness control risk for purchase transactions (high) and the existence and occurrence control risk for cash payments (moderate). The logic for this is as follows (notice that all of the following lead to potential existence problems in the balances):
  - A *completeness* problem with purchase transactions (a purchase has occurred but not recorded in the accounts) leads to a *completeness* problem in the payables balance. (The purchase was not recorded, so the payable was also omitted.)
  - For cash payments, an *occurrence* problem (cash payments have been recorded but no payment was made) leads to a *completeness* problem in the payables balance. (The payable exists but a payment has been recorded to reduce the payable to zero even though no payment was made.)
- Having assessed inherent risk and control risk, the auditor will now determine the acceptable level of detection risk that will allow the overall audit risk for existence and occurrence

to be low. Given that inherent risk is high and control risk is high, the auditor has determined that a low level of detection risk is appropriate to achieve the required audit risk. This level of detection risk will be used by the auditor to determine the nature, timing, and extent of substantive procedures that need to be performed. The level and detail of substantive procedures performed is a matter of professional judgement. Detection risk has been set low, so the auditor will be required to perform extensive substantive testing.

BEFORE YOU GO ON

10.5.1   What is the biggest risk with payables? Why?

10.5.2   Explain how accounts payable is affected by purchase and payment transactions

10.5.3   Explain how the control risk for completeness is impacted by the control risk assessments for purchases and cash transactions.

10.6 DESIGNING SUBSTANTIVE PROCEDURES

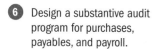

6 Design a substantive audit program for purchases, payables, and payroll.

The general framework for developing audit programs for substantive procedures was explained in previous chapters and it can also be used in designing substantive procedures for payables and payroll liabilities. Table 10.6 lists possible substantive procedures in an audit program developed on this basis. Note that each test in the table is linked to one or more of the specific account balance audit objectives from table 10.1. Also note that multiple procedures are keyed to each account balance audit objective.

The procedures are explained on the following pages, together with comments on how some tests can be tailored based on the acceptable level of detection risk to be achieved.

TABLE 10.6 **Possible substantive procedures for payables assertions**

CATEGORY	SUBSTANTIVE PROCEDURE	ACCOUNT BALANCE AUDIT OBJECTIVE (FROM TABLE 10.1)				
		EO4	C4	RO1	AV2	PD NO.
Initial procedures	1. Perform initial procedures on payables balances and records that will be subjected to further testing. (a) Trace the opening balance for payables to the previous year's working papers. (b) Review activity in the general ledger account for payables and investigate entries that appear unusual in amount or source. (c) Obtain a listing of accounts payable at the end of the reporting period and determine that it accurately represents the underlying accounting records by: • adding the listing and determining agreement with the total of the subsidiary ledger, or the accounts payable master file and the general ledger control account balance • testing the agreement of suppliers and balances on the listing with those included in the underlying accounting records				✓	
Analytical procedures	2. Perform analytical procedures. (a) Determine expectations. (b) Compare current and previous year balances. (c) Calculate significant ratios such as: • gross profit • accounts payable turnover (d) Obtain explanations for unexpected changes. (e) Corroborate explanations.	✓	✓		✓	

(continued)

TABLE 10.6 **Possible substantive procedures for payables assertions** (continued)

CATEGORY	SUBSTANTIVE PROCEDURE	EO4	C4	RO1	AV2	PD NO.
		ACCOUNT BALANCE AUDIT OBJECTIVE (FROM TABLE 10.1)				
Tests of details of transactions	3. Vouch a sample of recorded creditor transactions to supporting documentation.	✓	✓	✓	✓	✓1
	(a) Vouch credits to supporting suppliers' invoices, receiving reports, and purchase orders or other supporting documents.	✓	✓			
	(b) Vouch debits to payments.					
	4. Perform purchases cut-off test.					
	(a) Select a sample of recorded purchase transactions from several days before and after the year end and examine supporting vouchers, suppliers' invoices, and receiving reports to determine that purchases were recorded in the proper period.					
	(b) Observe the number of the last receiving report issued on the last business day of the audit period, and trace a sample of lower and higher numbered receiving reports to related purchase documents to determine whether transactions were recorded in the proper period.					
	(c) Examine subsequent payments between the end of the reporting period and the end of fieldwork and, when related documentation indicates the payment was for an obligation in existence at the end of the reporting period, trace to the accounts payable listing.	✓	✓			
	(d) Investigate unmatched purchase orders, receiving reports, and suppliers' invoices at the year end.					
	5. Perform cut-off test by tracing dates of cleared cheques on the subsequent period's bank statement to dates recorded.					
Tests of details of balances	6. Reconcile accounts payable to monthly statements received by the entity from suppliers.	✓	✓		✓	
	(a) Identify major suppliers by reviewing the accounts payable ledger or the accounts payable master file.					
	(b) Investigate and reconcile differences.	✓	✓	✓	✓	✓4
	7. Confirm payables with major suppliers whose monthly statements are unavailable.		✓			
	8. Perform a search for unrecorded liabilities.					
	(a) Investigate differences identified by analytical procedures.				✓	
	(b) Review agreements and long-term contracts requiring periodic payments for evidence of unrecorded liabilities.	✓	✓	✓	✓	✓6
	9. Recalculate accrued payroll liabilities.					
	10. Verify directors' and officers' remuneration.					
Presentation and disclosure	11. Compare financial statement presentation with applicable regulations and accounting standards.				✓	✓4, 7
	(a) Determine that payables are properly identified and classified as to type and expected period of payment.					
	(b) Determine whether there are debit balances that are significant in the aggregate and that should be reclassified.					
	(c) Determine the appropriateness of disclosures pertaining to related party payables.					
	(d) Inquire of management about existence of undisclosed commitments or contingent liabilities.					

10.6.1 Initial procedures

To begin verifying accounts payable:

- Trace the opening balance to the previous year's working papers, when applicable.
- Review activity in the general ledger account for any unusual entries.
- Obtain a listing of amounts owed at the end of the reporting period.

Usually the listing is prepared by the entity from the accounts payable records. The auditor must verify the mathematical accuracy of the listing by adding the total and verifying that it agrees with the underlying accounting records and the general ledger control account balance. In addition, the auditor selectively compares details of suppliers and amounts on the listing with the underlying records to determine that it is an accurate representation of the records from which the listing was prepared.

10.6.2 Analytical procedures

Tests of details are usually planned on the basis that the analytical procedures confirm expectations. It is best to perform analytical procedures early in the final audit so the auditor can determine any changes needed to tests of details before starting that part of the audit. The first stage in applying analytical procedures is to review the understanding of the entity obtained during the planning phase as to whether any changes to payables balances are to be expected. The second stage is to identify absolute changes in amounts between the current year and previous years. This is normally done in the course of preparing the lead schedule for payables and payroll balances. The third stage involves the use of more sophisticated relationships such as ratios and trends including the gross profit ratio. If it is higher than expected, then one explanation could be an understatement of purchases (such as by a deliberate cut-off error) in order to boost revenues.

Analysis of expense accounts is also important. The auditor usually undertakes this analysis by comparing the ratio of each expense to sales in the current year with that in previous years. In this way, the effect of changes in the level of activity is largely eliminated. An unusually low expense account may indicate unrecorded liabilities through cut-off error; for example, if the final quarter's electricity account has not been paid or allowed for, then the current year's electricity expense will appear unusually low compared with that for the previous year. Wherever a change in relationships cannot be readily explained, the auditor must seek an explanation from management and corroborate it, usually by conducting additional tests of details.

Analytical procedures are significant in achieving the desired level of detection risk for payroll balances. Particularly useful ratios are those of the average wages per employee, which should not be dissimilar from previous years, subject only to known wage rises, and payroll expenses as a percentage of sales.

10.6.3 Tests of details of transactions

As explained in chapter 9 in the case of receivables, balances affected by numerous transactions are more efficiently verified by tests of the closing balance and not by tests of the transactions making up that balance. When possible, the auditor performs the tests of details of transactions during the interim audit, commonly in the form of dual-purpose tests. No substantive tests of details of payroll transactions are described here, because the tests of controls described earlier may also constitute the main sources of substantive evidence for payroll transactions. The cut-off tests now described are always performed as part of year-end work and, although they are tests of transactions, they serve to verify the recorded balance at the end of the reporting period.

Vouching recorded payables to supporting documentation

The emphasis of these tests is on vouching purchase transactions to supporting documentation in the entity's files (such as purchase orders, receiving reports, and suppliers' invoices) to verify their occurrence as legitimate transactions. It is equally important, however, to test the numerical continuity of purchase orders and receiving reports, and to trace them to suppliers' invoices and accounts payable to verify completeness.

Performing purchases cut-off test

The purchases cut-off test involves determining that purchase transactions occurring near the end of the reporting period are recorded in the proper period. Most entities hold their books open for a certain period to ensure that purchase transactions are recorded in the correct accounting period. When the books are closed, unmatched receiving reports and purchase orders are scrutinised and, if they relate to the current period, they are recorded by way of journal entry.

Unlike receivables, it may take several weeks before all transactions occurring before the end of the reporting period are invoiced by the suppliers. Because cut-off is significant only at the end of the reporting period, most entities do not have effective controls to ensure an accurate distinction between the recording of transactions before and after that date. Acceptable detection risk is likely to be low, and extensive tests of details will be performed. The emphasis is on completeness, which is achieved by tracing receiving reports issued in the days immediately before the end of the reporting period to purchase journal entries or to the closing journal entry of purchase accruals. This procedure provides evidence that they are recorded in the current accounting period.

Because many purchases (such as services) do not result in the issue of a receiving report, purchases after the end of the reporting period are vouched to supporting documentation to ensure that they do not relate to goods or services received before the end of the reporting period.

Although the emphasis of the test is on completeness, the auditor also traces some receiving reports issued after the year end to suppliers' invoices, to ensure that they are recorded in the next period's purchase transactions file. In addition, the auditor vouches recorded purchases before the end of the reporting period to receiving reports dated before the end of the reporting period, to ensure that no transactions that occurred after the period are recorded before the end of the reporting period. This provides evidence as to the occurrence assertion. These tests usually cover a period of 5 to 10 business days before the end of the reporting period and as long after as appears necessary. In performing this test, the auditor should determine that a proper cut-off is achieved at the physical inventory count as well as in the recording of the purchase transactions. Where inventory is counted other than at the end of the reporting period, the auditor needs to check cut-off for purchases of inventory at the inventory count date as well as at the end of the reporting period.

Performing payments cut-off test

A proper cut-off of payment transactions at the year end is essential to the correct presentation of cash and accounts payable at the end of the reporting period. The usual method of verifying payments cut-off is to examine the date of presentation of cheques unpresented as at the end of the reporting period. This test is normally performed as part of the test of the bank reconciliation and the use of the next period's bank statement (see chapter 12).

10.6.4 Tests of details of balances

The three tests included in this category for payables are:

1. reconciling payables with monthly statements received by the entity from suppliers
2. confirming accounts payable
3. searching for unrecorded liabilities

The two tests for payroll balances are:

1. recalculating payroll liabilities
2. verifying directors' and executive officers' remuneration

Reconciling payables with suppliers' statements

In many cases, suppliers provide monthly statements that are available in entity files. As documentary evidence originating outside the entity, suppliers' statements provide reliable evidence as to suppliers' balances. However, because they are obtained from the entity, the auditor needs to be cautious that the statements have not been altered, and should not rely on photocopies and faxed statements. Where there is doubt, a copy should be requested directly from the supplier or the balance confirmed directly with the supplier.

In the selection of accounts for testing, the criterion should be the volume of business during the year, not the balance shown in the entity's accounts payable listing, because the main concern is that the recorded balance may be understated.

Discrepancies between suppliers' statements and the entity's accounts payable ledger need to be investigated. Most differences are likely to be due to goods and cash in transit and to disputed amounts. This procedure provides evidence as to the existence, completeness, and valuation assertions.

Confirming accounts payable

Unlike the confirmation of receivables, the **confirmation of accounts payable** is performed less frequently because:

- confirmation offers limited assurance that unrecorded liabilities will be discovered

- external evidence in the form of invoices and suppliers' monthly statements should be available to substantiate the balances

Confirmation of accounts payable is recommended (1) when detection risk is low and (2) for suppliers with which the entity undertook a substantial level of business during the current or previous years and that do not issue monthly statements, and for suppliers for which the statement at the end of the reporting period is unexpectedly unavailable.

As in the case of confirming receivables, the auditor must control the preparation and mailing of the requests and should receive the responses directly from the supplier. The auditor should use the positive form in making the confirmation request, as illustrated in figure 10.4. Note that the confirmation does not specify the amount due. In confirming a creditor, the auditor prefers to have the creditor indicate the amount due because that is the amount to be reconciled to the entity's records. Information is also requested regarding purchase commitments of the entity and any collateral for the amount due. This test produces evidence for all assertions relating to payables. However, the evidence provided about the completeness assertion is limited, given the possible failure to identify and send confirmation requests to suppliers with which the entity has unrecorded obligations.

Searching for unrecorded liabilities

The major procedure for identifying unrecorded liabilities is the examination of the next period's purchase and payment transactions and the review of unpaid invoices as described earlier under cut-off tests. Analytical procedures may also identify unexpected differences between the current year's and the previous year's expense or liability balances, which could indicate the presence of unrecorded liabilities. An analysis of rent expense, for example, may indicate that only three quarterly payments have been made, suggesting that the fourth quarter's rent needs to be allowed for. Similarly, a comparison of accruals and prepayments may identify differences arising from the failure to make a closing entry in the current year.

An examination of contractual commitments may also alert the auditor to the existence of liabilities not yet provided for, such as progress payments on long-term contracts or amounts accrued but not yet due or invoiced under a franchise agreement.

confirmation of accounts payable written inquiry of suppliers, requesting confirmation of the balance owed or a statement listing invoices owing at the confirmation date

---

FIGURE 10.4 Accounts payable confirmation

> PO Box 1777
> Halifax, Nova Scotia
>
> January 5, 2017
> Supplier Limited
> 2001 Lakeview Drive
> Halifax
>
> Dear Sir or Madam
>
> Will you please send directly to our auditors, W&S Partners, an itemized statement of the amount owed to you by us at the close of business on December 31, 2016. Please also supply the following information:
>
> Amount not yet due $..
>
> Amount past due $...
>
> Amount of purchase commitments $.......................................
>
> Description of any collateral held ....
>
> ....
>
> ....
>
> A business reply envelope addressed to our auditors is enclosed. A prompt reply will be very much appreciated.
>
> Yours faithfully
> Controller

Chapter 13 describes procedures known as the subsequent-events review and the review for contingent liabilities. Both procedures contribute to the search for unrecorded liabilities.

Recalculating payroll liabilities

It is necessary for many entities to make a variety of accrual entries at the end of the reporting period for amounts owed to officers and employees for salaries and wages, commissions, bonuses, holiday pay, and so on, and for amounts owed to government agencies for income tax and other deductions. Although the auditor's main concern regarding payroll expenses for the year is with overstatement, the main concern regarding the year-end accruals is with understatement. Also of concern is consistency in the methods of calculating the accrued amounts from one period to the next. In obtaining evidence concerning the reasonableness of management's accruals, the auditor should review management's calculations or make independent calculations. Additional evidence can be obtained by examining subsequent payments made for the accruals before the completion of fieldwork. Evidence obtained from these procedures relates mainly to the valuation assertion.

Verifying directors' and executive officers' remuneration

Directors' and executive officers' remuneration is audit-sensitive because directors and executive officers may be able to override controls and receive salaries, bonuses, share options, and other forms of compensation in excess of authorized amounts.

For these reasons, the auditor should compare the authorizations of the board of directors for directors' and executive officers' salaries and other forms of compensation with recorded amounts. This procedure relates to all assertions.

10.6.5 Disclosure

Each major class of creditors and borrowings must be disclosed. These are likely to include bank overdrafts, bank loans, accounts payable, lease liabilities, taxation, and employee benefits. In addition, disclosure must be made of the amount of each class of liability secured by a charge and the nature of the security. If accounts payable balances include material advance payments for future goods and services, such amounts should be reported as advances to suppliers and classified under current assets.

Cloud 9

Josh is now happy to be completing his work on the accounts payable, purchases, and payroll. He has reviewed the client's accounts payable supplier reconciliations. However, he still needs to perform cut-off testing and perform the search for unrecorded liabilities. He has asked Carla for the receiving reports issued immediately before the end of the year and he is planning to trace them back to the purchase journal entries or to the purchase accrual listing. He knows he has to complete these procedures before he can conclude on the completeness assertion for the accounts payable.

He has also asked Carla for copies of receiving reports issued for the first 10 days after year end. To get assurance over the occurrence assertion, he will trace a sample of receiving reports issued after the year end to suppliers' invoices, to ensure that they are recorded in the correct period. He is also planning to vouch purchases before year end to the receiving reports to ensure that purchases that occurred after the year end are recorded in the correct period (after December 31).

With the substantive procedures almost completed, Josh is hoping to sign off on the accounts payable procedures by the end of the day because he wants to see what is next.

BEFORE YOU GO ON

10.6.1   What is the purpose of payables cut-off testing?

10.6.2   What are three tests of details for accounts payable?

10.6.3   The confirmation of accounts payable is performed less frequently than the confirmation of receivables. Why?

SUMMARY

① Identify the audit objectives applicable to purchases, payables, and payroll.

In the auditing of purchases, the key issue is often to ensure that the purchases are all recorded and are not understated; therefore, the focus is on completeness, accuracy, and cut-off assertions. For payables that are derived from the purchases, the key issue is to ensure they are all fully recorded in the accounts as liabilities; therefore, the focus is on the completeness and valuation and allocation assertions. Lastly, the focus of the payroll expense is to ensure the expense has been properly recorded and the associated deductions for income tax, employee benefits, and related liabilities are properly recorded as liabilities. This means the focus is on the completeness, occurrence, and accuracy assertions as well as assertions related to balances of completeness, existence, and valuation and allocation.

② Describe the functions and control procedures normally found in information systems for processing purchase, payment, and purchase adjustment transactions.

The processing of purchase transactions involves the following functions: requisitioning goods and services, preparing purchase orders, receiving the goods, storing goods received in inventory, checking and approving the supplier's invoice, and recording the liability. Control procedures such as using pre-numbered cheques, approval of purchases by authorized personnel, and segregation of duties should be interwoven into each process to reduce the risk of material misstatement.

③ Describe the functions and control procedures normally found in information systems for payroll transactions.

The processing of payroll transactions involves the following functions: hiring employees, authorizing payroll changes, preparing attendance and timekeeping data, preparing the payroll, recording the payroll, paying the payroll, and protecting unclaimed wages. Control procedures such as limiting access to payroll records, independently reviewing the payroll, and making payments by direct deposit should be included in each process to reduce the risk of material misstatements.

④ Discuss considerations relevant to determining the audit strategy for purchases, payables, and payroll.

The audit process starts with obtaining an understanding of the purchases, payables, and payroll systems to help assess the inherent and control risks. For audit purposes, the most significant inherent risk is usually that of understatement of purchase transactions and accounts payable balances in order to boost reported profits and enhance liquidity. For the entity, the greatest inherent risk is that of improper purchasing and payments to fictitious employees. Next, the auditor assesses the control risk. Based on effectiveness of the internal controls, the auditor then drafts the audit program based on the preliminary assessment of control risk. The assessed level of control risk is confirmed on completion of the tests of operating effectiveness, which leads to the final determination of an audit strategy. For purchases and payroll, the audit strategy is likely to be one based on a combined approach.

⑤ Indicate the factors relevant to determining an acceptable level of detection risk for the audit of purchases, payables, and payroll.

Once the auditor assesses the inherent and control risks, detection risk is set to achieve the required audit risk. This detection risk will be used by the auditor to determine the nature, timing, and extent of substantive procedures that need to be performed. The level and detail of substantive procedures performed is a matter of professional judgement. If detection risk is set as low, the auditor will be required to perform extensive substantive testing. If the detection risk is set as high, the auditor may perform a combined audit.

⑥ Design a substantive audit program for purchases, payables, and payroll.

The final stage of the audit is the performance of substantive procedures. It is usually more cost-effective to test the balance of accounts payable than to test the transactions making up that balance. The most important test of transactions is that of cut-off at the year end. The major test of balances is the examination of suppliers' statements. Because these are documentary evidence received from third parties, they are moderately reliable; however, the auditor needs to be alert to the possibility that such statements may be forged or altered by the entity. Finally, the auditor must also verify directors' and officers' salaries.

KEY TERMS

Accounts payable master file, p. 359

Cheque register, p. 360

Confirmation of accounts payable, p. 378

Packing slip, p. 359

Payroll register, p. 364

Payroll transaction file, p. 364

Personnel authorization form, p. 362

Personnel file, p. 362

Personnel master file, p. 362

Purchase journal, p. 359

Purchase order, p. 358

Purchase requisition, p. 357

Receiving report, p. 358

Remittance advice, p. 361

Suppliers' invoice, p. 359

Termination notice, p. 363

MULTIPLE-CHOICE QUESTIONS

10.1 The auditor selects a sample of items from the purchase order file to determine that the goods and services were received and recorded. This relates to the:

(a) existence or occurrence assertion.

(b) completeness assertion.

(c) accuracy or valuation and allocation assertion.

(d) rights and obligations assertion.

10.2 The receiving department should be instructed not to accept goods without having on file a properly authorized:

(a) purchase requisition.

(b) invoice.

(c) receiving report.

(d) purchase order.

10.3 The audit objective of "All amounts included in accounts payable relate to amounts due to suppliers at the balance sheet date" relates to the account balances assertion of:

(a) completeness.

(b) accuracy.

(c) valuation and allocation.

(d) existence.

10.4 Responsibility for determining that unpaid suppliers' invoices are processed for payment on their due dates generally lies with the:

(a) chief financial officer's department.

(b) accounting department.

(c) purchasing department.

(d) internal audit department.

10.5 The following is a test of control that would provide audit evidence for the management assertion of occurrence of credit purchases:

(a) selecting a sample of purchase invoices and ensuring there is evidence of a check that the discount given agrees with supplier agreement records.

(b) selecting a sample of authorized purchase orders and agreeing to receiving report and purchase invoice.

(c) for a sample of purchase invoices, verifying that there are appropriately authorized purchase orders.

(d) selecting a sample of purchases and ensuring that the items purchased are included either in sales or inventories.

10.6 Controls over the preparation and signing of cheques include all of the following *except*:

(a) authorized personnel in the finance department should be responsible for signing the cheques.

(b) the cheque requisition and supporting documents should be cancelled (stamped) when the cheque is signed.

(c) the signed cheque and the supporting documents should be returned to the accounts payable clerk for review and mailing.

(d) pre-numbered cheques should be used.

10.7 Controls over the recording of cash payments include:

(a) an independent check by the accounting supervisor of the agreement of the amounts journalized and posted to accounts payable with the cheque summary received from the accountant.

(b) an independent check of the agreement of the total of cheques issued with a batch total of the vouchers processed for payment.

(c) the cheque signer should control the mailing of the cheques.

(d) pre-numbered cheques should be used.

10.8 Requiring a special supervisor's password in order to add a new employee to the personnel data master file relates to the:

(a) existence or occurrence assertion.

(b) completeness assertion.

(c) rights and obligations assertion.

(d) accuracy or valuation assertion.

10.9 A programmed routine in the edit run for payroll that lists all employees who worked more than 50 hours during the week for review is an example of:

(a) a reasonableness test.

(b) a validity test.

(c) a sequence test.

(d) a self-checking test.

10.10 When test data may be used to test application controls over accepting and recording data for unpaid suppliers' invoices, the following conditions would not be relevant:

(a) numerical characters in an alphanumeric field.

(b) missing or invalid supplier numbers.

(c) missing due date or payment terms.

(d) alphabetical characters in a numerical field.

REVIEW QUESTIONS

10.1 State the main audit objectives for: (a) purchases and payroll transactions and (b) accounts payable balances.

10.2 Explain the importance of segregating the personnel function from the payroll preparation.

10.3 Describe programmed application controls you would expect to find in a computerized payroll system. Explain the audit procedures for testing those controls.

10.4 Describe computer-assisted audit procedures that can be used in testing controls over purchasing.

10.5 Explain why the assessment of control risk for the occurrence of payment transactions affects the assessed level of control risk for the completeness of the accounts payable balance.

10.6 Describe the performance of the purchases cut-off test.

10.7 It is increasingly common for companies to program their computer information system to print and distribute cheques without further authorization. As an auditor, describe controls you would expect to find in place over such a system.

10.8 Explain why an unexpected change in the gross profit ratio leads the auditor to suspect a wide range of possible misstatements in recorded transactions and balances.

10.9 Cut-off procedures can be applied to receiving reports issued before the year end or to liabilities recorded after the year end. Consider the separate merits of each approach in assuring the completeness of recorded liabilities.

10.10 Explain why achieving an accurate cut-off of purchases and sales transactions is of critical importance in assuring the fairness of the financial statements. Illustrate your explanation with examples of the effect of cut-off errors.

PROFESSIONAL APPLICATION QUESTIONS

Basic ★   Moderate ★ ★   Challenging ★ ★ ★

10.1 Purchase controls ★ ★   ❶ ❷

Your firm is the external auditor of Bestwood Engineering Ltd., which manufactures components for motor vehicles and sells them to motor vehicle manufacturers and wholesalers. It has sales of $25 million and a profit before tax of $1 million. The company has a new financial controller who has asked your advice on controls in the company's purchasing system.

Bestwood has separate accounting, purchasing, and receiving departments. Most purchases are requisitioned by the production department, but other departments are able to raise requisitions for goods and services. The purchasing department is responsible for obtaining goods and services for the company at the lowest price that is consistent with the required delivery date and quality, and for ensuring their prompt delivery.

The accounting department is responsible for obtaining authorization of purchase invoices before they are input into the computer, which posts them to the accounts payable ledger and the general ledger. The accounting records are kept on a computer and a standard off-the-shelf accounting software is used. The accounting software maintains the accounts payable ledger, accounts receivable ledger, general ledger, and payroll. The company does not maintain inventory records because it believes the cost of maintaining these records outweighs the benefits.

The financial controller has explained that services include gas, electricity, telephone, repairs, and the short-term rentals of equipment and vehicles.

Required

(a) Describe the procedures that should be incorporated in the purchasing department to control the purchase and receipt of goods.

(b) Describe the controls the accounting department should exercise over obtaining authorization of purchase invoices before posting them to the accounts payable ledger.

(c) Explain how controls over the purchase of services, from creating the purchase requisition to posting the invoice to the accounts payable sub-ledger, may differ from the procedures for the purchase of goods, as described in your answers to parts (a) and (b).

Source: Adapted from ACCA Audit Framework, Paper 6(U), December 1998.

10.2 Internal control evaluation—cash payments ★

Management of Tarnawski Ltd. has requested a review of internal controls over cash payments for parts and supplies purchased at manufacturing plants. Cash payments are centrally processed at head office based on vouchers prepared and approved at manufacturing plants. Each manufacturing plant purchases parts and supplies for its own production needs. In response to management's request, a thorough evaluation of internal controls over payments for manufacturing plant purchases of parts and supplies is being planned. As a preliminary step in planning the engagement, the plant managers have been asked to provide a written description of their respective plant's procedures for processing payment vouchers for parts and supplies. The following are nine excerpts from one of the written descriptions.

1. The purchasing department acts on purchase requisitions issued by the stores department (which houses supplies).
2. Orders are placed on pre-numbered purchase order forms.
3. A complete purchase order copy is sent to the receiving department.
4. When goods are received, the receiving department logs the shipment in by stamping "order received" on its purchase order copy and forwards the annotated order to the accounts payable department.
5. Purchase orders, purchase order copies that have been annotated by the receiving department, and supplier invoices are matched by the accounts payable department.
6. Clerical accuracy of supplier invoices is checked by the accounts payable department.
7. A pre-numbered payment voucher is prepared and forwarded, along with supporting documentation, to the plant controller, who reviews and approves the voucher.
8. Supporting documents are returned to the accounts payable department for filing and approved payment vouchers are forwarded to head office for payment.
9. A report listing cheques issued by head office is received and promptly filed by the accounts payable department.

Required

For each of the payment system procedures listed above, state whether it is consistent with good internal control and describe how it strengthens or weakens internal control.

10.3 Segregation of duties and documentation ★ ★

Lise Couture is documenting the purchasing and cash payments processes at Hardies Wholesaling. Hardies Wholesaling imports garden and landscaping items, such as pots, furniture, fountains, mirrors, and sculpture, from suppliers in Southeast Asia. All items are non-perishable; are made from materials such as stone, concrete, metal, and wood; and are distributed to retailers throughout the country.

Purchases are denominated in U.S. dollars, which the company acquires under forward exchange contracts. The purchasing department initiates a purchase order when inventory levels reach reorder points or sales staff notify the department of large customer orders that need to be specially filled. The purchase order is approved and sent to suppliers selected from an approved supplier list. Goods are transported from Southeast Asia by ship and are delivered by truck to Hardies Wholesaling's central warehouse. A receiving report is generated by the receiving department and forwarded to the accounts department for matching with the copy of the original purchase order and the supplier's invoice. When the package of documents is completed, the purchase order and invoice are entered into the general ledger. The cash payments department initiates a voucher to request payment of the invoice according to the supplier's payment terms. The payment is approved and the cash payment is made.

Required
(a) Create a flowchart to represent the flow of transactions from the initiation of a purchase order to cash payment.
(b) Which duties in the above process should be segregated?

10.4 Payroll control and substantive testing ★★

You are reviewing the audit work for Online Ltd., a large Canadian company. Online uses a service bureau to process all wages. Time sheets are authorized by the appropriate supervisor, batched, and sent to the service bureau for processing. Detailed payroll reports, as well as the time sheets, are returned to the accountant, who reviews the reports for reasonableness and initials them as evidence of her review.

Your audit assistant performed a month-to-month comparison of wages and found no abnormal trends. The following conclusion was noted on the working paper: "I have checked that all payroll reports from the period were reviewed and initialled by the client. This, in conjunction with the results of analytical review, led me to conclude that the payroll expense is fairly stated."

Required
(a) Outline any queries you would raise with the audit assistant.
(b) Describe the additional audit procedures you believe should be performed to ensure that payroll is fairly stated.

Source: Adapted from ACCA Audit Framework, Paper 6Y, December 1997.

10.5 Computer information system controls—purchasing and cash payments ★★★

You are the auditor of Sofasellers Ltd., which buys furniture from manufacturers for sale to the public. You have been asked to audit certain aspects of the computerized purchasing and accounts payable system.

The company has a head office, a warehouse, and many shops throughout the country. Furniture from manufacturers may be delivered to the warehouse or directly to individual shops. Details of goods received are entered into computer terminals at the warehouse or shop, which are online with the head office main computer.

The computerized purchasing system involves the following six processes:
1. The user department (shop or warehouse) sends a purchase requisition to the purchasing department at head office.
2. The purchasing department issues a purchase order, which is sent to the supplier and recorded in the computer.
3. On delivery, the goods are checked by the receiving department in the warehouse and a receiving report is created, entered into the computer system, and allocated against the order.
4. On receipt of the invoice, the central accounting department forwards the invoice to the user department, which authorizes it and returns it to the accounting department. Invoice details are then recorded in the computer, which posts it to the accounts payable ledger.
5. The computer system allows payment only if the system has recorded:
   (a) the purchase order
   (b) receipt of the goods
6. When the purchase invoice is due for payment, the computer prints the cheque and remittance advice.

Cheques are automatically produced, so the partner in charge of the audit has asked you to identify controls over authorizing purchase invoices and changing suppliers' details on the computer's master file. He has explained that "application controls" comprise controls exercised by the company's staff and by the computer.

Required

(a) Describe the application controls you would expect to find in operation from creating the purchase requisition to the computer accepting the purchase invoice.

(b) Explain the controls that should be exercised over access to the main computer from terminals in the head office and at the retail locations.

(c) Describe the application controls that should be exercised over changing supplier details in the supplier master file in the computer. You should consider:

(i) why such controls are important and how a fraud could be perpetrated in the absence of effective controls.

(ii) the controls you would expect to find over changing supplier details and ensuring supplier details are correct. Your answer should include consideration of controls over access to the computer to perform these tasks.

Source: Adapted from ACCA Audit Framework, Paper 6, December 1994.

10.6 Strengths and weaknesses of controls ★ ★ ★

GGG Electronics builds shortwave radios. Its manufacturing plant is also a warehouse. When parts are received, the receiver compares the type of goods and quantity with a copy of the purchase order available online. If the quantity received differs from the quantity on the purchase order, the receiver adjusts the purchase order amount online. When the goods are checked by the receiver, she sends an e-mail to the accounting department, recording the type of goods, quantity, and date received. The accounting department uses the e-mail to create a receiver's report, and the purchase order is then printed and filed in the accounting department. The online system allows the company to reduce paper, because a hard copy is not needed until the goods are actually received. The company's order-entry and tracking system automatically assigns the next number in a series to the purchase order just before printing.

Inventory is physically moved to the warehousing area, which is located in a locked-up area at the end of the plant. There is a stores department in a separate area for supplies such as gloves, wire, and adhesives, all of which are used in significant quantities on a regular basis. When an assembly-line worker requires supplies, the supervisor fills out a serially pre-numbered requisition card, signs it, and gives it to the worker, who then takes it to the stores department to obtain the needed items. Each supervisor has a stock of requisition cards. When the supplier's invoice is received by the purchasing department, one of the purchasing department staff sends an e-mail to the accounting department, noting the invoice amount, supplier name, date of shipment, and type of goods. The accounting department then matches this to the purchase order and receiving report, and prepares a cheque for the controller to sign.

The controller does not sign the cheque until she also receives an e-mail from the accounting staff indicating that the purchase order, receiving report, and invoice have been matched.

Required

(a) List four internal controls that appear to be effective in GGG's system.

(b) List three examples of weak internal controls in GGG's system. Explain why each of your examples would be a weak control.

Source: © CGA-Canada, now CPA Canada. Reproduced with permission.

10.7 Transaction-level controls over the payroll cycle ★ ★ ★

Trillite Ltd. has had strong growth over the past three years. The company is involved in mining in northern Canada. While revenues have been increasing, the costs of mining at its remote locations have increased as well. An investigation revealed that the controller had added a fictitious employee and had defrauded Trillite by collecting and cashing false payroll cheques. The CEO fired the controller and, instead, hired a new accountant with a mandate to cut costs. The accountant eliminated a number of administrative staff, because these employees do not contribute to the income-earning process. Under the new office structure, only the personnel manager can authorize the hiring of new employees and their pay rate, and only the accountant will prepare and distribute the payroll cheques.

Required

Does the new accountant's plan provide strong internal controls over payroll? Justify your answer by stating the strength(s) and weakness(es) of the new plan.

Source: © CGA-Canada, now CPA Canada. Reproduced with permission.

10.8 Payroll—in-house payroll processing ★ ★ ★

Diamond Construction is an owner-managed entity with contracting revenues of $20 million in 2016. As construction is a labour-intensive industry, one of Diamond's largest expense accounts is labour and wages. You are a first-year auditor at Klein and Partners. You have been given the following information regarding the entity's payroll process for hourly employees at Diamond Construction:

1. The owner-manager is the only person who can authorize the hiring of a new employee.
2. When a new employee is hired, the payroll clerk prepares a new employee package that includes:
   (a) safety orientation
   (b) tax forms
   (c) benefits plan enrolment
3. Only the payroll manager has the ability to update the employee master list. This can only be done once the tax forms, a void cheque with direct deposit information, and the owner's approval have been received. All forms need to be returned before the payroll manager will update the payroll master list and add any new employees.
4. Hourly employees are paid biweekly.
5. Hours worked are tracked on time cards. Supervisors fill in the time cards for each individual day, noting the hours worked.
6. At the end of the pay period, time cards are provided to the payroll clerk, who compiles the total hours worked and codes the hours to the appropriate job number. Once compiled, the payroll clerk enters the hours worked per person in the payroll system.
7. The accounting system prepares the direct deposit information based on the rates of pay maintained in the payroll master list (listing of all authorized staff and approved wage rates). It also calculates the withholding taxes.
8. This is transferred to the bank and a record of the transmission is printed and attached to the front of the payroll run.
9. The payroll module is integrated with the general ledger. The payroll clerk prepares and posts the journal entry to the payroll expense accounts.
10. Remittance advices are given to the supervisors for distribution.
11. If an employee is terminated, Diamond just stops paying them as they no longer have time cards submitted.
12. When an employee has been promoted or their job classification has changed, the supervisor will verbally communicate this to payroll manager, who will then update the payroll master file. Therefore, source documentation in employee files will only relate to an employee's original job classification. The rationale for this was that most job classification changes would only result in an additional dollar or two per hour paid to the employee.

Required

(a) Identify the control strengths of the payroll process at Diamond Construction.
(b) Identify the control weaknesses of the payroll process at Diamond Construction. For each weakness, identify the implications of the weakness and recommend how to improve it.

10.9 Payroll at a not-for-profit entity ★ ★   ① ③ ④

Venture Volunteers for Troubled Teens is a not-for-profit entity that provides counselling services to troubled teens and adolescents. While the majority of its funding comes from the government, the group also participates in a variety of fundraising activities. To manage the fundraising activities and administer the various programs, there is an executive director, two accounting staff, and several youth counsellors. All staff are salaried and the payroll is processed biweekly. Employees are not paid overtime, but rather they use "flex" time to compensate for overtime. As a result, it is unusual for the payroll to change from pay period to pay period. All of the staff are on direct deposit, so no payroll cheques are issued. The responsibility for the payroll is split between the two accounting staff, Maddie and Ricardo. Maddie is responsible for preparing and posting the payroll while Ricardo is responsible for processing infrequent items such as staff terminations and administering the benefits program. The actual payroll processing is outsourced to a payroll service provider, Paystub Inc. Paystub processes the direct debit payments to employees and the remittance of all withholding taxes.

Maddie maintains a spreadsheet listing the employees with the approved pay rates. This is maintained in Excel and is password protected. The spreadsheet is sent to Paystub Inc., and it processes the payroll. Only Maddie and Ricardo have access to the spreadsheet and only Ricardo can add or remove employees. Paystub provides Maddie with the payroll register that details the individual pay amounts and totals. Based on this report, Maddie prepares the journal entry for posting to the general ledger. This is reviewed by Ricardo for accuracy, and once signed as reviewed, the journal entry is posted. Ricardo also reviews the payroll register for unusual amounts and significant fluctuations. Every quarter he prints a copy of the payroll master file and reviews it to ensure only actual employees are listed. He initials a copy of this master file to document this review.

When new staff are hired, they are provided with a new employee package. This package includes a signed offer letter, all tax and medical forms, a confidentiality package, an ethics statement, and a job description. These forms are maintained in an employee personnel file and stored in locked cabinets in the accounting area. Ricardo will update the employee master file when the employee begins work.

Maddie is notified of any staff terminations by the employee's manager. This is done via e-mail. No change can be made to the employee payroll file unless it is provided in writing and the organization deems e-mails adequate. There is a staff "leaving" checklist that needs to be completed and one of the requirements is to remove the employee from the payroll. Once completed, this is filed in the employee's personnel file.

All salary changes are requested by the departmental managers and sent to the executive director for approval. Once approved, an official letter is signed by the executive director and maintained in the employee's personnel file. Ricardo is provided with a copy so he can update the employee's salary in the master file.

Required

Identify *eight* strengths of the payroll process at Venture Volunteers. For each strength, identify what the test of that control could be.

CASES

10.10 Integrative Case Study—Blake Co.

Blake Co. assembles specialist motor vehicles such as freight trucks, buses, and delivery trucks. The company owns four assembly plants where parts are delivered and assembled into the motor vehicles.

The motor vehicles are assembled using a mix of robot and manual production lines. The assembly-line workers normally work a standard eight-hour day, although this is supplemented by overtime on a regular basis as Blake has a full order book. There is one shift per day; mass production and around-the-clock working are not possible due to the specialist nature of the motor vehicles being assembled.

Wages system—shift workers

Shift workers arrive for work at about 7:00 a.m. and "clock in" using an electronic identification card. The card is scanned by the time-recording system and each production shift worker's identification number is read from their card by the scanner. The worker is then logged in as being at work. Shift workers are paid from the time of logging in. The logging-in process is not monitored because it is assumed that shift workers would not work without first logging in on the time-recording system.

Shift workers are split into groups of about 25 employees, with each group under the supervision of a shift foreman.

Each day, each group of shift workers is allocated a specific vehicle to manufacture. At least 400 vehicles have to be manufactured each day by each work group. If necessary, overtime is worked to complete the day's quota of vehicles.

The shift foreman is not required to monitor the extent of any overtime working although the foreman does ensure workers are not taking unnecessary or prolonged breaks that would automatically increase the amount of overtime worked. Shift workers log off at the end of each shift by re-scanning their identification card.

Payment of wages

Details of hours worked each week are sent electronically to the payroll department, where hours worked are allocated by the computerized wages system to each employee's wages records. Staff in the payroll department compare hours worked from the time-recording system with the computerized wages system and enter a code word to confirm the accuracy of transfer. The code word also acts as authorization to calculate net wages. The code word is the name of a cat belonging to the department head and is therefore generally known around the department.

Each week the computerized wages system calculates:

1. gross wages, using the standard rate and overtime rates per hour for each employee,
2. statutory deductions from wages, and
3. net pay.

The list of net pay for each employee is sent over Blake's internal network to the accounting department. In the accounting department, an accounting clerk ensures that employee bank details are on file. The clerk then authorizes and makes payment to those employees using Blake's online banking systems. Every few weeks, the financial accountant reviews the total amount of wages paid to ensure that the management accounts are accurate.

Termination of employees

Occasionally, employees leave Blake. When this happens, the personnel department sends an e-mail to the payroll department detailing the employee's termination date and any unclaimed holiday pay. The receipt of the e-mail by the payroll department is not monitored by the personnel department.

Salaries system—shift managers

All shift managers are paid an annual salary; there are no overtime payments.

Salaries were increased in July by 3% and an annual bonus of 5% of salary was paid in November.

Required

(a) List four control objectives of a payroll system.
(b) As the external auditors of Blake Co., write a management letter to the directors regarding the shift workers' wages recording and payroll systems that:
    (i) identifies and explains four weaknesses in that system,
    (ii) explains the possible effect of each weakness, and
    (iii) provides a recommendation to alleviate each weakness.

(c) List three substantive analytical procedures you should perform on the shift managers' salary process. For each procedure, state your expectation of the result of that procedure.

(d) Audit evidence can be obtained using various audit procedures, such as inspection. Apart from this procedure, in respect of testing the accuracy of the time-recording system at Blake Co., explain four procedures used in collecting audit evidence and discuss whether the auditor will benefit from using each procedure.

Source: Adapted from ACCA Audit and Assurance (International), Paper F8, December 2008.

10.11 Integrative Case Study—Greystone Co.

Greystone Co. is a retailer of women's clothing and accessories. It operates in many countries around the world and has expanded steadily from its base in Canada. Its main market is 15- to 35-year-olds and its prices are mid to low range. The company's year end is September 30, 2016.

In the past the company has bulk-ordered its clothing and accessories twice a year. However, if the goods failed to meet the key fashion trends, this resulted in significant inventory write-downs. As a result, the company has recently introduced a just-in-time ordering system. The fashion buyers make an assessment nine months in advance as to what the key trends are likely to be. These goods are sourced from Greystone's suppliers but only limited numbers are initially ordered.

Greystone Co. has an internal audit department but at present its only role is to perform regular inventory counts at the stores.

Ordering process

Each country has a purchasing manager who decides on the initial inventory levels for each store; this is not done in conjunction with store or sales managers. These quantities are communicated to the central buying department at the head office in Canada. An ordering clerk amalgamates all country orders by specified regions such as Central Europe and North America, and passes them to the purchasing director to review and authorize.

As the goods are sold, it is the store manager's responsibility to reorder the goods through the purchasing manager. The stores are prompted weekly to review inventory levels because, although the goods are just in time, it can still take up to four weeks for goods to be received in store.

It is not possible to order goods from other branches as all ordering must be undertaken through the purchasing manager. If a customer requests an item of clothing that is unavailable in a particular store, then the customer is provided with other branch telephone numbers or recommended to try the company website.

Goods received and invoicing

To speed up the ordering to receipt of goods cycle, the goods are delivered directly from the suppliers to the individual stores. On receipt of goods, the quantities received are checked by a sales assistant against the supplier's delivery note, and then the assistant produces a receiving report. This is done at quiet times of the day so as to maximize sales. The checked receiving reports are sent to head office for matching with purchase invoices.

As purchase invoices are received, they are manually matched to receiving reports from the stores. This can be a very time-consuming process as some suppliers may have delivered to over 500 stores. Once the invoice has been agreed, then it is sent to the purchasing director for authorization. It is at this stage that the invoice is entered onto the purchase journal.

Required

(a) As the external auditors of Greystone Co., write a report to management in respect of the purchasing system that:

(i) identifies and explains four deficiencies in that system,

(ii) explains the possible implications of each deficiency, and

(iii) provides a recommendation to address each deficiency.

A covering letter is required.

(b) Describe substantive procedures the auditor should perform on the year-end trade payables of Greystone Co.

Source: Adapted from ACCA Audit and Assurance (International), Paper F8, December 2010.

10.12 Integrative Case Study—Blackburn Ltd.

You are the audit senior in charge of the audit of Blackburn Ltd., and you are auditing the company's trade creditors at December 31, 2016. A junior member of the audit team has been checking suppliers' statements against the balances in the accounts payable sub-ledger. He is unable to reconcile a material balance relating to Whitebone Ltd., and has asked for your help and suggestions on the audit work that should be carried out on the differences. The balance of Whitebone Ltd. in Blackburn's sub-ledger is shown below.

Supplier: Whitebone Ltd.

DATE	TYPE	REFERENCE	STATUS	DR	CR	BALANCE
April 10	Invoice	6004	Paid 1		2,130	
April 18	Invoice	6042	Paid 1		1,525	
April 23	Invoice	6057	Paid 1		2,634	
May 4	Invoice	6080	Paid 2		3,572	
May 15	Invoice	6107	Paid 2		1,632	
May 26	Invoice	6154	Paid 2		924	
May 31	Payment	Cheque	Alloc. 1	6,163		
	Discount		Alloc. 1	126		
June 14	Invoice	6285			2,156	
June 21	Invoice	6328			3,824	
June 30	Payment	Cheque	Alloc. 2	6,005		
	Discount		Alloc. 2	123		
June 30	Balance					5,980

Below are the details on Whitebone's suppliers' statement.

Customer: Blackburn Ltd.

DATE	TYPE	REFERENCE	STATUS	DR	CR	BALANCE
April 7	Invoice	6004	Paid 1	2,130		
April 16	Invoice	6042	Paid 1	1,525		
April 22	Invoice	6057	Paid 1	2,634		
May 2	Invoice	6080	Paid 2	3,752		
May 13	Invoice	6107	Paid 2	1,632		
May 22	Invoice	6154	Paid 2	924		
June 10	Receipt	Cheque	Alloc. 1		6,163	
June 4	Invoice	6210	Alloc. 1	4,735		
June 12	Invoice	6285		2,156		
June 18	Invoice	6328	Alloc. 2	3,824		
June 28	Invoice	6355	Alloc. 2	6,298		
June 30	Balance					23,447

Whitebone's terms of trade with Blackburn allow a 2-percent cash discount on invoices where Whitebone receives a cheque from the customer by the end of the month following the date of the invoice (i.e., a 2-percent discount will be given on November invoices paid by December 31).

On Blackburn's sub-ledger, under "Status," the cash and discount marked "Alloc. 1" pay invoices marked "Paid 1" (similarly for "Alloc. 2" and "Paid 2"). Blackburn's receiving department checks the goods when they arrive and issues a receiving report. A copy of the report is sent to the accounts payable department.

Required

(a) Prepare a statement reconciling the balance on Blackburn's payable sub-ledger to the balance on Whitebone's supplier's statement. (*Hint:* Look for errors and omissions.)

(b) Describe the audit work you will carry out on each of the reconciling items you have determined in your answer to part (a) to determine the balance that should be included in the financial statements.

(c) In relation to verifying trade creditors:

   (i) consider the basis you will use for selecting suppliers' statements to check against the balances on the purchase ledger.

   (ii) describe what action you will take if you find there is no supplier's statement for a material balance on the purchase ledger.

Source: Adapted from ACCA Audit Framework, Paper 6, June 1996.

10.13 Integrative Case Study—Integrated Measurement Systems Inc.

Integrated Measurement Systems Inc. (IMS) is a Canadian public company that manufactures high-end measuring devices used primarily in the oil and natural gas industries.

Ted Pollock, IMS's CEO, is a proponent of strong corporate governance. He has spent the last year strengthening IMS's internal control environment. He believes that organizations that demonstrate good corporate governance practices will be perceived favourably by the markets.

Ted has some concerns regarding the purchasing process. He has provided you with a description of the purchasing process in figure 10.5.

FIGURE 10.5 **IMS's purchasing process**

Control objectives that relate to the purchasing process

1. Proper approval of all transactions
2. Safeguarding of company assets
3. Prevention and detection of errors and irregularities
4. Accuracy and completeness of books and records
5. Appropriate use of information

Purchasing process documentation

The purchasing process has four major components, namely:

1. Vendor prequalification
2. Purchase of goods and/or services
3. Receipt of goods
4. Settlement

Process description

The purchasing process begins when there is a requirement for goods or services. A manually completed purchase request form is sent from the operating department (e.g., sales, marketing, manufacturing) to the purchasing department. The purchasing clerk numbers these documents and reviews each purchase request form to verify that a signature is present. Purchase request forms must be authorized by the signature of a person with the appropriate level of authority. The amount of the expenditure determines the level of authority required, and the expenditure authorization levels are organized in tiers. Because there are so many possible combinations of departments and authorization levels, the operating departments are responsible for ensuring that their purchase request forms are signed by individuals with the appropriate level of authority. This requirement eliminates the need for the purchasing clerk to check the specifics of the signatures.

The purchasing clerk sends the purchase requests to the purchasing manager for review and approval.

(continued)

FIGURE 10.5 **IMS's purchasing process** (continued)

The approved purchase request is then sent to the buyer, who sources the purchase. If the amount is below $5,000, selection of the vendor is left up to the buyer. For purchases in excess of $5,000 but less than $25,000, a vendor from the prequalification listing is selected, again at the discretion of the buyer. For purchases in excess of $25,000, a formal bidding process is performed. However, at the discretion of the buyer, the bid process can be waived if deemed to be cost inefficient.

Upon selection of the vendor, the buyer inputs the purchase request information into a purchase order form. The purchase order is forwarded to the purchasing manager for review and a photocopy is made and filed, in numerical order, with the appropriate photocopy of the purchase request. The original purchase order is then sent back to the buyer, who delivers it to the vendor.

All goods are received in the warehouse. All employees have access to the warehouse. The goods are checked against the packing slip and are examined for damage, amounts, and so on. If the goods are acceptable, the bill of lading is signed off by the receiver. A copy of the signed bill of lading is then forwarded to the purchasing clerk, who matches it to the file copy of the purchase request and purchase order. If there are differences in the details (over/under-shipment, wrong product, etc.), the bill of lading is forwarded to the buyer for resolution with the vendor. If no problems are noted, copies of the three documents are sent to the payables group for settlement.

The receiver, John Sang-hun (who was hired six months ago), sends the goods to the user department that made the original purchase request along with a photocopy of the bill of lading. The user department agrees the quantities noted by the receiver and files the bill of lading. User departments have noted that, recently, there have been an increasing number of manual adjustments to the quantities shipped versus received. Any unmatched purchase requests and purchase orders that remain outstanding for over 90 days are returned by the purchasing clerk to the user department that originally ordered the goods on the assumption that the goods have been received. It is then the responsibility of the user department to follow up and forward the paperwork to the payables group for settlement.

If a signed bill of lading is forwarded to the purchasing clerk for which there is no source documentation (i.e., no purchase request or purchase order exists), the purchasing clerk follows up with the buyer to understand the nature of the receipt. At the same time, a copy of the bill of lading is also sent to the payables group.

Required

(a) Identify the existing key internal controls within the purchasing process and relate each to the appropriate control objective.

(b) Identify the internal control weaknesses within the purchasing process and recommend improvements.

(c) To further strengthen the control environment, Ted Pollock is considering creating an internal audit department. Outline the kinds of things this group could be involved in.

Source: UFE 2004 Paper III, Simulation 1.

CASE STUDY—CLOUD 9

Answer the following question based on the information presented for Cloud 9 in Appendix B and in the current and earlier chapters. You should also consider your answers to the case study questions in earlier chapters.

Required

Prepare common-size statements for Cloud 9. Use total assets as the basis for the balance sheet, and revenue as the basis for the income statement. Comment on any audit implications revealed by your statements.

RESEARCH QUESTION 10.1

A generally accepted definition of earnings management is the planned timing of revenues, expenses, gains, and losses to smooth out earnings over a number of accounting periods. Generally speaking, earnings management is used to increase income in the current year at the expense of income in future years by, for example, prematurely recognizing sales before they are complete in order to boost profits. However, earnings management can also be used to decrease current earnings, so as to increase income in the future, a practice often referred to as "cookie jar" accounting. For example, WorldCom Inc., one of the greatest U.S. corporate bankruptcies, used so-called cookie jar accounting to inflate provisions for expected expenses and later reversed them to boost earnings.

Required

Consider the issues that lead to earnings management and, in particular, the reasons for companies adopting cookie jar accounting practices. How might auditors overcome such practices? In your discussion, refer to widely publicized corporate collapses such as WorldCom, which have used earnings management techniques.

SOLUTIONS TO MULTIPLE-CHOICE QUESTIONS

1. a, 2. d, 3. d, 4. b, 5. c, 6. c, 7. a, 8. b, 9. a, 10. d.

CHAPTER 11

Auditing inventories and property, plant, and equipment

LEARNING OBJECTIVES

After studying this chapter, you should be able to:

1 identify the audit objectives applicable to inventories

2 describe the functions and control procedures normally found for the custody and maintenance of inventory records

3 discuss considerations relevant to determining the audit strategy for inventories

4 design a substantive audit program for inventory

5 identify the audit objectives applicable to property, plant, and equipment

6 discuss considerations relevant to determining the audit strategy for property, plant, and equipment

7 design a substantive audit program for property, plant, and equipment.

AUDITING AND ASSURANCE STANDARDS

CANADIAN	INTERNATIONAL
CAS 315 *Identifying and Assessing the Risks of Material Misstatement through Understanding the Entity and Its Environment*	ISA 315 *Identifying and Assessing the Risks of Material Misstatement through Understanding the Entity and Its Environment*
CAS 501 *Audit Evidence—Specific Considerations for Inventory and Segment Information*	ISA 501 *Audit Evidence—Specific Considerations for Selected Items*
CAS 510 *Initial Engagements—Opening Balances*	ISA 510 *Initial Audit Engagements—Opening Balances*
CAS 540 *Auditing Accounting Estimates, Including Fair Value Accounting Estimates, and Related Disclosures*	ISA 540 *Auditing Accounting Estimates, Including Fair Value Accounting Estimates, and Related Disclosures*
CAS 600 *Special Considerations—Audits of Group Financial Statements (Including the Work of Component Auditors)*	ISA 600 *Special Considerations—Audits of Group Financial Statements (Including the Work of Component Auditors)*
CAS 610 *Using the Work of Internal Auditors*	ISA 610 *Using the Work of Internal Auditors*
CAS 620 *Using the Work of an Auditor's Expert*	ISA 620 *Using the Work of an Auditor's Expert*
IAS 2 *Inventories*	IAS 2 *Inventories*
IAS 16 *Property, Plant and Equipment*	IAS 16 *Property, Plant and Equipment*
IAS 17 *Leases*	IAS 17 *Leases*
IAS 36 *Impairment of Assets*	IAS 36 *Impairment of Assets*

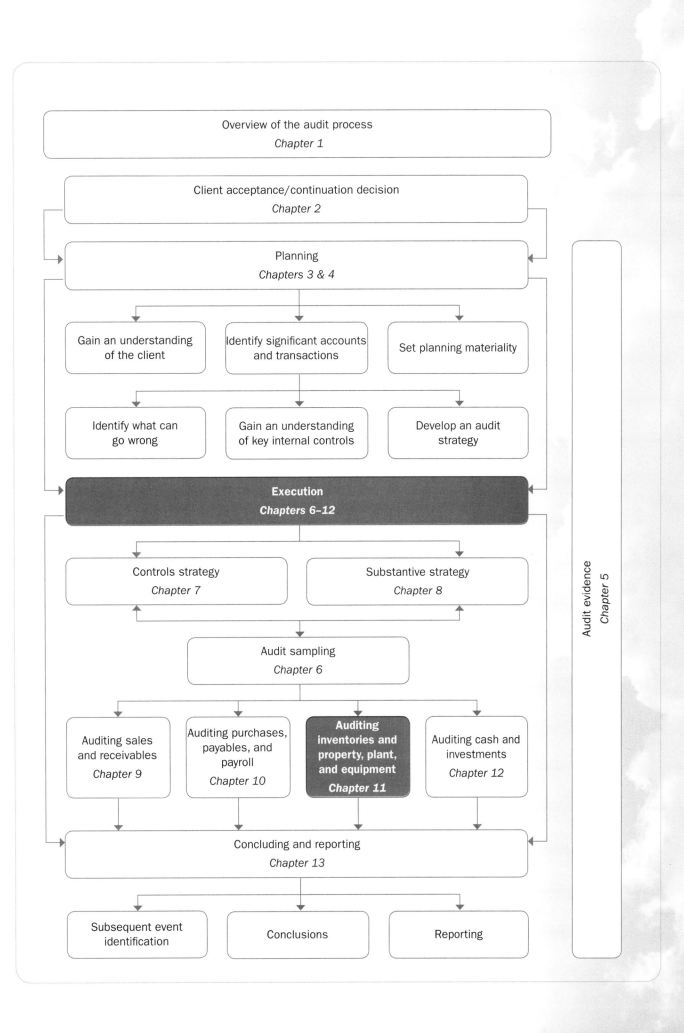

Cloud 9

Josh is now looking forward to focusing on the inventory of Cloud 9. He knows W&S Partners has a wide range of audit clients, including a department store, a chain of small retail shops, a construction company, a manufacturer of electronic goods, a farm, a jeweller, a private school, a mining company, a hotel, a chain of restaurants, and a car dealership. For each of these businesses, inventory is likely to be a significant asset.

Some of these companies, including Cloud 9, will have a perpetual inventory system where the receipt and shipping of goods are recorded as they happen. Regular inventory counts act as a check against the inventory recorded in the perpetual system and any discrepancies due to theft or other events will be adjusted for. While some businesses have very specialized products where specific expertise is required to understand the product and its worth, the running shoes at Cloud 9 are a relatively simple product to value. Regardless, for most clients, including Cloud 9, a significant amount of audit attention will be devoted to this area.

AUDIT PROCESS IN FOCUS

The purpose of this chapter is to examine the audit of inventories and property, plant, and equipment. The internal controls over the classes of transactions affecting both the inventory and property, plant, and equipment balances have already been considered. In chapter 10, we considered the purchase cycle, which included the acquisition of inventories and property, plant, and equipment assets, and in chapter 9, we considered the selling of inventory as part of the sales cycle. For this reason, the organization of this chapter differs from that of the two previous chapters. There is no separate section describing the functions and control procedures for inventory or property, plant, and equipment transactions. However, for inventory, there is a section describing functions and control procedures associated with the custody of inventory and the maintenance of inventory records. In the section on developing the audit plan, the significance of assessing the effectiveness of controls over inventory records is discussed in the context of determining the audit strategy.

For property, plant, and equipment, the auditor usually adopts a substantive approach. The nature of such records is described in the section on developing the audit plan, but there is rarely an assessment of controls. The explanation of the audit of property, plant, and equipment is followed by the design and execution of substantive audit procedures. Given the complex nature of intangible non-current assets, their audit is not dealt with in this text. The audit of non-current investments is the subject of chapter 12.

For both inventory and property, plant, and equipment the inherent risk is primarily over their existence and valuation. Thus, verification of the existence and valuation and allocation assertions for these assets receive special consideration.

11.1 AUDIT OBJECTIVES: INVENTORY

 Identify the audit objectives applicable to inventories.

The key issue in auditing inventories is to ensure the inventories actually exist, are owned, and are properly valued. Table 11.1 lists the main audit objectives for each assertion, referencing them to specific controls and audit procedures. More detail about assertions specific to the classes of transactions and account balances can be found in paragraph A111 of CAS 315 *Identifying and Assessing the Risks of Material Misstatement through Understanding the Entity and Its Environment*.

Note that, for occurrence and completeness, transfer transactions apply only to multi-location entities and manufacturing entities that distinguish between raw materials, work in process, and finished goods.

TABLE 11.1 **Selected specific audit objectives for inventory**

CLASSES OF TRANSACTION OBJECTIVES	
Occurrence (**OE**)	Recorded purchase transactions represent inventories acquired during the period (**OE1**).
	Recorded transfers represent inventories transferred between locations or categories during the period (**OE2**).
	Recorded sale transactions represent inventories sold during the period (**OE3**).
Completeness (**C**)	All inventory receipts during the period have been recorded as purchases (**C1**).
	All transfers of inventories between locations or categories during the period have been recorded (**C2**).
	All inventory shipped during the period has been recorded as sales (**C3**).
Accuracy (**AV**)	Inventory transactions are properly (accurately) recorded (**AV1**).
Cut-off (**CO**)	Inventories received before the period end are recorded as purchases in the current period and those received after the period end are included in the next accounting period (**CO1**).
	Inventories shipped before the period end are recorded as sales in the current period and those shipped after the period end are included in the next accounting period (**CO2**).
Classification (**PD**)	Inventory transactions are recorded in the correct accounts (**PD1**).
ACCOUNT BALANCE OBJECTIVES	
Existence (**OE**)	Inventories recorded represent items on hand at the end of the reporting period (**OE4**).
Rights and obligations (**RO**)	The entity has rights to the inventories included in the balance sheet (**RO1**).
Completeness (**C**)	Inventories include all materials, products, and supplies on hand at the end of the reporting period (**C4**).
Valuation and allocation (**AV**)	Inventories are properly stated at the lower of cost and net realizable value, determined in accordance with applicable accounting standards (**AV2**).
PRESENTATION AND DISCLOSURE OBJECTIVES (PD)	
Occurrence and rights and obligations	Disclosed inventories have occurred and pertain to the entity (**PD2**).
Completeness	All inventory disclosures that should have been included in the financial statements have been included (**PD3**).
Classification and understandability	Inventories are properly identified and classified in the financial statements (**PD4**).
	Inventories are appropriately presented and information disclosed is clearly expressed (**PD5**).
Accuracy and valuation	Inventories are disclosed accurately and at appropriate amounts (**PD5**).

Cloud 9

Because the same processes are used for the purchase and sale of all products and services, including inventory, Josh realizes that the audit team has already gathered some evidence about the inventory when they did the testing over the purchases and sales cycles. Josh can see from the audit file documentation that Weijing Fei, a first-year auditor with W&S, attended the inventory count at year end at Cloud 9's main warehouse. He is not sure if anyone was present for the inventory count at the retail location. He makes a note to ask Sharon about this.

Because W&S attended the count, he believes the audit team will plan a substantive approach in obtaining evidence as to the existence and completeness assertions of the inventory. He is uncertain what audit strategy they will use for the valuation assertion.

BEFORE YOU GO ON

11.1.1 What are two key issues auditors face when auditing inventory?

11.1.2 What is completeness with respect to inventory?

11.1.3 Define the audit objective of cut-off with respect to inventory.

11.2 CUSTODY OF INVENTORY AND MAINTENANCE OF INVENTORY RECORDS

2 Describe the functions and control procedures normally found for the custody and maintenance of inventory records.

In a merchandising entity, inventory consists of goods acquired for resale. In a manufacturing entity, inventory can be in one of three stages:

1. **raw materials** awaiting processing

2. partly manufactured items known as **work in process**

3. **finished goods** awaiting sale

Smaller entities, particularly those not engaged in manufacturing, may not maintain inventory records. Instead, inventory is determined at or near the end of the reporting period by a physical inventory count. The main audit procedure in such cases is observation of the count. At the other extreme, large manufacturing entities maintain comprehensive inventory records, with subsidiary inventory ledgers integrated with the general ledger. These records may be used as the basis for determining both the quantity and value of inventory at the end of the reporting period. To obtain sufficient audit evidence in such cases, the auditor must perform extensive tests of controls over the recording of inventory transactions and the maintenance of inventory records.

raw materials materials purchased from suppliers to be used in the manufacture of finished goods

work in process part-manufactured products consisting of materials, direct labour, and overhead applied to the stage of completion

finished goods manufactured inventory that is available for sale

11.2.1 Maintaining inventory records

The use of computer information systems has made it much easier for entities to maintain **perpetual inventory records**, and systems can maintain inventory records by quantity and value, which are fully integrated with the accounting records in an **inventory master file**. For merchandising entities, a single inventory record is required, although this may be subdivided by location. Manufacturing entities need to record separate inventories of raw materials, work in process, and finished goods, and to establish procedures for recording the movement of goods through production.

An important control over maintaining inventory records is the segregation of this function from the physical custody of the inventory. The custodian then has no opportunity to conceal an inventory shortage by manipulating the inventory records.

The separate functions are:

perpetual inventory records records of the movement of inventory items and the quantity on hand

inventory master file a file containing details of inventory items, their movement, and the quantity on hand

- recording the movement of goods into inventory

- recording the movement of goods from inventory

- recording transfers of inventory

- physically comparing inventory with inventory records

Movement of goods into inventory

In all cases, the initial entry into inventory is through the purchasing system (see chapter 10). The receiving clerk acknowledges receipt of the goods by initialling a copy of the receiving report. The receiving report then provides the source of the quantity and cost entries on the appropriate inventory record. These procedures relate mainly to the occurrence and completeness assertions (**OE1, C1**).

Movement of goods from inventory

When merchandise inventories or finished goods are sold, the shipping document serves as the basis for authorization of the release of the goods from inventory, and for the entry in inventory records reducing the quantity on hand. In retail stores, bar codes or security tags scanned at the cash register provide data for reducing recorded inventory. Control procedures as to the occurrence and completeness of sale transactions (see chapter 9) also relate to the occurrence and completeness of recorded inventory movements (**OE3, C3**).

Transfers of inventory

Further procedures are necessary where goods are transferred from one inventory location to another. In manufacturing entities, **inventory transfer requisitions** control the movement of goods from raw materials through work in process to finished goods. These pre-numbered documents are issued by production control and represent authorization to issue raw materials and to apply direct labour to process materials to produce the finished goods. Each transfer requisition consists of tickets identifying the specific material and labour requirements for the goods to be produced. Initialled copies of tickets represent acknowledgement, by inventory custodians, of the receipt of goods, or evidence of their proper delivery. They also provide the basis for accounting entries, relieving one inventory location and charging the other. Similar procedures, on a less elaborate scale, are required in retailing entities to record and control internal transfers. These procedures relate to the occurrence and completeness assertions for internal inventory movements (**OE2, C2**).

> **inventory transfer requisition** a document authorizing the requisitioning of materials and labour for the purpose of manufacturing

11.2.2 Physical comparison of inventory with inventory records

Perpetual inventory records need to be compared with actual inventory at regular intervals. The two functions involved are:

- an inventory count
- a comparison of the actual items on hand with the inventory records

Inventory count

Procedures for an inventory count are similar whether the purpose is to determine inventory at the end of the reporting period or to compare inventory with inventory records at an intermediate date. This section describes procedures applicable to a full inventory count. Procedures for **cyclical inventory counts** may be less thorough and involve counting only a portion of inventory items. Such counts are usually performed where a perpetual inventory system is in place and the cyclical counts act as a control. The sample selected for counting may be organized systematically, through different sections of the warehouse or different types of inventory, or by random sampling. Another approach is to count items at the reorder point when inventory levels are low, thus reducing both the cost of the count and the likelihood of count errors.

> **cyclical inventory counts** periodic inventory counts that count, over a year, all or most inventory items

The procedures for an inventory count involve:

- assigning and communicating responsibility
- preparing
- identifying
- counting
- checking
- clearing
- recording
- cut-off

These procedures are described as follows:

- *Assigning and communicating responsibility.* Overall responsibility for the count should be assigned to a person who has no responsibility for either the custody of inventory or the maintenance of inventory records. People involved in the count should also be suitably independent, although warehouse staff may be involved if supervised. The area containing inventory should be subdivided, with count teams assigned to specific sections. Instructions should be drawn up and responsibilities clearly explained to each person involved.

- *Preparing.* Before the count, areas such as the warehouse and shop floor should be tidied, with inventory neatly stacked and items not to be counted (such as scrap or goods held for third parties) removed or clearly marked. Arrangements need to be made to cease production, if possible, and receiving and shipping departments need to be alerted so as to avoid movement of goods to or from those departments during the count. In this way, cut-off errors can be avoided. If an accurate cut-off is not achieved, the physical count may include, for example, goods for which the purchase or production cost is not recorded by the information system until after the count. This could result in an overstatement of inventory.

- *Identifying.* Inventory to be counted must be properly identified. This is a particular problem with specialized items or work in process. With work in process, the problem is with identifying the stage of completion, which determines the costs accumulated against the items. Either the goods must be tagged in advance or count teams knowledgeable in the inventory must be assigned to the count in appropriate sections.

- *Counting.* Count teams usually work in pairs where any lifting or moving of items is necessary to ascertain the quantity. Forklift trucks and weighing scales may also need to be available. Instructions should ensure that count teams understand the unit of measurement (e.g., 25-kilogram bags). The degree of thoroughness also needs to be considered, such as whether cartons need to be opened at random or weighed to verify that they are full and the contents are as described.

- *Checking.* Sometimes all counts are double-checked and all discrepancies are re-counted. Where errors are unlikely, only spot checks need to be performed and only counts by those count teams making errors need to be double-checked.

- *Clearing.* As each item is counted, the count team should leave a mark to avoid duplicating the count. On completion of a section, a supervisor should tour the area to ensure no items appear to be uncounted.

- *Recording.* Control over count sheets is particularly important. Three systems are commonly used. First, where inventory items are standardized, pre-printed **inventory count sheets** containing descriptions are issued to the count teams, who then complete the sheets by entering the quantity. Another system is to issue blank, pre-numbered count sheets. The serial numbers issued to each count team must be noted and checked on completion to ensure that no sheets are missing. Half-filled sheets should be ruled off, and unused sheets should be identified as such to prevent items being added after the count. The third method involves attaching pre-numbered, three-part **inventory tags** to each inventory item before the count. The count team enters the description and quantity on the first part of the tag and removes it. The checkers do likewise with the second part, which is compared with the first part. The third part, the stub of the tag, remains attached to the item to enable the supervisor to verify the completeness of the count. Again, serial numbers should be fully accounted for. In each case, counters and checkers should be required to sign or initial each count sheet or tag.

- *Cut-off.* Serial numbers of the last pre-numbered receiving reports, shipping documents, and inventory transfer requisitions issued before the inventory count need to be recorded to ensure that the count is compared with inventory records based on the same documents.

Comparison with records

Comparison with the inventory records is of greater importance for cyclical counts, where the aim is to ensure the reliability of the inventory records and to establish the effectiveness of the procedures designed to ensure accountability for the custodianship and record-keeping of the inventory. With counts undertaken at or near the end of the reporting period, comparison with the records helps identify any major errors in quantities discovered by the count.

inventory count sheets prepared (usually pre-numbered) sheets for recording inventory description and quantity as counted

inventory tags three-part, tie-on tags for recording the inventory count of each item

Procedures should require a re-count of material differences. If the difference remains, further investigation is required to ascertain whether the inventory records are in error and why. A record should be maintained of differences and the causes (if known), and the inventory records should be adjusted to agree with the count. This list of errors provides evidence as to the reliability of the records and the possibility of reliance on inventory records in determining inventory at year end, without the need for a further count.

These procedures relate mainly to the existence assertion (**OE4**) but also contribute to the completeness assertion (**C4**).

11.2.3 Determining and recording inventory costs

For merchandise inventory, procedures relating to measurement in the recording of purchase transactions ensure that proper costs are recorded in inventory records. On sales, the cost of sales should be determined in accordance with the appropriate cost flow assumption, which would normally be either first-in, first-out or weighted average. Entities recording cost of sales on a continuing basis will usually rely on computer information systems, which should be programmed to determine the appropriate cost.

Costing of manufactured inventory is far more complex. Procedures are required to:

- determine the cost of materials entered into raw materials
- determine the cost of raw materials transferred to work in process at first-in, first-out or weighted average cost
- record costs of direct labour applied to work in process
- identify abnormal waste or spoilage in the production process
- identify manufacturing overhead costs and apportion costs to production departments
- assign overhead costs to work in process using an appropriate absorption rate
- apportion costs to by-products
- relieve work in process and charge finished goods on completion of manufacturing, based on costing procedures such as batch or process costing
- relieve finished goods with the cost of sales at first-in, first-out or weighted average

Some entities record inventory at standard cost and identify differences between standard and actual costs as variances.

In obtaining the understanding of the accounting system, the auditor needs to identify the entity's accounting policy and ascertain the procedures for ensuring that costs are recorded in accordance with that policy. It is also necessary for the auditor to ensure that the policy is consistent with the requirements of IAS 2 *Inventories*. These procedures relate to the accuracy (**AV1**) and valuation and allocation assertion (**AV2**), and contribute to the presentation and disclosure assertion (**PD5**).

Cloud 9

Josh is glad that Sharon had already arranged for Weijing to attend the physical inventory count at Cloud 9's warehouse at year end. He reviews Weijing's notes indicating there was no shipping or receiving at the warehouse the day of the count. The count was performed by count pairs who were assigned a specific area of the warehouse to count. Count tags and sequentially numbered count sheets were assigned and the warehouse was neat and tidy. The running shoes were neatly organized and stacked by item type. As items were counted, the count tags were ticked to prevent any double counting. Weijing noted that all count sheets were submitted at the end of the count. She also noted that Carla and the warehouse manager were present and supervised the count.

BEFORE YOU GO ON

11.2.1 What four functions should be segregated with respect to inventory?

11.2.2 Describe the eight procedures applicable to a full inventory count.

11.2.3 List the procedures required to cost manufactured inventory.

11.3 AUDIT STRATEGY: INVENTORY

3 Discuss considerations relevant to determining the audit strategy for inventories.

The selected approach to the audit of inventory depends on the availability and reliability of inventory records. Consideration of the internal control structure relating to inventory records, described in the previous section, is necessary only where such records exist. In all audits, consideration of the determination of cost records is important.

11.3.1 Inherent risk assessment

In a manufacturing entity, inventories and cost of sales are usually significant to both the entity's financial position and the results of its operations. Moreover, numerous factors contribute to the risk of misstatements in the assertions for these accounts, including those described below:

- The volume of purchase, manufacturing, and sale transactions that affect these accounts is generally high, increasing the opportunities for misstatements to occur.
- There are often contentious valuation and allocation issues, such as:
  - the identification, measurement, and allocation of indirect materials, labour, and manufacturing overhead
  - joint product costs
  - the disposition of cost variances
  - accounting for scrap and wastage
- Special procedures are sometimes required to determine inventory quantity or value, such as geometric volume measurements of stockpiles using aerial photography, and estimation of value by experts.
- Inventories are often stored at multiple sites, leading to difficulties in maintaining physical control over theft and damage, and in accounting for goods in transit between sites.
- Inventories are vulnerable to spoilage, obsolescence, and general economic conditions that may affect demand and saleability, and thus their valuation.
- Inventories may be sold subject to right of return and repurchase agreements.

In planning the audit, the auditor will be aware that the inherent risks are greater with respect to the existence assertion and the valuation and allocation assertion. Management typically has a greater incentive to overstate inventory, being an asset, than to understate it. It may do so by either inflating the quantity or overstating its value. There are numerous instances of such frauds discovered (and not discovered) by auditors. A lack of third-party evidence means it is also often easier to overstate inventories than assets such as cash or accounts receivable. Further, inventory is subject to theft both by employees and by outsiders. The depletion of inventory as a consequence of shoplifting is well known.

In verifying the existence (and completeness) assertions, the auditor has the choice of three audit strategies—a choice that depends on the entity's own policy for determining inventory quantity. The options are:

- Determine inventory quantity by perpetual inventory records where the entity does not intend to count inventory at or close to the end of the reporting period. The audit strategy requires assessing the control risk over inventory records as being low.
- Determine inventory quantities by a physical count near the end of the reporting period, adjusted to balance sheet quantities by reference to perpetual inventory records. This strategy requires assessing the control risk over inventory records, or of purchases and sales, as being less than high.
- Determine inventory quantities by a physical count at or within a few days of the end of the reporting period. This is a substantive approach in which the auditor does not test control over inventory records, which may not even exist.

The auditor may use all three methods for a single entity with different categories of inventory or for inventory at different locations. A manufacturing entity may, for example, determine the quantities of raw materials and finished goods at a year-end inventory count, but rely on perpetual records in determining the work-in-process inventory.

In developing the audit plan, the auditor needs to discuss the approach management intends to take. If management intends to rely solely on inventory records, then more extensive tests of controls will be necessary to confirm the required assessment of control risk. Moreover, this assessment must be completed before the end of the reporting period in the event that tests of controls fail to confirm the assessment of control risk as being low, and the auditor is required to advise management to undertake an inventory count at or near the end of the reporting period.

Specialized inventories may require the assistance of experts in determining either the quantity (as in the case of aerial measurement of stockpiles) or value (as in the case of antiques). In accordance with CAS 620 *Using the Work of an Auditor's Expert*, the type of expertise required will vary with different circumstances so the nature and scope of the work need to be clearly agreed between the expert and the auditor. The auditor must also ensure that they obtain sufficient understanding of the field of expertise to be able to evaluate the adequacy of the work performed; this includes an assessment of the expert's capabilities and objectivity.

For merchandise inventory, a substantive approach is usually more efficient in verifying the valuation and allocation assertion. For manufacturing entities, it is usually necessary for the auditor to have assessed control risk over the maintenance of costing records (used as the basis for costing closing inventory) as being less than high. This is an area that sometimes receives insufficient audit attention owing to a reluctance to unravel the complexities of the costing system.

Cloud 9

Josh understands that for the inventory account, the primary inherent risks are existence and valuation. This is because management has an incentive to overstate the quantity and/or value of inventories, athletic shoes are susceptible to theft, and the valuation of the shoes involves judgement and estimation by Cloud 9 management. He believes the work performed on the inventory count provides sufficient and appropriate evidence over the existence assertion.

PROFESSIONAL ENVIRONMENT

Inventory frauds

Inventory is an easy fraud target. For retailers, inventory is usually their biggest asset, while for manufacturers, inventory is a significant portion of their assets. Even service businesses have supplies on hand.

The most common type of inventory fraud is theft. Inventory items can be small and numerous, easily accessible, of small value, and not easily missed. Having few, large-value inventory items (like cars in a car dealership) is no guarantee of protection from such frauds. The loss is from the theft of business assets.

How is the fraud done?

Both employees and non-employees can easily steal inventory items. Many physical assets are not locked up, and many are freely available to employees without authorization or requisition, such as goods available to retail salespeople or materials needed by factory employees.

For smaller items or a one-time theft, employees will usually not bother to hide the theft, since it will probably go undetected in the business records or at the next inventory count. But for recurring inventory thefts, the employee will need to hide them in the business records.

In order to hide the inventory loss at the next inventory count, an employee would need to alter the accounting records, using one of four methods:

- False write off schemes involve writing off the stolen inventory as scrap or similar.
- False inventory counts involve falsifying the recorded stock count with the amount of inventory actually on hand.
- Perpetual record schemes involve falsifying the amount of inventory in the perpetual record when the inventory is stolen, so that the amount will match the inventory count later.
- False receiving documentation involves falsifying the amount of inventory received from suppliers in the records, to hide the actual amounts on hand and stolen.

How to reduce inventory fraud

There are several ways to reduce the risk of inventory fraud, including the following.

- Use physical security to secure inventory during and after business hours.
- Limit employee access to the business premises, especially the stockroom, after hours. This reduces the risk of them stealing things and also accessing records to alter and hide their theft.
- Require authorized employees to use passwords to access business records.
- Require independent authorization to write off inventory losses.
- Segregate duties regarding inventory, such as ordering, receiving, and invoicing.
- Conduct proper, verified inventory counts. Employees have even been known to stack empty boxes to try to fool auditors into thinking inventory is there when it isn't.

Sources: "Detecting and Deterring Business Asset Misappropriation by Employees," Business Owner's Toolkit, www.bizfilings.com, March 19, 2012; "Stock Fraud — Inventory Record Frauds: Description of Inventory Record Frauds," Worrells Solvency & Forensic Accountants, www.worrells.net.au, May 8, 2006; "Important Fraud Prevention Tips for Your Parts Department," The Mercadien Group, www.mercadien.com, n.d.

11.3.2 Control risk assessment

Assessment of control risk over inventory records is important where the entity does not intend to perform a full inventory count at or close to year end. In this case, a satisfactory assessment is vital. Assessment of control risk over the cost of inventory is always important for manufacturing entities.

Control risk over inventory records

Table 11.2 contains a partial listing of potential misstatements (WCGW), necessary controls, possible tests of the operating effectiveness of those controls, and the specific audit objective to which each belongs. As explained previously, the auditor assesses control risk over perpetual inventory records only where they are used in determining inventory at the end of the reporting period. If the preliminary assessment based on the design effectiveness of controls is that control risk is likely to be high, then the auditor would advise management not to rely on the records in determining inventory at the end of the reporting period.

If the preliminary assessment supports management's intended reliance on inventory records, then the auditor would draw up an audit program incorporating possible tests of the operating effectiveness of controls such as those identified in table 11.2.

Many of these tests are in the form of dual-purpose tests. It is important to remember that CAS 501 *Audit Evidence—Specific Considerations for Inventory and Segment Information* requires the auditor, where reliance is placed entirely on perpetual inventory records in determining inventory at the end of the reporting period, to perform procedures to ensure that changes in inventory between a count date and the period end are properly recorded. This includes procedures to ensure that:

- the design, implementation, and maintenance of internal controls over the recording of changes in inventory are effective

- significant differences between the physical count and the perpetual inventory records are properly adjusted

TABLE 11.2 **Control risk assessment considerations**

FUNCTION	"WHAT CAN GO WRONG"	NECESSARY CONTROL	POSSIBLE TEST OF OPERATING EFFECTIVENESS	RELEVANT AUDIT OBJECTIVE (FROM TABLE 11.1)				
				OE NO.	C NO.	AV NO.	CO NO.	PD NO.
Recording movement of goods into inventory	Failure to record goods	Use of pre-numbered receiving reports and inventory transfer requisitions	Re-perform test of numerical continuity.		✓1, 2		✓1	
		Independent reconciliation of inventory records with control account in general ledger	Re-perform.*	✓1, 2, 3	✓1, 2, 3	✓1	✓1, 2	
Recording movement of goods from inventory	Unauthorized removal of goods	Custodian required to acknowledge responsibility for receipt of goods into inventory	Inspect receiving reports and inventory transfer requisitions for custodian's initials.	✓1, 2			✓1	
		Custodian required to obtain receipt for all requests to move inventory out of storage	Vouch recorded removals with properly authorized shipping documents and inventory transfer requisitions.*	✓2, 3			✓2	
		Physical comparison of inventory with inventory records	Observe. Re-perform.*	✓1, 2, 3	✓1, 2, 3		✓1, 2	

(continued)

FUNCTION	"WHAT CAN GO WRONG"	NECESSARY CONTROL	POSSIBLE TEST OF OPERATING EFFECTIVENESS	RELEVANT AUDIT OBJECTIVE (FROM TABLE 11.1)				
				OE NO.	C NO.	AV NO.	CO NO.	PD NO.
Physical comparison of inventory with inventory records	Unreliable count procedures	Responsibility independent from maintenance of inventory records and custodianship of inventory	Observe.	✓4	✓4			
		Adequate instructions properly issued and followed	Observe. Re-perform.*	✓4	✓4			
	Inadequate investigation and correction	Proper record maintained of differences and their correction	Inspect. Re-perform.*	✓4	✓4			
	Insufficient extent of comparison	Prescribed procedures for systematic counts	Inspect.	✓4	✓4			
Determining inventory costs	Inappropriate basis	Approved by controller	Inquire. Compare with accounting standards.			✓1, 2		✓1, 4
	Improper calculation	Consistent with engineering specification	Inspect. Re-perform.*			✓1, 2 ✓1, 2		
		Program controls	Use test data.*					

* Usually performed as part of dual-purpose tests.

TABLE 11.2 **Control risk assessment considerations** (continued)

Close to the end of the reporting period, the auditor needs to consider the extent of test counts relative to total inventory, and to review the recorded differences between test counts and inventory records over the year and the explanations of those differences. If the auditor is not satisfied that results of test counts support an assessment of control risk as low, then the auditor must discuss with management the need for a complete inventory count.

Control risk over inventory cost

In a manufacturing entity, assessment of the reliability of the costing system to provide accurate costs of production that are correctly determined in accordance with acceptable accounting standards can constitute a substantial component of the interim audit.

Manufacturing costs are nearly always determined through the computer information system, and test data can be used to test the accuracy of processing and recording cost information. Where standard costs are intended to be used as the basis for valuing inventories, the tests must extend to the procedures used in developing standards from the engineering specifications as to the:

- quantities of labour and material required
- determination of standard prices for labour and materials

Cloud 9

Josh can see that the most important test of controls is the comparison of the results of the test counts to the accounting records. The extent and results of such test counts performed by the entity are important to the assessment of control risk. Where perpetual inventory records are used to determine inventory at the end of the reporting period, the auditor needs to obtain an understanding of the internal control structure and perform tests of controls. He knows this is not necessary for Cloud 9 because W&S Partners has planned a substantive audit strategy over the inventory.

BEFORE YOU GO ON

11.3.1 Describe some of the inherent risks for inventory.

11.3.2 In verifying the existence (and completeness) assertions, the auditor has the choice of which three audit strategies?

11.3.3 Is it possible for the auditor to rely on tests of controls for inventory?

11.4 SUBSTANTIVE PROCEDURES FOR INVENTORIES

④ Design a substantive audit program for inventory.

Except where perpetual records are used as the basis for determining inventory at the end of the reporting period, and for costing records in manufacturing entities, the audit for inventories is based mainly on substantive procedures applied to the account balance at the end of the reporting period.

The emphasis is on the assertions of existence and valuation, because the inherent risk of their misstatement is usually high. Acceptable detection risk for these two assertions is usually assessed as low, with detection risk for other assertions being low to moderate.

Table 11.3 lists possible substantive procedures to be included in the audit program, with each test referenced to the audit objectives shown in table 11.1.

TABLE 11.3 **Possible substantive procedures for tests of inventory assertions**

CATEGORY	SUBSTANTIVE PROCEDURES	RELEVANT AUDIT OBJECTIVE (FROM TABLE 11.1)					
		OE4	C4	RO1	AV2	CO	PD NO.
Initial procedures	1. Perform initial procedures on inventory balances and records that will be subjected to further testing. (a) Trace opening inventory balances to the previous year's working papers. (b) Review activity in inventory accounts and investigate entries that appear unusual in amount or source. (c) Verify totals of perpetual inventory records and their agreement with closing general ledger balances.				✓		
Analytical procedures	2. Perform analytical procedures. (a) Review industry experience and trends. (b) Examine an analysis of inventory turnover and gross profit. (c) Review relationships of inventory balances to recent purchasing, production, and sales activities.	✓	✓		✓	✓	
Tests of details of transactions	3. Test entries in inventory records to and from supporting documentation.	✓	✓	✓	✓	✓	
	4. Test the cut-off of purchases, inventory transfers, and sales.	✓	✓			✓	
Tests of details of balances	5. Observe the entity's physical inventory count. (a) Evaluate the adequacy of the entity's inventory-taking plans. (b) Observe physical inventory count and test compliance with prescribed procedures. (c) Make test counts. (d) Look for indications of slow-moving, damaged, or obsolete inventory. (e) Account for all inventory tags and count sheets used in the physical count. (f) Record cut-off data.	✓	✓	✓	✓	✓	

(continued)

CATEGORY	SUBSTANTIVE PROCEDURES	RELEVANT AUDIT OBJECTIVE (FROM TABLE 11.1)					
		OE4	C4	RO1	AV2	CO	PD NO.
	6. Test the clerical accuracy of inventory listings. (a) Recalculate totals and extensions of quantities times unit prices. (b) Trace test counts (from item 5(c)) to listings. (c) Vouch items on listings to and from count sheets and inventory tags. (d) Compare physical counts with perpetual inventory records. (e) Verify the adjustment of amounts for movements between the date of the physical count and the end of the reporting period.	✓	✓		✓		
	7. Test inventory pricing. (a) Examine suppliers' invoices for purchased inventories. (b) Examine the propriety of costing information, standard costs, and the disposition of variances relating to manufactured inventories. (c) Perform a lower of cost and net realizable value test.	✓	✓	✓	✓		
	8. Confirm inventories at locations outside the entity.			✓			
	9. Examine consignment agreements and contracts.						3
Disclosure	10. Compare statement presentation with applicable accounting standards. (a) Confirm agreements for assignment and pledging of inventories. (b) Review disclosures for inventories in drafts of the financial statements and determine conformity with applicable accounting standards.						✓2–6

TABLE 11.3 **Possible substantive procedures for tests of inventory assertions** (continued)

11.4.1 Initial procedures

In tracing opening inventory balances to working papers for the previous year, the auditor should make certain that any audit adjustments agreed on in the previous year were recorded. In addition, where perpetual inventory records are maintained, entries in the control accounts in the general ledger should be scanned to identify any postings that are unusual in amount or nature and thus require special investigation. Where perpetual inventory records are to be used as the basis for determining inventory at the end of the reporting period, the inventory listing must be test-checked to and from the records, added, and compared with the balance in the control account. Additional work on inventory listings is discussed in a later section on the tests of details of balances.

11.4.2 Analytical procedures

The application of analytical procedures to inventories is often extensive. A review of industry experience and trends may be essential in developing expectations to be used in evaluating analytical data for the entity. Knowledge of an industry-wide fall in inventory turnover, for example, will enable the auditor to expect a fall in the entity's inventory turnover ratio. If the ratio does not show the expected fall, then the auditor may suspect errors as to the existence or occurrence of the inventory balance, or in the completeness of the balance used in calculating the ratio. A review of relationships of inventory balances with recent purchasing, production, and sales activities should also help the auditor understand changes in inventory levels. An increase in the reported level of finished goods inventory when purchasing, production, and sales levels have remained steady, for example, could indicate misstatements relating to the existence or valuation of the finished goods inventory.

Important ratios are those of inventory turnover and gross profit. We previously explained the use of the gross profit ratio with respect to the audits of sales and purchases. An unexpectedly high inventory turnover ratio, or an unexpectedly low gross profit ratio, might be caused by an overstatement of cost of sales and a corresponding understatement of inventories. Conversely, conformity of these ratios with expectations provides assurance of the fairness of the data used in the calculations.

Where the physical inventory count is other than at the year end, the auditor should analyze totals of transactions in the intervening period for reasonableness.

11.4.3 Tests of details of transactions

With the exception of cut-off tests, tests of details of transactions are performed only where inventory at the end of the reporting period is determined wholly or partly from perpetual inventory records.

Testing entries in inventory records

Where inventory at the end of the reporting period is determined wholly by reference to perpetual inventory records, the tests of details of inventory transactions will be those described in table 11.2 as dual-purpose tests. Where inventory at the end of the reporting period is determined by a count other than at the year end and adjusted by reference to inventory records in the intervening period, such tests of details of transactions may be confined to the period between the date of the physical count and the year end.

Testing cut-off of purchase, manufacturing, and sale transactions

The purpose and nature of sales and purchases cut-off tests were explained in chapters 9 and 10, respectively, in connection with the audit of accounts receivable and accounts payable balances. Both tests are important in establishing that transactions occurring near the end of the year are recorded in the correct accounting period. Purchases in transit at year end, for example, should be excluded from inventory and payables, and inventory in transit to customers at year end should be included in sales and excluded from inventory. In a manufacturing entity, it must also be determined that entries are recorded in the proper period for the allocation of labour and overhead costs to work in process, and for goods moved between raw materials, work in process, and finished goods.

In each case, the auditor must ascertain, through inspection of documents and observation, that the paperwork cut-off and the cut-off for the physical inventory count are coordinated. If it is determined, for example, that an entry has reported the transfer of the cost of the final completed batch of the period to finished goods, then the auditor should determine that the goods, even if in transit, were included in the physical count of finished goods only; that is, that they were neither counted as part of work in process, nor double-counted, nor missed altogether. When attending the count, the auditor should note details of documentation relating to the movement of goods at the date of the count. Where the count is at a date other than at the end of the reporting period, the auditor must also check cut-off at the date of the count to ensure that movements between that date and the end of the reporting period exclude transactions before the count. Evidence from these cut-off tests relates to the occurrence, completeness, and accuracy assertions for inventory balances.

11.4.4 Tests of details of balances

As previously explained, the auditor reduces audit risk to the desired level mainly through the performance of substantive tests of details of balances.

In observing the inventory count, the auditor is not responsible for supervising the process. From this procedure, the auditor obtains direct knowledge of the reliability of management's inventory-counting procedures and, thus, the reliance that may be placed on management's assertions as to the quantities and physical condition of the inventories. In some cases, the entity may hire outside inventory specialists to do the count. Where the outside inventory specialists have no particular expertise in the type of inventory being counted, the auditor must be present to observe their counts, too, because, from an auditing standpoint, they are basically the same as entity employees. Where the specialists are experts in the particular type of inventory (such as precious stones), the auditor may be in a position to place a degree of reliance on the work of the expert in accordance with CAS 620 *Using the Work of an Auditor's Expert*.

As has been explained, the timing of the inventory count is negotiated with management in accordance with the entity's inventory system and the assessment of control risk. Except where reliance is placed wholly on perpetual inventory records, quantities are determined by physical count as at a specific date. The date should be at or near the end of the reporting period, and the auditor should be present on the specific date. For a multi-site entity, the auditor may vary locations attended each year, so long as the sample of inventory observed each year is of sufficient size. In such cases, the auditor may consider relying on internal audit for attendance at locations not visited, subject to the requirements of CAS 610 *Using the Work of Internal Auditors*. Such reliance, however, does not replace the requirement for the auditor to undertake sufficient personal observation of inventory counts. Other firms of auditors may also be engaged to observe an inventory count; for example, where another auditor is responsible for the audit of a subsidiary in a group, subject to the requirements of CAS 600 *Special Considerations—Audits of Group Financial Statements (Including the Work of Component Auditors)*.

Attendance at an inventory count involves performing tests of controls over entity procedures and substantive procedures applied directly by the auditor. Both procedures are performed simultaneously. Moreover, because there is no alternative audit strategy if the entity's inventory count procedures are found to be inadequate, the auditor should review and evaluate the entity's inventory count plans well in advance of the counting date. With ample lead time, the entity should be able to respond favourably to suggested modifications in the plans before the count begins. It is common for the auditor to help design a count plan that will facilitate both taking and observing the count.

Procedures are the same as for test counts in respect of perpetual inventory records (see section 11.2.2), except that the count is of all inventory, not just a sample.

In observing the inventory count to ensure prescribed procedures are being properly followed, the auditor should:

- observe entity employees performing their prescribed procedures
- determine that pre-numbered count sheets or inventory tags are properly controlled
- be alert to the existence of empty containers and hollow squares (empty spaces) that may exist when goods are stacked in solid formations
- observe that cut-off procedures are being followed and that the movement of goods, if any, is properly controlled
- see that all goods are marked as having been counted

In addition, the auditor should perform substantive procedures, including:

- making test counts and comparing quantities with the entity's count
- recording details of serial numbers of count sheets or tags used and unused (or taking copies of all used count sheets)
- appraising the general condition of the inventory, noting damaged, obsolete, and slow-moving items
- ensuring that partly used count sheets are ruled off to prevent additional entries being made
- identifying and noting the last receiving, production, and shipping documents used, and determining that goods received during the count are properly segregated

The extent of the auditor's test counts partly depends on the nature and composition of the inventory. Before the inventory count, the auditor may identify high-value items for test counting in addition to counting a representative sample of other items. In making test counts, the auditor should record the count and give a complete and accurate description of the item (identification number, unit of measurement, location, and so on) in the working papers, as shown in figure 11.1. Such data are essential for the auditor's comparison of the test counts with the entity's counts, and for the subsequent tracing of the counts to inventory summary sheets and perpetual inventory records.

On conclusion of the observation procedure, a designated member of the audit team should prepare a working paper detailing such matters as those listed below before reaching a conclusion as to the reliability of the count:

- departures from the entity's inventory count
- the extent of test counts and any material discrepancies resulting therefrom

FIGURE 11.1 **Inventory test counts working paper**

| Highlight Ltd.
Test counts
12/31/2016 | | | | | Prepared by: L.R.S
Date: 4/7/2017
Reviewed by: B.E.M.
Date: 4/10/2017 | |

Tag no.	Inventory sheet no.	Inventory		Count		
		Number	Description	Company	Auditor	Difference
6531	15	1-42-003	Olympic—Women's	125✓	125	
8340	18	1-83-012	Heavenly 456—Women's	93✓	93	
1483	24	2-11-004	Maximum Speed—Men's	1,321✓	1,325	4
4486	26	2-28-811	White Laces	220 ✓	220	
3334	48	4-26-204	Thunder 75—Men's	424✓	424	

Each difference was corrected by the company and the net effect of the corrections was to increase inventory by $840.

Total inventory values for which test counts were made and traced to inventory summaries without exception = $210,460 or 22% of the total. In my opinion, errors were immaterial.

✓ = Traced to company's inventory summary sheets (F–4), noting corrections for all differences.

- conclusions on the accuracy of the counts
- the general condition of the inventory

In the initial audit of an established entity, it is clearly impracticable for the auditor to have observed the physical inventory at the previous year end that established the opening inventory. ASA 510 *Initial Engagements—Opening Balances* (ISA 510) permits the auditor to verify the inventories by other auditing procedures. When the entity has been audited by another firm of auditors in the previous period, the auditor may review working papers of the predecessor audit firm and consider its competence and independence. If the entity has not been audited previously, the auditor may be able to obtain audit satisfaction by testing transactions from the previous period, reviewing the records of previous counts, or applying analytical procedures.

When sufficient evidence has not been obtained as to the existence of opening inventories, or when the auditor is unable to observe the taking of closing inventory counts or to obtain sufficient evidence from alternative procedures, the auditor cannot issue an unmodified auditor's report. We consider the specific effects on the auditor's report in chapter 13. Like the confirmation of accounts receivable, the observation of the entity's inventory count applies to many assertions. This procedure is the main source of evidence that the inventory exists. In addition, this procedure relates to the assertions detailed in table 11.4.

After the inventory count, the entity uses the count sheets or inventory tags to prepare a listing of all items counted. The inventory items are then priced to arrive at the total value of the inventory. Because this listing serves as the basis for the recorded inventory balance, the auditor must perform procedures to ensure that the listing is clerically accurate and that it accurately represents the results of the physical count.

ASSERTION	APPLICATION
Completeness	Procedures provide assurance that no items were omitted from the count.
Accuracy or valuation and allocation	Observation of the condition of goods as being damaged, obsolete, or apparently slow-moving provides evidence as to goods that may need to be valued at net realizable value.
Rights and obligations	Possession of goods on entity premises provides some evidence as to ownership.

TABLE 11.4 **Assertions for which attendance at an inventory count provides evidence**

To determine that the list accurately represents the results of the count, the auditor:

- compares his or her own test counts with the inventory listings
- identifies count sheets or tags used in the count according to records made by the auditor at the time of attendance, and tests items on those count sheets or tags to and from the listings
- compares the count, on a test basis, with amounts per perpetual records, when applicable, and inquires into any differences noted
- tests the clerical accuracy by recalculating the extensions of quantities times unit prices on a test basis, as well as the totals shown on the inventory listings

Cloud 9

Josh is reading the memo to file prepared by Weijing regarding the inventory count. She documented the item and serial numbers for all items included in her sample of test count. Weijing noted she vouched items from the count sheet to the inventory items to test for existence and traced items from the shelves back to the count sheets to test for completeness. Based on what he is reading, Josh believes the inventory count produced reliable results over the existence and completeness assertions. He can see that work on the valuation and allocation assertion must now be performed.

11.4.5 Testing inventory pricing

This procedure involves verifying the cost of inventory and the net realizable value of those items that management has determined need to be written down. It also involves considering whether other items, whose net realizable value may be below cost, need to be written down. Thus, it relates to the valuation and allocation assertion.

Inventory at cost

For merchandise inventory and raw materials valued on a first-in, first-out basis, this test involves examining suppliers' invoices covering the quantity in inventory.

For work in process and finished goods inventories, the auditor must test cost against costing records. The entity's costing system should have been evaluated during the interim audit, and controls over the determination of product cost assessed. Dual-purpose tests (table 11.2), serving as tests of both controls and substantive procedures, should provide sufficient evidence as to the reliability of product cost data. The auditor then vouches the costs that are applied to inventory to the costing records.

Where inventory is costed at standard cost, variances for the year need to be analyzed. When a variance account has a large balance, the auditor must consider whether fair presentation requires a pro rata allocation of the variance to inventories and to cost of sales, instead of charging the entire variance to cost of sales. A large adverse material price variance, for example, may indicate that the true cost of inventory is greater than the standard cost. If the variance is written off, then the cost of inventory is understated.

Inventory at net realizable value

IAS 2 *Inventories* requires inventory to be written down to net realizable value where below cost. The writedown constitutes an accounting estimate and the auditor must follow the procedures in CAS 540 *Auditing Accounting Estimates, Including Fair Value Accounting Estimates, and Related Disclosures.*

This requires the auditor to review and test the process used by management, use an independent estimate, and review subsequent events.

For items priced at net realizable value, the auditor must verify the basis for arriving at that value. In some cases, it will be the actual, current, or contracted selling price less an estimate of costs to be incurred in completion and selling. In other cases, a formula may be used, taking into account the age, past movement, and expected future movement of the inventory items. The auditor must examine the data and assumptions on which the estimates are based, check the calculations, consider previous period experience, and see that the estimates are properly approved by management.

In view of the inherent risk of understatement of the required writedown, the auditor should also carry out substantive procedures to identify the need for further writedowns. IAS 2 *Inventories* specifically identifies the following situations in which a writedown may be necessary:

- a fall in selling price
- physical deterioration of inventories
- obsolescence
- a decision to sell at a loss
- purchasing or production errors

  Specific procedures normally adopted by the auditor include:

- review of sales after the end of the reporting period
- observation of deterioration or obsolescence during the auditor's attendance at the physical count
- analysis of inventory holdings relative to recent or future budgeted turnover to identify excessive holdings; this is often performed with the use of generalized audit software
- inquiry of management and of sales and production personnel
- review of the minutes of the board of directors and executive committees

Use of an expert

When entity assertions about the value of the inventory relate to highly technical matters, the auditor may require the assistance of an outside expert. This may occur, for example, in an oil company with different grades of gasoline and motor oil, or in a jewellery shop with diamonds of varying quality. As explained in chapter 5, the auditor may use the work of an expert as an auditing procedure to obtain sufficient appropriate audit evidence when the auditor is satisfied as to the qualifications and independence of the expert.

11.4.6 Confirming inventories at locations outside the entity

When inventories are stored in public warehouses or with other third parties, the auditor should obtain evidence as to the existence of the inventory by direct communication with the custodian. This type of evidence is deemed sufficient except when the amounts involved represent a significant proportion of current or total assets. When this is the case, the auditor should apply procedures that include:

- considering the integrity and independence of the third party
- observing (or arranging for another auditor to observe) physical counts of the goods
- obtaining another auditor's report on the warehouse's control procedures relevant to physical counting and to custody of goods

Confirmation of inventories at outside locations also provides evidence about the rights and obligations assertion. In addition, it results in evidence as to the completeness assertion if the custodian confirms more goods on hand than stated in the confirmation request. It does not provide any evidence about the value of the inventory because the custodian is not asked to report on the condition of the goods stored in the warehouse.

11.4.7 Examining consignment agreements and contracts

Goods on hand may be held for customers, at their request, after a sale has occurred, and goods belonging to others may be held on consignment. A consignment "sale" is one made on a sale-or-return basis. Payment for the goods is required only on subsequent sale to a third party. For accounting purposes, such goods are included in the "seller's" inventory. Thus, management is requested to segregate goods not owned during the physical count. In addition, the auditor usually requests a written assertion on ownership of inventories in the representation letter (see chapter 5).

The auditor should also inquire as to whether any of the entity's own goods are held on consignment and included in inventory. If so, the auditor should review the documentation or, if the goods are material, confirm the existence of such goods directly with the other party.

Goods may also be assigned or pledged, usually as security for loans. The auditor must inquire of management as to the existence of such agreements and the appropriate disclosure should be checked in the financial statements. The auditor must also consider the possibility of window dressing. Substantial sales immediately before year end to an unlikely customer of goods that are not required to be delivered may, in reality, be a loan by the "customer," secured by the transfer of title to specified goods. Such a "transaction" enables the entity to reduce its inventories and increase its cash, thus enhancing the quick (or acid test) ratio. Further inquiry may reveal an agreement by the entity to repurchase the goods after the year end. Such a transaction should be accounted for in accordance with its substance: a loan secured by inventory.

Evidence obtained from this procedure relates to the rights and obligations assertion and the disclosure assertion.

11.4.8 Disclosure

It is appropriate to identify the major inventory categories in the balance sheet. In addition, there should be disclosure of the inventory costing method(s) used, the pledging of inventories, and the existence of major purchase commitments.

Inquiry of management is used to determine the existence of binding contracts for future purchases of goods. When such commitments exist, the auditor should examine the terms of the contracts and evaluate the fairness of the entity's accounting and reporting. When material losses exist on purchase commitments, they should be recognized in the financial statements, together with a disclosure of the attendant circumstances as noted in the discussion of accounts payable in chapter 10.

The substantive procedures described above provide evidence as to financial statement disclosure. Further evidence may be obtained, as needed, from a review of the minutes of board meetings and from inquiries of management. Based on the evidence, the auditor determines the fairness of the disclosures in accordance with the applicable accounting standards.

Cloud 9

Cloud 9 discloses that its inventory is valued at the lower of cost and net realizable value, which relates to the valuation and allocation assertion. Josh plans to test the inventory costing by looking at the most recent selling prices compared with the invoice costs for a sample of inventory items. He also plans to identify any slow-moving items and, using the most recent purchase invoices, verify if any writedowns to net realizable value are needed.

BEFORE YOU GO ON

11.4.1 What three possible strategies are available to the auditor to determine inventory quantity?

11.4.2 What are four controls that should be in place over inventory?

11.4.3 What is the auditor's responsibility with respect to a client's inventory count?

11.5 AUDIT OBJECTIVES: PROPERTY, PLANT, AND EQUIPMENT

⑤ Identify the audit objectives applicable to property, plant, and equipment.

There are various classes of property, plant, and equipment but all are tangible, non-current assets that are held to be used by the entity or to be rented out to others. Property includes:

- land and buildings, which may be freehold or leasehold
- plant and equipment, which includes machinery, vehicles, furniture, and equipment and may include items held under finance leases

The key issues in auditing property, plant, and equipment are ensuring that the property, plant, and equipment actually exist, are owned, and are properly valued with adequate provision for depreciation. The relevant audit objectives are presented in table 11.5. Note that, as discussed after table 11.1, further details on these assertions is provided in CAS 315 *Identifying and Assessing the Risk of Material Misstatement through Understanding the Entity and Its Environment*. A key focus in the audit of property, plant, and equipment relates to the transactions for purchasing new assets and disposing of old including profits or losses on sale. In addition, consideration is required in relation to depreciation charges, the treatment of leased assets, and asset revaluations.

TABLE 11.5 **Selected specific audit objectives for property, plant, and equipment**

CLASSES OF TRANSACTION OBJECTIVES	
Occurrence (**OE**)	Recorded additions represent property, plant, and equipment acquired during the period under audit (**OE1**).
	Recorded disposals represent property, plant, and equipment sold or scrapped during the period under audit (**OE2**).
Completeness (**C**)	All additions that occurred during the period have been recorded (**C1**).
	All disposals that occurred during the period have been recorded (**C2**).
Accuracy (**AV**)	Additions are correctly journalized and posted (**AV1**).
	Disposals are correctly journalized and posted (**AV2**).
Cut-off (**CO**)	Additions and disposals of property, plant, and equipment before the period end are recorded in the current period and those after the period end are included in the next accounting period (**CO1**).
Classification (**PD**)	Additions and disposals of property, plant, and equipment are recorded in the correct accounts (**PD1**).
ACCOUNT BALANCE OBJECTIVES	
Existence (**OE**)	Recorded property, plant, and equipment assets represent productive assets that are in use at the end of the reporting period (**OE3**).
Rights and obligations (**RO**)	The entity owns or has rights to all recorded property, plant, and equipment assets at the end of the reporting period (**RO1**).
Completeness (**C**)	Non-current asset balances include all applicable assets used in operations at the end of the reporting period (**C3**).
Valuation and allocation (**AV**)	Property, plant, and equipment are stated at cost or a valuation less accumulated depreciation (**AV3**).
PRESENTATION AND DISCLOSURE OBJECTIVES (PD)	
Occurrence and rights and obligations	Disclosed property, plant, and equipment transactions have occurred and pertain to the entity (**PD2**).
Completeness	Disclosures as to: • cost or valuation • depreciation methods and useful lives of each major class

(continued)

	• the pledging as collateral • the major terms of finance lease contracts of property, plant, and equipment assets are adequate (**PD3**).
Classification and understandability	The details of additions and disposals of property, plant, and equipment support their classification and disclosure in the financial statements (**PD4**).
Accuracy and valuation	Property, plant, and equipment transactions are disclosed accurately and at appropriate amounts (**PD5**).

TABLE 11.5 **Selected specific audit objectives for property, plant, and equipment** (continued)

Cloud 9

Josh sees that for Cloud 9, property, plant, and equipment represent the largest category of assets on the balance sheet and the expenses associated with property, plant, and equipment are material to the profit. He also notes that the property, plant, and equipment account balances are greater than last year's . He asks Sharon why this may be. She indicates she believes this is due to the addition of the new retail store, and part of their audit work will be to verify these additions.

BEFORE YOU GO ON

11.5.1 What items are considered property?

11.5.2 What are the key issues in auditing property, plant, and equipment?

11.5.3 Explain the completeness assertion for property, plant, and equipment.

11.6 AUDIT STRATEGY

Because transactions relating to property, plant, and equipment are usually few and individually material, assessment of control risk relating to these transactions is rarely necessary. Although the auditor rarely assesses controls over recording fixed asset transactions, the auditor generally uses a fixed asset continuity schedule as a source of evidence used in substantive procedures.

There may be significant variations in the inherent risk assessments for assertions relating to different property, plant, and equipment accounts. Inherent risk for the existence assertion may be low in a merchandising entity, for example, because the plant and equipment are not normally vulnerable to theft. However, it may be moderate or high in a manufacturing entity because scrapped or retired machinery may not be written off the books, or small tools and equipment used in production may be stolen. Similarly, the inherent risk in the accuracy or valuation and allocation assertions may be low when equipment items are purchased for cash, but high when items are acquired under finance leases. In the same way, the inherent risk may be high for the rights and obligations assertion and the disclosure assertion for plant and equipment acquired under finance leases.

Although material, the verification of property, plant, and equipment typically involves significantly less time and cost than the verification of current assets. Unlike receivables or cash balances, control risk assessments for non-current asset balances are usually less dependent on controls over major transaction classes.

The only transaction class with a significant effect on non-current asset balances is that of purchases, which we considered in chapter 10. When expenditures for smaller items (such as furniture, fixtures, and equipment) are processed as routine purchase transactions, the auditor may elect to use a combined approach. In such cases, the auditor's tests of controls of purchase transactions should include a sample of such assets. In assessing control risk for the plant and equipment assertions, the control risk assessments for purchase transactions are applicable. Other expenditures for land, buildings, and major capital improvements tend to occur infrequently and are not subject to the routine purchasing controls. These transactions may be subject to separate controls, including capital budgeting and specific authorization by the board of

6 Discuss considerations relevant to determining the audit strategy for property, plant, and equipment.

directors. Because such transactions are often individually material, a substantive approach is often adopted for the property, plant, and equipment assets, resulting in the specification of low acceptable levels of detection risk.

In determining detection risk for the valuation and allocation assertion for depreciation expense and accumulated depreciation, note that inherent risk is affected by both the degree of difficulty in estimating useful lives and residual values, and the complexity of the depreciation methods used. Control risk may be affected by the effectiveness of any controls related to these estimates and calculations.

Entities often maintain a **capital asset sub-ledger** detailing individual items of plant and equipment. The file records the cost of each asset and of any additions or alterations, and the accumulated depreciation charged against it. Balances in the sub-ledger reconcile with the written-down value of the plant and equipment account in the general ledger. The file may also contain additional information, such as serial number, supplier or manufacturer, insurance coverage, maintenance records and location, as well as other information relevant to management of the portfolio of plant and equipment. From time to time, the entity may carry out a physical verification of plant and equipment, mainly to identify the unrecorded disposals of fully depreciated items.

Control over maintenance of the sub-ledger is only of audit significance for assets that are vulnerable to misappropriation. Regular checking of such assets provides evidence of their existence and the auditor may not need to inspect such assets physically at the end of the reporting period. Procedures for understanding the internal control structure and assessment of control risk are similar to those for perpetual inventory records described in the first part of this chapter.

> **capital asset sub-ledger** a file containing plant and equipment information such as description, supplier, serial number, and location, as well as cost and depreciation charges that reconcile with the control account in the general ledger

PROFESSIONAL ENVIRONMENT

Ghost and zombie assets

When auditors determine the fair value of a company's assets, they need to locate and inspect them. Assets that can't be eyeballed are what auditors call "ghost and zombie assets." Ghosts are assets that appear in the books but can't be found. Zombies are assets that do exist but don't appear in the books. Neither is acceptable, of course.

Some companies don't periodically reconcile their fixed asset ledger to the property, plant, and equipment assets they actually have. That means auditors really can't certify that the internal controls over property, plant, and equipment are functioning. So by having ghost and zombie assets, an entity has a material weakness in internal controls. These controls could result in a missing computer (a ghost asset) or an item worth several million dollars that was unidentified in the books (a zombie asset).

The reasons for ghost assets include:

· unrecorded trade-ins
· parts of existing machines being used to repair other units
· factory rearrangement, with "unneeded" items scrapped
· not writing off old items when new items replace them

Sources: Alfred M. King, "Ghost and Zombie Assets— It's Midnight. Do You Know Where Your Assets Are?," Knowledge Leader provided by Protiviti, 2009; "The Benefits of Exorcising Ghost Assets from Your Books," Bloomberg BNA Software, www.bnasoftware.com, n.d.; "How Should We Handle Zombie Assets and Ghost Assets?", www.nacva.com, n.d.

Cloud 9

On determining the audit strategy, Josh assesses the inherent risk for property, plant, and equipment as being moderate to high, and control risk has not been not assessed at all (and thus is taken as being high). Substantive procedures will, therefore, be designed and performed so as to achieve the desired low level of detection risk. This will help the audit team achieve the required reduction in the audit risk of misstatements in the property, plant, and equipment balances.

BEFORE YOU GO ON

11.6.1 Why is a control risk assessment rarely performed for property, plant, and equipment?

11.6.2 What audit approach is generally used for property, plant, and equipment? Why?

11.6.3 Explain the purpose of a capital asset sub-ledger.

11.7 DESIGNING SUBSTANTIVE PROCEDURES FOR PROPERTY, PLANT, AND EQUIPMENT

In the first audit, evidence must be obtained as to the fairness of the opening balances and the ownership of the assets making up the balances. When the entity has previously been audited by another firm of auditors, this evidence may be obtained from a review of the predecessor auditor's working papers. If the entity has not been previously audited, the auditor must undertake an investigation of the opening balances. Information concerning opening balances obtained in the initial audit is usually recorded in the permanent audit file. This record is updated annually to record changes in the major assets, particularly property, including details of title deeds and registered charges such as mortgages.

In a recurring engagement, the auditor concentrates on the current year's transactions. The opening balances are verified through the preceding year's audit, and changes in the balance are usually few. This contrasts with the audit of current assets, which are subject to numerous transactions and for which the audit effort is concentrated on the closing balance. The auditor relies on the inspection of documentary evidence in verifying additions and disposals, and on mathematical evidence in verifying depreciation.

Possible substantive procedures for property, plant, and equipment balances, and the specific account balance audit objectives to which the tests relate, are shown in table 11.6. Risk considerations usually result in greater emphasis being placed on the existence or occurrence and the accuracy or valuation and allocation assertions. We explain each substantive procedure in a later section.

7 Design a substantive audit program for property, plant, and equipment.

TABLE 11.6 **Possible substantive procedures for property, plant, and equipment assertions**

CATEGORY	SUBSTANTIVE PROCEDURE	ACCOUNT BALANCE AUDIT OBJECTIVE (FROM TABLE 11.5)				
		OE3	C3	RO1	AV3	PD NO.
Initial procedures	1. Perform initial procedures on non-current asset balances and records that will be subjected to further testing. (a) Trace opening balances for plant assets and related accumulated depreciation accounts to and from the previous year's working papers. (b) Review activity in the general ledger, accumulated depreciation and depreciation expense accounts, and investigate entries that appear unusual in amount or source. (c) Obtain entity-prepared schedules of additions and disposals and determine that they accurately represent the underlying accounting records by: · adding and cross-adding the schedules and reconciling the totals with increases or decreases in the related general ledger balances during the period · testing the agreement of items on schedules with entries in related general ledger accounts	✓	✓	✓	✓	✓1, 2
Analytical procedures	2. Perform analytical procedures. (a) Calculate ratios. (b) Analyze ratio results relative to expectations based on previous year's results, industry data, budgeted amounts, or other data.	✓	✓		✓	
Tests of details of transactions	3. Compare asset additions with supporting documentation. 4. Compare asset disposals with supporting documentation. 5. Review repairs and maintenance and rental expense.	✓ ✓	✓ ✓ ✓	✓ ✓	✓ ✓	✓1 ✓2
Tests of details of balances	6. Examine title documents and contracts. 7. Review depreciation expense. 8. Consider the possibility of impairment. 9. Inquire into the valuation of property, plant, and equipment.	✓		✓	✓ ✓ ✓	✓3 ✓3

(continued)

TABLE 11.6 **Possible substantive procedures for property, plant, and equipment assertions** (continued)

CATEGORY	SUBSTANTIVE PROCEDURE	OE3	C3	RO1	AV3	PD NO.
						ACCOUNT BALANCE AUDIT OBJECTIVE (FROM TABLE 11.5)
Presentation and disclosure	10. Compare the statement presentation with applicable accounting standards. (a) Determine that property, plant, and equipment assets and related expenses, gains, and losses are properly identified and classified in the financial statements. (b) Determine the appropriateness of disclosures pertaining to the cost, value, depreciation methods, and useful lives of major classes of asset, the pledging of assets as collateral, and the terms of lease contracts.					✓2–5

11.7.1 Initial procedures

Before performing any of the other steps in the audit program, the auditor determines that the opening general ledger balances agree with the previous period's audit working papers. Among other functions, this comparison will confirm that any adjustments determined to be necessary at the conclusion of the previous audit and reflected in the previous period's published financial statements were also properly recorded and carried forward. Next, the auditor should test the mathematical accuracy of entity-prepared schedules of additions and disposals, and reconcile the totals with changes in the related general ledger balances for property, plant, and equipment during the period. In addition, the auditor should test the schedules by vouching items on the schedules to entries in the ledger accounts, and tracing ledger entries to the schedules to determine that they are an accurate representation of the accounting records from which they were prepared. The schedules may then be used as the basis for several other audit procedures. Figure 11.2 illustrates an auditor's lead sheet for property, plant, and equipment and accumulated depreciation.

FIGURE 11.2 **Property, plant, and equipment asset and accumulated depreciation lead schedule**

Cloud 9 Ltd.
Property, plant, and equipment and accumulated depreciation

Lead schedule

December 31, 2016

W/P ref.   G
Prepared by: C.J.G
Date: 03/25/17
Reviewed by: R.C.P
Date: 04/04/17

W/P REF.	ACCT NO.	ACCOUNT TITLE	BALANCE JAN. 1, 2016	ADDITIONS	DISPOSALS	ADJUSTMENTS DR/(CR)	BALANCE DEC. 31, 2016	BALANCE JAN. 1, 2016	DEPRECIATION EXPENSE	DISPOSALS	ADJUSTMENTS DR/(CR)	BALANCE DEC. 31, 2016
			ASSET COST					ACCUMULATED DEPRECIATION				
G–1	301	Land	450,000 (〰)				450,000					
G–2	302	Buildings	2,108,000 (〰)	125,000		⑳ (25,000)	2,208,000	379,440 (〰)	84,320		⑳ (1,000)	462,760
G–3	303	Mach. and equip.	3,757,250 (〰)	980,000	370,000	⑳ 25,000	4,392,250	1,074,210 (〰)	352,910	172,500	⑳ 1,000	1,255,620
G–4	304	Furn. and fixtures	853,400 (〰)	144,000	110,000		887,400	217,450 (〰)	43,250	21,000		239,700
			7,168,650 (〰)	1,249,000	480,000	0	7,937,650	1,671,100 (〰)	480,480	193,500	0	1,958,080
			F	F	F	F	FF	F	F	F	F	FF

(〰)Traced to general ledger and Dec. 31, 2015, working papers
F   Footed
FF   Cross-footed and footed

To reclassify cost and related accumulated depreciation for purchased addition recorded in Buildings account that should have been recorded in Machinery and Equipment account. See adjusting entry no. 21 on W/P AE–4.

11.7.2 Analytical procedures

Analytical procedures are less useful as a source of evidence as to property, plant, and equipment balances than they are for current assets and liabilities. This is because the balances can vary substantially as the result of relatively few transactions of which the auditor is already likely to be aware. A comparison of the annual depreciation charge with the cost or written-down value of the relevant class of assets should yield a measure comparable to the depreciation rate. Such evidence could provide some of the required evidence as to the valuation assertion. Comparison of repairs and maintenance expense with that for previous years or with net sales may indicate the possibility that some maintenance expenditures have not been recorded or that they have been capitalized in error.

11.7.3 Tests of details of transactions

These substantive procedures cover three types of transactions related to property, plant, and equipment: additions, disposals, and repairs and maintenance.

Substantiating additions

The auditor first needs to ascertain management's policy with regard to the distinction between capital and revenue expenditures. Most entities specify a cut-off value below which purchases are expensed regardless of their nature. A consistent policy also needs to be followed in distinguishing between improvements (which prolong the life or enhance the usefulness of existing assets) and repairs and maintenance (which are necessary for the asset to continue to function over its expected useful life). The auditor must ensure that additions are properly capitalized and that a consistent policy is followed.

The recorded amounts should be vouched to supporting documentation in the form of authorizations in the minutes, suppliers' invoices, and contracts. If there are numerous transactions, the vouching may be done on a test basis. In performing this test, the auditor ascertains that the amount capitalized includes installation, freight, and similar costs, but excludes expenses included on the supplier's invoice, such as a year's maintenance fee.

For construction in progress, the auditor may review the contract and documentation in support of construction costs. The auditor should physically inspect major items, ensuring that details of the asset inspected (such as its description and the manufacturer's serial number) agree with the documentation.

The auditor also needs to inquire about leases for property, plant, and equipment entered into during the period. Lease agreements convey, to a lessee, the right to use assets, usually for a specified period of time. For accounting purposes, leases may be classified as either capital leases or operating leases. The auditor should read the lease agreement to determine its proper accounting classification in accordance with IAS 17 *Leases*. When a finance lease exists, both an asset and a liability should be recognized in the financial statements. The cost of the asset and the related liability should be recorded at the present value of the future minimum lease payments. The auditor should do some recalculations to verify the accuracy of the entity's determination of the present value of the lease liability.

The vouching of additions provides evidence about the occurrence, rights and obligations, and accuracy assertions. In addition, the examination of lease contracts relates to the presentation and disclosure assertion, because of the disclosures that are required under IAS 17.

Substantiating disposals

Evidence of sales, disposals, and trade-ins should be available to the auditor in the form of cash remittance advices, written authorizations, and sales agreements. Such documentation should be carefully examined to determine the accuracy and propriety of the accounting records, including the recognition of gain or loss, if any.

The following procedures may also be useful to the auditor in determining whether all disposals have been recorded:

- analyzing the miscellaneous revenue account for proceeds from sales of property, plant, and equipment
- investigating the disposition of facilities associated with discontinued product lines and operations

- tracing disposal work orders and authorizations for disposals to the accounting records
- reviewing insurance policies for termination or reductions of coverage
- inquiring of management as to disposals

Inspection of the results of any inventory count of plant and machinery undertaken by the entity provides further evidence that all disposals have been recorded.

Evidence that all disposals or retirements have been properly recorded relates to the occurrence, rights and obligations, and accuracy assertions. Evidence supporting the validity of transactions that reduce property, plant, and equipment relates to the completeness assertion.

Reviewing repairs and maintenance and rental expenses

The auditor's objective in reviewing repairs and maintenance expenses is to determine the propriety and consistency of the charges to this expense. The auditor should scan the individual charges in excess of the entity's cut-off value for capitalization to ensure that they are properly expensed. This procedure is related to the examination of additions to ensure that they are properly capitalized.

This substantive procedure provides important evidence concerning the completeness assertion for property, plant, and equipment because it reveals expenditures that should be capitalized. In addition, the analysis may reveal misclassifications in the accounts that relate to the presentation and disclosure assertion.

Rental expenses are reviewed to ensure that such rents relate to assets under operating leases. Documentary evidence needs to be tested for evidence of leases that should be accounted for as finance leases. This procedure provides evidence as to the completeness assertion in that all assets acquired under finance leases are properly accounted for as additions to property, plant, and equipment.

11.7.4 Tests of details of balances

The auditor may conclude that the closing balance is correctly stated—with respect to the assertions of existence, completeness, and rights and obligations—after having tested the opening balance with the previous year's working papers, and verified additions and disposals. However, the auditor may examine documentary evidence as to the existence and rights and obligations assertions of the recorded balance.

The main tests of balances relate to valuation and disclosure. These test the accumulated depreciation, the need for provision for impairment, and the appropriateness of any revaluation.

Examining title documents and contracts

The auditor may establish ownership of vehicles by examining registration certificates and insurance policies. For plant and equipment, the "paid" invoice may be the best evidence of ownership. Evidence of ownership of freehold property is found in title deeds, property tax bills, mortgage payment receipts, and fire insurance policies. The auditor can also verify ownership of freehold property by reviewing public records. When this form of additional evidence is desired, the auditor may seek the help of a lawyer. The examination of ownership documents contributes to the existence assertion and rights and obligations assertion for property, plant, and equipment.

Reviewing accumulated depreciation

In this test, the auditor seeks evidence as to the reasonableness, consistency, and accuracy of depreciation charges.

- *Reasonableness.* The auditor determines the reasonableness of accumulated depreciation by considering such factors as the entity's past history in estimating useful lives and the remaining useful lives of existing assets. The auditor must also ensure that management has reviewed the depreciation rates during the year and adjusted the rates as necessary in accordance with IAS 16 *Property, Plant and Equipment.*
- *Consistency.* The auditor can ascertain the depreciation methods used by reviewing depreciation schedules prepared by the entity and inquiring of management. The auditor must then determine whether the methods in use are consistent with those used in the preceding year. On a recurring audit, this can be established by a review of the previous year's working papers.

- *Accuracy.* The auditor verifies accuracy through recalculation. Ordinarily, the auditor does this on a selective basis by recalculating the depreciation on major assets and testing depreciation taken on additions and disposals during the year.

These substantive procedures provide evidence about the valuation assertion.

Considering the possibility of impairment

The auditor must be satisfied that the carrying value of property, plant, and equipment does not exceed the greater of their realizable value or value in use in accordance with IAS 36 *Impairment of Assets.*

The auditor may derive evidence of overvalued assets by observing obsolete or damaged units during a tour of the plant, identifying assets associated with discontinued operations but not yet disposed of, and inquiring of management as to budgets and forecasts for specific activities in relation to the carrying value of assets associated with those activities.

Where amounts have been written off the carrying value of any item of property, plant, or equipment, the auditor must be satisfied, by inquiring of management and assessing management's documentation as to future plans, that the writedown is reasonable.

Inquiring into the valuation

Management may also choose to revalue property, plant, and equipment so as to reflect more fairly their value to the business. IAS16 *Property, Plant and Equipment* requires that any revaluation must be applied to a class of assets, not to individual assets within a class. Full valuations must be made or reviewed by an independent valuator. Interim valuations may be made by an internal valuator. The auditor would need to be satisfied as to the skill, competence, and objectivity of the valuator, whether that valuator is independent or an employee of the entity. In particular, it would be necessary for the auditor to:

- obtain a copy of the valuator's report
- determine the basis of valuation stated therein
- consider its appropriateness as the basis for determining the carrying amount of that class of assets in the financial statements

This substantive procedure provides evidence about the valuation assertion and the disclosure assertion.

11.7.5 Presentation and disclosure

The financial statement presentation requirements for property, plant, and equipment are extensive. The financial statements should show, for example, the depreciation expense for the year; the carrying value for major classes of property, plant, and equipment; and the depreciation method(s) used. For assets carried other than at cost, information that must be disclosed includes (1) the name and qualifications of the valuator and whether they are internal or independent, (2) the basis of valuation, and (3) the date and amounts of the valuation. The auditor acquires evidence concerning these matters through the substantive procedures described in the preceding sections.

Property pledged as security for loans should be disclosed. The auditor may obtain information on pledging by reviewing the board of directors' minutes and long-term contractual agreements; by confirming debt agreements; and by making inquiries of management. The auditor can determine the appropriateness of the entity's disclosures relating to assets under lease by referring to the authoritative accounting pronouncements and the related lease agreements.

Cloud 9

Josh now understands that transactions involving property, plant, and equipment tend to be infrequent and, where material, are usually subject to special treatment. For this reason, W&S Partners will adopt a substantive approach over the property, plant, and equipment and related financial statement accounts.

Josh realizes that, like inventory, the main inherent risks are over the existence and valuation assertions as management has an incentive to overstate the existence and/or value of property, plant, and equipment, and that valuation requires considerable estimation and judgement. He recognizes that for Cloud 9, property, plant, and equipment transactions are few and except for the new store costs, the makeup of the balance is relatively constant. Therefore, substantive procedures include verifying transactions to invoices and contracts and auditing any other items to reconcile the opening balance with the closing balance.

He also now sees that to gather evidence for the valuation assertion to consider the reasonableness, consistency, and accuracy of the year's accumulated depreciation, he must make sure all of the equipment is in use and, therefore, there are no impairments. Since Cloud 9 did not do any revaluations, no work is required in this area.

BEFORE YOU GO ON

11.7.1 What substantive procedures are normally performed over property, plant, and equipment additions?

11.7.2 Why does the auditor review the repairs and maintenance account?

11.7.3 What audit tests are normally performed over accumulated depreciation?

SUMMARY

1   **Identify the audit objectives applicable to inventories.**

The key issues in auditing inventory are usually to ensure the inventories actually exist, are owned, and are properly valued. The auditor's objective is to gather sufficient and appropriate evidence about each key assertion.

2   **Describe the functions and control procedures normally found for the custody and maintenance of inventory records.**

The key control over the maintenance of inventory is the segregation of duties. The duty of recording inventory movements should be segregated from the physical custody of inventory as goods move in and out of inventory and are transferred between areas.

A key control over the custody of the inventory is the performance of the cyclical and annual inventory counts. Inventory counts are the responsibility of management and they should be well planned to ensure count results are reliable. A comparison of the count results to the accounting records indicates whether the controls over inventory are effective.

3   **Discuss considerations relevant to determining the audit strategy for inventories.**

Inventories and cost of sales are usually significant to most entities' financial position and the results of their operations. The main inherent risks for inventory are the existence or occurrence assertion and the accuracy or valuation and allocation assertions. Numerous factors contribute to the inherent risk of misstatements, including the high volume of transactions, contentious valuation issues, and the high risk of theft and obsolescence.

Assessment of control risk is important where the entity does not plan to perform an inventory count at year end and for the cost of inventory for manufacturing entities. If test counts do not support an assessment of control risk as low, or if it is not an efficient audit strategy, the auditor will adopt a substantive audit strategy.

4   **Design a substantive audit program for inventory.**

Except where perpetual records are used as the basis for determining inventory at the end of the reporting period, and for costing records in manufacturing entities, the audit for inventories is based mainly on substantive procedures applied to the account balance at the end of the reporting period.

The emphasis is on the assertions of existence and valuation, because the inherent risk of their misstatement is always high. In verifying the existence of inventories, the auditor relies on physical inspection, whether through observation of cyclical counts verifying perpetual inventory records or through attendance at annual inventory counts. For valuation, the auditor verifies the cost of inventory against invoice prices or costing records.

The auditor also needs to ensure that the accounting basis adopted complies with applicable accounting standards and that required disclosures are properly made in the financial statements.

⑤ Identify the audit objectives applicable to property, plant, and equipment.

The key issues in auditing property, plant, and equipment are usually to gather sufficient and appropriate evidence as to the existence of the assets as well as whether the assets are owned and are properly valued with adequate provision for depreciation. Furthermore, a key focus in the audit of property, plant, and equipment relates to the purchasing of new assets and disposing of old assets, including any profits or losses on sale. In addition, consideration is required in relation to depreciation charges, the treatment of leased assets, and asset revaluations.

⑥ Discuss considerations relevant to determining the audit strategy for property, plant, and equipment.

There may be significant variations in the inherent risk assessments for assertions relating to different property, plant, and equipment accounts and the type of industry. For example, inherent risk for the existence assertion may be low in a merchandising entity because the plant and equipment are not normally vulnerable to theft.

Because transactions relating to property, plant, and equipment are few and usually individually material, assessment of control risk relating to these transactions is rarely necessary.

⑦ Design a substantive audit program for property, plant, and equipment.

In verifying property, plant, and equipment, the auditor relies on verifying changes in the recorded balance, including an inspection of additions. The auditor rarely inspects assets making up the balance, reflecting the incidence of transactions that are frequent for inventories, being a current asset, but infrequent for property, plant, and equipment.

Valuation is determined by the application of accounting procedures involving a high degree of judgement. For property, plant, and equipment, this involves estimating useful economic lives, residual value, and the basis of depreciation. The auditor needs to determine the appropriateness of the judgements made and the accuracy of the resulting calculations. The auditor also needs to ensure that the accounting basis adopted complies with applicable accounting standards and that required disclosures are properly made in the financial statements.

KEY TERMS

Capital asset sub-ledger, p. 416
Cyclical inventory counts, p. 399
Finished goods, p. 398
Inventory count sheets, p. 400

Inventory master file, p. 398
Inventory tags, p. 400
Inventory transfer requisitions, p. 399
Perpetual inventory records, p. 398

Raw materials, p. 398
Work in process, p. 398

MULTIPLE-CHOICE QUESTIONS

11.1   An important procedure for the conduct of a physical inventory count is to maintain control over the count records. The following is not a common count system:

(a) use of pre-printed inventory count sheets.

(b) use of blank inventory tags.

(c) use of blank, pre-numbered inventory count sheets.

(d) use of pre-numbered three-part inventory tags.

11.2   The following audit strategy would be most appropriate when an auditor has assessed that a substantive approach is necessary to determine inventory quantity:

(a) inventory quantities determined by physical count at or within a few days of the end of the reporting period.

(b) inventory quantities determined by physical count near the end of the reporting period, adjusted by reference to perpetual records.

(c) inventory quantities determined by reference to perpetual records, without a physical count at or near the end of the reporting period.

(d) inventory quantities determined by reference to perpetual records, with a sample of inventory items counted at each month end throughout the reporting period.

11.3   If preliminary assessment of control risk supports management's intended reliance on inventory records, the auditor is most likely to design an audit program that:

(a) excludes testing the operating effectiveness of those controls.

(b) includes testing the operating effectiveness of those controls.

(c) tests only inventory transactions and tests of details of the inventory balance.

(d) tests only inventory transactions and excludes tests of details of the inventory balance.

11.4   **Observation of an inventory count is a required audit procedure whenever:**

(a)   inventories are material.

(b)   it is practicable to do so.

(c)   inventories are material and it is practicable to do so.

(d)   inventories are material and the auditor considers it to be necessary.

11.5   **During the observation of the inventory count, the auditor has no responsibility to:**

(a)   observe the count by client personnel.

(b)   make some test counts of inventory quantities.

(c)   supervise the taking of the inventory count.

(d)   watch for damaged and obsolete inventory items.

11.6   **The auditor's strategy in performing test counts during the observation of the inventory count is to:**

(a)   test all large-dollar items.

(b)   randomly select all test items.

(c)   concentrate tests on high-dollar items with random selection of other items.

(d)   concentrate tests in areas where employees seem to be disregarding the inventory instructions.

11.7   **The auditor identifies the specific audit objective: "determine that property, plant, and equipment assets are in productive use at the end of the reporting period." This objective is derived from:**

(a)   the existence or occurrence assertion.

(b)   the completeness assertion.

(c)   the presentation and disclosure assertion.

(d)   the rights and obligations assertion.

11.8   **The following statement about inherent risk assessments for property, plant, and equipment is inaccurate:**

(a)   normally low for the presentation and disclosure assertion for plant assets acquired under capital leases.

(b)   normally low for the existence or occurrence assertion in a merchandising entity because plant assets are not generally vulnerable to theft.

(c)   normally moderate to high for the existence or occurrence assertion in a manufacturing entity because scrapped or retired plant assets may not be written off the books.

(d)   normally low for the accuracy or valuation and allocation assertions when plant assets are purchased for cash.

11.9   **When expenditures for property, plant, and equipment are processed as routine purchase transactions, the auditor:**

(a)   must include some of these transactions in the tests of controls over the expenditures cycle.

(b)   may elect to use a combined approach.

(c)   should use mainly a substantive approach on these and all major additions.

(d)   should normally assess control risk as high for these transactions.

11.10   **The following represents an existence test for property, plant, and equipment:**

(a)   select a sample of items of machinery in the factory and agree that they are correctly recorded in the machinery general ledger account.

(b)   review entries in the repairs and maintenance expense account for items of a capital nature.

(c)   obtain details of material asset disposals during the period and ensure that they are not included on the non-current assets master file at the period end.

(d)   select a sample of invoices relating to motor vehicle purchases and ensure they are correctly recorded on the non-current assets master file.

REVIEW QUESTIONS

11.1   Describe the alternative methods entities use to determine their inventory at the end of the reporting period and the possible effect of each method on audit strategy.

11.2   What steps should the auditor perform when observing the inventory count? Why should the auditor take test counts?

11.3   Discuss the different ways of identifying production overheads and methods of apportionment to determine the cost of inventory. Consider the audit implications of each method.

11.4   Many companies use standard costing as the basis for inventory costing. What audit procedures may be appropriate for establishing the fairness of the standard costs, for testing the maintenance of the standard cost records, and for determining the disposition of variances?

11.5   Overhead is to be absorbed into the cost of inventory on the basis of the normal level of activity. What evidence is available to the auditor in verifying management's determination of that level of activity?

11.6 Discuss the cut-off implications of the inventory count being before or after the year end and closing inventory being determined by adjusting the count by reference to purchases and sales records in the intervening period.

11.7 Why does the auditor usually adopt a substantive audit strategy for property, plant, and equipment assertions?

11.8 Discuss procedures that would be useful in ensuring that all disposals of property, plant, and equipment have been recorded.

11.9 What are the problems confronting the auditor in verifying both the rate and method of depreciation?

11.10 What steps can the auditor take to ensure that the disposal of fully depreciated assets is properly recorded? What are the implications if such assets are retained in the accounts?

PROFESSIONAL APPLICATION QUESTIONS

Basic ★   Moderate ★ ★   Challenging ★ ★ ★

11.1 Inventory: computer information system ★ ★   ❶ ❷

You are the auditor of Fenton Electronics Ltd., which has recently installed a computerized bar code system to record goods received, sales, and inventory quantities. The company is a retailer of electrical products.

1. When the goods are received, the receiving department:
   - either reads the bar code on the box containing the product or inputs the bar code number manually;
   - manually inputs the number of items received (e.g., a box may contain 100 CDs). The quantity of items received is added to the quantity of inventory recorded on the computer.

2. When goods are sold to a customer, the bar code of the product is either read or input manually, and the computer produces the sales invoice using the selling price of the product, as recorded on the computer's standing data file. The quantity of items sold is deducted from the inventory quantity recorded on the computer.

3. Periodically, the inventory is counted and these counts are compared with those on the computer. The inventory quantities on the computer are amended when significant differences are found.

4. The system allows:
   - details of new products and the selling prices of products to be added or amended
   - inventory quantities to be amended from differences found at the inventory count
   - special prices to be charged to customers (e.g., where the product is damaged or discontinued)

   The main products the company sells are:
   - slow-moving products, such as televisions, video recorders, digital cameras, and audio equipment
   - fast-moving, low-value products, such as batteries, blank CDs, and DVDs

Required

(a) Describe the edit checks that should be incorporated into the computer system to ensure that details of goods received are correctly entered into the computer.

(b) (i) Suggest how often inventory should be test counted.
   (ii) Describe the procedures the company should carry out to ensure the inventory quantities in the computer system are accurate.

(c) Describe the controls that should be used to ensure that the prices of the products on the computer file and on the products in the store are correct.

Source: Adapted from ACCA Audit Framework, Paper 6, December 1994.

11.2 Management of the physical inventory count ★ ★

Lily Window Glass Co. (Lily) is a glass manufacturer that operates from a large production facility, where it undertakes continuous production 24 hours a day, seven days a week. Also on this site are two warehouses where the company's raw materials and finished goods are stored. Lily's year end is December 31.

Lily is finalizing the arrangements for the year-end inventory count, which is to be undertaken on December 31, 2016. The finished windows are stored within 20 aisles of the first warehouse. The second warehouse is for large piles of raw materials, such as sand, used in the manufacture of glass. The following arrangements have been made for the inventory count.

The warehouse manager will supervise the count as he is most familiar with the inventory. There will be 10 teams of counters and each team will contain two members of staff, one from the finance and one from the manufacturing department. None of the warehouse staff, other than the manager, will be involved in the count.

Each team will count an aisle of finished goods by counting up and then down each aisle. As this process is systematic, it is not felt that the team will need to flag areas once counted. Once the team has finished counting an aisle, they will hand in their sheets and be given a set for another aisle of the warehouse. In addition to the above, to assist with the inventory counting, there will be two teams of counters from the internal audit department and they will perform inventory counts.

The count sheets are sequentially numbered, and the product codes and descriptions are printed on them but no quantities. If the counters identify any inventory that is not on their sheets, they are to enter the item on a separate sheet, which is not numbered. Once all counting is complete, the sequence of the sheets is checked and any additional sheets are also handed in at this stage. All sheets are completed in ink.

Any damaged goods identified by the counters will be too heavy to move to a central location; hence they are to be left where they are but the counter is to make a note on the inventory sheets detailing the level of damage.

As Lily undertakes continuous production, there will continue to be movements of raw materials and finished goods in and out of the warehouse during the count. These will be kept to a minimum where possible.

The level of work in process in the manufacturing plant is to be assessed by the warehouse manager. It is likely that this will be an immaterial balance. In addition, the raw materials quantities are to be approximated by measuring the height and width of the raw material piles. In the past this task has been undertaken by a specialist; however, the warehouse manager feels confident that he can perform this task.

Required

For the inventory count arrangements of Lily Window Glass Co.:

(a) Identify and explain six deficiencies.

(b) Provide a recommendation to address each deficiency.

11.3 Physical inventory: substantive procedures ★

Your firm is responsible for auditing the financial statements of Hucknall Manufacturing Ltd. for the year ended October 31, 2016. The company operates from a single site. Its sales are $5 million and the profit before tax is $110,000. There are no inventory records, so the inventory counts at year end will be used to value the inventory in the financial statements. Because Monday, October 31, is a normal working day, it has been decided that the inventory count should take place on Sunday, October 30, when there is no movement of inventory.

The company has produced the following schedule to determine the value of inventory at October 31, 2016, from that counted on October 30, 2016.

	$	$
Value of inventory counted at Oct. 30, 2016		583,247
Add Cost of goods received on Oct. 31, 2016	10,969	
Production labour on Oct. 31, 2016	3,260	
Overheads relating to labour at 120%	3,912	18,141
Less Cost of sales on Oct. 31, 2016		(36,740)
Value of inventory at Oct. 31, 2016		564,648

The company keeps basic accounting records using a standard software package. The following accounting procedures are used for sales, purchases, and wages.

1. The shipping department creates shipping documents when the goods are sent to customers. Sales invoices are produced based on the shipping documents. Sales invoices are input into the computer, which posts them to the accounts receivable ledger and the general ledger.
2. When goods are received, a receiving report is prepared. Purchase invoices are matched with the receiving reports and purchase orders, and authorized by the chief executive officer. After the purchase invoices have been authorized, they are input into the computer, which posts them to the accounts payable ledger and the general ledger.
3. For the wages system, the hours worked by each employee are input into the computer, which calculates the gross wages and deductions (e.g., for tax) and the net pay. All employees are paid weekly.

Required

(a) Describe the audit procedures you should perform to verify the accuracy of the inventory count:
   (i) before the inventory count
   (ii) on the day of the inventory count
   Include details of the matters you should record in your working papers for follow-up at the final audit.
(b) Explain the substantive procedures you should perform to check the company's schedule (as shown above) that adjust the value of inventory at October 30, 2016, to that at the company's year end of October 31, 2016. You are required to verify only the total value of inventory of $564,648 at October 31, 2016. You are not required to describe the procedures necessary to verify the accuracy of the individual values of raw materials, work in process, or finished goods.
(c) Describe the substantive procedures you should perform to check purchases cut-off at the year end.

Source: Adapted from ACCA Audit Framework, Paper 6, December 1998.

11.4 The audit of an inventory count: substantive procedures ★ ★

Refer to Professional Application Question 11.2 regarding Lily Window Glass Co. Now assume that you are the audit senior of Daffodil & Co. and are responsible for the audit of inventory for Lily. You will be attending the year-end inventory count on December 31, 2016. In addition, your manager wishes to use computer-assisted audit techniques for the first time for controls and substantive testing in auditing Lily's inventory.

Required

Describe the procedures to be undertaken by the auditor during the inventory count of Lily Window Glass Co. in order to gain sufficient appropriate audit evidence.

Source: Adapted from ACCA Audit and Assurance (International), Paper F8, December 2012.

11.5 Depreciation expense: substantive procedures ★

Pineapple Beach Hotel Co. (Pineapple) operates a hotel providing accommodation, leisure facilities, and restaurants. Its year end was April 30, 2016. You are the audit senior of Berry & Co. and are currently preparing the audit program for the year-end audit of Pineapple. You are reviewing the notes of last week's meeting between the audit manager and controller where the following material issue was discussed.

Pineapple incurred significant capital expenditure during the year on updating the leisure facilities for the hotel. The controller has proposed that the new leisure equipment be depreciated over 10 years using the straight-line method.

Required

Describe substantive procedures to obtain sufficient and appropriate audit evidence in relation to the above issue.

Source: Adapted from ACCA Audit and Assurance (International), Paper F8, June 2012.

11.6 Substantive testing of inventory ★

Securimax Limited has been an audit client of KFP Partners for the past 15 years. Securimax is based in Waterloo, Ontario, where it manufactures high-tech armour-plated personnel carriers. Securimax often has to go through a competitive market tender process to win large government contracts. Its main product, the small but powerful Terrain Master, is highly specialized, and Securimax does business only with nations that have a recognized, democratically elected government. Securimax maintains a highly secure environment, given the sensitive and confidential nature of its vehicle designs and its clients.

In September 2016, Securimax installed an off-the-shelf costing system to support the highly sophisticated and cost-sensitive nature of its product designs. The new system replaced a system that had been developed in-house, as the old system could no longer keep up with the complex and detailed manufacturing costing process that provides tender costings. The old system also had difficulty with the company's broader reporting requirements.

The manufacturing costing system uses all of the manufacturing unit inputs to calculate and produce a database of all product costs and recommended sales prices. It also integrates with the general ledger each time there are product inventory movements such as purchases, sales, wastage, and damaged inventory.

Securimax's financial year end is December 31.

Source: Adapted from the Institute of Chartered Accountants Australia's CA Program's Audit and Assurance Exam, May 2008. Provided courtesy of Chartered Accountants Australia and New Zealand.

Required

(a) What inventory items would you expect to see in Securimax's accounts? How would the cost of each item be calculated?

(b) Suggest some substantive procedures that you would use in the audit of inventory for Securimax. Justify your choices with respect to the risk assessment.

11.7 Property, plant, and equipment—substantive procedures ★ ★ ★

Your firm is auditing the financial statements of Newthorpe Manufacturing Ltd. for the year ended June 30, 2016. You have been assigned to the audit of the company's property, plant, and equipment, which includes freehold land and buildings, plant and machinery, fixtures and fittings, and motor vehicles.

The freehold land and buildings were purchased 12 years earlier (in July 2004) for $2 million. At the date of purchase, a valuator estimated that the land and the buildings each had a value of $1 million. Depreciation has been charged since 2004 on the buildings at 2 percent per year on cost. At June 30, 2016, the accumulated depreciation is $200,000 before the revaluation.

A qualified valuator, who is not an employee of the company, valued the land and buildings at $5 million ($2.9 million for the land and $2.1 million for the buildings). These values will be incorporated into the financial statements as at June 30, 2016.

The partner in charge of the audit is concerned at the large increase in the value of the land and buildings since they were purchased. She has asked you to check the reliability and accuracy of the valuation. She suggested that CAS 620 *Using the Work of an Auditor's Expert* could help you when carrying out this work.

In addition, you have been asked to verify the existence and completeness of plant and machinery recorded in the company's computerized non-current asset register, which records the description of each non-current asset, the original cost, the depreciation charge, and the accumulated depreciation.

Required

(a) Describe the audit work you will carry out to check whether the valuator has provided an accurate and independent valuation of the land and buildings.

(b) Describe the audit work you will carry out to check the existence and completeness of plant and machinery, as recorded in the company's non-fixed asset master file.

Source: Adapted from ACCA Audit Framework, Paper 6, June 1997.

11.8 Property, plant, and equipment—substantive procedures ★ ★

Your firm is the auditor of Daybrook Insurance Brokers Ltd., which operates from a number of branches and provides insurance for the general public and businesses. The company obtains insurance from large insurance companies and takes a commission for its services. You have been asked to audit certain aspects of the company's property, plant, and equipment for the year ended December 31, 2016.

The company's main property, plant, and equipment include:
· freehold land and buildings
· computers, printers, and related equipment, which are used by staff
· cars, which are provided to directors and salespeople who visit customers

The company has been operating for a number of years, and it maintains details of its office equipment and cars on a computerized fixed asset master file. The company uses the following depreciation rates:
· buildings (2 percent per year of cost)
· office equipment (including computers) (10 percent per year of cost)
· cars (25 percent per year of cost)

You are concerned that the depreciation rate for the computers may be inadequate.

Required

(a) Describe how you would verify the ownership of freehold land and buildings, computers, and cars.

(b) Explain how you would determine that the depreciation rate on the various assets is adequate.

Source: Adapted from ACCA Audit Framework, Paper 6, June 1997.

11.9 Property, plant, and equipment—audit objectives ★ ★ ★

Wear Wraith (WW) Co.'s main activity is the extraction and supply of building materials including sand, gravel, cement, and similar aggregates. The company's year end is December 31 and your firm has audited WW for a number of years. The main asset on the statement of financial position relates to non-current assets. The following draft non-current asset note for the financial statements has been prepared. The note has not been reviewed by the senior accountant and so may contain errors.

Depreciation rates stated in the financial statements are all based on cost and calculated using the straight-line basis. The rates are:
· land and buildings (2 percent)
· plant and machinery (20 percent)
· motor vehicles (33 percent)
· railway trucks (20 percent)

Disposals in the motor vehicles category relate to vehicles that were five years old.

	LAND AND BUILDINGS	PLANT AND MACHINERY	MOTOR VEHICLES	RAILWAY TRUCKS	TOTAL
COST	$	$	$	$	$
Jan. 1, 2016	100,000	875,000	1,500,000	–	2,475,000
Additions	10,000	125,000	525,000	995,000	1,655,000
Disposals	–	(100,000)	(325,000)	–	(425,000)
Dec. 31, 2016	110,000	900,000	1,700,000	995,000	3,705,000
Depreciation					
Jan. 1, 2016	60,000	550,000	750,000	–	1,360,000
Charge	2,200	180,000	425,000	199,000	806,200
Disposals	–	(120,000)	(325,000)	–	(445,000)
Dec. 31, 2016	62,200	610,000	850,000	199,000	1,721,200
Net book value					
Dec. 31, 2016	47,800	290,000	850,000	796,000	1,983,800
Net book value					
Dec. 31, 2015	40,000	325,000	750,000	–	1,115,000

– Land and buildings relate to company offices and land for those offices.
– Plant and machinery include extraction equipment such as diggers and dumper trucks used to extract sand and gravel, etc.
– Motor vehicles include large trucks to transport the sand, gravel, etc.
– Railway trucks are containers used to transport sand and gravel over long distances on the railway network.

Required

(a) List the audit work you should perform on railway trucks.

(b) You have just completed your analytical procedures of the non-current assets note.

  (i) Excluding railway trucks, identify and explain any issues with the non-current asset note to raise with management.

  (ii) Explain how each issue could be resolved.

Source: Adapted from ACCA Audit and Internal Review, June 2006.

CASE STUDY—CLOUD 9

Answer the following question based on the information presented for Cloud 9 in Appendix B of this book and in the current and earlier chapters. You should also consider your answers to the case study questions in earlier chapters.

While Cloud 9 maintains a perpetual inventory system, a full inventory count was done at year end. Weijing Fei, a junior W&S staff member, attended and observed the count. She subsequently prepared the following memo to file. Sharon is quite busy and she has asked you to critique the memo on her behalf.

Memo to File re: Inventory Test Count

By: Weijing Fei

On December 31, 2016, I attended the inventory count at Cloud 9 Ltd. warehouse located in Richmond, B.C. A perpetual inventory system is maintained and warehouse staff perform physical counts of the running shoes on a weekly basis. The year-end inventory count was done on December 31, 2016, in Richmond. The warehouse was closed to ensure the count would not be affected by incoming or outgoing orders.

The count was supervised by Carla Johnson and the warehouse manager. Count teams consisted of two employees. One person counted, while the other recorded the item. Count sheets were sequential. Each count team was provided with plain paper for items that may not have been listed on the count sheets. The inventory was arranged neatly and orderly, with all footwear stacked on shelves by type. The shelves are normally stacked five boxes high by shoe type. Count tags were used and the warehouse is organized. If there were too many shoes of the same type to fit on one shelf, then the excess was stacked on the shelf above, next to it, or in another marked shelf where room was available. Therefore, some shelves had more than one type of running shoe on them as a result of this. If shoes of the same kind were located on other shelves, then a tag was added to the shelf indicating where the rest could be located and how many were stacked there.

All footwear boxes were marked with labels that described the shoe style and type (model, size) and all of the shoes were arranged such that these labels were facing outward and could therefore be read by the counters.

Sample:
Chose a sample of 20 items for testing, 10 floor to sheet and 10 sheet to floor.

Results:
No errors were detected in the sample of inventory that was chosen.

Conclusion:
The year-end inventory listing has been adjusted to actual per-count results and can be relied upon.

Required
Critique the memo to file prepared by Weijing. Note both good and bad points.

RESEARCH QUESTION 11.1

Consider the following statement:
The audit of inventory is one of the riskiest areas of the audit. Management can manipulate the value of inventory through a variety of methods, such as through varying the provision for obsolescence or the method of valuation. It is therefore an area that can be "massaged" by management to achieve its required profit level.

Required
(a) Evaluate the statement and illustrate by researching the corporate collapse of Australian retailer Harris Scarfe, where inventory manipulation allowed the company to report "profits" for a number of years.
(b) Consider IAS 2 *Inventories* and the complementary auditing standard CAS 501. How is the issue of estimation in the recording of inventory considered and what audit procedures should have prevented the Harris Scarfe manipulation of inventory figures?

SOLUTIONS TO MULTIPLE-CHOICE QUESTIONS
1. b, 2. a, 3. b, 4. c, 5. c, 6. c, 7. a, 8. a, 9. c, 10. c.

CHAPTER 12

Auditing cash and investments

LEARNING OBJECTIVES

After studying this chapter, you should be able to:

1 identify the audit objectives applicable to cash

2 discuss considerations relevant to determining the audit strategy for cash

3 design and execute an audit program for cash balances

4 describe special considerations when auditing cash balances, including lapping, petty cash funds, and imprest bank accounts

5 identify the audit objectives applicable to investments

6 discuss considerations relevant to determining the audit strategy for investments

7 design and execute an audit program for investments

8 explain the special considerations applicable to the audit of investments in subsidiaries, associates, and joint ventures.

AUDITING AND ASSURANCE STANDARDS

CANADIAN	INTERNATIONAL
CAS 315 *Identifying and Assessing the Risks of Material Misstatement through Understanding the Entity and Its Environment*	ISA 315 *Identifying and Assessing the Risks of Material Misstatement through Understanding the Entity and Its Environment*
CAS 540 *Auditing Accounting Estimates, Including Fair Value Accounting Estimates, and Related Disclosures*	ISA 540 *Auditing Accounting Estimates, Including Fair Value Accounting Estimates, and Related Disclosures*
CAS 600 *Special Considerations—Audits of Group Financial Statements (Including the Work of Component Auditors)*	ISA 600 *Special Considerations—Audits of Group Financial Statements (Including the Work of Component Auditors)*
	IAPS 1012 *Auditing Derivative Financial Instruments*
IFRS 3 *Business Combinations*	IFRS 3 *Business Combinations*
IAS 7 *Statement of Cash Flows*	IAS 7 *Statement of Cash Flows*
IAS 21 *The Effects of Changes in Foreign Exchange Rates*	IAS 21 *The Effects of Changes in Foreign Exchange Rates*
IAS 24 *Related Party Disclosures*	IAS 24 *Related Party Disclosures*
IAS 27 *Consolidated and Separate Financial Statements*	IAS 27 *Consolidated and Separate Financial Statements*
IAS 28 *Investments in Associates*	IAS 28 *Investments in Associates*
IFRS 11 *Interests in Joint Ventures*	IFRS 11 *Interests in Joint Ventures*

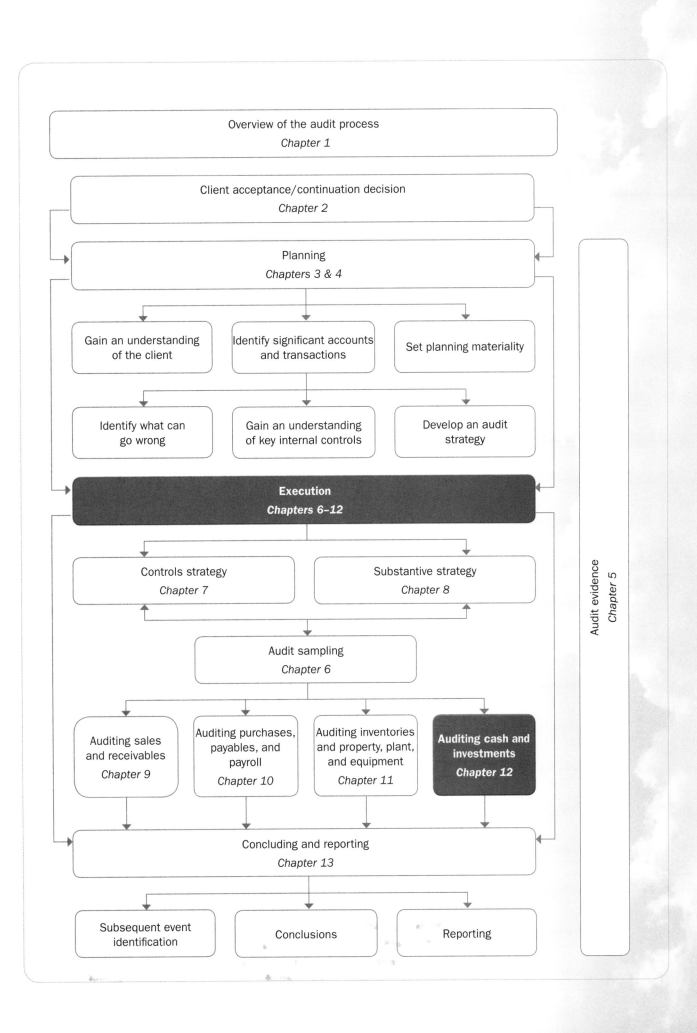

Cloud 9

Josh is reviewing the balance sheet and observes that cash and investments are the only assets on the balance sheet left to audit. He recognizes that, now that Cloud 9 operates a retail unit, there is cash on hand, and therefore, there is a greater risk of theft of cash. Sharon, the audit manager, indicated there is now a greater risk of skimming, a type of embezzlement that may occur when staff handle cash and have direct contact with the customer. With the use of a cash register at the Cloud 9 retail store, it is possible for employees to select the "no-sale" button on the till and keep the cash; therefore, it appears the employees are using the till but a sale has not been recorded. The cash in the till at the end of the day will still reconcile to the sales recorded. Josh wonders if the Cloud 9 management has disabled the no-sale button on the cash registers and implemented other strong controls over the cash processing to prevent this from happening.

AUDIT PROCESS IN FOCUS

Cash normally comprises cash balances at the bank or similar institutions and cash on hand. In some cases, cash can, in fact, be a negative balance and thus a liability, such as when an entity is operating a bank overdraft facility. Cash on hand includes undeposited receipts and petty cash. Cash at bank includes cash held in current and savings accounts and in imprest accounts, such as payroll bank accounts, that is available on demand. IAS 7 *Statement of Cash Flows* has an intermediate category of investments referred to as cash equivalents. Cash equivalents are highly liquid investments readily convertible to known amounts of cash within three months. These are included with cash in the statement of cash flows and may be included with cash in the balance sheet (also known as the statement of financial position).

Other bank balances that are not readily available do not meet the definition of cash equivalents (such as debenture sinking fund cash and other accounts that have restrictions on their use). These items should ordinarily be classified as investments, rather than as part of cash balances. Unlike other balance sheet account balances, cash may be either an asset or a liability. The latter arises where the bank or other institution with which the entity holds an account grants the entity an overdraft. That is, the entity is allowed to write cheques or transfer funds in excess of the balance in the account up to an agreed limit.

The internal control structures for transactions affecting both cash and investment assets in connection with the audits of sales and purchases were described in chapters 9 and 10, respectively. This chapter is concerned mainly with the application of substantive audit procedures aimed at verifying these account balances, but also considers two key control procedures over the safekeeping of these assets: (1) the use of bank reconciliations in the case of cash and (2) the maintenance of an investment register.

For each of these account balances, this chapter discusses the audit objectives, considerations when determining the audit strategy including controls, and applicable substantive procedures. Special consideration is given, in the audit of cash, to procedures designed to detect a fraud known as lapping and to the audit of petty cash balances and imprest bank accounts.

A particular feature of the audit of investments is the special disclosure requirement for investments in subsidiaries, associates, and joint ventures. It is usually in the form of consolidated financial statements. This chapter also explains the additional audit responsibilities in verifying investments in group entities, and the responsibilities for the consolidated financial statements.

12.1 AUDIT OBJECTIVES FOR CASH

1 Identify the audit objectives applicable to cash.

In the auditing of cash and investments, the key issues are to ensure that:

- The cash exists and is owned by the client and all cash transactions at the end of the reporting period are complete and properly disclosed.
- The investments exist, are owned, are properly recorded (including profits or losses on any sales) and disclosed, and are properly valued at the end of the reporting period.

CLASSES OF TRANSACTION OBJECTIVES	
Occurrence (**OE**)	Recorded receipt and payment transactions represent cash inflows and outflows during the period (**OE1**).
Completeness (**C**)	All cash inflows and outflows made during the period have been recorded (**C1**).
Accuracy (**AV**)	Payments and receipts are properly (accurately) recorded (**AV1**).
Cut-off (**CO**)	Year-end transfers of cash between banks and bank accounts are recorded in the proper period (**CO**).
Classification (**PD**)	Payments and receipts are recorded in the correct accounts (**PD1**).
ACCOUNT BALANCE OBJECTIVES	
Existence (**OE**)	Recorded cash balances exist at the end of the reporting period (**OE2**).
Rights and obligations (**RO**)	The entity has legal title to all cash balances shown at the end of the reporting period (**RO1**).
Completeness (**C**)	Recorded cash balances include the effects of all cash transactions that have occurred (**C2**).
Valuation and allocation (**AV**)	Recorded cash balances are realizable at the amounts stated on the balance sheet and agree with supporting schedules (**AV2**).
PRESENTATION AND DISCLOSURE OBJECTIVES (PD)	
Occurrence and rights and obligations	Lines of credit, loan guarantees, and other restrictions on cash balances are appropriately disclosed (**PD2**).
Completeness	Cash balances are properly identified and included in the balance sheet (**PD3**).
Classification and understandability	Cash balances are appropriately presented and information disclosed is clearly expressed (**PD4**).
Accuracy and valuation	Cash balances are disclosed accurately and at appropriate amounts (**PD5**).

TABLE 12.1 **Selected specific audit objectives for cash balances**

Internal control considerations and the related audit objectives for cash receipts and payments are covered in chapters 9 and 10, respectively. This chapter focuses mainly on verifying the cash account balance. Table 12.1 shows the account balance audit objectives. Assertions about presentation and disclosure in respect of account balance audit objectives include occurrence, rights and obligations, completeness, classification and understandability, and accuracy and valuation. Refer to paragraph A111 of CAS 315 *Identifying and Assessing the Risks of Material Misstatement through Understanding the Entity and Its Environment.*

BEFORE YOU GO ON

12.1.1 What items are included in cash balances?

12.1.2 What are cash equivalents?

12.1.3 What are the key issues when auditing cash and investments?

12.2 AUDIT STRATEGY FOR CASH

For many entities, cash balances represent only a small proportion of assets. However, the amount of cash flowing through the accounts over a period of time is usually greater than for any other account in the financial statements. Moreover, cash is vital to the survival of the business as a going concern. The inability of an entity to pay its debts as they fall due because it has a shortage of cash can render a company insolvent, despite the profitability of its operations. The cash

2 Discuss considerations relevant to determining the audit strategy for cash.

balance is material in a qualitative way even though it may not always be material in a quantitative way. Figure 12.1 illustrates the effect of the different transaction cycles on the cash balance, which shows that the cash account is affected by all of the business processes and therefore many accounting transactions affect the cash account.

The high volume of transactions contributes to a significant level of inherent risk for cash balance assertions, particularly existence and completeness. In addition, the nature of cash balances makes them susceptible to theft, as evidenced by numerous kinds of fraudulent schemes involving cash. In contrast to receivables or inventories, however, the risks pertaining to the rights and obligations assertion and the valuation and disclosure assertions for cash are minimal, given the absence of complexities involving these assertions.

When planning the audit, it is necessary to consider the effectiveness of control procedures that are designed to ensure the correctness of the recorded balance by way of regular bank reconciliations and the use of imprest accounts.

While the auditor generally adopts a substantive approach to the audit of cash balances, an understanding of procedures for maintaining accountability over cash is necessary in designing the substantive tests of details. The main procedures are:

- independently performed bank reconciliations
- the use of imprest accounts

12.2.1 Bank reconciliations

bank reconciliations schedules agreeing the balance of cash at the bank per the entity's records with the balance shown per the bank. The most common reconciling items are deposits in transit and outstanding cheques.

In the audit of cash receipts (chapter 9) and cash payments (chapter 10), the auditor will have obtained an understanding of **bank reconciliations** (see Appendix A, figure 15A) and tested controls relating to their preparation and use. This is a major internal control that relates to the audit of cash. It involves an independent comparison of the balance shown on the bank statement and the balance recorded in the entity's records. The difference between the two is reconciled by listing deposits in transit and outstanding cheques. Verifying the reconciliation of the bank account at the end of the reporting period is an important substantive procedure.

12.2.2 Imprest accounts

imprest petty cash fund petty cash fund maintained at a constant level via replenishment with the value of amounts paid out of the fund

An **imprest petty cash fund** is established by transferring a specified amount of cash, such as $500 or $750, to a petty cash box. When cash is paid out of the fund, an authorized voucher is placed in the petty cash box in its place. This voucher could be a supplier's invoice or a special petty cash voucher authorized by a responsible official. When the cash gets low, the vouchers are

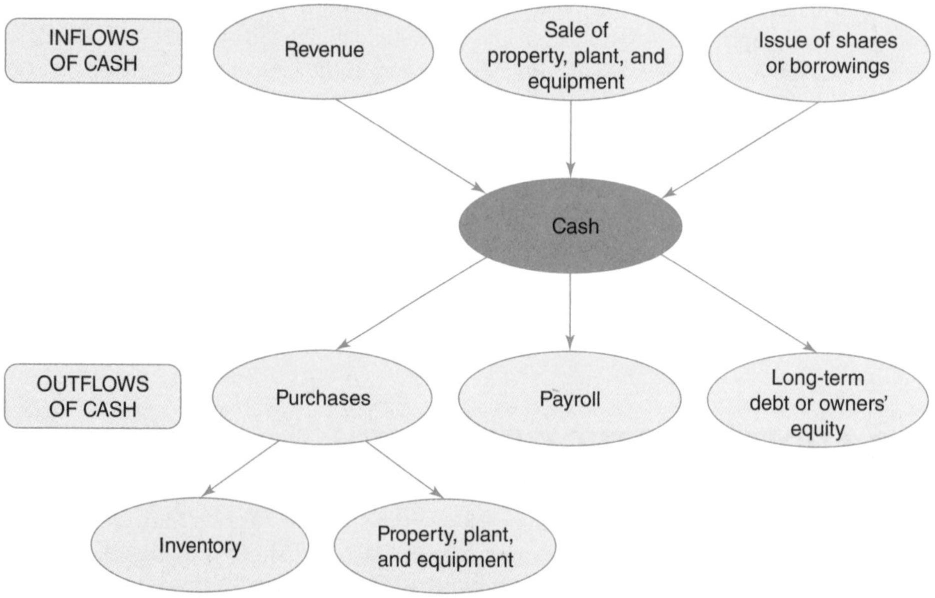

FIGURE 12.1 **The effects of major accounting transactions on cash**

used as support for a cheque requisition to replenish the fund. On replenishment, the cash in the petty cash box is restored to its imprest level.

The following internal control features apply to the management of an imprest petty cash fund:

- The fund should be maintained at the imprest level; that is, cash in the fund plus vouchers for payments should always equal the imprest amount.
- The fund should be in the custody of one person.
- The fund should be kept secure and stored in the safe when not in use.
- Payments from the fund should be for small amounts, and documentation should support each payment.
- The fund should not be mingled with other cash.
- Replenishment of the fund should be based on a review of supporting documentation.
- Upon payment, supporting documents should be stamped "paid" to prevent their reuse.

Certain bank accounts, typically payroll and dividend bank accounts, are sometimes also set up on an imprest basis. The **imprest bank account** is opened or replenished with the net payroll, dividends, and so on. When all cheques written on the account have been presented, the balance will be zero. Until such time, reconciliation can be achieved by comparing the balance per the bank statement with outstanding cheques. Internal controls over an imprest bank account include the following:

imprest bank account bank account funded with a sum sufficient to meet the payment of special-purpose cheques such as wages or dividends

- One person, such as a paymaster or the accountant, should be authorized to sign cheques drawn on the account.
- Only payroll cheques, dividend cheques, and so on should be written against the account.
- Each pay/dividend period, a cheque for the total net amount payable should be deposited in the imprest bank account.
- The imprest bank account should be independently reconciled each month.

Given the large volume of cash transactions tested in other cycles and the often small account balance, the audit strategy is invariably to concentrate on verifying the account balance. The approach is therefore usually substantive. The main procedures for cash balances are to audit the bank reconciliation and reconcile that balance to the confirmation from the bank. The auditor should thus be able to verify the balance exactly because no judgement is needed in determining the figure. Therefore, any differences found will almost always be considered material because of the ease with which the auditor should be able to verify the final balance and the materiality of the transactions that affect this balance.

In auditing the cash balance, the auditor should also be aware of the possibility of fraud. Cash is an area that is more susceptible to fraud than some other areas, so this increases the inherent risk of this part of the audit. This risk is one of the reasons even a small discrepancy in the audit of cash should be followed up. The following Professional Environment feature outlines a fraud in a large church at the hands of an unscrupulous bookkeeper.

PROFESSIONAL ENVIRONMENT

Asset misappropriation

More than 91 percent of internal corporate fraud involves asset misappropriation; of those cases, about 85 percent involve the misuse of cash and the rest involve the misappropriation of non-cash assets, according to the Association of Certified Fraud Examiners.

There are three types of asset misappropriation. Skimming involves misappropriation before the assets are recorded in the books. Larceny involves theft of cash or misuse of tangible assets such as equipment. The third type involves a scam while the organization is purchasing goods and services, such as fake invoices.

Asset misappropriation can happen where you least expect it, as shown in the following story of a bookkeeper at a large church who skimmed her employer. Her fraud went undetected for two years, even though there were controls in place, including having volunteers count the weekly cash collections together and oversee each other. The volunteers then submitted the cash plus a sheet documenting all the collections to the bookkeeper. But the bookkeeper never deposited the cash, and the documentation was never checked against the bank statements.

How was she found out? She took a sick day, and another employee happened to see a bank statement in an envelope that was open. She looked inside, and saw that the bookkeeper had made cheques payable to herself. The church investigated and uncovered the larger fraud.

Such frauds are not limited to churches and not-for-profit organizations. On a worldwide scale, the cost of fraud to companies is so large the numbers can seem hard to fathom. According to a 2014 global fraud survey published by the Association of Certified Fraud Examiners, "the typical organization loses five percent of its revenues each year to fraud. If applied to the 2013 estimated Gross World Product, this translates to a potential projected global fraud loss of nearly [US]$3.7 trillion."

Sources: Tracy Coenen, "Asset Misappropriation," *Essentials of Corporate Fraud*, John Wiley & Sons, 2009; Chad Albrecht, Mary-Jo Kranacher, and Steve Albrecht, "Asset Misappropriation Research White Paper for the Institute for Fraud Prevention," Institute for Fraud Prevention, 2008; "The Perils of Fraud," David Malamed, CPA Canada, November 1, 2014.

As previously discussed, liquidity is crucial to the company's survival. The cash adequacy and the flows of cash should be reviewed carefully by the auditor.

Cloud 9

Josh understands that Cloud 9 has a high volume of cash transactions, resulting in a high inherent risk. As he looks at the balance sheet, he can see that the overall cash balance is small; however, it is still a significant account given its impact on liquidity. Even though W&S Partners tested controls over cash transactions when auditing sales and purchases, they will still take a substantive approach to the audit of cash. The substantive procedures will include sending bank confirmations to all banks Cloud 9 does business with and testing the December 31 bank reconciliation.

BEFORE YOU GO ON

12.2.1 What are two control procedures over cash?

12.2.2 Explain an imprest petty cash fund.

12.2.3 What are the key issues when auditing cash and investments?

12.3 SUBSTANTIVE PROCEDURES FOR CASH BALANCES

 Design and execute an audit program for cash balances.

Procedures described in this section exclude those for petty cash and imprest bank accounts. The audit of these two accounts is considered separately.

As explained previously, the significance of cash to the entity's liquidity and the fact that the balance is relatively small mean that the acceptable level of detection risk in verifying cash balances is invariably set as low.

Table 12.2 lists possible substantive procedures to achieve the specific audit objectives for cash balances. The list is organized in accordance with the general framework for developing audit programs for substantive procedures. Note that several of the tests apply to more than one audit objective and that each objective is covered by multiple possible procedures. Not all of the procedures will be performed in every audit. Each procedure is explained in the sections that follow, including comments on when certain of the tests could be omitted and on how some tests can be tailored based on applicable risk factors.

12.3.1 Initial procedures

The starting point for verifying cash balances is to trace the current period's opening balances to the closing audited balances in the previous year's working papers. Next, the auditor should review the current period's activity in the general ledger cash accounts for any significant entries that are unusual in nature or amount and that may require investigation. In addition, the auditor obtains any schedules that might have been prepared by the entity showing summaries of undeposited cash receipts at different locations and/or summaries of bank balances. The auditor should determine the mathematical accuracy of such schedules and check their agreement with related

TABLE 12.2 **Possible substantive procedures for cash balance assertions**

CATEGORY	SUBSTANTIVE PROCEDURE	OE2	C2	RO2	AV2	CO	PD NO.
		CASH BALANCE AUDIT OBJECTIVE (FROM TABLE 12.1)					
Initial procedures	1. Perform initial procedures on cash balances and records that will be subjected to further testing. (a) Trace opening balances for cash on hand and in the bank to previous year's working papers. (b) Review activity in general ledger accounts for cash and investigate entries that appear unusual in amount or source. (c) Obtain entity-prepared summaries of cash on hand and in the bank, verify mathematical accuracy, and determine agreement with general ledger.				✓		
Analytical procedures	2. Perform analytical procedures by comparing cash balances with expected amounts.	✓	✓		✓		
Tests of details of transactions	3. Perform cash cut-off tests. (Note: These tests may have been performed as part of the audit programs for accounts receivable and accounts payable.) (a) Observe that all cash received by the close of business on the last day of the financial year is included in cash and that no receipts of the subsequent period are included, or (b) review documentation such as daily cash summaries, duplicate deposit slips, and bank statements covering several days before and after the year-end date to determine proper cut-off. (c) Observe the last cheque issued and mailed on the last day of the financial year and trace to the accounting records to determine the accuracy of the cash payments cut-off, or (d) compare dates on cheques issued for several days before and after the year-end date to the dates on which the cheques were recorded to determine proper cut-off.					✓	
	4. Trace bank transfers before and after the end of the reporting period to determine that each transfer is properly recorded as a payment and a receipt in the same accounting period.					✓	
Tests of details of balances	5. Confirm bank balances.	✓	✓	✓	✓		
	6. Confirm other arrangements with banks.	✓	✓	✓	✓		✓2
	7. Verify reconciliations as appropriate.	✓	✓	✓	✓		
	8. Obtain and use the subsequent period's statements to verify bank reconciliation items and look for evidence of window dressing.	✓	✓	✓	✓		
	9. Count undeposited cash on hand.	✓	✓	✓	✓		
Presentation and disclosure	10. Compare statement presentation with applicable accounting standards. (a) Determine that cash balances are properly identified and classified. (b) Determine that bank overdrafts are reclassified as current liabilities. (c) Make inquiries of management, review correspondence with banks, and review minutes of board meetings to determine matters requiring disclosure, such as lines of credit, loan guarantees, compensating balance agreements, or other restrictions on cash balances.						✓3–5 ✓3–5 ✓2

cash balances in the general ledger. This test provides evidence about the valuation assertion. The auditor should also obtain copies of all bank reconciliations for the year.

12.3.2 Analytical procedures

Cash balances do not normally show a stable or predictable relationship with other current or historical financial or operating data. As a result, the auditor will often not perform any analytical review procedures in this part of the audit. If the auditor does decide to perform some analytical review procedures, they are usually limited to comparisons with previous years' cash balances or with budgeted amounts.

12.3.3 Tests of details of transactions

Tests of details of cash receipt and cash payment transactions were discussed in chapters 9 and 10, respectively. The audit procedures discussed in these chapters give the auditor comfort over the assertions in relation to cash transactions. This chapter looks at tests of transactions around the end of the reporting period (cut-off) that help verify the balance as at that year-end date.

Cash cut-off tests

cash cut-off tests audit procedures verifying the agreement of cash receipts recorded in the accounting records at close of business with the physical movement of cash

A proper cut-off of cash receipts and cash payments at the end of the year is essential to the proper statement of cash at the end of the reporting period. Two **cash cut-off tests** are performed:

- a cash receipts cut-off test (see chapter 9)
- a cash payments cut-off test (see chapter 10)

The use of the subsequent period's bank statement (described below) is also helpful in determining whether a proper cash cut-off has been made. Cash cut-off tests are directed mainly at the financial statement assertions of existence and completeness.

Tracing bank transfers

kiting an irregularity overstating the cash balance by intentionally recording a bank transfer as a deposit in the receiving bank while failing to show a deduction from the bank account on which the transfer is drawn

bank transfer schedule a schedule prepared by the auditor listing bank transfers for a few days either side of the end of the reporting period, and the dates recorded in the records and the bank statement

Many entities maintain accounts with more than one bank. A company with multiple bank accounts may transfer money between bank accounts. Money may be transferred, for example, from a general bank account to a payroll bank account for payroll cheques (or for direct transfers to employees) that are to be distributed on the next payday. When a bank transfer occurs, several days will elapse before the cheque clears the bank on which it is drawn. Thus, cash on deposit per bank records will be overstated during this period because the cheque will be included in the balance of the bank in which it is deposited and will not be deducted from the bank on which it is drawn. Bank transfers may also result in a misstatement of the bank balance per books if the payment and receipt are not recorded in the same accounting period.

Intentionally recording a transfer as a deposit in the receiving bank while failing to show a deduction from the account on which the transfer cheque is drawn is an irregularity known as **kiting**. Kiting may be used to conceal a cash shortage or overstate cash at bank at the end of the reporting period.

The auditor identifies bank transfers by analyzing the cash book for a few days either side of the end of the reporting period, then enters these into a **bank transfer schedule**. The schedule is then completed by determining, from applicable bank statements, the dates on which the bank recorded the transfers, as illustrated in table 12.3.

TABLE 12.3 **Bank transfer schedule**

CHEQUE NUMBER	BANK ACCOUNTS		AMOUNT OF CHEQUE ($)	PAYMENT DATE		RECEIPT DATE	
	FROM	TO		PER BOOKS	PER BANK	PER BOOKS	PER BANK
4100	General	Payroll	50,000	Dec. 31	Jan. 4	Dec. 31	Jan. 3
4275	General	Branch 1	10,000	Dec. 31	Jan. 4	Jan. 3	Jan. 3
4280	General	Branch 2	20,000	Jan. 3	Jan. 3	Dec. 31	Dec. 31
B403	Branch 4	General	5,000	Jan. 3	Jan. 4	Jan. 3	Dec. 31

If we assume all cheques are dated and issued on December 31, cheque 4100 in table 12.3 has been handled properly because both book entries were made in December and both bank entries occurred in January. This cheque would be listed as an outstanding cheque in reconciling the general bank account at December 31 and as a deposit in transit in reconciling the payroll bank account. Cheque 4275 illustrates a transfer cheque in transit at the closing date. Cash per books is understated by $10,000 because the cheque has been deducted from the balance per books by the issuer in December, but has not been added to the Branch 1 account per books by the depositor until January. Thus, an adjusting entry is required at December 31 to increase the branch balance per books.

Cheques 4280 and B403 illustrate the likelihood of kiting because these December cheques were not recorded as payments per books until January, even though they were deposited in the receiving banks in December. Cheque 4280 results in a $20,000 overstatement of cash at bank because the receipt per the books occurred in December, but the corresponding book deduction was not made until January. Cheque B403 may illustrate an attempt to conceal a cash shortage because the bank deposit occurred in December, presumably to permit the reconciliation of bank and book balances, and all other entries were made in January. Similar issues can apply when transfers are done electronically, although this is much less likely because transactions are often completed on the same day, so the timing issues that relate to cheques around the end of the reporting period would seldom apply.

Kiting is possible when weaknesses in internal controls allow one person to issue and record cheques (that is, there is an improper segregation of duties) or when there is collusion between the people responsible for the two functions. In addition to tracing bank transfers, the auditor may detect kiting by:

- obtaining and using a subsequent period's bank statement, because the kited cheque clearing in January will not appear on the list of outstanding cheques for December
- performing a cash cut-off test, because the last cheque issued in December will not be recorded in the cheque register

The tracing of bank transfers provides reliable evidence concerning the existence and completeness assertions.

12.3.4 Tests of balances

There are five commonly used substantive tests for cash balances in this category:

1. confirming bank balances
2. confirming other arrangements with banks
3. verifying bank reconciliations
4. obtaining and using the subsequent period's bank statement
5. counting cash on hand

Confirming bank balances

The auditor normally confirms the bank balance directly with the bank through a **bank confirmation**. This letter is sent to all banks with whom the auditor is aware that the client has a relationship. The form requests information about account balances, securities, loan documents, and other related information held by the bank on behalf of the entity.

The accepted practice is that bank confirmation requests are sent on every audit and it would be considered highly unusual not to send one. The client must sign a letter of authorization to the bank requesting completion of the form. The auditor (in consultation with the client) fills in the account information and the bank is then responsible for completing the information requested. See Appendix A, figure 1A for an example of a bank confirmation.

The confirming of cash on deposit provides evidence mainly of the existence of cash at bank (because there is written acknowledgement that the balance exists) and of rights and obligations (because the balances are in the name of the entity). The response from the bank also provides some evidence for the valuation assertion for cash in that the confirmed balance is used in arriving at the correct cash balance at the end of the reporting period.

bank confirmation written confirmation of the balance at bank and other matters received directly by the auditor from the entity's bank

The confirming of overdraft and loan balances provides evidence of:

- existence, because there is written acknowledgement that the loan balance exists
- rights and obligations, because the loan is a debt of the entity
- valuation, because the response indicates the amount of the loan balance

This test also contributes to the completeness assertion in the same manner as for confirming deposit balances.

Confirming other arrangements with banks

The bank confirmation form also requests information as to other arrangements with the bank, such as loans and other contingent liabilities.

The confirmation of other arrangements with the banks is helpful in meeting the disclosure assertion. It also provides evidence for each of the other assertions. However, the evidence for the completeness assertion is limited to information known by the branch officer who is completing the confirmation.

Where the auditor believes there may be material accounts, agreements, or transactions that he or she is unaware of, the auditor should contact the bank and request further information.

Verifying bank reconciliations

Testing of a client's bank reconciliation is central to the audit of cash balances. This testing verifies that the balance confirmed with the bank agrees with the bank balance per the client's records. Follow the steps below by referring to the reconciliation shown in figure 12.2.

1. Check the mathematical accuracy (✗) and compare with the general ledger |(✳).
2. Verify the bank balance per the bank confirmation with the bank balance per the reconciliation (∿).
3. Trace outstanding cheques on the bank reconciliation to the subsequent period's bank statement (✓).
4. Trace deposits in transit on the bank reconciliation to the subsequent period's bank statement (✓).
5. Verify any bank charges or errors on the reconciliation with the bank statement or other supporting documentation (ϕ).

Testing or preparing a bank reconciliation establishes the correct cash at the end of the reporting period. Thus, it is a primary source of evidence for the valuation assertion. It also provides evidence for the existence, completeness, and rights and obligations assertions.

Obtaining and using the subsequent period's bank statement

subsequent period's bank statement the first bank statement issued after the end of the reporting period, which is used by the auditor to verify the existence of outstanding deposits and uncleared cheques listed on the bank reconciliation as at the end of the reporting period

The **subsequent period's bank statement** is normally issued at the end of the month following the entity's financial year end. In most situations, this timeframe will be sufficient. However, if the audit deadline does not permit waiting for the issue of this statement, then a special statement can be requested. The date should be at a point in time that will permit most of the year-end uncleared cheques to clear the bank, usually 7 to 10 business days following the end of the entity's financial year. On receipt of the subsequent period's bank statement, the auditor should:

- trace all cheques and bank transfers dated but not cleared in the previous financial year to the outstanding cheques and bank transfers listed on the bank reconciliation
- trace deposits or bank transfers in transit on the bank reconciliation to deposits on the statement
- scan the statement for unusual items such as large transfers close to year end

The tracing of cheques is designed to verify the list of outstanding cheques. In this step, the auditor may also find that a cheque dated in the previous period that is not on the list of outstanding cheques has cleared the bank and that some of the cheques listed as outstanding have not cleared the bank. The former may be indicative of the irregularity known as kiting, which we explained earlier in connection with bank transfers; the latter may be due to delays in the entity mailing the cheques or in the payees depositing the cheques. The auditor should investigate any unusual circumstances.

FIGURE 12.2 **Review of entity-prepared bank reconciliation**

Bates Ltd.
Bank reconciliation—City Bank
Dec. 31, 2016
(PBC)

Prepared by: C.J.W.
Date: Jan. 7, 2017

Reviewed by: A.C.E.
Date: Jan. 11, 2017

Account no. 110 Dec. 31, 2016
Bank acc. no. 12345-642

Balance per bank				120,262.47 ↶
Deposits in transit:	*Per books*	*Per bank*		
	Dec. 29	Jan. 2	8,425.15 ✓	
	Dec. 30	Jan. 7	17,844.79 ✓	26,269.94 ✗
Outstanding cheques:		1047	225.94 ✓	
		1429	21,600.00 ✓	
		1435	47.25 ✓	
		1436	1,428.14 ✓	
		1437	1,000.00 ✓	
		1440	832.08 ✓	
		1441	41.08 ✓	(25,174.49) ✗
Add NSF cheque—ZIM Dec. 28				200.00 ɸ
Balance per books				121,557.92 ∣(✗)
Adjusting entry—AJE4				200.00
Balance as adjusted				121,357.92
				To A ✗

Adjusting entry		
Dr Accounts Receivable ZIM	200	
Cr Cash in Bank		200
NSF cheque charged by bank		
Dec. 28.		

↶ Verified with bank statement and bank confirmation
✓ Traced to January bank statement
✗ Footed (added)
ɸ Traced to statement and debit memoranda
∣(✗) Traced to general ledger

When the aggregate effect of outstanding cheques is material, it may indicate an irregularity known as **window dressing**. This is a deliberate attempt to enhance a company's apparent short-term solvency. (Assume that the entity's balances at the end of the reporting period show current assets of $800,000 and current liabilities of $400,000. If $100,000 of cheques to short-term creditors have been prematurely entered, then the correct totals are current assets of $900,000 and current liabilities of $500,000, which results in a 1.8:1 current ratio instead of the reported 2:1.) Window dressing is normally perpetrated by writing cheques on the last day of the financial year but not mailing them until several weeks later, when cleared funds are available at the bank to meet those cheques. If none of a sequence of cheques is presented for payment on the bank statement for more than two weeks after the end of the reporting period, then the auditor should make inquiries of the treasurer. Recipients do not usually delay depositing cheques once received, and it is normal for most cheques to clear the bank statement within a week of issue. Where the evidence is clear that the company has engaged in material window dressing, the auditor should recommend appropriate adjustments to the cash balance.

The tracing of deposits in transit to the subsequent period's bank statement is normally a relatively simple matter because the first deposit on that statement should be the deposit in transit shown on the reconciliation. When this is not the case, the auditor should determine the underlying circumstances for the time lag from the accountant, and corroborate his or her explanations. Delays in depositing cash receipts could indicate the practice of lapping. Generally, deposits in transit would be expected to be minimal because of the use of electronic transfers and the speed of processing.

window dressing a deliberate attempt to enhance some aspect of a company's apparent short-term solvency, such as by misstating the cut-off of cash receipts and payments

In scanning the subsequent period's statement for unusual items, the auditor should be alert for such items as unrecorded bank debits and credits, and bank errors and corrections. Figure 12.2 illustrates a deposit made before the year end returned by the drawer's bank after the year end, marked "not sufficient funds" (NSF) and requiring adjustment.

Counting cash on hand

cash count audit procedure of counting cash on hand and agreeing the balance with the accounting records

Cash on hand consists of undeposited cash receipts and change. To perform **cash counts** properly, the auditor should:

- control all cash and negotiable instruments held until all funds have been counted
- insist that the custodian of the cash be present throughout the count
- obtain a signed receipt from the custodian on return of the funds
- ascertain that all undeposited cheques are payable to the order of the entity, either directly or through endorsement

The control of all funds is designed to prevent transfers by entity personnel of counted funds to uncounted funds. The sealing of funds and the use of additional auditors are often required when cash is held in many locations. Having the custodian present and requiring his or her signature on return of the funds minimizes the possibility, in the event of a shortage, of the custodian claiming that all cash was intact when released to the auditor for counting.

This procedure provides evidence of each of the financial statement assertions except disclosure. Note that the evidence about rights is weak because the custodian of the fund may have substituted personal cash to cover a shortage.

Companies generally try to keep cash on hand to a minimum and therefore this amount is often very immaterial. As a result, in many audits this procedure is not performed, although this should be reassessed when there are circumstances indicating a higher risk of fraud associated with cash.

12.3.5 Disclosure

Cash should be correctly identified and classified in the balance sheet. Cash on deposit, for example, is a current asset, but a fixed-term deposit may be a long-term investment. In addition, there should be appropriate disclosure of arrangements with banks, such as lines of credit, compensating balances, and contingent liabilities.

The auditor determines the appropriateness of the statement presentation from a review of the draft of the entity's financial statements and the evidence obtained from the foregoing substantive procedures. In addition, the auditor should review the minutes of board meetings and inquire of management for evidence of restrictions on the use of cash balances.

Cloud 9

Josh reviews the cash account at Cloud 9. He notes that there are several bank accounts that make up the cash balance on the balance sheet. For each bank account, he has obtained the bank reconciliation from Carla, the controller, and he has checked that it is mathematically correct. He has also agreed the balance per the bank with the bank confirmation. He has just obtained the subsequent bank statement from the bookkeeper and he is verifying that the deposits in transit and outstanding cheques have cleared since year end. He knows this will verify their existence at year end.

BEFORE YOU GO ON

12.3.1 Why are analytical procedures not often useful when auditing the cash balance?

12.3.2 What is kiting?

12.3.3 Describe the purpose of the subsequent bank statement.

12.4 SPECIAL CONSIDERATIONS FOR CASH BALANCES

This section covers three topics: (1) testing to detect an irregularity known as lapping, (2) auditing imprest petty cash funds, and (3) auditing imprest bank accounts.

12.4.1 Detecting lapping

Lapping is an irregularity that results in the deliberate misappropriation of cash receipts, either temporarily or permanently, for the personal use of the individual perpetrating the unauthorized act. Lapping is usually associated with collections from customers, but it may also involve other types of cash receipts. Conditions conducive to lapping exist when the same person handles cash receipts and maintains the accounts receivable ledger. The auditor should assess the likelihood of lapping in obtaining an understanding about the segregation of duties in the receiving and recording of collections from customers.

4 Describe special considerations when auditing cash balances, including lapping, petty cash funds, and imprest bank accounts.

lapping an irregularity concealing the misappropriation of cash by using subsequent cash receipts to conceal the original misappropriation

An example of lapping

Assume on a given day that cash register receipts totalled $600 and mail receipts opened by the defrauder consisted of one payment on account by cheque for $200 from customer A (total actual receipts = $800). The lapper would steal $200 in cash and destroy all evidence of the mail receipt, except for the customer's cheque. The cash receipts journal entry would agree with the register ($600), and the deposit slip would show cash of $400 and customer A's cheque for $200. These facts can be tabulated as shown in figure 12.3.

ACTUAL RECEIPTS		DOCUMENTATION	CASH RECEIPTS JOURNAL ENTRY		BANK DEPOSIT SLIP	
Cash	$600	Cash tape	$600	Cash sales	$600	Cash	$400
Customer A's cheque	200		—		—	Customer A's cheque	$200
	$800		$600		$600		$600

FIGURE 12.3 **Sample cash receipts journal entry—customer A**

To conceal the shortage, the defrauder usually attempts to keep bank and book amounts in daily agreement so a bank reconciliation will not detect the irregularity. The defrauder will also need to ensure that customer A's account is correct. This can be done by allocating some of the payment received from another customer (customer B) to customer A's account. As shown in figure 12.4, a cheque for $300 is received from customer B, enabling the defrauder to steal another $100 and cover the amount missing from customer A's account. The total shortage is now $300: $200 from the first example plus $100 from the second example.

There will, of course, now be a shortfall in customer B's account that will eventually be covered by a cheque from someone else. To enable this to continue, the same person must always deal with cash receipts. Thus, when the person involved with cash receipts never takes holidays, the auditor needs to take extra care.

ACTUAL RECEIPTS		DOCUMENTATION		CASH RECEIPTS JOURNAL ENTRY		BANK DEPOSIT SLIP	
Cash	$500	Cash tape	$500	Cash sales	$500	Cash	$400
Customer B's cheque	300	Customer A's cheque	200	Customer A's cheque	200	Customer B's cheque	$300
	$800		$700		$700		$700

FIGURE 12.4 **Sample cash receipts journal entry—customer B**

A greater risk of fraud occurs when the person in cash receipts is able to make adjustments to the accounts receivable subsidiary ledger. In this situation, the defrauder can take cash as described above, but does not need to cover up because it is a simple matter to record a credit note against the customer's balance. (This may be queried by the customer when a detailed statement is sent at the end of the month, as it would show a credit note reducing an amount owing rather than a payment made.)

Auditing procedures

Tests to detect lapping are performed only when the control risk for cash receipts transactions is moderate or high. There are three procedures that should detect lapping:

1. *Confirm accounts receivable on a surprise basis at an interim date.* Confirming at this time will prevent the person engaged in lapping from bringing the "lapped" accounts up to date. Confirmation at the end of the reporting period may be ineffective because the "defrauder" may anticipate this procedure and adjust the lapped accounts to their correct balances at this date.

2. *Make a surprise cash count.* The cash count will include coin, currency, and customer cheques on hand. The auditor should oversee the deposit of these funds. Subsequently, the auditor should compare the details of the deposit shown on the duplicate deposit slip with cash receipts journal entries and postings to the customers' accounts.

3. *Compare details of cash receipts journal entries with the details of corresponding daily deposit slips.* This procedure should uncover discrepancies in the details such as those shown in the above two examples.

As has been outlined so far in this chapter, cash in the bank is an area where the risk of fraud is higher than in some other parts of the audit. This is particularly the case where cash registers and actual cash are involved.

The following Professional Environment box provides tips for prevention of cash register fraud.

PROFESSIONAL ENVIRONMENT

How to prevent cash register fraud

For retailers, cash register fraud is a huge concern. Many employees might have access to the cash drawer with little stopping them from "dipping their hands into the cookie jar" or ringing up only part of the merchandise and letting their friends walk away with unpaid goods. Customers can just lean over and help themselves to cash when no one is looking. And the public can even walk away with the entire register if it's not secured to the countertop. Cash is hard to trace.

Here are some tips for preventing cash register fraud and theft by employees and the public.

1. Use codes. Purchase more expensive cash registers that require each employee to have their own security code to use it. This makes it easier to trace missing cash and sales to a particular employee.
2. Lock it down. Secure the cash register to the countertop.
3. Install cameras. Use CCTV cameras to keep an eye on staff and customers, and post signs indicating that there are cameras in use, which deters theft.
4. Clear the drawer. Periodically remove large bills and sums of cash and store in a safe or deposit in the bank.

5. Buddy up. Assign at least two staff on every shift to be responsible for the cash registers and to watch over each other.
6. Look out. Train staff to be alert to possible scams, such as thieves who try to distract employees at the till. In one recent case, a CCTV camera in a clothing retailer caught thieves who distracted staff and installed a device on the cash register that recorded employees' credit card information and defrauded the customers and the store.
7. Check receipts. Carefully monitor cash register receipts to see if there's anything fishy. An internal auditor reviewing register receipts uncovered employee fraud by noticing that customer refunds were always in even amounts, such as $300 or $400, when sales are normally in uneven amounts. An investigation uncovered the fact that an employee rang up fictitious refunds and removed that amount of cash from the till after almost every shift.

Sources: Herb Weisbaum, "New Security Threat: Cash Register Skimmers," CNBC, October 16, 2013; Barry Fish, "How Safe Is Your Money? Top 10 Tips to Prevent Cash Register Fraud and Theft," September 18, 2009, www.a2boffice.co.uk/; Joseph T. Wells, "Control Cash-Register Thievery," *Journal of Accountancy*, June 2002.

12.4.2 Auditing imprest petty cash funds

The balance of petty cash is rarely material and for this reason the majority of audits do not involve an audit of petty cash. Generally, the only time this part of the audit is performed is when the company expects or requests petty cash to be audited. If the auditor does happen to audit petty cash, it is often a good "litmus test" for the controls that operate throughout the entity. For this reason, the auditor may sometimes document the controls that operate over petty cash, particularly for small clients. If substantive testing of petty cash is done, the following substantive procedures are performed.

In auditing petty cash, the auditor performs tests of details of transactions and tests of balances. The auditor tests a number of replenishing transactions, including reviewing supporting documentation, accounting for all pre-numbered receipts, and determining that the reimbursement cheque was for the correct amount. The test of balances involves counting the fund. The count is usually made by surprise at an interim date rather than at the end of the reporting period. The auditor may also count the fund at the end of the reporting period, along with all other cash funds, to avoid the possibility that petty cash may be used to conceal a shortage elsewhere.

12.4.3 Auditing imprest bank accounts

An entity may use an imprest bank account for payroll and dividends.

The substantive tests should include confirming the balance with the bank, reviewing the reconciliation prepared by the entity, and using the subsequent period's bank statement. The adjusted or true cash balance at the end of the reporting period should be the imprest amount. The only reconciling items on the bank statement will be unpresented payroll or dividend cheques. Employees usually cash their paycheques promptly, so all the unpresented cheques should clear the bank on the subsequent period's bank statement. Unpaid dividends are more likely to be a problem. However, larger entities with quoted share capital (which are more likely to experience uncleared dividend cheques) usually employ an independent share registrar, one of whose functions is to distribute dividends. In such cases, the entity pays the total dividend to the registrar in a single cheque, and it is the registrar's responsibility to pay individual dividends and to maintain records of uncleared dividend cheques.

Cloud 9

Now that the bank reconciliations have been audited, Josh is reviewing the sales processes at the new Cloud 9 retail store. He has specifically asked Carla how cash and credit card sales are processed at the retail location. Carla explains all sales are recorded using the cash register, which includes the recording of the amount of each sale and the items removed from inventory sold. The sales data from the cash register are transferred electronically to the accounting department at the end of each day. The cash is counted by two sales associates and the store manager takes the daily deposits to the bank, while the total cash deposited is agreed to the sales information that has been transferred from the store. Total cash received is then recorded in the cash receipts journal, and then the general ledger.

Carla explains that the process is similar for credit card sales, whereby payments by credit cards are authorized at the retail location when the customer swipes their credit card to pay for the goods purchased. The credit card sales are transferred electronically to the accounting department and recorded for each credit card company in an accounts receivable sub-ledger account. When payment is received from the credit card companies, the accounting clerk agrees the total sales to the amounts received from the credit card companies, less the commission payable to those companies. The receivables ledger is updated with the payments received.

Carla explains that the store managers perform surprise cash counts.

Josh is glad to hear they have processes in place over the cash and credit card sales.

BEFORE YOU GO ON

12.4.1 What is lapping?

12.4.2 What are three auditing procedures for lapping?

12.4.3 Describe substantive procedures relevant for imprest bank accounts.

12.5 AUDIT OBJECTIVES FOR INVESTMENTS

⑤ Identify the audit objectives applicable to investments.

Entities commonly invest in other entities. These investments take a variety of forms: equity securities such as preference or ordinary shares, or debt securities such as corporate debentures or government bonds. Investments may be held for one of two reasons:

- to hold surplus funds or funds earmarked for a future purpose
- to secure a long-term relationship with the other party

A special category of this latter type of investment is investment for the purpose of acquiring influence or control over the activities of the other entity. Such entities may be classified as subsidiaries, associates, or joint ventures, and are regarded as part of the economic entity. The financial statements of the investing or "parent" entity are required to include appropriate balances relating to these other entities, so as to present a consolidated picture of the group or reporting entity. The audit of such investments extends to the verification of the balances in the separate entity financial statements, which are then consolidated with the parent entity's accounts.

Investment transactions involve cash receipts, such as dividends and interest received on investments, and proceeds on their disposal. Control considerations for cash receipts were discussed in chapter 9. Investment transactions also involve cash payments for the purchase of investments. Control considerations for payment transactions were discussed in chapter 10. This chapter considers additional controls applicable to investing transactions only. We discuss these controls in the course of discussing the development of the audit plan.

For the five categories of financial statement assertions, table 12.4 lists specific account balance audit objectives relating to accounts affected by investing transactions. The following sections explain considerations and procedures relevant to meeting these objectives.

TABLE 12.4 **Selected specific audit objectives for investments**

CLASSES OF TRANSACTION OBJECTIVES	
Occurrence (**OE**)	Investment revenues, gains, and losses resulted from transactions and events that occurred during the period (**OE1**).
Completeness (**C**)	All purchases of investments during the period have been recorded as additions (**C1**). All sales of investments during the period have been recorded as disposals (**C2**).
Accuracy (**AV**)	Investment revenues, gains, and losses are reported at proper amounts (**AV1**).
Cut-off (**CO**)	Investment transactions are recorded in the proper period (**CO**).
Classification (**PD**)	Investment transactions are recorded in the correct accounts (**PD1**).
ACCOUNT BALANCE OBJECTIVES	
Existence (**OE**)	Recorded investment balances represent investments that exist at the end of the reporting period (**OE2**).
Rights and obligations (**RO**)	All recorded investments are owned by the reporting entity (**RO1**).
Completeness (**C**)	The income statement includes the effects of all investment transactions and events during the period (**C3**).
Valuation and allocation (**AV**)	Recorded cash balances are realizable at the amounts stated on the balance sheet and agree with supporting schedules (**AV2**).
PRESENTATION AND DISCLOSURE OBJECTIVES (PD)	
Occurrence and rights and obligations	Disclosed investment pertains to the entity (**PD2**).
Completeness	All required disclosures are made concerning (1) related party investments, (2) the bases for valuing investments, and (3) the pledging of investments as collateral (**PD3**).
Classification and understandability	Investment balances are properly identified and classified in the financial statements (**PD4**).
Accuracy and valuation	Investments are disclosed accurately and at appropriate amounts (**PD5**).

Cloud 9

Cloud 9 reports a significant investment balance as part of its current assets. These investments are material to Cloud 9's short-term solvency, but income from such securities is much less significant. Josh believes there are inherent risks relating to how investments are accounted for because they must be reported at market value. One reason for this risk is the difficulties in accounting for investments depending on whether they are considered strategic or non-strategic investments. If the investment is non-strategic, it should be reported at the lower of cost and net realizable value. If the investment is strategic, the method of accounting depends on how many shares are held. If the company does not have "significant influence," the method of accounting is the same as it is for a non-strategic investment.

BEFORE YOU GO ON

12.5.1 Describe the various types of investments.

12.5.2 Define the rights and obligations assertion with respect to investments.

12.5.3 Explain completeness with respect to presentation and disclosure for investments.

12.6 AUDIT STRATEGY FOR INVESTMENTS

Often the purchases and sales of investments are processed separately from other purchases and sales, especially for entities holding substantial investment portfolios where specific control procedures over investments are likely implemented.

6 Discuss considerations relevant to determining the audit strategy for investments.

12.6.1 Control environment

The understanding of several control environment factors is relevant to the audit of the investments. The authority and responsibility for investing transactions, for example, should be assigned to a company officer such as the treasurer. This individual should be a person of integrity, with appropriate knowledge and skills, who realizes the importance of observing all prescribed control procedures and can help other participating members of management make initial and ongoing assessments of the risks associated with individual investments.

The information system must include provision for capturing the data required for each method of accounting for the various categories of investment in equity and debt securities, both at acquisition date and at the end of subsequent reporting periods. Accounting personnel must be familiar with these requirements and capable of implementing them.

In addition, internal auditors and the audit committee of the board of directors should closely monitor the effectiveness of controls over investing activities.

12.6.2 Functions and related controls

Activities in the investing cycle include the following investing functions and related controls.

Purchases and sales should be made in accordance with management's authorizations. The purchase and sale of investments intended to be retained as non-current assets normally require board approval. Where substantial investments are held, a separate **investment subsidiary ledger** or **investment register** may be maintained. This records details of acquisitions and disposals, the receipt of interest and dividends, and market values.

- Dividend and interest cheques must be promptly deposited intact, and the completeness of recorded investment income must be independently verified.

- Transactions should be recorded on the basis of appropriate supporting documentation, and the duties of recording of transactions and custody of the securities should be segregated.

- Securities should be stored in safes or vaults, with access restricted to authorized personnel. Periodically, relevant documents should be independently compared with recorded balances.

investment subsidiary ledger (investment register) a subsidiary ledger recording individual investments in shares and debentures. Entries show purchases and sales, the cost of each bundle purchased, and the quantity and the cost of the balance owed.

- Changes in value and in circumstances relating to the appropriate classification of investments should be periodically analyzed.
- Management should undertake performance reviews to detect poor investment performance and/or incorrect reporting.
- Periodically, the classification of individual investments should be reviewed.

The auditor should obtain an understanding of the entity's prescribed procedures to identify potential misstatements that could occur in investment balances and to design substantive procedures accordingly. If investment certificates are kept in the entity's safe and not independently verified, for example, then the audit program must call for physical inspection at or close to the end of the reporting period.

The most important audit risk where the investment is non-strategic or there is no significant influence is in relation to ensuring that the market value has been properly assessed. This is not a problem for investments that relate to shares listed on the stock exchange, as there is an active market. When the shares are in unlisted companies, more judgement is required by the auditor and there is a higher level of inherent risk, particularly in relation to the valuation assertion. Where the assessment of market value is below cost, an adjustment may not be warranted if management can provide good reasons for believing the carrying amount of the investment will eventually be recovered. If management does make this assertion, the auditor needs to assess the reasonableness of the assertion.

However, if the company does have significant influence, the investment should be accounted for using the equity method of accounting. Where the company has "control," which means it can dominate (directly or indirectly) the decision-making processes of another company in relation to its financial and operating policies, the company must consolidate the investment into its financial statements.

Another difficulty for the auditor is that there are judgements associated with assessing significant influence and control and sometimes the company may be unwilling to adopt a certain treatment because of the effect that it may have on its financial statements.

For most companies, the volume of investing transactions is quite low. For this reason it is generally more efficient to use a substantive approach in the audit of investment balances. That is the approach discussed in this chapter. As with any transaction cycle, of course, the auditor should still obtain an understanding of the internal control structure applicable to investments.

Because of the complexity of accounting for some investments, there is also a heightened risk of fraud in this area, which the auditor should take into consideration when planning the audit.

Another risk arising from investments that affects the overall audit strategy is that associated with related party transactions when these investments meet the definition of related parties in accordance with IAS 24 *Related Party Disclosures*. The auditor should ensure that all transactions between related parties and the company are at arm's length and that all other requirements of IAS 24 are complied with.

As demonstrated, inherent risk and control risk assessments can vary widely, owing to the various types of investments and circumstances across entities. However, the small number of transactions means that it is not usually cost-effective to test controls. Acceptable detection risk is usually set as being low, and most evidence is obtained through the performance of substantive procedures.

Cloud 9

Josh is relieved that Cloud 9 does not have any strategic investments; therefore, he doesn't have to worry about the equity method of accounting or consolidation. However, because Cloud 9 Ltd. is a subsidiary of Cloud 9 Inc., the separate entity financial statements will be consolidated with those of the parent company. Sharon has advised the audit team that the work to be performed on the consolidation will be done by another team of auditors.

After reviewing the balance sheet, Josh notes that Cloud 9 does hold some non-strategic investments for the purpose of generating investment income. He understands these types of investments should be reported at fair value. He is certain that part of the substantive audit work will involve testing the market values of these investments.

BEFORE YOU GO ON

12.6.1 What is an investment subsidiary ledger?

12.6.2 List six controls that should be implemented over investments.

12.6.3 What is the most important audit risk when investments are classified as non-strategic?

12.7 SUBSTANTIVE PROCEDURES FOR INVESTMENTS

For most entities, investment transactions are infrequent, but individual transactions are usually for substantial amounts. Investment transactions rarely present cut-off problems so the auditor may perform many substantive procedures before or after the end of the reporting period. Income statement account balances relating to investments are usually verified at the same time.

Table 12.5 lists possible substantive procedures for investment balances and the specific audit objectives to which they relate. Procedures are explained as follows.

7 Design and execute an audit program for investments.

TABLE 12.5 **Possible substantive procedures for investment balance assertions**

CATEGORY	SUBSTANTIVE PROCEDURE	INVESTMENT BALANCE AUDIT OBJECTIVE (FROM TABLE 12.4)					
		OE NO.	C NO.	RO1	AV NO.	CO	PD NO.
Initial procedures	1. Perform initial procedures on investment balances and records that will be subjected to further testing. (a) Trace opening balances for investment accounts to the previous year's working papers. (b) Review activity in all investment-related balance sheet and income statement accounts, and investigate entries that appear unusual in amount or source. (c) Obtain entity-prepared schedules of investments and determine that they accurately represent the underlying accounting records from which they are prepared by: • adding and cross-adding the schedules and reconciling the totals with the related subsidiary and general ledger balances • testing the agreement of items on schedules with entries in related subsidiary and general ledger accounts				✓1, 2		
Analytical procedures	2. Perform analytical procedures by analyzing interest and dividend yields relative to expectations.	✓1, 2	✓1–3	✓1, 2			
Tests of details of transactions	3. Vouch entries in investment and related income and equity accounts.	✓1, 2	✓1–3	✓	✓1, 2	✓	✓1, 2, 5
Tests of details of balances	4. Inspect and count securities on hand. (Note: The majority will be held with registries.)	✓2	✓3	✓		✓	✓1, 2, 5
	5. Confirm securities held by others (e.g., share registries).	✓2	✓3	✓	✓1		
	6. Recalculate investment revenue earned.	✓1	✓1, 2		✓1, 2		
	7. Review documentation concerning fair values.						
Presentation and disclosure	8. Compare statement presentation with the applicable accounting standards. (a) Determine that investment balances are properly identified and classified in the financial statements. (b) Determine the appropriateness of disclosures concerning the valuation basis for investments, realized and unrealized gains or losses, related party investments, and pledged investments.					✓4 ✓2, 3	

12.7.1 Initial procedures

First, the auditor verifies the agreement of opening investment balances with audited amounts in the previous year's working papers. Next, the auditor reviews the activity in investment-related accounts to identify entries that are unusual in nature or amount and that should be investigated. Then the auditor checks entity-prepared schedules of investment additions and disposals in the period for mathematical accuracy and agreement with the underlying accounting records. This procedure includes determining that schedules and subsidiary investment ledgers agree with related general ledger control account balances. The schedules can then serve as the basis for additional substantive procedures.

12.7.2 Analytical procedures

It is rarely possible to obtain much evidence from the application of analytical procedures to investment balance sheet accounts. Current asset investments tend not to have any predictable relationship with other balances, and non-current investments are subject to so few transactions that it is easier to proceed directly to tests of details. Analytical procedures can be applied in comparing interest and dividend revenues with investment balances. Unexpected differences in interest or dividend yields may indicate misstatements; for example, a higher-than-expected rate of return may be found to have been caused by erroneously recording the unrealized gain from an increase in the value of non-current securities in the income statement rather than as a revaluation reserve.

12.7.3 Tests of details of transactions

Auditors usually vouch purchases and sales of investments by examining brokers' advices and evidence of appropriate approval. Purchases and sales of non-current investments, for example, should be vouched to authorizations in the minutes of directors' meetings. These tests provide evidence about the occurrence of transactions, the transfer of ownership of securities, and the valuation of the securities at the transaction date.

Evidence as to the completeness of recorded purchases is determined through verification of purchase and payment transactions. Evidence as to the completeness of sales of investments is determined through verification of the existence of recorded investment assets as one of the tests of details of balances.

The auditor can vouch dividend and interest receipts to remittance advices accompanying the payment. A problem often arises as to completeness. Receipt of dividends cannot always be foreseen, and the misrecording or even misappropriation of a dividend payment may not be readily detected by the information system. Interest can normally be verified by analytical procedures. Dividends paid by listed companies can normally be checked against reference works recording dividend payments. For substantial investments in unlisted companies, the auditor may need to verify dividends received against copies of the companies' financial statements.

12.7.4 Tests of details of balances

Tests of details of balances involve inspecting or confirming recorded investments, verifying income from investments, and checking their market value. There may also be a need to assess controls of a service organization if the entity hires the services of a custodian or broker. The work done will depend on whether the securities are listed or unlisted. If they are listed, the following will apply.

Where the securities relate to listed companies, the auditor may inspect broker statements to provide evidence on the existence and the rights and obligations assertions. However, depending on the materiality of the shareholdings, the auditor may obtain a confirmation directly from the broker at the end of the financial year. This provides evidence on the existence, completeness, rights and obligations, and presentation and disclosure assertions.

Securities held at the entity's own premises should be inspected and counted at the same time as the count of cash and other negotiable instruments. In performing the test, the custodian of the securities should be present throughout the count, a receipt should be obtained from the custodian when the securities are returned, and the auditor should control all securities until the count is completed.

For securities stored for safekeeping in bank safety deposit boxes, the banks will generally seal the boxes on the nominated date of the count at the entity's request and will confirm to the auditor that there was no access to the box, other than by the auditor, until all locations have been counted. When the count is not made at the end of the reporting period, the auditor should prepare a reconciliation from the date of the count to the year-end date by reviewing any intervening security transactions.

In inspecting securities, the auditor should observe such matters as the:

- certificate number on the document
- name of the owner (which should be the entity, either directly or through endorsement)
- description of the security
- number of shares (or debentures)
- value of the shares (or debentures)
- name of the issuer

These data should be recorded as part of the auditor's analysis of the investment account. All securities should be checked against the records in the investment register and, for securities purchased in previous years, the details should be compared with those shown on the previous year's working papers. A lack of agreement between the certificate numbers may indicate unauthorized transactions for those securities.

This substantive procedure provides evidence about the existence, completeness, rights and obligations, and presentation and disclosure assertions.

Securities held by outsiders for safekeeping must be confirmed as of the date on which securities held by the entity are checked. The steps in the confirmation process for securities are identical to those for confirming receivables. Thus, the auditor must control the mailings and receive the responses directly from the custodian. The data confirmed are the same as the data that should be noted when the auditor is able to inspect the securities.

Securities may also be held by creditors as collateral against loans. In such cases, the confirmation should be sent to the indicated custodian. The confirmation of securities held by third parties provides evidence as to the existence or occurrence and the rights and obligations assertions. It also furnishes evidence about the completeness assertion if the confirmation response indicates more securities on hand than recorded.

The auditor verifies income from investments by use of documentary evidence and recalculation. Dividends on all shares listed on stock exchanges and many others are included in dividend record books published by investment services. The auditor can independently verify the dividend revenue by referring to the declaration date, amount, and payment date as shown in the record book. The verification of dividend income is usually incorporated into the schedule of investments.

The auditor can verify the interest earned in relation to debentures by examining the interest rates and payment dates indicated on the debenture certificate. This substantive procedure is directed mainly at the valuation and completeness assertions for interest revenue. However, it also provides evidence about the existence assertion for interest receivable.

Where they are held as current assets, quoted equity securities and marketable securities (i.e., ordinary shares, government bonds, and corporate debentures) are normally valued at the lower of aggregate cost and market value. Investments held as non-current assets are usually stated at the lower of cost and impaired value, but may be carried at valuation. In any event, disclosure is also required of the valuation of quoted securities. The auditor should verify market quotations by referring to published security prices on stock exchanges. For infrequently traded securities, the auditor may need to seek advice from an independent broker as to the estimated market value at the end of the reporting period. When market quotations are based on a reasonably broad and active market, they ordinarily constitute sufficient appropriate audit evidence as to the current market value of the securities.

Audited financial statements of the entity in which investments are held help in the valuation of unquoted shares, debentures, and similar debt obligations.

12.7.5 Presentation and disclosure

To conform to the requirements of the accounting standards, the presentation of investments in securities in the financial statements requires the following:

- analysis of investments as either current or non-current
- bonds
- recognition of dividends, interest, and realized gains and losses in the income statement
- recognition of impairment write offs in the income statement
- disclosure of the basis and methods of accounting

- disclosure of the market value of quoted investments
- disclosure of any liens

The foregoing substantive procedures should provide evidence of the first four of the above items. Inspection of the minutes and loan agreements should reveal the existence of liens. In addition, the auditor should inquire of management as to its intent in holding the securities. On the basis of the evidence obtained, the auditor then determines whether the proposed presentations and disclosures are appropriate.

BEFORE YOU GO ON

12.7.1 List four substantive procedures usually performed for investments.

12.7.2 When inspecting securities, what things should the auditor note?

12.7.3 Describe the disclosure requirements over investments.

12.8 AUDITING CONSOLIDATED FINANCIAL STATEMENTS

8 Explain the special considerations applicable to the audit of investments in subsidiaries, associates, and joint ventures.

Where a company (or other entity) controls another company (or other entity), consolidated financial statements must be prepared for the economic entity. The economic entity comprises both the parent company and the controlled entities (unless the company or entity is itself a controlled entity) (IAS 27 *Consolidated and Separate Financial Statements*). The auditor is required to report on the consolidated financial statements. To do so, the auditor must identify the controlled companies (or other entities) constituting the reporting entity, verify the amounts pertaining to the other companies (or entities) to be consolidated, and verify the accuracy of the preparation of the consolidated financial statements.

Similar but less extensive disclosure requirements apply in respect of investments in associates (AASB 128 *Investments in Associates*; IAS 28) and in joint ventures (IAS 31 *Interests in Joint Ventures*). The same audit procedures with respect to subsidiaries also apply to investments in associates and joint ventures. The parent entity and its subsidiaries, associates, and joint ventures are referred to collectively as group entities.

Auditors should be sure to gather sufficient appropriate audit evidence in the following areas:

- representations made by those charged with governance of the investor as to the existence and ownership of the investment, and the existence or otherwise of significant influence
- the appropriateness of the carrying amount of an investment
- the appropriateness of adjustments to the carrying amount of an investment
- the adequacy of financial report disclosure
- the appropriateness of other equity accounting adjustments such as adjustments for dissimilar accounting policies and elimination of unrealized profits and losses
Some of this guidance is also relevant to the audit of subsidiaries and joint ventures.

12.8.1 Audit strategy for consolidated financial statements

It is difficult to make generalizations about the level of inherent risk for related account balance assertions. Sometimes the investment will be very passive and very low risk. However, there will also be instances where the relationship is very complex and high risk. This may give rise to uncertainty as to the existence of control over the related entities, in which case the inherent risk for the completeness assertion may be high. Sometimes, too, the consolidation adjustments may be particularly complex and involve a significant degree of management estimation. This can happen with the consolidation of foreign group entities whose financial statements may be prepared on accounting bases different from those appropriate to the parent entity, or with new acquisitions requiring determination of the fair value of their net assets at the acquisition date. In such cases, the inherent risk as to the valuation or measurement assertion may be moderate or high.

Another reason related account balances can be risky is if the investor company does not closely monitor the actions of the subsidiary or associate but provides guarantees over its activities. There have been many examples where the unchecked activities of subsidiaries or associates have resulted not only in their own failure but also in the failure of the investor company.

Given the materiality of the amounts involved, the audit approach will be predominantly substantive. Detection risk will, therefore, be inversely related to the relevant inherent risk assessments.

Sometimes there will be an additional risk in the audit of investments in associates or subsidiaries, because the audit may be performed by another auditor. In these situations, the auditor should consider the requirements of CAS 600 *Special Considerations—Audits of Group Financial Statements (Including the Work of Component Auditors)*. As part of the review of the other auditor's work, the head office auditor may sometimes send a very detailed questionnaire to the other auditor for completion.

Outlined below are some of the substantive procedures involved in performing an audit of consolidated financial statements.

12.8.2 Substantive procedures

Table 12.6 shows a list of possible substantive procedures for the consolidated financial statements, together with the assertions to which each test relates.

Identifying the reporting entity

Where an entity has investments in entities that it controls, and where that entity is a reporting entity, it must prepare consolidated financial statements of the economic entity comprising the parent entity and its subsidiaries. The auditor ensures that all entities included in the consolidated financial statements are properly recognized as subsidiaries and that no such entities are excluded.

The auditor must make an assessment as to whether the entity's investment in other entities constitutes control, thereby requiring consolidation. IFRS 10 provides a definition of control as follows: *Control is the power to govern the financial and operating policies of an entity so as to obtain benefits from its activities.*

The auditor needs, therefore, to exercise judgement on the appropriateness of management's assertions about control (or lack thereof) of other entities.

The auditor also investigates the possibility that cumulative investments by the entity and its subsidiaries enable the economic entity to exercise control over other entities. If, for example, the parent holds 15 percent of the shares of another entity and one of its subsidiaries holds 40 percent, then that other entity is controlled by the group and is to be accounted for as a subsidiary. In obtaining an understanding of the business in the planning stage and in reviewing related party transactions, the auditor should be alert for evidence of the existence of control over other entities other than through ownership of voting rights. The auditor will need to obtain and verify an explanation as to why such entities are excluded from the consolidation.

This procedure provides evidence as to the existence assertion and the rights and obligations assertion with respect to entities consolidated as controlled entities, and to the completeness assertion that all controlled entities are included in the consolidation.

Verifying the financial statements of other group entities

To verify the amounts included in the consolidated financial statements, the auditor must obtain and verify the financial statements of each group entity. Where the auditor is not also the auditor of another group entity, CAS 600 *Special Considerations—Audits of Group Financial Statements* recommends that the principal auditor should:

- obtain information regarding the professional competence of the other auditor
- advise the other auditor of the independence requirements and obtain representation as to the other auditor's compliance

TABLE 12.6 **Possible substantive tests of consolidated financial statement assertions**

SUBSTANTIVE PROCEDURE	ASSERTIONS					
	OE	C	RO	AV	CO	PD
Identify the reporting entity.	✓	✓	✓			
Verify the financial statements of other group entities.	✓	✓		✓		
Verify the consolidating adjustments.				✓	✓	
Compare the statement presentation with applicable accounting standards.						✓

- communicate to the other auditor any special requirements, such as identification of inter-company transactions
- advise the other auditor as to applicable accounting and auditing requirements and obtain representation as to the other auditor's compliance
- consider the findings of the other auditor

This procedure provides evidence as to the existence assertion and the completeness assertion with respect to assets, liabilities, and transactions with entities consolidated with those of the parent entity.

Verifying the consolidating adjustments

Consolidation adjustments fall into four categories: (1) acquisitions and disposals, (2) the elimination of inter-entity balances and transactions, (3) the standardization of accounting policies, and (4) the translation of foreign currencies.

1. *Acquisitions and disposals.* On the acquisition of an interest in an associate or subsidiary, its assets are consolidated (directly or by way of equity accounting) in the group accounts at their fair value at the acquisition date (IFRS 3 *Business Combinations*). The difference between the fair value of the parent entity's ownership interest in the net assets and the consideration paid constitutes purchased goodwill. It is important that the auditor verify the amounts recorded as fair value. CAS 540 *Auditing Accounting Estimates, Including Fair Value Accounting Estimates, and Related Disclosures* provides some guidance for auditors in this area. The auditor should test the entity's fair value measurements and disclosures and, where applicable, evaluate whether the assumptions used by management provide a reasonable basis for the fair value measurements. This involves testing management estimates and evaluating the work of experts. Of particular concern are valuations placed on intangibles not recorded in the books of the controlled entity. Adjustments on the disposal of a controlling interest must be verified against the carrying amount of the controlled entity's net assets immediately before disposal.

2. *Elimination of inter-entity balances and transactions.* In the course of auditing each group entity, the auditor ensures that inter-entity transactions are properly identified and recorded. Where group entities are audited by other auditors, they must be asked to ensure that all such transactions are properly accounted for. At year end, the auditor obtains an analysis of inter-entity balances, verifies their reconciliation to one another, and ensures that they are properly eliminated. Inter-entity transactions that require particular scrutiny by auditors are those that occur around the year end. The auditor should also ensure that any inter-entity profit in assets held by any of the group entities is properly identified and eliminated on consolidation.

3. *Standardization of accounting policies.* Where the financial statements of group entities have been prepared using accounting policies inconsistent with those of the reporting entity, appropriate adjustments must be made on consolidation. When auditing group entities or when communicating with other auditors of group entities, the auditor must identify any accounting policies inconsistent with those of the reporting entity, and verify the consolidating adjustment.

4. *Translation of foreign currencies.* Where a group entity's financial statements are prepared in a foreign currency, they must be translated for purposes of consolidation. The auditor must verify the exchange rates used, check the translations, and ensure that the accounting treatment conforms to the requirements of IAS 21 *The Effects of Changes in Foreign Exchange Rates*.

These substantive procedures provide evidence as to the existence, completeness, and valuation assertions.

The auditor should ensure that the disclosures in the consolidated financial statements conform to the requirements of applicable accounting standards and the Corporations Act. Particular requirements are explanations as to why control exists over entities in which the parent entity's ownership interest is 50 percent or less, and why control does not exist over entities in which the ownership interest is greater than 50 percent.

BEFORE YOU GO ON

12.8.1 What is the common audit approach for auditing consolidated financial statements?

12.8.2 What things should the auditor consider when group entities are audited by other auditors?

12.8.3 Discuss the substantive procedures normally performed over intercompany balances.

SUMMARY

❶ Identify the audit objectives applicable to cash.

Cash normally includes cash balances at the bank or similar institutions, cash on hand, and cash equivalents. In the auditing of cash, the key issues are to ensure that the cash exists and is owned by the client and that all cash transactions at the end of the reporting period are complete and properly disclosed.

❷ Discuss considerations relevant to determining the audit strategy for cash.

The verification of cash balances is an important part of the financial statement audit. Even though the balances at the end of the reporting period may appear immaterial, the amount of cash flowing through the accounts can be very material. The high volume of transactions contributes to a significant level of inherent risk for cash balance assertions, particularly existence and completeness. While the audit approach to cash is usually substantive, the auditor should understand the procedures the client uses for maintaining accountability over cash. This often includes independently performed bank reconciliations and the use of imprest accounts.

❸ Design and execute an audit program for cash balances.

Several types of substantive procedures to test cash balances are performed during most audits, including conducting cash cut-off tests, tracing bank transfers, counting cash on hand, confirming certain balances and other arrangements with banks, reviewing bank reconciliations, obtaining and using subsequent period bank statements, and determining the adequacy of management's disclosures for cash balances.

❹ Describe special considerations when auditing cash balances, including lapping, petty cash funds, and imprest bank accounts.

Lapping is an irregularity that results in the misappropriation of cash receipts for personal use. The auditor should assess the likelihood of lapping in obtaining an understanding about the segregation of duties in the receiving and recording of collections from customers. Three procedures that should detect lapping include confirming accounts receivable on a surprise basis at an interim date, making surprise cash counts, and comparing details of cash receipts journal entries with the details of corresponding daily deposit slips.

The balance of petty cash is rarely material and for this reason the majority of audits do not involve an audit of petty cash. Generally, the only time this part of the audit is performed is when the company expects or requests petty cash to be audited. When auditing petty cash, the auditor performs tests of details of transactions and tests of balances. The auditor tests a number of replenishing transactions.

An entity may use an imprest bank account for payroll and dividends. Substantive tests should include confirming the balance with the bank, reviewing the bank reconciliations, and using the subsequent period's bank statement.

❺ Identify the audit objectives applicable to investments.

In the auditing of investments, the key issues are to ensure that the investments exist, are owned, are properly recorded (including profits or losses on any sales) and disclosed, and are properly valued at the end of the reporting period.

❻ Discuss considerations relevant to determining the audit strategy for investments.

Investing transactions occur infrequently and internal control over the processing of transactions is generally good. However, because transactions are infrequent and usually individually significant, it is common for the auditor to use a substantive approach.

❼ Design and execute an audit program for investments.

Auditors usually vouch purchases and sales of investments by examining brokers' advices and evidence of appropriate approval. Tests of details of balances involve inspecting or confirming recorded investments, verifying income from investments, and checking their market value.

8 Explain the special considerations applicable to the audit of investments in subsidiaries, associates, and joint ventures.

Where a company controls another company, consolidated financial statements must be prepared. The auditor generally uses a substantive approach in verifying the consolidation of investments in group entities in the consolidated financial statements of the economic entity.

KEY TERMS

Bank confirmation, p. 441
Bank reconciliations, p. 436
Bank transfer schedule, p. 440
Cash counts, p. 444
Cash cut-off tests, p. 440

Imprest bank account, p. 437
Imprest petty cash fund, p. 436
Investment subsidiary ledger (investment register), p. 449
Kiting, p. 440

Lapping, p. 445
Subsequent period's bank statement, p. 442
Window dressing, p. 443

MULTIPLE-CHOICE QUESTIONS

12.1 In the planning of an audit, it was decided that cash would not be audited because it made up only 1 percent of total assets. You respond to this decision by saying:

(a) Whether or not this was acceptable would depend on the company and the type of industry.

(b) Cash is always going to be material, no matter what amount it is.

(c) An amount of 1 percent of total assets is likely to be immaterial.

(d) It is probable that this amount would still be considered material, because of the nature of cash.

✗ 12.2 The main evidence regarding year-end bank balances is documented in the:

(a) bank deposit schedule.

(b) interbank transfer schedule.

(c) bank reconciliation.

(d) standard bank confirmation.

12.3 In reviewing the bank reconciliation prepared by the client, the auditor finds a "miscellaneous reconciling item." From discussion with the client, the auditor is told that this relates to foreign exchange fluctuations. The auditor should:

(a) accept the client's explanation.

(b) accept the client's explanation, provided it is also noted in the management representation letter.

(c) ask the client to provide a detailed schedule of the amounts that make up this variance for subsequent review.

(d) try to find what constitutes the difference personally.

12.4 The following would be the best protection for an entity that wishes to prevent the lapping of trade accounts receivable:

(a) ask that customers' payment cheques be made payable to the entity and addressed to the treasurer.

(b) have customers send payments directly to the entity's bank.

(c) segregate duties so that no employee has access to both the cheques from customers and currency from daily cash receipts.

(d) segregate duties so that the bookkeeper in charge of the general ledger has no access to incoming mail.

12.5 The assertion that is the highest risk for an auditor in auditing investments is:

(a) valuation.

(b) existence.

(c) completeness.

(d) presentation and disclosure.

12.6 The control that would be the most effective in assuring that the proper custody of assets in the investing cycle is maintained is:

(a) the purchase and sale of investments are executed on the specific authorization of the board of directors.

(b) the recorded balances in the investment subsidiary ledger are periodically compared with the contents of the safety deposit box by independent personnel.

(c) direct access to securities in the safety deposit box is limited to only one corporate officer.

(d) personnel who post investment transactions to the general ledger are not permitted to update the investment subsidiary ledger.

12.7 When the client company does not maintain its own share register, the auditor should obtain written confirmation from the transfer agent and registrar concerning:

(a) the number of shares subject to agreements to repurchase.

(b) guarantees of preferred share redemption values.

(c) the number of shares issued and outstanding.

(d) restrictions on the payment of dividends.

12.8 An auditor testing the reasonableness of long-term investments would ordinarily use analytical procedures to ascertain the reasonableness of the:

(a) existence of unrealized gains or losses in the portfolio.

(b) completeness of recorded investment income.

(c) classification of current and non-current portfolios.

(d) valuation of marketable equity securities.

12.9 If a client is not deemed to have "significant influence" in an investee company, to obtain audit evidence to verify the investment balance, the auditor should:

(a) review the audited accounts of the investee company.

(b) get an independent valuation of the assets and liabilities of the investee company.

(c) perform the audit of the investee company.

(d) obtain the market value of the investee company's shares.

12.10 When the client has control over an investee company, the most appropriate audit procedure to obtain evidence to verify the investee company's accounts is to:

(a) re-perform the audit of the investee company.

(b) get an independent valuation of the assets and liabilities of the investee company.

(c) if satisfied as to the reliability of the investee company's auditor, rely on his or her work.

(d) obtain the market value of the investee company's shares.

REVIEW QUESTIONS

12.1 Explain the use and audit of imprest accounts.

12.2 Explain why the balance of cash on hand and at bank is always audited, and why a substantive approach is preferred.

12.3 Explain why it is important to trace transfers between bank accounts on either side of the end of the reporting period.

12.4 Describe the procedures for counting cash on hand.

12.5 Outline the procedures involved in verifying the bank reconciliation.

12.6 Explain lapping. Describe appropriate audit procedures to perform where it is suspected.

12.7 What substantive tests apply to the existence and valuation assertions for investment balances?

12.8 When inspecting securities on hand, what things should the auditor observe?

12.9 Explain the financial reporting principle underlying the audit verification of the existence and completeness assertions with respect to entities consolidated into group financial statements.

12.10 Describe procedures to be undertaken where group entities are audited by other auditors.

PROFESSIONAL APPLICATION QUESTIONS

Basic ★   Moderate ★★   Challenging ★★★

12.1 Substantive procedures for cash balances ★

You are an audit senior performing the audit of Stella's Stars Ltd., a talent agency. In performing the audit, Stella informs you of the following:

1. She does not want you to send the bank a confirmation because she objects to the cost and feels that the year-end bank statement issued by the bank should be sufficient.

2. She would like you to prepare the bank reconciliation at the end of the year.

3. She would like the audit done within one month of the end of the financial year.

Required

Write a memo to your audit manager outlining any concerns you might have with any of Stella's requests.

12.2 Bank reconciliation errors ★★

You have spent two years working as an auditor. In that time, you have come across a number of errors in performing bank reconciliations. Outlined below are some of them:

1. An unreconciled item of $340 was on the final bank reconciliation of the client and was deemed by the client to be immaterial.

2. Two deposits totalling $4,070 relating to accounts receivable were collected on July 2 (the company has a June 30 year end) but recorded as cash receipts on June 30.

3. An amount from an associated company of $40,000 was deposited two days before the end of the year in the client's bank account and then paid back one week after the end of the year.

4. A cheque for $6,000 was omitted from the outstanding cheque list on the bank reconciliation at December 31. It cleared the bank on January 14.

5. A bank transfer of $20,000 was included as a deposit in transit at December 31 in the accounting records.

Required

(a) What control could be implemented to reduce the likelihood of each of the above?

(b) What is an audit procedure to detect each of the above?

12.3 Cash control system ★ ★

Shiny Happy Windows Co. (SHW) is a window cleaning company. Customers' windows are cleaned monthly and the window cleaner then posts a stamped addressed envelope for payment through the customer's front door.

SHW has a large number of receivable balances and these customers pay by cheque or cash, which is received in the stamped addressed envelopes in the post. The following procedures are applied to the cash received cycle:

1. A junior clerk from the accounting department opens the mail and if any cheques or cash have been sent, she records the receipts in the cash received log and then places all the monies into the locked cash box.

2. The contents of the cash box are counted each day and every few days these sums are deposited at the bank by whichever member of the accounting team is available.

3. The cashier records the details of the cash received into the cash receipts journal and also updates the sales ledger.

4. Usually on a monthly basis, the cashier performs a bank reconciliation, which he then files. If he misses a month, he then catches this up in the following month's reconciliation.

Required

(a) For the cash cycle of SHW:
  (i) Identify and explain three deficiencies in the system.
  (ii) Suggest controls to address each of these deficiencies.
  (iii) List tests of controls the auditor of SHW would perform to assess if the controls are operating effectively.

(b) Describe substantive procedures an auditor would perform in verifying this company's bank balance.

Source: Adapted from ACCA Audit and Assurance Paper F8, June 2010.

12.4 Banking of cash receipts ★

Your firm is the auditor of Trojan Trading Ltd. The audited financial statements for the year ended December 31, 2016, show the company's revenue was $5 million and the profit before tax was $320,000. The part of the working papers that records audit work on the bank reconciliation at December 31, 2016, noted cash receipts of $14,000 recorded in the cash book before the year end that were not credited to the bank statement until a week after year end. No further work was carried out because the amount was not considered material, and that conclusion was noted in the audit working papers. In February 2017, the company investigated delays in depositing cash receipts and discovered a fraud of $36,000. The fraud was carried out by the cashier who was responsible for depositing all receipts and preparing the bank reconciliation.

Required

(a) What further work should the auditor have done in this situation (if any)?

(b) Should this have been reported? If so, to whom?

Source: Adapted from ACCA Audit Framework, June 1998.

12.5 Substantive procedures for investments ★★

Ingrid Shalansky, an audit senior, was given the task of auditing Crabapple Ltd., an investment company. Her firm had not performed the audit before; however, from a discussion with the previous year's auditors, she found out that the following transactions occurred during the previous year:

- payment of debenture interest
- accrual of debenture interest, payable at the year end
- redemption of outstanding debentures
- purchase of a portfolio of shares

Ingrid has been asked to detail audit procedures for this year's audit based on the assumptions that similar transactions will occur.

Required

(a) Identify a substantive procedure that Ingrid would need to perform to verify each of the above transactions, and the assertion to which each relates.
(b) Indicate the type of evidence obtained from each of the procedures noted in part (a).

12.6 Audit of consolidated financial statements ★ ★ ★

Oxford Ltd. is a reporting entity of which your firm of accountants is the auditor. Oxford's consolidated financial statements incorporate the financial statements of its four subsidiaries. Three subsidiaries are incorporated in Canada and audited by your firm. The fourth subsidiary is located in another country and audited by another firm of professional accountants.

Required

(a) Explain how you would verify the intercompany balances.
(b) Describe other audit adjustments you would expect to find and explain how you would verify each of them:
   (i) where the subsidiary had been acquired *before* the financial year under audit.
   (ii) where the subsidiary had been acquired *during* the financial year under audit.
(c) Describe the procedures necessary to determine the level of reliance to be placed on the audited financial statements of the foreign subsidiary.

12.7 Audit of investments ★ ★ ★

Your firm is the auditor of Zhao's Charity for Pensioners. The charity was formed many years ago from a large gift by the Zhao family, the income from which is used to pay pensions to needy people. The original gift has been invested in fixed-interest investments and shares in listed companies. The trustees manage the charity, and the full-time administrator keeps the accounting and other records.

The draft summarized income and expenditure account for the year ended September 30, 2016, and an extract from the balance sheet are shown below, together with the audited figures for 2015.

The following information has been provided:

1. During the year, some shares were sold at a profit of $182,900 and the proceeds were reinvested in shares of other companies.
2. There were no purchases or sales of fixed-interest investments in the year ended September 30, 2016. In the year ended September 30, 2016, some of the fixed-interest investments were sold and others were purchased using the proceeds of sale.
3. The charity is managed by voluntary trustees who meet four times a year, and the administrator keeps the minutes of the meetings.
4. The administrator keeps the accounting records.
5. As auditor of the charity, you prepare the financial statements from the accounting records kept by the administrator and audit those financial statements. Your auditor's report is addressed to the trustees of the charity.

INCOME AND EXPENDITURE ACCOUNT FOR YEAR ENDED SEPTEMBER 30

	2016 $	2015 $
Income		
From fixed-interest investments	44,200	41,900
From shares in listed companies	123,900	123,500
	168,100	165,400
Expenditure		
Payments to pensioners	141,300	144,300
Administration costs	21,600	20,500
Audit and accounting	4,700	4,500
Sundry expenses	2,800	2,600
	170,400	171,900
Net (deficit) for the year	(2,300)	(6,500)

EXTRACT FROM BALANCE SHEET AS AT SEPTEMBER 30

Cost of investments	$	$
Fixed-interest investments	511,200	511,200
Shares in listed companies	1,445,600	1,262,700
	1,956,800	1,773,900

Required

Describe the audit work you would carry out to verify:

(a) income from investments: your audit tests should verify that all the income from the investments has been received by the charity and included in the financial statements, including dividends from the shares in listed investments bought and sold during the year.

(b) the ownership of the fixed interest investments and shares in listed companies.

Source: Adapted from ACCA Audit Framework, Paper 6, December 1996.

12.8 Controls over petty cash ★★ ❹

Mathias Co. sells cars, car parts, and gasoline from 25 different locations in one country. Each branch has up to 20 staff working there, although most of the accounting systems are designed and implemented from the company's head office. All accounting systems, apart from petty cash, are computerized, with the internal audit department frequently advising and implementing controls within those systems.

Mathias has an internal audit department of six staff, all of whom have been employed at Mathias for a minimum of five years and some for as long as 15 years. In the past, the chief internal auditor appointed staff within the internal audit department, although the chief executive officer is responsible for appointing the chief internal auditor. The chief internal auditor reports directly to the chief financial officer (CFO). The CFO also assists the chief internal auditor in deciding on the scope of work of the internal audit department.

You are an audit manager in the internal audit department of Mathias. You are currently auditing the petty cash systems at the different branches. Your initial systems notes on petty cash contain the following information:

1. The average petty cash balance at each branch is $5,000.
2. Average monthly expenditure is $1,538, with amounts ranging from $1 to $500.
3. Petty cash is kept in a lock box on a bookcase in the accounts office.
4. Vouchers for expenditures are signed by the person incurring that expenditure to confirm they have received reimbursement from petty cash.
5. Vouchers are recorded in the petty cash book by the accounting clerk; each voucher records the date, reason for the expenditure, amount of expenditure, and person incurring that expenditure.
6. Petty cash is counted every month by the accounting clerk, who is in charge of the cash. The petty cash balance is then reimbursed using an imprest system and the journal entry produced to record expenditure in the general ledger.

7. The cheque to reimburse petty cash is signed by the accountant at the branch at the same time as the journal entry to the general ledger is reviewed.

Required

Explain the internal control weaknesses in the petty cash system at Mathias Co. For each weakness, recommend a control to overcome that weakness.

Source: Adapted from ACCA Audit and Assurance (International), Paper F8, December 2007.

12.9 Substantive procedures for investments ★★

You are performing the audit of Toledo Ltd. for the financial year ended December 31, 2016. Under the terms of a major loan contract, Toledo is required to maintain certain financial ratios. If the ratios are breached, then the loan is immediately due for repayment. This would create significant cash flow problems. To comply with the loan covenant and maintain the ratios, Toledo must continue to hold its 100-percent shareholding in Granada Ltd. as a long-term investment.

You have obtained a management representation letter from the client, which says in part: "Toledo Ltd. warrants for the period January 1, 2016, to December 31, 2016, that it intends to retain ownership of its entire parcel of ordinary shares in Granada Ltd. Toledo has not entered into any discussions with any party, directly or indirectly, regarding the sale of these shares."

On February 24, 2017, you noted an article in the financial press that described the rumoured sale of Granada's business assets to a foreign investor.

Required

(a) Does the management representation letter from Toledo regarding its shareholding in Granada constitute sufficient appropriate audit evidence? Give reasons for your answer.

(b) Describe the procedures you need to perform in relation to this situation before signing the auditor's report.

Source: Adapted from Professional Year Programme of the ICAA, 1997, Advanced Audit Module. Provided courtesy of Chartered Accountants Australia and New Zealand.

12.10 Performing a bank reconciliation ★★★

Your firm is the auditor of Thai Textiles Ltd. and you are auditing the financial statements for the year ended June 30, 2016. The company has sales of $2.5 million and a before-tax profit of $150,000. The company has supplied you with the following bank reconciliation at year end. You have entered the "date cleared" on the bank statement (the date on which the cheques and deposits appeared on July's bank statement).

Required

(a) List the matters that cause you concern on the client's bank reconciliation. Describe the investigations that you will carry out on these items.

(b) Explain what adjustments to the financial statements would be required from part (a).

Source: Adapted from ACCA Audit Framework, Paper 6Y, December 1997.

			$	$
Balance per bank statement at June 30, 2016				**(9,865)**
Add: deposits not credited				
CJ date	**Type**	**Date cleared**		
June 30	ARL	July 4	11,364	
June 24	CS	July 4	653	
June 27	CS	July 5	235	
June 28	CS	July 6	315	
June 29	CS	July 7	426	
June 30	CS	July 8	714	
June 30	CS	July 11	362	14,069

				$	$
Less: uncleared cheques					
CJ date	**Cheque no.**	**Type**	**Date cleared**		
June 29	2163	CP	July 4	1,216	
June 30	2164	APL	July 18	10,312	
June 30	2165	APL	July 19	11,264	
June 30	2166	APL	July 18	9,732	
June 30	2167	APL	July 20	15,311	
June 30	2168	APL	July 21	8,671	
June 30	2169	APL	July 19	12,869	
June 30	2170	APL	July 21	9,342	
June 30	2171	CP	July 4	964	(79,681)
Balance per cash journal at June 30, 2016					(75,477)

Notes

- "CJ date" is the date on which the transaction was entered into the cash journal.
- Type of transaction: ARL (accounts receivable receipt); CS (receipt from cash sales); APL (accounts payable payment); CP (cheque payment [for other expenses]).
- All cheques for accounts payable payments are written out at the end of the month.

12.11 Substantive procedures for cash balances ★ ★ ★

You have been asked by the financial controller, Walid Hossain, of Potter Ltd. to carry out an investigation of a suspected fraud by the company's cashier. The cashier, Alfred Blyton, has left the firm without notice.

Potter Ltd. is a small company, and there were few controls and checks over Alfred's work because the company had employed him for a number of years. You are aware that the auditor found a discrepancy in the bank reconciliation for the company's year end of December 31, 2016, and that Alfred left the day on which it was discovered. Walid has asked you, rather than the company's auditor, to carry out the investigation. He is not happy with the auditor because he believes he should have found the fraud earlier or at least warned that there were control weaknesses.

Walid says that Alfred was responsible for:

- receiving cash from customers for both credit and cash sales
- making all payments, including purchase journal and sundry payments
- drawing the cash for wages
- recording all receipts and payments in the cash book and preparing a bank reconciliation
- making and approving petty cash payments and recording these transactions in the petty cash book

The computerized sales and purchase ledgers are maintained by the staff in the accounting department, who post all transactions to these ledgers. Alfred used to send the sales clerk a schedule showing the cash he had received. The remittance advices from customers were attached to this schedule, and they showed the invoices that were being paid.

The purchases clerk would inform Alfred of the payments she wished to make, and Alfred would then prepare the cheques, which Walid signed. A remittance advice was attached to the payment that was sent to the supplier. Alfred would prepare the purchases and sales ledger control accounts each month and the reconciliation of these balances to the total balances on the respective ledgers.

For cash sales, the sales department raises a sales order, which is sent to the shipping department, which, in turn, raises a shipping note. The first copy of the shipping note is given to the customer, the second copy is sent to the accounting department, and the third copy is retained in the shipping department. The accounting department then prices the invoice. The customer would pay the cash to Alfred, who retained a copy of the invoice for his records. Alfred would record the sales details in his analyzed cash book, and the month's cash sales were posted from the total in the cash book to the ledger.

The payroll department calculates the wages. Alfred would draw the cheque to pay the wages and receive the cash. The payroll department makes up the wage packets and pays the wages to employees. Alfred would retain any wages not given to employees.

Walid is the authorized signatory for cheques; however, Alfred was the signatory when Walid was on holiday.

Required

Describe what checks you would conduct to

(a) determine whether a fraud has actually taken place and

(b) quantify the loss. Consider:

    (i)   bank reconciliations

    (ii) cash receipts

    (iii) cash payments

    (iv) petty cash

Source: Adapted from ACCA Audit Framework, Paper 3.4, December 1991.

CASE STUDY—CLOUD 9

Answer the following questions based on the information presented for Cloud 9 in Appendix B of this book and in the current and earlier chapters. You should also consider your answers to the case study questions in earlier chapters.

The worksheet you completed for the case study question in chapter 8 includes your estimates of the overall risk assessment (ORA) and the acceptable detection risk (DR) in the sales to cash receipts process.

Required

Based on your ORA and DR estimates, design substantive audit procedures for Cloud 9 that would address the DR for cash.

RESEARCH QUESTION 12.1

The audit of short-term investments can be a high-risk area for auditors. A case in Australia (*AWA Ltd v. Daniels t/a Deloitte Haskins & Sells & Ors* (1992) 10 ACLC 933) found the auditors negligent for failing to report weaknesses in the foreign exchange trading to an adequate level of management. The collapse of Barings Bank in Singapore also focused questions on whether adequate attention was paid to reviewing internal controls over foreign currency transactions. Consider, for example, the following extract:

> The refusal of Coopers & Lybrand's Singapore partnership to cooperate with the inquiry into the collapse of Barings Bank has left gaping holes in the explanation of the auditors' role in the affair. The inquiry by the Board of Banking Supervision concluded that the collapse could be attributed to concealed and unauthorized trading by Nick Leeson, which the bank's management and the external auditors and regulators failed to notice.

Crucial from the auditors' point of view is why they failed to notice the "absolute failure" of Barings' internal controls. Some indication of the crisis was picked up by Barings' internal auditors in 1994, but their recommendations were never implemented, and the external auditors subsequently ruled the company's controls acceptable.

Source: Extract from "Auditors' Silence Leaves Questions Unanswered," *Accountancy* 116(1224), August 1995, p. 11.

Required

(a) For one of the above two cases mentioned, research the alleged or actual deficiencies of the work performed by the auditor.

(b) What are specific issues of importance in performing an audit of short-term investments?

SOLUTIONS TO MULTIPLE-CHOICE QUESTIONS

1. d, 2. d, 3. c, 4. b, 5. a, 6. b, 7. c, 8. b, 9. d, 10. c.

CHAPTER 13

Completing and reporting on the audit

LEARNING OBJECTIVES

After studying this chapter, you should be able to:

1 explain the procedures performed as part of the engagement wrap-up, including gathering and evaluating audit evidence

2 understand the considerations when assessing the going concern assumption used in the preparation of the financial statements

3 understand the purpose of and the procedures performed in the review for contingent liabilities and commitments

4 compare the two types of (material) subsequent events to determine what effect they have on the financial statements (if any)

5 analyze misstatements and explain the difference between quantitative

and qualitative considerations when evaluating misstatements

6 evaluate conclusions obtained during the performance of the audit and explain how these conclusions link to the overall opinion formed on the financial statements

7 describe the components of an audit report

8 identify the types of modifications to an audit report

9 explain what reporting is required to management and those charged with governance.

10 understand the various types of other engagements that auditors may be asked to perform (Appendix 13).

AUDITING AND ASSURANCE STANDARDS

CANADIAN	INTERNATIONAL
CAS 230 *Audit Documentation*	ISA 230 *Audit Documentation*
CAS 240 *The Auditor's Responsibilities Relating to Fraud in an Audit of Financial Statements*	ISA 240 *The Auditor's Responsibilities Relating to Fraud in an Audit of Financial Statements*
CAS 250 *Consideration of Laws and Regulations in an Audit of Financial Statements*	ISA 250 *Consideration of Laws and Regulations in an Audit of Financial Statements*
CAS 260 *Communication with Those Charged with Governance*	ISA 260 *Communication with Those Charged with Governance*
CAS 265 *Communicating Deficiencies in Internal Control to Those Charged with Governance and Management*	ISA 265 *Communicating Deficiencies in Internal Control to Those Charged with Governance and Management*
CAS 320 *Materiality in Planning and Performing an Audit*	ISA 320 *Materiality in Planning and Performing an Audit*
CAS 450 *Evaluation of Misstatements Identified During the Audit*	ISA 450 *Evaluation of Misstatements Identified During the Audit*
CAS 500 *Audit Evidence*	ISA 500 *Audit Evidence*
CAS 501 *Audit Evidence—Specific Considerations for Selected Items*	ISA 501 *Audit Evidence—Specific Considerations for Selected Items*
CAS 520 *Analytical Procedures*	ISA 520 *Analytical Procedures*
CAS 560 *Subsequent Events*	ISA 560 *Subsequent Events*
CAS 570 *Going Concern*	ISA 570 *Going Concern*
CAS 580 *Written Representations*	ISA 580 *Written Representations*
CAS 700 *Forming an Opinion and Reporting on Financial Statements*	ISA 700 *Forming an Opinion and Reporting on Financial Statements*
CAS 705 *Modifications to the Opinion in the Independent Auditor's Report*	ISA 705 *Modifications to the Opinion in the Independent Auditor's Report*
CAS 706 *Emphasis of Matter Paragraphs and Other Matter Paragraphs in the Independent Auditor's Report*	ISA 706 *Emphasis of Matter Paragraphs and Other Matter Paragraphs in the Independent Auditor's Report*
CAS 720 *The Auditor's Responsibilities Relating to Other Information in Documents Containing Audited Financial Statements*	ISA 720 *The Auditor's Responsibilities Relating to Other Information in Documents Containing Audited Financial Statements*
CAS 800 *Special Considerations— Audits of Financial Statements Prepared in Accordance with Special Purpose Frameworks*	ISA 800 *Special Considerations— Audits of Financial Statements Prepared in Accordance with Special Purpose Frameworks*
CAS 805 *Special Considerations—Audits of Single Financial Statements and Specific Elements, Accounts or Items of a Financial Statement*	ISA 805 *Special Considerations—Audits of Single Financial Statements and Specific Elements, Accounts or Items of a Financial Statement*
CAS 810 *Engagements to Report on Summary Financial Statements*	ISA 810 *Engagements to Report on Summary Financial Statements*
Rules of professional conduct of each provincial institute/order	*Code of Ethics for Professional Accountants*
IAS 1 *Presentation of Financial Statements*	IAS 1 *Presentation of Financial Statements*
IAS 10 *Events After the Reporting Period*	IAS 10 *Events After the Reporting Period*
ASPE Section 3820 *Subsequent Events*	
CSAE 5815, 7050, 7600, 8500, 8600, 9100, 9110, AuG-16.	

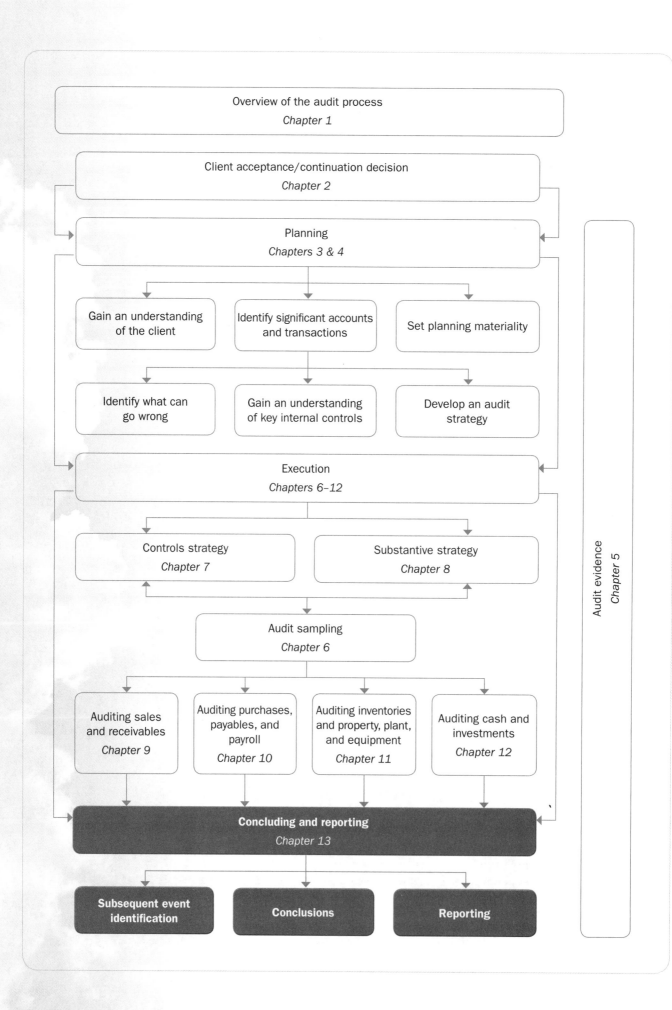

Cloud 9

The partner on the Cloud 9 Ltd. audit, Jo Wadley, has called a meeting with the senior staff (Sharon Gallagher, Josh Thomas, Suzie Pickering, and Mark Batten) to discuss the completion of the audit. The partner wants to be sure that all issues are "in hand" and that she is briefed on all contentious matters so that she can resolve them at the scheduled meetings with Cloud 9's board and management. Meetings with clients at the end of the audit can be quite difficult. Sometimes the audit partner considers qualifying the audit report if the client's management will not adjust the financial statements to reflect errors found during the audit.

Sharon, Josh, Suzie, and Mark decide to hold a preliminary meeting to prepare for the meeting with the partner. On the agenda are:
- final evidence and misstatements evaluation
- going concern procedures and assessment
- subsequent events procedures and evidence
- overall conclusion and audit opinion
- legal issues
- communication with Cloud 9's board

What issues have arisen with Cloud 9's audit? How can they make sure that the partner is fully prepared for the meeting with the client's management?

AUDIT PROCESS IN FOCUS

During the completion phase of the audit a number of procedures are performed. First, the auditor evaluates the audit evidence obtained and reviews the documentation to ensure that it is of a sufficient quality and quantity. Before drawing an overall conclusion on the audit, the auditor also reassesses the going concern assumption, considers the existence of contingent liabilities and subsequent events, performs any additional wrap-up procedures, and assesses any misstatements (sometimes referred to as audit differences) identified throughout the audit and the effect they may have on the overall conclusion (and opinion). The auditor also performs analytical procedures on the adjusted financial statements as a means of assessing their fair presentation.

The final step in the audit process is to evaluate the conclusions drawn from the audit evidence obtained (which will form the basis for the auditor's opinion on the financial statements) and to prepare an appropriately worded audit report. At the same time, a management representation letter is obtained from the client and appropriate communication with those charged with governance is prepared. Consideration is given to compliance with laws and regulations throughout the audit and again as part of the wrap-up and conclusion procedures.

13.1 ENGAGEMENT WRAP-UP

During the wrap-up of an engagement, the auditor finalizes any open items before issuing the audit report, including determining if any remaining procedures are to be completed for the audit. Any remaining audit procedures are assigned to team members, with due dates for completion of the open items. This includes determining that the audit team has properly completed and executed the audit procedures that were planned (as described in chapters 3 and 4) and that all relevant matters have been appropriately considered.

The following areas are ordinarily covered during the wrap-up of an engagement:

1. Review the audit file to ensure that the planned audit procedures were executed properly and completely. The file is typically reviewed in detail by the manager or above and high-risk areas are typically reviewed by the partner. During the review process, the reviewer makes a list of "review comments" identifying issues not yet resolved, issues requiring further clarification, and any audit procedures not yet completed. As each working paper is reviewed, it is initialled and dated as evidence that the review was performed.

2. Determine that all necessary matters have been appropriately considered. All significant issues should be documented and conclusions reached. For open items that are no longer

1 Explain the procedures performed as part of the engagement wrap-up, including gathering and evaluating audit evidence.

relevant to the audit (or necessary to complete), the auditor documents in the audit working papers this fact and the reason(s) why they are no longer relevant.

3. Clear all outstanding review notes and "to-do" items and perform any audit procedures not yet completed. At this stage, if additional audit attention is needed, the auditor performs the necessary audit procedures to resolve open items and issues until they are cleared to the reviewer's satisfaction.

4. Remove all unnecessary documentation, drafts, and cleared review notes from the engagement files. The auditor retains records relevant to the audit, such as audit working papers and other documents that form the basis of the audit opinion, including memoranda, correspondence, communications, and other documents and records (including electronic records) that (1) are created, sent, or received in connection with the audit and (2) contain conclusions, opinions, analyses, or financial data related to the audit. Superseded working papers and financial statements, notes that reflect incomplete or preliminary thinking, and duplicates of documents should be removed.

5. For multi-location engagements, check to ensure that all documents requested from other audit teams have been obtained and reviewed.

6. Consider the amount used for materiality. The auditor considers whether the amount that was used for **materiality** (as discussed in chapter 4 and addressed in CAS 320 *Materiality in Planning and Performing an Audit*) when planning the audit and detecting misstatements (rather than evaluating them) is still appropriate as the basis for their conclusion on the fair presentation of the financial statements taken as a whole. They consider whether, during the course of the audit, they have identified any factors or conditions about the client or its environment (for example, a significant change in anticipated operating results) that would cause them to determine that a different (lower) amount would have been appropriate in establishing their planning materiality. It is important to revisit the amount used for materiality when evaluating misstatements, taking into consideration qualitative as well as quantitative factors.

    When the amount considered material at the end of the audit is significantly lower than at the beginning of the audit (for example, because the basis used for calculating materiality at the planning stage was substantially higher), the auditor considers whether the procedures used throughout the audit were sufficient and whether additional audit procedures need to be performed. To avoid possible surprises at the end of an audit, the auditor should reassess the appropriateness of the materiality set throughout the audit to make sure that sufficient audit procedures are being performed.

7. Reconsider the assessments of internal control at the entity level and the risk of fraud. When planning an audit, the auditor identifies the presence or absence of factors related to the five components of internal control (as discussed in chapter 7) and the risk of fraud and makes an initial assessment of control and fraud risk. They then consider throughout the audit whether additional factors or risks are present and whether they need to revise their conclusion of control risk at the entity level and whether the controls are supportive of the prevention and correction of material misstatements whether due to fraud or error (as discussed in chapters 3 and 7). The auditor specifically reconsiders the assessment of internal control at the entity level when they become aware of significant changes in the client's system of internal controls and after they perform tests of controls. Their conclusions about the effectiveness of internal control at the entity level may be affected by control exceptions that they identify when executing their tests of controls.

    When the results of their audit tests identify misstatements in the financial statements, the auditor considers whether such misstatements may be indicative of fraud. The auditor's consideration of fraud risk, and the results of their audit procedures, may indicate that they need to consider withdrawing from the engagement. For example, the auditor may determine that the fraud is so pervasive in the business that they will be unable to complete their audit procedures, or that the fraud will have such an impact on the client's reputation that they no longer wish to have them as a client. In these rare cases, any decision to withdraw from the engagement is not taken lightly and extensive consultation both internally within the audit firm as well as externally with legal counsel will occur before any action is taken. Whether or not the decision is taken to withdraw from the audit engagement depends on (1) whether

materiality information that has an impact on the decision-making of users of the financial statements

the evidence suggests that management has been involved in perpetrating the fraud (or there are concerns regarding management's integrity, based on how it dealt with the fraud once it was identified) and (2) the diligence and co-operation of management in investigating the circumstances of the fraud and taking appropriate action.

At the conclusion of the audit, the auditor formally reconsiders their assessment of internal control and fraud risk by considering whether the accumulated results of their audit procedures and other observations affect the assessments they made when planning the audit. This evaluation also considers qualitative matters based on the engagement team and audit team executives' **professional judgement**. (Quantitative and qualitative considerations for materiality are discussed in chapter 4.)

professional judgement the auditor's professional characteristics, such as expertise, experience, knowledge, and training

8. Revisit the planning documentation to ensure that all significant issues identified during the planning phase have been addressed.

9. Perform analytical procedures on the adjusted financial statements. Analytical procedures are used at the end of the audit to evaluate whether the final financial statements are consistent with the knowledge of the business obtained during the audit. Analytics are employed to corroborate the conclusions formed on the individual financial statement elements and the financial statements overall.

10. Perform a review for contingent liabilities and commitments to ensure that they are properly accounted for or disclosed. Specific audit procedures are performed in this area, usually toward the end of the audit. This is discussed further in section 13.3.

11. Perform subsequent events procedures. During the wrap-up of the engagement the auditor performs what is referred to as subsequent events procedures. The objective of subsequent events procedures is to identify those events occurring between year end (that is, the reporting date) and the date of the audit report that may require adjustment to or disclosure in the financial statements. Subsequent events procedures are normally performed through to and including the date of the audit report. Subsequent events are discussed in more detail in section 13.4.

12. It is important that the audit file be completed on a timely basis. The audit quality control standards (CSQC 1) require engagement teams to assemble the final engagement file on a timely basis after the audit report has been finalized. Many firms refer to this as "archiving" the audit file. Once a file is "archived" nothing is to be removed, deleted, or discarded from the file. If the auditor finds it necessary to modify existing audit documentation or add new audit documentation, the nature of the modifications, why the changes were made, and by whom they were made must be documented.

13.1.1 Sufficient appropriate audit evidence

As discussed in chapter 1, the objective of an audit is to obtain sufficient appropriate evidence to reduce the risk of material misstatement in the financial statements to an acceptably low level.

What constitutes **sufficient appropriate evidence** is ultimately a matter of professional judgement. It will be based on the satisfactory performance of audit procedures designed to address the assessed risk of material misstatement (as discussed in chapters 1, 3, and 4 and addressed in CAS 500 *Audit Evidence*). This includes any additional or modified procedures performed to address changes identified in the original assessment of risk. Factors to consider in evaluating the sufficiency and appropriateness of audit evidence (assuming the tests were appropriate to the type of account and assertions most at risk) include:

sufficient appropriate evidence quantity (sufficiency) and quality (appropriateness) of audit evidence gathered

- materiality of misstatements
- management responses
- previous experience
- results of audit procedures performed
- quality of information obtained
- persuasiveness of the audit evidence
- whether the evidence obtained supports or contradicts the results of the risk assessment procedures

If it is not possible to obtain sufficient appropriate audit evidence, the auditor should express a qualified, adverse, or disclaimer of opinion, as described in CAS 705 *Modifications to the Opinion in the Independent Auditor's Report.*

13.1.2 Evaluating audit evidence

The goal in evaluating audit evidence is to decide, after considering all the relevant data obtained, whether:

1. the assessments of the risk of material misstatement at the assertion level are appropriate, and

2. sufficient evidence has been obtained to reduce the risk of material misstatement in the financial statements to an acceptably low level.

An audit is an ongoing, cumulative, and iterative process of gathering and evaluating evidence. This requires an attitude of professional scepticism to be applied by each member of the audit team, ongoing discussions among the audit team members throughout the engagement, and timely modifications being made to planned procedures to reflect any changes to the original risk assessments.

When misstatements or deviations from controls are found in planned procedures, consideration should always be given to:

- the reason for the misstatement or deviation
- the impact on risk assessments and other planned procedures
- the need to modify or perform further audit procedures

Before evaluating the results of procedures and any misstatements identified, as discussed previously, consideration should be given to whether the materiality levels established during the planning phase need to be revised. A change in materiality could be a result of:

- new information—for example, the bank supplying the company with funding may have decided to refinance the debt during the year and put in place very restrictive covenants relating to certain balances
- a change in the auditor's understanding of the entity and its operations
- new circumstances—for example, actual profit may be significantly lower than expected profit at the planning stage of the audit

Cloud 9

Sharon suggests that the members of the team ask themselves whether they believe that sufficient appropriate evidence on which to base an audit opinion has been gathered. Which issues are not satisfactorily resolved? Where do they need to gather additional evidence? Which notes can be cleared and removed from the files? Are assessments of risk and materiality still valid given evidence obtained from substantive procedures?

The team members have performed a final review of the audit evidence on the audit sections they were assigned, and have identified the major audit differences that the partner will need to resolve with Cloud 9's management. It appears that the only other major outstanding items are the going concern assessment, the search for contingent liabilities, and the subsequent events procedures. None of these can be finalized prior to year end, and certain procedures need to be performed up until the audit report date.

BEFORE YOU GO ON

13.1.1 Explain why it is important to reassess materiality at the end of the audit.

13.1.2 What is the goal in evaluating audit evidence?

13.1.3 Provide three considerations when evaluating the sufficiency and appropriateness of audit evidence.

13.2 GOING CONCERN

As discussed in chapter 3 and CAS 570 *Going Concern*, the going concern assumption is a fundamental principle in the preparation of the financial statements. Under the **going concern** assumption, an entity is viewed as continuing in business for the foreseeable future with neither the intention nor the need for liquidation, ceasing trading, or seeking protection from creditors pursuant to laws or regulations. As a result, assets and liabilities are recorded on the basis that the entity will be able to realize its assets and discharge its liabilities in the normal course of business.

Some financial reporting frameworks contain an explicit requirement for management to make an assessment of the entity's ability to continue as a going concern. For example, IAS 1 *Presentation of Financial Statements* requires management to make an assessment of an entity's ability to continue as a going concern, and when management is aware of material uncertainties related to events or conditions that may cast significant doubt upon the entity's ability to continue as a going concern, to disclose those uncertainties.

Under other financial reporting frameworks (for example, preparing information in accordance with a joint venture or sale agreement), there may be no explicit requirement for management to make a specific assessment of the entity's ability to continue as a going concern. Nevertheless, since the going concern assumption is a fundamental principle in the preparation of the financial statements, management has a responsibility to assess the entity's ability to continue as a going concern even if the financial reporting framework does not include an explicit requirement to do so.

The following factors are relevant when management is assessing the going concern assumption:

- Generally, the further into the future an event is likely to take place, the greater the uncertainty surrounding that event. For that reason, most financial reporting frameworks specify the period for which management is required to assess all available information when making its going concern assessment. In Canada, this is typically 12 months from the date of the financial statements.

- Any judgement about the future is based on information available at the time at which the judgement is made. Subsequent events can contradict a judgement that was reasonable at the time it was made. Management of clients in industries subject to frequent change face more difficulty when assessing the going concern assumption.

- The size and complexity of the entity, the nature and condition of its business, and the degree to which it is affected by external factors all affect judgement regarding the outcome of events or conditions.

CAS 570 *Going Concern* requires that the auditor consider the appropriateness of management's use of the going concern assumption in the preparation of the financial statements. Consideration of management's use of the going concern assumption is based on knowledge of conditions or events obtained through planning and performing the audit. The auditor considers whether their procedures identify conditions and events that, when considered in the aggregate, indicate that there could be substantial doubt about the entity's ability to continue as a going concern.

The auditor also considers whether there are material uncertainties about the entity's ability to continue as a going concern that need to be disclosed in the financial statements. Usually, material uncertainties relate to an entity's inability to meet obligations as they become due without substantial disposals of assets outside the ordinary course of business, restructuring of debt or equity, or major operational improvements.

The going concern assumption does not apply to the financial statements prepared on a liquidation basis. For example, when owners decide to dissolve the business or bankruptcy proceedings reach a point at which liquidation is probable, they prepare the financial statements on a liquidation basis. When the financial statements are not prepared on a going concern basis, that fact needs to be disclosed, together with the basis on which the financial statements have been prepared and the reason why the entity is not considered to be a going concern.

 2 Understand the considerations when assessing the going concern assumption used in the preparation of the financial statements.

going concern the viability of a company to remain in business for the foreseeable future

Cloud 9

Sharon and the team discuss whether there are any issues causing doubt on the appropriateness of the going concern assumption at Cloud 9. The financial ratios indicate no problems with solvency, and the major borrowings are not due to be repaid or refinanced for another four years. However, a loss is expected for this financial year. Cloud 9's management is anticipating a loss because of the costs associated with the new store opening and the sponsorship deal. The team makes a note that these issues have been formally reviewed and they conclude that there are no significant issues casting doubt on the going concern assumption.

BEFORE YOU GO ON

13.2.1 Provide one consideration management should take into account when assessing the going concern assumption.

13.2.2 Provide one consideration the auditor should take into account when assessing the going concern assumption.

13.2.3 Does the going concern assumption always apply to all audits?

13.3 CONTINGENT LIABILITIES

3 Understand the purpose of and the procedures performed in the review for contingent liabilities and commitments.

Contingent liabilities are existing or possible obligations on the balance sheet date when the final outcome is uncertain and contingent upon a future event. Most financial reporting frameworks require an entity to record or disclose such contingent liabilities, depending on whether they are "likely" or "probable" and "measureable." While it is management's responsibility to determine the appropriate accounting treatment, given the financial reporting framework under which the financial statements will be prepared, CAS 501 *Audit Evidence—Specific Considerations for Selected Items* requires the auditor to "search" for any litigation and claims involving the entity that the auditor may not be aware of but which may give rise to a material misstatement. The auditor is required to perform the following procedures:

- Inquire of management and others within the entity, including in-house legal counsel, if there are any unreported contingent liabilities.

- Review minutes of meetings of **those charged with governance** and correspondence between the entity and its external legal counsel.

- Review correspondence with taxation authorities.

- Review legal expense accounts for unexpected fluctuations.

- Include in the managment representation letter the fact that all contingent liabilities have been disclosed to the auditor.

those charged with governance generally the board of directors, and may include management of an entity

If the auditor has assessed a risk of material misstatement regarding litigation and claims, they are required by CAS 501.10 to request permission from the client to contact the entity's external counsel. This is usually done via the legal letter, as discussed in chapter 5. If the client does not grant permission for this communication, then the auditor will look to gather evidence by performing alternative procedures. If the alternative procedures do not provide sufficient and appropriate evidence, then the auditor will need to modify the opinion in the auditor's report.

The procedures for contingent liabilities are usually performed at the end of the audit to ensure that there is sufficient and appropriate evidence in the audit file to support not only contingent liabilities but also the work performed for subsequent events, as described in the next section. While performing the procedures for contingent liabilities, the auditor will also look for evidence that the entity has entered into long-term commitments that have not been appropriately disclosed.

13.4 SUBSEQUENT EVENTS

The financial statements are prepared on the basis of conditions existing at year end (that is, the reporting date). However, significant events, both favourable and unfavourable, can occur after year end but before the issuance of the audit report that, unless reflected in the financial statements or suitably disclosed therein, could make the financial statements misleading. Therefore, the auditor is responsible for gathering evidence for subsequent events up to the date of the audit report. Once the audit report has been signed, the auditor is no longer responsible for detecting subsequent events.

There are three key dates that are important when considering subsequent events:

1. The date on which the financial statements are approved. This is the date on which those with the recognized authority assert that they have prepared the entity's complete financial statements, including the related notes, and that they have taken responsibility for the financial statements. The audit report cannot be dated before this date.

2. The date of the audit report. This is the date on which the auditor signs the audit report on the financial statements. The audit report is not dated earlier than the date on which the auditor has obtained sufficient appropriate audit evidence on which to base their opinion on the financial statements. Sufficient appropriate audit evidence includes evidence that the entity's complete financial statements have been prepared and that those with the recognized authority have asserted that they have taken responsibility for the statements.

3. The date on which the financial statements are issued. This is the date on which the audit report and audited financial statements are made available to third parties, which may be, in many circumstances, the date on which they are filed with a regulatory authority.

Each of these terms becomes important when considering the date when field work is completed. They are further explained below.

CAS 560 *Subsequent Events* establishes standards and provides guidance on the auditor's responsibility regarding subsequent events. This standard describes the two types of **subsequent events** that require consideration and evaluation:

1. events that provide additional evidence with respect to conditions that existed at the date of the financial statements (type 1 subsequent events)

2. events that provide evidence with respect to conditions that arose subsequent to the date of the financial statements (type 2 subsequent events)

The two types of subsequent events are also defined in IAS 10 *Events After the Reporting Period* and ASPE Section 3820 *Subsequent Events*. Each of these is now discussed in more detail.

13.4.1 Type 1 subsequent events

Type 1 subsequent events provide additional evidence with respect to conditions that existed at year end. Such events may affect the estimates inherent in the financial statements or indicate that the going concern assumption in relation to the whole or a part of the entity is not appropriate. Therefore, the financial statements should be adjusted to reflect any material type 1 subsequent event up to the date of the audit report. This may include revisions to estimates where new information is now available. Examples of type 1 subsequent events (requiring changes of amounts in the financial statements) are:

- the bankruptcy of a customer subsequent to year end, which would be considered when evaluating the adequacy of the allowance for doubtful accounts

4 Compare the two types of (material) subsequent events to determine what effect they have on the financial statements (if any).

subsequent events both events occurring between year end and the date of the audit report, and facts discovered after the date of the audit report

- an amount received with respect to an insurance claim that was being negotiated at year end
- deterioration in operating results and financial position after year end that is so significant that it may indicate that the going concern assumption is not appropriate to use in the preparation of the financial statements
- the settlement of a lawsuit after the reporting period for an amount different from what was originally estimated

13.4.2 Type 2 subsequent events

Type 2 subsequent events are those events that do not result in changes to amounts in the financial statements. However, these events may be of such significance as to require disclosure in the financial statements. Examples of type 2 subsequent events (not requiring adjustment but possibly requiring disclosure in the financial statements) are:

- the uninsured (or underinsured) loss of plant or inventory as a result of a fire or flood subsequent to year end
- the purchase of a business
- the issuance of shares or debt securities

13.4.3 Procedures used when conducting a subsequent events review

The subsequent events review performed for identifying type 1 or type 2 events requires the auditor to perform specific audit procedures different from the usual examination of transactions after year end (for example, the verification of the cut-off of sales or the collection of trade receivables). However, when the usual examination of transactions after year end is performed as part of the substantive tests of certain account balances, primarily to ensure that routine transactions are recorded in the proper period, or to review the appropriateness at year end of the carrying amounts of assets and the adequacy of provisions for losses or expenses, the auditor will be alert for items that may indicate significant subsequent events. When performing these procedures, the auditor may become aware of significant events occurring subsequent to the balance sheet date that may require adjustment to or disclosure in the financial statements.

The procedures performed to identify events that may require adjustment of or disclosure in the financial statements are performed as near as practicable to the date of the audit report and include some or all of the following:

- gaining an understanding of and evaluating processes that management has established to determine that subsequent events are identified and dealt with
- reading minutes of meetings of the board of directors and executive committees held after year end and inquiring about matters discussed at meetings for which minutes are not available
- reading and analyzing the latest available interim financial statements and, as considered necessary and appropriate, budgets, cash flow forecasts, and other related management reports for events such as changes in accounting principles, significant changes in results or working capital, and non-compliance with loan terms, and reviewing sales, receipts, journals, and other accounting records relating to transactions that have occurred subsequent to the date of the financial statements
- inquiring, or extending previous oral or written inquiries, of the entity's legal counsel concerning litigation and claims
- assessing continued compliance with borrowing limits and loan covenants
- inquiring of those charged with governance as to whether any subsequent events have occurred that might affect the financial statements
- inquiring of management as to whether any subsequent events have occurred that might affect the financial statements. Examples of inquiries of management on specific matters are:
  - whether new commitments, borrowings, or guarantees have been entered into or any other factors have changed the classification of any liabilities

- whether sales of assets have occurred or are planned, or any other plans have been made that may affect the carrying value or classification of assets
- whether new shares have been issued, long-term debt financing instruments have been put in place, or an agreement to merge or liquidate has been made, or any of these events are planned
- whether any change of ownership has occurred or is contemplated
- whether any assets have been seized (or appropriated) by the government or destroyed—for example, by flood or fire
- whether there have been any developments regarding risk areas and contingencies
- whether any unusual adjustments have been made since the date of the financial statements or are contemplated
- whether any significant changes in foreign exchange rates have occurred that could affect the entity
- whether there has been any change in the status of related party transactions, including those entered into subsequent to the date of the financial statements
- whether any significant assessments have been made by tax authorities with respect to tax assessments, fines, and penalties
- the current status of items involving subjective judgement or that were accounted for on the basis of preliminary information, such as provisions for litigation in progress
- whether any events have occurred or are likely to occur that will bring into question the appropriateness of accounting policies used in the preparation of the financial statements; for example, if such events call into question the validity of the going concern assumption
- sales and profit trends, industry and general economic climate, exceptional bad debt losses, decreases in raw material prices or possible inventory losses, renegotiation of prices under contract, or sales of inventory at a loss

The auditor obtains written representations (as covered in CAS 580 *Written Representations*) from management as part of the management representation letter (as illustrated in chapter 5) confirming oral representations made with respect to subsequent events and that it is not aware of other relevant subsequent events.

The extent to which the results of these procedures will need reviewing and updating immediately prior to issuing the audit report depends on the length of time that has elapsed since the procedures were carried out and the susceptibility of the matters under consideration to change over time.

Figure 13.1 shows the subsequent event timeline and the responsibility of the auditor to gather evidence up to the release of the audited financial statements.

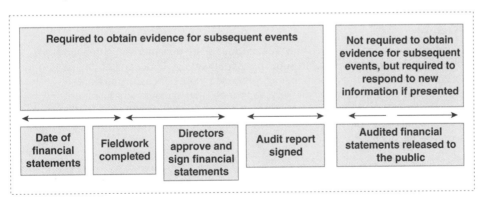

FIGURE 13.1 **Subsequent event timeline**

13.4.4 Auditor responsibility for subsequent events

Subsequent events may require adjustments to the financial statements. For subsequent events occurring *up to the date of the auditor's report*, if the client indicates that it will not change the financial statements in a situation where the auditor believes they should be changed, a qualified or adverse opinion is issued. When the audit report has been released to the entity (but not released to the public), the auditor would notify those charged with governance (generally the board of directors and management) not to issue the financial statements and audit report to any third parties. If the financial statements have been released or are subsequently released anyway (without being changed), the auditor must take action to prevent reliance on the audit report. This is usually done by withdrawing the audit report and the company issuing a communication to those third parties that have received the report.

After the audit report is signed, the auditor is not required to perform any further procedures relating to subsequent events. But if *after the financial statements have been issued* the auditor becomes aware of a fact that existed at the date of the audit report and that, if the auditor had known at that date, could have caused them to modify the audit report, the auditor should:

1. consider whether the financial statements need revision.
2. discuss the matter with management and those charged with governance.
3. consider whether the actions taken are appropriate in the circumstances. This would include performing any additional audit procedures necessary, and reviewing and approving any revisions to the financial statements. In addition, anyone in receipt of the previously issued financial statements and audit report should be informed of the situation and advised that a new audit report has been issued on the revised financial statements.

The revised audit report may be dated no earlier than the date on which the new financial statements are approved and should include an emphasis of matter paragraph referring to the note in the financial statements that more extensively outlines the reason(s) for the revision to the previously released financial statements. If the impact of the item requiring adjustment is not pervasive to the financial statements overall, the auditor may alternatively choose to double-date the audit report. In this case, the audit report date would be the original date and a new date would be added for the change to the financial statements. For example, if the original audit report was signed and issued on March 15, 20X6, and subsequently the auditor became aware of a lawsuit that should have been disclosed but was not, the financial statements should be amended to include the note disclosure of the contingent liability. As the impact of the subsequent event in this example can be isolated, the auditor can still date the financial statements March 15, 20X6, adding "except for note X dated April 15, 20X6."

When management does not take the necessary steps, the auditor should notify those charged with governance (such as the audit committee or board of directors) of the entity that action will be taken by the auditor to prevent future reliance on the auditor's report. As discussed above, this is usually done through communication with regulatory filers and through the entity's company website.

Cloud 9

Procedures to search for subsequent events at Cloud 9 are documented in the audit program. These include a review of minutes of board meetings in December, January, and February, and analysis of the interim results for these months (including analytical procedures). The partner on the audit will also formally ask management about any subsequent events that have come to its attention in the meetings to be held between year end and the audit report date. The team will also search for additional borrowings or other matters involving significant contracts.

BEFORE YOU GO ON

13.4.1 Describe the two types of subsequent events that are required to be considered as part of the audit of the financial statements.

13.4.2 Provide two types of procedures an auditor may perform to identify a subsequent event.

13.4.3 What should an auditor do when, after the discovery of a subsequent event, the client does not take appropriate action?

13.5 MISSTATEMENTS

As noted in chapter 8, when performing substantive testing the key objective is to determine whether there are material errors within each account balance and to quantify any identified errors. A **misstatement** is a difference between the amount, classification, presentation, or disclosure of a reported financial statement item and the amount, classification, presentation, or disclosure that is required for the item to be in accordance with the applicable financial reporting framework. An **error** is an unintentional misstatement in the financial statements, including the omission of an amount or a disclosure. When an error or exception is identified during substantive testing, the first response is to find out why the error or exception has arisen. It may require an increase to the sample size to ensure that there are no other errors in the balance (unless the total error in the account balance is able to be quantified without performing additional testing). It is important when errors are identified to continue testing until the error can either be accurately quantified or the balance has been fully tested to an extent that proves that a material error can no longer exist within the balance.

In reaching a conclusion as to whether the misstatements need to be corrected by the client, the auditor evaluates whether the misstatement either causes the financial statements to be materially misstated or requires additional disclosure. This evaluation involves considerable professional judgement. Both quantitative and qualitative considerations are taken into account, including:

- the risk of additional misstatements remaining undetected
- the effects of identified misstatements on the client's compliance with covenants under debt or similar agreements
- whether the proposed corrections result from an error or are the result of a **judgemental misstatement** between the client's and the auditor's application of accounting policies
- the reversing effect of uncorrected misstatements identified in the prior year on the current year's financial statements (see section 13.5.2)
- the likelihood that recurring differences, which currently are immaterial, will have a material effect in the future
- the sensitivity of the circumstances surrounding the misstatements—for example, the implications of differences involving fraud and possible illegal acts, or violations of contractual provisions
- the significance of the financial statement elements affected by the misstatements
- the significance of the misstatements relative to known user needs—for example, the magnifying effects of the misstatements on the calculation of a purchase price in a transfer of interests (buy/sell agreement)
- the effect of the misstatements on segment information or on another portion of the client's business that has been identified as playing a significant role in the client's operations or profitability
- the effects of offsetting misstatements in different financial statement captions (or balance names within the financial statements—for example, cash at bank, prepayments, or payables)

13.5.1 Current-year misstatements

When misstatements identified during the audit are not corrected by the client, the auditor prepares a working paper (sometimes referred to as a schedule or summary of audit differences) that accumulates all identified misstatements in order to be able to consider their aggregate effect on the financial statements as a whole. The auditor also considers these misstatements against individual items or balances, such as profit before tax or net income, trend of earnings, working capital, shareholders' funds, and loan covenants.

When evaluating the materiality of misstatements, the auditor considers the cumulative effect of the misstatements at the end of the current year on pre-tax income and/or net income, working capital, and shareholders' equity. The auditor also considers whether the matters underlying the misstatements could cause a material misstatement in future years' financial statements if the client

 5 Analyze misstatements and explain the difference between quantitative and qualitative considerations when evaluating misstatements.

misstatement a difference between the amount, classification, presentation, or disclosure of a reported financial statement item and the amount, classification, presentation, or disclosure that is required for the item to be in accordance with the applicable financial reporting framework. Misstatements can arise from error or fraud.

error an unintentional misstatement in the financial statements, including the omission of an amount or a disclosure

judgemental misstatement a misstatement that arises as a result of a difference in the application of judgement by the client and the auditor, such as the use of an estimate the auditor considers unreasonable or the inappropriate application of an inappropriate accounting policy. A judgemental misstatement is not the same as an error

December 31, 2016
Worksheet—Summary of identified misstatements (CORE)

Objectives
To document misstatements identified during the audit and to evaluate:
• The effect of identified misstatements on the audit.
• The effect of uncorrected misstatements, if any, on the financial statements.

Performance materiality $_____42,500 Insignificant misstatements under $_____1,000 need not be recorded below.

Description	Circumstances of occurrence	Amount of over (under) misstatement in the financial statements					Corrected? Yes/No	W/P Ref
		Assets	Liabilities	Income	Equity	F/S disclosures		
Accrue audit fee for the year	Missed Accrual	–	(15,000)	(15,000)	–		No	
Reverse revenue not earned	Cut-Off Error	25,000	–	25,000	–		No	
Total identified misstatements during the audit		25,000	(15,000)	10,000	–			
Misstatements corrected by management		–	–	–	–			
Total uncorrected misstatements		25,000	(15,000)	10,000	–			
Effect of income taxes on uncorrected misstatements				–	–			
Effect of uncorrected **misstatements** from prior periods				(15,000)	–			
Uncorrected misstatements to be carried forward				(5,000)	–			

FIGURE 13.2 **Summary of audit differences**

Source: CPEM Form 335: Worksheet—Summary of Identified Misstatements (CORE) *2013*

should decide to correct all the misstatements in one year, even though the misstatements are not material to the current year's financial statements. This is particularly relevant when the misstatements represent recurring, and generally increasing, differences in particular areas or accounts, such as certain expense accruals. See figure 13.2 for an example of a summary of audit differences.

13.5.2 Prior-year misstatements

Misstatements may not have been corrected by the client in the prior period because they did not cause the financial statements for that period to be materially misstated. As described in CAS 450 *Evaluation of Misstatements Identified During the Audit*, the cumulative impact of immaterial uncorrected misstatements related to prior periods may have a material effect on the current period's financial statements.

When these misstatements in the prior year have been identified, they are considered by the auditor to "reverse" in the following reporting period. For example, if payables are understated due to a cut-off error in the prior period, the misstatement is considered to "reverse" in the following period and therefore overstates payables in that period. Misstatements that are due to errors (or fraud) are always considered to reverse in the following period, whereas misstatements that arise due to judgemental misstatements between the client and the auditor may not necessarily reverse. Assessing prior-period judgemental misstatements is a complex area that requires a high level of professional judgement and experience, and is considered an advanced auditing concept.

The identification and resolution of misstatements is one of the most important responsibilities in an audit and is a critical step in the formulation of the opinion on the fairness of the client's financial statements. Considerable judgement is required when reaching a conclusion on the materiality of unrecorded misstatements, and is influenced by the evaluation of the needs of a reasonable person who will rely on the financial statements. This requires the evaluation of the total mix of information available, both quantitative (the dollar amounts of the misstatements relative to the position and results of the entity) and qualitative (other considerations that are not influenced by the dollar amount of the misstatements). This is why the final evaluations and conclusions formed regarding misstatements are always performed by the partner responsible for the audit engagement. Figure 13.2 shows a summary of audit differences.

PROFESSIONAL ENVIRONMENT

Forensic accounting

One of the more popular television genres in recent years has been crime with a heavy reliance on forensic science to solve cases (for example, the *CSI* franchise). The programs are so popular there are claims that they have led to a jump in enrolments in forensic science courses. According to Long, demand for forensic accounting has also never been higher, although this is more likely due to the fallout from Enron and WorldCom than from any television program. These cases have made boards of directors more aware of their liability for fraud. If a problem is brought to their attention, they appear to be more willing to order an investigation, and forensic accountants are called in to do the work.

Another potential cause of the increased interest in forensic accounting is terrorism. Since the tragedy of 9/11, tracing the money trail behind terrorism has been a high priority for security agencies. Forensic accounting expertise is similar to auditing in the sense that both rely on a deep understanding of double-entry accounting plus a large dose of other skills and attributes; in the case of forensic accounting, these include expert knowledge of legal systems and interview techniques. However, at its heart, forensic accounting relies on accounting knowledge because some fraudsters go to great lengths to hide their trail and a knowledge of double-entry bookkeeping is necessary to keep up.

Forensic accountants need to have an eye on how their findings will be used in court. In fact, "forensic" means something that will be used in, or is suitable to be used in, courts of law. In the past, most forensic accounting work related to accountants appearing in court as expert witnesses for personal injury or divorce cases. Now, forensic accounting practices are focusing more on investigation, fraud risk management, anti-money laundering, and computer forensics.

The world's largest anti-fraud organization and premier provider of anti-fraud training and education, the Association of Certified Fraud Examiners (ACFE), has experienced a sharp rise in membership over the last few years. The fraud investigators say they have been trying for years to get regulators interested in investigating potential fraud cases, such as the Bernard Madoff Ponzi scheme. Now they say they have noticed a recent increase in community appreciation of their work.

Sources: C · PEM, "Amending Audit Reports" (Chapter 13), 2010; C. Long, "Forensic Frenzy," *Charter*, June 2007.

13.5.3 Qualitative considerations

Qualitative considerations may cause misstatements of quantitatively immaterial amounts to be considered material to the financial statements. Examples of this are when correcting the misstatement would affect:

- the client's compliance with regulatory requirements or covenants under debt or similar agreements
- the client's compliance with contractual requirements of operating and other agreements
- management's satisfaction of requirements for the awarding of bonuses or other forms of incentive compensation
- the reported profit, by changing it to a loss or vice versa
- individual line items, subtotals, or totals, by a material amount
- key ratios monitored by analysts or other key users of the financial statements

Cloud 9

Numerous misstatements have been found during the Cloud 9 audit. Sharon and the team review these items individually as they arise and collectively at the completion of the audit field work.

For any matters they believe are material, either quantitatively or qualitatively, they will prepare a summary for the partner. The partner needs to understand the nature of the item, including the probable cause of the error and whether it is an indicator of more serious issues in the client's systems. The summary will outline the nature of the evidence gathered and the additional work completed to verify the size and nature of the misstatement, including whether there was an expansion of the sample size and the results of any alternative procedures performed. The summary will make a recommendation and outline why the audit team believes that an adjustment should or should not be made to the client's financial statements.

BEFORE YOU GO ON

13.5.1 What does an auditor do when misstatements identified during the audit are not corrected by the client?

13.5.2 Why is it important to consider the prior-year unadjusted misstatements?

13.5.3 Name two qualitative considerations that may be taken into account when assessing misstatements.

13.6 EVALUATING THE CONCLUSIONS AND FORMING AN OPINION

6 Evaluate conclusions obtained during the performance of the audit and explain how these conclusions link to the overall opinion formed on the financial statements.

The final phase of the audit is to assess all of the audit evidence obtained and determine whether it is sufficient and appropriate to reduce the risk of material misstatement in the financial statements to an acceptably low level. Forming an opinion on the financial statements involves the following four steps:

1. evaluating the audit evidence obtained

2. evaluating the effects of unrecorded misstatements identified and the qualitative aspects of the entity's accounting practices

3. evaluating whether the financial statements have been properly prepared and presented in accordance with the applicable reporting framework

4. evaluating the fair presentation of the financial statements

13.7 COMPONENTS OF THE AUDIT REPORT

7 Describe the components of an audit report.

The format of an audit report for general purpose financial statements is governed by CAS 700 *Forming an Opinion and Reporting on Financial Statements*. For audit reports that are not prepared for general purpose financial statements but are instead provided on other historical financial information or special purpose financial statements, CAS 800 *Special Considerations—Audits of Financial Statements Prepared in Accordance with Special Purpose Frameworks*, CAS 805 *Special Considerations—Audits of Single Financial Statements and Specific Elements, Accounts or Items of a Financial Statement*, and CAS 810 *Engagements to Report on Summary Financial Statements* detail the required components of the audit report, which are the same as those required by CAS 700.

The main components of the auditor's report, which is required by CAS 700 to be in writing, include:

1. Title

2. Addressee

3. Introductory paragraph:
   - identifies the entity whose financial statements have been audited
   - states that the financial statements have been audited
   - identifies the title of each of the statements that comprise the complete financial statements
   - refers to the summary of significant accounting policies and other explanatory notes
   - specifies the date and period covered by the financial statements

4. Management's responsibility for the financial statements. Management's responsibility includes establishing and maintaining internal controls relevant to the preparation and fair presentation of the financial statements that are free from material misstatements, whether due to fraud or error; selecting and applying appropriate accounting policies; and making accounting estimates that are reasonable in the circumstances.

5. Auditor's responsibility for the financial statements. The auditor must state that the responsibility of the auditor is to express an opinion on the financial statements based on the audit, state that the audit was conducted in accordance with auditing standards (including compliance with relevant ethical requirements), describe the audit, and state that the auditor

believes that the audit evidence obtained is sufficient and appropriate to provide a basis for the auditor's opinion.

6. Auditor's opinion on whether the financial statements give a true and fair view or is presented fairly, in all material respects, in accordance with the applicable financial reporting framework

7. Other reporting responsibilities; for example, in some cases auditors may be required to report on other matters

8. Auditor's signature either in the firm's name, the personal name of the auditor, or both (depending on the legislative requirements)

9. Date of the report

10. Auditor's address

The standard wording used when providing an opinion on the financial statements in accordance with an applicable accounting framework and expressing an unqualified opinion is provided in CAS 700. A sample audit report is provided in chapter 1.

PROFESSIONAL ENVIRONMENT

Changes coming for auditor reporting?

The International Auditing and Assurance Standards Board (IAASB) commissioned a research study in 2006 on user perceptions of the contents of the auditor's report. Findings from this research, as well as input from various stakeholders around the world, have led to the same conclusion: the status quo is not an option. There is a demand for auditors to provide greater transparency about significant matters. As a result, the IAASB released an exposure draft regarding proposed changes to the auditor report. The exposure draft included new proposed ISA titled *Communicating Key Audit Matters in the Independent Auditor's Report.* Recommended changes included the following:

· Additional information in the form of an "auditor commentary" to highlight matters that are likely to be important to users. This would be required for publicly traded entities but could be at the discretion of the auditor for other entities.

· An explicit statement as to whether material uncertainties in relation to going concern have been identified and an overall conclusion on the appropriateness of management's use of the going concern assumption.

· A statement as to whether any material inconsistencies between the audited financial statements and other information have been identified.

· The prominent placement of the auditor's opinion and other entity-specific information in the auditor's report

· Further measures to provide transparency about the audit performed and to clarify the responsibilities of the auditor, management, and those charged with governance in an ISA audit.

"The proposed changes would move the auditor's report away from a standardized one-page report to one that is longer and more entity specific," said Eric Turner, Principal at the Canadian Institute of Chartered Accountants (now with the Chartered Professional Accountants of Canada). He believed that Canadian opinion to this proposal was mixed. Some were concerned about the additional time and cost required to discuss and reach agreement on what goes into the auditor's report. Others supported the auditor providing more transparency about what has been discussed with the audit committee, but were concerned that auditors would not provide useful information due to liability concerns, resulting in a longer but more standard "boilerplate" report.

Regardless, significant changes are likely. Prof. Arnold Schilder, the IAASB Chairman, said, "These changes are critical to the perceived value of the financial statement audit and thus to the continued relevance of the auditing profession."

Sources: "Improving the Auditor's Report: Invitation to Comment," Auditing and Assurance Standards Board, July 2012; Eric Turner, "Dramatic Changes to the Auditor's Report Will Affect Companies Large and Small (but Is It Worth It?)," Conversations about Audit Quality (www.cica.ca/focus-on-practice-areas/audit-and-assurance/conversations-about-audit-quality/entries/item75424.aspx), August 15, 2013; "IAASB Proposes Standards to Fundamentally Transform the Auditor's Report; Focuses on Communicative Value to Users," IAASB, July 25, 2013.

BEFORE YOU GO ON

13.7.1 Name two factors included in the description of management's responsibility for the financial statements, as included in the audit report.

13.7.2 Name five components of the audit report.

13.7.3 What is the auditor's responsibility for the financial statements, as included in the audit report?

13.8 IDENTIFICATION OF THE TYPES OF MODIFICATIONS TO AN AUDIT REPORT

8 Identify the types of modifications to an audit report.

In some situations, the auditor's report will require modified wording to emphasize a certain matter or to express a qualified, adverse, or disclaimer of opinion (as outlined in CAS 705 *Modifications to the Opinion in the Independent Auditor's Report* and CAS 706 *Emphasis of Matter Paragraphs and Other Matter Paragraphs in the Independent Auditor's Report*). This usually happens when:

1. a significant uncertainty exists that should be brought to the reader's attention,
2. there is an inability to obtain appropriate audit evidence, or
3. the financial statements are materially misstated.

13.8.1 Emphasis of matter

An emphasis of matter does not affect the auditor's opinion and applies where the resolution of a matter is dependent on future actions or events not under the direct control of the entity, but that may affect the financial statements, and the matter is disclosed in the financial statements. The most common emphasis of matter is one relating to an entity's ability to continue as a going concern, which may depend on finance arrangements still in negotiation or the financial support of the parent entity.

See figure 13.3 for an unqualified audit report with an emphasis of matter.

FIGURE 13.3 **Unqualified audit report with an emphasis of matter**
Source: EY, 2014

Ernst & Young LLP
Ernst & Young Tower
222 Bay Street, PO Box 251
Toronto, ON M5K 1J7

Tel: +1 416 864 1234
Fax: +1 416 864 1174
ey.com

Building a better working world

INDEPENDENT AUDITORS' REPORT

To the Board of Directors of Skyward Ltd.

We have audited the accompanying consolidated financial statements of Skyward Ltd., which comprise the consolidated statements of financial position as at December 31, 2016 and 2015, and the consolidated statements of comprehensive income, changes in equity and cash flows for the years then ended, and a summary of significant accounting policies and other explanatory information.

Management's responsibility for the consolidated financial statements
Management is responsible for the preparation and fair presentation of these consolidated financial statements in accordance with International Financial Reporting Standards, and for such internal control as management determines is necessary to enable the preparation of consolidated financial statements that are free from material misstatement, whether due to fraud or error.

Auditors' responsibility
Our responsibility is to express an opinion on these consolidated financial statements based on our audits. We conducted our audits in accordance with Canadian generally accepted auditing standards. Those standards require that we comply with ethical requirements and plan and perform the audit to obtain reasonable assurance about whether the consolidated financial statements are free from material misstatement.

An audit involves performing procedures to obtain audit evidence about the amounts and disclosures in the consolidated financial statements. The procedures selected depend on the auditors' judgment, including the assessment of the risks of material misstatement of the consolidated financial statements, whether due to fraud or error. In making those risk assessments, the auditors consider internal control relevant to the entity's preparation and fair presentation of the consolidated financial statements in order to design audit procedures that are appropriate in the circumstances, but not

(continued)

for the purpose of expressing an opinion on the effectiveness of the entity's internal control. An audit also includes evaluating the appropriateness of accounting policies used and the reasonableness of accounting estimates made by management, as well as evaluating the overall presentation of the consolidated financial statements.

We believe that the audit evidence we have obtained in our audits is sufficient and appropriate to provide a basis for our audit opinion.

Opinion

In our opinion, the consolidated financial statements present fairly, in all material respects, the financial position of Skyward Ltd. as at December 31, 2016 and 2015, and its financial performance and its cash flows for the years then ended in accordance with International Financial Reporting Standards.

Emphasis of matter

Without qualifying our opinion, we draw attention to Note 4 in the financial statements which indicates that Skyward Ltd. incurred a net loss of $600,000 during the year ended December 31, 2016 and, as of that date, Skyward Ltd.'s current liabilities exceeded its total assets by $1,220,000. These conditions, along with other matters as set forth in Note 4, indicate the existence of a material uncertainty that may cast significant doubt on Skyward Ltd.'s ability to continue as a going concern.

Toronto, Canada

February X, 2017

"Ernst & Young LLP"

Chartered Professional Accountants

Licensed Public Accountants

A member firm of Ernst & Young Global Limited

FIGURE 13.3 **Unqualified audit report with an emphasis of matter** (continued)

13.8.2 Inability to obtain appropriate audit evidence

A limitation on the scope of the auditor's work could result from an inability to perform procedures (the most common form of scope limitation) or an imposition by the entity (rare). The auditor may not be able to perform procedures believed necessary due to factors such as timing, damage to accounting records, and lack of or restricted access to key personnel, accounting records, or operating locations; or the absence of adequate accounting records to provide sufficient and appropriate audit evidence upon which to rely. For example, it may not be possible for the auditor to verify the existence of inventory if the client has not held an inventory count, or does not have particularly reliable perpetual inventory records. If this is material but not pervasive to the financial statements overall, this would then form the basis for a qualified opinion due to a scope limitation. Figure 13.4 shows a sample audit report with a qualification due to a scope limitation. Where a scope limitation is material and pervasive to the financial statements overall, a disclaimer of opinion would be issued. For example, if there was a flood at the client's office and

Ernst & Young LLP
Ernst & Young Tower
222 Bay Street, PO Box 251
Toronto, ON M5K 1J7

Tel: +1 416 864 1234
Fax: +1 416 864 1174
ey.com

INDEPENDENT AUDITORS' REPORT

To the Board of Directors of Skyward Ltd.

We have audited the accompanying consolidated financial statements of Skyward Ltd., which comprise the consolidated statements of financial position as at December 31, 2016 and 2015, and the consolidated statements of comprehensive income, changes in equity and cash flows for the years then ended, and a summary of significant accounting policies and other explanatory information.

FIGURE 13.4 **Sample audit report with a qualification due to a scope limitation**

Source: EY, 2014

(continued)

FIGURE 13.4 **Sample audit report with a qualification due to a scope limitation** (continued)

Management's responsibility for the consolidated financial statements

Management is responsible for the preparation and fair presentation of these consolidated financial statements in accordance with International Financial Reporting Standards, and for such internal control as management determines is necessary to enable the preparation of consolidated financial statements that are free from material misstatement, whether due to fraud or error.

Auditors' responsibility

Our responsibility is to express an opinion on these consolidated financial statements based on our audits. We conducted our audits in accordance with Canadian generally accepted auditing standards. Those standards require that we comply with ethical requirements and plan and perform the audit to obtain reasonable assurance about whether the consolidated financial statements are free from material misstatement.

An audit involves performing procedures to obtain audit evidence about the amounts and disclosures in the consolidated financial statements. The procedures selected depend on the auditors' judgment, including the assessment of the risks of material misstatement of the consolidated financial statements, whether due to fraud or error. In making those risk assessments, the auditors consider internal control relevant to the entity's preparation and fair presentation of the consolidated financial statements in order to design audit procedures that are appropriate in the circumstances, but not for the purpose of expressing an opinion on the effectiveness of the entity's internal control. An audit also includes evaluating the appropriateness of accounting policies used and the reasonableness of accounting estimates made by management, as well as evaluating the overall presentation of the consolidated financial statements.

We believe that the audit evidence we have obtained in our audits is sufficient and appropriate to provide a basis for our qualified audit opinion.

Basis for qualified opinion

Skyward Ltd.'s investment in Cumulus Inc., a foreign associate acquired during the year and accounted for by the equity method, is carried at $450,000 on the consolidated balance sheet as at December 31, 2016, and Skyward Ltd.'s share of Cumulus Inc.'s net income of $90,000 is included in Skyward Ltd.'s income for the year then ended. We were unable to obtain sufficient appropriate audit evidence about the carrying amount of Skyward Ltd.'s investment in Cumulus Inc. as at December 31, 2016 and Skyward Ltd.'s share of Cumulus Inc.'s net income for the year because we were denied access to the financial information, management, and the auditor of Cumulus Inc. Consequently, we were unable to determine whether any adjustments to these amounts were necessary.

Qualified opinion

In our opinion, except for the possible effects of the matter described in the basis for qualified opinion paragraph, the consolidated financial statements present fairly, in all material respects, the financial position of Skyward Ltd. as at December 31, 2016 and 2015, and its financial performance and its cash flows for the years then ended in accordance with International Financial Reporting Standards.

Toronto, Canada

February X, 2017

"Ernst & Young LLP"

Chartered Professional Accountants
Licensed Public Accountants

A member firm of Ernst & Young Global Limited

all of the accounting records were not recoverable, the auditor would not be able to gather sufficient and appropriate evidence for many of the financial statement accounts, and therefore, a disclaimer of opinion would be issued. The disclaimer indicates that the auditor could not gather enough evidence to form an opinion. See an example in figure 13.5.

13.8.3 Material misstatement of financial statements

The auditor may disagree with those charged with governance about matters such as the acceptability of accounting policies selected, the method of their application, or the adequacy of disclosures in

Ernst & Young LLP
Ernst & Young Tower
222 Bay Street, PO Box 251
Toronto, ON M5K 1J7

Tel: +1 416 864 1234
Fax: +1 416 864 1174
ey.com

FIGURE 13.5 **Sample audit report with a disclaimer of opinion**
Source: EY, 2014

INDEPENDENT AUDITOR'S REPORT

To the Board of Directors of Skyward Ltd.

We were engaged to audit the accompanying financial statements of Ltd. which comprise the statement of financial position as at December 31, 2016, and the statement of comprehensive income, statement of changes in equity and statement of cash flows for the year then ended, and a summary of significant accounting policies and other explanatory information.

Management's responsibility for the consolidated financial statements

Management is responsible for the preparation and fair presentation of these financial statements in accordance with International Financial Reporting Standards, and for such internal control as management determines is necessary to enable the preparation of financial statements that are free from material misstatement, whether due to fraud or error.

Auditor's responsibility

Our responsibility is to express an opinion on these financial statements based on conducting the audit in accordance with Canadian generally accepted auditing standards. Because of the matters described in the Basis for Disclaimer of Opinion paragraph, however, we were not able to obtain sufficient appropriate audit evidence to provide a basis for an audit opinion.

Basis for disclaimer of opinion

Due to a flood after year end, management was unable to provide appropriate supporting documentation for the majority of the transactions selected for audit. We were unable to satisfy ourselves by alternative means concerning the assets, liabilities, revenues and expenditures reported by Skyward Ltd. As a result of these matters, we were unable to determine whether any adjustments might have been found necessary in respect of the assets, liabilities, revenues and expenditures making up the statement of financial position as at December 31, 2016, and the statement of comprehensive income, statement of changes in equity and statement of cash flows for the year then ended.

Disclaimer of opinion

Because of the significance of the matters described in the Basis for Disclaimer of Opinion paragraph, we have not been able to obtain sufficient appropriate audit evidence to provide a basis for an audit opinion. Accordingly, we do not express an opinion on the financial statements.

Toronto, Canada
February X, 2017

"Ernst & Young LLP"
Chartered Professional Accountants
Licensed Public Accountants

A member firm of Ernst & Young Global Limited

the financial statements. Where these disagreements are material to the financial statements, a qualified or adverse opinion is expressed. Where the financial statements include a material misstatement that is not pervasive to the overall financial statements, a qualified opinion may be issued. For example, if management refuses to depreciate the capital assets as required by GAAP, but the rest of the financial statements are free from material misstatements, the auditor may issue a qualified opinion due to a GAAP departure. See figure 13.6 for an example. If however, management refuses to consolidate a subsidiary under its control as required by GAAP, this will impact many of the revenue and expense accounts in the financial statements. In this case the auditor may issue an adverse opinion. See figure 13.7 for an example. Table 13.1 outlines the circumstances in which a modification would be issued and the type of modification appropriate in the circumstances.

FIGURE 13.6 **Sample audit report with a qualification due to a GAAP departure**

Source: EY, 2014

INDEPENDENT AUDITOR'S REPORT

To the Board of Directors of Skyward Ltd.

We have audited the accompanying financial statements of Skyward Ltd., which comprise the statement of financial position as at December 31, 2016, and the statement of comprehensive income, statement of changes in equity, and statement of cash flows for the year then ended, and a summary of significant accounting policies and other explanatory information.

Management's responsibility for the financial statements

Management is responsible for the preparation and fair presentation of these financial statements in accordance with Canadian Accounting Standards for Private Enterprises, and for such internal control as management determines is necessary to enable the preparation of financial statements that are free from material misstatement, whether due to fraud or error.

Auditor's responsibility

Our responsibility is to express an opinion on these financial statements based on our audit. We conducted our audit in accordance with Canadian generally accepted auditing standards. Those standards require that we comply with ethical requirements and plan and perform the audit to obtain reasonable assurance about whether the financial statements are free from material misstatement.

An audit involves performing procedures to obtain audit evidence about the amounts and disclosures in the financial statements. The procedures selected depend on the auditor's judgment, including the assessment of the risks of material misstatement of the financial statements, whether due to fraud or error. In making those risk assessments, the auditor considers internal control relevant to the entity's preparation and fair presentation of the financial statements in order to design audit procedures that are appropriate in the circumstances, but not for the purpose of expressing an opinion on the effectiveness of the entity's internal control. An audit also includes evaluating the appropriateness of accounting policies used and the reasonableness of accounting estimates made by management, as well as evaluating the overall presentation of the financial statements.

We believe that the audit evidence we have obtained is sufficient and appropriate to provide a basis for our qualified audit opinion.

Basis for qualified opinion

As discussed in Note 8 to the financial statements, no depreciation has been recorded in the financial statements, which in our opinion, is not in accordance with Canadian Accounting Standards for Private Enterprises. The depreciation expense for the year ended December 31, 2016, should be $100,000 calculated using the straight-line method and annual rates of 10% for the building and 25% for the equipment. Accordingly, the property, plant, and equipment should be reduced by accumulated depreciation of $100,000 and the loss for the year and accumulated deficit should be increased by $100,000.

Qualified opinion

In our opinion, except for the effects of the matter described in the Basis for Qualified Opinion paragraph, the financial statements present fairly, in all material respects, the financial position of Skyward Ltd. as at December 31, 2016, and its financial performance and its cash flows for the year then ended in accordance with Canadian Accounting Standards for Private Enterprises.

Toronto, Canada
February X, 2017

"Ernst & Young LLP"
Chartered Professional Accountants
Licensed Public Accountants

A member firm of Ernst & Young Global Limited

Ernst & Young LLP
Ernst & Young Tower
222 Bay Street, PO Box 251
Toronto, ON M5K 1J7

Tel: +1 416 864 1234
Fax: +1 416 864 1174
ey.com

FIGURE 13.7 **Sample audit report with an adverse opinion**
Source: EY, 2014

INDEPENDENT AUDITOR'S REPORT

To the Board of Directors of Skyward Ltd.

We have audited the accompanying consolidated financial statements of Ltd. and its subsidiaries, which comprise the consolidated statement of financial position as at December 31, 2016, and the consolidated statement of comprehensive income, statement of changes in equity, and statement of cash flows for the year then ended, and a summary of significant accounting policies and other explanatory information.

Management's responsibility for the consolidated financial statements

Management is responsible for the preparation and fair presentation of these consolidated financial statements in accordance with International Financial Reporting Standards, and for such internal control as management determines is necessary to enable the preparation of financial statements that are free from material misstatement, whether due to fraud or error.

Auditor's responsibility

Our responsibility is to express an opinion on these consolidated financial statements based on our audit. We conducted our audit in accordance with Canadian generally accepted auditing standards. Those standards require that we comply with ethical requirements and plan and perform the audit to obtain reasonable assurance about whether the consolidated financial statements are free from material misstatement.

An audit involves performing procedures to obtain audit evidence about the amounts and disclosures in the consolidated financial statements. The procedures selected depend on the auditor's judgment, including the assessment of the risks of material misstatement of the consolidated financial statements, whether due to fraud or error. In making those risk assessments, the auditor considers internal control relevant to the entity's preparation and fair presentation of the consolidated financial statements in order to design audit procedures that are appropriate in the circumstances, but not for the purpose of expressing an opinion on the effectiveness of the entity's internal control. An audit also includes evaluating the appropriateness of accounting policies used and the reasonableness of accounting estimates made by management, as well as evaluating the overall presentation of the consolidated financial statements.

We believe that the audit evidence we have obtained is sufficient and appropriate to provide a basis for our adverse audit opinion.

Basis for adverse opinion

As explained in Note 10, the company has not consolidated the financial statements of its subsidiary Cumulus Inc. that it acquired during 2016 because the fair values of certain of the subsidiary's material assets and liabilities at the acquisition date are unknown. This investment is therefore accounted for on a cost basis. Under International Financial Reporting Standards, the subsidiary should have been consolidated because it is controlled by the company. Had Cumulus Inc. been consolidated, many elements in the accompanying financial statements would have been materially affected. The effects on the consolidated financial statements of the failure to consolidate have not been determined.

Adverse opinion

In our opinion, because of the significance of the matter discussed in the Basis for Adverse Opinion paragraph, the consolidated financial statements do not present

(continued)

FIGURE 13.7 **Sample audit report with an adverse opinion** (continued)

fairly the financial position of Skyward Ltd. and its subsidiaries as at December 31, 2016, and their financial performance and their cash flows for the year then ended in accordance with International Financial Reporting Standards.

Toronto, Canada   "Ernst & Young LLP"
February X, 2017   Chartered Professional Accountants
                                            Licensed Public Accountants

A member firm of Ernst & Young Global Limited

TABLE 13.1 **Types of qualified and unmodified audit reports**

NATURE OF MATTER THAT DOES NOT GIVE RISE TO A QUALIFICATION	UNMODIFIED REPORT	
Significant uncertainty—going concern	Emphasis of matter	
Significant uncertainty—litigation	Emphasis of matter	
Additional disclosures with which the auditor concurs	Emphasis of matter	
Early adoption of a new accounting standard with a significant impact on the financial statements	Emphasis of matter	
A major catastrophe that has had or continues to have an impact on the entity	Emphasis of matter	
Subsequent event resulting in a new auditor's report on revised financial statements	Emphasis of matter	
NATURE OF MATTER GIVING RISE TO THE QUALIFICATION	**AUDITOR'S JUDGEMENT ABOUT THE PERVASIVENESS OF THE EFFECTS OR POSSIBLE EFFECTS ON THE FINANCIAL REPORT**	
	MATERIAL BUT NOT PERVASIVE	**MATERIAL AND PERVASIVE[a]**
Financial statements are materially misstated	Qualified opinion	Adverse opinion
Inability to obtain sufficient appropriate audit evidence	Qualified opinion	Disclaimer of opinion

[a]Where the circumstances are so material and pervasive that the auditor has been unable to obtain sufficient appropriate audit evidence, or where a qualified opinion is inadequate to disclose the misleading or incomplete nature of the financial statements.

Cloud 9

Sharon prepares the draft audit report for the partner. The partner will discuss the audit report with Cloud 9's management at their meetings. If management refuses to amend the financial statements for the material misstatements found during the audit, the audit report may need to be revised and a qualified report may be issued. It is possible that a subsequent event could still occur that would require an emphasis of matter. However, there have been no scope limitations.

13.8.1 Provide an example of a common emphasis of matter included in audit reports.

13.8.2 Does the inclusion of an emphasis of matter in the audit report result in the report being qualified?

13.8.3 Describe one situation in which scope limitation may be appropriate in the audit report.

13.9 COMMUNICATION WITH THOSE CHARGED WITH GOVERNANCE

Communication with those charged with governance is covered in CAS 260 *Communication with Those Charged with Governance*, which requires that the auditor communicate audit matters of governance interest arising from the audit of the financial statements with those charged with governance. Communication with those charged with governance, with management, and with third parties, when applicable, is also covered in several other auditing standards. For example, if the auditor has identified a fraud, or has information that indicates the existence of a fraud, they are required to communicate these matters to an appropriate level of management by CAS 240 *The Auditor's Responsibilities Relating to Fraud in an Audit of Financial Statements*. Similarly, when the auditor has identified material non-compliance with laws and regulations, they are required to communicate their findings to those charged with governance in accordance with CAS 250 *Consideration of Laws and Regulations in an Audit of Financial Statements*.

"Governance" is the term used to describe the role of people entrusted with the supervision, control, and direction of an entity. Those charged with governance are accountable for ensuring that the entity achieves its objectives, with regard to reliability of financial reporting, effectiveness and efficiency of operations, compliance with applicable laws, and reporting to interested parties. Those charged with governance includes management only when it performs such functions.

"Audit matters of governance interest" are those that arise from the audit of the financial statements and, in the auditor's opinion, are both important and relevant to those charged with governance in overseeing the financial reporting and disclosure process. Audit matters of governance interest include only those matters that have come to the auditor's attention as a result of the performance of the audit. The auditor is not required to design audit procedures for the specific purpose of identifying matters of governance interest.

Figure 13.8 shows a sample letter to the board of directors where no significant issues were noted.

9 Explain what reporting is required to management and those charged with governance.

13.9.1 Audit matters of governance interest to be communicated

The auditor meets with management and those charged with governance to discuss the results of the audit. The matters that they discuss are those that arise from the audit and that, in the auditor's opinion, are both important and relevant to those charged with governance. As previously stated, the auditor is not required to design audit procedures for the specific purpose of identifying matters of governance interest.

Matters of governance interest that the auditor may wish to discuss with those charged with governance include:

- the general approach and overall scope of the audit, including any expected limitations thereon, or any additional requirements

- the selection of, or changes in, significant accounting policies and practices that have, or could have, a material effect on the entity's financial statements. (The auditor considers the appropriateness of the accounting policies to the particular circumstances of the entity. They judge these against the objectives of relevance, reliability, comparability, and understandability, but having regard for the need to balance the different objectives and the cost of providing information with the likely benefit to users of the entity's financial statements. They also discuss the appropriateness of accounting estimates and judgements—for example, in

To the Members of the Board of Directors,

The matters raised in this report arise from our financial statement audit and relate to matters that we believe need to be brought to your attention.

We have substantially completed our audit of Cloud 9 Ltd. financial statements in accordance with Canadian generally accepted auditing standards.

Our audit is performed to obtain reasonable assurance as to whether the financial statements are free of material misstatements. Absolute assurance is not possible due to the inherent limitations of an audit and of internal control, resulting in the unavoidable risk that some material misstatements may not be detected.

In planning our audit, we consider internal control over financial reporting to determine the nature, extent, and timing of audit procedures. However, a financial statement audit does not provide assurance on the effective operation of internal control at Cloud 9. However, if in the course of our audit, certain deficiencies in internal control come to our attention, these will be reported to you. Please refer to Appendix A1 to this letter.

Because fraud is deliberate, there are always risks that material misstatements, fraud, and other illegal acts may exist and not be detected by our audit of the financial statements.

The following is a summary of findings resulting from the performance of the audit:

1. We did not identify any material matters (other than the identified misstatements already discussed with you that have now been corrected) that need to be brought to your attention.
2. We received good co-operation from management and employees during our audit. To the best of our knowledge, we also had complete access to the accounting records and other documents that we needed to carry out our audit. We did not have any disagreements with management and we have resolved all auditing, accounting, and disclosure issues to our satisfaction.

Please note that Canadian auditing standards do not require us to design procedures for the purpose of identifying supplementary matters to communicate with those charged with governance. Accordingly, an audit would not usually identify all such matters.

This communication is prepared solely for the information of management and those charged with governance and is not intended for any other purpose. We accept no responsibility to a third party who uses this communication.

Yours truly,

W & S Partners

March 15, 20X6

FIGURE 13.8 Sample letter where no significant issues are noted

Source: PEM Audit Engagements Phase III- Reporting. *C·PEM*, Electronic Templates, Form 515, 2010–2011

relation to provisions, including the consistency of assumptions and degree of prudence reflected in the recorded amounts.)

- the potential effect on the financial statements of any material risks and exposures, such as pending litigation, that are required to be disclosed in the financial statements
- misstatements, whether or not recorded by the entity, that have or could have a material effect on the entity's financial statements
- material uncertainties related to events and conditions that may cast significant doubt on the entity's ability to continue as a going concern
- disagreements with management about matters that, individually or in aggregate, could be significant to the entity's financial statements or the audit report. (These communications include consideration of whether the matter has or has not been resolved and the significance of the matter.)

- expected modifications to the audit report. The auditor discusses any expected modifications to the audit report on the financial statements with those charged with governance to confirm that:
  - those charged with governance are aware of the proposed modification and the reasons for it before the report is finalized
  - there are no disputed facts with respect to the matter(s) giving rise to the proposed modification (or that matters of disagreement are confirmed as such)
  - those charged with governance have an opportunity, where appropriate, to provide further information and explanations with respect to the matter(s) giving rise to the proposed modification
- any practical difficulties encountered in performing the audit
- any irregularities or suspected non-compliance with laws and regulations that came to the auditor's attention during the audit
- comments on the design and operation of the internal controls and suggestions for their improvement, particularly if the auditor has identified material weaknesses in internal control during the audit. (This is sometimes separately communicated in a management letter, as discussed in chapter 7.)
- any other matters agreed upon in the terms of the audit engagement

The auditor also informs those charged with governance of those uncorrected misstatements aggregated by the auditor during the audit that were determined by management to be immaterial, both individually and in the aggregate, to the financial report taken as a whole.

13.9.2 Documentation considerations

The auditor retains a copy of the communication with those charged with governance in their working papers, together with details of any responses from management and/or those charged with governance and their intended action(s). If the communication takes the form of a presentation at a meeting or meetings, the auditor files a copy of the presentation material and also gives a copy of the material to management to prevent disputes at a later date. Depending on the nature, sensitivity, and significance of the matters communicated, the auditor may decide to confirm oral communications in writing.

As soon as practicable, the auditor should communicate deficiencies in internal controls to management or those charged with governance. The reporting of internal control deficiencies should always be documented; the most common form is a letter (as discussed in chapter 7). However, depending on the circumstances, documentation in the form of a file note (minutes of meetings) may be appropriate as evidence of the discussion held on internal control deficiencies.

Cloud 9

Sharon also prepares a draft letter to be used for communication with those charged with governance at Cloud 9. The letter is incomplete but will be finalized after the completion of subsequent events procedures and the final meetings between the partner and Cloud 9's management.

BEFORE YOU GO ON

13.9.1 Name five items of governance interest that would be communicated to those charged with governance.

13.9.2 Is communication with those charged with governance always in the form of a letter?

13.9.3 If communication is not always in the form of a letter, what other forms of communication could the auditor use?

13.10 APPENDIX 13—OTHER ENGAGEMENTS

10 Understand the various types of other engagements that auditors may be asked to perform.

An auditor in public practice primarily performs audit, review, and compilation engagements of financial information as well as a variety of tax engagements. However, clients may have other information needs. They may ask the auditor to prepare or to provide an opinion on information other than general purpose financial statement information. This information may be financial or non-financial information. Depending on the type of engagement, a particular Canadian Auditing Standard (CAS) or Canadian Standard on Assurance Engagements (CSAE) may apply. However, in all cases, the auditor should obtain an engagement letter to clearly identify the terms of the engagement as well as the form and content of the report. This is to ensure both the auditor and the client understand the purpose of the engagement and the specific reporting requirements.

We will now briefly discuss some of the common special engagements an auditor may be asked to perform.

13.10.1 Reports prepared in accordance with a special purpose framework

An auditor may be asked to provide assurance on financial information prepared on a basis of accounting other than GAAP, or in accordance with a special purpose framework. Examples of these types of reports include financial statements prepared in the following situations: in accordance with the terms of a contract, in accordance with the requirements of a regulation, or in applying a tax basis of accounting. If an audit level of assurance is required, then the engagement should be performed in accordance with CAS 800 *Special Considerations—Audits of Financial Statements Prepared in Accordance with Special Purpose Frameworks*. If a review engagement is performed, then the auditor must ensure compliance with the standards of CSAE 8500 —*Reviews of Financial Information Other than Financial Statements*.

When accepting this type of engagement, the auditor must understand the nature of the agreement or contract, and the form and content of the assurance report. As this type of report is usually issued for a specific user with a specific purpose, these are not general purpose financial statements. As a result, the report often includes a restriction on distribution. The report should also specifically indicate the basis of accounting used.

13.10.2 Reports on a component of the financial statements

A report on a component of the financial statements is a report issued on a single financial statement line item. This is appropriate when a user wants some assurance over a particular financial statement account such as sales, accounts receivable, or inventory to meet a particular financial reporting need. For example, auditors are sometimes asked to prepare a report on gross sales. This is common in the retail industry because landlords often include a percentage rent clause in a tenant's lease agreement. This means that a portion of the rent may be based on the retailer's gross sales. To get some assurance that the sales are not materially misstated, the landlord may request an audit or a review of this information.

An audit report of this nature falls under CAS 805 —*Audits of Single Financial Statements and Specific Elements, Accounts or Items of a Financial Statement*, while a review engagement would again fall under the requirements of CSAE 8500 —*Reviews of Financial Information Other than Financial Statements*. When performing this type of engagement, the auditor must consider the related financial statement items that may have a material impact on the specific account being reported on. For example, if the auditor is reporting on sales, then the accounts receivable and allowance for doubtful accounts should be considered. Again, the report issued should indicate the basis of accounting.

13.10.3 Reports on compliance with contractual agreements

This type of report may be requested when a specific user is looking for assurance on compliance with specific requirements of a contractual agreement, such as covenants, dividend restrictions, or sinking fund provisions. If an audit report is required, it would fall under CSAE 5815—*Audit Reports on Compliance with Agreements, Statutes and Regulations*, while a review engagement would fall under CSAE 8600—*Reviews in Compliance with Agreements and Regulations*. The auditor must ensure they have the professional competence to perform such an engagement. The report should indicate that the entity has complied with the provisions of the agreement.

13.10.4 Review engagements on interim financial statements

All publicly reportable entities are required to file quarterly financial statements with the appropriate regulator. For entities listed on a Canadian stock exchange, a review of the interim financial information is not required, whereas for entities listed on a stock exchange in the United States, it is required. Even though an interim review is not required for Canadian-listed companies, some may elect to have their interim financial statements reviewed. If this is the case, the engagement falls under the requirements of CSAE 7050 —*Auditor Review of Interim Financial Statements*. The purpose of this engagement is to provide moderate assurance that the interim financial statements are prepared using the same basis of accounting as the annual financial statements.

13.10.5 Reports on applying specified procedures to financial information other than financial statements

This report is issued when the auditor has performed agreed-upon procedures relating to the entity's financial information other than the financial statements. The auditor performs specific procedures requested by the client over specific financial information and then reports the factual results of these procedures. As a result, no assurance is provided. For example, a government agency may provide expense reimbursement to a housing agency to subsidize low-income families. The government may want to ensure the organization is recording the expenditures accurately, and ask an auditor to agree invoice amounts to the amounts recorded in the general ledger. The auditor then issues a report on the results of applying these specified procedures stating the number of invoices reviewed and how many were recorded correctly. This type of engagement is covered by CSAE 9100—*Reports on the Results of Applying Specified Audit Procedures to Financial Information Other Than Financial Statements*.

13.10.6 Reports on agreed-upon procedures regarding internal control over financial reporting

This report is issued when the auditor has performed agreed-upon procedures relating to the entity's financial reporting process. The auditor performs specific procedures requested by the client and then reports the factual results of the specific controls tested. For example, the client may request a report on whether internal controls exist over posting journal entries. The auditor would do that by attempting to post unauthorized journal entries and then reporting the factual results of this test. As a result, the auditor does not provide any assurance over the adequacy or effectiveness of internal controls over financial reporting. Also, this report only relates to the results on the specific controls considered and it does not encompass or report on all of the controls over the financial reporting process. This falls under CSAE 9110—*Agreed-Upon Procedures Regarding Internal Control over Financial Reporting*.

13.10.7 Compilation of a forecast or a projection

Management may ask the auditor to prepare a forecast or a projection. A forecast is generally prepared for a one-year time frame, while a projection is usually prepared for more than one year. The auditor prepares this information based on the assumptions provided by management. The engagement generally requires calculating and assembling the information; therefore, no assurance is provided. Guidance over this type of engagement is provided in AuG-16—*Compilation of a Financial Forecast or Projection*.

13.10.8 Reports on the application of accounting principles

This report is covered under CSAE 7600—*Reports on the Application of Accounting Principles*. This refers to a report on the application of accounting principles to either a specific transaction or to the financial statements overall. It only applies to actual transactions and it does not relate to hypothetical transactions. The auditor should understand the form and substance of the transaction, ensure it is in accordance with GAAP, and if needed consult with other professionals, specifically the incumbent accountant. All relevant facts, circumstances, and assumptions should be obtained in writing.

BEFORE YOU GO ON

13.10.1 Provide three examples of when an auditor may issue an audit report on a special purpose framework.

13.10.2 What is a report on a component of the financial statements?

13.10.3 Does the auditor provide any assurance when he or she performs agreed-upon procedures relating to the entity's financial information other than the financial statements?

SUMMARY

❶ Explain the procedures performed as part of the engagement wrap-up, including gathering and evaluating audit evidence.

During the engagement wrap-up, the auditor reviews planned audit procedures to ensure they are completed, finalizes any open items (including review notes and to-do items), ensures that all necessary documentation is in the working paper files and removes any unnecessary documentation, reconsiders their risk assessment and fraud risk, reconsiders materiality, performs analytical procedures, assesses misstatements, and performs subsequent events procedures.

❷ Understand the considerations when assessing the going concern assumption used in the preparation of the financial statements.

The auditor is required to consider whether the going concern assumption is the correct basis upon which the financial statements have been prepared. That is, is the entity viewed by the auditor, management, and those charged with governance as continuing into the foreseeable future with neither the intention nor the need to liquidate, to cease trading, or to seek protection from creditors?

❸ Understand the purpose of and the procedures performed in the review for contingent liabilities and commitments.

It is the auditor's responsibility to perform procedures to verify that there are no unrecorded or undisclosed lawsuits or claims that could result in the financial statements being materially mistated.

❹ Compare the two types of (material) subsequent events to determine what effect they have on the financial statements (if any).

There are two types of subsequent events. Type 1 subsequent events are those that provide additional evidence with respect to conditions that existed at year end. These are required to be adjusted for in the financial statements. Type 2 subsequent events are those that provide evidence with respect to conditions that developed subsequent to year end; these are not required to be recorded in the

financial statements, but are considered for inclusion as a disclosure note.

❺ Analyze misstatements and explain the difference between quantitative and qualitative considerations when evaluating misstatements.

Quantitative and qualitative considerations of misstatements include the risk of undetected errors remaining, the effect of the misstatements on compliance with covenants or agreements, whether the misstatements are errors or judgemental misstatements, whether any prior-period unadjusted misstatements exist and could affect the current period's results, the likelihood that these differences will become material in the future, the sensitivity of the misstatements, the significance of the misstatements for the known users of the financial statements, the effect of offsetting differences in financial statement captions, and the dollar amount (quantity) of the misstatements.

❻ Evaluate conclusions obtained during the performance of the audit and explain how these conclusions link to the overall opinion formed on the financial statements.

The final phase of the audit is to assess all of the audit evidence obtained and determine whether it is sufficient and appropriate to reduce the risk of material misstatement in the financial statements to an acceptably low level. Based on the evidence gathered, the audit opinion on the financial statements will be determined.

❼ Describe the components of an audit report.

The audit report includes a title, addressee, introductory paragraph, management's and the auditor's responsibility for the financial statements, audit opinion, other matters including other reporting responsibilities, auditor's signature, date of the report, and auditor's address.

❽ Identify the types of modifications to an audit report.

The overall conclusion reached at the end of the audit can be unmodified, unmodified with an emphasis of matter, modified with a qualification, modified with an adverse opinion, or modified with a disclaimer of opinion.

9 **Explain what reporting is required to management and those charged with governance.**

All audit matters of governance interest—that is, items that are important and relevant to those charged with governance in overseeing the financial reporting and disclosure process—should be reported to management and those charged with governance by the auditor. This is a required communication that can be provided verbally or in writing, with written communications (or evidence of such communications) preferred.

10 **Understand the various types of other engagements that auditors may be asked to perform.**

An auditor may be asked to perform engagements other than those involving financial information and tax engagements. These other engagements include reports prepared in accordance with a special purpose framework or a basis of accounting other than GAAP; reports on a single financial statement line item, such as inventory or gross sales; reports on compliance with contractual agreements, such as covenants; reviews of interim financial statements, such as for companies listed on a stock exchange in the United States; reports on applying specified procedures to financial information other than financial statements, such as reports on the accuracy of expenditures: reports on agreed-upon procedures regarding internal control over financial reporting, such as controls over posting journal entries; a compilation of a forecast or projection, generally for a one-year time frame; and reports on the application of accounting principles to either a specific, actual transaction or to the financial statements overall.

KEY TERMS

Error, 479
Going concern, 473
Judgemental misstatement, 479

Materiality, 470
Misstatement, 479
Professional judgement, 471

Subsequent events, 475
Sufficient appropriate evidence, 471
Those charged with governance, 474

MULTIPLE-CHOICE QUESTIONS

13.1 **At the conclusion of the audit, the wrap-up process involves:**
(a) review of proper and complete execution of planned audit procedures.
(b) determination that all necessary matters have been appropriately considered.
(c) revisiting open review notes, to-do items, and open audit procedures.
(d) all of the above.

13.2 **If an auditor finds any misstatements or deviations in planned procedures:**
(a) the auditor should consider the reason for the misstatement or deviation.
(b) the auditor should not revise the risk assessment.
(c) the auditor should not alter any planned procedures.
(d) the auditor does not have to consider the need to perform further audit procedures.

13.3 **The going concern assumption means:**
(a) the entity is facing difficulties continuing as a going concern.
(b) the entity is viewed as continuing in business for the foreseeable future with no need for liquidation.
(c) assets and liabilities are stated at liquidation values.

(d) the auditor is concerned about whether the entity is going to change locations.

13.4 **Subsequent events are:**
(a) events subsequent to the start of the financial year.
(b) events subsequent to the appointment of the auditor.
(c) events subsequent to the end of the financial year.
(d) events subsequent to the going concern assumption.

13.5 **The following is a valid type of subsequent event:**
(a) an event that provides additional evidence with respect to conditions that existed at year end.
(b) an event that occurred after the start of the year but before the end of the year.
(c) legal action that was settled in the last month of the financial year.
(d) all of the above.

13.6 **If an auditor becomes aware after the date of the auditor's report but before the financial statements are issued of a fact that may materially affect the financial statements, the auditor should:**
(a) consider whether the financial statements need changing.
(b) discuss the matter with management.
(c) take the action appropriate in the circumstances.
(d) all of the above.

13.7 The following is an example of an event that provides evidence with respect to conditions that developed subsequent to year end:

(a) bankruptcy of a customer subsequent to year end, which would be considered when evaluating the adequacy of the allowance for uncollectable accounts.

(b) loss of plant as a result of fire or flood after year end.

(c) deterioration in financial results after year end, which may indicate doubt about the going concern assumption in the preparation of the financial statements.

(d) an amount received with respect to an insurance claim that was in the course of negotiation at year end.

13.8 Management's responsibility for the financial statements includes:

(a) selecting internal controls tests.

(b) selecting samples for audit testing.

(c) selecting and applying appropriate accounting policies.

(d) selecting experts to assist with testing asset valuations.

13.9 Emphasis of matter is used without an accompanying qualification of the audit report when:

(a) a significant uncertainty exists that should be brought to the reader's attention.

(b) an extreme limitation of the scope of the engagement exists.

(c) there is a disagreement with those charged with governance regarding the selection of accounting policies.

(d) all of the above.

13.10 Communication with those charged with governance:

(a) means that the auditor should write to the board of directors about any matters of governance interest arising from the audit of the financial statements.

(b) is done at the start of the audit.

(c) is done through the audit report.

(d) requires the auditor to write to the CEO at the conclusion of the audit.

REVIEW QUESTIONS

13.1 List and describe the engagement wrap-up process. Why is it important?

13.2 What is the accounting assumption of "going concern"? Why is it of interest to auditors?

13.3 What procedures must the auditor perform to search for contingent liabilities?

13.4 Explain the difference between the two types of subsequent events. Discuss the auditor's responsibility for detecting subsequent events (a) prior to the completion of field work, (b) prior to signing the audit report, and (c) between the date of the audit report and the issuance of the financial statements.

13.5 What options does an auditor have when material errors are found? Do these options vary for current-year misstatements and prior-year misstatements?

13.6 Why do audit reports contain paragraphs outlining (a) management's responsibility for the financial statements and (b) the auditor's responsibility for the financial statements? What is contained in these paragraphs?

13.7 What is "modified wording" in an audit report? What are the different types of modified wording and when are they used?

13.8 Explain the difference between limitation of scope and disagreement with those charged with governance.

13.9 CAS 260 stresses the importance of communication with "those charged with governance." Who are these people and why is it important that the auditor communicate with them (and not others)?

13.10 What matters does an auditor communicate at the end of an audit to those charged with governance? Why are these matters important?

PROFESSIONAL APPLICATION QUESTIONS

Basic ★	Moderate ★★	Challenging ★★★

13.1 Audit wrap-up ★

Lucy Huang has just finished her first audit assignment. She is now assisting her audit manager, Tom Lucas, in wrapping up the engagement. He has asked Lucy to make a list of all uncleared review notes, to-do items, and audit procedures, and to note for each whether the matter requires more attention, has been resolved (but is not yet noted on file), or is no longer relevant because of other events.

Tom has also asked Lucy to go through the files and remove all unnecessary documentation, drafts, and review notes. Lucy is very nervous about this task because she believes her inexperience will mean that she will not be able to distinguish "unnecessary" from "necessary." She has heard that in a famous case in the United States an audit firm was prosecuted because it shredded files that should have been kept.

Required

(a) What additional attention would open matters require?

(b) Explain why documents in a client's audit files would be "unnecessary." Give examples.

13.2 Going concern ★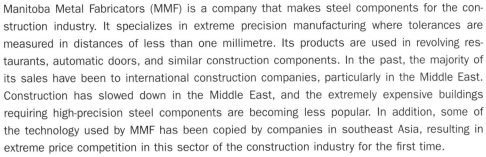

Phil Nanere is the partner in charge of the audit for a new client, Western Wonderland (WW). The client engaged Phil's audit firm in November 2015, in preparation for the 2016 audit. From January 30, 2016, onwards, WW has consistently paid its suppliers late, well in excess of the suppliers' agreed credit terms. This has resulted in some suppliers demanding cash on delivery from WW. Phil is also aware from his review of correspondence between WW and its bank that the company has been experiencing cash flow problems since 2014.

Required

Identify any significant events or conditions that individually or collectively may cast significant doubt on WW's ability to continue as a going concern.

Source: Adapted from the Institute of Chartered Accountants Australia's CA Program's Audit and Assurance exam, December 2010. Provided courtesy of Chartered Accountants Australia and New Zealand.

13.3 Assessing going concern ★ ★

Manitoba Metal Fabricators (MMF) is a company that makes steel components for the construction industry. It specializes in extreme precision manufacturing where tolerances are measured in distances of less than one millimetre. Its products are used in revolving restaurants, automatic doors, and similar construction components. In the past, the majority of its sales have been to international construction companies, particularly in the Middle East. Construction has slowed down in the Middle East, and the extremely expensive buildings requiring high-precision steel components are becoming less popular. In addition, some of the technology used by MMF has been copied by companies in southeast Asia, resulting in extreme price competition in this sector of the construction industry for the first time.

MMF is highly leveraged. Two years ago the company borrowed a large sum of money to fund the purchase of new premises and the latest laser cutting equipment. The loan is due for renewal three months after year end. One week before the audit report is to be signed, the bank has still not agreed to renew the loan and MMF's management has begun negotiations with another bank.

Required

(a) Identify the factors that would raise questions about the going concern assumption for MMF. Are there any mitigating factors?

(b) What reporting options are available to the auditor of MMF? Discuss. Refer to CAS 570 in your answer.

13.4 Subsequent events procedures ★ ★

Mitch Ziegel and Rosie Punter are discussing the audit plan for a large manufacturing company. The company has two main manufacturing plants plus several warehouse and distribution centres (one in each province). The company has a large investment in trade receivables and there are additional concerns this year about whether the tough economic conditions have affected the collectability of the trade receivables. The agenda for the board of directors' monthly meeting includes an item to discuss the effect of the economic crisis on customers. The board is also negotiating a takeover with a competing company. The discussions have been ongoing for some time and one month before year end the board of the other company indicated it would like more progress to be made on this deal. Another matter concerning senior management at the manufacturing company is a threatened labour dispute by the largest union representing workers at the distribution centres. A number of safety issues have been identified for the company, explaining the union's demands for better working conditions and a pay increase. The company management is disputing most of the safety concerns.

Mitch and Rosie are reviewing the draft plan to ensure that adequate procedures are included to meet their obligations for detecting subsequent events during the period from year end to the date of signing the audit report. Mitch is the engagement partner on the audit and Rosie is an audit manager. Rosie admits to Mitch that she has always had trouble distinguishing the two types of subsequent events in IAS 10 and therefore has some trouble applying CAS 560. She also admits to Mitch that she has never been involved in an audit where there was a subsequent event arising after the date of the audit report, so she doesn't know what the auditor is supposed to do in these circumstances.

Required

(a) Explain the difference between the two types of subsequent events. Give an example of each and explain the type of adjustment (if any) to the financial statements that would be required.

(b) List some audit procedures that should be in the audit plan for this company for the detection of subsequent events occurring prior to the date of the audit report.

(c) Explain the auditor's responsibilities for subsequent events that arise after the date of the audit report (after the date the financial statements are issued). What is the difference in the auditor's responsibilities between these events and those arising before the date of the audit report?

13.5 Reporting subsequent events ★ ★

Brad Gokool is reviewing the results of the subsequent events audit procedures. Brad is writing a report for his audit partner based on these results and will be attending a meeting tomorrow with the partner and representatives of the company to discuss them. The issue will be whether the financial statements should be amended or additional notes should be included for these subsequent events.

Many of the items are not material and Brad will recommend that no action be taken with respect to these. However, there are several items that Brad believes are material and should be discussed at the meeting. These are:

· The board is planning to issue shares in a private placement on August 15.

· The share issue is to fund the purchase of a 60-percent stake in another company. The negotiations are in the final stages and although the contract is not yet signed, it will be signed by August 15.

· A statement of claim was lodged in court in the week after year end claiming damages for illness allegedly caused by chemicals used at a subsidiary company's manufacturing plant in the 1990s. This is the tenth such claim lodged and the client has denied responsibility in all cases because it was unreasonable to believe at that time that these chemicals had adverse health effects. The claimant has new scientific evidence that counters this defence.

· The review of subsequent cash receipts has revealed that several of the accounts receivable that were considered doubtful have now been paid. However, the audit procedures have shown that a large customer with a significant receivable balance considered safe on June 30 unexpectedly declared bankruptcy on July 20.

· The year end for the company is June 30 and the audit report is due to be signed on August 20.

Required

For each item above:

(a) What type of subsequent event is it?

(b) What is the appropriate treatment in the financial statements?

13.6 Events after balance date ★

Martin Rorke is reviewing the results of the review of subsequent cash receipts. There are several receipts listed from customers that were considered doubtful at the end of the year (June 30). Martin is also reviewing evidence that shows that another customer that had a large balance at year end was unexpectedly declared bankrupt on July 10.

Required

How should this information be reflected in the financial report?

13.7 Disclosure of subsequent events ★ ★ ★

In connection with your examination of the financial statements of Martinson Inc. for the year ended December 31, your post-balance sheet date audit procedures disclosed the following items:

1. January 5: The funds for a $50,000 loan to the corporation made by Mr. Martinson on May 18 were obtained by him with a loan on his personal life insurance policy. The loan was recorded in the account Loan Payable to Officers. The source of the funds obtained by Mr. Martinson was not disclosed in the company records.

2. January 9: The mineral content of a shipment of ore en route on December 31 was determined to be 80 percent. The shipment was recorded at year end at an estimated content of 50 percent by a debit to Raw Material Inventory and a credit to Accounts Payable in the amount of $41,200. The final liability to the vendor is based on the actual mineral content of the shipment.

3. January 31: As a result of reduced sales, production was curtailed in mid-January and some workers were laid off. On February 5, all the remaining workers went on strike. To date, the strike is unsettled.

4. February 20: A contract was signed whereby Whitworth Enterprises purchased from Martinson Inc. all of its capital assets, inventories, and the right to conduct business under the name "Martinson Inc. Division." The transfer's effective date will be March 1. The sale price was $800,000.

Required

Assume that the above items came to your attention prior to completion of your audit work on February 28. For each of the above items, discuss the disclosure that you would recommend for the item.

13.8 Approaches to reporting contingent liabilities ★ ★

Hatami and Partners completed the field work for the December 31, 2016, audit of Harbinger Corporation on March 1, 2017. The financial statements and auditor's report were issued and mailed to shareholders on March 15, 2017.

Required

In each of the two situations below, select from the list of possible actions the choices that would be appropriate for an auditor to make under those circumstances. Assume both situations are material.

Situations

1. On January 5, 2017, a lawsuit was filed against Harbinger for a copyright infringement action that allegedly took place in early 2016. In the opinion of Harbinger's lawyers, there is a reasonable (but not probable) danger of a significant loss to Harbinger.

2. On February 15, 2017, Harbinger settled a lawsuit out of court that had originated in 2016 and is currently listed as a contingent liability.

Possible Actions

(a) Adjust the December 31, 2016, financial statements.

(b) Disclose the information in a footnote in the December 31, 2016, financial statements.

(c) Request that the client revise and reissue the December 31, 2016, financial statements. The revision should involve an adjustment to the December 31, 2016, financial statements.

(d) Request that the client revise and reissue the December 31, 2016, financial statements. The revision should involve the addition of a footnote, but no adjustment, to the December 31, 2016, financial statements.

(e) No action is required.

13.9 Emphasis of matter paragraph ★

Springsteen Ltd. is a new audit client for the 2016 financial year. Springsteen's financial report for the 2015 year, the last with the previous auditor, was prepared on the assumption of a going concern. An unmodified audit opinion with an emphasis of matter paragraph was included in the auditor's report because of a going concern issue. The issue identified by the auditor was that Springsteen was due to refinance a material amount of debt shortly after the prior year end. You are aware that Eastcoast Bank appeared unwilling to extend further financing, and Springsteen had taken no steps to secure other financing. Springsteen did not disclose any information about the debt refinancing matter in its financial report.

Required

Was the opinion in the auditor's report appropriate? Explain.

Source: Adapted from the Institute of Chartered Accountants Australia's CA Program's *Audit and Assurance Exam*, May 2010. Provided courtesy of Chartered Accountants Australia and New Zealand.

13.10 Audit documentation for going concern ★

It is August 2016 and the first audit for Springsteen Ltd. with your audit firm (refer to question 13.9) for the 2015–16 year is almost complete. Prior to reaching your final conclusions, you are reviewing the working papers for the year ended June 30, 2016. The material bank loan with Eastcoast Bank was extended in September 2015 for another 12 months.

Required

Given the history of the bank loan, outline two types of documentation you would expect to see included in the audit file to provide audit evidence that this year's financial report can be prepared on a going concern basis.

Source: Adapted from the Institute of Chartered Accountants Australia's CA Program's *Audit and Assurance Exam*, May 2010. Provided courtesy of Chartered Accountants Australia and New Zealand.

13.11 Misstatements and the audit report ★ ★ ★

Katrina Lukacs is the engagement partner of the audit of Champion Securities, an investment company. Most of Champion's assets and liabilities are financial and their valuation is critical to the assessment of the company's solvency and profitability. Katrina has employed two outside experts to value the financial assets and liabilities because they are extremely complex to value, particularly the energy market derivatives and the instruments traded in foreign markets. In addition, the valuations are highly dependent on market conditions and the specific and detailed requirements of the recently revised accounting standards.

Throughout this year's audit, Katrina has had difficulties with the CEO of Champion Securities. He is vehemently opposed to any asset writedowns she has suggested. The CEO has the backing of the chair of the board and Katrina has been unable to get the CEO to listen to her concerns about the valuations of the financial assets and liabilities the company has made. In past years, Katrina has had an amicable relationship with both the CEO and the chair and the audits have run very smoothly. Katrina has now realized that this harmonious relationship was mainly due to the boom in the market. It was unlikely that there would be arguments about writing up the value of the company's assets during these good times.

Katrina, with the help of the experts, has prepared a summary of the relevant items, detailing the revised values for the assets and liabilities and the associated effects on income and retained earnings. The CEO has dismissed this summary and the audit recommendations with the comment, "The market has hit the bottom and is recovering. There is no need to show these writedowns because by the time the financial statements are published the values will be back to where they were before the market fell. It is all a waste of time. In fact, I think you are just being difficult to deal with. I think we need an auditor who is a bit more realistic."

Required

(a) Discuss the ethical issues Katrina faces and explain what she needs to do to comply with the code of professional conduct independence requirements.

(b) Explain Katrina's audit report options.

(c) Recommend a course of action for Katrina.

13.12 Misstatements and the audit report ★ ★ ★

The staff at Nguyen and Partners have completed the necessary audit work for Manitoba Metal Fabricators. The partner responsible for the audit is now reviewing the audit file. She has come across the Schedule of Unadjusted Differences and is considering the type of audit report to issue. Referring to figure 13.2, answer the following:

Required

(a) If overall materiality for the engagment were set at $50,000, what type of audit report would be issued? Why?

(b) If overall materiality for the engagment were set at $100,000, what type of audit report would be issued? Why?

(c) Why does the current year Schedule of Unadjusted Differences include entries from the prior year? Explain the impact these entries have on the current year financial statement balances.

13.13 Audit reports and other communication at the end of an audit ★ ★

Steven Erasmus has had difficulties throughout the audit of Kingston Catering. The company is a long-standing client of the audit firm and there have been no problems in the past. However, four months into the start of the financial year the company's computer systems failed. Subsequent diagnostic tests revealed that a particularly nasty virus had infected the computer system and corrupted all the processed data. The IT manager called in an IT specialist for advice as soon as the problem was discovered. The specialist installed a new computer system and additional security programs and the IT manager is confident that the problem will not recur.

The processed data had been backed up and stored in a secure location, but when a restoration was attempted it was discovered that the virus had also corrupted the backups. The Kingston Catering staff tried to reconstruct the computer files based on paper records, but the reconstruction was incomplete because some paper documents had been inadvertently destroyed.

Steven is particularly concerned about sales and trade receivables. Kingston Catering has many "one-time" customers as well as several large accounts. The first four months of the year corresponded with the busiest time of the year for the company. Staff attended many corporate and private functions during this time and made numerous sales of catering equipment to wholesale and retail customers. Or at least they think they did, and they believe that they collected all the accounts. Steven is not so sure. He thinks the chaos caused by the computer virus meant that deliveries were being made in a rush without the completion of the appropriate paperwork and the attempts to collect accounts were ineffectual as customers took advantage of the situation to claim that they had either already paid or had returned goods for credit. Other customers simply "fell off" the system and were never billed.

Required

(a) Discuss Steven's audit report options and recommend the appropriate wording for the audit report.

(b) What matters would Steven include in the letter to those charged with governance at Kingston Catering?

Questions 13.14 and 13.15 are based on the following case.

Fabrication Holdings Ltd. (FH) has been a client of KFP Partners for many years. You are an audit senior and have been assigned to the FH audit for the first time for the financial year end, December 31, 2016.

FH's financial statements for the year ended December 31, 2016, show land and buildings at fair value of $20.8 million. As part of your subsequent events procedures, you become aware that FH sold the property in January 2017 when an independent third party made an unexpected offer of $24.5 million. The difference between the sale price and the amount stated in the financial statements (which has not been adjusted) is material. You have not yet signed the audit report.

Source: Adapted from the Institute of Chartered Accountants Australia's CA Program's *Audit and Assurance exam,* May 2008. Provided courtesy of Chartered Accountants Australia and New Zealand.

13.14 Subsequent events ★ ★   ❸

Required

Analyze the events surrounding the sale of FH's land and buildings. Is it a subsequent event? If so, which type?

13.15 Audit reports and subsequent events ★ ★   ❼

Required

Based on your answer to question 13.14, explain what type of audit opinion you would issue. Why?

Questions 13.16 and 13.17 are based on the following case.

Fellowes and Associates Chartered Accountants is a successful mid-tier accounting firm with a large range of clients across Canada. In 2016, Fellowes and Associates gained a new client, Health Care Holdings Group (HCHG), which owns 100 percent of the following entities:
- Shady Oaks Centre, a private treatment centre
- Gardens Nursing Home Ltd., a private nursing home
- Total Laser Care Limited (TLCL), a private clinic that specializes in the laser treatment of skin defects

Year end for all HCHG entities is June 30.

You are the audit partner reviewing the audit work papers for HCHG for the year ended June 30, 2016. Today is July 13, 2016, and the audit report is due to be signed in three weeks' time.

During your review you note that the fixed-term borrowings of HCHG totalling $75 million are approaching maturity and HCHG does not seem to have renegotiated any terms of refinancing. You are aware, from your experience with other clients, that banks are reluctant to extend financing on the same terms in the current market. The financing of HCHG was historically managed by the group's treasurer, who left the group six months ago and has not been replaced.

HCHG's financial controller, who has been with the group for nine months, has advised you that he has been busy renegotiating with some of HCHG's key suppliers who recently requested cash on delivery for all orders, rather than extending the normal credit terms.

You are also aware that a fire that occurred in the Shady Oaks cafeteria last week was not adequately covered by insurance. Fortunately, no one was seriously injured in the fire, but the cafeteria was so badly damaged that it had to be closed. When you are discussing this matter with HCHG's law firm, they reveal that the centre is unlikely to have adequate professional indemnity insurance to meet the current demands of several malpractice cases that have been brought against it in the last 12 months.

Source: Adapted from the Institute of Chartered Accountants Australia's CA Program's *Audit and Assurance Exam*, December 2008 and March 2009. Provided courtesy of Chartered Accountants Australia and New Zealand.

13.16 Final review issues—subsequent events ★ ★

Required

(a) Explain your responsibilities with respect to the Shady Oaks cafeteria fire.

(b) How will this event be handled in the HCHG financial statements and the audit report?

13.17 Final review issues—going concern and reporting ★ ★ ★

Required

(a) Are there any going concern issues for HCHG? Explain. If so, what are the mitigating circumstances?

(b) How will you recommend that the issues be handled in the financial statements and the audit report?

13.18 Types of audit reports and modifications ★

Required

For each of the following situations, indicate what type of modification/audit report is most appropriate.

(a) There is a scope limitation and it is material. However, the overall financial statements are still presented fairly.

(b) There is a departure from GAAP and it is pervasively material.

(c) The auditor lacks independence in fact, but not necessarily in appearance.

(d) The uncorrected misstatements are immaterial.

13.19 Assurance report over gross sales ★

Beautiful Shoes Inc. is a high-end ladies shoe store. It has recently expanded its operations and signed a long-term lease in a popular shopping centre. The owner, Beverly Hung, is concerned because the lease agreement requires that she submit to the landlord a percentage of her gross sales at the end of the calendar year. The lease indicates she must also provide a report on the gross sales. This report should have an assurance report attached. Beverly has no idea what this means or how she will come up with such a report. She has asked you, her CPA, to explain what may be required.

Required

Explain to Beverly what is needed to satisfy the requirements of the new lease agreement.

13.20 Special engagement reporting ★ ★

You, a recently designated CPA, have agreed to serve on a committee that is organizing a sports adventure race as a fundraiser for Far West Camp, a camp for teenagers from all economic backgrounds. Far West Camp has obtained support from two sponsors that have specified criteria that must be met before they will contribute. They have also asked for an independent opinion that their criteria have been fulfilled. The following is a list of the sponsors and their stated criteria.

Sponsor	Contribution Criteria
Sports Wear Unlimited to provide $10 per participant	Confirmation of the number of participants
Department of Tourism to provide a grant for publicity	Independent confirmation that the funds are spent on eligible activities, and that there is no direct benefit to individuals involved in organizing the race or operating the camp. Final approval for the grant is expected in the next couple of weeks.

The chair of the committee has asked you to explain to the committee what it can do to satisfy the sponsor's requests.

Required

Explain to the committee chair the various report options for both sponsors.

Source: Adapted from 2008 UFE, Day 3, Problem 3.

CASES

13.21 Integrative Case Study—Ball Construction Corporation ★ ★ ★

You are the audit senior of Ball Construction Corporation (BC), a small public company that enters into construction contracts with individuals and developers and builds to their specifications. BC is a Canadian company, but recently opened a branch in the southwestern United States.

It is September and the audit fieldwork for this year's audit engagement has just been completed. You are in the process of finalizing the audit file. The following is documented in the audit file:

Risk Assessment

Although BC's audit is recurring and we are familiar with its operations and systems, we determined that the audit risk for this year has increased from medium to high. There are three main reasons for the change:

- Recent declines and instability in the U.S. housing market have created a high credit-risk situation.
- BC's controller left in March 2016, and the position had not been filled by year end.
- The bank increased the interest rate on the company's operating line during the year, suggesting that it views BC as a higher risk than before.

Audit Approach

No information systems issues were noted in prior years. While we identified isolated control weaknesses in this year's review of the systems, overall the controls appear reliable. We will use a combined approach, and, because of the increased risk, we will increase the amount of substantive work.

Materiality

Planning materiality was set at $242,000.

1. Internal control
   (a) When the controller left, the finance department staff took on additional duties. We noted that during the latter part of the year, the same individual was creating purchase orders, entering invoices into the system, and preparing the cheque runs. The CFO said the situation was unavoidable, and noted that the accounting manager reviewed the cheque runs and prepared the bank reconciliations.
   (b) We noted that many journal entries had not been approved. The CFO said that he trained most of the employees responsible for the entries, so he knows what the entries are for. He also said, "Our management review of reports and financial statements would uncover any incorrect entries."
   (c) The CFO relies on senior management to review, approve, and sign reports generated by the finance department, such as the costing report by project. Testing of a sample of reports indicated that most reports had been appropriately approved. However, some reports were found on a construction manager's desk. When asked about them, she explained, "I'm so busy managing the jobs that I have that I haven't had time yet to look them over." The signed reports were given to the audit team the next day and the audit testing was completed.

2. Accounts receivable and allowance for doubtful accounts

We sent confirmations to a sample of accounts receivable and noted the following issues based on the responses received:

- One confirmation was returned stating that a receivable balance, related to a $1,542,000 contract, was overstated based on the progress report. Upon examination of the relevant report, we noted that a transposition error had occurred (86 percent completion was used when it should have been 68 percent). This represents a known error of $277,560. The CFO agreed that it was an error, but was satisfied that this was an isolated issue and would normally have been caught by the supervisor's review. The CFO does not want to adjust for this error.

- The CFO was quite adamant that no adjustments be made to the financial statements, declaring that "the statements fairly and accurately represent the financial situation of BC."

Required

(a) What type of audit report should be prepared, assuming the CFO does not change his position? Discuss.

(b) Prepare the draft management letter.

Source: Uniform Final Exam (UFE), The Institutes of Chartered Accountants in Canada and Bermuda, Paper 2, 2008.

CASE STUDY—CLOUD 9

Answer the following questions based on the information presented for Cloud 9 in Appendix B of this book and the current and earlier chapters. You should also consider your answers to the case study questions in earlier chapters.

Required

Based on everything you know about the audit of Cloud 9, finalize the audit by preparing the audit report and the letter to those charged with governance of the company.

RESEARCH QUESTION 13.1

The global financial crisis led to increasing legal action against auditors as company managers searched for scapegoats and potential places to recover their losses. The tough economic times also likely caused companies that would otherwise have survived to fail, exposing bad management and poor-quality auditing.

Required

Conduct a literature search for reports of threatened and actual legal action against auditors as a result of the global financial crisis. Include in your search articles raising questions about auditors and the quality of their work even though legal action may not have commenced.

Write a summary of your findings and comment on the merits of the cases against auditors. Is there any evidence of poor-quality auditing?

SOLUTIONS TO MULTIPLE-CHOICE QUESTIONS

1. d, 2. a, 3. b, 4. c, 5. a, 6. d, 7. b, 8. c, 9. a, 10. a.

APPENDIX A: SAMPLE DOCUMENTS

BANK CONFIRMATION

(Areas to be completed by client are marked §, while those to be completed by the financial institutions are marked †)

FINANCIAL INSTITUTION (Name, branch and full mailing address) § Regional Bank of Canada 1234 West Street Toronto, Ontario M5J 2X8	CLIENT (Legal name) § ABC Company Ltd. 987 South Road Toronto, Ontario M8G 3R1 The financial institution is authorized to provide the details requested herein to the below-noted firm of accountants § _John Smith_____ Client's authorized signature
CONFIRMATION DATE § December 31, 2016 (**All information to be provided as at this date**) (See Bank Confirmation Completion Instructions)	Please supply copy of the most recent credit facility agreement (initial if required) § _____

1. LOANS AND OTHER DIRECT AND CONTINGENT LIABILITIES (If balances are nil, please state)

NATURE OF LIABILITY/ CONTINGENT LIABILITY†	INTEREST (Note rate per contract) RATE † DATE PAID TO †	DUE DATE †	DATE OF CREDIT FACILITY AGREEMENT †	AMOUNT AND CURRENCY OUTSTANDING †

ADDITIONAL CREDIT FACILITY AGREEMENT(S)

Note the date(s) of any credit facility agreement(s) not drawn upon and not referenced above †

2. DEPOSITS/OVERDRAFTS

TYPE OF ACCOUNT §	ACCOUNT NUMBER §	INTEREST RATE §	ISSUE DATE (If applicable)§	MATURITY DATE (If applicable)§	AMOUNT AND CURRENCY (Brackets if Overdraft)†

EXCEPTIONS AND COMMENTS
(See Bank Confirmation Completion Instructions)†

STATEMENT OF PROCEDURES PERFORMED BY FINANCIAL INSTITUTION †
The above information was completed in accordance with the Bank Confirmation Completion Instructions.

_____
Authorized signature of financial institution

_____
BRANCH CONTACT - Name and telephone number

Please mail this form directly to our chartered accountant in the enclosed addressed envelope.

Name:	Jason Power, Staff Accountant EY
Address:	222 Bay Street Toronto, Ontario M5K 1J7
Telephone:	(416) 864-1234
Fax:	(416) 864-1174

Developed by the Canadian Bankers Association and The Canadian Institute of Chartered Accountants

FIGURE 1A Bank confirmation

Source: The Bank Confirmation form is copyrighted to CaseWare International Inc., all rights reserved.

Skyward

January 5, 2017

ACT Supply Company
456 North Avenue
Toronto, Ontario
M8G 4C9

Dear Sir or Madam:

Our auditors, EY, are auditing our financial statements and wish to obtain direct confirmation of amounts owed to us as at **December 31, 2016**. Compare the information below with your records on that date and confirm that this information agrees with your records on that date or note the details of any discrepancies in the space provided below. Then please sign this request and return it in the enclosed reply envelope directly to our auditors.

Our records on December 31, 2016, showed **$87,425** as receivable from you. This is not a request for payment and remittances should not be sent to EY.

Your prompt attention to this request will be appreciated.

Sincerely,

John Smith
Controller

(Please do not detach)

CONFIRMATION

The information as stipulated above by Skyward is correct except as noted below.

_____

_____

_____

Signed: _____   Date: _____

Title: _____   Customer #: ACT-1

Company: _____

FIGURE 2A **Accounts receivable confirmation—positive balance**

Skyward

January 5, 2017

ACT Supply Company
456 North Avenue
Toronto, Ontario
M8G 4C9

Dear Sir or Madam:

Our auditors, EY, are auditing our financial statements and wish to obtain direct confirmation of amounts owed to us as at **December 31, 2016**. If the information is incorrect, please report the details of any discrepancies directly to our auditors in the space provided below. Then please sign this request and return it in the enclosed reply envelope directly to our auditors. If no differences are reported to the auditors, this statement will be considered correct.

Our records on December 31, 2016, showed **$87,425** as receivable from you. This is not a request for payment and remittances should not be sent to EY.

Your prompt attention to this request will be appreciated.

Sincerely,

John Smith
Controller

———————————————————————————————————
(Please do not detach)

CONFIRMATION

The information as stipulated above by Skyward is correct except as noted below.

_____

_____

_____

Signed: _____   Date: _____

Title: _____   Customer #: ACT-1

Company: _____

FIGURE 3A **Accounts receivable confirmation—negative balance**

Skyward

January 5, 2017

ACT Supply Company
456 North Avenue
Toronto, Ontario
M8G 4C9

Dear Sir or Madam:

Our auditors, EY, are auditing our financial statements and wish to obtain direct confirmation of amounts owed to us as at **December 31, 2016**. Compare the information attached with your records on that date and confirm that this information agrees with your records or note the details of any discrepancies in the space provided below. Then please sign this request and return it in the enclosed reply envelope directly to our auditors.

Our records on December 31, 2016, showed the attached list of invoices totalling $4,790 as receivable from you. Please note that these invoices may not represent the entire balance owed to us as at that date. This is not a request for payment and remittances should not be sent to EY.

Your prompt attention to this request will be appreciated.

Sincerely,

John Smith
Controller

(Please do not detach)

CONFIRMATION

The information as stipulated above by Skyward is correct except as noted below.

_____

_____

_____

Signed: _____   Date: _____

Title: _____   Customer #: ACT-1

Company: _____

FIGURE 4A **Accounts receivable confirmation—positive invoice**

Skyward

January 5, 2017

ACT Supply Company
456 North Avenue
Toronto, Ontario
M8G 4C9

Dear Sir or Madam:

Our auditors, EY, are auditing our financial statements and wish to obtain direct confirmation of amounts owed to us as at **December 31, 2016**. If the information is incorrect, please report the details of any discrepancies directly to our auditors in the space provided below. Then sign this request and return it in the enclosed reply envelope directly to our auditors. If no differences are reported to the auditors, this statement will be considered correct.

Our records on December 31, 2016, showed the attached list of invoices totalling $4,790 as receivable from you. Please note that these invoices may not represent the entire balance owed to us as at that date. This is not a request for payment and remittances should not be sent to EY.

Your prompt attention to this request will be appreciated.

Sincerely,

John Smith
Controller

_____

(Please do not detach)

CONFIRMATION

The information as stipulated above by Skyward is correct except as noted below.

_____

_____

_____

Signed: _____   Date: _____

Title: _____   Customer #: ACT-1

Company: _____

FIGURE 5A **Accounts receivable confirmation—negative invoice**

Soft Soles Inc.
Trial Balance

Account Number	Account Description	Debits	Credits
1020	Cash Operating Account	84,679.00	0.00
1030	Cash Saving Account	2,400.00	0.00
1050	Petty Cash	786.00	0.00
1055	Store Locations	500.00	0.00
1200	Accounts Receivable	145,180.50	0.00
1205	Allowance for Doubtful Accounts	0.00	14,518.05
1320	Prepaid Expenses	3,004.00	0.00
1520	Inventory	60,389.00	0.00
1530	Goods in Transit	4,530.00	0.00
1540	Allowance for Obsolescence	0.00	417.00
1820	Office Furniture & Equipment	17,689.00	0.00
1825	Accum. Amort.—Furn. & Equip.	0.00	12,838.00
1860	Building	13,248.00	0.00
1865	Accum. Amort.—Building	0.00	3,606.00
1880	Land	1,704,933.00	0.00
2100	Accounts Payable	0.00	56,984.00
2120	Other Accrued Expenses	0.00	49,875.00
2130	Warranty Provision	0.00	9,145.00
2160	Corporate Taxes Payable	0.00	35,854.00
2170	Vacation Payable	0.00	15,654.00
2180	EI Payable	0.00	14,935.00
2185	CPP Payable	0.00	20,909.00
2190	Federal Income Tax Payable	0.00	35,833.00
2370	HST Charged on Sales	0.00	246,900.00

Account Number	Account Description	Debits	Credits
2375	HST Paid on Purchases	123,450.00	0.00
2620	Bank Loans	0.00	787,500.00
3350	Common Shares	0.00	100.00
3560	Retained Earnings—Previous Year	0.00	599,622.45
4200	Sales	0.00	2,057,500.00
4440	Interest Revenue	0.00	4,543.00
5020	Cost of Sales (COS) Stores	1,028,750.00	0.00
5300	Freight Expense	11,511.00	0.00
5410	Wages & Salaries	653,345.00	0.00
5610	Accounting & Legal	16,536.00	0.00
5615	Advertising & Promotions	15,643.00	0.00
5620	Bad Debts	5,423.00	0.00
5625	Business Fees & Licences	1,357.00	0.00
5660	Amortization Expense	2,580.00	0.00
5680	Income Taxes	27,807.00	0.00
5685	Insurance	2,065.00	0.00
5690	Interest & Bank Charges	563.00	0.00
5700	Office Supplies	2,450.00	0.00
5760	Rent	23,187.00	0.00
5765	Repair & Maintenance	2,643.00	0.00
5780	Telephone	1,458.00	0.00
5784	Travel & Entertainment	1,654.00	0.00
5790	Utilities	8,973.00	0.00
		3,966,733.50	3,966,733.50

FIGURE 6A **Trial balance**

Skyward Ltd.
Excerpt from General Ledger
Sorted by: Transaction Number

	Date	Comment	Source #	Trans. No.	Debits	Credits	Balance
1020 Cash Operating Account							80,000.00 Dr
	1/13/2016	Bank deposit	1	J25	40,254.00	0.00	120,254.00 Dr
	1/13/2016	Soft Soles Inc.	1	J28	0.00	35,575.00	84,679.00 Dr
					40,254.00	35,575.00	
1200 Accounts Receivable							0.00 Dr
	1/1/2016	Sports Galore	1	J1	565.00	0.00	565.00 Dr
	1/1/2016	Cross Country Sports	200	J5	13,750.00	0.00	14,315.00 Dr
	1/4/2016	Grandview Sportswear	201	J6	39,000.00	0.00	53,315.00 Dr
	1/5/2016	Meyer Sports	202	J7	4,950.00	0.00	58,265.00 Dr
	1/5/2016	Meyer Sports	203	J8	15,500.00	0.00	73,765.00 Dr
	1/5/2016	Rebel Sports	204	J9	31,000.00	0.00	104,765.00 Dr
	1/5/2016	Sports Galore	205	J10	19,097.00	0.00	123,862.00 Dr
	1/5/2016	Sports Galore	206	J11	1,864.50	0.00	125,726.50 Dr
	1/9/2016	Rebel Sports	207	J12	13,250.00	0.00	138,976.50 Dr
	1/9/2016	Meyer Sports	208	J13	19,500.00	0.00	158,476.50 Dr
	1/9/2016	Rebel Sports	209	J14	7,125.00	0.00	165,601.50 Dr
	1/9/2016	The Soccer Store	210	J15	19,500.00	0.00	185,101.50 Dr
	1/11/2016	Cross Country Sports	211	J16	20,580.00	0.00	205,681.50 Dr
	1/11/2016	Meyer Sports	212	J17	8,000.00	0.00	213,681.50 Dr
	1/13/2016	Rebel Sports	213	J18	13,850.00	0.00	227,531.50 Dr
	1/13/2016	Grandview Sportswear	1	J20	0.00	4,000.00	223,531.50 Dr
	1/13/2016	Rebel Sports	2	J21	0.00	679.00	222,852.50 Dr
	1/13/2016	Rebel Sports	3	J22	0.00	7,125.00	215,727.50 Dr
	1/13/2016	Meyer Sports	4	J24	0.00	28,450.00	187,277.50 Dr
	1/13/2016	Meyer Sports	5	J29	0.00	19,500.00	167,777.50 Dr
	1/13/2016	Sports Galore	6	J30	0.00	21,526.50	146,251.00 Dr
	1/13/2016	Grandview Sportswear	7	J31	0.00	1,070.50	145,180.50 Dr
					227,531.50	82,351.00	

FIGURE 7A **General ledger**

Soft Soles Inc.
Aged Overdue Sales Invoices Summary
As at 1/13/2016

Name	Total Due	Total Current	Total Overdue	1 to 30 Overdue	31 to 60 Overdue
Cross Country Sports	26,979.00	26,979.00	0.00	0.00	0.00
Grandview Sportswear	31,000.00	30,000.00	1,000.00	1,000.00	0.00
Meyer Sports	17,950.00	17,950.00	0.00	0.00	
Rebel Sports	35,225.00	13,850.00	21,375.00	11,375.00	10,000.00
Sports Galore	21,526.50	11,526.50	10,000.00	10,000.00	0.00
The Soccer Store	12,500.00	12,000.00	500.00	500.00	0.00
Total outstanding:	145,180.50	94,355.50	50,825.00	22,875.00	10,000.00

FIGURE 8A **Subsidiary ledger**

Soft Soles Inc.
Customer Master File

Customer Number	Name	Contact	Street	City	Province	Postal Code	Balance Approved Credit Limit
12001	Cross Country Sports	Jack Williams	106 Ave	Vancouver	British Columbia	V2S 9G2	25,000.00
12002	Grandview Sportswear	Frank Johnstone	2315 Erie Road	Toronto	Ontario	L4S 9G3	15,000.00
12003	Meyer Sports	Franklin White	100 Brand Road	Winnipeg	Manitoba	R3W 1Q6	50,000.00
12004	Rebel Sports	Elizabeth Franklin	PO Box 22, Station A	Toronto	Ontario	L4D 9G3	25,000.00
12005	Sports Galore	John Johnson	65 How Street	Guelph	Ontario	N3E 9H2	10,000.00
12006	The Soccer Store	Cindy Black	66 Charlottetown Place	St. John's	NL	A1A 9N0	15,000.00

FIGURE 9A **Master file**

Soft Soles Inc.

PURCHASE REQUISITION

Req. No.	322
Date:	Jan. 2, 2016

SUPPLIER NAME	ADDRESS - CITY, PROVINCE, POSTAL CODE:
Skyward Ltd.	Toronto, Ontario

Department	Purchasing
Method of Shipment	
Ship to Attention of:	Merchandising Division
Required Delivery Date:	Jan. 16, 2016
Authorization Number	TBD

Item	Quantity	Part No.	Description	UM	Price	Total
238902	100		Cloud Comfort Walking Shoe	ea		

REQUESTED BY: John King, Merchandising Manager

APPROVED BY:

FIGURE 10A **Purchase requisition**

PURCHASE ORDER

Soft Soles Inc.

100 Anywhere Street
Vancouver, BC

P.O. NO.   322
DATE   January 6, 2016
CUSTOMER ID   CLO9

VENDOR   Skyward Ltd.
Toronto, Ontario
(416) 999-9999

SHIP TO   Soft Soles Inc.
100 Anywhere Street
Vancouver, BC
604-555-5566

SHIPPING METHOD	SHIPPING TERMS	DELIVERY DATE
Courier		1/16/16

QTY	ITEM #	DESCRIPTION	JOB	UNIT PRICE	LINE TOTAL
100 each	238902	Cloud Comfort Walking Shoe		$ 50.00	$ 5,000.00
				SUBTOTAL	$ 5,000.00
				SALES TAX	600.00
				TOTAL	$ 5,600.00

1. Please send two copies of your invoice.
2. Enter this order in accordance with the prices, terms, delivery method, and specifications listed above.
3. Please notifiy us immediately if you are unable to ship as specified.
4. Send all correspondence to:

    Soft Soles
    100 Anywhere Street
    Vancouver, BC

Authorized by   Date

FIGURE 11A **Purchase order**

Packaging Slip/Shipping Document

Skyward Ltd.
Toronto, Ontario
Phone 416-999-9999
Fax 416-999-9991

Date: January 12, 2016
Customer ID: SoftSo

Ship to: Soft Soles Inc.
           100 Anywhere Street
           Vancouver, BC
           604-555-5566

Bill to: Same as Ship To

Order Date	Order Number	
1/6/16	322	

Item #	Description	Quantity
238902	Cloud Comfort Walking Shoe	100 ea

Please contact Customer Service at (416) 999-9999 with any questions or concerns.

Thank you for your business!

FIGURE 12A **Packaging slip/Shipping document**

Skyward Ltd.
Toronto, Ontario
Phone 416-999-9999   Fax 416-999-9991

INVOICE

DATE: 01/16/2016
INVOICE #   214

Bill To:
Soft Soles Inc.
100 Anywhere Street
Vancouver, BC
604-555-5566

Ship To:
Same as Bill to

Comments or Special Instructions: None

SALESPERSON	P.O. NUMBER	SHIP DATE	SHIP VIA	F.O.B. POINT	TERMS
	322	16-Jan-16	Courier		2/10, net 30

QUANTITY	DESCRIPTION	UNIT PRICE	AMOUNT
100	238902 Cloud Comfort Walking Shoe	$ 50.00	$ 5,000.00

SUBTOTAL	$ 5,000.00
TAX RATE	12.00%
SALES TAX	600.00
SHIPPING & HANDLING	–
TOTAL	$ 5,600.00

Make all cheques payable to Skyward
If you have any questions concerning this invoice, call Barbara, Skyward, 604-999-9998

THANK YOU FOR YOUR BUSINESS!

FIGURE 13A **Sales invoice**

Skyward Ltd.
Toronto, Ontario
Phone 416-999-9999
Fax 416-999-9991

Date: 1/5/2016
Statement # 101

To:

Soft Soles Inc.

100 Anywhere Street

Vancouver, BC

604-555-5566

Please Attach with Payment					

Remittance:

Statement #	101
Date	
Amount Enclosed	

Make all cheques payable to Skyward Ltd.

Thank you for your business!

FIGURE 14A **Remittance advice**

C3
Skyward
9/30/2016

BANK RECONCILIATION   DATE October 7, 2016

Prepared by Client   LEDGER ACCOUNT   1006-0-00
                            DESCRIPTION   CHEQUING ACCOUNT
                            BANK NAME   LOCAL BANK
                            RECONCILIATION DATE   Sept. 30, 2016
                            PERFORMED BY   Bill Reds, Oct. 2, 2016
                            REVIEWED BY   Noel Smith, Oct. 3, 2016

RECONCILIATION   —

BALANCE PER BANK Sept. 30, 2016	200,448.90	B
DEDUCT		
Wire transfer to Supplier XX - recorded by us in Sept 2016	41,909.00	A
Wire transfer to Supplier XX - recorded by us in Sept 2016	63,621.20	A
Wire transfer to Supplier XX - recorded by us in Sept 2016	6,575.00	A
ADD Service charge - recorded by us in Oct 2016	55.80	i C
Net interest expense for September 2016 - recorded by us in Oct 2016	752.40	i C
BALANCE PER BOOKS Sept. 30, 2016 C1 lead	89,151.90	

A   Traced to bank cut-off statements. Processed by bank in Oct 2016. Noted agreement to description and amounts.

B   Traced to bank's statement of accounts at 9-30-2016. Traced to bank response summary in C5.

[i]   C   Not recorded by client. Amount is, however, immaterial. Pass further review.

☑ checked totals

FIGURE 15A **Sample bank reconciliation**

Sample Client Ltd.
Dec-31-16
PPE Continuity Schedule

ASSETS

A/C NO	DESCRIPTION	PY BALANCE Dec. 31, 2015	ADDITIONS	CIP reclass	RETIREMENTS	TB BALANCE Dec. 31, 2016
1400	LAND	45,000.00	264,000.00 K2			309,000.00
1410	LAND IMPROVEMENTS	86,096.73	6,292.50			92,389.23
1420	BUILDING	3,170,144.64	1,545,451.90			4,715,596.54
1430	PRODUCTION EQUIPMENT	6,204,856.31	777,197.95 K2	225,152.13 K2	156,142.37	7,051,064.03
1440	DIES & MOULDS	8,420,714.52	440,422.57 K2	254,489.66 K3	117,585.00	8,998,041.75
1450	TOOL ROOM EQUIPMENT	147,767.42				147,767.42
1460	OFFICE EQUIPMENT	28,673.10				28,673.10
1470	FURNITURE & FIXTURE	134,348.55	102,264.95			236,613.50
1475	VEHICLES	81,554.93				81,554.93
1480	ENGINEERING EQUIPMENT	54,171.15	29,927.42			84,098.57
1485	QC EQUIPMENT	14,691.29	3,987.00		3,906.00	14,772.29
1490	COMPUTER EQUIPMENT	283,657.56	53,591.42		13,546.59	323,702.39
1540	CONSTRUCTION IN PROGR	479,641.79	133,489.35	−479,641.79 K3		133,489.35
		19,151,317.99	3,356,625.06	0.00	291,179.96	22,216,763.10

ACCUMULATED DEPRECIATION

A/C NO	PY BALANCE Dec. 31, 2015	PROVISION	RETIREMENTS	TB BALANCE Dec. 31, 2016	PY FY 15 DEPREC	DIFF	%	NBV Dec. 31, 2016	NBV Dec. 31, 2015
1610								309,000.00	45,000.00
1620	84,229.19	1,177.32		85,406.51	2,974.65	(1,797.33)	−60.4%	6,982.72	1,867.54
1630	1,296,544.40	133,014.21		1,429,558.61	126,655.17	6,359.04	5.0%	3,286,037.93	1,873,600.24
1634	3,877,675.68	522,430.78 K4	138,939.71 K3	4,261,166.75	420,787.95	101,642.83	24.2%	2,789,897.28	2,327,180.63
1650	5,762,463.15	1,200,780.56 K4	117,585.00 K3	6,845,658.71	1,123,205.04	77,575.52	6.9%	2,152,383.04	2,658,251.37
1660	140,273.72	4,995.30		145,269.02	7,311.33	(2,316.03)	−31.7%	2,498.40	7,493.70
1670	22,786.89	2,351.67		25,138.56	1,291.38	1,060.29	82.1%	3,534.54	5,886.21
1675	97,107.81 K4	20,102.28		117,210.09	14,797.82	5,304.46	35.8%	119,403.41	37,240.74
1680	5,831.18	11,662.35		17,493.53	5,831.18	5,831.17	100.0%	64,061.40	75,723.75
1685	19,549.79	18,814.88		38,364.67	6,916.01	11,898.87	172.0%	45,733.90	34,621.36
1690	13,715.55	1,633.74 K3	3,906.00	11,443.29	1,943.70	(309.96)	−15.9%	3,329.00	975.74
1635	84,196.73 K4	58,826.31	13,546.59 K3	129,476.45	46,833.23	11,993.08	25.6%	194,225.94	199,460.83
						0.00		133,489.35	479,641.79
	11,404,374.09	1,975,789.40	273,977.30	13,106,186.19	1,758,547.46	217,241.94	12.4%	9,110,576.91	7,746,943.90

EXPENSE BREAKDOWN

A/C NO		
5370	PROD EQ	1,740,402.80
5371	PROD EQ-NEW	117,000.00
5375	LEASED EQ	0.00
5570	TOOL ROOM	4,995.30
5990	SHIPPING	11,662.35
6170	R&D	18,814.88
6170	QC	1,633.80
7170	SALES	11,414.39
8170	OFFICE EQ	69,865.88
		1,975,789.40

Notes

A   All amounts traced to the Fixed Asset Depreciation-Book Purposes Report (PP&E detail register) for the applicable asset classification.

Tickmarks

☑ Clerical accuracy checked. Re-calculated formulas.
PY Agreed to prior year
TB Agreed to trial balance

FIGURE 16A **Example working paper (PPE continuity schedule)**

CLIENT: Sample Client Ltd
Period-end: 12/31/2016
Currency/Unit: $ 000's

NO4 - SEARCH FOR UNRECORDED LIABILITIES

Reference **NO4**

Section 1: review of subsequent disbursements

| Disbursement type (disbursements after year end) | Disbursement reference | Disbursement | | | Invoice details | | | TM/Ref | Delivery Date/ Date of service provided | TM/Ref | Accrued at year end? | TM/Ref | Comments |
		Recipient	Amount	Date	Date	Amount	Description						
Wire transfer	123 456	ABC	(700)	Jan. 31, 2017	Jan. 12, 2017	(500)	Electricity bill 12/16	▣	2016	✓	Yes	✓*	
Wire transfer	654 293	DEF	(1,500)	Jan. 31, 2017	Jan. 13, 2017	(1,000)	Lawyer's invoices 12/16	▣	2016	✓	Yes	✓*	
Cheques	754 633	GHI	(2,001)	Jan. 31, 2017	Jan. 13, 2017	(2,001)	Flight to Las Vegas in FY17	▣	2017	✓	N/A	N/A	
etc...													

Section 2: Review of invoices received after year end

| Date | Invoice details | | TM/Ref | Delivery date/ date of service provided | TM/Ref | Accrued at year end? | TM/Ref | Comments |
	Amount	Description						
Jan. 5, 2017	(900)	Raw material	▣	200N+1	✓	N/A	N/A	
Jan. 3, 2017	(1,000)	Lawyer's invoices 12/10	▣	200N	✓	Yes	✓*	
Jan. 4, 2017	(1,500)	Temporary workers Dec 2010	▣	200N	✓	Yes	✓*	
Jan. 4, 2017	etc...							

Key to audit tickmarks:
▣ Agrees to Invoice details
✓ Agrees to delivery note/details of service provided
✓* Agrees to details of accrued liabilities

Comments: No error detected (in addition to the one detected during our cut-off procedures)

FIGURE 17A **Completed working paper (search for unrecorded liabilities)**

CLIENT: Sample Client
Period-end: 12/31/2016
Currency/Unit: $ 000's

F01.2 - OBSERVATION OF PHYSICAL INVENTORIES_COUNTS

EY

Reference F01.2

EY Attendee:	Max Power
Location of Count:	Location C
Date:	Nov. 30, 2016
Account balance at the date of physical inventory:	50,000

F04

Section 1: Procedures to complete before and during the physical counts

Comments: Please refer to F01.3 for the documentation of our work relating to review of the client's procedures and details of observation during the physical counts. No issue noted

Section 2: Review of entity's counts and test of compilation

Test #	Selection number/tag reference	Item #	Description	Measurement in units	[A] Quantity per EY	[B] Quantity per count teams	TM/Ref	[B] - [A] Variance	[C] Final quantity verified with the client	[D] Quantity per inventory compilation	TM/Ref	[D] - [C] Variance	Comments
Count Sheets to Floor													
1	123 453	ABC		Unit	10	10	⬡			10	✗	-	
2	124 556	DEF		Unit	15	15	⬡	5	15	15	✗	-	
3	244 537	GHI		Unit	10	10	⬡			9	✗	(1)	A
4	982 345	F450D		Unit	45	45	⬡	-		45	✗	-	
5	123 444	234F5G		Unit	32	32	⬡	-		32	✗	-	
6	124 567	WOE902		Unit	78	78	⬡	-		78	✗	-	
7	128 919	XE9901		Unit	12	12	⬡	-		12	✗	-	
8	234 001	V34ER		Unit	42	42	⬡	-		42	✗	-	
9	236 013	B7829D		Unit	111	111	⬡	-		111	✗	-	
10	878 130	W2340KD		Unit	54	54	⬡	-		54	✗	-	
11	124 904	1209KKI8		Unit	45	45	⬡	-		45	✗	-	
12	765 432	72DIKMD		Unit	67	67	⬡	-		67	✗	-	
13	232 224	0987234		Unit	89	89	⬡	-		89	✗	-	
Floor to Count Sheets													
1	245 367	JKL		Unit	10	10	⬡			10	✗	-	
2	653 452	MNO		Unit	10	15	⬡	5	15	15	✗	-	
3	765 342	PQR		Unit	10	10	⬡	-		10	✗	-	
4	546 737	12OPEP		Unit	19	19	⬡	-		19	✗	-	
5	345 792	RED56W2		Unit	102	102	⬡	-		102	✗	-	
6	932 842	F4O2OXC		Unit	10	10	⬡	-		10	✗	-	
7	123 591	FS234VTE		Unit	92	92	⬡	-		92	✗	-	
8	876 761	AS3290F		Unit	43	43	⬡	-		43	✗	-	
9	988 238	NNO0S		Unit	56	56	⬡	-		56	✗	-	
10	234 912	MPO02D		Unit	43	43	⬡	-		43	✗	-	
11	123 479	AD129MK		Unit	56	56	⬡	-		56	✗	-	
12	567 230	120LLK		Unit	2	2	⬡	-		2	✗	-	

FIGURE 18A **Example of an inventory working paper**

(continued)

Key to audit tickmarks:

　Agrees to count sheet
　↗ Agrees to inventory compilation

Comments:

* In two instances, our counts differed from client's. After further investigation, we agreed with the client's original counts.
* At after inventory counts, the client further investigated reference 244 537 and identified an error in the part number for one of the items and corrected after inventory stock taking. This correction has no impact on total inventory (reference 432 567 was also modified for the same amount), and we do not need to reconsider the quality of the client's counts.

FIGURE 18A **Example of an inventory working paper (continued)**

APPENDIX B: CLOUD 9 LTD.

W&S Partners is a Canadian accounting firm with offices located in each of the major cities. W&S Partners has just won the December 31, 2016, statutory audit work for Cloud 9 Ltd. The audit team assigned to the client is Partner, Jo Wadley; Audit Manager, Sharon Gallagher; Audit Seniors, Josh Thomas and Suzie Pickering; IT Audit Manager, Mark Batten; and Audit Juniors, including Ian Harper, Weijing Fei, and you.

Prior-year audits were conducted by Ellis & Associates. As part of the change of auditors process, Jo Wadley met with R.J. Ellis (Managing Partner, Ellis & Associates) to discuss acceptance of Cloud 9 Ltd. as a client and to inquire about access to Ellis & Associates' workpapers. In the discussion, R.J. Ellis stated that there were no issues that W&S Partners should be aware of before accepting the client or commencing the work.

CLOUD 9 LTD. COMPANY BACKGROUND

Originally founded in 1980 by Ron McLellan, the Toronto-based company was a manufacturer and retailer of customized basketball shoes. In 1993, Cloud 9 Inc. (a publicly listed Canadian company) purchased the original company from Ron McLellan and renamed it Cloud 9 Ltd. As part of the sale agreement, Ron McLellan was appointed to the Cloud 9 Ltd. board of directors.

The parent company, Cloud 9 Inc., has wholly owned subsidiaries in the United Kingdom, Germany, United States, China, and Brazil, and has built a reputation around the fact that its shoes are comfortable and durable. The company promotes itself using its now well-known tagline, "Our shoes are so comfortable, it's like walking on Cloud 9." Currently, Cloud 9 Ltd. is primarily a wholesaler of athletic shoes to its main customers: David Jones, Myer, Foot Locker, and Rebel Sports.

Cloud 9 Ltd. receives the majority of its inventory from the China production plant, with the remainder coming from the United States. All inventory is purchased on free on board (FOB) shipping terms, which means Cloud 9 Ltd. takes ownership of the products once the international courier accepts the goods for delivery. The inventory is sent to the main warehouse in Richmond, B.C., which is linked to retailers through an electronic inventory system. When retail inventory levels get low, the company ensures that deliveries are made using their own transport trucks, thus ensuring control throughout the entire process.

In February 2014, Cloud 9 Ltd. launched its new product line, which included the "Heavenly 456" walking shoe. Advertising campaigns and media coverage have been very successful and sales for this style of shoe have steadily increased. For Cloud 9 Ltd., the "Heavenly 456" now makes up 20 percent of total sales.

A specific marketing campaign was initiated in 2016 to promote and build the Cloud 9 brand in Canada. The Canadian company was granted permission from its parent entity to sponsor a new soccer team, the Thompson Thunders, for the 2016 season. Under this sponsorship agreement, Cloud 9 Ltd. is to provide all the athletic footwear for the team, as well as having sole merchandising rights. The agreement also includes general advertising rights at the stadium.

In a separate contractual arrangement, Cloud 9 Ltd. has signed Kevin McDonald, the captain of the Thompson Thunders, as spokesperson for the brand. This arrangement allows Cloud 9 Ltd. to use Kevin's image to promote and build the brand in Canada.

To further establish the brand, the first Cloud 9 retail store was opened in Toronto, Ontario, on June 1, 2016. The store operates on a just-in-time inventory system linked with the main warehouse in Richmond, B.C. However, the management team reports that there have been a few hiccups in determining ideal inventory quantities for the store to allow optimum availability of merchandise to the customers. There have also been some thefts of merchandise from the store and in order to reduce inventory loss by theft, the company has installed closed-circuit television cameras.

Personnel

Cloud 9 Ltd. has 52 full-time employees. In the retail store, the company employs part-time staff, with casual employees enhancing staff levels in the busier retail period.

To administer the company's finances, Cloud 9 Ltd. employs Finance Director David Collier, Financial Controller Carla Johnson, and Business Systems Manager Justin Reeves. These three employees are entitled to participate in the employee stock-purchase plan and receive stock options in Cloud 9 Inc. if revenue targets are met.

Financial information

Responding to pressure from its parent company, Cloud 9 Ltd. set a goal of increasing its revenue by 3 percent for the 2016 fiscal year. One of the critical success factors for the company achieving this 3-percent increase is to grow its share of the North American footwear market. However, with the new store opening and the subsequent increase in costs, as well as the costs related to the sponsorship deals, the management team is projecting a loss for the year.

In addition, to build customer loyalty and promote sales in the retail store, Cloud 9 Ltd. introduced a loyalty program whereby customers earn one point for every $10 that they spend. Customers can then redeem points by going online to receive coupons that can be exchanged for merchandise in the store.

On October 1, 2015, the company took out an additional loan of $2 million with Ontario Bank to help fund the store costs and to purchase additional delivery trucks and vans. This loan is repayable over five years. The company's other debt relates to loans issued five years ago from a company that is majority-owned by one of the directors.

All inventory is purchased in U.S. dollars, which the company acquires under forward exchange contracts. The company provides a 12-month warranty on all footwear. Historical claims have been 2 percent of total sales.

The prior-year income statement and balance sheet are included below.

CLOUD 9 LTD.
Income Statement
Year ended December 31, 2015

	2015	2014
Revenue	$34,038,192	$32,114,278
Cost of goods sold	16,393,394	16,378,281
Gross profit	17,644,798	15,735,997
Other expenses	16,277,979	14,540,408
Income from operations	1,366,819	1,195,589
Other income	312,447	269,489
Income before taxes	1,679,266	1,465,078
Income tax expenses	378,074	452,064
Net income	1,301,192	1,013,014

CLOUD 9 LTD.		
Balance Sheet		
As at December 31, 2015		
	2015	**2014**
Assets		
Current assets		
Cash	$ 1,653,765	$ 534,938
Accounts receivable	10,554,937	9,608,742
Inventory	6,163,242	6,796,990
Prepaids	666,054	1,135,416
Total current assets	19,037,998	18,076,086
Due from parent	482,306	482,306
Plant and equipment	852,965	627,885
Total assets	20,373,269	19,186,277
Liabilities and Shareholders' Equity		
Current liabilities		
Accounts payable	1,215,219	4,354,152
Accrued liabilities	2,751,332	2,072,075
Total current liabilities	3,966,551	6,426,227
Long-term debt	9,560,224	7,560,224
Deferred taxes	170,284	136,794
Total liabilities	13,697,059	14,123,245
Equity		
Share capital	5,448,026	5,448,026
Retained earnings	1,228,184	(384,994)
	20,373,269	19,186,277

Following are the December 2016 trial balance for Cloud 9 Ltd., a draft statement of income for 2016, a transcript of a meeting with Carla Johnson (Cloud 9 Ltd. financial controller), and sales and cash control testing support.

	CLOUD 9 LTD. Trial Balance			
	December 31, 2016		December 31, 2015	
	DR	CR	DR	CR
Cash—operating account	184,679		551,583	
Cash—savings account	60,000		1,100,000	
Petty cash	1,786		2,182	
Cash—store locations	500			
Trade receivables—stores	217,649			
Trade receivables—wholesales	10,604,933		11,118,837	
Allowance for doubtful accounts		468,197		637,167
Miscellaneous receivables	44,789		49,372	
HST receivable	31,457		23,895	
Inventory	5,788,922		6,057,752	
Goods in transit	453,002		629,235	
Allowance for inventory obsolescence		417,788		523,745
Amounts receivable from parent	482,306		482,306	
Prepaid rent	300,450		211,699	
Prepaid insurance	765,702		417,603	
Other prepaid expense	45,876		36,752	
Furniture and equipment	1,768,954		1,098,290	
Accumulated depreciation— furniture and equipment		1,283,848		757,958
Leasehold improvements	1,324,875		722,302	
Accumulated depreciation— leasehold improvements		360,650		209,669
Deferred tax assets	278,074			
Trade payables		2,179,603		1,215,219
Accrued bonuses		300,000		250,000
Sales commissions payable		423,786		398,074
Other accrued expenses		1,949,875		1,203,470
Inter-company payables		593,457		494,361
Accrued vacation payable		156,548		111,937
Loyalty program provision		62,456		
Provision for current tax liabilities		159,866		207,893
Warranty provision		91,456		85,597
Long-term debt		8,872,482		9,560,224
Provision for deferred tax liabilities		198,647		170,284
Share capital		5,448,026		5,448,026
Retained earnings		1,375,887		(73,008)
Revenue—stores		854,376		
Revenue—wholesale		36,340,556		34,038,192

(continued)

(continued)

CLOUD 9 LTD. Trial Balance				
	December 31, 2016		December 31, 2015	
	DR	CR	DR	CR
Interest from bank		60,576		28,642
Foreign exchange gain/loss		47,289		29,568
Proceeds on disposals				7,714
Other revenue		251,453		246,523
Cost of goods sold—stores	640,781			
Cost of goods sold—wholesale	16,453,395		16,393,394	
Salaries and employee benefits	5,084,460		4,842,343	
Storage—rent expense, store	166,667		—	
Storage—rent expense, warehouse	2,959,257		2,959,257	
Distribution expenses	2,068,255		2,008,015	
Telephone	99,537		—	
Computer and IT costs	252,469		298,583	
Advertising and promotion—print	2,085,812		1,046,668	
Trade shows	327,687		384,934	
Advertising and promotion—TV	1,741,901		496,996	
Advertising and promotion—sponsorships	1,713,008		—	
Rent expense—office	309,170		309,170	
Bad debt expenses	75,712		120,000	
Depreciation—furniture and equipment	701,187		339,852	
Depreciation—leasehold improvements	201,309		96,326	
Entertainment	220,576		320,703	
Professional fees	318,205		458,903	
Insurance expense	2,753,461		1,597,463	
Recruitment	352,436		297,190	
Interest expense—loan from bank	1,017,583		701,576	
Income tax expense	0		378,074	
	61,896,822	61,896,822	55,551,255	55,551,255

Draft Income Statement December 31, 2016	
Revenue	37,194,932
Cost of goods sold	17,094,176
Gross profit	20,100,756
Other expenses	22,448,693
Loss from operations	(2,347,937)
Other income	359,319
Loss before taxes	(1,988,618)
Income tax expense	—
Net loss	(1,988,618)

TRANSCRIPT OF MEETING WITH CARLA JOHNSON
Present: Carla Johnson, Financial Controller, Cloud 9 Ltd.,
Josh Thomas, Audit Senior, W&S Partners

JT: **Thanks for seeing me, Carla.**

CJ: You're welcome, Josh. What can I do for you?

JT: **I need to ask you some questions around Cloud 9's process for recording wholesale revenue transactions, including the trade receivables and cash receipts aspects. After I understand the process, I'll need to select a sample transaction to confirm my understanding of the process as you have explained.**

CJ: Well, I can tell you what should be happening, but you may want to go and speak to the sales manager or warehouse managers to confirm that they do what the company policy and procedures say.

JT: **Good point, I'll make appointments to see them. Thanks. So let's start at the beginning—how does a sales transaction get initiated?**

CJ: We've got a pretty complex inventory management software system called Swift. It was designed by some of our tech guys in the United States. It tracks and does everything!

JT: **Sounds impressive!**

CJ: Anyway, the customers—let's say the Sport Mart store in Toronto—complete a purchase order online through a site that is linked to Swift.

JT: **How do the customers decide the quantity and know the price?**

CJ: Swift is linked (don't ask me how) and sends an alert when their inventory balance of our products gets below the predetermined limit they set with us. They can select the quantity based on their needs, but the prices are set in the system. They get sent price lists from the sales manager so they know the current prices.

JT: **How often are prices changed?**

CJ: Depends on the market, really. I don't think they change too frequently.

JT: **What if you don't have the products?**

CJ: The system doesn't allow them to place an order greater than our current inventory levels. If they need more, they need to fill out a separate request form that gets e-mailed to our warehouse manager so he can place the order with China.

JT: **OK, so they complete a purchase order. Then what?**

CJ: The submitted purchase order goes through a credit check and then becomes a sales order. That's all done behind the scenes in the system. We really don't see anything on our side until the sales order stage.

JT: **Guess that saves a lot of time and trees!**

CJ: Yeah, there's so much that we rely on the system to do for us, it's scary. If we were hit by an electrical storm, we'd be in trouble.

JT: **What happens to the sales orders—how do they get filled?**

CJ: Every day, the warehouse manager downloads the outstanding sales orders to these little hand-held computer/scanner thingies. It's very Star Trek. Warehouse personnel use these to select the items off the shelves onto pallets. The pallets are taken to a staging area where each product is then scanned. This establishes the shipping document in Swift, which then gets printed for the delivery.

JT: **Are the shipping documents approved before the goods go out the door? How do you know that what got sent is what was ordered?**

CJ: Swift matches the quantities and products on the shipping document to the sales order. Once they match, the approval box is activated and the shipping supervisor can enter his pass code. This officially approves the shipping document and it gets printed.

JT: **How many orders do you fill in a day? It sounds like a lot for one person to do.**

CJ: We probably complete about 50 orders a day. Shoes aren't perishable items, you know, so it's not like we are sending products to every store, every day. We're trying out the "pit crew" concept, where there's two shipping supervisors with about four to five warehouse employees in their crew team. So they are in the staging area with them and do it right there with the hand-held devices. They like to have little contests to see who can do it the fastest. You should go down there; it's quite a lively group. David encourages it and it's been great for productivity and morale.

JT: **Sounds like a great working environment. Better than being stuck in a broom closet sifting through invoices!**

CJ: Ah, the life of an auditor. I remember the good old days . . .

JT: **And the goods are sent out on your own trucks?**

CJ: That's right. We've bought our own trucks and vans rather than relying on couriers. The drivers pick up their loads in the morning and bring back anything undelivered. Because shoes are an easy product to off-load, we have to be careful about theft. So nothing can be left in the back of a truck at the end of the day. It comes back here and gets locked up in the shipping cage until it can be delivered again.

JT: **Why would goods be undelivered?**

CJ: Sometimes the drivers get behind or the store is closed unexpectedly. So there are occasions when all the goods won't get delivered in the day.

JT: **OK, so once the goods are delivered to the customer, how do you bill them?**

CJ: The drivers have the customers sign for the goods and then give us the signed copy. We go into the billing system and pull up the draft invoice that was generated when the shipping document was approved. We match the quantities in the invoice against the shipping document and confirm customer sign-off. This way, we only bill for those goods that were actually received by the customer. At 4 p.m., we do a batch run for the day. The copy is stapled to the signed shipping document and put on file. The running of the batch run posts the invoices to the sales journal and accounts receivable subledger.

JT: **Does finance ever go back to the sales order?**

CJ: No. Since a shipping document can't get generated unless it agrees to the sales order, we don't go back that far into the process. Why, do you think we have to?

JT: **I wouldn't say so at this stage. But you'd have to be sure to have some tight controls around Swift, given that it seems to do everything.**

CJ: Like I said, it does everything.

JT: **What is the cash receipts process?**

CJ: We get most payments via EFT, so my AR clerk downloads the previous day's receipts from online banking. She then goes into the subledger to post the receipts against the customer accounts. When she's finished posting each entry, she runs a batch report of all postings and reconciles it back to the bank statement. I review that reconciliation and sign off.

JT: **Are bank reconciliations done in a timely manner?**

CJ: I do bank recs each month for the operating and savings accounts. David reviews and approves them. Keep in mind what I just explained is for the wholesale transactions. We have separate procedures for the store regarding daily cash balance reconciliations to the deposits in the operating bank account.

JT: **Yes, our graduate will be handling the store side of the sales to cash receipts process. They will probably come and talk to you in a day or two. Well, I think that should do it for now. I may have some follow-up questions for you as I start getting my head around all of this.**

CJ: Door's always open.

JT: **Thanks for your time.**

SALES CONTROL TESTING SUPPORT

CLOUD 9 LTD.
SALES INVOICE

TO: David Jones
    23 Main St, Shop 43
    Toronto, Ontario

October 13, 2016

132811
Swift Purchase order reference: P00132811
Shipping reference: D00132811

Code	Description	Qty	Price per unit	Total price
786541	Heavenly 456 — Women 9	5	$114.74	$573.70
786540	Heavenly 456 — Women 8	3	$114.74	$344.22
	Total			$917.92
	HST			$119.33
	TOTAL			**$1,037.25**

Payment due on November 27, 2016

CLOUD 9 LTD.
SHIPPING DOCUMENT

TO: David Jones
    123 Main St, Shop 43
    Toronto, Ontario

October 12, 2016

D00132811
Swift Purchase order reference:
P00132811
Authorized: YES

Code	Description	Qty
786541	Heavenly 456 — Women 9	5
786540	Heavenly 456 — Women 8	3

Driver: R. Williams

I declare that all goods were received and no damage noted.

Customer Signature: .... *Sally Rose* .... 12/10/16 ....

CLOUD 9 LTD.
SALES INVOICE

TO: Rebel Sports — World Square
     680 George Street, Shop 12
     Barrie, ON

October 27, 2016

133410
Swift Purchase order reference: P00133410
Shipping reference: D00133410

Code	Description	Qty	Price per unit	Total price
587241	Maximum Speed — Men 12	4	$123.56	$494.24
786540	Heavenly 456 — Women 8	2	$114.74	$229.48
	Total			$723.72
	HST			$94.08
	TOTAL			**$817.80**

Payment due on December 13, 2016

CLOUD 9 LTD.
Shipping Document

TO: Rebel Sports — World Square
     680 George Street, Shop 12
     Barrie, ON

October 25, 2016

D00133410
Swift Purchase order reference:
P00133410
Authorized: YES

Code	Description	Qty
587241	Maximum Speed — Men 12	4
786540	Heavenly 456 — Women 8	2

Driver: R. Williams

I declare that all goods were received and no damage noted.

Customer Signature: _Jenna Hennesey_ . 26/10/16

CLOUD 9 LTD.
SALES INVOICE

TO: Myer — Burnaby
328 Elizabeth Ave
Burnaby, BC

134063
Swift Purchase order reference: P00134063
Shipping reference: D00134063

November 4, 2016

Code	Description	Qty	Price per unit	Total price
649852	Olympic — Women 6	4	$109.21	$436.84
475125	Thunder 75 — Men 14	2	$157.68	$315.36
	Total			$752.20
	GST and PST			$90.26
	TOTAL			**$842.46**

Payment due on December 19, 2016

CLOUD 9 LTD.
SHIPPING DOCUMENT

TO: Myer — Burnaby
328 Elizabeth Ave
Burnaby, BC

D00134063
Swift Purchase order reference:
P00134063
Authorized: YES

November 3, 2016

Code	Description	Qty
649852	Olympic — Women 6	4
475125	Thunder 75 — Men 14	2

Driver: Ted McGinty

I declare that all goods were received and no damage noted.

Customer Signature: *Julie Brown*   3/11/16

CLOUD 9 LTD.
SALES INVOICE

TO: Cross Country Sports
769 First Avenue
St. John's, NL

November 6, 2016

134104
Swift Purchase order reference: P00134104
Shipping reference: D00134104

Code	Description	Qty	Price per unit	Total price
786541	Heavenly 456 — Women 9	2	$114.74	$229.48
	Total			$229.48
	HST			$29.83
	TOTAL			**$259.31**

Payment due on December 21, 2016

CLOUD 9 LTD.
SHIPPING INVOICE

TO: Cross Country Sports
769 First Avenue
St. John's, NL

November 5, 2016

D00134104
Swift Purchase order reference:
P00134104
Authorized: YES

Code	Description	Qty
786541	Heavenly 456 — Women 9	2

Driver: D. Bredbenner

I declare that all goods were received and no damage noted.

Customer Signature: _Olivia Villagran_   5/11/16

CLOUD 9 LTD.
SALES INVOICE

TO: Wide Road Specialty Retailer
    74 Shore Highway
    Fredericton, NB

    December 12, 2016

135215
Swift Purchase order reference: P00135215
Shipping reference: D00135215

Code	Description	Qty	Price per unit	Total price
587240	Maximum Speed — Men 10	3	$123.56	$370.68
475123	Thunder 75 — Men 12	3	$157.68	$473.04
347586	Heat Seeker — Men 15	2	$174.21	$348.42
	Total			$1,192.14
	HST			$154.98
	TOTAL			**$1,347.12**

Payment due on January 15, 2017

CLOUD 9 LTD.
SHIPPING DOCUMENT

TO: Wide Road Specialty Retailer
    74 Shore Highway
    Fredericton, NB

    December 11, 2016

D00135215
Swift Purchase order reference:
P00135215
Authorized: YES

Code	Description	Qty
587240	Maximum Speed — Men 10	3
475123	Thunder 75 – Men 12	3
347586	Heat Seeker – Men 15	2

Driver: R. Jones

I declare that all goods were received and no damage noted.

Customer Signature: _Sharon J Jones_ 11/12/16

CLOUD 9 LTD.
SALES INVOICE

TO: Foot Locker — Pitt St Mall
435 Pitt St, Shop 4
London, ON

December 20, 2016

135947
Swift Purchase order reference: P00135947
Shipping reference: D00135947

Code	Description	Qty	Price per unit	Total price
649852	Olympic — Women 6	2	$109.21	$218.42
786540	Heavenly 456 — Women 8	5	$114.74	$573.70
786539	Heavenly 456 — Women 7.5	2	$114.74	$229.48
	Total			$1,021.60
	HST			$132.81
	TOTAL			**$1,154.41**

Payment due on January 31, 2017

CLOUD 9 LTD.
SHIPPING DOCUMENT

TO: Foot Locker — Pitt St Mall
435 Pitt St, Shop 4
London, ON

December 18, 2016

D00135947
Swift Purchase order reference:
P00135947
Authorized: YES

Code	Description	Qty
649852	Olympic — Women 6	2
786540	Heavenly 456 — Women 8	5
786539	Heavenly 456 — Women 7.5	2

Driver: R. Williams

I declare that all goods were received and no damage noted.

Customer Signature: .... 18/12/16 ....

CLOUD 9 LTD.
System 01 version 1.9
Daily Reconciliation of AR Posting to Bank
as at September 19, 2016

Description	Source	Amount
Cash receipts posted to accounts receivable	Subledger	10,577.23
Total bank deposits	Bank statement	10,577.23
Difference		0.00
		OKAY

Prepared: _Jessica Williams_ .... 19/9/16 ....

Approved: _Carla Johnson_ .... 19/9/16 ....

ON_Bank_

CLOUD 9 LTD.
Online Banking
EFT payments for September 19, 2016
Passcode accepted:
Carla Johnson

EFT 427	David Jones	$7,856.46
EFT 428	Cross Country	$2,720.77
Total		$10,577.23

CLOUD 9 LTD.
System 01 version 1.9
Daily Reconciliation of AR Posting to Bank Report
as at October 8, 2016

Description	Source	Amount
Cash receipts posted to accounts receivable	Subledger	8,765.49
Total bank deposits	Bank statement	8,765.49
Difference		0.00
		OKAY

Prepared: _Jessica Williams_ 8/10/16

Approved: _Carla Johnson_ 8/10/16

ONBank

CLOUD 9 LTD.
Online Banking
EFT payments for October 8, 2016
Passcode accepted:
Carla Johnson

EFT 445	Rebel Sport	$2,963.54
EFT 446	Foot Locker	$1,964.71
EFT 447	Myer	$3,837.24
Total		$8,765.49

CLOUD 9 LTD.
System 01 version 1.9
Daily Reconciliation of AR Posting to Bank Report
as at October 23, 2016

Description	Source	Amount
Cash receipts posted to accounts receivable	Subledger	5,490.61
Total bank deposits	Bank statement	5,490.61
Difference		0.00
		OKAY

Prepared: *Jessica Williams*   23/10/16

Approved: *Carla Johnson*   23/10/16

ON*Bank*

CLOUD 9 LTD.
Online Banking
EFT payments for October 23, 2016
Passcode accepted:
Carla Johnson

EFT 501	David Jones	$1,237.89
EFT 502	Cross Country	$4,252.72
Total		$5,490.61

CLOUD 9 LTD.
System 01 version 1.9
Daily Reconciliation of AR Posting to Bank Report
as at November 12, 2016

Description	Source	Amount
Cash receipts posted to accounts receivable	Subledger	9,302.20
Total bank deposits	Bank statement	9,302.20
Difference		0.00
		OKAY

Prepared: _Jessica Williams_ 12/11/16

Approved: _Carla Johnson_ 12/11/16

ONBank

CLOUD 9 LTD.
Online Banking
EFT payments for November 12, 2016
Passcode accepted:
Carla Johnson

EFT 534	David Jones	$2,179.52
EFT 535	Dick's Sports	$1,095.48
EFT 536	Running Shop — Calgary	$2,304.00
EFT 537	Myer	$2,612.72
EFT 538	Foot Locker	$1,110.48
Total		$9,302.20

CLOUD 9 LTD.
System 01 version 1.9
Daily Reconciliation of AR Posting to Bank Report
as at December 3, 2016

Description	Source	Amount
Cash receipts posted to accounts receivable	Subledger	12,567.33
Total bank deposits	Bank statement	12,567.33
Difference		0.00
		okay

Prepared: _Jessica Williams_   3/12/16

Approved: _Carla Johnson_   3/12/16

ON_Bank_

CLOUD 9 LTD.
Online Banking
EFT payments for December 3, 2016
Passcode accepted:
Carla Johnson

EFT 576	Myer	$3,684.53
EFT 577	Foot Locker	$2,087.45
EFT 578	Rebel Sport	$1,832.12
EFT 579	Rebel Sport	$1,971.03
EFT 580	David Jones	$2,992.20
Total		$12,567.33

CLOUD 9 LTD.
System 01 version 1.9
Daily Reconciliation of AR Posting to Bank Report
as at December 19, 2016

Description	Source	Amount
Cash receipts posted to accounts receivable	Subledger	13,874.85
Total bank deposits	Bank statement	13,874.85
Difference		0.00

OKAY

Prepared: _Jessica Williams_   19/12/16

Approved: _Carla Johnson_   19/12/16

ONBank

CLOUD 9 LTD.
Online Banking
EFT payments for December 19, 2016
Passcode accepted:
Carla Johnson

EFT 635	Wide Road Specialty Retailer	$6,130.61
EFT 636	Cross Country	$1,456.18
EFT 637	Foot Locker	$6,288.06
Total		$13,874.85

Glossary

accountability relationship a situation in which one party is answerable to another for the subject matter, p. 5.

accounts payable master file a computer file containing details of suppliers, transactions with suppliers, and the balance owing, p. 359.

accounts receivable master file a computer file containing customer details in terms of contact information, address, and approved credit limit, p. 316.

accounts receivable subsidiary ledger a ledger recording the details of transactions by customer and balances owing by invoice, p. 317.

accounts receivable trial balance a listing of individual customer balances at a particular date on the accounts receivable master file or accounts receivable sub-ledger, p. 332.

accuracy assertion that amounts and other data relating to recorded transactions and events have been recorded appropriately, pp. 153, 213.

adverse opinion opinion provided when the auditor concludes that there is a pervasive material misstatement in the financial statements, p. 19.

advocacy threat the threat that can occur when a firm or its staff acts on behalf of its assurance client, p. 43.

aged trial balance an accounts receivable trial balance in which customer balances are analyzed by the period since each sales transaction was entered, p. 332.

analytical procedures an evaluation of financial information made by studying plausible relationships among both financial and non-financial data, pp. 127, 173, 293.

applicable financial reporting framework the financial framework chosen by management to prepare a company's financial statements. For example, an applicable framework for a reporting issuer would be International Financial Reporting Standards (IFRS). An applicable framework for a private enterprise could be Accounting Standards for Private Enterprises (ASPE), or it could be IFRS, p. 6.

application controls manual or automated controls that operate at a business process level and apply to the processing of transactions by individual applications, p. 90.

assertion statement made by management regarding the recognition, measurement, presentation, and disclosure of items included in the financial statements, pp. 6, 111, 153.

asset-test (quick) ratio liquid assets to current liabilities, p. 130.

association what occurs when a public accountant is involved with financial information, p. 41.

assurance engagement an engagement performed by an auditor or consultant to enhance the reliability of the subject matter, p. 5.

attribute sampling a sampling technique used to reach a conclusion about a population in terms of a rate (frequency) of occurrence, p. 251.

audit committee a sub-committee of the board of directors. The audit committee enhances auditor independence and ensures that the financial statements are fairly presented and that the external auditor has access to all records and other evidence required to form their opinion, p. 50.

audit evidence information used by the auditor to support the audit opinion, p. 6.

audit file the file where the evidence and documentation of the work performed is kept as a permanent record to support the opinion issued, p. 6.

audit plan a plan that details the audit procedures to be used when testing controls and when conducting detailed substantive audit procedures, pp. 6, 198, 211.

audit program a detailed listing of the audit procedures to be performed, with enough detail to enable the auditor to understand the nature, timing, and extent of testing required, p. 287.

audit risk the risk that an auditor expresses an inappropriate audit opinion when the financial statements are materially misstated, pp. 6, 110, 212, 231, 284.

audit sampling the application of audit procedures to less than 100 percent of items within a population, pp. 198.

audit strategy a strategy that sets the scope, timing, and direction of the audit and provides the basis for developing a detailed audit plan, pp. 75, 121, 211.

authorized price list a list of selling prices for each product, p. 317.

bank confirmation a letter sent directly by an auditor to their client's bank requesting information such as the amount of cash held in the bank (or overdraft), details of any loans with the bank, and interest rates charged, pp. 157, 441.

bank reconciliations schedules agreeing the balance of cash at the bank per the entity's records with the balance shown per the bank. The most common reconciling items are deposits in transit and outstanding cheques, p. 436.

bank transfer schedule a schedule prepared by the auditor listing bank transfers for a few days either side of the end of the reporting period, and the dates recorded in the records and the bank statement, p. 440.

block selection the selection of items that are grouped together within the population of items available, p. 203.

board of directors the group that represents the shareholders and oversees the activities of a company and its management, p. 41.

capital asset sub-ledger a file containing plant and equipment information such as description, supplier, serial number, and location, as well as cost and depreciation charges that reconcile with the control account in the general ledger, p. 416.

cash count audit procedure of counting cash on hand and agreeing the balance with the accounting records, p. 444.

cash cut-off test an audit test performed to obtain reasonable assurance that cash receipts and payments are recorded in the correct accounting period, p. 440.

cash receipts cut-off test a substantive procedure designed to obtain reasonable assurance that cash receipts are recorded in the accounting period in which they are received, p. 334.

cash receipts journal a journal recording cash receipt transactions for posting to the ledgers, p. 319.

cheque register a listing of all cheques issued, p. 360.

classification assertion that transactions and events have been recorded in the proper accounts, pp. 154, 213.

closing procedures processes used by a client when finalizing the books for an accounting period, p. 76.

combined audit strategy a strategy used when the auditor obtains a detailed understanding of their client's system of internal controls and plans to rely on that system to identify, prevent, and detect material misstatements, p. 122.

common-size analysis a comparison of account balances with a single line item, p. 128.

compilation engagement an engagement in which an auditor compiles a set of financial statements based on the information provided by the client, ensuring mathematical accuracy, p. 16.

completeness assertion that all transactions, events, assets, liabilities, and equity items that should have been recorded have been recorded, pp. 153, 213.

compliance audit an audit to determine whether the entity has conformed with regulations, rules, or processes, p. 12.

component auditor an auditor who, at the request of the group engagement team, performs work on financial information related to a component for the group audit, p. 171.

comprehensive audit an audit that encompasses a range of audit and audit-related activities, such as a financial statement audit, operational audit, and compliance audit, p. 12.

computational evidence evidence gathered by an auditor checking the mathematical accuracy of the numbers that appear in the financial report, p. 165.

confidentiality the obligation that all members of the professional bodies refrain from disclosing information that is learned as a result of their employment to people outside of their workplace, p. 39.

confirmation of accounts payable written enquiry of suppliers requesting confirmation of the balance owing at the confirmation date, p. 378.

consulting firms non-audit firms that provide assurance services on non-financial information, such as corporate social responsibility and environmental disclosures, p. 13.

control activities policies and procedures that help ensure that management directives are carried out. Control activities are a component of internal control, pp. 238.

control environment the attitudes, awareness, and actions of management and those charged with governance concerning the entity's internal control and its importance in the entity, p. 233.

control exception an observed condition that provides evidence that the control being tested did not operate as intended, p. 252.

control risk the risk that a client's system of internal controls will not prevent or detect a material misstatement, pp. 111, 212, 236, 285.

corporate governance the rules, systems, and processes within companies used to guide and control, pp. 46, 76.

corporate social responsibility (CSR) a range of activities undertaken voluntarily by a corporation. CSR disclosures include environmental, employee, and social reporting, p. 13.

current file a file that contains client information that is relevant for the duration of one audit, p. 176.

current ratio current assets to current liabilities, p. 130.

customer order a document indicating the goods requested by a customer that provides evidence of authenticity, p. 315.

cut-off assertion that transactions and events have been recorded in the correct accounting period, pp. 153, 213.

cyclical inventory counts periodic inventory counts that count all or most inventory items over a year, p. 399.

debt to equity ratio liabilities to equity, p. 131.

deposit slip a listing of cash, coins, and individual cheques for deposit with the bank, endorsed by the bank teller, a copy of which is retained by the entity, p. 319.

detection risk the risk that the auditor's testing procedures will not be effective in detecting a material misstatement, pp. 114, 236, 285.

disclaimer of opinion opinion provided when the impact of a scope limitation is so extreme that an auditor is unable to obtain sufficient appropriate evidence to base an opinion, p. 19.

documentary evidence information that provides evidence about details recorded in a client's list of transactions (for example, invoices and bank statements), p. 161.

dual purpose tests procedures that provide evidence for both tests of controls and substantive procedures, p. 291.

due care the obligation to complete each task thoroughly, document all work, and finish on a timely basis, p. 39.

earnings per share (EPS) profit to weighted average ordinary shares issued, p. 125.

electronic evidence data held on a client's computer, files sent by e-mail to the auditor, and items scanned and faxed, p. 166.

embedded audit facility procedures written directly into the program of a specific computer application allowing the auditor intervention to capture or process data for audit purposes, p. 326.

emphasis of matter what results when an auditor will issue an unmodified audit opinion when there is a significant issue that is adequately disclosed and there is a need to draw the attention of the user to it, p. 18.

engagement letter a letter that sets out the terms of the audit engagement, to avoid any misunderstandings between the auditor and their client, p. 57.

entity-level controls the collective assessment of the client's control environment, risk assessment process, information system, control activities, and monitoring of controls, pp. 233.

error an unintentional misstatement in the financial statements, including the omission of an amount or a disclosure, p. 479.

evidence information gathered by the auditor that is used when forming an opinion on the fair presentation of a client's financial statements and to confirm amounts recorded in client records, pp. 156, 167.

execution stage the audit stage involving detailed testing of controls and substantive testing of transactions and accounts, pp. 75, 127.

executive directors employees of the company who also hold a position on the board of directors, p. 49.

existence assertion that recorded assets, liabilities, and equity interests exist, pp. 154, 214.

expert someone with the skills, knowledge, and experience required to aid the auditor when gathering sufficient appropriate evidence, p. 169.

extent of audit testing the amount of audit evidence gathered when testing controls and conducting detailed substantive procedures, p. 217.

external confirmation evidence obtained as a direct written response to the auditor from a third party, in paper form, or by electronic or other medium, p. 157.

externally generated evidence information created by a third party (for example, supplier statements, bank statements), p. 168

fair presentation the consistent and faithful application of accounting standards when preparing the financial statements, p. 10.

familiarity threat the threat that can occur when a close relationship exists or develops between the assurance firm (staff) and the client (staff), p. 43.

financial statement audit an audit that provides reasonable assurance about whether the financial report is prepared in all material respects in accordance with the financial reporting framework, p. 10.

financial statements a structured representation of historical financial information, including the related notes, p. 6

finished goods manufactured inventory that is available for sale, p. 398.

fraud an intentional act through the use of deception to obtain an unjust or illegal advantage, p. 75.

general controls controls that apply to a company's IT system as a whole. They include policies and procedures for the purchase, maintenance, and daily operations of an IT system, security, and the staff training, p. 90.

generalized audit software software auditors use under a variety of data organization and processing methods, p. 326.

going concern the viability of a company to remain in business for the foreseeable future, pp. 75, 473.

gross profit margin gross profit to net sales, p. 129.

group engagement partner the auditor responsible for signing the audit report, p. 171.

haphazard selection the selection of a sample without use of a methodical technique, p. 203.

imprest bank account bank account funded with a sum sufficient to meet the payment of special purpose cheques such as wages or dividends, p. 437.

imprest petty cash fund petty cash fund maintained at a constant level via replenishment with the value of receipts paid out of the fund, p. 436.

independence the ability to act with integrity, objectivity, and professional scepticism maintaining an attitude that includes a questioning mind, being alert to conditions that may indicate possible misstatement due to error or fraud, and a critical assessment of audit evidence, p. 41.

independent auditor's report the auditor's formal expression of opinion on whether the financial statements are in accordance with the applicable financial reporting framework, p. 6.

independent directors non-executive directors without any business or other ties to the company, p. 46.

information risk the risk that users will rely on incorrect information to make a decision, p. 8.

information technology the use of computers to store and process data and other information, p. 89.

inherent risk the susceptibility of the financial statements to a material misstatement without considering the internal controls, pp. 110, 212, 236, 285.

inquiry an evidence-gathering procedure that involves asking questions verbally or in written form to gain an understanding of various matters throughout the audit, p. 173.

inspection an evidence-gathering procedure that involves checking documents and physical assets, pp. 166, 173.

integrated test facility a type of test of controls that requires using a fictitious entity and entering fictitious transactions for that entity with the regular transactions, and then comparing the result with the expected output, p. 326.

integrity the obligation that all members of the accounting professional bodies be straightforward and honest, p. 39.

internal audit an independent service within an entity that generally evaluates and improves risk management, internal control procedures, and elements of the governance process, p. 12.

internal auditors employees of the company who evaluate and make recommendations to improve risk management, internal control procedures, and elements of the governance process, p. 50.

internal control the process designed, implemented, and maintained by those charged with governance, management, and other personnel to provide reasonable assurance about the achievement of the entity's objectives with regard to reliability of financial reporting, effectiveness and efficiency of operations, and compliance with applicable laws and regulations, pp. 6, 230.

internally generated evidence information created by the client (for example, customer invoices, purchase orders), p. 167.

intimidation threat the threat that can occur when a member of the assurance teams feels threatened by client staff or directors, p. 44.

inventory count sheets prenumbered count sheets used to record inventory on hand and quantity counted, p. 400.

inventory master file a file containing details of inventory items, their movement, and the quantity on hand, p. 398.

inventory tags three-part, tie-on tags for recording the inventory count of each item, p. 400.

inventory transfer requisition a document authorizing the requisitioning of materials and labour for the purpose of manufacturing, p. 399.

inventory turnover cost of sales to average inventory, p. 130.

investment subsidiary ledger (investment register) a subsidiary ledger recording individual investments in shares and debentures. Entries show purchases and sales, the cost of each bundle purchased, and the quantity and the cost of the balance owed, p. 445.

judgemental misstatement a misstatement that arises as a result of a difference in the application of judgement by the client and the auditor, such as the use of an estimate the auditor considers unreasonable or the inappropriate application of an inappropriate accounting policy. A judgemental misstatement is not the same as an error, p. 475.

judgemental selection the selection of items that an auditor believes should be included in their sample for testing, p. 203.

key performance indicators (KPIs) measurements, agreed to beforehand, that can be quantified and that reflect the success factors of an organization, p. 125.

kiting an irregularity overstating the cash balance by intentionally recording a bank transfer as a deposit in the receiving bank while failing to show a deduction from the bank account on which the transfer is drawn, p. 440.

lapping an irregularity concealing the misappropriation of cash by using subsequent cash receipts to conceal the original misappropriation, p. 445.

legal letter a letter sent to a client's lawyer asking them to confirm the details of legal matters outstanding identified by management, p. 162.

liens legal claims of one person on the property of another person to secure the payment of a debt or the satisfaction of an obligation, p. 345.

liquidity the ability of a company to pay its debts when they fall due, p. 125.

listed entity an entity whose shares, stock, or debt are listed on a stock exchange, p. 10.

management letter a document prepared by the audit team and provided to the client that discusses internal control weaknesses and other matters discovered during the course of the audit, p. 263.

management representation letter a letter from the client's management to the auditor acknowledging management's responsibility for the preparation of the financial statements and details of any verbal representations made by management during the course of the audit, p. 164.

material an amount or disclosure that is significant enough to make a difference to a user, p. 6.

materiality information that has an impact on the decision-making of users of the financial statements, p. 470.

misstatement a difference between the amount, classification, presentation, or disclosure of a reported financial report item and the amount, classification, presentation, or disclosure that is required for the item to be in accordance with the applicable financial reporting framework. Misstatements can arise from error or fraud, pp. 205, 301, 479.

moderate assurance assurance that provides negative assurance on the reliability of the subject matter, p. 14.

monthly customer statement a listing sent to each customer of transactions with that customer that have occurred since the date of the previous statement, which shows the closing balance due, p. 317.

nature of audit testing the purpose of the test and the procedure used, p. 215.

negative confirmation a letter sent directly by an auditor to a third party, who is asked to respond to the auditor on the matter(s) included in the letter only if they disagree with the information provided, p. 158.

negligence failure to exercise due care, p. 51.

no assurance what results when an auditor completes a set of tasks requested by their client and they report factually on the results of that work to their client, p. 16.

non-executive directors board members who are not employees of the company. Their involvement on the board is limited to preparing for and attending board meetings and relevant board committee meetings, p. 49.

non-sampling risk the risk that the auditor reaches an inappropriate conclusion for any reason not related to sampling risk, p. 200.

non-statistical sampling any sample selection method that does not have the characteristics of statistical sampling, p. 201.

Notice to Reader the communication issued when the auditor performs a compilation engagement, p. 16.

objectivity the obligation that all members of the professional bodies not allow their personal feelings or prejudices to influence their professional judgement, p. 39.

observation an evidence-gathering procedure that involves watching a procedure being carried out by another party, p. 173.

occurrence assertion that transactions and events that have been recorded have occurred and pertain to the entity, pp. 153, 213.

operational audit an assessment of the economy, efficiency, and effectiveness of an organization's operations, p. 12.

packing slip a form that details the quantity of goods delivered to the entity. This is signed by the receiver as evidence that the goods were actually received, p. 359.

payable confirmation a letter sent directly by an auditor to their client's lender or supplier requesting information about amounts owed by the client to the lender or supplier, p. 158.

payroll register a document that contains details of wages paid, withholding taxes, and a cumulative record of wages paid per employee, per department, and in total, p. 364.

payroll transaction file a file recording details of hours worked, wage rates, and wages paid per employee, p. 364.

performance materiality an amount less than materiality that is set to reduce the likelihood that a misstatement in a particular class of transactions, account balances, or disclosures, in aggregate, do not exceed materiality for the financial statements as a whole, p. 119.

permanent file a file that contains client information that is relevant for more than one audit, p. 175.

perpetual inventory records records of the movement of inventory items and the quantity on hand, p. 398.

personnel authorization form a form issued by the personnel department indicating the job classification and wage rate for all approved positions, p. 362.

personnel file a file maintained by the personnel department recording details of individual employees, such as the job classification, wage rate, and date of hiring, p. 362.

personnel master file a computer file containing details of employees, such as approved wage rate and date of hiring, p. 362.

physical evidence inspection of a client's tangible assets, such as its inventory and fixed assets, p. 166.

planning stage the audit stage involving gaining an understanding of the client, identifying risk factors, developing an audit strategy, and assessing materiality, p. 75.

positive confirmation a letter sent directly by an auditor to a third party, who is asked to respond to the auditor on the matter(s) included in the letter in all circumstances (that is, whether they agree or disagree with the information included in the auditor's letter), p. 158.

price–earnings (PE) ratio market price per share to earnings per share, p. 125.

professional behaviour the obligation that all members of the professional bodies comply with rules and regulations and ensure that they do not harm the reputation of the profession, p. 39.

professional competence the obligation that all members of the accounting professional bodies maintain their knowledge and skill at a required level, p. 39.

professional judgement the exercise of the auditor's professional characteristics such as their expertise, experience, knowledge, and training, pp. 263, 284, 471.

professional scepticism maintaining an independent questioning mind, p. 83.

profit margin profit to net sales, p. 130.

profitability the ability of a company to earn a profit, p. 125.

projected error extrapolation of the errors detected when testing a sample to the population from which the sample was drawn, p. 210.

purchase journal a computer file listing details of all purchase transactions, p. 359.

purchase order a form showing the description of the goods, the quantity ordered, and other relevant data. This is signed by the purchasing officer as evidence of the approval of the purchase, p. 358.

purchase requisition a form issued by authorized personnel detailing the goods and services required, p. 357.

qualified opinion an opinion provided when the auditor concludes that the financial report contains a material (significant) misstatement, p. 19.

quantitative materiality information that exceeds an auditor's preliminary materiality assessment, p. 118.

random selection process whereby a sample is selected free from bias and each item in a population has an equal chance of selection, p. 202.

rate of deviation when testing controls, the proportion of items tested that did not conform to the client's prescribed control procedure, p. 206.

raw materials materials purchased from suppliers to be used in the manufacture of finished goods, p. 398.

reasonable assurance high but not absolute assurance on the reliability of the subject matter, p. 14.

recalculation an evidence-gathering procedure that involves checking the mathematical accuracy of client records, p. 173.

receivable confirmation a letter sent directly by an auditor to their client's credit customers requesting information about amounts owed to the client by the debtor, p. 158.

receivables turnover net credit sales to average net receivables, p. 131.

receiving report a form issued by the receiving department detailing the description and quantity of the goods delivered by the supplier, p. 358.

relevance extent to which information is logically connected to an assertion, p. 157.

reliability extent to which information reflects the true state of the information, p. 157.

remittance advice a form accompanying cash or cheques paid by a customer, indicating the customer's details and the items being paid, p. 318, 361.

re-performance an evidence-gathering procedure that involves redoing processes conducted by the client, p. 173.

reporting issuer a public company with a market capitalization and a book value of total assets greater than $10 million, p. 44.

reporting stage the audit stage involving evaluating the results of the detailed testing in light of the auditor's understanding of their client and forming an opinion on the fair presentation of the client's financial statements, p. 75.

return on assets (ROA) profit to average assets, p. 130.

return on equity (ROE) profit to average equity, p. 130.

review engagement an engagement in which the auditor does adequate work to report whether or not anything came to their attention that would lead them to believe that the information being assured is not fairly presented, p. 14.

rights and obligations rights to assets held or controlled by the entity, and liabilities (obligations) of the entity, pp. 154, 214.

risk assessment process the entity's process for identifying and responding to business risks, p. 236.

roll-forward procedures procedures performed during the period between an interim date and year end (the roll-forward period) to provide sufficient and appropriate audit evidence to base conclusions on as at year end when substantive procedures are performed at an interim date, p. 290.

sales cut-off test a substantive procedure designed to obtain reasonable assurance that sales and accounts receivable are recorded in the accounting period the transaction occurred, and that the corresponding cost of sales and inventory entries are made in the same period, p. 334.

sales invoice a form detailing the goods or services supplied to a customer and the amount owing, p. 316.

sales journal a journal listing completed sales transactions, p. 317.

sales order a form showing the description of the goods, the quantity ordered, and other relevant data, which serves as the basis for the internal processing of the customer order, p. 315.

sales return cut-off test a substantive procedure designed to obtain reasonable assurance that sales returns are recorded in the period the original sale occurred, p. 334.

sales transactions file a computer file listing details of all sales transactions, p. 317.

sampling risk the risk that the sample chosen by the auditor is not representative of the population available for testing and, as a consequence, the auditor arrives at an inappropriate conclusion, p. 199.

self-interest threat the threat that can occur when an accounting firm or its staff has a financial interest in an assurance client, p. 42.

self-review threat the threat that can occur when the assurance team needs to form an opinion on their own work or work performed by others in their firm, p. 43.

shareholders owners of the company, p. 49.

shipping document a form authorizing the release of goods from inventory and the delivery of the goods to the customer, p. 316.

significant account an account or group of accounts that could contain material misstatements based on their materiality and/or relationship to identified inherent and financial statement risks, pp. 284.

significant risk an identified and assessed risk of material misstatement that, in the auditor's judgement, requires special audit consideration, p. 111.

specific materiality information that is relevant when some areas of the financial statements are expected to influence the economic decisions made by users of the financial statements, p. 119.

statistical sampling an approach to sampling where random selection is used to select a sample and probability theory is used to evaluate the sample results, p. 201.

stratification the process of dividing a population into groups of sampling units with similar characteristics, p. 202.

subsequent events both events occurring between year end and the date of the audit report, and facts discovered after the date of the audit report, p. 475.

subsequent period bank statement the first bank statement issued after the end of the reporting period used by the auditor to verify the existence of deposits in transit and outstanding cheques listed on the bank reconciliation at the end of the reporting period, p. 442.

substantive audit procedures procedures used when the auditor plans to get a minimum knowledge of the client's controls and conducts extensive substantive procedures that involve intensive testing of year-end account balances and transactions from throughout the year, p. 211.

substantive audit strategy a strategy used when the auditor does not plan to rely on the client's controls and increases the reliance on detailed substantive procedures that involve intensive testing of year-end account balances and transactions from throughout the year, p. 121.

substantive procedures (substantive testing or **tests of details)** audit procedures designed to detect material misstatements at the assertion level, pp. 213, 254, 287.

sufficient appropriate evidence quantity (sufficiency) and quality (appropriateness) of audit evidence gathered, pp. 75, 156, 471.

suppliers' invoice a form issued by the supplier detailing the goods or services supplied and the amount owing, p. 359.

systematic selection the selection of a sample for testing by dividing the number of items in a population by the sample size, giving sampling interval (n) and then selecting every nth item in the population, p. 202.

systems control audit review file an embedded audit facility that enables auditors to specify parameters of interest, such as transactions meeting specified criteria, which are then recorded on a special audit file for subsequent review by the auditors, p. 326.

technical competence the skills, training, and ability of the internal audit team, p. 51.

termination notice a form issued by the personnel department to document the termination of an employee, p. 363.

test data approach a method of testing controls in a computerized information system environment, where the auditor prepares fictitious transactions and tests the fictitious data using the entity's software. The output is then compared with the expected output, p. 325.

tests of controls (controls testing) the audit procedures designed to evaluate the operating effectiveness of controls in preventing, or detecting and correcting, material misstatements at the assertion level, pp. 212, 242.

tests of details of balances tests that support the correctness of an account ending balance, p. 292.

tests of details of transactions tests predominantly designed to verify a balance or a transaction back to supporting documentation; therefore, they usually include vouching and tracing, p. 291.

third parties anyone other than the client and its shareholders who uses the financial statements to make a decision, p. 53.

those charged with governance generally the board of directors, and may include management of an entity, pp. 12, 474.

times interest earned profit before income taxes and interest expense, p. 131.

timing of audit testing the stage of the audit when procedures are performed and the date, such as within or outside the accounting period, that audit evidence relates to, p. 216.

tolerable error or misstatement the maximum error an auditor is willing to accept within the population tested, p. 205.

tracing tracking a source document back to the underlying accounting records, p. 291.

transaction-level controls controls that affect a particular transaction or group of transactions, pp. 242.

trend analysis a comparison of account balances over time, p. 128.

unmodified opinion a clean audit opinion; the auditor concludes that the financial statements are fairly presented, pp. 6, 18.

valuation and allocation assertion that assets, liabilities, and equity interests are included in the financial statements at appropriate amounts and any resulting valuation or allocation adjustments are appropriately recorded, pp. 154, 214.

verbal evidence responses of key client personnel to auditor enquiries throughout the course of the audit, p. 165.

vouching taking a balance or transaction from the underlying accounting records and verifying it by agreeing the details to supporting evidence outside the accounting records of the company, p. 291.

walkthrough tracing a transaction through a client's accounting system, p. 122.

WCGWs areas where material misstatements due to error or fraud could occur in a flow of transactions or in the sourcing and preparation of information that affects a relevant financial report assertion, p. 243.

window dressing a deliberate attempt to enhance some aspect of a company's apparent short-term solvency, such as by misstating the cut-off of cash receipts and payments, p. 443.

work in process part-manufactured products consisting of materials, direct labour, and overhead applied to the stage of completion, p. 398.

working papers paper or electronic documentation of the audit created by the audit team as evidence of the work completed, pp. 6, 175.

Index